Strategies for Teaching Students with Learning and Behavior Problems

Strategies for Teaching Students with Learning and Behavior Problems

Second Edition

Candace S. Bos
University of Arizona

Sharon Vaughn
University of Miami

Allyn and Bacon
Boston   London   Toronto   Sydney   Tokyo   Singapore

To Bob and Jim

Series Editor: Ray Short
Series Editorial Assistant: Carol Craig
Production Administrator: Annette Joseph
Production Coordinator: Susan Freese
Editorial-Production Service: Spectrum Publisher Services, Inc.
Text Designer: Denise Hoffman, Glenview Studios
Manufacturing Buyer: Louise Richardson
Cover Administrator: Linda K. Dickinson
Cover Designer: Suzanne Harbison

Copyright © 1991, 1988 by Allyn and Bacon
A Division of Simon & Schuster, Inc.
160 Gould Street
Needham Heights, Massachusetts 02194

Library of Congress Cataloging-in-Publication Data

Bos, Candace S.
   Strategies for teaching students with learning and behavior
problems / Candace S. Bos, Sharon Vaughn.—2nd ed.
      p. cm.
   Includes bibliographical references and index.
   ISBN 0-205-12970-6
   1. Learning disabled children—Education—United States.
  2. Problem children—Education—United States. 3. Remedial
teaching—United States. I. Vaughn, Sharon. II. Title.
LC4705.B67 1991
371.9—dc20   90-23623
                                                       CIP

Printed in the United States of America

10 9 8 7 6 5 4   96 95 94 93 92

Photo credits: Pages 1, 24, 58, 90, 138, 176, 212, 254, 290, 324, 348, and 382 © Frank Siteman 1990.

Brief Contents

Contents

Chapter Five
Reading: Fluency and Comprehension   *138*

Chapter Eight
Mathematics   *254*

Chapter Nine
Socialization   *290*

Chapter Eleven
The Special Education Teacher: Consultant, Collaborator, and Manager   348

Appendix D
Educational Computer Software Producers and Distributors   *464*

Preface

While traveling by car on a typical Arizona scorcher between Phoenix and Tucson following a state Association for Children and Adults with Learning Disabilities meeting, we were discussing the content and assignments to the methods courses we teach at our respective universities. The topic inevitably drifted to what we would like to do better. Since both of us are responsible for preparing teachers and potential teachers to work effectively with students who have learning and behavior problems, we spend a considerable amount of time considering the content of our classes. We concluded that we would like the class and the textbook for the class to provide adequate background in procedures for teaching skill and content areas such as reading, math, oral and written expression, and social and study skills. We also would like our students to understand which methods are most effective with what types of students and why.

Like many good ideas, this book is the result of that initial lengthy discussion, focusing on the ideal content of a book designed to prepare teachers to meet the needs of elementary and secondary students with learning and behavior problems. What followed was many more lengthy discussions aimed at preparing a book that would provide learning strategies and techniques as well as the foundation for using these strategies and techniques.

Audience and Purpose

We have written this book for graduate and undergraduate students who are developing expertise in teaching students with learning and behavior problems. This book is also intended for professionals in the field, including special and regular education teachers, school psychologists, language specialists, and school administrators who are interested in learning more about working successfully with students who have learning and behavior problems.

The purpose of this book is to provide:

1. Information about general approaches to learning and teaching so the foundation for the methods and procedures for teaching all learners can be better understood.
2. Descriptions of methods and procedures that include sufficient detail so that teachers and other professionals can read about them and know how to use them.
3. Information regarding classroom management, consultation, and working with parents and professionals so that beginning teachers can develop a plan of action for the school year and experienced teachers can refine these skills.

Organizational Overview

First we deal with foundational concepts. Chapter One describes the characteristics of the target population, a range of alternative learning environments, the teaching-learning process, and strategies for evaluating and monitoring progress, including individual educational programs.

Chapter Two presents approaches to learning and teaching: operant learning, cognitive behavior modification, sociocultural theory of cognitive development, and information processing and schema theories. These learning models provide the basis for the methods and strategies presented later in the book.

We then focus on learning and teaching in specific skill and content areas. The emphasis in Chapters Three through Ten is on methods and procedures for effectively teaching skills, strategies, and content to students with learning and behavior problems. Information is presented not only on how to teach but also on why and when to use different instructional strategies and techniques.

Because of the extensive problems experienced in the area of literacy by special learners, Chapters Three through Six deal specifically with oral language, reading, and writing. The content of these chapters is organized to provide background in the content areas and detailed descriptions of strategies for teaching specific skills and processes. Due to the increasing focus on study skills and content area learning (e.g., social studies, science, career/vocational education) at the upper-elementary and secondary levels, Chapter Seven deals with teaching content area subjects and teaching study skills, including time and notebook management, memorization and test-taking skills, listening and notetaking skills, and textbook usage skills. Chapter Eight deals with mathematics, covering such areas as measurement, time, verbal math problem solving, and computational skill development. Chapter Nine focuses on teaching social skills as well as information related to the social and affective development of students, including anorexia nervosa, suicide, and drug-related problems. Chapter Ten discusses the use of computers as a means of shaping and reinforcing instruction.

Next, we focus on managing the classroom and communicating with parents and professionals. Chapter Eleven discusses such issues as arranging the instructional environment and scheduling. Strategies for effective mainstream-ing and collaborating with regular classroom teachers are also discussed, since the majority of these students spend most of their school day in regular education classes. Chapter Twelve focuses on effective communication and making and maintaining professional relationships with regular classroom teachers, special education teachers, and other specialists such as school psychologists, language and occupational therapists, and school administrators. Parents, the most effective agents for change, and their special needs are also presented.

In revising this book we have heeded the suggestions of students and professors who have used it, and we have updated the text based on new intervention research and practice. The most significant changes we made are in the chapters on reading and socialization. To the sections on reading we have added information on whole language, literature-based reading programs, and Reading Recovery. We have also expanded our discussion on reciprocal teaching. In the chapter on socialization we have described a number of new intervention techniques designed to foster prosocial behavior and social problem solving. In the chapter on approaches to learning and teaching and throughout the book, we have highlighted learning strategies, metacognition and self-regulation, and the use of interactive teaching and learning. Finally, we have expanded the section on collaboration, consultation, and strategies for mainstreaming and renamed Chapter Eleven to emphasize the change (The Special Education Teacher: Consultant, Collaborator, and Manager). We hope this new edition will prove to be a valuable resource to special education teachers.

Acknowledgments

Many people deserve a great deal more acknowledgment than their names appearing here will provide. We wish to acknowledge and thank the teachers whom we have written about in this book. The time we have spent in their classrooms—observing, discussing, and teaching—

has afforded us the ability to write a book that is grounded in classroom experiences and practices. These teachers include Judy Cohen, Joan Downing, Louise Fournia, Joan Gervasi, Linda Jones, Tom Lebasseur, Marynell Schlegel, and Mary Thalgott.

We also wish to acknowledge those individuals who reviewed the manuscript at various stages for Allyn and Bacon: Anthony DeFeo, University of Arizona; Linda Patriarcha, Michigan State University; and Cynthia Wilson, University of Miami. Special thanks go to Carol Sue Englert, Michigan State University, and to Corrine Roth Smith, Syracuse University, for their expert comments.

We also want to thank the students in our methods classes who field-tested the book and provided us with valuable ideas. Our appreciation and thanks go to Kathy Haagenson, Pauline Havens, and Kathy Madsen for their assistance in reviewing the literature. To our secretaries, Mary Kord and Sandy Richards, we are most appreciative.

Special thanks also to our husbands, Jim and Bob, who wondered if we would ever come out from behind our word processors.

Most important of all, we would like to thank the teacher whose observations, research, and thinking has done more to guide our development and the field or special education than any other, Samuel Kirk.

Last, we want to thank each other. Many people start off coauthoring a book as friends—we still are. For this, we are grateful.

Chapter One

The Teaching-Learning Process

Chapter Questions

- *What are some of the characteristics of students with learning and behavior problems?*
- *What factors should be considered when determining how serious a learning or behavior problem is?*
- *What is the teaching-learning process and how can it be applied to students with learning and behavior problems?*
- *How do the individualized educational program (IEP) and student and teacher involvement relate to the instructional cycle?*
- *What measures can be used to evaluate student progress?*

This book is about children and adolescents who have difficulty learning and interacting appropriately in school. If you saw these children in school you would not be able to identify them by how they look. You would, however, be able to identify them by what they do. What are these students like? Teachers describe them this way:

> *Servio has a very poor self-concept. He is extremely sensitive and gets upset at the least little thing. For example, yesterday he noticed that his red crayon was broken and he started to cry. When I told him he could have another red crayon, he still continued to cry, saying that he wanted this red crayon fixed. He often says he can't do things, that he doesn't care, and that he is bad. When he has problems at home he says he's going to be bad. He often says that he was punished at home for being bad and he's going to be bad today at school. He used to throw things at school but he doesn't do that anymore. He doesn't have any friends in the class and most of the other students don't pay attention to him.*

> *Dana has a great deal of difficulty with her work. She appears to have trouble remembering. Well, not always. Sometimes she remembers how to read a word; other days she looks at the same word and it's like she has to scan all of the information in her head to try to locate the name of the word. I know she is trying, but it is very frustrating because her progress is so slow. She is also very easily distracted. Even when the aide is working with her alone she will look up and stop working at the littlest things. Something like the air conditioning going on and off will distract her from her work. I know she is bright enough but she seems to have serious problems learning.*

> *Tina is more work for me than the rest of my class put together. She has both academic problems and behavior problems. For example, after I have explained an assignment to the class, Tina always asks me several questions about the assignment. It's like I have to do everything twice, once for the class and then again for Tina. She has a terrible time with reading. She reads so slowly and she often reads the wrong word. For example, she will say* carrot *for* circus *and* monster *for* mister. *She often doesn't know what she's read after she's finished reading it. Also, she can never sit still. She is always moving around the room, sharpening her pencil, getting a book, looking out the window. It is hard for her to do the same thing for more than a few minutes. She's always "bugging" the other students. She's not really a bad kid, it's just that she is always doing something she's not supposed to be doing, and she takes a lot of my time.*

The purpose of this book is to acquaint you with the teaching skills and strategies necessary to understand and teach students like Servio, Dana, and Tina. This chapter provides background information on students with learning and behavior problems and an overview of the teaching-learning process.

What Are the Characteristics of Students with Learning and Behavior Problems?

Most professionals are able to recognize with little difficulty those students with learning and behavior problems. They are students who call attention to themselves in the classroom because they have difficulty learning and interacting appropriately. Students with learning and/or behavior problems manifest one or more of the following behaviors:

- *Poor academic performance.* These students display significant problems in one or more academic areas such as spelling, reading, and mathematics.
- *Attention problems.* These students seem to have difficulty working for extended periods of time on a task. They may have trouble focusing on the teacher's directions. These students are often described by teachers as being easily distracted.
- *Hyperactivity.* These students are overactive and have a difficult time staying in their seats and completing assigned tasks. They move from task to task, often from location to location in the classroom. They can be working on an assignment and the least little noise will distract them.
- *Memory.* These students have a hard time remembering what they were taught. Often their difficulty remembering is associated with symbols such as letters and numbers. These students may remember something one day but not the next.
- *Poor motor abilities.* These students have poor coordination, are awkward, and show spatial problems as well as fine-motor problems, such as the inability to use scissors, manipulate pencils and pens, open a combination lock, and so on.
- *Poor perceptual abilities.* These students have auditory and/or visual perception problems. For example, visual discrimination difficulties may be evidenced in a student's inability to tell one letter from another even after extensive instruction. Auditory discrimination problems may be evidenced when a student cannot distinguish one letter sound from another.
- *Poor language abilities.* These students have language difficulties that are manifested in a number of ways. Often these language problems can be corrected through speech therapy. Students may have difficulty with vocabulary, understanding the concept, using language to adequately express themselves, or producing correct sounds.

- *Aggressive behavior.* These students are physically or verbally assaultive. They may hit, kick, get into fights, and/or verbally threaten or insult others. These children are easily upset and cope with being upset by acting out.
- *Withdrawn behavior.* These students seldom interact with others. Unlike shy students, who may have one or two friends, these students are real loners who avoid involvement with others.
- *Bizarre behavior.* These students display very unusual patterns of behavior. They may stare for long periods of time at objects they hold in the light, they may sit and rock, or they may display aggressive behaviors at times and withdrawn behaviors at other times.

Students with learning and/or behavior problems often exhibit more than one of these behaviors. Yet, some students exhibit these behaviors and are not identified as having learning and behavior problems. There are other factors teachers consider when determining how serious a learning and behavior problem is.

What Factors Should Be Considered When Determining How Serious a Learning and Behavior Problem Is?

Approximately 15 to 25 percent of all students have some type of learning or behavior problem. There are several factors to be considered when determining how serious the problem is.

1. *Persistence of the problem.* Sometimes a student has a learning or behavior problem for a short period of time, perhaps while there is some type of crisis in the family, and then it disappears. Other students display persistent learning and behavior problems throughout their schooling experience. These persistent learning and behavior problems have more serious consequences for the student.

2. *Severity of the problem.* Is the student's learning or behavior problem mild, moderate, or severe? Is the student performing slightly below or significantly below what would be expected of him or her? Is the behavior slightly different or substantially different from the student's peers?

3. *Speed of progress.* Does the student appear to be making steady progress in the classroom despite the learning and behavior problem? We do not expect all students to learn at the same rate. In fact, in an average fourth-grade classroom the range of performance varies from second-grade level to seventh-grade level. The teacher must assess whether the student's progress is steady and if it appears to reflect his or her capabilities.

4. *Motivation.* How interested in learning is the student? Does the student persist at tasks and attempt to learn? Does he or she initiate and complete tasks without continual praise and encouragement?

5. *Parental response.* How do the parents feel about their child's academic and/or behavioral progress? How do they think it compares with his or her progress in the past? Are they concerned about how their child's abilities compare with other children the same age? How have siblings performed in school?

6. *Other teachers' responses.* How did the student perform in previous classes? What do previous or other teachers say about learning style, academic abilities, and behavior?

7. *Relationship with the teacher.* What type of relationship does the student have with his or her present teacher? Sometimes there is a poor interpersonal match between the student and the teacher that may interfere with the student's academic performance and/or behavior.

8. *Instructional modifications and style.* What attempts has the present teacher made to modify the student's academic and/or behavioral program? Does the student seem responsive to

attempts at intervention? If the student is not performing well in a traditional reading program, has the teacher tried other instructional approaches to reading? Has the student had opportunities to work with different students in the class? If the problem is behavior, what type of behavior change programs have been implemented? Are any successful?

What kind of match is there between the student's learning style and the learning style in the educational setting? Some children function best in a highly structured classroom where the rules, expectations, and assignments are very clearly stated. Other children function better in a learning environment where there is more flexibility.

9. *Adequate instruction.* Has the student had adequate exposure to the material and time to learn? Some students have little experience with school learning situations before coming to school. Other students have multiple experiences, including preschool programs that teach letters and letter sounds. Students who have less exposure to school learning situations, or whose parents provide few schoollike learning experiences, may need more time and exposure to the learning environment before gains are made.

10. *Other factors.* Are there other factors that may be contributing to the student's learning and/or behavior problems? For example, how closely does the student's background experiences, culture, and language match those of the teacher and other students in the class?

Are there any health-related factors that may be interfering with the student's learning or behavior?

Has the student's vision and hearing been adequately assessed to determine whether they may be affecting the student's learning or behavior?

Considering these ten factors should assist in identifying how serious the problem is.

FIGURE 1.1   *Model of the Continuum of Educational Program Alternatives*

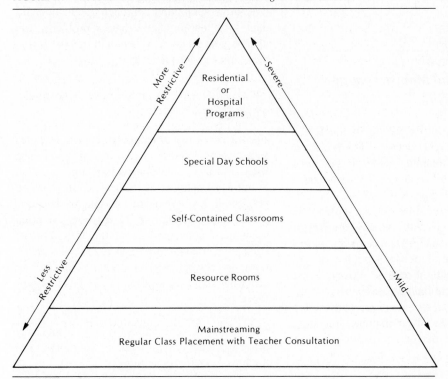

Source: J. W. Lerner, *Learning Disabilities: Theories, Diagnosis, and Teaching Strategies.* 4th ed. (Boston: Houghton Mifflin, 1985).

What Learning and Educational Environments Are Available for Students with Learning and Behavior Problems?

Most students with learning and behavior problems receive their educational program in the regular classroom. Students whose learning and behavior problems are so severe that they warrant special assistance may be involved in a range of support services. These support services include remedial reading or math, counseling, individualized instruction with a teaching assistant, and special education.

PL 94-142, Education for All Handicapped Children Act, assures that a continuum of alternative placements is available for students. This continuum is conceptualized from the least to the most restrictive. Figure 1.1 presents a model of the continuum of alternative educational placements. Restrictive, in an educational sense, refers to the extent to which the student is educated with nonhandicapped peers. A most restrictive setting is one in which the student spends no part of his or her educational program with nonhandicapped peers. In a less restrictive setting, the student may spend part of his or her educational day with nonhandicapped peers. PL 94-142 mandates that all students should be educated in the least-restrictive educational system possible.

Are Least-Restrictive Environment and Mainstreaming the Same Concept?

Mainstreaming is an extension of the least-restrictive environment concept, but it is not the same thing. Mainstreaming is the placement of handicapped students in classes with nonhandicapped students for part of the school day. Although PL 94-142 requires that all students be educated in the least-restrictive environment, it does not require that all students be mainstreamed; the intent of the law is not to place all handicapped students in regular classes. Thus, any one of the educational placements presented in Figure 1.1 may serve as the least-restrictive environment for a particular student, depending on the severity of his or her learning and/or behavior problem.

How Do Teachers Teach Students with Learning and Behavior Problems?

Instruction for students like Servio, Dana, and Tina needs to be carefully orchestrated to take into account the interactive nature of the *teaching-learning process*. The teaching-learning process is a model of teaching and learning that takes into account the complexity of the learning environment or context, the beliefs and characteristics of the learner and teacher, and the instructional cycle the teacher orchestrates to facilitate learning. It is based on notions of *individual programming*. Although students may be instructed in groups, the teacher studies and plans for each student individually, realizing that students have both common and unique needs. The teaching-learning process is represented in Figure 1.2. It is the foundation upon which the

rest of this book rests in that it presents a reflective, problem-solving approach to teaching students with learning and behavior problems. Let us look first at the key players in this process—the learner and the teacher.

The Learner

The learner brings to school beliefs and attitudes about learning and the world in which he or she lives, a variety of skills and knowledge on which to build, and strategies to assist in the learning process. In a way, we are speaking of the *characteristics of the learner*. As teachers, we often seem most concerned about the *skill level* of students. Our assessment process focuses on determining at what level the student is functioning and what skills the student can and cannot perform. However, *knowledge, attitudes,* and *strategic learning* can also provide us with a wealth of information concerning the learner and may prove to be the critical features when determining how to facilitate learning.

The following example illustrates the importance of the student's knowledge. Read the passage once. Your purpose for reading is so you can tell someone else what it was about when you have finished.

> If the balloons popped, the sound would not be able to carry since everything would be too far away from the correct floor. A closed window would also prevent the sound from carrying since most buildings tend to be well insulated. Since the whole operation depends on a steady flow of electricity, a break in the middle of the wire would also cause problems. Of course the additional problem is that a string could break on the instrument. Then there could be no accompaniment to the message. It is clear that the best situation would involve less distance. Then there would be fewer potential problems. With face to face

FIGURE 1.2   *The Teaching-Learning Process*

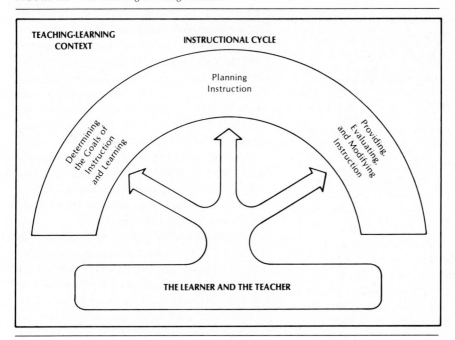

contact, the least number of things could go wrong.

Bransford and Johnson (1972) presented this passage to a group of students and asked them to rate the passage for comprehensibility and then to recall the passage from memory. Most students in the group rated the passage as incomprehensible and their recalls were short and disorganized. However, the same passage becomes comprehensible if you are supplied with the necessary background knowledge, in this case, the picture presented in Figure 1.3. Students who looked at this picture before reading rated the passage much higher for comprehensibility and they recalled twice as many ideas from the passage.

If the learner has little *knowledge* of the topic being studied, then you, the teacher, can assist the student by providing activities that build background knowledge and help the

student link this new knowledge to current knowledge.

Skills and knowledge not only play an important role in learning, but they also influence the learner's *attitudes* about learning and the world. Randy and Tamara illustrate this point. In fifth grade, Randy was determined to learn how to read, although at the time he was struggling with beginning reading books. He worked all year on his reading and at the end of the year he had grown in his reading skill by about one grade level. Still, he carried with him the attitude that reading was important and that he should continue to struggle with a process that for him was quite difficult. Tamara, on the other hand, was a sixth grader who was reading at about the third-grade level. For her, learning to read was a much easier process, yet she finished the year making only marginal gains. Why? She believed that reading simply was not necessary for her life and that her future goal, being a mother, just didn't

FIGURE 1.3   *Context for the Balloon Passage*

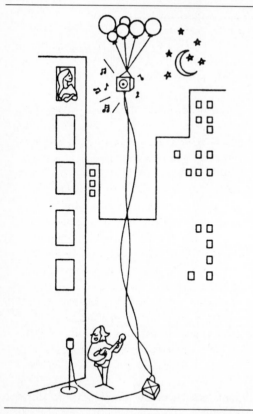

Source: From J. D. Bransford and M. D. Johnson, Contextual prerequisites for understanding: Some investigations of comprehension and recall. *Journal of Verbal Learning and Verbal Behavior, II* (1972):719. Copyright 1972 Academic Press. Reprinted by permission.

require her to be a good reader. These students' attitudes influenced their rate of learning.

A student's *strategies for learning* also affect the teaching-learning process. When you are told to read a chapter in a textbook and study for a test, what strategies do you employ? Do you preview the chapter before reading? Do you ask questions as you read to check your comprehension? Do you underline or take notes? Do you review your notes before the test, rehearsing the important points? These are all strategies that make you a more effective student.

The Teacher

The second player in the teaching-learning process is you, the teacher. Just like the student, you bring to the learning situation your teaching knowledge and skills, your beliefs and attitudes about teaching, learning, and the world, and your strategies for teaching. One purpose of this chapter is to heighten your awareness of your beliefs and attitudes about teaching.

As you read this section, reflect on your beliefs and attitudes about teaching, learning, and students who experience learning and behavior problems. What is the nature of learning and what is your role as a teacher?

Learning can be perceived as changes in behavior that result in a student demonstrating new knowledge and skills. The role of the teacher is that of an educational technician who engineers or arranges the environment so that the probability of learning is increased. This is accomplished by providing the student with the cues to trigger learning and the rewards for learning. The student is the receiver of the new knowledge and skills, whereas the teacher imparts them or arranges the context so that they are imparted by others. An effective teacher is one who conveys knowledge and skills in a systematic, explicit manner. This perception of learning and teaching is probably best reflected in behavior theory and cognitive behavior modification, both of which are discussed in the next chapter. It is also reflected in instructional strategies and materials that are based on systematic ordering and teaching of skills. You will find that some of the strategies and materials presented in the content chapters reflect this perspective on learning and teaching.

Learning can also be perceived as a dynamic process in which the student plays an active role, constantly interacting with the environment and people around him or her. Not only do the student's notions, ideas, and skills change in the learning process but so does the environment in which the learning takes place. Thus, learning is not merely the accumulation of knowledge and skills but it is the active construction and transformation of ideas based on observations and experiences. This perception of learning is represented in information processing and schema theories, which are presented in Chapter Two. The teacher, serving as a facilitator for learning, creates an environment in which the students can take risks and develop flexible learning and thinking strategies as they acquire skills and knowledge. You will also find this perspective represented in the content chapters.

Just as the *characteristics of the learner* affect the teaching-learning process, so will your *beliefs and attitudes* as a teacher. And since the teaching-learning process is dynamic and interactive in nature, your beliefs and attitudes will change, depending on the needs of the learner. For example, Ms. Kranowski, a special education teacher who works with students who have learning and behavior problems, has eleven students, fourth through sixth grade, in her self-contained class. Each day after lunch they practice writing. Ms. Kranowski uses a process approach to teaching writing in which students select their own topics and write about them, sometimes taking several weeks to complete a piece. Students usually write multiple drafts, sharing their work with other students and the teacher.

At first, the learners in Ms. Kranowski's class needed to develop a process for writing. They needed to develop purposes for their writing other than to please the teacher or to complete the worksheets. As the students became more confident of their drafts, they needed to learn such skills as how to organize a descriptive paragraph and a story, and how to use dialogue and quotation marks. Although Ms. Kranowski continues with this process approach to writing, she now also spends some time teaching skills to small groups. She uses systematic skill lessons whereby she models a skill, then has the students practice it in their own writing and in published and teacher-made materials. Whereas the first approach to teaching represents an interactive model of teaching and learning, during skill lessons Ms. Kranowski serves as the conveyor of

knowledge by explicitly teaching systematic skill sequences. Ms. Kranowski's instruction shifts to reflect the needs of the students in her class.

How does Ms. Kranowski explain her simultaneous use of these different approaches to the teaching-learning process?

Well, when I first began using a process approach to teaching writing, I found that the students really learned to like writing. For me, that was a big accomplishment, since most of these kids had previously hated writing. But I also found that because these students have so many learning problems and take so much practice to learn a new skill, they just weren't getting enough opportunities to practice intensely a new writing skill when they were first trying to learn it. Consequently, they never learned the skills very well. Now, two days a week we take about twenty minutes for a skill lesson. I select the skill based on the needs of the students as a group. Right now we are working on dialogue and quotation marks. I introduce the skill and show how I use it in my writing. Then several of the students demonstrate how they can use it in their writing. We use an overhead projector, and they project their writing on the screen. We talk about how to add quotation marks, and they add them right then. For the next several weeks when they are writing their pieces, I encourage them to use dialogue, and we make an effort to compliment each other when the quotation marks are right. If the students need additional practice, I provide them with stories where they have to add quotations marks to the writing. We also take turns reading stories and books that have lots of dialogue and the students identify the dialogue and tell where the quotes go. I realize that this is really mixing two philosophies of teaching and learning, but for me its the best way to get the job done.

The Instructional Cycle

Within the teaching-learning process, the instructional cycle helps to shape and sequence teaching and learning. Ms. Kranowski uses this cycle in her teaching as she sets instructional goals, plans instruction, and provides, evaluates, and modifies instruction based on evaluation. She uses this cycle in a flexible way, taking into account the *characteristics of the learner,* her *teaching beliefs and attitudes,* and the *context* in which the teaching and learning are happening. Sometimes she changes her instructional goals based on input from the students or on feedback regarding rate of learning. Sometimes she modifies her plans and the way in which she instructs to reach her instructional goals more effectively. When Ms. Kranowski added skill lessons to the writing curriculum, she changed her plans, which resulted in changes in instruction. Let's look to see what we might want to consider when developing and implementing each part of the instructional cycle.

Determining the Goals of Instruction and Learning

Setting goals for instruction helps you know where you are going. Several questions you may want to ask when you are setting goals for instruction and learning are:

- Have I used the information I have about the characteristics of the learner?
- Have I taken into account my beliefs and attitudes?
- Have I involved the students in setting the goals?
- Have I set goals that are realistic yet challenging to both the learner and myself?
- How do these goals fit with the larger teaching-learning context (e.g., goals of the

school, curriculum, long-range career goals of the student)?

When Ms. Kranowski set her instructional goals for writing she decided that she had two major objectives: (1) to have the students enjoy writing and feel good about themselves as authors, and (2) to have the students develop writing skills that would help them in school and later in life. She wanted very much to involve the students in setting goals, believing that if they set shared goals then the students would have a greater commitment to reaching those goals. She began the year by telling the students about "the way that writing works" in the classroom. She shared the importance of supporting each other, for she wanted students to set a goal of working together. As they worked together, shared their writing, and got to know each other better, Ms. Kranowski would sit down with each one of them and help them select skills for improvement. By analyzing the students' written products, observing the students as they wrote, talking with the students about their writing, and using her knowledge about the scope and sequence of writing skills, she felt comfortable working with students in selecting goals. In this way, Ms. Kranowski's instructional goals were interwoven with the students' learning goals.

Planning Instruction

When you plan instruction you are selecting the instructional content and procedures to use for instruction. This book provides many ideas for the *content of instruction* within each content chapter (e.g., oral language, reading, word identification, written expressions, and socialization). It provides *procedures for instruction,* using generalized principles and theories such as those discussed in chapters Two (Approaches to Learning and Teaching), Eleven (The Special Education Teacher as Manager), and Twelve

FIGURE 1.4 *Questions for Evaluating the Instructional Process*

- *Student motivation* Am I creating a context in which learning is valued?
- *Student attention* Am I creating an environment in which students can and are encouraged to attend to the learning task?
- *Encouragement* Am I creating a setting in which students are encouraged to take risks and be challenged by learning?
- *Modeling* Are the students given the opportunity to watch, listen, and talk to others so that they can see how the knowledge or skill is learned?
- *Activating prior knowledge* Am I getting the students to think about what they already know about a skill or topic, and are they given the opportunity to build upon that information in an organized fashion?
- *Rate, amount, and manner of presentation* Are the new skills and knowledge being presented at a rate and amount that allows the students time to learn, and in a manner that gives them enough information yet does not overload them?
- *Practice* Are the students given ample opportunity to practice?
- *Feedback* Are the students given feedback on their work so they know how and what they are learning?
- *Acquisition* Are the students given the opportunity to learn skills and knowledge until they feel comfortable with them and to the point they do or know something almost automatically?
- *Maintenance* Are the students given the opportunity to continue to use their skills and knowledge so that they can serve as tools for further learning?
- *Generalization* Are the students generalizing the skills and knowledge to other tasks, settings, and situations? Are the students, other teachers, or parents seeing the learning?
- *Application* Are the students given the opportunity to apply their skills and knowledge in new and novel situations, thereby adapting their skills to meet the new learning experiences?

(Communicating with Parents and Professionals). Specific procedures for instruction can be found in the content chapters.

Providing, Evaluating, and Modifying Instruction

Even though you approach instruction with a plan of action, it is important to remember that your plan will need to be modified and changed. Effective instruction is obtained when the instructional procedures and content match the overall teaching-learning process. Since the teaching-learning process is dynamic and flexible, the instructional process must also be dynamic and flexible.

Earlier, Ms. Kranowski had talked about how her writing instruction had changed. She

had started with a plan of action, but had found that her plan wasn't allowing the students to develop the writing skills they needed. She had determined this through evaluation. She had watched and listened to the students and analyzed their written products over time. She had even administered a standardized test to measure skills in capitalization, punctuation, spelling, and grammar. All these evaluative measures had led her to the same conclusion—her students' writing skills were not improving at a rate she considered adequate.

In determining how to modify her instruction, Ms. Kranowski thought about the ideas presented in Figure 1.4. She felt she had adequately addressed the first four questions. Student motivation, attention, encouragement, and modeling had been good. She did not feel as comfortable about her answers to the next three questions: prior knowledge, manner of presentation, and practice. Sometimes she thought she wasn't focused enough on one or two writing skills. She tended to present too much and not allow for enough practice and feedback. Ms. Kranowski decided her modifications had to alleviate the problems with presentation, practice, and feedback. Her solution was the skill lessons that focused on teaching specific writing skills twice a week. For Ms. Kranowski and her students, this solution was successful. Her students began acquiring and maintaining the targeted writing skills. Now she is asking questions and planning for generalization and application.

Developing an Individualized Education Program

For those students who have been identified as handicapped (including students who are learning-disabled and emotionally handicapped) and who receive special education services, procedures for setting goals and planning instruction have been designated by law. The yearly determination of learning and instructional goals is orchestrated through an individualized education planning meeting as required by PL 94-142, the Education for All Handicapped Children Act of 1975. At this meeting the parent(s), the student (if appropriate), the student's teachers (usually the special education teacher), other relevant professionals (e.g., school psychologist, speech/language therapist), and a representative of the school district other than the students' teacher who is qualified to provide or supervise special education (e.g., principal, school psychologist, another special education teacher) meet to plan the annual education program for the student (Strickland and Turnbull, 1990). According to law, this educational plan must include:

1. The student's current level of performance in the areas of concern (e.g., reading, written expression, social skills, study skills)
2. Annual and short-term objectives
3. The specific education services to be provided and the extent to which the student will participate in regular education
4. The projected date for initiation of the program and anticipated duration of such services
5. A description of the schedule and evaluation procedures for determining whether objectives are being met

This program must be reviewed at least on an annual basis.

In addition to the areas mentioned above, the students' strategies for learning, and other relevant factors such as student motivation, prior knowledge, previous learning experiences, the teacher's attitudes and teaching style are generally taken into consideration when developing an individualized education program (IEP).

Figure 1.5 presents a sample IEP form completed for Derek, one of the students in Ms. Shiller's class. Ms. Shiller works with emotionally handicapped junior-high students in a self-contained setting. Derek, a student in Ms. Shiller's class, not only has serious emotional and behavior problems but is also several years below grade level and his expected achievement level in reading, written expression, and math. Derek has difficulty with oral language in the area of language use in that he does not vary his language style to match the context and the person to whom he is speaking. Consequently, Derek has goals and objectives written not only for behavior and social skills but also for reading, written expression, math, and language use. A major goal for Derek is to learn successfully in the regular classroom. Therefore, one annual goal is to attend regular classes for art, home economics or shop, math, and science by the end of the year. At this point, his social skills and behavior preclude him from attending any regular classes.

A major part of the IEP includes the annual goals and short-term objectives. The goals of an IEP usually cover the entire school year; short-term objectives usually cover a six- to nine-week period. Completion of a related set of the short-term objectives should lead to the accomplishment of the annual goal as demonstrated by the objectives and goals developed for Derek in the area of math. Whether writing annual goals or objectives, they should contain enough information so that they can be evaluated to determine if they have been met. This includes:

1. A description of the behavior the student will demonstrate once the objective or goal is accomplished
2. A description of the conditions under which the behavior will occur
3. The level of performance necessary to accomplish the objective or goal (Mager, 1975)

During the IEP meeting, Ms. Shiller shared the goals and objectives with Derek and his mother. Ms. Blake, Derek's mom, suggested two additional goals for Derek, which Ms. Shiller incorporated into the IEP.

Parental Involvement

The people who formulated PL 94-142 felt much like Ms. Shiller in their conviction that parents need to be actively involved in their handicapped child's education. Therefore, the following procedures, according to law, should be followed to encourage parent attendance and participation:

1. Parents should be notified well in advance of the meeting. The purpose, time, and location of the meeting and the persons who will be in attendance should be included in the notice. Parents should be informed that the student may attend.

2. Schedule the meeting at an agreed-upon time and place.
3. If neither parent can attend, the meeting should be rescheduled. If a parent still cannot attend, the school should use other methods to involve the parent such as telephone calls or home visits.
4. If a meeting is held without a parent in attendance, the school must document their attempts to involve the parent.
5. The parents must sign and receive a copy of their child's IEP.

This essentially describes what the law requires in involving parents. Chapter Twelve describes strategies teachers can use for actively involving parents in their child's education, including the planning aspects.

Student Involvement

By law, students only need to attend the IEP meetings if appropriate. In practice many students with learning and emotional handicaps do not attend these meetings, even when these students are in secondary-level settings. Yet involving students in this decision-making process assists them in developing a commitment to learning and helps them develop a sense of responsibility and control over the decisions made regarding their learning.

Why do many students not attend the conference? In interviewing junior-high, learning-disabled students and their parents, two major reasons are evident (Van Reusen and Bos, 1990). First, frequently parents are not aware that students can attend. Second, even when students are invited to attend, they choose not to because they feel that they do not know what to say or do and they are afraid that the major topic of discussion will be ''how bad they are doing.''

To alleviate these two concerns, Van Reusen and his colleagues developed an education planning strategy (I PLAN) that is designed to inform students and prepare them to partici-

FIGURE 1.5 *Individualized Education Program Form*

INDIVIDUALIZED EDUCATIONAL PLAN

Student's Name __Blake__ __Derek__ ___
                  Last   First   MI

Matric _____
Birthdate 5/10/79
Ethnic Code 1
Grade 7th

Student's Address 1948 Ford Street 85719 NA
                                   (Zip) Telephone Number

☑ Original
___ Addendum

Reason for Conference:
___ Staffing ___ Review ☑ IEP
___ IEP was interpreted in _____
Language _____ by _____

Interpreter's Name _____
The handicapping condition is __Emotionally Handicapped__ Initiation Date __Sept. 3, 1991__ Duration Date __12 months__
The delivery system shall be ___ Resource ☑ Self-Contained ___ Other _____
School __Wilcox Middle School__
The child shall participate in Special Education services approximately __4__ hour(s) per (day) / week, the balance of time will be spent in regular education.
                                                                          (circle one)

Related Service	Recommended Yes	No	Date	Init. Date		Related Service	Recommended Yes	No	Date	Init. Date
Speech Assessment		✓				Medical Svs.		✓		
Speech/Lang. Therapy		✓				Interpreter		✓		
Occupational Therapy		✓				Transportation	✓			7/3/88
Physical Therapy		✓				Other				
Counseling	✓			7/3/88						

Related Service	Recommended Yes	No	Date	Init. Date
Adaptive PE		✓		
Psychological Svs.		✓		
Vocational Ed.		✓		
Audiology Assessment		✓		
Audiology Svs.				

The child's current level of education performance (functioning levels in Intellectual Ability, Academic Achievement, Performance, Psychological Processes and Behavior) including strengths and weaknesses. Include name and levels of tests.

Woodcock-Johnson-R
	Grade Equiv
Reading	5.6
Math	3.4
Written Lang	3.2
Knowledge	7.8

IQ   FS-WISC-R   108

Behavior-conduct disorder
loses temper
hits others

Will work in class for two-week periods without losing temper or being inappropriately disruptive
Math 5.0   Written Lang 7.0
Reading 7.0

The recommendation is to ___ Add ___ Delete ☒ Continue The following service(s) of __self-contained services with counseling__

Those involved in the decision are as follows:

(Anyone who disagrees with placement recommendations should write "disagree" after his/her signature.)

Mrs. Cotterell 9/2/88	_Mr. Schiller_ 9/2/88	
Building Adm./Designee Date	Special Education Teacher Date	
	Mrs. Blake 9/2/88	
Derek Blake	Parent/Guardian Date	
Special Education Adm./Designee Date		
	Name/Position Date	
Student Date	Evaluator/Reviewer Date	
	Classroom Teacher Date	
	Name/Position Date	

The nature and content of the program has been explained to me. I also understand that: (1) all Special Education placements are on a temporary basis; (2) there will be a semester review by the staff; (3) a review of the placement and records relating to the placement can be made at any time; (4) a Special Education placement will not be made without my written consent; (5) I may obtain an independent evaluation; (6) all Special Education placements are subject to due process procedure; and (7) I may withhold my consent by refusing to sign this placement statement or withdraw my consent to the placement at any time. I approve of placement and I understand my rights.

(✓) I received prior written notice of the staffing.

Mrs. Blake 9/2/91
Signature of Parent or Guardian   Date

( ) I waive prior written notice of the staffing.
Date given to parent

For parent not attending: Notified by: _____   ( ) Conference   ( ) Phone   ( ) Other _____   Date _____

14

LONG TERM GOAL:

Attain a grade equivalent of 5.0 in math.

PROGRAM OR RELATED SERVICE _E.H. self contained_
PERSON(S) RESPONSIBLE _Ms. Schiller_
DURATION OF SERVICE (DAY/WEEK/YEAR) _4 hours_ PER _day_
FREQUENCY ___✓___ Min./Hrs./Days _____ DAY/WEEK/MONTH _____ OTHER

_____ ORIGINAL _____ ADDENDUM

SHORT TERM OBJECTIVES

The student will:	EVALUATION CRITERIA	METHOD OF EVALUATION	START DATE	DATE(S) OBJECTIVE EVALUATED	COMMENTS: TM=TOTALLY MET PM=PARTIALLY MET UM=UNMET NA=NOT ATTEMPTED
learn multiplication facts to automatic level with 95% accuracy		Teacher-made test	9/3/91		
learn division facts to automatic level with 95% accuracy		same			
learn to add and subtract fractions with 90% accuracy		same	10/1/91		
learn to complete 2-step story problems using +, -, x, ÷ with whole #s to 90% accuracy		same	9/15/91		
learn to measure in 1/8 inch increments with 90% accuracy					

MATERIALS USED OR ADDITIONAL COMMENTS:
use computer-drill and practice software for learning facts
teach strategy for solving story problems
use manipulative for fractions

Apply the Concept 1.1

I PLAN: AN EDUCATIONAL PLANNING STRATEGY

Purpose: To provide students with the skills and knowledge to participate effectively in an educational planning conference.

Target Audience: The strategy can be taught to students in upper elementary or secondary settings who will be participating in an educational planning conference. This could include an IEP conference as well as other educational planning conferences.

Type of Instruction: Small group to large group instruction, usually three to ten students.

Time: Five to six hours of instruction.

Description of Strategy: The strategy the students learn consists of five steps. They complete the first step prior to the conference and use the remaining steps during the conference. The steps are:

Step 1: Inventory your
            learning strengths
            learning weaknesses
            goals and interests
            choices for learning
Step 2: Provide your inventory information
Step 3: Listen and respond
Step 4: Ask questions
Step 5: Name your goals

To help the students remember the steps in the strategy, the acronym *I PLAN* can be made from the first letter in each step.

The teacher and students participate in activities that assist the students in creating an Inventory Sheet. This sheet lists their learning strengths, learning weaknesses to improve, learning and career goals and interests, and ways they learn best (e.g., size of group, type of activity, type of test).

The students are also taught to use *Share Behaviors* to help with effective communication during the conference. They are:

Sit up straight
Have a pleasant tone of voice
Activate your thinking
    Tell yourself to pay attention
    Tell yourself to participate
    Tell yourself to compare ideas
Relax
    Don't look uptight
    Tell yourself to stay calm
Engage in eye communication

Teaching the Strategy: The strategy is taught by using the acquisition and generalization steps used to teach motivation strategies. Motivation strategies are techniques and procedures that involve the learner in the learning process, and they are used to increase the students' commitment to learn. They represent processes that learners can acquire and use to increase their interest and efforts in learning and to gain greater control over their own learning progress (Van Reusen, Bos, Deshler, and Schumaker, 1987). The strategies are based on research in motivation and are adapted from the learning strategies model (Alley and Deshler, 1979).

The teacher uses seven steps to teach the strategy:

Step 1: Orient and Obtain Commitment
Step 2: Describe
Step 3: Model and Prepare
Step 4: Verbal Rehearsal
Step 5: Group Practice and Feedback
Step 6: Individual Practice and Feedback
Step 7: Generalization

During the first step, the teacher and students discuss how involvement in education planning conferences will empower students by giving them more control over what they are learning. The importance and purpose of these conferences are discussed and the teacher obtains the students' commitment to learn the *I PLAN* strategy.

During the second step, *Describe,* the strategy is described to the students and the students begin to memorize the steps in the strategy and the *SHARE* behaviors.

During the third step, *Model and Prepare,* the students work with the teacher to prepare their Inventory Sheets. Through modeling and discussion, they systematically develop lists of learning strengths and weaknesses in the areas of reading, math, writing, study skills, social skills, and vocational skills. Based on these same areas and their current classes, they also identify weaknesses to improve. They also inventory their learning and career goals and interests and their preference for learning. In addition to preparing the Inventory Sheet, the teacher models the rest of the steps in the strategy (*PLAN*) and the *SHARE* behaviors.

During the fourth step, *Verbal Rehearsal,* students learn the steps in the *I PLAN* strategy and the *SHARE* behavior to an automatic level.

During the fifth step, *Group Practice and Feedback,* students review the steps in the strategy and practice using the strategy by providing feedback to each other during a simulated planning conference.

During the sixth step, *Individual Practice and Feedback,* students practice the strategy with the teacher during a simulated conference.

During the seventh step, *Generalization,* students use the steps in the strategy during the scheduled educational planning conference. Once the strategy has been taught, it can be reviewed for each additional educational planning conference scheduled and the Inventory Sheet can be updated or redeveloped.

A teaching manual has been developed that explicitly describes how to teach the *I PLAN* strategy (Van Reusen, Bos, Deshler, and Schumaker, 1987).

---

pate in educational planning conferences (Van Reusen, Bos, Deshler, and Schumaker, 1987). Teachers can teach students this strategy in about five to six hours over a one- to two-week period. We have found that junior-high and high-school learning-disabled students who learn this strategy provide more information during IEP conferences than students who are only told about the IEP conference but not taught the strategy (Bos and Van Reusen, 1986; Van Reusen and Bos, 1990). Apply the Concept 1.1 describes this strategy and how to teach it.

Evaluating Student Progress

According to the instructional cycle (Figure 1.2), once learning and instructional goals have been established and instruction has been planned, then instruction is implemented. However, instruction is more effective and efficient if, at the same time the instruction is being implemented, it is also being evaluated and modified based on the evaluation information.

As teachers, we evaluate student progress in our heads all the time. Think for a minute about the last time you listened to a student read aloud or watched a student complete a math word problem. Did you listen to the student's reading fluency, noticing whether or not he or she read with expression and meaning? Did you take note of the type of word identification errors the student made and the skills and strategies the student used when he or she tried to figure out an unknown word? Did you watch as the student read the word problem, analyzed the problem, and set up the computational problem? Did you notice what steps the student used to compute the answer, and if he or she checked the answer? Did you check the correctness of the answer? If you answered these questions affirmatively, then you were evaluating the student and his or her progress.

Evaluating students and making instructional decisions based on those evaluations are important for effective instruction, whether we evaluate "in our heads" or "on paper." Some general guidelines for evaluating student progress are:

1. Observe the process as well as the product. A correct product does not necessarily indicate that the student understands the process.
2. Have the student talk about what he or she is doing. Sometimes you may have difficulty understanding the process a student is using to complete a task. Asking the student to explain what he or she is doing and thinking can assist in evaluation.
3. Observe not only if the student can complete the task, but how comfortable or proficient the student is in completing it.

4. Evaluate not only for learning, but for maintenance, generalization, and application of the skill or knowledge.

As we evaluate, it is important to keep some type of written record of student progress. The written record provides a means for objectively reflecting on the data to determine if progress is evident (Deno, 1985; Fuchs, Deno, and Mirkin, 1984; Haring, Liberty, and White, 1980; Isaacson, 1988; Utley, Zigmond, and Strain, 1987). This written record also provides a means for communicating with others regarding student progress. Sharing progress with parents, principals, other teachers, and, most importantly, the student provides a sense of accomplishment and satisfaction for all involved. Having students monitor their own progress can increase their motivation toward learning and give them a sense of pride in learning. Self-monitoring procedures have been used with students who have learning and behavior problems (e.g., Frith and Armstrong, 1986; Hallahan, Lloyd, Kosiewicz, Kauffman, and Graves, 1979; Jackson and Boag, 1981; Swanson, 1985).

Types of Evaluation Measures

Although there are many methods a teacher or student can use to evaluate progress, generally these methods can be divided into three types: progress graphs, progress charts, and performance records. The first two types are frequently used for measuring daily progress on individual skills or knowledge, and the third type is usually used for measuring overall progress across a considerable length of time (e.g., grading period, semester, year).

Progress Graphs
Progress graphs are generally used to measure progress on one behavior or skill. Graphs seem particularly suited for self-monitoring because the results are displayed in such a manner that they are easy to interpret (see Figures 1.6 and 1.7). To use a progress graph, the behavior,

skill, or knowledge must be quantifiable, either by time or by occurrence. For example, Ms. Shiller, the junior-high teacher for a self-contained classroom of emotionally handicapped students, uses progress graphs for the following activities:

1. Silent reading rate
2. Speed in completing math facts
3. Percent of questions answered correctly for the social studies assignment
4. Number of times student disrupted other students during the morning independent learning activity
5. Student and teacher rating of written pieces based on interest and readability

With a progress graph the measurement unit is marked on the vertical axis. For example, time would be marked on the vertical axis for silent reading rate and speed in completing math facts. Percent would be marked on the vertical axis for the percent of social studies questions answered. On the horizontal axis, the occurrence unit is marked (e.g., date, teaching session, social studies assignment number). It is relatively easy to plot progress data on either a line graph, as depicted in Figure 1.6 or a bar graph (Figure 1.7).

Progress Charts
Progress charts are usually used in the same manner as progress graphs, to measure progress on one skill or behavior. The difference between a progress chart and graph is that with a chart you report the score but do not present it in a relational manner (see Figure 1.8). Although progress charts are generally more efficient in the use of space, they do not provide the clear visual representation of the student performance; therefore, student progress or lack of it is not so automatically apparent. Consequently, graphing is generally recommended for student self-monitoring over charting.

Performance Records
Performance records are often used to record student progress across a set of skills or knowl-

FIGURE 1.6   *Timing Chart Using a Line Graph*

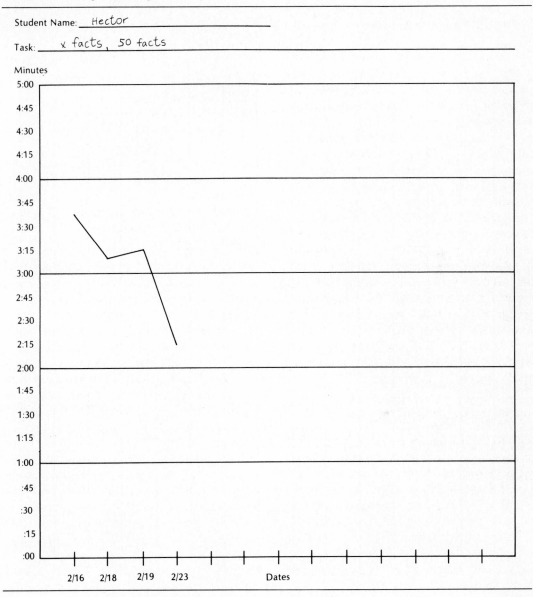

Student Name: *Hector*

Task: *x facts, 50 facts*

edge and for a significant length of time. An IEP is a performance record in that annual goals and short-term objectives are written, and evaluation of the goals and objectives is recorded on the IEP (see Figure 1.5). Many school districts have developed skill and knowledge competencies or objectives that students need to attain at various grade levels. These are often arranged on an individual student performance record so that as a student becomes proficient in a listed competency, it can be noted (see Figure 1.9). Many commercial

FIGURE 1.7   *Timing Chart*

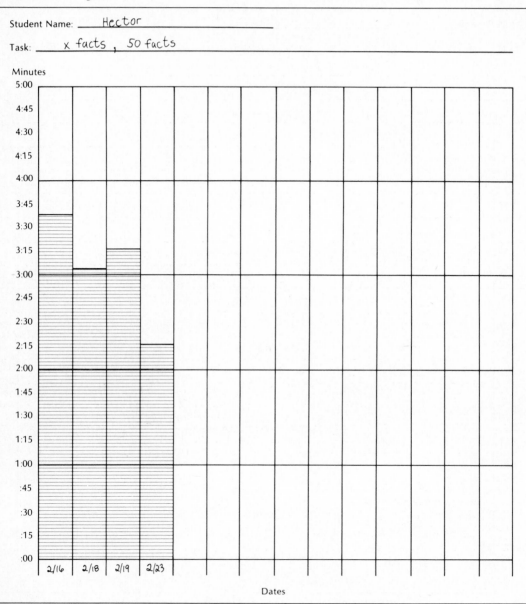

Student Name: ___Hector___

Task: ___x facts , 50 facts___

reading, math, writing, and other content area programs publish performance records so that student progress can be recorded. One caution in using such performance records is that although most of them measure proficiency they do not measure maintenance, generalization, or application. Consequently, a teacher may receive a performance record on a student and find that the student cannot perform some of the skills listed as mastered.

FIGURE 1.8　*Progress Chart for Sight Words*

Name:　Lisa

	3/12	3/14	3/15	3/18
sometimes	+　+　+	+　+　+	+　+　+	+　+　+
everyone	−　−　o	−　o　+	o　+　+	+　+　+
when	−　−　−	o　o　+	−　o　+	o　+　+
themselves	−　o　+	o　+　+	o　+　+	+　+　+
mystery	−　o　o	o　o　+	+　o　+	+　o　+
hurry	o　o　+	+　+　+	+　+　+	+　+　+
their	−　o　−	o　+　o	+　o　+	+　+　+
friend	+　o　+	+　+　+	+　+　+	+　+　+
mountain	−　o　o	o　o　+	+　+　o	+　+　+
trail	−　+　−	−　o　−	−　+　+	+　o　+
route	−　−　o	o　+　o	o　+　o	o　o　+

+　Correct and Automatic

o　Correct but Not Automatic

−　Incorrect

Another type of performance record is permanent products of performance. Collecting writing, reading, and math samples or the progress graphs and charts collected across a school year can provide the teacher with data for evaluating progress. Whereas reading samples can be collected on audiotape, sample written products of math and written pieces can be collected. The teacher may want to set up a portfolio for each student in the class. Have the students help select which pieces to place in the folder, and then review the products with them periodically, identifying areas of progress and areas that need further improvement.

In addition to collecting permanent products, the teacher and/or the students may want to

FIGURE 1.9 *Sample Competency-Based Performance Record*

Student: Karen

Competency Area and Skill	Date of Mastery
Reading	
Early Reading	
Identifies letters of alphabet	10/87
Names letters of alphabet	12/87
Holds book and turn pages one at a time	9/87
Looks first at the left page and then at right	9/87
Distinguishes print from pictures	9/87
Scans in left to right, top to bottom directions	9/87
Reads along when listening to a familiar book	9/87
Rhymes words	11/87
Identifies words in a familiar book	10/87
Beginning Reading	
Reads simple stories (preprimer/primer level)	3/88
Identifies consonant sounds	2/88
Identifies short vowel sounds	2/88
Identifies long vowel sounds	4/88
Identifies simple sight words in isolation	2/88
Recognizes that "s" makes sounds plural	4/88
etc.	

keep progress journals. Usually this journal accompanies a portfolio and provides the student or teacher a space where each can write comments concerning progress. Ms. Shiller found that progress journals were particularly helpful for documenting progress regarding students' behavior. She used this in combination with graphs to evaluate several students' progress. She found that her dated journal entries provided insights into how she might modify the instructional context and the instruction.

One of the major obstacles in evaluating student progress is planning and organizing an evaluation system. Early in the school year:

1. Determine what you want to evaluate.
2. Determine how you will evaluate it (e.g. progress graphs, charts, permanent product records, progress journals).
3. Determine if and when you will use student self-monitoring.

4. Develop the forms you need for evaluation.
5. Set up the system so that it is easy to collect, file, and retrieve progress data.

Coordinate your evaluation system with the school system, and then collect and use the data to make instructional decisions.

Invitation for Learning

As you read this book, we encourage you to reflect on how the information presented can be interwoven into your beliefs and thoughts about the teaching-learning process. We also encourage you to use the reflective, problem-solving orientation to teaching that Ms. Kranowski did in her classroom. A reflective, problem-solving model of teaching and learning is critical for success with students who have learning and behavior problems.

Chapter Two

Approaches to Learning and Teaching

Chapter Questions

- *Within the operant learning model, what procedures can be used to increase desirable behavior? Decrease undesirable behavior?*
- *What are the stages of learning and how can they be applied using the operant learning model?*
- *What are the common characteristics of most cognitive behavior modification interventions?*
- *Using principles associated with cognitive behavior modification, design a strategy that one could use to solve subtraction problems with regrouping.*
- *What implications does a sociocultural perspective have on teaching and learning?*
- *How does long-term memory relate to working memory and perception?*
- *Using implications from information processing and schema theories, what could you do to assist a student who is having difficulties remembering the information needed to pass an objective social studies test?*

Models and theories for learning can assist us in understanding and explaining how students learn. They also guide us in modifying our teaching and the learning context to promote effective and efficient learning. This chapter overviews four theories or approaches to learning and teaching: operant learning, cognitive behavior modification, a sociocultural theory of learning, and information processing and schema theory. The models are sequenced in the chapter from less cognitively oriented, operant learning, to more cognitively oriented, information processing and schema theory. Many of the general principles presented in this chapter will be applied to specific content areas in the subsequent chapters. As you read this chapter, we encourage you to think about students who you know are not succeeding in school and who have learning and behavior problems. How are their learning patterns and habits explained by the various approaches to learning described in this chapter? What general teaching principles do the different approaches suggest to help such students? We will begin by looking at operant learning, a theory that has provided educators with a variety of techniques for improving student behavior and learning.

Operant Learning

Operant learning theorists believe that behavior is learned and, for this reason, it can be unlearned or the student can be taught new behaviors. Operant learning focuses on identifying observable behaviors and manipulating the antecedents and consequences of these behaviors to change behavior. Operant learning theory is not concerned with what you think or tell yourself during the learning process.

In this section on operant learning we will discuss how to increase behaviors we want to see continued and how to eliminate undesirable behaviors through extinction, reinforcing incompatible behaviors, punishment, and time-out, and how to teach to different levels of learning.

Increasing Desirable Behaviors

During the past few weeks, Ms. Glenn has focused on teaching Marjorie, Sheila, and Jose subtraction with regrouping. During this time she demonstrated many of the principles by using "ten packs" of sticks. The students recently practiced applying the principles on the chalkboard. Ms. Glenn then asked the students to practice the skills independently by completing a math paper with twelve subtraction-with-regrouping problems. She watched them complete the first problem correctly. She then needed to teach another group, yet she wanted to be sure that these three students would continue the desirable behavior of working on their math while she was working with her other group.

According to operant learning, behavior is controlled by the consequences that follow it. Ms. Glenn needed to decide what consequences would follow "math performing behavior" in order to maintain or increase its occurrence. She told Marjorie, Sheila, and Jose, "If you complete this math sheet with 80 percent or better accuracy, I will let you have five minutes of free time in the Fun Corner." Free time in the Fun Corner was very reinforcing to all three students, and they accurately completed the math sheet while she worked with other students.

There are several principles to apply when attempting to maintain or increase behavior:

1. The behavior must already be in the student's repertoire. In the preceding example, Ms. Glenn's students knew how to perform the math task. Reinforcing them with free time in the Fun Corner would have been an ineffective consequence if they did not know how to perform the assigned task. If you want to maintain or increase social or academic behaviors, you must first be sure the student knows how to perform the target behaviors.

2. A consequence must follow the precise behavior you want to change or be linked to it through language. For example, "Because you completed all of your math assignments this week, I'll let you select a movie to watch on the VCR.''

3. A reinforcer is whatever follows a behavior and maintains or increases the rate of the behavior.

4. To be most powerful, reinforcement should occur immediately following the behavior.

Thus, to control behavior all we need to learn is to control the consequence that follows the behavior. Consequences that increase behavior, such as reinforcement and the Premack Principle, will be discussed next.

Reinforcement

Reinforcement is the most significant means of increasing desirable behavior. There are two types of reinforcement, positive and negative; both increase responding. How do they differ? The major difference between positive and negative reinforcement is that *positive reinforcement* is the presentation of a stimulus to increase responding, whereas *negative reinforcement* is the removal of a stimulus to increase responding.

Positive reinforcement increases responding by following the target behavior with activities, objects, food, and social rewards, which include such things as ice cream, toys, clothes, and privileges such as helping the teacher or having an extra recess.

When using reinforcers it is important to start with more *intrinsic reinforcers* such as using activities that are reinforcing to the student (e.g., listening to records, coloring) and move to more *tangible reinforcers* such as tokens and food only as necessary. For example, Christian (1983) suggests a seven-level hierarchy of reinforcers, ranging from food and hugs to internal self-reinforcement (''I did a good job''). This hierarchy is presented in Table 2.1.

The practice of negative reinforcement is often misused because the term *negative* is misinterpreted to mean harmful or bad and, therefore, the implication is that positive reinforcement is good and negative reinforcement is bad. Negative reinforcement means taking away something unpleasant or punishing contingent on the performance of a specific behavior. If a teacher scowls at a student until the student works, removing the scowl is negative reinforcement. The learning that takes place through negative reinforcement is avoidance learning. A

TABLE 2.1   *A Practical Reinforcement Hierarchy for Classroom Behavior Modification*

	A Infantile Physical Contact	B Food	C Toys	D School Implements	E Privileges	F Praise	G Internal Self-Reinforcement
Consequence Level							
Examples	Hugs	Milk	Balloon	Eraser	Free Time	Verbal Comments	"I did well."
	Pats	Raisins	Marble	Ruler	Errands	Grades	"My work's all complete."
	Physical Proximity	Crackers	Kite	Notepad	Collect Papers	Certificate	
		Gum	Clay	Crayon			
	<— — — — — — — — Concreteness				Abstractness — — — — —>		

Source: B. T. Christian, ''A Practical Reinforcement Hierarchy for Classroom Behavior Modification,'' *Psychology in the Schools 20* (1983): 83–84. Reprinted with permission.

common use in schools is the completion of work assignments to avoid staying after school. The completion of work assignments is reinforced by the removal of the unpleasant task of staying after school. Children often use negative reinforcement with adults. An example is a child who throws a temper tantrum until he or she gets what he or she wants.

Secondary Reinforcer

A *secondary reinforcer* is a previously neutral behavior that is paired with a reinforcer and therefore takes on reinforcing properties of its own. Thus if the teacher always calls a student up to the teacher's desk prior to rewarding him or her, then being called to the teacher's desk becomes reinforcing—a secondary reinforcer.

Sincere praise and attention are the most frequently used secondary reinforcers. Teachers are often quite skillful at using such subtle but effective secondary reinforcers as a hand on the shoulder, a pat on the head, a smile, or a wink. Many teachers position themselves carefully in the room to be near students whose behavior they want to reinforce with their attention.

Token reinforcement systems are frequently used by special education teachers. Briefly, a *token system* is an economy in which a symbol (e.g., points, chips, or stars) is given contingent on designated behaviors. Tokens are symbols in that they usually have little inherent value themselves but can be exchanged for valuable things or privileges. Token systems can be very simple (e.g., receiving stars for completing writing assignments, with each star worth three minutes of extra recess); they can also be very complicated and may even involve a level system with rewards and privileges varying according to the level the student is on. Students are assigned to levels contingent upon their behavior. Being raised or lowered to a different level occurs as points are accumulated. Points are awarded and deducted for a full range of behaviors. More complicated token systems are typically used to manage aggressive behaviors displayed by severely disturbed students.

Shaping

If reinforcement maintains or increases the rate of behavior already occurring, what does the teacher do if the behavior is occurring at a very low rate or not at all?

For example, Mr. Kladder's goal is to shape Rhonda's behavior so that she is performing multiplication facts quickly and automatically. During the initial teaching phase Mr. Kladder rewards her for computing 3 × 5 by adding five threes. After Rhonda demonstrates she can perform this behavior with high accuracy, Mr. Kladder no longer reinforces her for adding the numbers but only for skip counting 5, 10, 15, and then writing the answer. After Rhonda is successfully able to skip count she is reinforced for computing the answer in her head and writing it down. Now Mr. Kladder begins to give Rhonda timed tests in which she is reinforced only for beating her best time. Like most good teachers, Mr. Kladder is *shaping* his student's behavior by reinforcing responses that more and more closely approximate the target response.

Premack Principle

If one activity occurs more frequently than another, the more frequently occurring activity can be used as a reinforcer to increase the rate of the less frequently occurring activity (Premack, 1959). For example, Adam more frequently participates in outdoor play than in writing stories. His teacher can make outdoor play contingent on completing the writing assignment. The advantage of the Premack Principle is that a teacher can use events that are already occurring in the classroom. One possibility is to inventory the student and rank behaviors from most liked to least liked, for example, (1) reading, (2) math, (3) spelling. Thus reading could be contingent on completing spelling. A more appropriate list for most students with learning and behavior problems might include five minutes of free time contingent on completing spelling. Reinforcing activities such as talking quietly with friends or listening to music can be used to increase the rate of less desirable activities such as completing a book report. Students who prefer activities that involve movement can be informed that they can engage in these behaviors contingent on their performance in less desirable activities such as sitting still and listening to the teacher.

Group Contingencies

Group contingencies can be used to increase desirable behavior or decrease undesirable behavior. When using *group contingencies,* a group of students, or an individual student, is either reinforced or loses reinforcement, contingent on the behavior of the entire group or a target student in the group. For example, the teacher could establish a twenty-minute block of free time at the end of the school day. Every time the noise level of the classroom exceeds the teacher's limits she subtracts one minute from the allocated free time. In addition to changing group behavior, group contingencies can be used to change the behavior of one student in the class. For instance, Carla is a twelve-year-old child who has been mainstreamed into a regular sixth-grade class. During Carla's first couple of weeks in the class she continually got into fights with her classmates during recess. The teacher told the class that she would extend their recess by ten minutes if Carla did not get into any fights during recess. The class included Carla in their group play and fighting was eliminated. However, there are dangers in group contingencies being dependent on the behavior of an individual. It is possible the individual will use his or her position to manipulate the behavior of others in the class. For example, Carla could say to the other students in the class, ''You better let me be captain of the team. Otherwise I'll get into a fight and you won't get extra recess.'' It is also possible that the individual will view himself or herself negatively because of this position.

Contingency Contracting

Contingency contracting is an agreement between two or more persons that specifies their behaviors and consequences. A common example of a contingency contract is the agreement

FIGURE 2.1 *Contingency Contract*

We agree that there will be no math homework on any school day in which 100% of the math assignment is completed with 80% accuracy during the time allotted for math during the school day.

Signed _____ (teacher)

                 _____ (student)

between parent and child regarding an allowance. The child agrees to perform certain behaviors in return for a specified amount of money each week. The objective of a contingency contract is to delineate the exchange of reinforcers between two or more persons (Hall, 1975).

The contingency contract should specify who is doing what, when, under what conditions, and for what consequences. The contract in Figure 2.1 was set up by a teacher and her learning-disabled student.

Decreasing Undesirable Behaviors

Unfortunately, students manifest behaviors that interfere with their learning or the learning of others. Techniques for decreasing these undesirable behaviors include: extinction, reinforcing incompatible behaviors, punishment, and time-out.

Extinction

Extinction is the removal of reinforcement following the behavior. For example, a teacher wants to extinguish a student's behavior of shouting out and determines that telling the student to raise his hand is reinforcing the shouting out. To extinguish shouting out, the teacher removes the reinforcer (''Raise your hand'') and ignores the student's shouting out.

Extinction can be an effective means of decreasing undesirable behaviors, but it is often slow and can be impractical for many behaviors that occur within the classroom because the reinforcers for the undesirable behavior are often difficult for the teacher to control. For example, let's return to the student who continually shouted out in class. In this situation the student was being reinforced not only by the classroom teacher's attention ("Raise your hand") but also by other students who looked and attended to him when he shouted out. A teacher attempting to reduce this behavior through extinction would have to eliminate both the teacher's reinforcement and the reinforcement of others in the class. To compound the difficulty, slip-ups by the teacher or students would intermittently reinforce the behavior and maintain it for a long time. As we discussed in the section on reinforcement schedules, intermittent reinforcement is a powerful way to maintain behavior and it is difficult to extinguish behaviors maintained on an intermittent schedule.

Another characteristic of extinction is its effect on the rate the target behavior continues to occur. During extinction the target behavior will increase in rate or intensity before decreasing. Thus a teacher attempting to eliminate tantrums through extinction will observe the tantrums occurring more frequently, lasting longer, and perhaps even being louder and more intense than before extinction. As long as the teacher continues to withhold reinforcement, usually attention, the rate and intensity will decrease and tantrums can be eliminated. For this reason it is extremely important to chart behavior when using extinction. Taking *baseline*, a record of the frequency and/or duration of the behavior before implementing the intervention, and continuing to take data after intervention is implemented, will document behavior change.

Although extinction can be an effective means of decreasing undesirable behaviors, it requires patience and the ability to control all of the reinforcers. Ignoring, the most frequently applied form of extinction in the classroom, is an important skill for teachers to learn. A summary of points to remember about using ignoring as a means of decreasing undesirable behavior follows:

1. Ignoring can be effective when the behavior is being reinforced by the teacher's attention.
2. If the teacher attempts to eliminate a behavior through ignoring, the behavior must be ignored every time it occurs.
3. Ignoring will not be effective if the behavior is being maintained by other reinforcers, such as the attention of classmates.

Reinforcing Incompatible Behavior

Ignoring can be most effective when it is paired with reinforcing an incompatible behavior. *Reinforcing an incompatible behavior* requires the teacher to target the undesirable activity. For example, while ignoring the out-of-seat behavior of a student, the teacher targets and reinforces the desirable behavior that is incompatible, in this case, in-seat behavior. Therefore, when Scott is sitting in his seat the teacher is quick to catch his appropriate behavior and reinforce. In addition, the teacher would intermittently reinforce Scott for being in his seat. Reinforcing incompatible behavior requires you, the teacher, to do four things:

1. Identify the behavior you want to change (interfering behavior).
2. Identify the incompatible behavior.
3. Discontinue reinforcing the interfering behavior.
4. Reinforce the desirable behavior in the target child or others who are displaying it.

Punishment

Punishment, the opposite of reinforcement, is following a behavior with a consequence that decreases the strength of the behavior or reduces the likelihood the behavior will continue to occur. Unfortunately, punishment does not assure the desired behavior will occur. For example, a student who is punished for talking in class may stop talking, but may not attend to his or her studies for the remainder of the day.

There are many significant arguments against the use of punishment:

1. Punishment is ineffective in the long run.
2. Punishment often causes undesirable emotional side effects such as fear, aggression, and resentment.
3. Punishment provides little information to the person as to what to do, teaching the individual only what not to do.
4. The person who administers the punishment is often associated with it and also becomes aversive.
5. Punishment frequently does not generalize across settings, thus it needs to be readministered.
6. Fear of punishment often leads to escape behavior.

If there are so many arguments for not using punishment, why is it so frequently used as a means for changing behavior? There are many explanations, including lack of familiarity with the consequences of punishment and the inability to effectively use a more positive approach. Also, punishment is often reinforcing to the punisher, reducing the occurrence of the undesirable behavior, therefore reinforcing its use.

Punishment should be used only when behaviors are harmful to the child or others. In this case, the student should be told ahead of time what the consequence (punishment) for exhibiting the behavior will be. When the undesirable behavior occurs, the punishment should be delivered quickly and as soon as the inappropriate behavior is initiated. Punishment should be applied consistently every time the designated behavior occurs. If you choose to use punishment you should identify several other behaviors you would like to see maintained and give extensive reinforcement for their occurrence.

Time-Out

Time-out occurs when the student is removed from the opportunity to receive any reinforcement. Time-out occurs when the teacher asks a student to sit in the hall during the remainder of a lesson, when a young child is asked to leave the group, or when a student is asked to sit in a quiet chair until he or she is ready to join the group.

Unfortunately, time-out is frequently used inappropriately. The underlying principle behind the successful use of time-out is that the environment the student is leaving must be reinforcing and the time-out environment must be without reinforcement. This may not be as easy to achieve as you might think. For example, when Elizabeth was talking and interfering with others during the science lesson, her teacher thought she would "decrease" Elizabeth's behavior by sending her to time-out, which was a chair in the back of the room away from the group. The teacher became discouraged when Elizabeth's inappropriate behavior during science class increased in subsequent lessons rather than decreased. A likely explanation for the ineffectiveness of time-out in this situation is that Elizabeth did not enjoy science class and she found sitting in a chair in the back of the room looking at books and toys reinforcing. The efficacy of time-out is strongly influenced by environmental factors. If the environment the student is leaving is unrewarding, then time-out is not an effective means of changing the student's behavior.

Teachers who use secluded time-out areas or contingent restraint (holding the student down plus withdrawal, exclusion, and seclusion) should be aware of the legal implications of such intervention, and should obtain the necessary authorization from within the school setting and from parents or guardians. Recommended procedures for successfully implementing time-out are listed in Apply the Concept 2.1.

Levels of Learning

One way the principles of operant learning can be applied is through stages of learning. The stages of learning (see Figure 2.2) are the levels a student may pass through in acquiring proficiency in learning. For example, the first stage of learning, *entry,* is the level of performance the student is presently performing. During the second stage, *acquisition,* the components of the

Apply the Concept 2.1

PROCEDURES FOR IMPLEMENTING TIME-OUT

Time-out, like punishment, should be used as a last resort. Teachers should discuss this intervention with school administrators and parents before implementing it.

1. The student should be told in advance which behaviors will result in time-out.
2. The amount of time the student will be in time-out should be specified ahead of time.
3. The amount of time the student is in time-out should be brief (between one to five minutes).
4. The student should be told once to go to time-out. If the student does not comply, the teacher should unemotionally place the student in time-out.
5. Time-out must occur every time the undesirable behavior occurs.
6. Contingencies should be set in advance for the student who fails to comply with time-out rules.
7. Do not leave the time-out area unmonitored.
8. When time-out is over, the student should return to the group.
9. Reinforce positive behaviors that occur after time-out.

FIGURE 2.2 *Stages of Learning*

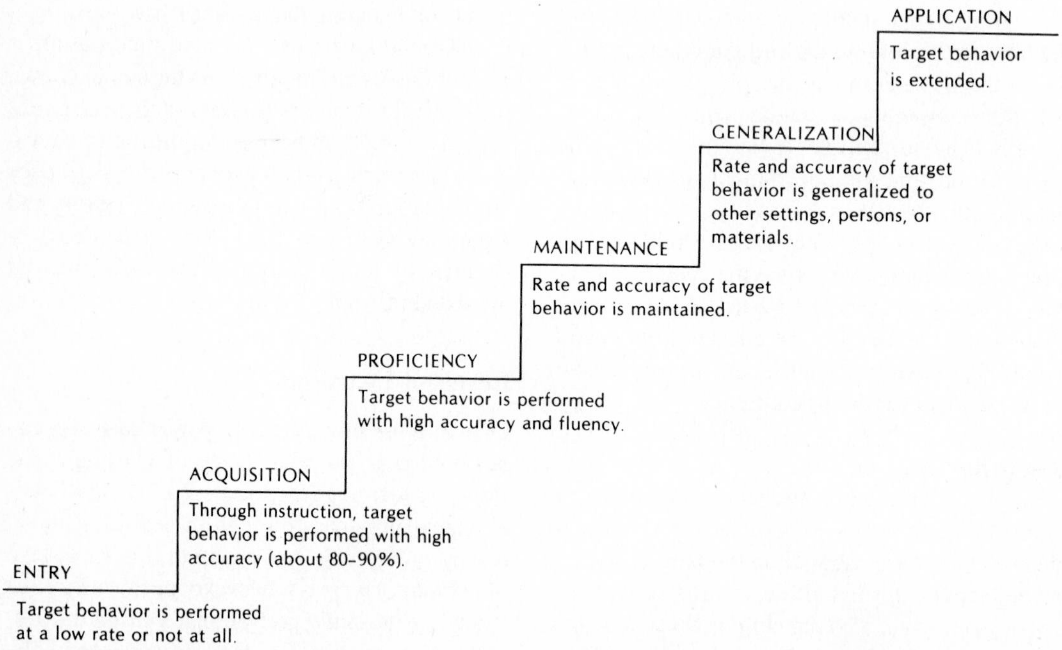

APPLICATION
Target behavior is extended.

GENERALIZATION
Rate and accuracy of target behavior is generalized to other settings, persons, or materials.

MAINTENANCE
Rate and accuracy of target behavior is maintained.

PROFICIENCY
Target behavior is performed with high accuracy and fluency.

ACQUISITION
Through instruction, target behavior is performed with high accuracy (about 80–90%).

ENTRY
Target behavior is performed at a low rate or not at all.

target behavior are sequenced into teachable elements. Each teachable element is taught to mastery through a high rate of reinforcement, shaping, and consistent use of cues. After the behavior is occurring at a high level of accuracy, the focus of the learning is on *proficiency*. During this level the teacher's goal is to increase the student's accuracy and fluency in performing the behavior. At the next level, *maintenance,* the goal is for the behavior to be maintained at the target level of accuracy and proficiency with intermittent reinforcement and a reduction in teacher assistance and cues. With reduced reinforcement and assistance, many students with learning and behavior disorders have difficulty maintaining behaviors. The next stage is *generalization*, in which the target behavior transfers across settings, persons, and materials. Stokes and Baer (1977) suggest that generalization may be a separate skill that needs to be taught. Apply the Concept 2.2 provides further information on how to teach for generalization. At the final level, *application*, the learner is required to extend and utilize the materials in new situations. Application is a difficult skill for special learners, and the teacher's role may be to demonstrate and delineate a range of opportunities for applying the newly acquired skill.

In summary, the principles of operant learning are applicable within the classroom for both instructional and classroom management purposes. Teachers can use such principles as positive and negative reinforcement, token reinforcement, shaping, the Premack Principle, and group contingencies to increase desired behaviors. Teachers who want to decrease undesirable behaviors can apply such principles as extinction, reinforcing incompatible behaviors, punishment, and time-out. (See Apply the Concept 2.3.)

Cognitive Behavior Modification

Cognitive behavior modification integrates notions from operant, social, and cognitive learning theories, and assumes that cognitive behavior (thinking processes), like observable behaviors, can be changed. This model of teaching and learning incorporates many of the principles of operant learning, but it adds some additional techniques that seem relevant when the goal of instruction is to change the way one thinks. Let's look at how Mrs. Neal uses cognitive behavior modification to help Marlow and his classmates better understand their science textbooks.

Marlow, a seventh grader in a class for emotionally handicapped students, and several of his classmates consistently have difficulty comprehending the important ideas from their textbooks, particularly in science. Even though they can identify most of the words in the text, they only remember a few details from what they read. Mrs. Neal wants to teach Marlow and his classmates how to understand and remember the major points. She decided that if she wants to teach the students this cognitive behavior, she will have to give them a consistent set of steps to use in completing the process, much in the same way we use a consistent set of steps to tie shoes. She also knows that for the students to learn what to do, they need to observe someone else. But how can she do this?

Mrs. Neal uses cognitive behavior modification. First, she selects the steps she wants to teach Marlow and the other students to use when they read their science text. Next, she and the students discuss the strategies the students currently use and their effectiveness. They also discuss the importance of improving this skill and the payoff for improvement. Mrs. Neal then tells the students about the steps she uses when she reads. To model these steps, she reads and explains what she is thinking. Then she gets the students to try the steps as she talks them through the steps. Finally, Mrs. Neal gives the students lots of opportunities to practice the steps when reading their textbooks, encouraging them at first to say the steps aloud as they work through them. She provides feedback on how they are doing and she also teaches them how to evaluate their own performance.

Apply the Concept 2.2 _____

GENERALIZATION STRATEGIES

Change Reinforcement

Description/Methods	*Examples*
Vary amount, power, and type of reinforcers.	
• Fade amount of reinforcement.	• Reduce frequency of reinforcement from completion of each assignment to completion of day's assignments.
• Decrease power of reinforcer from tangible reinforcers to verbal praise.	• Limit use of stars/stickers and add more specific statements, e.g., ''Hey, you did a really good job in your math book today.''
• Increase power of reinforcer when changing to mainstreamed setting.	• Give points in regular classroom although not needed in resource room.
• Use same reinforcers in different settings.	• Encourage all teachers working with student to use the same reinforcement program.

Change Cues

Description/Methods	*Examples*
Vary instructions systematically.	
• Use alternate/parallel directions.	• Use variations of cue, e.g., ''Find the . . .''; ''Give me the . . .''; ''Point to the . . . .''
• Change directions.	• Change length and vocabulary of directions to better represent the directions given in the regular classroom, e.g., ''Open your book to page 42 and do the problems in set A.''
	• Move from real objects to miniature objects.
• Use photograph.	• Use actual photograph of object or situation.
• Use picture to represent object.	• Move from object/photograph to picture of object or situation.
• Use line drawing or symbol representation.	• Use drawings from workbooks to represent objects or situations.
• Use varying print forms.	• Vary lower and upper case letters; vary print by using manuscript, boldface, primary type.
	• Move from manuscript to cursive.

Change Materials

Description/Methods	*Examples*
Vary materials within task.	
• Change medium.	• Use unlined paper, lined paper; change size of lines; change color of paper.
	• Use various writing instruments such as markers, pencil, pen, typewriter.
• Change media.	• Use materials such as films, microcomputers, filmstrips to present skills/concepts.
	• Provide opportunity for student to phase into mainstream.

Change Response Set

Description/Methods	*Examples*
Vary mode of responding.	
• Change how student is to respond.	• Ask child to write answers rather than always responding orally.
	• Teach student to respond to a variety of question types such as multiple choice, true/false, short answer.
• Change time allowed for responding.	• Decrease time allowed to complete math facts.

Change Some Dimension(s) of the Stimulus

Description/Methods	*Examples*
Vary the stimulus systematically.	
• Use single stimulus and change size, color, shape.	• Teach colors by changing the size, shape, and shade of "orange" objects.
• Add to number of distractors.	• Teach sight words by increasing number of words from which child is to choose.
• Use concrete (real) object.	• Introduce rhyming words by using real objects.
• Use toy or miniature representation.	• Use miniature objects when real objects are impractical.

Change Setting(s)

Description/Methods	*Examples*
Vary instructional work space.	
• Move from structured to less structured work arrangements.	• Move one-to-one teaching to different areas within classroom.
	• Provide opportunity for independent work.
	• Move from one-to-one instruction to small-group format.
	• Provide opportunity for student to interact in large group.

Change Teachers

Description/Methods	*Examples*
Vary instructors.	
• Assign child to work with different teacher.	• Select tasks so that child has opportunities to work with instructional aide, peer tutor, volunteer, regular classroom teacher, and parents.

Source: S. Vaughn, C. S. Bos, and K. A. Lund, *Teaching Exceptional Children* (Spring 1986): 177–178.

Apply the Concept 2.3 _____

THE CLASSROOM BASED ON OPERANT LEARNING

In a classroom based on operant learning theory, the teacher has behavioral objectives that specify the behavior the students need to perform to be judged successful. If the target response does not occur naturally, then it is important for the teacher to develop a method of shaping the behavior. The behaviors are sequenced from the simple to the more difficult. A full range of reinforcers, such as verbal praise, smiles from the teacher, gold stars, tokens, free time, and other specialized reinforcers that are effective with students, are used. Students are dealt with individually, with target behaviors reflecting the needs of the student. Behaviors are initially taught through continuous reinforcement; after acquisition of these behaviors, they are maintained through intermittent reinforcement. Teachers reduce inappropriate behavior by ignoring it and reinforcing incompatible behavior. Teachers avoid the use of punishment. Behaviors are discussed in observable terms and learning is measured by the acquisition of new behaviors.

Using these systematic techniques, Mrs. Neal finds that in several weeks Marlow and his classmates are improving in their ability to remember the important information from their science text. In addition, they are beginning not to rely so much on the strategy she taught them. It is almost as if they are using it automatically, without having to consciously remember to use it. Mrs. Neal feels that she has taught her students a good strategy for thinking about what they are reading and that she has changed their cognitive behavior (thinking processes).

Mrs. Neal used *cognitive behavior modification* (CBM). This approach includes an analysis of the task as well as an analysis of the thinking processes involved in performing the task. It also includes a training regimen that utilizes modeling, self-instructional techniques, and evaluation of performance (Meichenbaum, 1977, 1983).

Several key learning and teaching principles are associated with CBM. One principle of CBM is *cognitive modeling*. When Mrs. Neal explained what she was thinking as she read, she was using cognitive modeling. Another principle is *guided instruction*. Mrs. Neal used this principle when she guided the students through the reading task by telling them the steps in the process as they read. *Self-instruction* is another principle. When learners use language to guide their performance, they are using self-instruction. For instance, if you talk or think through the steps in solving a complex algebra problem while completing it, you are using self-instruction. If you talk aloud, it is called *overt self-instruction;* if you think to yourself, it is referred to as *covert self-instruction*.

Self-evaluation and self-regulation are two more principles of CBM. *Self-evaluation* refers to making judgments concerning the quality or quantity of performance. Mrs. Neal had Marlow and his classmates judge the quality of their performance by having them pause at the end of each section of the science text and comment on how they were doing. *Self-regulation* refers to the learner monitoring his or her own thinking strategies through language mediation. Self-regulation also occurs when the learner corrects or uses fix-up strategies when he or she detects a problem. For example, Mrs. Neal taught Marlow and his classmates to say to themselves what the main idea was when they finished reading each paragraph or section of the text. If the students could not give the main idea, then she demonstrated and encouraged them to use a fix-up strategy. In this case, she showed them how to go back and reread the first sentence in the paragraph to see if that helped them to remember the main idea. If this did not work, she demonstrated how to review the paragraph quickly.

Origins of Cognitive Behavior Modification

Cognitive behavior modification has origins from several theories in the psychology of learning (Harris, 1982, 1985). From operant learning come the principles of behavior modification. Behavior modification techniques such as task-analyzing the skill to be learned, providing cues to the learner, and using reinforcement and corrective feedback have been incorporated into many CBM training programs.

Social learning theory (Bandura, 1977) has also influenced CBM. A major assumption of social learning theory is the notion that affective, cognitive, and behavior variables interact in the learning process. For example, the extent to which Eva understands the cognitive concepts of place value will affect how well she performs the behavior of computing three-digit subtraction problems with regrouping. Motivation and other affective variables also interact. Eva will probably perform the subtraction more accurately and carefully if she is determining whether there is enough money in her bank to buy a new record than if she is doing the twenty-fifth problem on a page of assigned subtraction problems.

The notion that we learn through watching others is another assumption that comes from social learning theory (Bandura, 1977). In social learning theory the importance of modeling is emphasized in relation to social behaviors (e.g., aggressive and cooperative behaviors). In CBM, modeling has been expanded to include cognitive modeling. When Mrs. Neal "talked aloud" what she was thinking as she read, she was using cognitive modeling.

Cognitive theory and cognitive training have also had a strong influence on CBM. Like cognitive training, CBM explicitly teaches problem solving and relies heavily on principles of self-regulation and self-evaluation.

Common Features of CBM Interventions

Cognitive behavior modification interventions or training regimens have been used to develop a range of academic and social skills. Lloyd (1980) identified five common features found in most CBM techniques: strategy steps, modeling, self-regulation, verbalization, and reflective thinking.

Strategy Steps

A series of steps is usually identified for the student to work through when solving a problem or completing a task. These steps are based on a task analysis of the cognitive and observable behaviors needed to complete the task. Before Mrs. Neal began teaching, she determined the steps in the reading strategy she wanted to teach Marlow and his classmates.

Graham and Harris and their colleagues have developed a series of writing strategies to assist students in writing stories and other pieces (e.g., Graham and Harris, 1989a, 1989b; Harris and Graham, 1985). Each strategy has steps that the students learn to assist them with specific aspects of writing. For example, to help students write a story Graham and Harris (1989a) used the following strategy steps:

1. Look at the picture (picture prompts were used.)
2. Let your mind be free.
3. Write down the story part reminder (W-W-W; What = 2; How = 2). The questions for the story part reminder were:
   - Who is the main character? Who else is in the story?
   - When does the story take place?
   - Where does the story take place?
   - What does the main character want to do?
   - What happens when he or she tries to do it?

- How does the story end?
- How does the main character feel?

4. Write down the story part ideas for each part.
5. Write your own story; use good parts and make sense.

Modeling

In CBM, modeling is used as a primary means of instruction. Research in social learning theory as well as in CBM supports the notion that modeling is a very effective teaching technique. With CBM, students are asked not only to watch observable behaviors as the instructor performs the task, but also to listen to the instructor's self-talk. In this way the instructor is modeling both observable behaviors and the unobservable thinking processes associated with those behaviors. Being able to model unobservable thinking processes is an important component for teaching such cognitive skills as verbal math problem solving, finding the main idea in a paragraph, editing written work, and solving social problems. In most instances the person modeling is the teacher or a peer, but video and puppets have also been used effectively for modeling. Vaughn, Ridley, and Bullock (1984) used puppets as models for teaching interpersonal social skills to young, aggressive children. The puppets were used to demonstrate appropriate social behaviors and strategies for solving interpersonal problems.

Self-Regulation

Self-regulation refers to the learner monitoring his or her thinking and actions through language mediation. When Meichenbaum (1977) developed his CBM training for improving the self-control of hyperactive children, he used Vygotsky's notions about how language affects socialization and learning processes. Luria (1961) and Vygotsky (1962) suggest that children become socialized using verbal self-regulation. Children first use language to mediate their actions by overtly engaging in self-instruction

and self-monitoring. Later, this language mediation becomes covert.

Using self-regulation, students act as their own teachers. Students are expected to take active roles in the learning process and to be responsible for their own learning. Although they work under the guidance of a teacher, students are expected to monitor their learning, change or modify strategies when difficulties arise, evaluate their performance, and in some cases provide self-reinforcement. For example, Kosiewicz, Hallahan, Lloyd, and Graves (1982) used self-instruction in combination with self-correction to improve the handwriting legibility of a ten-year-old, learning-disabled boy. The self-instruction consisted of having the child do the following:

1. Say aloud the word to be written.
2. Say the first syllable.
3. Name each of the letters in the syllable three times.
4. Repeat each letter as it is written.
5. Repeat steps 2 through 4 for each syllable.

For self-correction, the student was asked to judge each letter and circle the errors in a list or paragraph he had copied on the previous day. Both of these techniques reflect self-regulation in that the student is performing the techniques independently and is responsible for his learning.

Verbalization

Verbalization is typically a component of self-instruction and self-monitoring with overt verbalization being faded to covert verbalization. Many CBM programs rely on a "talk aloud" or "think aloud" technique. After listening to the teacher think aloud as he or she performs the targeted processes and task, students are encouraged to talk aloud as they initially learn the strategy. For example, Ramon might say the following as he completes a two-digit subtraction problem without regrouping, "Start at the one's place and take the bottom number away from the top. Write the answer in the one's place. Now go to the ten's place. Do the same thing.'' Usually these overt verbalizations only occur during the initial stages of learning. As the strategy becomes more automatic, students are encouraged to ''think to themselves'' instead of ''aloud.''

In addition to verbalization concerning the learning processes, students are also encouraged to make self-statements about their performance. For example, ''That part is done. Now go to the next part.'' or ''I'm getting much faster at this.'' or ''I need to think about all my choices before I decide.'' Figure 2.3 presents examples of coping self-statements rehearsed by clients participating in a CBM program to control anger. This training (Novaco, 1975) was used to assist clients in coping with their negative emotions. As part of the training, clients were asked to imagine various anger-engendering situations and to rehearse self-statements such as the ones given in Figure 2.3.

Meichenbaum (1977) has suggested several ways to encourage students to use self-talk:

1. The teacher can model self-talk and self-statements as he or she performs the task.

2. The teacher can begin with tasks for which the students are already somewhat proficient. Later, as the students are comfortable with self-talk, the teacher can switch to the targeted tasks.

3. Students can develop and use cue cards to help them remember the steps they are to talk through. For example, Camp, Blom, Herbert, and Van Doorninck (1977) used the pictures in Figure 2.4 as cue cards when teaching self-control to twelve aggressive second-grade boys. The program began by using a ''copy-cat'' game in which the boys learned to ask themselves the four questions depicted in Figure 2.4. The cue cards were used as reminders to self-verbalize as the boys applied these questions first to cognitive and then to interpersonal tasks.

Reflective Thinking

Reflective thinking requires students to take the time to think about what they are doing. Teaching students who have learning and behavior problems to ''stop and think'' is an important skill to include in instruction. Many of these students are impulsive in their actions, seeming to act without thinking (Blackman and Goldman, 1982; Kauffman, 1985; Keogh and Donlon, 1972). These students have limited and ineffective strategies for approaching academic tasks or social situations. They approach these tasks and situations in a disorganized, haphazard way, and often without thinking about the consequence of the actions (Torgesen, 1982; Torgesen and Licht, 1983; Wallace and Kauffman, 1986). In using CBM training programs, teachers assist students in using reflective thinking.

Let's look at how Wong, Wong, Perry, and Sawatsky (1986) encouraged reflective thinking when they taught seventh-grade students to use self-questioning when summarizing social studies texts. After teaching the students how to identify the main idea of paragraphs and how to summarize paragraphs, Wong and colleagues taught the students a summarization strategy. The summarization form (see Figure 2.5) and the steps in this strategy required the students to be reflective in their reading. The questions the students asked themselves were:

1. In this paragraph, is there anything I don't understand?
2. In this paragraph, what's the most important sentence (main-idea sentence)? Let me underline it.
3. Let me summarize the paragraph. To summarize, I rewrite the main-idea sentence, and add important details.
4. Now, does my summary statement link up with the subheading?
5. When I have written summary statements for a whole subsection:
   a. Let me review my summary statements for the whole subsection. (A subsection is one with several paragraphs under the same subheading.)
   b. Do my summary statements link up with one another?

FIGURE 2.3 *Examples of Self-Statements Rehearsed in Controlling Anger*

Preparing for an Angering Situation

This is going to upset me, but I know how to deal with it.
What is it that I have to do?
I can work out a plan to handle this.
I can manage the situation. I know how to regulate my anger.
If I find myself getting upset, I'll know what to do.
Try not to take this too seriously.

Encountering the Angering Situation

Stay calm. Just continue to relax.
As long as I keep my cool, I'm in control.
Just roll with the punches; don't get bent out of shape.
Think of what I want to get out of this.
I don't need to prove myself.
There is no point in getting mad.
I'm not going to let him get to me.

Coping with Anger

Getting upset won't help.
It's just not worth it to get so angry.
I'll let him make a fool of himself.
It's time to take a deep breath.
I can't expect people to act the way I want them to.
Take it easy; don't get pushy.

Reflecting on an Angering Situation

(When the conflict is unresolved)

Forget about the aggravation. Thinking about it only makes me upset.
These are difficult situations, and they take time to straighten out.
Try to shake it off. Don't let it interfere.
Don't take it seriously.

(When the conflict is resolved)

I handled that one pretty well. It worked!
That wasn't as hard as I thought.
It could have been a lot worse.
I actually got through that without getting angry.
I'm doing better at this all the time.

Source: Adapted from R. Novaco, *Anger Control: The Development and Evaluation of an Experimental Treatment* (Lexington, Mass.: D. C. Heath, 1975), pp. 95–96. Adapted with permission.

6. At the end of an assigned reading section: Can I see all the themes here? If yes, let me predict the teacher's test question on this section. If no, let me go back to step 4 (Wong et al., 1986, pp. 25–26).

Teaching Implications of CBM

Cognitive behavior modification is designed to actively involve students in learning. Meichenbaum (1977, 1983) characterizes the student as a

FIGURE 2.4 *Cue Cards Used for Teaching Self-Control*

What is my problem?

How can I do it?

Am I using my plan?

How did I do?

Source: Reprinted with permission from Camp B. W., and Bash, M. A. S. (1985). *Think Aloud: Increasing Social and Cognitive Skills—A Problem-Solving Program for Children. Classroom Program: Grades 1–2* (pp. 48–51). Champaign, IL: Research Press.

collaborator in learning. General guidelines to consider when using CBM include:

1. Analyze the target behavior carefully.
2. Determine if and what strategies the student is already using.
3. Select strategy steps that are as similar as possible to the strategy steps used by good problem solvers.
4. Work with the student in developing the strategy steps.

5. Train the prerequisite skills.
6. Train the strategy steps using modeling, self-instruction, and self-regulation.
7. Give explicit feedback.
8. Teach strategy generalization.
9. Help the students maintain the strategy.

Guidelines for assessing the effects of training (see Table 2.2) have also been suggested (Rooney and Hallahan, 1985).

A substantial and growing body of research supports the use of cognitive behavior modification for developing academic, cognitive, and social skills in students with learning and behavior problems (Deshler, Warner, Schumaker, and Alley, 1983; Graham and Harris, 1989a; Hallahan, Hall, Ianna, Kneedler, Lloyd, Loper, and Reeve, 1983; Montague and Bos, 1986b; Palincsar and Brown, 1987; Paris and Oka, 1986; Schumaker, Deshler, and Ellis, 1986; Vaughn, Ridley, and Bullock, 1984; Wong and Wilson, 1984). As discussed in Apply the Concept 2.4, researchers at the Kansas Institute for Research in Learning Disabilities have developed a teaching model as well as a number of task-specific strategies that employ the principles of CBM.

Sociocultural Theory of Cognitive Development

The sociocultural theory of cognitive development (Vygotsky, 1978) is similar to cognitive behavior modification in that it highlights the importance of modeling and the use of language to facilitate learning. However, the theory also assumes that learning is a social activity highly influenced by the resources that learners bring to the learning environment.

One concept associated with this theory is that the teacher needs to consider and utilize these resources (Diaz, Moll, and Mehan, 1986), which include such aspects as culture and lan-

FIGURE 2.5   *Summarization Form Used in Teaching Summarization Skills*

Name: *Theresa*

Chapter Title: *From Sea to Sea*

Main Section Title: *The View From West to East*

Subsection (1): *The Spanish in California*

Paragraph 1   Main idea sentences(s)

Spain paid little attention to this land   called New Spain in 1800.

Important details

(a) *only small settlements there*

(b) *as far north as Montana*

(c) *settlements prevent other nations from claiming land*

(d)

Summary sentence: *In 1800 New Spain had very few settlements and wasn't considered very important by countries, even Spain.*

Source: Summarization Form reprinted from B. Y. L. Wong, R. Wong, N. Perry, and D. Sawatsky. "The Efficacy of a Self-Questioning Summarization Strategy for Use by Underachievers and Learning Disabled Adolescents in Social Studies," *Learning Disabilities Focus,* 2 (Fall, 1986), p. 25. Used by permission of the Division of learning Disabilities.

TABLE 2.2   *Guidelines for Assessing Strategy Effectiveness*

Behavior	*Assessment Questions*
Independence	Can the student use the strategy without cues or assistance?
	Can the student match the appropriate strategy to the task?
	Can the student adapt the strategy if necessary?
Spontaneity	Does the student use the strategy without being asked or cued to do so?
Flexibility	Can the student modify and adapt the strategy to match the situation?
	Can the student pick out the cues in the situation to guide strategy use?
Generalization	Does the student use the strategy appropriately in various situations?
	Does the student use the strategy across different class periods?
Maintenance	Does the student continue to use the strategy after direct instruction of the strategy has stopped?
Reflective Thinking	Does the student stop and think about how to do a task before beginning?
	Does the student think about which strategy to use before beginning?
	Does the student reflect on his or her performance and adjust the strategy if necessary?
Improved Performance	Has the student's performance on the targeted task improved?
	Is there improvement in the student's productivity, accuracy, and task completion?
Improved Self-Concept	Does the student see himself or herself as an active participant in learning?
	Does the student see himself or herself in control of his or her learning?
	Does the student regard himself or herself as more successful?

Source: Adapted from K. J. Rooney and D. P. Hallahan, "Future Directions for Cognitive Behavior Modification Research: The Quest for Cognitive Change," *Remedial and Special Education* 6 (2) (1985): 49. Copyright © 1985 by Pro-Ed. Reprinted with permission.

guage as well as background knowledge the learners can apply to the task being completed or the problem to be solved. For example, Moll (in press) in assisting Hispanic elementary students in developing literacy began by first exploring the "funds of knowledge" that could be gained from the community and the Hispanic and southwestern cultures. He also examined how literacy functioned as a part of community and home life. He brought this information into the schools and used it to build a literacy program. In this way, culturally diverse students were given the opportunity to use sources of knowledge that are not often highlighted in traditional school curriculums.

Another important theoretical concept is the premise that learning occurs during social interactions; that is, learning is a social event in which language plays an important role. Using this concept, teachers and students discuss what they are learning and how they are going about learning. Such interactive dialogue between teachers and learners provides language models and tools for guiding one's inner talk about learning (Moll and Diaz, 1987). Initially, a more expert person may model the self-talk and vocabulary related to the cognitive processes. However, this gives way to a collaborative or social dialogue in which the learner assumes increasing responsibility. This type of teaching allows for the instruction of cognitive and metacognitive strategies within purposeful, meaningful discussions and also provides a means for selecting, organizing, and relating the content matter being discussed. For example, in reciprocal teaching (Palincsar and Brown, 1984), a technique designed to foster comprehension and comprehension monitoring, the teacher and students take turns leading dialogues which focus on their knowledge of the information they are studying and on the processes they are using for understanding and for checking their understanding.

Another concept of the sociocultural theory of learning relates to the role of the teacher or the expert, who encourages learners by providing temporary and adjustable support as they develop new skills, strategies, and knowledge. The instruction is referred to as *scaffolded instruction* (Tharp and Gallimore, 1988). The metaphor of a scaffold captures the idea of an adjustable and temporary support that can be removed when no longer necessary. Vygotsky (1978) describes

learning as occurring in the "zone of proximal development" or "the distance between the actual developmental level as described by independent problem solving and the level of potential development as determined through problem solving under adult guidance or in collaboration with more capable peers" (p. 86).

Thus, the sociocultural theory of learning implies the following for instruction:

1. Instruction is designed to facilitate scaffolding and cooperative knowledge sharing among students and teachers within a context of mutual respect and critical acceptance of others' knowledge and experiences.
2. Learning and teaching should be a meaningful, socially embedded activity.
3. Instruction should provide opportunities for mediated learning with the teacher or expert guiding instruction within the students' zones of proximal development.

Information Processing and Schema Theories

Whereas operant learning focuses on observable behaviors and views learning as the establishing of functional relationships between a student's behavior and the stimuli in the environment, cognitive learning theory focuses on what happens in the mind and views learning as changes in the learner's cognitive structure.

Information processing theory, one of several cognitive theories, attempts to describe how sensory input is perceived, transformed, reduced, elaborated, stored, retrieved, and used (Hunt, 1985; Neisser, 1976; Swanson, 1987). Psychologists and educators studying information processing attempt to understand how thinking processes operate to allow humans to complete such complex cognitive tasks as summarizing a chapter in a textbook, solving

Apply the Concept 2.4 _____

APPLICATION OF COGNITIVE BEHAVIOR MODIFICATION:
THE LEARNING STRATEGIES CURRICULUM

Can the principles of cognitive behavior modification be applied to academic tasks in such a way that learning-disabled adolescents can be successful in performing the skills required for secondary school settings? This is one of the major questions that was addressed by Don Deshler, Gordon Alley, Jean Schumaker, and their colleagues at the Kansas University Institute for Research in Learning Disabilities. The Learning Strategies Intervention Model (Deshler and Schumaker, 1986; Ellis, Deshler, Lenz, Schumaker, and Clark, in press) developed at this research institute is one of the most comprehensive examples of an intervention model based on cognitive behavior modification.

The goal of the Learning Strategies Intervention Model is "to teach learning disabled adolescents strategies that will facilitate their acquisition, organization, storage, and retrieval of information, thus allowing them to cope with the demands of social interaction" (Alley and Deshler, 1979, p. 8). Learning strategies are techniques, principles, or routines that enable students to learn to solve problems and complete tasks independently. Learning strategies instruction focuses on how to learn and how to use what has been learned.

The *Learning Strategies Curriculum* (e.g., Lenz, Schumaker, Deshler, and Beals, 1984; Nagel, Schumaker, and Deshler, 1986; Schumaker, Denton, and Deshler, 1984; Schumaker and Sheldon, 1985) contains three strands of academic, task-specific strategies. The Acquisition Strand enables students to gain information from written materials. The Storage Strand consists of strategies to assist students in organizing, storing, and retrieving information. The Expression and Demonstration of Competence Strand contains strategies that enables students to complete assignments, express themselves, and take tests.

Each strategy uses a teaching model that incorporates principles of cognitive behavior modification. The stages in the teaching model are:

Acquisition

Stage 1   **Pretest and Make Commitments**

Obtain measure(s) of current functioning
Make students aware of inefficient/ineffective habits
Obtain students' commitments to learn

Stage 2   **Describe the Strategy**

Give rationales for using the strategy
Give general characteristics of situations
Solicit example situations

Describe results that can be expected
Supervise goal setting
Describe the steps of the strategy

Stage 3   **Model the Strategy**

Demonstrate the entire strategy "Thinking Aloud"
Involve the students in a demonstration

Stage 4   **Verbal Elaboration and Rehearsal**

Have students describe intent of strategy and strategy steps
Have students name strategy steps at an automatic level
Require mastery

Stage 5   **Controlled Practice and Feedback**

Supervise practice in "easy" materials
Provide positive and corrective feedback
Move from guided practice to independent practice
Require mastery

Stage 6   **Advanced Practice and Feedback**

Supervise practice in materials from regular coursework
Provide positive and corrective feedback
Fade prompts and cues for strategy use and evaluation
Move from guided practice to independent practice
Require mastery

Stage 7   **Confirm Acquisition and Make Generalization Commitments**

Obtain measure(s) of progress
Make students aware of progress
Obtain the students' commitment to generalize

Stage 8   **Generalization**

Phase I   **Orientation**

Discuss situations, settings, and materials in which the strategy can be used
Evaluate appropriateness of strategy in various settings and materials
Identify helpful aspects of the strategy and adjustments
Make students aware of cues for using the strategy

Phase II   **Activation**

Program the students' use of the strategy in a variety of situations
Provide feedback
Reinforce progress and success

(continued)

Apply the Concept 2.4 *continued*

Phase III	**Adaptation**
	Discuss how the strategy can be modified to meet differing demands
	Assist students in applying the modifications
Phase IV	**Maintenance**
	Set goals related to long-term use
	Conduct periodic reviews
	Identify self-reinforcers and self-rewards
	Provide feedback (Deshler and Schumaker, 1986; Ellis, Deshler, Lanz, Schumaker, and Clark, in press)

This teaching model relies heavily on modeling, self-instruction, and self-regulation. It encourages students to assume an active and collaborative role in learning. The teaching model has been validated with a number of specific learning strategies, for example, a strategy for learning information from textbooks (MULTIPASS) (Schumaker, Deshler, Alley, Warner, and Denton, 1982), a strategy for listening to lectures and taking notes (LINKS) (Schumaker, Deshler, Alley and Warner, 1983), a strategy for remembering information (FIRST) (Nagel, Schumaker, and Deshler, 1986), and a strategy for paraphrasing text (RAP) (Schumaker, Denton, and Deshler, 1984). Several of the specific learning strategies are presented in the chapters on reading, written expression, and content areas learning and study skills.

The University of Kansas Institute for Research in Learning Disabilities requires that persons planning to implement the Learning Strategies Model obtain training available through the Institute, University of Kansas, Lawrence, KA 66045.

---

complex math problems, writing a mystery novel, and comparing and contrasting theories of learning.

A visual model depicting the sequence of stages in which information is processed or learned is presented in Figure 2.6. Although the figure implies that each activity is relatively separate, these processes are highly interactive. This processing system is controlled by *executive functioning* or *metacognition,* which assists the learner in coordinating, monitoring, and determining which strategies the learner should employ for effective learning (Campione, Brown, and Ferrara, 1982; Swanson, 1987).

We can use this model to explain how Greg, a learning-disabled, high-school student, might acquire and remember some new information about "seizure" as it relates to the Fourth Amendment of the United States Constitution. Mr. Gomez is explaining the concepts of "search and seizure" to Greg and the rest of the students in government class. He writes the word *seizure* on the board and says, "Seizure is when the police take your possessions away from you because those possessions are illegal. Sometimes the police need a search warrant to seize your possessions and sometimes they do not.

As you read this chapter see if you can determine the rules for when the police need a search warrant."

According to the model presented in Figure 2.6, the first step in learning and remembering the information on the concept of "seizure" is to receive the information through the senses or sensory receptors. Mr. Gomez exposed Greg to both visual and auditory information by writing the word on the board and by talking about it.

Next, the information is transported to the sensory store. Here, both the visual representation of "seizure" and the auditory information is stored. At this point Greg has neither attended to the information nor connected meaning to it.

Now Greg can attend to the information, but he has only a limited capacity for attending and he can selectively attend to some sensory information and not to other information. If most of Greg's attention is allocated to thoughts about a Friday night date or a comic book he is reading, the information Mr. Gomez shared with Greg cannot be learned because Greg has not selectively attended to it. For our example, we will assume that Greg was attending to Mr. Gomez.

FIGURE 2.6 *An Information Processing Model of Learning*

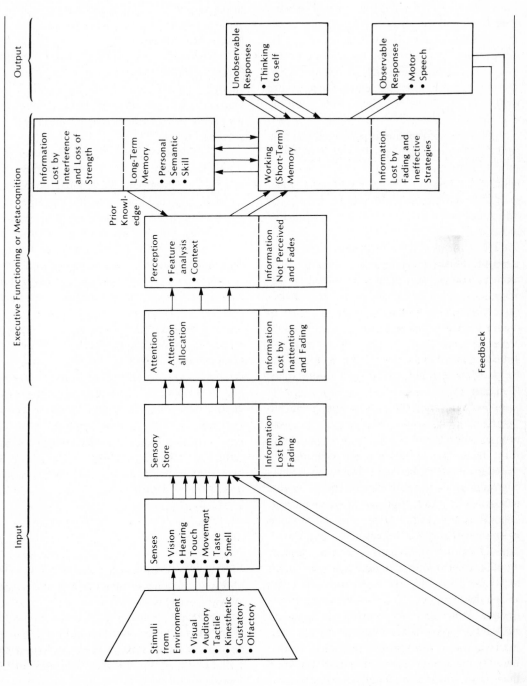

Next, Greg can recognize or perceive the information by detecting the salient features in the information and using the context and his prior knowledge to assist in perception. For example, Greg can use salient visual features in the word *seizure,* his sight word recognition for the word (prior knowledge), and Mr. Gomez's discussion of seizure (context) to perceive the word written on the board as *seizure* rather than the word *leisure* or *search.*

Once the information is perceived it can be held for a short period of time in working or short-term memory. However, if Greg wants to learn the information, he can either transfer and store the information in long-term memory or utilize a strategy to keep the information active in short-term memory. Unless some effort is made to remember the information, it will fade in about fifteen seconds. We can use a variety of memory strategies to keep information active. We can rehearse it (repeat it aloud and to ourselves), chunk it (group it together to make fewer pieces of information to remember), elaborate on it (expand on it by using information we already know), and so on. Greg rehearses the word and its definition by saying it several times to himself.

Greg is aware that the information related to "seizure" needs to be remembered for a long time or at least until the test next week. Therefore, the information must be meaningfully stored in long-term memory to become part of his cognitive structure. This way, he should be able to retrieve the information next week for the test. One efficient means of storing new information is to relate the new information to old information. Greg retrieves from his memory a story about a senior who tried to raise marijuana in his backyard. The police found it, arrested him, and seized the marijuana. This is a good example of seizure. When he hears or reads the word *seizure,* he can think of the senior having the marijuana seized. Greg also retrieves from his memory that search and seizure are discussed in the Fourth Amendment. Greg can relate the new information to old information almost as if he were filing it away in an organized filing system. Greg can store the new information about seizure in the same file as the one containing the story about the marijuana and the information on the Fourth Amendment.

When the exam is given next week, and Mr. Gomez asks for the definition of seizure, Greg should be able to retrieve the information from long-term memory into working memory and then write the definition because he filed it in a meaningful way.

Throughout the process, learning is orchestrated by executive functioning or metacognition. For example, when Greg decided to rehearse the word and its definition rather than write them down, he was using his executive functioning to coordinate the learning process.

Although we process information in a logical sequence (see Figure 2.6), we generally process information very quickly and don't think consciously about what we are doing. We do not necessarily say to ourselves, "Now I need to rehearse this so I won't forget it," or "I have to relate this information to what I already know so that I can remember it." Information processing is also very interactive. Feedback is possible both from observable responses we make and unobservable thinking responses. These interactions are depicted by the bi-directional arrows in Figure 2.6. Let's explore information processing further by looking at each component and at the overall coordinating processes of executive functioning and metacognition.

Sensing

Sensing involves the use of one or more of our senses to obtain information. It refers to our system's capacity to use the sensory processes to obtain information, not our system's ability to attend or discriminate. Stimuli from the environment are received through all our senses. However, much of the information we learn in school-related tasks is received through visual and auditory senses.

Sensory Store

The *sensory store* holds all incoming information for approximately a second, just long enough for us to attend and perceive it (Loftus and Loftus, 1976). Although we have the ability to retain large amounts of information in the sensory store, the information quickly fades unless we actively attend to and perceive it (Sperling, 1960).

Attention

Most of us use the term *attention* to refer to a wide range of behaviors. We speak of attending to details when we are concerned about the quality of a job, we ask people if they are attending to us when we want them to hear what we are about to say, and we measure students on the amount of time they attend to tasks. Attention is the capacity to focus awareness on selected incoming stimuli. At any one time a variety of information is being received by the senses and held in sensory store. However, as depicted in Figure 2.6, we attend only to some of the information, depending on the task demands. In other words, we selectively attend.

The importance of *selective attention* can be demonstrated in relation to the reading process. You have probably experienced reading a text by going through the mechanical motions (identifying the words) only to realize suddenly that you are not attending and cannot remember what you were reading. Instead, your mind has drifted to thoughts about a friend's problems, the music playing in the background, or how good the apple pie baking in the oven smells. All of these stimuli are being received by your senses and funneled into the sensory store. An effective learner must selectively attend to the relevant stimuli.

Attention can only be allocated to a few cognitive processes at a time. However, the more proficient you are at a process, the less attention it will require. Well-practiced processes require little attention and are said to be *automatic,* whereas processes requiring considerable attention have been referred to as *deliberate* (Anderson, 1980; Kolligian and Sternberg, 1987). LaBerge and Samuels (1974; Samuels, 1987) have applied these principles to the reading process. Poor readers, including many students with learning and behavior problems, must allocate so much of their attention to identifying the words in the text that little is left to allocate toward comprehension. Good readers, however, have word recognition at an ''automatic'' level, and therefore have more attentional capacity to allocate to understanding what they read.

Many students with learning and behavior disabilities have some sort of automation failure (e.g., Ackerman and Dykman, 1982; Samuels, 1987; Spear and Sternberg, 1986). As a result, the disabled students must allocate attention and exert effort to task and task components that nondisabled individuals have already mastered.

Not only do these students have to allocate more attention to some tasks than nondisabled students, they also have difficulty selectively attending to the relevant stimuli and attending for sustained periods of time (Anderson, Halcomb, and Doyle, 1973; Ross, 1976; Tarver, Hallahan, Cohen, and Kauffman, 1977).

Perception

Once we allocate our attention to incoming stimuli, the next step in processing is to recognize or perceive the information. *Perception* can be defined as ''the process of 'recognizing' a raw, physical pattern in sensory store as representing something meaningful'' (Loftus and Loftus, 1976, p. 23). *Perceptual learning* is the increased ability to gain new information from the environment (Gibson, 1969). Students who have perceptual disabilities usually have trouble interpreting and obtaining meaning from the stimuli in the environment (Schiff, 1980).

One explanation of how perception works entails the perceiver using feature analysis and the context in which the stimulus is presented to give the stimulus meaning. In *feature analysis,*

FIGURE 2.7   *Effect of Context on Letter Recognition*

THE CAT

the perceiver uses the critical features to recognize the stimuli. For example, the critical feature between *n* and *u* and *p* and *b* is orientation. We process more slowly and are prone to confuse letters that have minimal feature differences such as *C* and *G* or *b* and *d* (Kinney, Marsetta, and Showman, 1966). Similar findings have been shown with speech sounds (phonemes). Feature analysis is used across a variety of contexts. For instance, a listener might use the salient clue "Once upon a time" to recognize that she is listening to a story.

The perceiver also uses the *context* in which the stimulus is presented to assist in perception. Read the two words presented in Figure 2.7. Did you have any difficulty reading *THE CAT*? Now look closely at the *H* and the *A*. They are the exact same visual image. The context provided by the words facilitates the appropriate interpretation (Neisser, 1967). Context also plays an important role in perceiving auditory stimuli. Warren and Warren (1970) asked individuals to listen to sentences in which a nonspeech sound replaced a speech sound. The sentences were similar to the following:

It was found that the *eel was on the axle.
It was found that the *eel was on the shoe.
It was found that the *eel was on the orange.
It was found that the *eel was on the table.

In each case, the * represented a nonspeech sound. The individuals did not report hearing the nonspeech sound or the word *eel*, but they used the context to assist in perception and reported hearing the words *wheel*, *heel*, *peel*, and *meal*, respectively. Our store of background information, as represented in long-term memory (see

Figure 2.6), interacts with the incoming stimuli to assist us in the perception process.

Perception involves the simultaneous use of both feature analysis and use of context and prior knowledge. Feature analysis has been referred to as *bottom-up processing* "because information flows from little perceptual pieces (features), which serve as the foundation of perception, to larger units built from them (e.g., letters, words, pictures)" (Anderson, 1980, p. 43). If we processed every feature of every letter when reading a page, it is estimated that we would be making an average of 100 feature analyses per second. But because we can also use context and prior knowledge to assist in perception, we do not need to detect every feature, every letter, or even every word (Smith, 1978; Goodman, Smith, Meredith, and Goodman, 1987). When context or prior knowledge guide perception, we refer to the processing as *top-down processing*, since high-level general knowledge determines the interpretation of low-level perceptual units (Anderson, 1980). It is the interaction of bottom-up and top-down processing that makes for efficient perceptual processing (Anderson, 1977; Rumelhart, 1980).

Working Memory

Once information is perceived it can move into working or short-term memory. *Working memory* can be thought of as activated memory since it represents the information that is easily accessible. Working memory has a limited capacity in that we have the ability to store only a small amount of information in working memory at any one time (i.e., seven bits of information plus or minus two bits) (Miller, 1956). However, much of the information that enters through our senses is already lost (see Figure 2.6). We lose some information because we do not attend to it; we lose other information because we do not perceive it or because it will not fit into working memory.

Working memory can be contrasted with long-term memory. Long-term memory represents the information passively stored outside the attentional spotlight (Rumelhart, 1977). An example can clarify the difference between short-term and long-term memory.

Study the following numbers so that you can remember them: 9-6-5-8-2-4-1-7. Now cover the numbers, wait for at least fifteen seconds, and then write them. After you attended and perceived the numbers, you probably studied them to keep them active in your working memory and then you wrote them. To keep the numbers active you may have rehearsed the numbers, closed your eyes and tried to visualize them, or used some other memory strategy.

Now write the phone numbers of your two best friends. This information is stored in long-term memory. You had to search your long-term memory for your two best friends. You probably used their names in searching, although you could have used their appearances or an idiosyncratic characteristic. Then you retrieved their phone numbers and transferred them to working memory. Once the information was in working memory you were ready to use the information, so you wrote their phone numbers.

Now, without looking back, write the numbers you were asked to remember earlier. You will probably have difficulty with this task. Since information fades from working memory if you do not work with it, and since you filled your working memory with the phone numbers of your two best friends, you probably cannot write the original numbers. If you had stored the original numbers in long-term memory, you might be able to retrieve them, but the task did not require you to do this. Consequently, they are lost forever.

Several concepts were demonstrated by this example:

1. Working or short-term memory is activated memory.

2. Working memory has a limited capacity. We can keep a limited amount of information in working memory (i.e., seven pieces of information plus or minus two pieces). These pieces can be of various size or comprehensiveness. For example, they may be seven single digits, seven phone numbers, seven sentences, or seven major concepts.

3. The more we cluster or group information into larger related concepts, the more information we can keep in working memory.

4. If we do not actively work with the information in working memory, it will fade rapidly (in about fifteen seconds).

5. We can use various strategies to keep information active in working memory. For example, we can rehearse the information, elaborate on it, create visual images of it, and so on.

6. Information in working memory is easily replaced by new incoming information (e.g., recalling your friends' phone numbers).

7. Information not stored in long-term memory cannot be retrieved.

8. Information that is stored in long-term memory is sometimes retrievable. How the information is organized in long-term memory affects how easily it can be retrieved.

9. Information from long-term memory is transferred to working memory. Then you can use that information (e.g., writing the phone numbers of your best friends).

Like attention and perception, some students with learning and behavior problems have difficulties with tasks requiring them to listen to or look at numbers, pictures, letters, words, or sentences, hold them in working memory, and then recall them (e.g., Howe, Brainerd, and Kingma, 1985; Swanson, 1985, 1987; Torgesen, Rashotte, Greenstein, Houck, and Portes, 1987).

Long-Term Memory and Schemas

We have already discussed the role that long-term memory plays in learning. Using Figure 2.6 as a reference, we see that *long-term memory* aids us in perceiving incoming stimuli. It provides the context that allows us to use top-down processing when perceiving information (e.g., to perceive the stimuli *THE CAT* even though the visual images of the *H* and the *A* are the same). It helps us fill in the words or speech sounds of a conversation that we do not fully hear because we are at a noisy party. Long-term memory also interacts with working memory. Information is retrieved from long-term memory and transferred to working memory before it can be used to make responses.

If long-term memory plays such an important part in the information processing system, how is it organized? If it has to hold all the information we know, including our store of knowledge about the world, procedural information on how to do numerous skills such as tie shoes and play basketball, and information about our goals and values, how does long-term memory keep all this information straight? Like the rest of the information processing system, cognitive psychologists do not know just how this vast array of information is organized, but they do have some logical hunches.

According to one theory, schema theory, our knowledge is organized into schemas. *Schemas* can be defined as organized structures of stereotypic knowledge (Schank and Abelson, 1977). They are higher-order cognitive structures that assist in understanding and recalling events and information.

It is hypothesized that we have innumerable schemas for events and procedures and it is our schemas that allow us to make inferences about the events that happen around us (Rumelhart, 1980; Spiro, 1980). These schemas are organized in our cognitive structure is such a way that they can be retrieved and utilized in working memory to aid in understanding new events and ideas (Brewer and Nakamura, 1984).

Read the following short passage about an event John experienced.

John had been waiting all week for Friday evening. He skipped lunch just to get ready for the occasion. At 6:30 P.M. he got

in his car and drove to the restaurant. He planned to meet several friends when he arrived. When he arrived, he got out of his car and waited outside for his friends.

At this point you are probably using a general schema for restaurants. You could answer such questions as "Is John going to eat dinner?" "Will John eat dinner with his friends?" However, you have not been given enough information to utilize a more specific restaurant schema. Now read on to see how your schema is sharpened by the information given in the rest of the passage.

After a few minutes, John's friends arrived. They entered the restaurant and walked up to the counter. John placed his order first. After everyone ordered, they carried the trays of food to a booth.

How has your schema changed? You should be using a more specific schema for fast-food restaurants. Now you can probably answer more specific questions such as "What kind of food did John and his friends probably eat?" "Did John leave a tip?" Utilizing schemas (e.g., our prior knowledge about stereotypic events) allows us to make inferences, thereby filling in the gaps and giving meaning to incoming information. Schemas serve a crucial role in providing an account of how old or prior knowledge interacts with new or incoming information (Anderson, 1977; Rumelhart, 1980; 1985).

The early work in schema theory is usually credited to Bartlett (1932) who, in his book *Remembering,* argued that memory is not simply recalling what one remembers almost in a templatelike fashion, but it is *reconstructive.* In other words, in comprehending and recalling information, our prior knowledge interacts with incoming information, and to some extent it changes the information to fit with our prior knowledge. In this way we reconstruct the meaning in relation to our schemas. To verify his premise about schemas, Bartlett had English subjects read and then recall a folktale from another culture. He had the individuals recall the tale immediately after they read it and again at later times.

If you want to join in Bartlett's experiment, read the folktale in Apply the Concept 2.5 and then in several hours, write what you remember about the tale.

Bartlett's subjects showed clear distortions in their memory of the story. These inaccuracies appear to be systematic in that the individuals distorted the folktale to fit with their own cultural stereotypes. Many of the people omitted proper names, unfamiliar details, and hard-to-interpret aspects of the tale. They made the tale shorter, more coherent, and more consistent with their cultural expectations. In other words, understanding and memory do not simply reflect a rote recall process but a *reconstructive* process, resulting in the interaction of a person's schemas with the new information.

Within and across schemas, concepts or ideas are organized so as to promote understanding and retrieval. Information can be stored in semantic networks composed of concepts and relationships between concepts (Kintsch, 1974; Rumelhart, 1980). Figure 2.8 presents a representation of the concept of *bird*. (Your network for *bird* is probably more extensive than the one presented in this figure.) The closer together the concepts are in the network, the better they serve as cues for each other's recall (Ratcliff and McKoon, 1978; Weisberg, 1969). For example, *wings* should serve as a better recall cue for *bird* than should *two*. Concepts do not exist in isolation in semantic memory but are related to other concepts at higher, lower, or the same levels. In the case of *birds*, it could be filed along with *reptiles* and *mammals*, under the superordinate concept of *animals*.

Schemas and semantic networks allow us to organize our knowledge in such a way that we

Apply the Concept 2.5 ⸻

ACTIVATING SCHEMA

Read the following folktale:

"War of the Ghosts"

One night two young men from Egulac went down to the river to hunt seals, and while they were there it became foggy and calm. Then they heard war-cries, and they thought: "Maybe this is a war-party." They escaped to the shore, and hid behind a log. Now canoes came up, and they heard the noise of paddles, and saw one canoe, and they said: "What do you think? We wish to take you along. We are going up the river to make war on the people."

One of the young men said: "I have not arrows."

"Arrows are in the canoe," they said.

"I will not go along. I might be killed. My relatives do not know where I have gone. But you," he said, turning to the other, "may go with them."

So one of the young men went, but the other returned home.

And the warriors went on up the river to a town on the side of Kalama. The people came down to the water, and they began to fight, and many were killed. But presently the young man heard one of the warriors say: "Quick, let us go home. That Indian has been hit."

Now he thought: "Oh, they are ghosts." He did not feel sick, but they said he had been shot.

So the canoes went back to Egulac, and the young man went ashore to his house, and made a fire. And he told everybody: "Behold, I accompanied the ghosts, and we went to fight. Many of our fellows were killed, and many of those who attacked us were killed. They said I was hit, and I did not feel sick."

He told it all, and then he became quiet. When the sun rose he fell down. Something black came out of his mouth. His face became contorted. The people jumped up and cried.

He was dead.

In an hour or so, write what you remember about this folktale and then compare it to the original passage. Does your retelling differ from the passage? If so, how does it differ? Does your retelling reflect your culture better than the culture depicted in the passage?

Source: R. C. Bartlett, *Remembering* (Cambridge, England: Cambridge University Press, 1932). Reprinted with the permission of Cambridge University Press.

FIGURE 2.8 *A Semantic Network for the Concept of "Bird"*

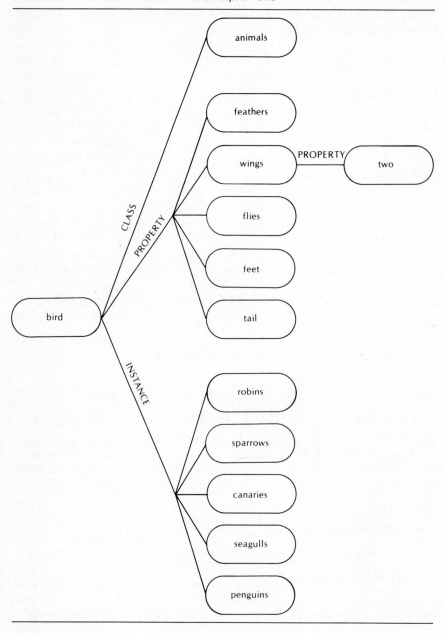

can retrieve information and effectively add new information to long-term memory. They also assist us in determining the relationship among ideas.

Executive Functioning and Metacognition

The specific processes in the information processing system (i.e., attention, perception, working memory, and long-term memory) are controlled or coordinated by what has been referred to as *executive functioning* (see Figure 2.6). In the same way that a business executive has many departments that he or she has to coordinate, and many decisions that have to be made regarding how best to use those various departments, the learner has to coordinate his or her various learning processes and strategies and make decisions regarding learning. For example, as learners, we must decide (1) which stimuli to attend to (e.g., the book we are reading and/or the smell of the apple pie baking); (2) whether to rely more on feature analysis or context and prior knowledge when perceiving information; (3) what memory strategies are more effective for keeping the information active in working memory; and (4) what is an effective and efficient way to store the information so that we can retrieve it later. Making decisions allow us to control the learning process.

This executive functioning or control and coordination of our learning processes has also been referred to as metacognition (Brown, 1980; Flavell, 1976). *Metacognition* is generally considered to have two components (Brown, 1980):

1. An awareness of what skills, strategies, and resources are needed to perform a cognitive task
2. The ability to use self-regulatory strategies to monitor the thinking processes and to

undertake fix-up strategies when processing is not going smoothly

In many ways, metacognition and executive functioning are similar to the concepts of self-evaluation and self-regulation presented in the section on cognitive behavior modification.

Flavell, one of the first cognitive psychologists to focus his research in the area of executive functioning, explains:

> For example, I am engaging in metacognition (metamemory, metalearning, metaattention, metalanguage, or whatever) if I notice that I am having more trouble learning A than B; if it strikes me that I should double-check C before accepting it as a fact; if it occurs to me that I had better scrutinize each and every alternative in any multiple-choice type task situation before deciding which is the best one; if I sense that I had better make a note of D because I may forget . . . (1976, p. 232).

Metacognition and executive functioning require the learner to monitor the effectiveness of his or her learning and, based on feedback, regulate learning by activating task-appropriate strategies. Read the short essay in Apply the Concept 2.6 and see how you use your metacognition.

Students with learning and behavior problems certainly have potential for having difficulties with executive functioning or metacognition. For example, the essay you read in Apply the Concept 2.6 was also read by groups of learning-disabled and average-achieving seventh graders. They were asked to read the essay to see if it made sense. Although most of the average-achieving students recognized the inconsistency, most of the learning-disabled students reported that there was nothing wrong with the essay (Bos and Filip, 1984). Others have found similar metacognitive deficits for these students in reading, memory, and math tasks (Cherkes-Julkowski, 1985; Montague and Bos, 1986b; Torgesen, 1985; Torgesen and Houck, 1980; Wong, 1979, 1980).

Teaching Implications from Information Processing and Schema Theories

Information processing and schema theories have definite educational implications for students with learning and behavior problems. As you read the content chapters in this book, think about how information processing theory helped to shape the instructional techniques. When teaching, think about how you can modify your teaching and the learning environment to facilitate directing a student's attention to the relevant stimuli and his or her perception of the incoming information. What strategies can you teach students so that information can stay active in working memory, and how can you present information to facilitate its storage and organization of long-term memory? How can you teach students to use executive functioning to coordinate the various learning and memory strategies? Several general implications are:

1. *Provide cues to students so they might be guided to the relevant task(s) or salient features of the task.* For instance, when giving a lecture, provide cues to assist the students in attending to the key points by giving an overview of the lecture, writing important concepts on the board, providing the students with a written outline of the lecture, or teaching the students how to listen and look for behaviors that signal important information (e.g., raised voice, repetition).

2. *Have students study the critical feature differences between stimuli when trying to perceive differences.* For example, highlight the "stick" part of the letters *b* and *d;* provide instances and noninstances when discussing a concept.

3. *Have the students use the context to aid in perception.* Students are not likely to substitute *bog* for *dog* if they are reading a story or sentence about a dog.

4. *Facilitate the activation of schemas and provide labeled experiences.* In this way students can develop adequate schemas and modify their current schemas for better understanding of the concepts being presented in both skill and content area subjects.

5. *Teach students to use memory strategies.*

6. *Use organization techniques to assist students in organizing their long-term memories.*

7. *Teach students to be flexible thinkers and how to solve problems, thereby encouraging them to use executive functioning.*

Much work is still to be completed before we fully understand how learners process infor-

---

Apply the Concept 2.6 _____

COMPREHENSION MONITORING

Read the following short essay:

> There are some things that almost all ants have in common. For example, they are all very strong and can carry objects many times their own weight. Sometimes they go very, very far from their nest to find food. They go so far away that they cannot remember how to go home. So, to help them find their way home, ants have a special way of leaving an invisible trail. Everywhere they go, they put out an invisible chemical from their bodies. This chemical has a special odor. Another thing about ants is they do not have noses to smell with. Ants never get lost (Bos and Filip, 1984, p. 230).

As you read the first part of this essay, you probably read along smoothly and quickly, comprehending the information and confirming that in fact what you are reading makes sense. However, when you read the last couple lines of the essay, you probably slowed your reading rate, possibly went back and reread, and/or stopped and thought about what you were reading. If these are the type of cognitive strategies in which you engaged, then you were using your executive functioning or metacognition to monitor your information processing system.

mation. Still, there is an accumulated body of research from which we, as educators, can draw implications for effective teaching and learning.

Summary

This chapter presents approaches to learning and teaching for guiding the teaching-learning process. The models provide principles that influence the way you, as a teacher, observe, record, interact, and evaluate the teaching-learning process with students.

The first model, operant learning theory, focuses on observed behavior and the antecedents and consequences that control the behavior. In this model the teacher is able to increase or maintain desirable behaviors through positive and negative reinforcement, secondary reinforcers, the Premack Principle, shaping, and group contingencies. Through operant learning the teacher is also able to decrease undesirable behaviors by using extinction, reinforcement of incompatible behavior, punishment, and time-out. Teachers can use the principles from operant learning to enhance students' progress through the stages of learning. These include entry, acquisition, proficiency, maintenance, generalization, and application. The teaching-learning process in the operant learning model is highly teacher directed.

The second model, cognitive behavior modification, utilizes principles from both operant learning theories and cognitive-oriented theories. Key features of cognitive behavior modification interventions are that they include strategy steps, modeling, self-regulation, verbalization, and reflective thinking. Through cognitive behavior modification the student and the teacher have a more interactive role in the teaching-learning process.

The third model, a sociocultural theory of learning, emphasizes the social nature of learning and encourages interactive discussions between students and teachers. In these discussions the teacher is encouraged to use the students' funds of knowledge and to provide the needed support for the student to acquire new strategies, skills, and knowledge.

The fourth model, information processing and schema theories, is a pair of cognitive theories that attempt to explain how information is received, transformed, retrieved, and expressed. Key features of information processing are sensing, sensory store, attention, perception, memory, executive functioning, and metacognition. The information processing model focuses on an interactive role between the teacher and the student, with the concentration on activating prior background knowledge in the student, relating new learning to information the learner already has learned, and maintaining the student as an active learner who thinks about how he or she thinks, studies, and learns.

Throughout the remaining chapters you will see many examples of the principles for teaching and learning that were presented in this chapter. These examples will assist you in understanding how the different approaches to learning and teaching can be applied when interacting with students. In a sense, this chapter provides the theoretical underpinnings for the strategies presented in the subsequent chapters. As you read the subsequent chapters, think about how theory guides the instructional practices and how it will guide your teaching as you work with students experiencing learning and behavior problems.

Chapter Three

Oral Language

Chapter Questions

- *What are the three major components of oral language? Listen to a conversation between two students and think about how the components function.*
- *What three general teaching strategies can you easily employ when building oral language skills? Converse with a young child and use these strategies (i.e., parallel talk, expansion, and elaboration).*
- *Name at least five different functions for which we use language. Observe students as they play and note the different ways they use language.*
- *Using several of the principles recommended for teaching content, plan how to teach students to categorize ideas about a topic.*
- *What is word-finding difficulty? Describe several strategies you could use to help a student who has word-finding difficulty.*
- *When planning instruction for students whose first language is not English, what considerations should you keep in mind?*

Jerry is a handsome second grader who is good at sports. He seems bright until you hear him talk. Whether he is having a conversation with you or trying to read, he has difficulty thinking of the right words. Yesterday he was trying to describe the work that he and his dad had done on his go-cart. He could not think of the words *screwdriver, hammer, sand, wheels, axle, steering wheel,* and *engine.* Sometimes he attempted to describe what he was trying to say, for example, when he could not think of *screwdriver,* he said, "It's the thing you use to put in things that are kind of like nails." Sometimes he can only think of a word that is similar to the word he is trying to say, for example, "I was using the hitter to hit some nails." Jerry also has trouble remembering words when he reads. He does not remember simple sight words and consequently has to resort to attempting to sound out the words. Often the words he cannot remember are not phonetic (e.g., *come, are, was, very*), so his strategy is only somewhat useful. Jerry is currently in a regular second grade but he receives speech and language therapy for his language problems and services from the special education resource teacher for his reading difficulties.

Debbie is in eighth grade. If you just listen to Debbie, you would not necessarily recognize that she has a language problem. Her vocabulary is adequate for a student her age, and she uses fairly sophisticated sentences. But Debbie's language frequently seems to get her in trouble. Debbie is growing up in a tough neighborhood, and she is bused across town. She has difficulty switching her language style to match this new context. She continues to use her "street language," resulting in the interpretation that she is both arrogant and disrespectful to teachers. Debbie also has other problems using language effectively. She has difficulty determining when the listener is not understanding what she is trying to explain. Instead of reexplaining her point, she continues with her description or explanation. When the listener asks her to clarify a point, Debbie implies the listener is stupid. She also fails to take turns easily during conversations.

She either monopolizes the conversation or expects the other person to do all the talking while she gives little feedback to let the other person know that she is listening. Consequently, Debbie is perceived as a student with behavior problems, although there is no indication of any serious emotional problems. She sees her counselor once a week and has a special education English class. In the last several months, the speech/language pathologist has been consulting with the special education teacher and counselor concerning Debbie. They are working with Debbie to help her use language more effectively and to vary it across contexts. It will be interesting to see if this will help to eliminate some of the social and behavior problems Debbie is currently experiencing.

Teddy is a language-delayed child. He started talking at age three and a half, and now, as a third grader, his language seems more like that of a first grader. He began receiving speech and language therapy at age four. Although he is currently placed in a self-contained class for learning-disabled students, he receives speech and language therapy for thirty minutes, four days a week. Teddy is delayed in all aspects of language. His vocabulary is limited, he uses simple sentence patterns, and he uses language primarily to obtain information and attention and to inform others of his needs. He rarely initiates a conversation, but he will carry on a conversation if the other person takes the lead. Mrs. Borman, his self-contained, special education teacher, is working closely with the speech/language pathologist to help ensure that Teddy is receiving the structured language programming he needs throughout the school day. One of Mrs. Borman's roles in this programming is to provide Teddy with many opportunities to practice and receive feedback on the skills he is learning in speech/language therapy.

As special education teachers, we will undoubtedly work with students like Jerry, Debbie, and Teddy. To assist these students in developing effective language and communication skills, we need to understand the *content of lan-*

guage instruction and *procedures for teaching language.*

Content of Language Instruction

Language is a vehicle for communicating our ideas, beliefs, and needs. It is ''a code whereby ideas about the world are represented through a conventional system of arbitrary signals for communication'' (Bloom and Lahey, 1978, p. 4). Language allows us to share our knowledge with others and, as discussed in Chapter Two, organize the knowledge in our long-term memory so that we can retrieve it and use it to communicate.

The major purpose for language is communication. Both in school and in our society language is a powerful resource. We use language to maintain contact with others, gain information, give information, persuade, accomplish goals, and even monitor our own behavior when we talk to ourselves. Language functions as an integral part of the communication process because it allows us to represent ideas by using a conventional code.

A person's ability to understand what is being communicated is referred to as *comprehension* or *receptive language,* whereas a person's ability to convey the intended message is referred to as *production* or *expressive language.* A basic assumption for the communication process to be effective is that both the speaker and the listener use the same code and know the same rules of language. Perhaps you have had the experience of trying to explain a need to someone who speaks a different language. You probably found yourself using many more gestures than usual. This is because although your listener could not understand your verbal communication code, he or she could understand your nonverbal code (gestures).

Some students with learning and behavior problems experience developmental delays in *comprehension* or receptive language. They frequently ask for information to be repeated or clarified. In school these students have difficulties with:

- Following directions
- Understanding the meaning of concepts (particularly temporal and spatial concepts and technical or abstract concepts)
- Seeing the relationship among concepts
- Understanding humor and figurative language
- Understanding multiple meanings
- Understanding less common and irregular verb tenses
- Understanding compound and complex sentences
- Detecting breakdowns in comprehension

Students with learning and behavior problems also have delays in *production* or expressive language. Sometimes these students choose not to communicate as frequently as other students. Students with delays in expressive language have difficulty:

- Using correct grammar
- Using compound and complex sentences
- Thinking of the right word to convey the concept (*word finding*)
- Discussing abstract, temporal, or spatial concepts
- Changing the communication style to fit various social contexts
- Providing enough information to the listener (e.g., starting a conversation with, ''He took it to the fair,'' when *he* and *it* have not been previously identified)
- Maintaining the topic during a conversation
- Repairing communication breakdowns

Although some students with learning and behavior problems have difficulty with both receptive and expressive language, other students experience difficulty primarily with expressive language. Students who have only expressive language difficulties generally understand much more than they are able to communicate.

Relationship of Oral and Written Communication

We use language when we read and write and when we communicate orally. In written communication, the writer is similar to the speaker in that the person is responsible for sending the message. The reader is similar to the listener, whose job it is to interpret the message. The relationship of speaking and listening to writing and reading is presented in Figure 3.1. Since both oral and written communication are language based, if a student is having difficulty in oral communication (e.g., understanding figurative language), he or she will also have difficulty in written communication. However, there are differences between oral and written communication. For example, a speaker can obtain imme-

diate feedback from a listener. Consequently, the speaker can adjust the way in which the message is expressed (e.g., lower the vocabulary level, reexplain, or restate) more easily than in the writing or reading processes. This chapter presents methods for teaching students who have difficulty with oral communication; the next three chapters describe ways for teaching students who have difficulty with written communication. Some of the instructional ideas will be similar because of the underlying language base of both oral and written communication. In some instances an instructional strategy that is suggested as a reading comprehension strategy can also be used as a listening or writing strategy (e.g., teaching students to ask themselves the questions of Who, What, When, Where, Why, and How as they read, write, or listen). We encourage you to keep in mind the close relationship of oral and written communication as you read the next four chapters.

FIGURE 3.1   *Modes of Communication*

A Model of the Communication Process

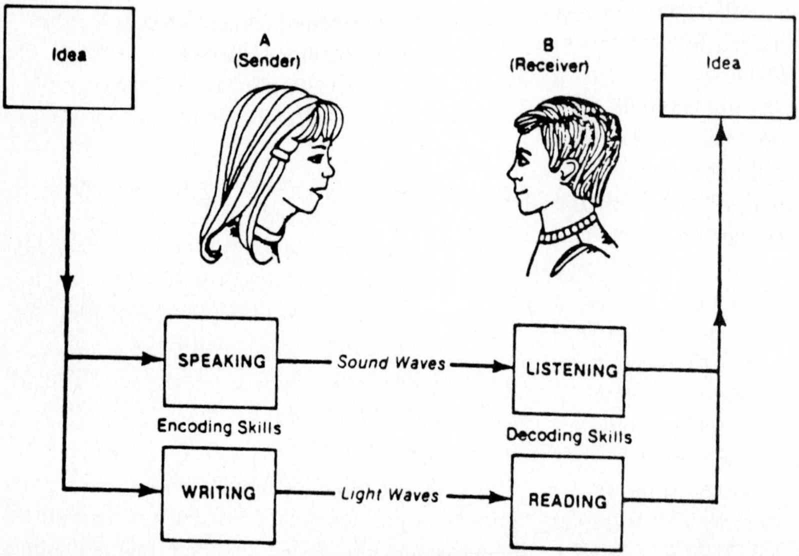

Source: Janet Lerner, *Learning Disabilities: Theories, Diagnosis, and Teaching Strategies,* 4th ed. (Boston: Houghton Mifflin, 1985), p. 320. Adapted by permission.

Components of Language

The content of language instruction for students with learning and behavior problems focuses on teaching the language code, the rules of the code, and how to use the code to communicate. To help us understand language so that we can more effectively plan the content of language instruction, we will consider several components of language.

Content

Content, also called *semantics,* refers to the ideas or concepts we are communicating. Elsa can communicate her desire for two chocolate chip cookies in numerous ways. For example, she can say, ''I want two chocolate chip cookies,'' or ''Me want choc-chip cookies'' (while pointing to the cookie jar and then holding up two fingers). In both cases, the content or ideas are the same.

When we teach content, we are teaching concepts and helping students learn the labels (vocabulary) for those concepts. When a young child asks such questions as ''What's that?'' or ''What are you doing?'' we often respond by giving the label for the object (e.g., spoon, blanket, shirt) or the action (i.e., stirring, making the bed, ironing). In this way we are teaching the labels for the ideas or concepts.

We are also teaching content when we help students see the relationships among the ideas or concepts. The diagram or semantic network of the concept of ''bird,'' as depicted in Figure 2.8 (page 54), is one way to demonstrate how ideas are related. In this case, we used a network that represented the concept of ''bird'' in terms of its class, properties, and examples or instances. Much of education, whether teaching about fruits and vegetables in primary grades or the characteristics of capitalism and communism in high school, centers on teaching about ideas, the relationships among the ideas, and the vocabulary that labels the ideas (Anders and Bos, 1986; Reed, 1986).

Form

Form refers to the structure and sound of language. In the example of Elsa wanting two chocolate chip cookies, two different forms were presented for the underlying meaning of the message. Form is usually further divided into phonology, morphology, and syntax.

Phonology. *Phones* are the actual sounds produced by speakers. *Phonemes* are the smallest linguistic units of sound that can signal a meaning difference. In the English language there are approximately forty-five phonemes or speech sounds that are classified as either vowels or consonants. Learning the speech sounds and their relationships to the written letters can help students identify unknown words when they read. *Phonology* refers to the rules for combining and patterning phonemes within the language. Phonology also includes the control of vocal features (timing, frequency, duration) that influence the meaning we express when talking. Without changing any words, we can vary the underlying meaning of a sentence simply by the way we change our voice (e.g., intonation, pitch, and stress). For example, try saying, ''I like *that?*'' and ''I *like* that.'' Depending on the intonation, stress, and pitch, the first statement can mean ''I don't like that'' and the second one can mean ''I do like that.''

Morphology. *Morphemes* are the smallest units of language that convey meaning. There are two different kinds of morphemes: free and bound. *Free morphemes,* or root words, can stand alone (e.g., *cat, run, small, drive*), whereas *bound morphemes,* or affixes, that change the meaning when attached to words (e.g., cat*s*, *re*run, small*est,* driv*ing*). The word *recaptured* is composed of three morphemes: the root *capture,* the prefix *re,* and the inflectional ending *ed,* which signals past tense. Helping elementary and secondary students learn the various affixes (prefixes, suffixes, and inflectional endings) and their meanings can assist them in determining the meaning of words. For example, the word *predetermina-tion* is composed of the root word *determine* (to decide), the prefix *pre* (before), and the suffix *tion* (which makes a verb into a noun). By combining these different meanings, we can generate the meaning of *predetermination* as a decision made in advance.

Syntax. *Syntax* refers to the order of words in sentences and the rules for determining the order. Just as phonemes combine to form words, words combine to form phrases and sentences. In the same way that rules determine how phonemes can be combined, rules also determine how words can be combined. The basic syntactical structure for English is subject + verb + object (e.g., Mike eats cereal).

The rules for combining words vary across languages. For example, in English, adjectives almost always precede the noun they modify (e.g., a delicious apple), whereas in Spanish, adjectives generally follow the noun they modify (e.g., *una manzana deliciosa*—an apple delicious).

Use

Use, also called *pragmatics,* refers to the way in which we use language to communicate and to carry out social functions (McLean and Snyder-McLean, 1978).

One aspect of use relates to the *goals of language*. We use language for many different purposes (Halliday, 1975). Young children often use language simply for vocal play, as reflected in babbling. This helps children learn the rules of the sound system as well as intonation and pitch. We also use language for getting attention, commenting on our own or other's actions (past, present, or future), requesting objects, obtaining information, giving information, asking questions, and regulating our own or other's behavior.

A second aspect of use is related to the context in which the language is used. We use language differently, depending on the social situation in which we are placed (Prutting, 1982). For example, a student will use much more casual language when discussing a book with a friend over lunch than when giving an oral report in literature class. Different sets of circumstances determine how a speaker will use language to accomplish a goal (Bloom and Lahey, 1978). For instance, depending on who the listener is and the relationship the speaker has with the listener, a speaker could say any of the following to accomplish the goal of getting the air conditioner turned down:

> Turn <u>down</u> the thermostat.
> When you get up, will you please turn down the thermostat.
> I'm really getting hot.

The way a speaker uses language will also be influenced by the knowledge the speaker thinks the listener has about the topic being discussed. If you are describing how to hang a picture on a wall, your language is quite different if the listener is familiar with a plastic anchor and screw. The manner in which a topic is introduced, maintained, and changes, as well as how we reference topics, is governed by pragmatic rules.

School-Age Language Development and Difficulties

Knowing how language develops during the school-age years and what difficulties students with learning and behavior problems demonstrate during these years will further help us make decisions concerning the content and focus of language instruction.

Much of the research in language development has focused on the preschool child. Between the ages of zero to five, most children become amazingly facile with their language and communication (Brown, 1973; deVilliers and deVilliers, 1978; Owens, 1988). Due to the quantity and quality of development that occurs during this period, the preschool child has been the center of focus for most language researchers. However, during the last ten years there has been a growing interest in the language development that takes place during the school years

(Nippold, 1988; Wallach, 1984; Wallach and Miller, 1988) and in the difficulties that students encounter with language in school settings (Scott, 1988; Spinelli and Ripich, 1985).

Although not enough research is available to support a comprehensive scope and sequence for school-age language development, there is enough information to assist us in planning the content of language instruction.

Knowing about school-age language development is particularly important for teachers of students who have learning and behavior problems. There is a growing amount of evidence to suggest that these students have mild to moderate language problems (Camarata, Hughes, and Ruhl, 1988; McDonough, 1989; Snyder, 1984; Wallach, 1984; Wiig and Semel, 1984). The largest subgroup of learning-disabled students are those who experience language difficulties (McKinney, 1984; Simon, 1985; Wiig and Semel, 1984).

Let's examine the development of content, form, and use at the school-age level and the difficulties that students with learning and behavior problems demonstrate.

Content

During the school-age period, children increase the size of their vocabularies and their ability to understand and talk about abstract concepts.

Vocabulary Growth. Children's vocabulary continues to expand as they enter and participate in school. In general, the size of the vocabulary for six-year-old children is estimated to be about 2,500 words (Wiig and Semel, 1984). In comparison, when technical words are discounted, average adult speakers converse in everyday conversation using about 10,000 words, and an estimated 60,000 to 80,000 words are known and used by the average high-school graduate (Carroll, 1964). School provides students with the opportunities to listen, read, and learn, thus increasing their vocabularies. Think for a moment about the vocabulary that students develop as they learn math. Table 3.1 presents sample math vocabulary from math curricula. Even math,

which is often considered less language-based than social studies and science, contains a significant number of concepts and words to learn.

In addition to learning more words, there is also an increase in the breadth and specificity of meaning. For example, the word *bird* to a preschooler may refer to animals that fly. However, most children later learn a whole set of specific vocabulary that defines different types of birds and their characteristics. The semantic network that was depicted in Figure 2.8 (page 54) grows more and more complex and more interrelated as a student's knowledge of birds increases.

During school-age years, the ability for students to understand and organize abstract concepts increases significantly (Anglin, 1970). This results in the ability to group words by such abstract features as animate or inanimate, spatial (location) or temporal (time) relationships, and so on. For example, in learning about fossils, students learn to simultaneously classify different types of fossils (e.g., trilobites, crinoids, brachiopods) according to plant/animal, extinct/not extinct, and location (e.g., sea, lake, or land).

Multiple meanings of many common words are acquired during the school-age years (Menyuk, 1971). For example, *bank* has several meanings and can function as both a noun and verb:

> Lou sat on the *bank* fishing.
> You can *bank* on him to be there.
> Put your money in the *bank* for now.

Students with learning and behavior problems generally have vocabularies that are more limited, and their word meanings are generally more concrete and less flexible. For example, in teaching a group of seventh-grade learning-disabled students about fossils, we found the students sometimes had difficulty considering three different characteristics of fossils simultaneously (Bos and Anders, 1990). Questions such as "Which fossils are extinct sea animals?" required them to juggle too much information. In

TABLE 3.1   *Sample Vocabulary in Math Curricula*

Third Grade	Sixth Grade	Eighth Grade
addition	numeral	absolute value
area	digit	associative property
circle	exponents	axis
cone	place value	binary operation
customary system	addends	bisector
distance	difference	circumference
equivalent	estimating	collinear points
fraction	products	communicative property
line of symmetry	multiples	composite number
metric	factors	diagonal
perimeter	divisible	disjoint sets
ordinal	numerator	equation
quotient	denominator	finite set
regroup	decimals	
remainder	centimeter	
rounding	perpendicular	
sum	acute angle	
	equilateral	
	median	
	probability	
	integers	
	positive/negative numbers	

comparison, the students could easily answer questions in which they had to deal with only one characteristic at a time, for example, "Which fossils live in the sea?" "Which fossils are animals?" and "Which fossils are extinct?"

These students also have greater difficulty understanding that words can have multiple meanings and knowing which meaning to apply. In the question, "Was the *fare* that you paid for your taxi ride to the *fair* a *fair* price?" students are required to have and use several different meanings for the word *fair*.

Figurative Language. During the school-age years, students gain greater understanding and ability to use figurative language. This allows children to use language in truly creative ways (Owens, 1988). The primary types of figurative language include:

- Idioms (I had to break my date. It is raining cats and dogs. Let's throw a party.)

- Metaphors (She had her eagle-eye watching for him.)
- Similes (He ran like a frightened rabbit.)
- Proverbs (The early bird catches the worm.)

Students with learning and behavior problems oftentimes have difficulty with figurative language. As these students move into adolescence, where figurative language plays an important role in both school and social activities, their concrete interpretations are quite evident. For example, Ivan, a high-school student in a self-contained class for emotionally handicapped students, showed up at his girlfriend's house and lost his temper because he didn't understand what "breaking a date" meant.

Word Retrieval. Some students with learning and behavior problems also experience difficulties with *word retrieval* or *word finding* (German, 1979, 1982; McGregor and Leonard, 1989;

Rudel, Denckla, and Broman, 1981). A word retrieval problem is like having the word on the tip of your tongue but not being able to think of it. The following dialogue presents a conversation between two third-grade students—one with normal language and the other with word retrieval problems.

Setting:	Third-grade classroom
Topic:	Discussion about how to make an Easter basket
Susan:	Are you going to make, uh, make, uh . . . one of these things (pointing to the Easter basket on the bookshelf)?
Cori:	Oh, you mean an Easter basket?
Susan:	Yeah, an Easter basket.
Cori:	Sure, I'd like to but I'm not sure how to do it. Can you help me?
Susan:	Yeah, first you'll need some, uh, some, uh, the things you cut with, you know . . . .
Cori:	Scissors.
Susan:	Yeah, and some paper and the thing you use to stick things together with.
Cori:	Tape?
Susan:	No, uh, uh, sticky stuff.
Cori:	Oh, well let's get the stuff we need.
Susan:	Let's go to, uh, uh, the shelf, uh, where you get, you know, the stuff to cut up.
Cori:	Yeah, the paper, and let's also get the glue.

It is obvious from the conversation that both students were frustrated by the communication process. Susan's language is filled with indefinite words ("thing") ("dealie"), circumlocutions ("The things you cut with"), and filler ("Let's go to, uh, the shelf, um, where you get, you know, the stuff to cut up.") At first, students like Susan may seem very talkative because of their overuse of descriptions, circumlocutions, and fillers (Swafford and Reed, 1986); however,

after listening for a while, their language seems "empty in information."

Form

During the school-age years, students continue to grow in the ability to use more complex sentence structures (Scott, 1988). Although by age five most students understand and generate basic sentences (McNeill, 1970), first graders produce sentences that are neither completely grammatical (*He'll might go to jail*) nor reflect the syntactical complexities of the English language. Table 3.2 shows the percentage of correct usage for various sentence types by first graders (Menyuk, 1969). Table 3.3 presents the sequence for selected syntactical structures (Carrow, 1973). Some of the most difficult structures require the use of complex sentences using causals (*because*), conditional (*if*), and enabling relationships (*so that*).

Another later-developing sentence structure is the passive sentence (*The boy is chased by the dog*), which is usually not established until ages five to seven (Chomsky, 1969; Owens, 1988).

As sentence complexity increases, so does the average length of sentences. Table 3.4 demonstrates the growth in the number of words per sentence or communication unit.

Children also continue to increase in their ability to use inflectional endings, suffixes, and prefixes. Table 3.5 presents the order of and age ranges for the acquisition of selected suffixes and inflectional endings. Although the major time for the development of rules for forming regular noun plurals appears to be during kindergarten and first grade, irregular plurals (e.g., *men, mice, sheep*) may be delayed by two or three years (Koziol, 1973). In contrast, students with language problems are generally delayed in their development of irregular verbs (*He goed with me*), plurals, comparatives, and possessives (Vogel, 1983).

Students with language problems are slower to develop advanced syntactic structures (Andolina, 1980), and these delays are most evident in the elementary grades (Swafford and Reed, 1986).

TABLE 3.2 *Percentages of First Graders Who Produced Well-Formed Sentences*

Percentage	Sentence Type	Examples
100	Infinitival complement.	I want *to have it.*
100	Adjective, nominal compound and possessives.	The *boy and girl* danced. It is the *boy's* hat.
97	Adverb inversion.	Sometimes boys like to cook.
95	"And" conjunction.	The boy ran *and* the girl jumped.
90	Imperative sentences.	*Go* to the cafeteria!
89	Conjunction deletion.	The boy *drank* the tea *and ate* the pie.
89	Separation with verb and particle construction.	The boy *took* the dog *out.*
87	Relative clauses.	That's the boy *who lives next door.*
69	Reflexive structure.	The man shaved *himself.*
66	Substitution and embedding.	The man *who was sick* went home.
64	Passive construction.	The car *was bought by* the man.
41	Pronominalization.	*You* take it.
37	"Cause" conjunction.	She ate it *cause* she was hungry.
29	Nominalization.	They went *fishing.*
20	Participle complement.	The *roaring* river disturbed me.
20	"If" conjunction.	*If* it rains, I won't play outside.
19	"So" conjunction.	She bought it *so* she could play with it.

Source: E. H. Wiig and E. M. Semel, *Language Assessment and Intervention for the Learning Disabled,* 2nd ed. (Columbus, Ohio: Charles E. Merrill, 1984), p. 299. Reprinted by permission of the publisher.

Use

The area of most important linguistic growth during the school-age years is language use or pragmatics (Owens, 1988). During the school years the child becomes quite adept in using communication for a variety of functions. During later school years students become proficient in using language in sarcasm, jokes, and double meanings (Schultz, 1974). Throughout the schooling years students become more empathetic toward the listener and able to understand a variety of perspectives. Older children are much more aware of and take into account the listener's knowledge concerning a topic (Krauss and Glucksberg, 1967).

According to White (1975), young school-age children use language to:

1. Gain and hold adult attention in a socially acceptable manner.
2. Use others, when appropriate, as resources for assistance or information.
3. Express affection or hostility and anger appropriately.
4. Direct and follow peers.
5. Compete with peers in storytelling and boasts.
6. Express pride in himself or herself and in personal accomplishments.
7. Role play.

By adolescence, students reflect communicative competence (Allen and Brown, 1977; Wiig and Semel, 1984) in that they can:

1. Express positive and negative feelings and reactions to others.
2. Present, understand, and respond to information in spoken messages related to persons, objects, events, or processes that are not immediately visible.
3. Take the role of another person.
4. Understand and present complex messages.

TABLE 3.3   *Developmental Sequence for Comprehension of Sentence Types*

Syntactic Structure	Sentence	Age of Comprehension		
		By 75%		*By 90%*
Simple imperative	Go!	4–6*	to	6–0 years
Negative imperative	Don't cross!	5–6	to	7–0+ years
Active declarative				
Regular noun and present progressive	The girl is jumping.	3–0	to	3–0 years
Irregular noun and present progressive	The sheep is eating.	6–6	to	7–0 years
Past tense	The man painted the house.	5–6	to	7–0+ years
Past participle	The lion has eaten.	6–0	to	7–0+ years
Future	He will hit the ball.	7–0	to	7–0+ years
Reversible	The car bumps the train.	6–6	to	7–0+ years
Perfective	The man has been cutting trees.	7–0+	to	7–0+ years
Interrogative				
Who . . .	Who is by the table?	3–0	to	3–0 years
What . . .	What do we eat?	3–6	to	5–0 years
When . . .	When do you sleep?	3–6	to	5–6 years
Negation				
Explicit	The girl isn't running.	5–6	to	7–0+ years
Inherent	These two are different.	6–6	to	7–0+ years
Reversible passive	The boy is chased by the dog.	5–6	to	6–0 years
Conjunction				
If . . .	If you're the teacher, point to the dog; if not, point to the bear.	7–0+	to	7–0+ years
. . . then	Look at the third picture; then point to the baby of his animal.	7–0+	to	7–0+ years
neither . . . nor	Find the one that is neither the ball nor the table.	7–0+	to	7–0+ years

*4–6 = 4 years, 6 months.

Source: E. H. Wiig and E. M. Semel, *Language Assessment and Intervention for the Learning Disabled,* 2nd ed. (Columbus, Ohio: Charles E. Merrill, 1984), p. 300. Reprinted by permission of the publisher.

5. Adapt messages to the needs of others.
6. Based on prior experience, approach verbal interactions with expectations of what to say and how to say it.
7. Select different forms for their messages based on the age, status, and reactions of the listeners.

Some students with learning and behavior disorders also experience difficulties with language *use* or pragmatics. The following dialogue demonstrates how Brice, an adolescent with behavior disorders and subsequent learning problems, has difficulty using language effectively in a conversation with a peer. He tends to switch topics (lack of topic maintenance), does not provide enough context for his listener, does not provide adequate referents for his pronouns, and does not respond to his listener's requests for clarification.

TABLE 3.4 *Average Number of Words per Communication Unit*

| Grade | Average Number of Words per Communication Unit (mean) | | |
	High Group	Random Group	Low Group
1	7.91	6.88	5.91
2	8.10	7.56	6.65
3	8.38	7.62	7.08
4	9.28	9.00	7.55
5	9.59	8.82	7.90
6	10.32	9.82	8.57
7	11.14	9.75	9.01
8	11.59	10.71	9.52
9	11.73	10.96	9.26
10	12.34	10.68	9.41
11	13.00	11.17	10.18
12	12.84	11.70	10.65

Source: W. Loban, *Language Development: Kindergarten through Grade Twelve,* Res. Report #18 (Urbana, Ill.: National Council of Teachers of English, 1976), p. 27. Reprinted by permission of the publisher.

Setting: Computer Lab
Topic: Brice is explaining to Reid how to play a computer game
Brice: Did you get in trouble for last night?
Reid: What do you mean for last night?
Brice: You know, for what you did.
Reid: I'm not sure what you are talking about.
Brice: Want to learn how to play Chopperlifter?
Reid: Yeah, I guess, but what about last night?
Brice: Well, one thing you do is put it in the slot and turn on the computer.
Reid: What thing? Do you mean the disk?
Brice: Sure I do. Now watch. (Brice boots the disk and selects Chopperlifter from a game menu.) You got to take it and go pick up the men.

Reid: You mean the helicopter?
Brice: Yeah, aren't you listening?
Reid: Yeah, but you're not telling me enough about the game.
Brice: Yes I am. You're just like my brother, you don't listen.
Reid: I'm not going to put up with this. I'll see you around.

Although not reflected in his language sample, Brice also has difficulty varying his language for different audiences. Like other students with pragmatic language problems (Soenksen, Flagg, and Schmits, 1981), he sometimes sounds disrespectful to adults because he does not vary his language to suit different speakers or speaking environments. Finally, Brice and other students with pragmatic language difficulties tend to misinterpret emotions or meanings indicated by nonverbal communication, including facial expressions and body language, more frequently than their normal peers (Axelrod, 1982; McDonough, 1989; Wiig and Harris, 1974).

However, it is important to remember that content, form, and use are related. Sometimes students who appear to have difficulties with language use, have these difficulties because of limited content and form. For these students, it would be important to focus instruction in the areas of content and form and see if language use automatically improves. These students tend to lack the content and form devices for looking good pragmatically.

Conclusion

Even though students enter school with many language skills already mastered, there are still many skills that develop during the school years. Students' vocabulary grows significantly both in number and abstractness. They learn to use and control more difficult sentence structures such as compound, complex, and passive sentences, and they learn how to use prefixes, suffixes, and inflectional endings to modify root words. Students' uses for language expand and their ability to communicate increases as they become more aware of the listener and his or her needs in the communication process. In short, language development in the areas of content, form, and use increase measurably during the school-age years. Whereas this process happens almost automatically for most students because of the opportunities that school and expanding environments afford for learning language, students with learning and behavior problems are often delayed in this development and require more explicit instruction. We will now focus on the procedures for language instruction.

Procedures for Language Instruction

In educating students with learning and behavior problems, we have traditionally focused on teaching academic skills and have placed less emphasis on the development of oral language skills. However, it is clear that language continues to develop during the school-age years and that students with learning and behavior problems evidence difficulties in oral language that affect oral as well as written communication. Let's look at some general principles and proce-

dures for teaching oral language skills to these students.

General Procedures for Teaching Language

Opportunities for teaching oral language abound in the school setting. When we teach students new concepts and vocabulary in content area subjects we are teaching oral language. When students learn how to give oral reports or retell a story, how to introduce themselves, or how to use irregular verbs, they are learning language. A list of general procedures or guidelines for teaching language to students with learning and behavior problems is presented in Figure 3.2 and discussed in this section. The principles can serve as guidelines for teaching. You will also find that the speech/language pathologist is a good source for additional guidelines, techniques, and teaching ideas.

1. *Teach language in context.* Whether you are teaching a student to use causal relationships (form), to categorize fossils (content), or how to use the telephone to request information (use), it

TABLE 3.5 *Order of Acquisition of Word Formation Rules*

Word Formation Rule	Application	Age Range of Acquisition	
		by 75%	*by 90%*
Regular noun plurals	balls	3–6	to 6–0 years
	coats	5–6	to 6–6 years
	chairs	6–6	to 7–0+ years
Present progressive tense	running, hitting	3–0	to 3–6 years
Present progressive tense	going	3–6	to 5–6 years
Adjective forms			
Comparative	smaller, taller	4–0	to 5–0 years
Superlative	fattest	3–0	to 3–6 years
Noun derivation			
-er	hitter	3–6	to 5–0 years
	painter	4–0	to 6–0 years
	farmer	5–0	to 6–6 years
-man	fisherman	5–6	to 6–0 years
-ist	bicyclist, pianist	7–0	to 7–0+ years
Adverb derivation			
-ly	easily, gently	7–0+	to 7–0+ years

Source: E. H. Wiig and E. M. Semel, *Language Assessment and Intervention for the Learning Disabled,* 2nd ed. (Columbus, Ohio: Charles E. Merrill, 1984), p. 294. Reprinted by permission of the publisher.

FIGURE 3.2   *General Principles for Teaching Language*

Teach language in context.

In most cases, follow the sequence of normal language development.

Teach comprehension and production.

Use effective teaching strategies when presenting a new concept or skill.

Use self-talk to explain what you are doing or thinking.

Use parallel talk to describe what others are doing.

Use modeling to help students get practice and feedback on a specific language skill.

Use expansion to demonstrate how an idea can be expressed in a slightly more complex manner.

Use elaboration to demonstrate how more information can be expressed.

Use structured language programs to provide intensive practice and feedback.

Reinforce language learning theory by using intrinsic reinforcers and naturally occurring consequences.

Systematically plan and instruct for generalization.

is important to teach language in context. It is difficult to imagine teaching someone how to use a hammer, drill, or saw unless we had nails, boards, and probably the goal of making a simple wood project in mind. The same should apply when teaching students to use language. Rote practice of sentence structures or rehearsal of word definitions will teach the student little about how to use language.

To foster teaching language in context, plan activities that highlight the language skill you are teaching. For example, Mr. Cardoni used the context of following a recipe for chocolate cookies and building bird feeders to teach the vocabulary related to fractions (e.g., half, one-quarter, two-thirds, part, whole, fraction). During the activities the students measured and compared the different fractional parts (e.g., determining what fraction one teaspoon is of one tablespoon). This allowed Mr. Cardoni and his students to talk about the concepts of fractions in a situation where they played an important role in the proj-

ect and to demonstrate with concrete examples the differences between fractions.

2. *In most cases, follow the sequence of normal language development.* Determining the content of instruction is a major part of the teaching-learning process, whether it be in language, academics, content areas, or social areas. Although the developmental sequence of language skills for students with learning and behavior problems is not well-documented, there is some evidence to suggest that these students develop language knowledge and skills in the same sequence as normal-achieving students but at a slower rate (Reed, 1986; Wiig and Semel, 1984). They may also have more difficulty in one component of language: content, form, or use. For example, Susan, the third grader with word-finding problems (see page 67) has difficulty primarily in the area of content. On the other hand, Brice (see page 70) appears to have adequate content and form in his language, but has difficulty with use. Therefore, in planning a language program, begin by determining what skills the student has already acquired in the areas of content, form, and use, and then target the subsequent skills in the development process. For instance, if a student is already using past tense (*The boy ate the cake.*), then you might next focus on past participle (*The boy has eaten the cake.*) (see Table 3.3). A speech/language pathologist should be an excellent resource for helping to determine what skills to teach next.

3. *Teach comprehension and production.* Be sure to give the students opportunities to develop both their understanding (comprehension) and their ability to express (production) the new skill you are teaching. For example, when teaching students to comprehend the past participle, you will want to label examples of events that have already happened (e.g., *Juan has sharpened his pencil. Kim has finished her math assignment.*). When providing intensive practice and feedback, you could show the students picture-sequence cards (see Figure 3.3) and have the students identify the picture that demonstrates that something "has hap-

FIGURE 3.3 *Sequence Cards to Assist Students in Comprehending and Producing Tenses*

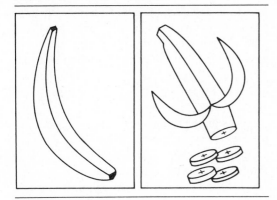

porated into language instruction. Figure 3.4 lists key strategies that should be used when teaching language.

5. *Use self-talk to explain what you are doing or thinking.* Self-talk is simply talking about what you are doing or thinking, emphasizing the concepts or skills you are trying to teach. For example, Ms. Schmidt wants to teach future tense to a group of first-grade language/learning-disabled students. To emphasize the difference between present progressive tense (a tense the students were already using successfully) and future tense, she uses self-talk while she demonstrates the art activity for the day. Before she does something (e.g., gets the scissors and paper) she says, "I *will get* the paper and scissors." She continues this throughout the activity, each time emphasizing the verb tense. As suggested by the principles of cognitive behavior modification (Chapter Two, pages 37 to 39) do not limit yourself to only talking about what you are doing. Using self-talk to let students know what you are thinking can help them understand how to use language to think.

pened.'' To teach production, have the students label events that have happened by using the past participle form. For example, you could ask students, "What *have* you just done?''

4. *Use effective teaching strategies when presenting a new concept or skill.* Based on the teaching-learning process, there are a number of effective teaching strategies that should be incor-

FIGURE 3.4 *Effective Teaching Strategies for Presenting a New Concept or Skill*

When teaching new language concepts or patterns, keep the following strategies in mind:

1. Gear the activities to the students' interests and cognitive level.
2. Get the students' attention before engaging in communication activities.
3. Bombard the student with the concept or skill frequently throughout the day in a functional manner.
4. When speaking, place stress on the target concept or language pattern.
5. Pause between phrases or sentences so that the student has time to process the new concept or language pattern.
6. Decrease the rate or presentation when first introducing the concept or language pattern.
7. When introducing a new concept or language pattern, use familiar, concrete vocabulary and simple sentence patterns (Bloom, Miller, and Hood, 1975; Reed, 1986).
8. If possible, present the new concept or language pattern by using more than one input mode (e.g., auditory, visual, kinesthetic). Gestures and facial expressions that are paired with a specific language pattern often assist students in understanding the form. For example, giving a look of puzzlement or wonder when asking a question can serve as a cue to the students.
9. Pair written symbols with oral language. For instance, demonstrating morphological endings such as *s* (plurals) and *ed* (past tense) can be done in writing. The students can then be cued to listen for what they see.

6. *Use parallel talk to describe what others are doing.* Whereas self-talk focuses on what you are doing or thinking, parallel talk emphasizes what the student is doing or what is about to happen to the student or his or her environment (Van Riper and Emerick, 1984). The purpose of parallel talk is to demonstrate to the student how language can be used to talk about his or her actions and the surrounding environment. For example, Mr. Fong is trying to get students to understand causal relationships by demonstrating how temperature affects water. First, he has the students heat water until it boils. As they complete this task Mr. Fong labels their actions by using sentences containing causal connectives (e.g., "Heat *causes* the water to get hotter and hotter." "Water boils and turns to steam *because* it gets too hot to stay a liquid.").

7. *Use modeling to help students get practice and feedback on a specific language skill.* Modeling plays an important role in learning language. For example, Ms. Simon is teaching Carlos to use present progressives. She models the following as she and Carlos play with toy cars and trucks.

Ms. Simon: The blue car *is going*. The red car *is going*. The yellow truck *is going*. What is the green truck doing?

Carlos: Truck is going.

Some evidence suggests that the critical component is the modeling, and that it is not always necessary to have the student respond as Carlos did in the example (Ellis-Weismer and Murray-Branch, 1989).

Peer modeling can also prove effective because the student hears the language being modeled by other students.

8. *Use expansion to demonstrate how an idea can be expressed in a slightly more complex manner.* The purpose of expansion is to facilitate the development of more complex language form and content. It demonstrates to the students how their thoughts can be expressed in a slightly more complex manner. For example, Mr. Lee is trying to get his students to use more precise terms when explaining size. Currently, they restrict their descriptions to "big" and "small" or "little." When Jennie describes the elephant and mouse in the story they were reading as being "big" and "small," Mr. Lee expands her vocabulary by stating, "Yes, the elephant was *enormous* and the mouse was *tiny*."

Expansion is a technique that is also frequently used when trying to get a student to give a more complex language form. For example, Rob rarely uses adverbs in his language, a form Mr. Lee is trying to get Rob to develop. Rob sometimes substitutes adjectives for adverbs. During the day, whenever Rob explains what he is doing, Mr. Lee repeats what Rob said but adds an adverb.

Rob: I got the first one easy. The second one was hard."

Mr. Lee: Oh, you got the first one *easily*. The second one was hard."

Note that with expansion you do not want to imply that you are correcting the student, but simply showing him or her a more complex way of expressing the thought. It is also important only to expand slightly on the content or form and focus on only one or two target areas of instruction. For example, if Mr. Lee had expanded by responding, "Oh, so you got the first math problem easily, but the second one was a real killer," then the expansion probably would have been too complex for Rob to profit from it.

9. *Use elaboration to demonstrate how more information can be expressed.* When we elaborate on an idea we provide more detail or context for the idea. The language of learning-disabled students frequently reflects limited detail and context (Wiig and Semel, 1984). For example, Chris, a fourth-grade, learning-disabled student, was explaining that snakes have rough skin. Ms. Anderson elaborated on his idea by commenting, "Snakes have rough skin and so do lizards, gila monsters, and alligators. They all have rough skin.''

10. *Use structured language programs to provide intensive practice and feedback.* Teaching in context is critical for learning and generalization. However, sometimes by teaching in context we do not provide the students with adequate opportunities to practice a new skill. Students who have learning problems need the practice and feedback provided in many language programs and activities to gain mastery of the skill. For example, both *DISTAR Language* (Engelmann and Osborn, 1987) and the *Monterey Language Program* (Gray and Ryan, 1973) provide intensive practice in different language forms (e.g., sentence structures, inflectional endings, etc.). However, these programs should not serve as the students' entire language program. Although they provide practice and feedback, they generally do not teach the skill within the relevant contexts that are needed for learning and generalization.

11. *Reinforce language learning by using intrinsic reinforcers and naturally occurring consequences* (Holland, 1975; Hubbell, 1977). Because language is such an enabling tool, it carries a great deal of intrinsic reinforcement for most children. Rather than using praise (''I like the way you said that'' or ''Good talking''), we can capitalize on the naturally reinforcing nature of language. For example, during a cooking activity Mr. Warren asks the students, ''How can we figure out how much two-thirds of a cup plus three-fourths of a cup of flour is?'' After Lydia explained, Mr. Warren comments, ''Now we know how to figure that out. Shall we give it a try?'' Later, the teacher asks how to sift flour. After Rona explained, he says, ''I've got it. Do you think we can sift it just the way Rona explained to us?'' Rather than commenting on how ''good'' their language was and disrupting the flow of communication, Mr. Warren complimented Lydia and Rona by letting them know how useful the information was. When a student's purposes and intents are fulfilled because of the language he or she uses, those lan-

guage behaviors are naturally reinforced. The student learns that appropriate language use is a powerful tool in controlling the environment (Reed, 1986).

12. *Systematically plan and instruct for generalization.* As is the case when teaching other skills, language instruction must incorporate into the instructional sequence a variety of contexts, settings, stimuli, and persons with which the student interacts if he or she is to generalize the language skills.

Because language is a tool that is used across so many contexts, it is relatively easy to incorporate generalization into language instruction. Mrs. McDonald, the self-contained special education teacher, and Ms. Cortez, the speech/language pathologist, are working with Julie, a second-grade, learning-disabled child, on sequencing events and using sequence markers (e.g., first, second, next, last). When Julie goes to language, Mrs. McDonald sends a note that lists, in order, the activities Julie participated in thus far during the day. When Julie returns from language, Ms. Cortez sends back a note that lists her language activities. Each teacher then converses with Julie about what she did in the other teacher's class, emphasizing sequence and sequence markers. Other activities also build generalization for Julie. Whenever either teacher or Julie's mom reads Julie a story, Julie is asked sequence questions. During the weekly cooking activity, Julie and the other students are asked the steps in making the food for the day, and these steps are written on large chart paper with numbers listed beside them. Julie also arranges picture sequence cards and is then asked to describe them. In this way Julie is receiving numerous opportunities to generalize this language skill to a variety of contexts, persons, and settings.

Teaching Content

We teach language content throughout the day. For example, one of the major goals in teaching a new unit in social studies and science is for the students to understand and use the new vocabulary. What are some of the basic vocabulary categories that we may want to teach? Table 3.6 lists some general categories of words and word relationships. Let us look at some strategies for teaching content or vocabulary, whether it be the more general vocabulary listed in Table 3.6, or the specific vocabulary found in content area instruction.

1. *Emphasize the distinguishing and critical features of the concepts being taught.* When teaching new concepts, emphasize the features that are important to the meaning. For example, when teaching the concepts of ''mountains'' and ''hills'' the distinguishing or critical features to emphasize are ''size'' and ''height.'' In comparison, the ''texture of the land'' is not important since it is not a feature that usually helps us distinguish between hills and mountains.

2. *Concepts should be introduced in a number of different ways.* When teaching the concept of ''precipitation,'' for instance, present pictures of different types of precipitation (e.g., snow, rain, sleet, hail, and mist). Have the students tell about a time when they remember each type of precipitation. Discuss what is happening to the water in the atmosphere when it is precipitating and discuss what the weather is like when it is precipitating.

3. *Present examples and nonexamples of the concept.* For example, when learning about cactus, have the students generate two lists of plants, one that represents examples of cacti and one that represents nonexamples. Then talk about and list the features that make the cacti different from the nonexamples.

4. *Categorize new concepts so that students understand how the concept relates to other concepts.* If the concept of ''melancholy'' is being taught, the students should learn that this is an example of a feeling or emotion. Other feelings are ''gladness,'' ''relief,'' and ''hurt.'' Characteristics of people who are melancholy are ''not happy,'' ''quiet,'' ''not talkative,'' and ''somber.'' These ideas can be positioned in a visual diagram, such as a *semantic map,* which shows how the different concepts relate to one another (see Figure 3.5).

5. *Present new vocabulary in simple sentences or phrases.* It is harder to learn a new concept or idea if the teacher is using difficult language to explain what it means. The rule of thumb is to use simple sentences or phrases to introduce new concepts (i.e., four- to seven-word sentences and two- to four-word phrases.)

6. *Use games and other activities to reinforce newly introduced concepts.* For example, Twenty Questions is a good game to use to get students to think about the characteristics of a concept and the categories in which it falls. This game is played by having one person think of an idea or concept (e.g., parakeet) and having the rest of the students ask questions that can be answered with ''yes'' or ''no'' in order to guess the concept (e.g., Is it a plant? Is it smaller than a person?). The object of the game is to guess the concept before twenty questions have been asked.

Oral or written cloze passages, as shown in Figure 3.6, can be used to highlight a particular set of concepts being taught.

Name that Category is a game that can be played similarly to Name that Tune, except the object of the game is to earn points by naming the category when examples of a category are given. The sooner the category is named, the more points the player(s) receives. For instance, one team or group of students thinks of a category and five examples (e.g., mammals: bears, dogs, kangaroos, rats, and humans). They tell the other team the examples one at a time, with the other team guessing the category after each example is given. If the other team gets the category after the first example, they get 30 points. If it takes two examples, then the team gets 20 points, then 15, 10, and 5 for each additional example given.

Idioms, metaphors, and similes can be used when playing Charades, with the students acting out the literal meanings of the phrases (e.g., catch a plane, blow your stack).

TABLE 3.6   *Categories of Words and Word Relationships*

Categories	School-Related Examples
Existence/Nouns	science, math, reading, vowels, consonants, sentences, paragraphs
Actions/Verbs	Verbs often used in instruction—draw, write, circle, underline, discuss, compare, critique, defend
Attributes/Adjectives	Words that describe such attributes as size, shape, texture, weight, position (high/low, first/last), color, age, speed, affect, attractiveness
Attributes/Adverbs	Words that describe actions such as easily, hurriedly, friendly, willingly
Prepositions	locative (in, on, under, beside, in front of, ahead of, behind), directional (off, out of, away from, toward, around, through), temporal (before, after, between), for, from, at, of, to, with, without

Personal pronouns

Subjective	Objective	Possessive
I	me	my, mine
you	you	your
she, he, it	her, him, it	her, his, its
we	us	our
they	them	their

Categories	School-Related Examples
Demonstrative pronouns	this, that, these, those
Indefinite and negative pronouns	a/an, someone, somebody, something, somewhere, anyone, anybody, anything, anywhere, no one, nobody, nothing, nowhere, the
Antonyms	full/empty, boiling/freezing, easy/hard, soft/hard
Synonyms	pants/slacks/trousers/britches laugh/giggle/chuckle happy/glad/pleased/elated/tickled pink
Homonyms	sail/sale, bear/bare
Multiple-meaning words	run fast, run in your stocking, go for a run, in the long run
Comparative relationships	taller than, shorter than
Spatial relationships	See Prepositions
Temporal-sequential relationships	Words connoting measurement, time (days of the week, minutes, seasons), temporal prepositions, first, last, next, then
Conditional relationships	if . . . then
Causal relationships	because, therefore, since
Conjunctive relationships	and
Disjunctive relationships	either . . . or
Contrastive relationships	but, although
Enabling relationships	in order that, so that
Figurative language	*Idioms:* catch a plane; hit the road *Metaphors:* her eagle-eye *Similes:* her eyes twinkled like stars; busy as a beaver

FIGURE 3.5   *A Semantic Map of the Concept of "Melancholy"*

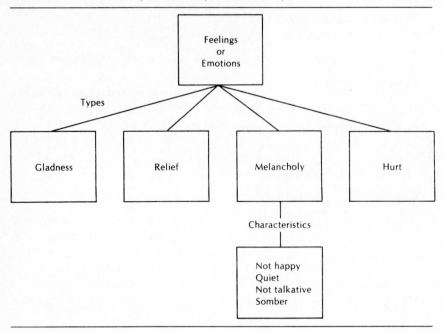

Additional ideas for teaching new concepts and the relationships among those concepts, particularly as they relate to teaching content area subjects (i.e., science, social studies, vocational areas), are discussed in Chapter 7. A number of language materials and programs are available for teaching concepts to school-age students. Chapter Appendix 3.1 presents the names and short descriptions for several of these programs and materials.

Increasing Word-Finding Ability

Another difficulty that some students with learning and behavior problems encounter is word finding. These students know the word but are unable to recall it automatically. Most frequently, these words are nouns. Several techniques (McGregor and Leonard, 1989) can be used to assist students in increasing their ability to recall words, thereby increasing the accuracy and fluency of their expressive language.

1. *Teach students to classify and categorize words.* Teaching students to classify and categorize words should improve their long-term memory and thus help them recall and retrieve specific words. In a sense, you are strengthening how well a student "knows" a word. When learning new concepts, students should be encouraged to name the category and then rapidly name the vocabulary in the category. Pictures, written words, and graphic representations such as a semantic map (see Figure 3.5) may help with this activity.

2. *Teach students to use visual imagery.* Getting students to "see" in their minds the objects they are trying to retrieve can sometimes help them think of the word. To help students develop these mental images, encourage them to picture new words in their minds. For example, when students are trying to learn the parts of a flower, have them picture a flower in their minds, with the labels for the parts written on the different parts. Have them talk about the kind of flower

FIGURE 3.6 *Sample Cloze Emphasizing Prepositions*

Cloze passages can be used either as an oral or written activity or combined with the oral activity reinforcing the written.

> More than anything else, Robert wanted _____ climb _____ the top _____ the mountain. Everyday _____ his way home _____ school he looked up _____ the mountain. It was so high that the few trees _____ the top looked very small. He had heard that it would take a day _____ climb _____ the summit, and a day to get back _____ the mountain. One evening when he was looking _____ his window, he saw a campfire burning _____ the top of the mountain. He knew _____ only he practiced hiking, he could make it.
>
> Well, this spring he would start practicing. He and his friend, Jim, could join the Young Hikers' Club and _____ early summer they would be ready _____ the climb. Robert could hardly wait _____ spring _____ come.

they pictured, discussing the parts as they describe the flower.

3. *Teach students to use word association clues to help in retrieving words.* Activities in which students learn and practice word associations can facilitate word retrieval. These activities may be as broad as asking students to name as many things as they can think of in a given amount of time. But generally the teacher will want to focus the associations. Figure 3.7 presents a variety of association tasks that are more focused. If students have established strong word associations, then when they cannot think of the correct word, providing an associative clue may assist them in retrieving the correct word.

Increasing Elaboration in Language

Some students with learning and behavior problems use language that is not very elaborated. When asked to retell stories or events, or to give descriptions, these students provide only the most basic information. Three steps can be used to teach students how to elaborate on an object

or pictured object, on an event or pictured event, and on an event sequence or a pictured event sequence: (1) model the elaboration, (2) ask questions to the students so that they elaborate, and (3) have the students produce spontaneous elaborations.

Wiig and Semel (1984) suggest that the teacher begins with objects or pictured objects, then moves to events or pictured events, and finally focuses on event sequences or pictured event sequences. The three steps for teaching elaboration of an object or pictured objects are:

1. *Model elaboration by introducing familiar objects or pictured objects and by demonstrating verbal descriptions of their attributes and functions.* In this step you are describing the object, noting its attributes and functions. In some instances you may want to contrast it to similar or related objects. For example, describe a cactus and compare it to a rosebush.

2. *Have students elaborate in response to direct questions.* After modeling, ask the students direct questions about the object that require the student to focus on its attributes and functions. For example: What kind of stem does a cactus have? Why does it have such a chunky stem?

3. *Have students spontaneously describe the object or pictured object.* Ask the student to describe the object, using such cues as: Tell me about the cactus. What else can you tell me about it? Are there any other things about it that are important? In what way is a cactus like a rosebush?

The sequence for teaching events and the event sequences would be the same.

Teaching Form

Form refers to the structure of language. Table 3.7 presents morphological and syntactical forms that seem most relevant when teaching school-age students with language and learning problems. Some procedures and activities for teaching these language forms are:

1. *Teach new sentence structures or prefixes, suffixes, and inflectional endings according to developmental sequences or the order of difficulty.* Table 3.7, as well as language programs and activities designed to teach form (see Chapter Appendix 3.2), can assist the teacher in deciding the order in which to teach the various sentence and morphological forms.

2. *When teaching a new structure or form, use familiar, concrete examples and vocabulary.* For example, Mrs. Ogle wants to have her students work on passive sentences. She begins by having her students act out simple events (e.g., Julio tagged Maria during a relay race). Then she asks the students to tell her a sentence about the event. She writes it on the board (*Julio tagged Maria*). Next she shows the students how she can

say what had happened in a different way (*Maria was tagged by Julio*). Then the students act out other events and give passive sentences. In this way, Mrs. Ogle starts with concrete experiences and uses familiar, simple vocabulary to teach the new sentence structure.

3. *Use simple sentences when teaching a new sentence or morphological form.* When Mrs. Ogle initially taught her students passive sentences, she used very simple sentences. She could have said, "Julio chased Maria while playing tag," but this sentence would have been much more difficult for the students to put in the passive form.

4. *Once the students have learned the new form using simple sentences and familiar, concrete vocabulary, then it should be extended to*

FIGURE 3.7   *Associative Tasks for Improving Word Retrieval and Developing Vocabulary*

Free Association Tasks

Name as many things as you can in a specified amount of time (usually one to three minutes).

Controlled Association Tasks

Name as many foods, animals, things you take hiking, kinds of fish, etc., as you can think of in a specified amount of time (usually one to three minutes).

Antonym Association Tasks

Listen to each word and tell me the word that means the exact opposite.
  girl
  man
  hot
  inside
  happy

Synonym Association Tasks

Listen to each word and tell me the word that means about the same thing.
  small
  giggle
  mad
  rapid

Categorization Tasks

Listen to these words and tell me what they are.
  dog, cat, fish, alligator
  bread, fruit, vegetables, chicken
  robin, sparrow, eagle

Temporal Relationship Tasks

Listen to each word and tell me what you think of.
  winter   (ice skating, skiing, sledding)
  evening   (watching TV, supper, homework)
  Christmas (gifts, Santa Claus, carols)

Agent-Action Relationship Tasks

Listen to the names of these animals and objects. Each of them goes with a special action. Tell me what special thing each one of these does.
  plane   (flies)
  lion   (roars)
  doorbell (rings)

Action-Object Relationship Tasks

Listen to these actions. Each one goes with special objects. Tell me what the objects are.
  fly   (planes, helicopters, kites)
  run   (animals, insects)
  button (shirts, jackets)

Source: Adapted from E. H. Wiig and E. M. Semel, *Language Assessment and Intervention for the Learning Disabled,* 2nd ed. (Columbus, Ohio: Charles E. Merrill, 1984), pp. 274–276. Adapted by permission of the publisher.

TABLE 3.7 *Intervention Areas in Morphology and Syntax for Students with Learning Disabilities*

Intervention Areas	School-Related Examples
Morphology	
Regular noun plurals	pencils, pens, lunches
Noun-verb agreement for singular and plural forms of regular nouns and verbs in present tense	This girl bakes good cookies. Ants build homes quickly. I like the oranges best.
Regular noun possessives in the singular and plural forms	the boy's eraser
Irregular noun plurals	the sheep in the field
Irregular noun possessives	the children's books
Present progressive tense	Jose is sharpening his pencil.
Regular past tense of verbs	Susan wanted to end the story.
Irregular past tense of verbs	Bill went to the gym.
Comparative and superlative forms of adjectives	Joan's is larger than Chad's. This is the best paper of all.
Derivation and derivational affixes	teach/teacher read/reader science/scientist/scientific thought/thoughtful easy/easily mind/mindless
Prefixes	uncover/recover/discover
Syntax	
Word order in simple sentences	Helen on the paper wrote. or Helen wrote on the paper.
Negative sentences	John is not sitting at his desk. The book is not in her desk.
Passive sentences	The book was read by the girl.
Yes/No interrogatives	You finished your work, didn't you? Did you finish your work? Is your work finished?
Indirect requests	I sure am cold.
Wh- interrogative	In the story, why was Melissa sick?
Coordinating conjunction	Charlie and Jerry want to do their math together. Bob reads well and writes interesting stories.
Subordinating conjunctions	

Order of difficulty:

cause/because	Jane goes on dates *because* she wants to.
if	Jane goes on dates *if* she wants to.
so	Jane goes on dates *so* she can meet Jim.
when	Jane goes on a date *when* she wants to.
after	Jane went on a date *after* Jim called.
before	Jane went on a date *before* Jim called.
until	Jane did not go on a date *until* Jim called.
since	Jane went on a date *since* she was bored.
although	Jane went on a date *although* she was tired.
as	Jane went on a date *as* she was bored.

(Wiig and Semel, 1984)

(continued)

TABLE 3.7   *continued*

Intervention Areas		*School-Related Examples*
Relative clauses		

Order of difficulty:

Relative Pronoun	*Sentence Category*	*Example*
Whose	Appended, object-related relative clause	Joe saw the girl *whose* hair was blonde.
What	Free relatives	Joe read what the teacher told him.
Which	Appended, object-related relative clause	Joe read the book which he bought.
Who	Appended, object-related relative clause	Joe worked with the boy who got good grades.
Deleted	Appended, object-related relative clause with pronoun deletion	Joe saw the boy he wanted for his partner.

Source: Adapted from E. H. Wiig and E. M. Semel, *Language Assessment and Intervention for the Learning Disabled.* 2nd ed. (Columbus, Ohio: Charles E. Merrill, 1984).

situations that require more elaborated and complex sentences and less familiar vocabulary. For example, when teaching the morphological ending *er,* move from familiar vocabulary such as *teacher, reader,* and *writer,* to less familiar vocabulary such as *painter, plumber, framer,* and *landscaper* in the context of house construction, and to the exceptions in this area, such as *mason* and *electrician.*

5. *Use actual objects and events or pictures of them when initially teaching a new structure or form. Also, pair oral communication with written communication.* Mrs. Ogle uses the event of playing tag in order to teach passive sentences. She also pairs the oral sentences with the written sentences by writing them on the board. Word and sentence boundaries are clarified by written language, and pictures or actual experiences can assist the students in focusing on the target language pattern. Figure 3.8 demonstrates how pictures and written words demonstrate possessives.

6. *New sentence or word forms should be introduced in a variety of ways.* For example, when teaching comparative and superlative forms of adjectives during a measuring activity, Ms. Kamulu has the students determine who has the ''long/longer/longest'' pencils,

pens, scissors, shoelaces, hair, and so on. Numerous comparisons can be made by using items found in a classroom, and the various comparisons may be depicted on a chart such as the one shown in Table 3.8. Students can then use the examples and the chart to discuss the comparisons and to practice the targeted language skills.

Teaching Use

Instruction in language use may be one of the most important areas for students with learning and behavior problems. One way to organize pragmatic language instruction is based on five ways in which language is used (Wells, 1973). These include ritualizing, informing, controlling, feeling, and imagining. Table 3.9 presents the five areas with a list of pragmatic skills related to each area. These skills are drawn from *Let's Talk for Children* (Wiig and Bray, 1983), a language program designed to assist preschool and early elementary-level children to acquire, use, maintain, and generalize communication functions, and *Let's Talk: Developing Prosocial Communication Skills* (Wiig, 1982a), a language program designed for preadolescents, adolescents, and young adults.

In addition to these areas, other pragmatic skills that can be taught include:

- Ability to vary language to match the person to whom one is talking (e.g., speaking differently to a young child, a peer, and an adult)
- Ability to vary language to match the context in which the language is occurring (e.g., school, playground)
- Ability to maintain a topic during a conversation
- Ability to take turns during a conversation
- Ability to recognize when the listener is not understanding and to take clarifying actions to assist the listener
- Ability to be a considerate speaker and listener (i.e., attending to the cognitive, affective, and language needs of the other person).

Several teaching guidelines can be used when teaching the various skills associated with language use.

1. *Use role playing to simulate different situations in which the targeted pragmatic skills are required.* Ms. Peterson uses role playing in her class so that students will have some idea what it will feel like when they are put in a situation that requires them to communicate in a certain way or for a specific purpose. Last week the students had to ask each other for directions to their houses during "pretend" telephone conversations. This week students are practicing how to ask questions during a "pretend" science lecture.

2. *Use pictures or simulations to represent feelings.* Some students have difficulty discriminating different nonverbal and verbal communication that accompanies various feelings. By using pantomime or pictures, students can determine what feelings are being expressed and can discuss the cues that helped them determine the feelings. Encourage students to attend to other students' feelings by using such statements as, "You look like you're feeling. . . ." or "I bet you feel really. . . ." or "I can't tell how you're feeling."

FIGURE 3.8 *Visual Representations Depicting Possessive Marker*

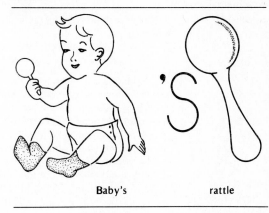

Baby's   rattle

3. *Use conversations as a framework for teaching functional language.* Conversations about topics familiar to the students or about common experiences can serve as ideal situations for building students pragmatic skills (Hoskins, 1990). The teacher can serve as a facilitator by assisting the students in using the following conversational skills:

- **a.** introducing a topic
- **b.** maintaining a topic
- **c.** introducing a topic in an elaborated form
- **d.** extending a topic
- **e.** changing a topic
- **f.** requesting clarification
- **g.** responding to requests for clarification (Hoskins, 1987)

TABLE 3.8 *Comparison Chart*

Item	Long	Longer	Longest
red pencils	Susan	Kim	Danny
blue pencils	Susan	Cori	Ken
yellow pencils	Kim	Danny	Ken
white shoelaces	Kim	Danny	Ken
black shoelaces	Cori	Susan	Kim
brown hair	Cori	Kim	Susan
blond hair	Danny	Ken	Steve

TABLE 3.9   *Intervention Areas in the Functional Use of Language*

Area	*Examples*
Ritualizing	Greetings and farewells
	Introductions
	Requests to repeat and requests to clarify
	Initiating and responding to telephone calls
Informing	Asking for and telling name, address, and telephone number
	Asking for and telling about size, color, amounts, tastes and flavors, sounds, and textures
	Asking for and telling about actions of people and animals
	Asking for and telling about the actions and functions of objects
	Asking for and telling about the location of objects
	Asking for and telling about the actions of people and animals
	Asking for and giving directions
	Asking for and telling about the time of events
	Asking for and telling about conditions and states
	Asking for and telling about reasons and causes
	Asking for and telling about preferences
	Asking for and telling about abilities
	Asking for and telling about information on using a telephone
Controlling	Asking for and telling about wants and needs
	Asking for and offering favors, help, or assistance
	Giving and responding to warnings
	Suggesting and responding to suggestions
	Asking for and giving permission
	Asking for and telling about intentions
	Promising and responding to promises
	Negotiating and responding to negotiations for an exchange
	Reminding and responding to reminders
	Asking and responding to requests to discontinue, change actions, or states
	Making and responding to a complaint
	Asking for and telling about terms
Feeling	Expressing and responding to affection
	Expressing and responding to expressions of appreciation
	Expressing and responding to expressions of approval, support, congratulations, or compliments
	Asking for and telling about feeling states and conditions
	Asking for, telling about, and responding to expressions of attitudes and reactions
	Apologizing and responding to apologies
	Expressing and responding to agreements and disagreements
Imagining	Understanding and telling a story
	Understanding and telling a fantasy
	Understanding and telling a joke
	Using speculation

Planning Instruction for Children with Language Diversity

A growing number of children with language and literacy difficulties may not speak English as their first language (L1), and may be in the process of developing English as their second language (L2). It is important that these children receive an evaluation which is sensitive to their cultural diversity. Without such sensitivity, diversity may be interpreted as language and literacy difficulties (Duran, 1989; Rueda, 1989). It is also important that cultural and language diversity and principles of second language acquisition be taken into consideration when planning instruction for these children (Cummins, 1984, 1989).

In planning for children whose first language is not English, it is important to consider their proficiency in English. In this regard, a number of educators have suggested that it is helpful to think about two types of language proficiency. The first type, basic interpersonal communicative skills (BICS) refers to the use of language in everyday communicative contexts. When children converse as they play a familiar game on the playground, they are relying on their BICS. The context is rich in that they are talking about what they are currently playing and can rely on familiar phrases and gestures to assist in their communication. As teachers, when we greet children and converse about what they did the previous evening, the children rely heavily on BICS. Research in second language acquisition would suggest that it is BICS, or conversational proficiency, that is the first to develop for children who begin school learning a second language. Typically these conversational skills are functional within two years (Cummins, 1981; Saville-Troike, 1984).

The second type of language proficiency, cognitive/academic language proficiency (CALP), refers to the children's ability to manipulate language in decontextualized academic situations. For example, when children are reading and discussing concepts associated with the weather cycle using their second language, they are expected to use their second language to make generalizations and draw conclusions about ideas which are abstract. In comparison to the language skills required when playing a familiar game or having a morning conversation with the teacher, a more sophisticated level of language proficiency is required. In effect, CALP develops more slowly than BICS, with proficiency establishing itself within four to seven years (Cummins, 1981; Saville-Troike, 1984; Wong Fillmore, 1983).

What implications does this information have for us as teachers? Several seem particularly relevant:

1. Do not assume that if children can converse with you fluently in their L2 (English), they are ready to learn academic and other cognitive skills in English.

2. Initial instruction in L2 should be highly contextualized and focus on familiar experiences.

3. When teaching abstract or unfamiliar concepts, provide rich contexts, many examples, and opportunities for the children to experiment with the concepts.

4. Provide labels for concepts in L1 as well as L2.

5. Capitalize on the culture represented by the children's first language. Use this culture to provide familiar and rich contexts in which to embed instruction. For example, using a language experience story about Cinco de Mayo with a group of children whose parents immigrated from Mexico would capitalize on their culture and background in comparison to reading a story from a basal reader about games children play in the winter in North America.

While these instructional implications are relevant for all children learning a second language, they are even more important for children who also have language learning disabilities (Cummins, 1984; Langdon, 1989).

Instructional Activities

Appendix B provides instructional activities that are related to oral language. Some of the activities teach new skills; others are best suited for practice and reinforcement of already acquired skills. For each activity, the objective, materials, and teaching procedures are described.

Summary

Language is a vehicle for communicating our ideas, beliefs, and needs. We use language to gain and give information, accomplish goals, support interpersonal relationships, and monitor our own behavior and thinking. Although most children enter school with many language skills already mastered, language continues to develop throughout the school years. Students realize significant growths in vocabulary, the ability to represent abstract concepts in language, and the ability to use figurative language, sarcasm, and humor. They communicate easily, using complex sentences and other more advanced sentence and word forms. They also increase in the ability to use language to accomplish goals.

Some students with learning and behavior problems experience considerable difficulty in the development of language skills during the school-age years. Some of these students may have problems primarily focused in one of the three components of language (content, form, and use), but because of the interactive nature of these components such students generally have difficulty in all three areas.

In planning instruction for students with language difficulties, we should take into consideration what language skills the students have already developed, what skills developmentally come next, and whether English is the students' first or second language. In this way we can target skills that will build directly on the students' current skills. When implementing instruction, we should present new skills in context, using intensive practice to reinforce the skills being taught. This means that we have to plan activities in which the language will be a functional and useful tool for communication.

Given the complexity of language at the school-age level and the need to teach language in context, providing language instruction for students with learning and behavior problems is a challenge. As you work on this challenge we encourage you to work with a speech/language pathologist. You should find this specialist willing to participate in collaborative language programs for students. Recent trends in intervention call for a consultative model of service delivery in the schools (Marvin, 1987) and increasingly emphasize integrating language across the school curriculum (Wolf Nelson, 1989). Such efforts will help to make your instruction consistent and integrative. Finally, we encourage you to accept the challenge of teaching language. Providing students with the language skills to be effective communicators in school and other life settings may be one of the most important tasks we undertake as special education teachers.

APPENDIX 3.1

Selected Programs for Teaching Language

Communicative Competence: A Functional-Pragmatic Language Program (1980) by C. S. Simon. Tucson, Az.: Communication Skill Builders.

Communicative Competence is designed for use by speech-language pathologists and learning disabilities specialists. Its purpose is to provide a conceptual model for a comprehensive approach to expressive communicative competence and the materials to implement the model. There are three components of the program:

1. A theoretical monograph that discusses the author's clinical model and rationale for the procedures suggested
2. A set of stimulus materials consisting of color photographs of actions, objects, and people; filmstrips with sequential stories; stimuli to elicit modifying adjectives and phrases; and support materials (spinners, graphs, etc.) that enable the clinician to implement the theoretical model
3. A manual that offers some specific programming suggestions to the clinician for use with these and other materials

The main focus is on the development of structurally adequate, nonegocentric, coherent communication skills. Communicative competence refers to competence in the *use* of language in ways that are appropriate to the situation. The author assumes that language needs to be a flexible, social, and cognitive tool that serves the individual in his or her various roles. Pragmatic considerations that are involved in conversations are emphasized with techniques for teaching the "rules for conversation" (Grice, 1975).

The program provides for sequential development of the communicative skills with sample IEP forms included. The companion diagnostic instrument for this language program is *Evaluating Communicative Competence: A Functional-Pragmatic Procedure* (rev. ed.) (1984) by C. S. Simon. Tucson, Az.: Communication Skill Builders.

Let's Talk for Children (1983) by E. H. Wiig and C. M. Bray. Columbus, Ohio: Charles E. Merrill.

This language program is designed to help preschool, kindergarten, and early elementary-level children acquire, use, maintain, and generalize speech acts and communication functions relevant to early childhood. It consists of the following compnents:

1. Professional's Guide
2. Communication Situation Cards
3. Communication Activity Cards
4. Hand Puppets and Barney Bag
5. Home Activities Manual
6. Progress Checklist
7. Let's Talk Stickers

The components are coordinated for instruction in the communication categories of:

1. Ritualizing function, with emphasis on rituals expected in the early grades
2. Informing function, with emphasis on speech act sequences encountered in the early grades.
3. Controlling function, with emphasis on social skills relevant for the early grades
4. Feeling function, with emphasis on intents relevant to early and middle childhood

Some of the activities associated with each function are described in Table 3.9 (page 84). The activities and materials are designed to facilitate and develop accurate understanding, recall, selection, and formulation and expression of the speech acts featured in each function. Each activity card provides a title, objectives, prerequisite concepts, materials, set-the-stage instructions, modeling demonstration, discrimination training, and activities.

Conversations: Language Intervention for Adolescents (1987) by Barbara Hoskins. Allen, Tex.: Developmental Learning Materials.

This program provides a framework for utilizing conversations as a means of building language comprehension and production. The program helps students increase the basic social/cognitive skills and linguistic/conceptual skills that are necessary to draw upon when engaging in conversations. These include such skills as concept development, sentence structure, mutual focus, taking another's perspective, and nonverbal communication.

The teacher acts as a facilitator in structuring the situation and guiding the students as they learn the basic conversation moves of:

1. Introducing a topic
2. Maintaining a topic
3. Introducing a topic in an elaborated form
4. Extending a topic
5. Changing a topic
6. Requesting clarification
7. Responding to requests for clarification

(continued)

APPENDIX 3.1   *continued*

The topics and content of the conversations is mutually determined by the teacher and students. The program consists of conversation move cards, foundation skills activity cards, and a teacher's guide.

Let's Talk: Developing Prosocial Communication Skills (1982a) by E. H. Wiig. Columbus, Ohio: Charles E. Merrill.

The *Let's Talk* program is designed to meet a need for social communication training in preadolescents, adolescents, and young adults with language delays, language disorders, or language differences. The *Let's Talk* program consists of the following components:

1. A manual that features background materials and communication skill training activities
2. Five communication card games that emphasize communication skills in functional situations and contexts, and the score sheets for each of the card games
3. Four communication card games that emphasize different communication intents, and the score sheets for these games

The *Let's Talk* communication skill training activities feature thirty-three selected speech acts and speech act sequences, representing the communicative functions of ritualizing, informing, controlling, and feeling. Each skill training session features objectives, instructions to students, modeling and demonstration, discrimination training where appropriate, and a variety of activities that employ group interaction and role-playing formats. See Table 3.9 for the types of activities included. The companion assessment instrument is *Let's Talk Inventory for Adolescents* (1982b) by E. H. Wiig. Columbus, Ohio: Charles E. Merrill.

Making Conversation Idiomatic (1987) by Anthony DeFeo, Diann Grimm, and Patricia Paige. Tucson, Az.: Communication Skill Builders.

This program facilitates the comprehension and use of idiomatic expressions in conversations and narrations. It is designed for students ages nine through adult and is appropriate not only for students with language difficulties but also for students who are in the process of learning English as a second language.

The program consists of ninety-five illustrated idiom cards and an activities manual. The manual includes oral and written language tasks, objectives, measurement protocols, and a section on strategy teaching.

Activities in the program are designed to proceed through four levels of language knowledge: (1) indicating awareness of an idiom, (2) comprehending the idiomatic meaning, (3) generatively expressing an idiom, and (4) providing definition of an idiom.

Peabody Language Development Kits (rev. ed.) (1981) by L. M. Dunn, J. O. Smith, L. M. Dunn, K. B. Horton, and D. D. Smith. Circle Pines, Minn.: American Guidance Service.

This language program is designed to stimulate overall oral language skills in Standard English and to advance children's cognitive skills. It consists of four kits—one each for preschool/kindergarten, first, second, and third grades. Each kit contains:

1. Lesson Manuals
2. Teacher's Guide
3. Card deck consisting of colorful pictures and photographs grouped according to a variety of categories
4. Puppets to demonstrate concept and language skills
5. Posters that depict different scenes and stories
6. Sound books that contain sound and song activities designed to reinforce various language concepts
7. Colored chips for counting, sequencing, grouping, and providing reinforcement

The activities emphasize the skills of *reception* through sight, hearing, and touch; *expression* through vocal and motor behavior; and *conceptualization* through divergent, convergent, and associative thinking. Each lesson includes three or more activities with a focus statement for each activity and guidelines for teaching each lesson.

APPENDIX 3.2

Selected Programs for Teaching Syntax and Morphology

Fokes Sentence Builder and *Fokes Sentence Builder Expansion* (1984) by Joann Fokes. Allen, Tex.: DLM/Teaching Resources.

This program is designed to provide systematic practice in the comprehension and production of various sentence constructions. The program provides a systematic approach to sentence construction through the ordering of five grammatical categories: who and what (subject and direct object), is doing (verb), which (adjective), and where (prepositional phrase). Each category is designated by a colored box that contains line drawings (with the written word) representing items within the word class. Children learn the items represented in each box and arrange them in specific order to generate sentences. Lessons are presented in a developmental sequence, with sentence constructions moving from simple to complex. *Fokes Sentence Builder Expansion* provides three additional categories: whose, how, and when.

Teaching Morphology Developmentally (1981) by K. G. Shipley and C. J. Banis. Tucson, Az.: Communication Skill Builders.

This developmental program for teaching word formation is designed for students whose language age is between two and a half to ten years. The color stimulus cards can be used to teach more than a thousand free morphemes and seven hundred bound morphemes. Specific morphemes that are focused on include present progressives, plurals, possessives, past tenses, third-person singulars, and derived adjectives. Reproducible lists of curriculum items, pre- and posttest forms, and suggestions for developing behavioral objectives are included in the instructional guide.

WH-Questions (1982) by Rebecca Alsup. Allen, Tex.: DLM/Teaching Resources.

This program is designed to teach the comprehension, discrimination, and formulation of WH-question forms. The program consists of three levels: beginning level (preschool through primary grades); intermediate level (middle grades); and advanced level (junior high and above). Students not only learn to comprehend and discriminate among basic question words but also among question constructions that contain negatives, pronouns, adverbs, adjectives, and many other common structures. The materials consist of colored photographs with ten questions written on the back.

Chapter Four

Reading:
Word Identification

Chapter Questions

- *What are the characteristics of the reading process and how are oral language and written expression related to reading?*
- *What are the types of cues and knowledge that a reader uses to identify words? Listen to a primary-grade student reading a book. Listen and watch for the types of cues and knowledge the child uses.*
- *Compare and contrast meaning-emphasis and code-emphasis approaches or strategies for teaching word recognition. Look at reading materials representative of each orientation to help you make your comparisons.*
- *What are the similarities and differences between the Fernald method and the Gillingham-Stillman method?*
- *When would a student most likely profit from learning the word identification strategy DISSECT?*
- *Describe how using a language experience story for reading could be used to build oral language.*

In the elementary school day more time is spent teaching reading than any other subject. As students move into upper elementary, middle, and high school, reading becomes a major avenue through which information is provided. Listen to teachers as they discuss curricular issues. The reading process and how to accommodate students who are struggling with the reading process are frequently central issues in the discussions. It is not surprising that more students are referred for special education services because of problems in reading than for difficulties in any other academic area.

In this chapter we will look at the reading process, its relationship to metalinguistics, metacognition, and writing, and some selected approaches and techniques for teaching students how to use strategies for learning and identifying unknown words. In the next chapter we will discuss instructional strategies for assisting students to become fluent readers and active comprehenders as they read.

Although we have divided our discussion of reading and writing instruction into three chapters (Chapters Four through Six), we stress the importance of the relationships between reading and writing. Critical to successful instruction for students with learning and behavior problems are opportunities for them to write about what they are reading and learning and to write stories similar in structure to the ones they are reading, to read each other's writing and discuss the role of the author, and to talk about the processes and strategies involved in reading and writing. As you read the next three chapters, think about how reading and writing are related and can be taught in such a way that one complements and supports the other. Also think about how the strategies and instructional ideas that were discussed in the previous chapter are related to reading and writing and could be incorporated into your teaching.

The Reading Process

"Reading can be compared to the performance of a symphony orchestra," according to Anderson, Hiebert, Scott, and Wilkinson (1985, p.7). These authors explain that, like a symphony's performance, reading is a holistic act. Even though reading is sometimes characterized by specific skills, such as discriminating letters, identifying words, and understanding specific vocabulary, performing the subskills one at a time does not constitute reading. Reading can take place only as an integrated performance. Like a good performance, excellence comes with participating in the activity over long periods of time. Interest in the activity is increased when it is shared as a social event and discussed with other participants. Like a musical score, there may be more than one interpretation of the text. Just as the interpretation depends on the musicians and the conductor, meaning is dependent on the background of the reader, the purpose for reading, and the context in which reading occurs. Reading, therefore, is meaning-based, entails the active construction of meaning, and requires the reader to be strategic and to interact with the text. Reading, like other language-learning activities, is mediated by others. Let's look at these five concepts in greater detail.

1. *Reading is an active search for meaning.* "Reading is not walking on the words; it's grasping the soul of them" (Freire, 1985, pp. 18–19). Since reading entails constructing meaning, it requires the reasoning and thinking processes sometimes called *comprehension*. It is understanding what one reads.

2. *Reading is the process of constructing meaning from text.* Remember what happened in Chapter Two when you, like Bartlett's subjects, read and recalled "War of the Ghosts"? You took the information presented in the folktale and constructed the meaning. That meaning was affected not only by the information presented by the author but also by your background knowledge. In fact, you might want to take a few minutes to write again what you remember about the legend and then compare it to the text and to what you wrote the last time. You will probably find that as your specific memory of the "War of the Ghosts" becomes less clear, you have to construct more and more of the legend, and that this last construction more closely resembles your schema for legends and your cultural beliefs. When we read, the author does not simply convey ideas to the reader but stimulates the reader to construct meaning from his or her experiences (Horn, 1937). This construction of meaning does not occur necessarily in a straightforward manner. Instead, the reader gradually constructs meaning or makes hypotheses, tests them, and then confirms, modifies, or rejects the hypotheses (Goodman, 1967, 1984).

3. *Reading is a strategic process.* When we say that reading is strategic, we mean that reading requires the reader to use a variety of thinking strategies to derive meaning from the text. Some of those strategies are related to *comprehending* the text. For example, you use different comprehension strategies if you are reading an article from a popular magazine while in a waiting room than you do when reading a textbook for a test. When something is unclear, you have other strategies upon which you can rely. You can go back and reread the information, or you can continue on to see if further clarification is provided. Knowing about these strategies and knowing in which situations to apply different strategies is called *metacognition*. As discussed in the section on information processing in Chapter Two, it is these metacognitive processes that make us effective and efficient thinkers, or in the case of reading, comprehenders.

Not only does reading entail strategies for comprehending, it also entails the attentional, perceptual, and memory processes necessary to identify or recognize words in the text. Remember in Chapter Two how you had no difficulty reading "THE CAT" even though the "H" and the "A" were exactly the same? You used selective attention, feature analysis, context, and your background knowledge from long-term memory to help you interpret these words. This process of recognizing words, sometimes referred to as *word identification* or *decoding*, involves understanding and utilizing a variety of strategies to translate printed words into meaning.

4. *Reading is an interactive process.* When we read we interact with the ideas presented by the author of the text. Reading is not simply starting with letters or words, translating them into sounds or language, and combining them to obtain meaning from the text. Instead, the reader uses his or her knowledge about oral and written language to guide the reading process so that it is not necessary to perceive every letter or word. In this way, reading is a predictive process in which the reader is constantly establishing and evaluating hypotheses about what the author is saying. Goodman (1967, 1984) has referred to this as a psycholinguistic guessing game, since the reader utilizes his or her knowledge about the topic and about language to predict the author's meaning for the text.

Several types of knowledge (Rumelhart, 1985) or cue systems (Goodman, 1984) are available for the mature reader to use as he or she interacts with the author's ideas and to guide the reading process.

Grapho-phonic knowledge has to do with understanding the written symbols (orthography) of language and their complex relationships to the sound system of the language. When we teach these relationships, we often refer to this as teaching *phonics*, which entails learning the relationship between written letters (graphemes) and their speech sounds (phonemes). This system is relatively complex because in the English language these relationships do not necessarily have a one-to-one correspondence. For example, the letter *a* sounds different when you say the words *all, at,* and *ate.* Instructional strategies that teach students these relationships (as presented in this chapter) can improve word identification skills, thereby providing students with strategies for identifying unknown words.

Syntactic knowledge refers to the reader's understanding of the grammar of the language. In English, the syntactic rules that apply to oral language (as discussed in Chapter Three) also apply, for the most part, to our written language. However, our written language generally reflects a more *formal* grammar than our oral language. Teaching students syntactic patterns presented in the last chapter can assist students in understanding what they read.

Semantic knowledge refers to the reader's understanding of concepts and the relationships among those concepts. If you are reading a technical medical journal you will probably have difficulty interacting with the text and constructing meaning because you do not have enough knowledge of the topic being discussed. In the same vein, when children are asked to read about a topic in which they have little background knowledge, they also will have difficulty constructing the meaning. Therefore, prereading activities that provide opportunities for the students to gain more background knowledge (as discussed in the next chapter) can facilitate comprehension and reading.

An effective reader flexibly uses all three types of information to confirm his or her hypotheses about the meaning of the text.

5. *Reading as a language learning activity is socially mediated.* Learning to read, like learning to listen, speak, and write, is socially mediated (Vygotsky, 1978). When children and teachers talk about what they are reading, they share what they already know related to the topic and integrate their knowledge with that of the text, thus constructing meanings that are relevant to them. When children and teacher talk about reading, they are sharing the strategies they use

to construct meaning from the semantic, syntactic, and grapho-phonic cues.

Integrating Language Instruction: Literacy and Whole Language

As discussed in Chapter Three, listening, speaking, reading, and writing are highly related activities and are reciprocal in nature. Whereas for the past several decades, elementary and middle school curriculums have separated instruction in reading, writing, and oral language, recently there has been a growing emphasis on curriculums which integrally tie instruction in reading to writing and build in strong oral language components. For example, newly published literature-based reading series (see Chapter Five) closely tie the teaching of reading to process-oriented approaches to teaching writing (see Chapter Six). Teaching literacy (reading and writing) involves instructional activities that increase children's ability to relate language meaning to printed symbols (Lindfors, 1984). By design, writing complements and supports reading whether writing is the scribbles and early writing of preschool children after they visit and listen to stories about visiting the zoo or the fantasies and reports about safaris written by elementary children as they read a series of stories about African animals.

A number of literacy educators have stressed importance of integrating reading and writing with oral language (e.g., Cambourne, 1988; Goodman, 1986; Goodman, Goodman, and Hood, 1989; Hansen, Newkirk, and Graves, 1985; Harste, 1990; Harste, Woodward, and Burke, 1984; Rhodes and Dudley-Marling, 1988). One of the best examples of this orientation is represented in whole language (Goodman, 1986). Whole language is a perspective on instruction that is based on the following ideas:

1. Language is for making meanings, for accomplishing purposes.

2. Written language is language—thus what is true for language in general is true for written language.
3. The cuing systems of language are always simultaneously present and interacting in any instance of language use.
4. Language use always occurs in a situation.
5. Situations are critical to making of meaning (Altwerger, Edelsky, and Flores, 1987, p. 145).

The overriding considerations in classrooms using whole language is that the reading and writing experiences be embedded in meaningful situations and use literature that is authentic, not textbooks or instructional activities specifically designed to "teach" literacy. Typically, a strong emphasis is placed on the use of literature and on trade and reference books about topics related to content areas such as science, social studies, or art.

Instructional Implications

What does this concept of reading say to those of us who work with students who have difficulty learning to read and have difficulty using their reading skills to learn in other content areas? First, we need to assist students in developing a concept of reading that focuses on meaning or comprehension rather than word identification. Second, our instruction should provide students with opportunity to develop semantic, syntactic, and grapho-phonic knowledge. Third, by using some of the teaching procedures presented in the section of Chapter Two (e.g., modeling, thinking aloud, interactive discussions, and systematic practice and feedback), we can assist students in learning how to use their semantic, syntactic, and grapho-phonic knowledge. This knowledge can help them actively search for meaning, construct meaning, and use strategic and interactive processes. Fourth, linking reading and writing using meaningful learning situations can provide students with a context for learning that is both meaningful and motivational.

The questions we can ask as we make teaching decisions regarding reading are related to the general instructional questions we asked in Chapter One.

— What is the student's concept of reading based on observations and discussions with the student?
— What attitudes does the student have toward reading and how does the student perceive himself or herself as a reader?
— What purposes does reading serve for the student?
— What processes and strategies related to reading does the student currently have and use?
— What prior knowledge concerning the topics of the text does the student bring to the reading experience?
— What is the student's reading level and how does this compare to his or her cognitive abilities?
— What are the student's oral language and writing skills?
— How has and is the reading process being taught?
— How are reading and writing integrated in the classroom?
— How does teaching style match the student's learning characteristics?

Using these questions as a framework, let's apply these concepts to some students and see how this information guides our teaching (see Apply the Concept 4.1).

Metalinguistics and Reading

Metalinguistics refers to an awareness that learners develop about language and its use. It is knowing that language is an object that can be talked about, thought about, and manipulated. It requires the learner to shift attention from the meaning of language to the form of language. In the development of young readers and writers,

Apply the Concept 4.1 _____

*DEVELOPING INSTRUCTIONAL PLANS FOR STUDENTS WITH
READING DIFFICULTIES*

Shawn talks about reading as "saying the words right."
When you listen to Shawn read aloud, he seems to call
out the words, paying little attention to meaning. Even
his intonation reflects his definition of reading. He
doesn't read with expression, nor does he pay attention
to punctuation. What he does when he mispronounces a
word tells us about the type of knowledge that he relies
on to identify words. His errors usually sound or look
similar to the words, but they don't necessarily make
sense nor are they always the correct part of speech. For
example, when reading a passage about living in China,
Shawn sometimes said *horse* for *house, mate* for *mat,*
and *bool* for *bowl.* He rarely went back to reread. When
he was encouraged to reread a sentence, he usually read
it the same way. When he was asked to try to figure out
a word in a sentence, he attempted to give each letter a
sound and then said the sounds quickly. These attempts
sometimes resulted in nonsense words and rarely the
correct word.

Even though Shawn has adequate language skills
and cognitive abilities, sometimes he cannot even give
the gist of what he has read. He tends to remember a few
of the isolated facts. Shawn is in third grade and he reads
comfortably in books at the first- to beginning
second-grade level. It is this low achievement in reading,
despite adequate language and cognitive skills, that
caused Shawn's regular third-grade teacher to refer
Shawn for special education services.

Shawn says he likes to read, but he rarely selects
reading as a free-time activity. He does not make regular
trips to the library, nor does reading appear to play an
important role in his home. His major way of gaining
information is through television.

The reading emphasis in Shawn's first- and
second-grade classes was on word identification,
particularly phonics.

What should be our plan of action for Shawn?
First, we need to help him gain a different understanding
of what reading is about and how to use his semantic
and syntactic knowledge when reading. Helping Shawn
learn to ask himself questions about the meaning as he
reads or teaching him to summarize what he has read
(techniques described in the next chapter) could assist
him in changing his ideas about reading. We may also
want to use prereading activities in order to assist Shawn
in setting purposes for reading, and to encourage him to
predict as he reads (techniques presented in the next
chapter). At the same time, we may want to model how
to use the meaning (context clues) to assist in identifying
unknown words (described in this chapter). We also

want to provide opportunities for him to read for
pleasure, listen to others read, and read along with
others. Taped books may assist us in this endeavor. After
Shawn has modified his definition of reading and is
using semantic and syntactic knowledge more
effectively, we may find it necessary to build his
knowledge of phonics.

On the other hand, when you listen to Leila read
her sixth-grade social studies text, it appears that her
definition of reading is right on target. She reads quickly
and with expression, and she rarely hesitates. But rather
than just listening, follow along as she reads. You will
find that she is miscalling 30 to 40 percent of the words,
resulting in major changes in the meaning. Sometimes
by the end of a paragraph, you think she is not attending
to the text at all. When you ask Leila about her definition
of reading, she tells you that reading is "getting the main
point." But Leila also lets you know that when she does
not recognize a word she will "just make something up
that sounds good." She confides, "This way people
don't know I don't read very well." Leila also reports
that she doesn't "particularly like to read because it is
hard for me to remember the words." However, if
someone reads to her, she can "get what the author is
trying to say." When asked how she figures out words
she can't remember, she says "I think of a word that
makes sense."

There are lots of positive aspects of Leila's reading
(e.g., her ideas about reading, her use of semantic
knowledge). She has an adequate definition of reading
and relies (to a point of overrelying) on her semantic and
syntactic knowledge when she reads. In working with
Leila it seems important that, for a while, she reads text
in which she can use her semantic and syntactic
knowledge more effectively. She needs to feel successful
and change her perception about her reading ability. As
a resource teacher in an elementary school, we could
facilitate this by having her read text that is more
predictable, for which she has more background
knowledge, and for which she can recognize more of
the words. Library books of interest in the areas of social
studies and science, with an estimated readability of
about third to fourth grade might be one suggestion. At
the same time, we want to help Leila develop her
grapho-phonic knowledge. Ideas and programs
presented in the "Word Structure Techniques" section
of this chapter might prove helpful. Finally, Leila reports,
"I just can't remember the words." In working with
Leila, if we find that she does seem to struggle with
remembering words even after she has had the

opportunity to read them multiple times in text, then we may want to use whole-word techniques for memorizing the words (described in this chapter).

As Leila becomes more confident of her reading and as her repertoire of reading skills increase, we will want Leila to move back to reading the sixth-grade social studies and science texts. This transition should be just as systematic as our initial instruction with Leila.

If we expect her to *generalize* her confidence and skills to the sixth-grade texts and classroom, then we want to systematically plan for her success.

Both Shawn and Leila are experiencing difficulties in reading. What we learn by studying their reading strategies and beliefs, their knowledge and skills, and the context and format for teaching lets us know that these two students need different instructional plans.

---

attention is shifted to the form of language. As children encounter print in their environment, they ask questions and learn about how language is represented in its written form.

One aspect of metalinguistics that seems particularly relevant to learning the sound-symbol relationships and how they are applied in reading is knowing that meaning or ideas can be segmented into words and that words can be broken into syllables and individual phonemes. For example, Mary, a beginning reader, was asked to give the first letter in the word *dog* when her teacher said the word. In terms of metalinguistic skills, Mary must understand that *dog* is a word, that words are divided into sounds, and that giving the first letter in the word means giving the letter name for the first sound in the word *dog*. Scott, a first grader, was asked by his teacher to tell if the words *dog/bog* and *pat/pan* are the same or different. When Scott could not successfully complete this task, the teacher assumed that Scott had auditory discrimination problems (i.e., could not perceive the differences between speech sounds). To successfully complete this task, Scott not only must perceive the differences between speech sounds as they are presented in words, but metalinguistically Scott must know the concepts of "same" and "different" as they apply to words, and to understand that as little as one different sound makes the words different. When Scott's teacher taught him the meaning of "same" and "different" as they apply to discriminating words such as *dog* and *bog*, his difficulty in telling if two words were the same or different

was resolved. In this case, Scott lacked the necessary metalinguistic skills to allow him to manipulate his language.

Research in the area of metalinguistics is relatively new but it does indicate that several metalinguistic skills are related to successful acquisition of early reading skills (Lenchner, Gerber, and Routh, 1990; Liberman and Shankweiler, 1987; Mann, 1986; Mann and Liberman, 1984; Williams, 1986). These skills include:

- segmentation (dividing ideas into words, and words into syllables and phonemes)
- phonemic analysis (breaking or analyzing words into phonemes or speech sounds)
- blending (putting the sounds or phonemes together to form words)

Lewkowicz (1980) conducted an intensive analysis of the metalinguistic skills that have been used in both research and instruction. She concluded that segmentation and blending were the basic metalinguistic tasks that should be included in instructional programs that teach students how to identify words using the sound-symbol relationships.

How do students who struggle with learning to read deal with these metalinguistic skills? There is substantial evidence to suggest that these students are deficient in segmentation and phonemic awareness and analysis (Fox and Routh, 1980; Liberman and Shankweiler, 1987; Stanovich, 1986; Torgesen, Rashotte, Greenstein, Houck, and Portes, 1987). This research suggests that it is important that we teach these metalinguistic skills to students who encounter difficulties in learning how to read. How do we as teachers provide for the opportunities to learn these metalinguistic skills? The Report of the Commission on Reading, *Becoming a Nation of Readers* (Anderson et al., 1985), indicates that these skills develop by providing students with opportunities to talk and learn about written language. This includes:

- Reading aloud with students and showing them how oral language relates to written language (Chomsky, 1972; Durkin, 1987)
- Providing students opportunities to write and experiment with written language through their writing (Durkin, 1966, 1987; Graves, 1985)
- Providing instruction in phonics within meaningful contexts (Clay, 1985; Johnson and Baumann, 1984; Williams, 1985).

Metacognition and Reading

As discussed in Chapter Two, *metacognition* refers to the knowledge we have about our thinking processes or strategies, and our ability to regulate these processes or strategies to ensure successful learning. For example, metacognition in reading is deciding whether associating the word with a picture, or rehearsing the word, or both associating and rehearsing the word will be most helpful in remembering the word. It is actively checking comprehension when reading and, if understanding is not adequate, then instigating strategies to alleviate the problem. These include such strategies as rereading, slowing down, and holding the inconsistency in memory while reading further for clarification.

Students who have reading difficulties tend to have difficulty with metacognitive skills, including efficient memory processing for words (Bauer 1987; Mann and Liberman, 1984; Torgesen, 1985) and comprehension monitoring (Bos and Filip, 1984; Palincsar and Brown, 1987; Wong, 1979, 1980, 1987). Research in the area of memory processing indicates that these students do not effectively use elaborative encoding strategies, such as rehearsals, categorization, and association, when trying to remember words or word lists. Studies with good and poor readers suggest that the poor readers do not automatically monitor their comprehension or engage in strategic behavior to restore meaning when there is a comprehension breakdown.

Like metalinguistic skills, metacognitive skills seem amenable to instruction. Using the teaching and learning principles of cognitive behavior modification and cognitive training, metacognitive skills in the area of reading have been successfully taught (Bos, 1988; Palincsar and Brown, 1984, 1986; Schumaker, Deshler, Alley, Warner, and Denton, 1982; Wong and Wilson, 1984; Wong and Wong, 1988). Wong and Wilson (1984) applied the concept to teaching passage organization (see Apply the Concept 4.2).

Strategies for Identifying Words

What do you do when you are reading and come to a word you cannot identify? Your response varies according to your purposes for reading and the type of text you are reading. When you are reading a Russian novel and you come to a name you cannot read, perhaps you skip it, use a nickname or initials, or use your knowledge of dividing words into syllables (*syllabication*) and phonics to pronounce it. When you are reading a science textbook and come to the name of a chemical process that you will need to discuss in class, you will probably use the grapho-phonic cuing system in terms of your knowledge of syllables, phonics, *structural analysis* (analyzing words according to root words, prefixes, and suffixes), and, if necessary, the dictionary to figure out the word. When you are reading the description of a character and come to an adjective you do not recognize, you will probably rely heavily on your semantic and syntactic knowl-

Apply the Concept 4.2

TEACHING METACOGNITION

After Wong and Wilson (1984) showed that learning-disabled students were less sensitive to passage organization than nondisabled students, they taught the metacognitive skill of organizing a passage to twenty-four learning-disabled students who could not successfully complete this task. The researchers taught the students a five-step strategy:

1. Sort the sentences into groups (paragraphs).
2. Check the sentences. Is any sentence in the wrong group (paragraph)?

3. Put the sentences in the right order in each group (paragraph)
4. Think: What does each group of sentences say about the topic?
5. Get ready to tell the story.

Results of the posttest indicate that these learning-disabled students readily learned how to organize sentences around the topic and subtopics of a passage. More importantly, the acquisition of this metacognitive skill increased their retention of the passage.

---

edge to aid in identifying the word. In other words, you can draw upon a variety of cues and strategies to recognize an unfamiliar word. The language cuing systems can be discussed in relation to seven strategies used to identify words: visual configuration, picture clues, semantic clues, syntactic clues, structural analysis, phonic analysis, and syllabication (Ives, Bursuk, and Ives, 1979). In addition to these, a person may choose to check another source such as asking someone or looking up the word in the dictionary. Remember, readers use these strategies in concert with one another to identify words necessary to promote comprehension.

1. *Visual configuration* refers to using graphic or distinctive visual features to recognize a word or a group of words such as a phrase or whole clause. When using this skill we are attending to visual information and using our graphic knowledge to help us identify the word. We often use visual configuration to recognize words automatically. We can also use visual configuration at a less automatic level. For example, we might think to ourselves, "Does this look similar to another word?" "This is a long word." "This word has tall letters at the beginning and the end." Generally the types of visual configuration clues we use to identify a word are word length; word shape; presence of double letters and repetition of letters; use of capitals, hyphens,

apostrophes, and periods; and the graphic characteristics of individual letters.

2. *Picture clues* refer to using pictures, graphs, diagrams, maps, and other types of pictured representations that surround the text to aid in word recognition. If a child is reading about an airplane and the sentence reads, "The pilots sat in the cockpit," a picture of pilots in a cockpit may help the reader identify the word *cockpit*. Picture clues can sometimes be helpful and sometimes distracting, particularly if the pictures do not fit well with the text. Some students with reading difficulties tend to overrely on picture clues.

3. *Semantic clues* refer to using the words in the text and the meaning of the text to help identify the word. When we ask a reader "what word makes sense?" we are asking the individual to use semantic clues and his or her semantic knowledge. Semantic clues also help readers determine which meaning of a word to apply. For example, context helps in determining the meaning of "lead" in the following sentences: "Put the dog on a *lead*." "Susan had the *lead* in the school play."

4. *Syntactic clues* refer to using grammatical information to aid in identifying a word. In the sentence, "John walked down the _____ ," the reader knows that the word in the blank must be a noun. The individual is applying syntactic knowledge or knowledge of grammar and word order. Syntactic clues also help readers determine which meaning of a word to apply. For example: "The safe was made of *lead.*" "John *led* his friend down the path."

It is next to impossible not to use semantic and syntactic clues simultaneously. *Context clues* refer to the combination of semantic and syntactic clues. Using context clues requires the reader to rely on linguistic information that is at the sentence and text (discourse) level. The next three techniques require the reader to rely on linguistic information at the word level.

5. *Structural analysis or morphemic analysis* refers to using the meaningful subunits of a word as identification clues. For example, the word *reeducation* can be broken into the meaningful parts of *re*, meaning to do again, *educate*, meaning the process of teaching knowledge or skills, and *tion*, which changes the root word from a verb to a noun. Morphemes, the smallest written or spoken units of meaning, can be classified into the categories of roots or root words (e.g., *educate, run, class*), prefixes, suffixes, and inflections or inflectional endings (e.g., *-s, -ed, -ing*). White, Sowell, and Yanagihara (1989) suggest teaching *un-, ne-, in-,* and *dis-* as the most frequently used prefixes; *-s/es, -ed,* and *-ing* as the most common inflectional endings; and *-ly, -er/or,* and *-tion/ion* as the most common suffixes.

Appendix A provides a list of prefixes and suffixes along with examples of their use and their common meaning. Teaching students prefixes, suffixes, and their meaning can not only aid in the identification of a word, but also in understanding its meaning.

6. *Phonic analysis* or *phonics* refers to using the sound of letters as word identification clues. Phonic analysis focuses on the relationship between *phonemes* (speech sounds) and *graphemes* (letter symbols used in written language). As discussed earlier, phonic analysis depends on the student's ability to segment words into sounds

and to blend the sounds together to orally pronounce the word. Appendix A provides an instructional sequence for teaching phonic analysis skills as well as lists of words containing typical word patterns or phonograms.

7. *Syllabication* refers to using the sounds of words to divide them into pronunciation units. A *syllable* is a unit of pronunciation, and it may include one or more sounds. Because syllabication is strictly an oral language phenomenon, it does not have a written language parallel. Consequently, its application as a word identification technique is somewhat limited. Nevertheless, dividing a word into segments or syllables is often an aid to applying phonic analysis in multisyllabic words. Rude and Oehlkers (1984) suggest teaching three common rules for syllabication:

  a. When two consonants (C) come between two vowels (V), as in *supper* or *lumber*, divide the word between the two consonants: *sup-per* (VC-CV pattern).

  b. When a single consonant comes between the two vowels, divide the word after the first vowel, as in *ba-con* (V-CV pattern).

  c. When a word ends in a consonant followed by *le*, as in *cable*, the final syllable is made up of the consonant and the *le* (Cle pattern) (p. 149).

Appendix A presents a suggested scope and sequence for word identification skills by reading level. We can use such information to determine what to teach. Scope and sequences for word identification skills can also be found in the teachers' editions of most reading series.

Teaching Word Identification

Bradley, a third grader, is in the lowest reading group and is still not making progress in reading. When he reads orally from his first-grade reader, the teacher pronounces about 30 percent of the words for him. He reads slowly and when he comes to a word he cannot identify, he applies inconsistent strategies. Sometimes Bradley seems to use the context (semantic cues) to assist him, and other times he appears to make wild guesses. Sometimes he attempts to sound out the letters, but usually he is not successful beyond the first two letters. Even when he does make correct sound-symbol associations, he does not successfully blend the sounds together. Even though Bradley struggles to decode the individual words, he appears to understand what he has read by successfully answering questions about the story. Bradley has average intelligence, understands what he hears, and communicates effectively with his peers and teachers. His math skills are at a third-grade level.

Teaching students like Bradley to read fluently and to automatically recognize the words necessary to promote comprehension requires the teacher to closely observe the students when reading and to assist them in developing and using the various word identification strategies flexibly. The rest of this chapter focuses on teaching strategies and approaches that promote the development and use of word identification strategies. The first section presents meaning-emphasis strategies and approaches to word identification and early reading. These strategies and approaches emphasize teaching word identification within the context of meaningful stories and books. The second section presents code-emphasis strategies and approaches to teaching word identification and early reading, stressing systematic introduction of phonic and structural analysis. Typically the associated reading materials are controlled for the phonic and structural patterns they use. The third section presents several activities that provide students with repeated opportunities to practice identifying words in isolation and to use associative clues to assist in word recognition. The fourth section presents a strategy for word identification that has proven particularly successful with older students who

are having difficulty identifying multisyllabic words.

When beginning to work with a student who has difficulty in learning and remembering words (acquiring a sight word vocabulary) and who has limited word identification strategies, it is helpful not only to determine the student's current strategies but also to determine what approaches he or she has previously tried, how consistently, for how long, and with what success. Taking into consideration the student's current reading strategies and metalinguistic and metacognitive skills as well as the previous instructional history, you can better select a strategy or approach that encourages the student to become a flexible, competent reader.

Meaning-Emphasis Strategies for Teaching Word Identification

Meaning-emphasis strategies and approaches to word identification and early reading emphasize teaching word identification within the context of meaningful stories and books. This section presents four related approaches that have been used with students who experience difficulties in developing fluent word recognition and effective word identification strategies.

Modified Language Experience Approach
This approach to teaching initial reading and word identification strategies capitalizes on the linguistic, cognitive, social, and cultural knowledge and abilities of the child so that the transfer from oral language to written language can be made (Stauffer, 1970). It encourages the student to rely on repetition, visual configuration, and context clues to identify words. This approach is often considered a language arts approach, since it integrates oral language, writing, and reading (Allen, 1976). Several methods for teaching language experience approaches have been developed (Allen, 1976; Allen and Allen, 1966–68, 1982; Ashton-Warner, 1958, 1963, 1972; Cunningham, 1979; Stauffer, 1970). The modified

language experience approach we describe is designed for students who have limited experiences or success with reading and little or no sight vocabularies. The objectives are:

1. To teach the concept that text is talk written down
2. To teach the metalinguistic skills of sentence and word segmentation
3. To teach left-to-right progression
4. To teach use of semantic and syntactic clues
5. To teach recognition of words both within the context of the experience story and in isolation

The approach is built on the idea that oral and written language are interdependent and that oral language can serve as the base for the development of written language skills (see Figure 4.1).

— Procedures: The procedures for this modified language experience approach are similar to those suggested by Stauffer (1970). However, more structure and practice have been incorporated into this modification to provide for the needs of students who experience difficulties in learning to read. It is designed to be used individually or with small groups of two to five students. At the heart of this approach is the language experience story, a story written by the students about events, persons, or things of their choice (see Figure 4.2).

For the *first day* of instruction, guidelines for developing a language experience story are:

1. *Provide or select an experience.* Provide or have the students select an experience of interest to them. Ideally this should be an experience for which the students have ample background knowledge. Sometimes a picture can help stimulate ideas, but be sure the students have experiences related to the picture. Remember—you are relying on the students' memory of the experience and their memory for the language used to describe the experience.

FIGURE 4.1   *Relationship of Reading and Writing to Oral Language*

I can think about what I have experienced and imagined.

I can talk about what I think about.

What I can talk about I can express in some other form.

Anything I can record I can tell through speaking or reading.

I can read what I can write by myself and what other people write for me to read.

As I talk and write, I use some words over and over and some not so often.

As I talk and write, I use some words and clusters of words to express my meanings.

As I write to represent the sounds I make through speech, I use the same symbols over and over.

Each letter of the alphabet stands for one or more sounds that I make when I talk.

As I read, I must add to what an author has written if I am to get full meaning and inherent pleasure from print.

Source: R. V. Allen, *Language Experiences Communication* (Boston: Houghton Mifflin, 1976), pp. 51–55. Reprinted by permission.

FIGURE 4.2   *Dictated Language Experience Story*

Woody Woodpecker was driving a jet to outerspace and saw some aliens. And he got on his jet and went to Jupiter and saw some people from outerspace and they were driving jets, too.

2. *Explain the procedure to the students.* Explain that the students are going to be dictating a story about the selected experience. This story will then become their reading text or book.

3. *Discuss the experience.* Discuss the experience with students so that they can begin to think about what they want to put in the dictated story. Students with learning and behavior problems sometimes have difficulty organizing their thoughts. The discussion can serve as time for the students to plan what they want to say. To facilitate the planning process you may want to write notes.

4. *Write the dictated story.* Have the students dictate the story. Students should watch as you write or type it. If you are working with several students you may want to write the story on large chart paper. Have each of the students contribute to the story. If you are working with an individual, sit next to the student so that he or she can see what you write. Encourage the students to use natural voices. Write the story as the students tell it. The language experience story presented in Figure 4.2 was dictated by Sam, a third grader reading at the primer level.

5. *Read the story to the students.* Ask the students to listen to the story to see if they want to make any changes. Make changes accordingly.

6. *Have students read the story.* First have the students read the story together with you (choral reading) until they seem comfortable with the story. When you are choral reading you may want to point to the words so that the students focus on the text as they read. Next have the students read individually and pronounce words they cannot identify. In some cases a student may give you a lengthy story, yet his or her memory for text is limited. When this occurs, you may work on the story in parts, beginning with only the first several sentences or first paragaph.

7. *Encourage the students to read the story to others.* This is often a very intrinsically reinforcing activity.

8. *Type the story.* If not already typed, type the story and make one copy for each student. Also make a second copy for each student to keep and use for record keeping.

For the *second day* of instruction, guidelines for reading the story are:

1. *Practice reading the story.* Have the students practice reading the story using choral reading, individual reading, and reading to one another. When the students are reading individually and they come to a word they do not recognize, either pronounce the word or encourage the students to look at the word and think of what word would make sense.

2. *Focus on individual words and sentences.* Have the students match, locate, and read individual sentences and words in the story. Discuss what markers are used to denote sentences and words. Finally, have the students read the story to themselves and underline the words they think they know.

3. *Check on known words.* Have each student read the story orally. Record the words the student knows on your copy of the story.

4. *Type the words from the story on word cards.* Type the words each student knows from the story on word cards.

Guidelines for the *third day* are:

1. *Practice reading the story.* Repeat the type of activities described in step 1 of the Second Day.

2. *Focus on individual sentences and words.* Repeat the type of activities described in step 2 of the Second Day.

3. *Check on known words.* With the word cards in the same order as the words in the text, have each student read the word cards, recording the words the student knows.

FIGURE 4.3   *Suggested Activities for Word Box Cards*

1. Alphabetize words in word banks.

2. Match the word with the same word as it occurs in newspapers, magazines, etc.

3. Make a poster of the words known. A profile of the student can be drawn from the known words.

4. Complete sentences using word banks. Provide students with a stem or incomplete sentences and have students fill slot with as many different words as possible. Example:

    He ran to the _____. The _____ and _____ ran into the park.

5. Find or categorize words in word banks:

naming words	science words
action words	color words
descriptive words	animal words
words with more than one meaning	names of people
words with the same meaning	interesting words
opposites	funny words
everyday words	happy words
people words	exciting words

6. Organize words into small books or posters. Have pupils make a dictionary, picture dictionary, or books for certain categories of words.

7. Locate words beginning the same, ending the same, or meaning the same.

8. Locate words with various endings.

9. Complete sentences using different-category words. Example: Today I am _____ (feeling word). Juan _____ (action word).

10. Match sentences in stories with words from word bank.

11. Make punctuation cards. Locate and match punctuation in stories.

12. Describe cartoon captions with words from word banks.

    Where are you _____?
    I am leaving for the _____.
    I wonder what they _____.

13. Organize captions and titles for pictures and cartoon frames, using words from word banks.

14. Organize words from word banks into complete sentences.

We	drove	to	the	farm	.

15. Organize words into sentences, commands, and questions.

We	went	to	the	farm	.
Where	are	we	going	?	
Go	to	the	farm	!	

16. Have students describe someone or something, using words from the word banks separately or organized into sentences. Have other students guess the person or thing.

17. Have students select a word from their word bank and use it in as many different sentences as possible.

18. Have students play dominoes with each other's words.

pot	Tom	mother

19. Use word bank cards for matching-card games, such as grab and bingo.

20. Form phrases using words from different categories. For example, select a color word and have students find as many words as they can which match.

21. Organize words into a story. Students might need to borrow words for this use and may wish to illustrate or make a permanent record of it.

22. Delete words from a story. Have other students use words from their word banks to complete the story.

23. Scramble the sentences in the story and have students rearrange them in an appropriate order.

24. Scramble the words in a student's sentence and have other students unscramble them.

25. Illustrate different stories and have students describe a story with their word cards. Have students match the illustration with the word cards.

26. Complete stories with sentences formed by the word cards.

27. Create a silent movie with word cards for captions.

28. Create advertisements with word cards.

29. Organize words or sentences into a "Top 40" list based upon popularity. Students can vote which of the sentences used in class seemed the most interesting. This can be done with words, phrases, or imaginary book and song titles.

30. Establish class word banks for different classroom centers, such as science words, number words, weather words, house words, family words.

Source: R. J. Tierney, J. E. Readence, and E. K. Dishner, *Reading Strategies and Practices: Guide for Improving Instruction* (Boston: Allyn and Bacon, 1980), pp. 285–287. Reprinted with permission.

Guidelines for the *fourth day* are:

1. *Practice reading the story.* Repeat the type of activities described in step 1 of the Second Day.

2. *Focus on sentences and words.* Repeat the type of activities described in step 2 of the Second Day.

3. *Check on known words.* With the cards in random order, have each student read the words, recording the words each student knows.

Guidelines for the *fifth day* are:

1. *Check on known words.* Repeat step 3 from the Fourth Day, using only the words the student knows from the previous day.

2. *Enter known words in word bank.* Each student should make word cards (5 x 7 index cards or scraps of poster board work well) for the words that he or she can identify in step 1. These words should be filed by the student in his or her word bank (index card box). Words the student cannot identify should not be included.

3. *Read, illustrate, and publish the story.* Have the students read the story and decide if they want to illustrate it and/or put it into a language experience book. Books can be developed for individual students or one book can be made for the group. These books can then be shared with each other, with other interested persons, and placed in the library.

Once the students have completed at least one story and have developed fifteen to twenty words in their word banks, they can begin to use the banks for a variety of activities, such as generating new sentences, locating words with similar parts (i.e., inflectional endings, beginning sounds, shapes), and categorizing words by use (e.g., action words, naming words, describing words).

As the number of sight words continues to increase students can write their own stories, using the words from the word bank to assist them. More suggestions for developing activities based on the word bank are given in Figure 4.3.

━ Comments: The modified language experience approach provides a method for teaching children initial skills in reading, including the recognition of sight words. The approach utilizes the students' memory and oral language skills as well as visual configuration and context clues. Once the initial sight vocabulary has been built to between 50 and 150 words, students should be encouraged to read other books and stories.

Activities are incorporated into the approach to encourage the development of the metalinguistic skills of sentence and word segmentation. However, this approach does not present a systematic method for teaching phonic and structural analysis. For students who have difficulty inducing these relationships, a more sturctured method of teaching phonic and structural analysis may need to be used after students have developed an initial sight vocabulary. This approach may not provide some students with enough drill and practice to develop a sight vocabulary. In those cases, it will be necessary to supplement this approach with activities presented in the section on word recognition activities.

Patterned Language Approach

One of the major problems for students who have difficulty learning to read is that they get little practice reading. Many of the books these children attempt to read, including the reading series, contain too many words they do not recognize. Therefore, they do not get the opportunity to let the flow of the language assist them in identifying unknown words or to experience the success of reading. The patterned language approach (Bridge and Burton, 1982; Bridge, Winograd, and Haley, 1983; Heald-Taylor, 1987; Martin and Brogan, 1971; Martin, 1990; Rhodes, 1979, 1981; Trachtenburg and Ferruggia, 1989) uses highly predictable reading materials and provides many opportunities for the teacher and students to read together (choral reading). It is based on assumptions that repetition of predictable language and choral reading will assist the students in learning to make the connections between oral language and the printed word (Smith, 1988; Goodman, 1986).

▬ *Procedures:* The procedures for the patterned language approach are built on many of the principles discussed earlier in this chapter. They rely heavily on the students making predictions and on using predictable reading materials to increase the likelihood that the predictions will be logical. Many predictable reading materials are available, as listed in Chapter Appendix 4.1. In addition, a number of education companies publish series of easy, predictable books (e.g., DLM, Rigby Education, Scholastic, The Wright Group).

Bridge, Winograd, and Haley (1983) used the following steps when using the patterned language approach with low first-grade readers:

1. Read the book aloud to the students. Reread the book, inviting the students to join in when they can predict what will come next. Have the students take turns choral reading the book.
2. Put the text of the book on a large paper without the book's picture cues. Read and choral read the story from the chart. Give the students sentence strips with sentences from the story. Have them match the strips to the chart and then read the sentences.
3. Give the students individual word cards from the story, in order. Have the children place each card under the matching word in the chart.
4. Read and choral read the story from the chart. Place the individual word cards from sections of the story in random order at the bottom of the chart. Have the students match the word cards to the words in the story.

The sentence and word matching procedures are used so that the students will attend to the grapho-phonic clues as well as the semantic and syntactic clues. An important aspect of instruction is having the students discuss the patterns and compare the language patterns (Lynch, 1986). Also, using patterned language and predictable books provide easy entry into writing: Students can expand the books by furnishing more examples of the patterns presented, or they can develop and write their own books.

▬ *Comments:* Bridge, Winograd, and Haley (1983) coupled this approach with a language experience approach (Cunningham, 1979) then compared it to the standard procedures in a basal reader. When they compared the reading of the low first-grade readers in the study, they found the students that used the patterned language approach learned significantly more words.

Reading Recovery

Reading Recovery is a preventative program designed for children who are having difficulty learning to read during their first year of reading instruction. The program was developed and researched by Marie Clay (1982, 1985), a leading educator and psychologist in New Zealand. The program is short-term, usually lasting from twelve to fifteen weeks, and uses one-on-one instruction for thirty minutes each day to provide children strategies for reading. Supplemental to the reading and writing instruction that occurs in the classroom, the program ties reading and writing activities. Children are taught how to use a variety of word identification and comprehension strategies and how to orchestrate the strategies while attending to the meaning of the text (Pinnell, DeFord, and Lyons, 1988). The materials include hundreds of simple books, particularly predictable and patterned language books, that progress in difficulty from early reading picture books and wordless books to books adept first-grade readers can read by the end of the year (see Chapter Appendix 4.2 for a list of sample books). Teachers using the program participate first in staff development that focuses on observing children as they learn to read and write, learning how to teach literacy strategies, and learning how to use the lead of the child to focus instruction.

▬ *Procedures:* In New Zealand children enter school on their fifth birthday and begin immediately to participate in reading and writing activities that generally highlight language experience and whole language approaches to reading. At the end of the first year of instruction, children having difficulty are individually assessed by a Reading Recovery teacher using the Diagnostic Survey (Clay, 1985) to determine which children are having the most difficulty with literacy development. This survey affords the teacher the opportunity to closely observe the child completing a variety of literacy activities including letter identification, word recognition of a simple word list, reading a simple book, writing a story or words the child knows, and writing a dictated sentence. In addition, children participate in the evaluative activity, *Concepts about Print* (Clay, 1982), which includes left-to-right and top-to-bottom directionality, word segmentation, sound segmentation, punctuation, and capitalization (Clay, 1985, 1989).

When a child begins the program, the child and teacher spend the first two weeks of instruction "roaming around the known" (Clay, 1985).

The teacher does not systematically teach but rather explores reading and writing with the child. Together they enjoy books, write collaborativly, and get to know each other. Generally, the teacher selects tasks that are easy for the child, using them to increase his or her knowledge of the child and to build a sense of trust.

After the first two weeks, the teacher begins using a consistent lesson framework to assist the child in discovering the patterns and strategies associated with literacy.

1. *Rereading familiar books.* The teacher and child begin the thirty-minute lessons by rereading books that are familiar to the child. After a book has been introduced and read by the child, it is placed in the child's reading box. During this part of the lesson both the child and teacher select familiar books to read. Some of the books may be selected by the teacher because they provide opportunities for teaching and reviewing certain strategies (Pinnell, Fried, and Estice, 1990). Other books may be selected by the child. Rereading allows the child to participate in fluent reading in much the same way that using language experience stories written by the child allows for the reading of familiar text. During this time the teacher observes closely to see if the child is using such strategies as rereading sentences when miscalled words change the meaning of the text.

2. *Rereading the previous lesson's new book and taking a running record.* During this part of the lesson, the teacher takes the role of observer and recorder to determine how the child is using word identification, comprehension, and monitoring strategies when reading the book that was introduced and read once the previous day. This reading is to be independent, although the teacher may provide a word when the child is completely stopped. "The child is not expected to read this book with complete accuracy, but it should not be so difficult that the child has to struggle. An accuracy check [on word recognition] confirms the teacher's selection of the right level of difficulty. If the child is reading at about 90 percent to 95 percent accuracy, the text is probably in the appropriate range (Pinnell, Fried, and Estice, 1990, p. 284).

3. *Working with letters.* If a child does not recognize and write the upper- and lowercase letters, the teacher works with the child, generally using plastic or magnetic letters. Clay (1985) suggests that when a child knows more than 10 letters, an alphabet book can be made with the upper- and lowercase letters and a key picture the child associates with the letter. Leaving blank pages for the letters the child does not know gives the child some idea of the size of the task as well as a sense of accomplishment as the letters are learned and entered in the book.

4. *Writing a story.* The child composes a brief message or story usually one to two sentences in length. This is done with assistance from the teacher, using a writing book in which the binding is turned horizontally so the top page can be used as a practice area and the bottom page used to write the message. Sometimes related messages are written over several lessons, thus composing a story. The message is written word by word with the child or teacher saying the words slowly. When appropriate, the child is encouraged to predict the letters that represent the sounds. The teacher may also draw empty boxes on the practice page to represent each letter in a word. The child then listens to predict the letters; written or magnetic letters may be used. In this supported situation, the child discovers sound/symbol relationships and participates in structural and phonic analyses. The child then reads the message. The teacher then writes the message on a sentence strip and cuts the strip so the child can reassemble it and compare it to the sample in the writing book.

5. *Reading a new book.* At each lesson the teacher introduces a new book to the child, who then reads it. By way of introduction, the teacher and child look through the book and talk about it. They look at the pictures, make predictions, talk about their knowledge and experiences related to the story, introduce the characters, draw

attention to the important ideas or new vocabulary, and "give opportunities for the child to hear the new words which he [or she] will have to guess from the pictures and language context" (Clay, 1985, p. 68). After introducing the book, the teacher then assists the child in reading it. The teacher supports the child by encouraging the use of various strategies for word identification and comprehension, models and reinforces the use of strategies, and discusses and enjoys the book with the child. For example, when a child comes to a word that he or she cannot identify, the teacher might encourage using the pictures to assist. Or, depending upon the word (e.g., *bunny*) and the child's skills, the teacher might use magnetic letters to make a known word that looks similar (e.g., *funny*) and then substitute letters so the child can compare the two words by seeing and saying the differences. The teacher might also have the child reread the sentence and think about what word would make sense.

This format is generally used for each lesson. Critical to the success of the lesson is a teacher who is watching and listening to the child and then varying the instruction to assist the child in developing strategies for reading. The teacher also relies heavily on modeling and talking about the reading strategies as they are applied by the teacher and child. Children continue in the program until they have developed the kind of independent reading system that good readers use. This is usually twelve to fifteen weeks after beginning the program. Clay comments, "There is no fixed set of strategies nor any required levels of text nor any test score that must be attained to warrant discontinuing. It is essential that the child has a system of strategies which work in such a way that the child learns from his [or her] own attempts to read (Clay, 1985, p. 82). Figure 4.4 presents some of the strategies that a child ready to discontinue the program will use when reading and writing.

▬ Comments: The effectiveness of this preventative program has been investigated, first in New Zealand (Clay, 1985) and more recently in

FIGURE 4.4   *Strategies Used by Children Ready to Discontinue Reading Recovery and Teaching Ideas to Encourage Strategy Development*

Strategy	Teaching Ideas
Directional Movement The child has control over left-to-right and top-to-bottom progression or will be aware of his or her tendency to lose control and will check his or her own behavior.	*Directional Movement* • Point to the starting position on the page or line. • Assist the child in using hand movements that match voice to text.

One-to-One Matching
The child uses a controlled one-to-one matching of spoken to written words for checking purposes.
	One-to-One Matching
	• Point with your finger to match the child's voice and fail to move on when he or she makes an error that you feel he or she could self-correct.
	• Cue: Read with your finger?
	    Did that match?
	    Were there enough words?

Self-Monitoring
The child checks on himself or herself, noticing miscues and checking for meaning.
	Self-Monitoring
	• Cue to child to reread and point to each word or "Use a pointer and make them match."
	• Direct the child's attention to the meaning:
	    "Look at the picture to see what is happening?"
	• When the child self-corrects:
	    "I like the way you did that, you found the hard part."
	• When child gives signs of uncertainty even though he or she takes no action:
	    "Was that OK?"
	    "Why did you stop?"
	    "What did you notice?"

Use of Multiple Cue Sources
The child uses the different cues in concert (syntactic, semantic, and grapho-phonic cues).
	Use of Multiple Cue Sources
	Use the following questions in flexible ways:
	    "You said, _____ . Does that sound right?"
	    "You said, _____ . Does that make sense?"
	    "You said, _____ . Does it look right?"
	When a child uses multiple cue sources and self-corrects, say "I like the way you found out what was wrong all by yourself."

Cross-checking
The child monitors his or her own reading and notices discrepancies in his or her own responses by comparing one kind of cue with another cue.
	Cross-checking
	• Point up discrepancies between the two cue sources:
	    "It could be _____ by the way it looks, but does it make sense?"
	• Talk with the child about the cues he or she is using:
	    "What lets you know that the word was _____ ? What other cues did you use to help you know the word?"

Source: Adapted from Clay, M. M. (1985). *The Early Detection of Reading Difficulties* (3rd ed.). Portsmouth, N. H.: Heinemann.

Ohio (Pinnell, DeFord, and Lyons, 1988). In both cases the results have been encouraging, not only at the end of the program but several years afterward. Several years after the end of the program, a group of ethnically mixed New Zealand children who were originally selected in first grade as being the lowest 20 percent of their class in reading and writing, were achieving at a level commensurate with that of a randomly selected group of children who served as a control (Clay, 1985). An initial study in Columbus, Ohio, and then one statewide study demonstrated similar results. In the Columbus study (Pinnell, DeFord, and Lyons, 1988), students participating in Reading Recovery scored substantially higher throughout a three-year study than a comparison group of children participating in other compensatory programs and scored about the same as a random sample of children in the same grade level. Similar results have been reported for a larger-scale statewide study.

Critical to the success of this program is the training and staff development. Teachers participate in intensive staff development for a year in which they meet weekly to learn the program, observe each other teaching, reflect on their teaching, and fine-tune their diagnostic and teaching skills. The role of the teacher-leader is to get the teachers thinking and analyzing their own teaching decisions for each child they teach (Gaffney and Anderson, in press; Pinnell, Fried, and Estice, 1990).

Fernald (VAKT) Method

The Fernald method (Fernald, 1943, 1988) uses a multisensory or visual-auditory-kinesthetic-tactile (VAKT) approach to teach students to read and write words. This method was used by Grace Fernald and her associates in the clinic school at the University of California at Los Angeles in the 1920s. It is designed for students who have severe difficulties learning and remembering words when reading, who have a limited sight vocabulary, and for whom other

methods have not been successful. It is usually taught on an individual basis.

➤ *Procedures:* The Fernald method consists of four stages through which students progress as they learn to identify unknown words more effectively. The first stage, which is the most laborious, requires a multisensory approach and utilizes a language experience format. By the final stage, the students are reading books and are able to identify unknown words from the context and their similarity to words or word parts already learned. At this stage, the students are no longer tracing or writing a word to learn it.

Stage One: Guidelines for Stage One are as follows:

1. *Solicit the student's commitment to learn.* Tell the student that you are going to be showing him or her a technique for learning to read unknown words that has been successful with many students who have not learned in other ways. Inform the student that this method will take concentration and effort on his or her part, but it should be successful.

2. *Select a word to learn.* Have the student select a word (regardless of length) that he or she cannot read but would like to learn to read. Discuss the meaning of the word and listen for the number of syllables.

3. *Write the word.* Sitting beside the student, have him or her watch and listen while you:
  a. Say the word.
  b. Using a broad-tipped marker on a piece of unlined paper approximately 4'' × 11'', write the word in blackboard-size script, or in print if cursive writing is not used by the student. Say the word as you write it.
  c. Say the word again as you smoothly move your finger underneath the word. See Figure 4.5 for a model.

4. *Model tracing the word.* Model how the student is to trace the word so that he or she might learn it. Do not explain the process but simply say to the student, ''Watch what I do and listen to what I say.''

a. Say the word.

b. Trace the word using one or two fingers. The fingers should touch the paper in order to receive the tactile stimulation. As you trace the word, say the word. When discussing this process, Fernald (1943) stresses that the student must say each part of the word as he or she traces it. This is necessary to establish the connection between the sound of the word and its form, so that the student will eventually recognize the word from the visual stimulus alone. it is important that this vocalization of the word be natural; that is, it should be a repetition of the word as it actually sounds — not a stilted, distorted sounding-out of letters or syllables in such a way that the word is lost in the process. The sound for each letter is never given separately nor overemphasized. In a longer word, like *important,* the student says *im* while tracing the first syllable, *por* while tracing the second syllable, and *tant* as he or she traces the last syllable.

c. Say the word again while moving the tracing finger(s) underneath the word in a sweeping motion.

Model this process several times and then have the student practice the process. If the student does not complete the process correctly, stop the student when he or she makes an error and cue, ''Not quite. Watch me do it again.'' Continue this procedure until the student is completing the three-stage process correctly.

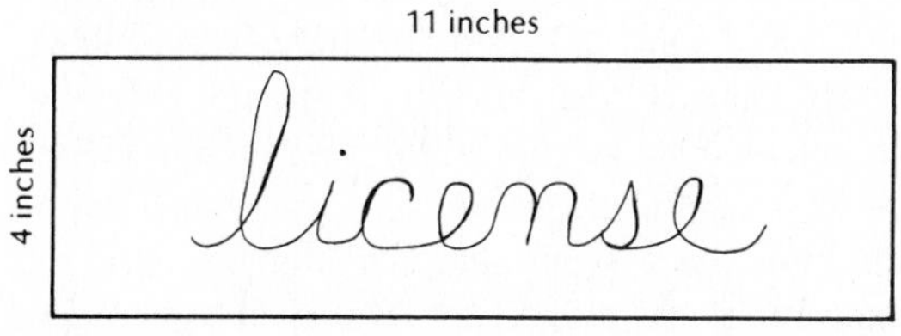

5. *Trace until learned.* Have the student continue tracing the word until the student thinks he or she can write the word from memory.

6. *Write from memory.* When the student feels he or she is ready, remove the model and have the student write the word from memory, saying the word as he or she writes. Fernald (1943) stresses that the student should always write the word without looking at the copy. She comments:

> When the child copies the word, looking back and forth from the word he is writing to the copy, he breaks the word up into small and meaningless units. The flow of the hand in writing the word is interrupted and the eye movements are back and forth from the word to the copy instead of those which the eye would make in adjusting to the word as it is being written. This writing of the word without the copy is important at all stages of learning to write and spell. The copying of words is a most serious block to learning to write them correctly and to recognize them after they have been written (pp. 37–39).

It is also important that the student write the word as a unit. If the student makes an error in writing the word or hesitates unduly between letters, stop the student immediately, cross out the word, and have him or her again practice tracing the large model. The word is never erased and rewritten. Fernald states, ''The reason for this procedure is that the various movements of erasing, correcting single letters or syllables, and so forth, break the word up into a meaningless total which does not represent a word'' (p.39). It also can interfere with the student's motor memory for the word. The student should write the word from memory correctly at least three consecutive times.

FIGURE 4.5   *Sample Word Using Fernald Technique*

11 inches

4 inches

license

7. *File the word.* After the word has been written three times correctly, the student should place it in his or her word bank.

8. *Type the word.* Within an interval of twenty-four hours, each word learned using this process should be typed and read by the student. This helps establish the link between the written and typed word.

The number of words learned per session using this VAKT process depends on the number of tracings a student needs to learn a new word. This number varies greatly among students. We have worked with students who need less than five tracings to learn a new word, whereas other students required over fifty tracings when first beginning this approach.

Fernald (1943) reports, ''As soon as a child has discovered that he can learn to write words, we let him start 'story writing' '' (p.33). As the student writes a story and comes to a word he or she cannot spell, the tracing process is repeated. These stories should be typed within twenty-four hours so that the student may read the newly learned words in typed form within the context of the story.

Fernald suggests no arbitrary limit be set for the length of the tracing period (Stage One). The student stops tracing when he or she is able to learn without it. This is usually a gradual process, with the student sometimes feeling the need to trace a word and sometimes thinking the word does not need to be traced.

Stage Two: When the student no longer needs to trace words to learn them, he or she moves to Stage Two. In this stage, the teacher writes the requested word in cursive (or manuscript) for the student. The student then simply looks at the word, saying it while looking at it, and then writes it without looking at the copy, saying each part of the word as he or she writes it from memory. As with Stage One, words to be learned are obtained from words the student requests while writing stories. The word bank continues to function as a resource for the student, but a smaller word box can be used since the teacher is writing the words in ordinary script size.

Stage Three: The student progresses to the third stage when he or she is able to learn directly from the printed word without having it written. In this stage the student looks at the unknown printed word, and the teacher pronounces the word. The student then says the word while looking at it and then writes it from memory. Fernald reports that during this stage, students still read poorly but are able to recognize quite difficult words almost without exception after once writing them.

During this stage the student is encouraged to read as much as and whatever he or she wants. Unknown words are pronounced, and when the passage is finished, the unknown words are learned by using the technique described in the preceding paragraph.

Stage Four: The student is able to recognize new words from their similarity to words or parts of words he or she has already learned. At first, a student may need to pronounce the word and write it on a scrap of paper to assist in remembering it, but later this becomes unnecessary. The student continues to read books of interest to him or her. When reading scientific or other difficult material, the student is encouraged to scan the paragraph and lightly underline each word he or she does not know. These words are then discussed for recognition and meaning prior to reading.

▬ Comments: Empirical evidence lends support to this approach for teaching word identification to severely reading-disabled students (Berres and Eyer, 1970; Coterell, 1972; Fernald, 1943; Kress and Johnson, 1970; Meyers, 1978; Thorpe and Borden, 1985). Although this approach tends to be successful with such readers, the first several stages are very time-consuming for both the teacher and the student. Consequently, it should be used only if other approaches have not been successful.

Code-Emphasis Strategies for Teaching Word Identification

Some students with reading difficulties are successful in developing a basic sight vocabulary and strategies for identifying words using the approaches discussed in the previous section. Some students, however, may profit from teaching strategies and approaches which systematically emphasize phonic and structural analysis for assisting them in "cracking the code." Typically, the reading material associated with these approaches are controlled for the phonic and structural patterns they use. Apply the Concept 4.3 describes how word structure techniques are applied in each instance.

Let's look at several approaches for teaching phonic and structural analysis skills.

Analytic Method for Teaching Phonics

The analytic method for teaching phonics relies on the students' abilities to see the similarities among the words they can already identify and to induce from those words the sound-symbol relationships between oral and written language. This method of teaching phonics requires that the students already have a pool of sight words.

▬ *Procedures:* The steps in the analytic method for teaching phonics as adapted from Karlin (1980), are as follows:

1. *Select a sound-symbol relationship to teach, using the developmental sequence presented in Appendix A as a guide.* Write a list of words on the chalkboard that have the target sound-symbol relationship. Tell the children to look at the words as you read them aloud. For example:

> pat
> pill
> purse
> pottery

Through discussion, help the students to induce the following generalizations:
    a. The words all start with the same letter.
    b. The words all sound alike at the beginning.
    Tell the students to underline the letter that is the same in the words.

Next, have the students listen to other words that begin the same as the words in the list. (These words should be in the student's listening vocabulary.) For example, *poison, pillow, pin, pollution, pot,* and *pepper.* Ask the students to think of new words that start with the selected phonic element.

Finally, have the students listen to new words, only some of which begin with the target sound. Ask the students to judge which words begin with the target sound.

2. *Sound substitution.* In this step students are asked to apply their new generalization about the sound-symbol relationship to help identify unknown words. To do this, write a sight word on the chalkboard; below it write a similar word with the target sound. For example:

> day
> pay

Ask the students what is similar about the two words. Now refer the students to the list of words on the chalkboard that begin with *p.* Model as you think aloud how to take away the *d* in *day* and write a *p* in its place. Cue the students, "Remember how words that start with a *p* sound? So now *day* is changed to _____ ."

Repeat this procedure with other words, each time getting the students to note the likenesses and differences and to substitute letters or sounds to identify the unknown word.

3. *Contextual application.* This step requires the students to apply their new rule when reading in context. The new words that were learned in step 2 are put in sentences, and the students are asked to read the sentences. If the students cannot remember the new words, they are asked to think of a word that makes sense and begins with the sound that *p* makes. Finally, this activity is completed with reading other sentences that contain new words that start with *p.*

Apply the Concept 4.3

USING CODE-EMPHASIS TECHNIQUES TO TEACH INITIAL READING

Cassandra first began to feel successful about her reading in the second half of second grade. Cassandra did not attend either preschool or kindergarten and had limited reading experiences when she entered first grade. During first grade Cassandra worked in a basal reading series along with the other students in her class. Her teacher augmented this series with language experience stories and read to the students quite frequently. The reading series focused on learning basic sight vocabulary and then later introducing sound-symbol relationships. In first grade Cassandra never could learn more than ten words that she regularly remembered. She did learn some sound-symbol relationships but she did not use them to help her figure out unknown words. At the beginning of second grade Cassandra began receiving help from a resource teacher, Ms. Kaufman. Ms. Kaufman wanted Cassandra to feel good about reading and began by using a combination of the modified language experience approach and patterned language approach. Even though Cassandra learned to identify more words, she seemed to forget the words quickly and she rarely transferred them to different texts. Ms. Kaufman lamented, "Sometimes I felt like all my teaching was to no avail. When I was sure Cassandra knew a story one day, the next day she looked at me like she had never seen it before." Despite this difficulty in remembering printed words, Cassandra had adequate oral language skills and enjoyed listening to and discussing stories.

Right after the winter holiday, Ms. Kaufman decided it was time to make a change in Cassandra's reading program. She was going to systematically teach Cassandra a few sound-symbol relationships and then teach her how to blend these sounds together to make words. Cassandra could then practice using controlled text that contained words with the sound-symbol relationships she already knew. Ms. Kaufman realized that this approach portrayed reading as "reading the words or cracking the code" rather than "reading for meaning." However, Cassandra was having so much difficulty with natural and predictable text, she decided to try this systematic phonic approach using controlled text.

To help Cassandra continue to develop her "reading for meaning" skills, Ms. Kaufman read to Cassandra or had Cassandra listen to taped books at least twice a week. Then they discussed the reading. Cassandra made progress as a result of this

approach, which focused on the structure of the words rather than on the words as wholes. When she came to a word she did not know she could sound it out. Eventually she recognized the words without sounding them out, and through systematic instruction in phonics she learned how to apply and use more and more sound-symbol relationships. Ms. Kaufman felt that two factors accounted for Cassandra's success with this approach to beginning reading. First, it was very systematic and provided for a lot of practice and repetition. Second, it gave Cassandra a strategy for figuring out words that did not rely so heavily on her memory skills.

Ms. Kaufman used an approach to teaching initial reading that started with the smallest units (sound-symbol relationships) and then taught the student to combine these units together to form words. Words were then combined to form sentences, sentences combined to form paragraphs, and so on.

Sergio is a third grader who reads books with an estimated readability of high first grade. Ms. Kaufman has been working with Sergio for the last year. She has used lots of predictable books, augmented by the sight word association procedure and the cloze procedure to initially teach Sergio to read. Sergio is making good progress and is now reading less predictable reading materials. He is using context and picture clues quite effectively, but Sergio needs more strategies for identifying unknown words. Therefore, Ms. Kaufman wants to teach Sergio how to use phonic and structural analysis.

Ms. Kaufman began to teach Sergio phonic and structural analysis skills using an *analytic method*. This method teaches these word analysis skills through inductive reasoning. Using this method, Ms. Kaufman began to point out the phonic and structural similarities among Sergio's sight words, encouraging him to generate the phonic and structural analysis rules. However, Sergio had difficulty generating these rules.

Now Ms. Kaufman is using a *synthetic method* for teaching phonic and structural analysis skills. This method uses deductive reasoning. In other words, Ms. Kaufman first teaches Sergio specific sound-symbol relationships. Then she teaches Sergio how to apply these rules to identify unknown words by sounding out the word and then blending the sounds together until Sergio recognizes the word. This is the same method to teaching phonics that Ms. Kaufman used with Cassandra.

The analytic and synthetic methods for teaching phonic and structural analysis skills capitalize on a student's ability to utilize such metalinguistic skills as segmentation and blending. If a student does not have these skills, then instruction in these metalinguistic skills should be built into the reading program.

Initially you may want to control the position of the sound-symbol relationship within the word, for example, by introducing a consonant sound first in the initial position, then final position, and then medial position. Later you can introduce the sound in different positions simultaneously.

■ *Comments:* When using this method of teaching phonics, it is recommended that the sound *p* not be said in isolation (Tierney, Readence, and Dishner, 1985). However, Karlin (1980) notes that this may be necessary for some students to understand the association between the grapheme and phoneme. Using this approach has the advantages of teaching students to use phonic analysis skills in conjunction with other word identification skills and of directly teaching students that words are composed of sounds. However, this approach does require the students to generate rules when they are given examples and then apply those rules in novel situations. This inductive reasoning process may be difficult for some students with reading and learning problems.

Linguistic Approach

The linguistic approach uses highly controlled text and an analytic method of teaching phonics to introduce word families of phonograms (e.g., *at: sat, fat, rat, bat, cat*). This approach was introduced by linguists Bloomfield and Barnhart (1961) and Fries (1963) in the early 1960s, and it gained popularity as an approach to teaching beginning reading in the late sixties and early seventies. Today this approach is used with students for whom traditional basal reading approaches have not proven successful. This approach is based on several assumptions delineated in *Let's Read* (Bloomfield and Barnhart, 1961):

1. Language is primarily speech. Instruction in reading should be based upon the oral language acquired by the child in the first five years of his or her life.
2. English has an alphabetic writing system whose code is easily broken. The child's immediate task when he or she starts to read is to master that code.
3. Language is systematic. It employs contrasting patterns that consistently represent differences in meaning . . . taking advantage of the patterns and contrasts.

The linguistic approach is based on the notion that English is technically an alphabetic language, even though (1) the alphabet has only twenty-six letters to represent the forty-four sounds; (2) the alphabet contains cases where two letters represent the same phoneme (e.g., *cent* and *sent*); and (3) there are cases where a single grapheme may represent several phonemes (e.g., *at, all, ate*).

■ *Procedures:* The procedures for using this approach are outlined in a number of linguistic reading materials (see Figure 4.6). Linguistic readers provide extensive exposure and practice for each word family or phonogram, using highly controlled vocabulary (see Figure 4.7). The vocabulary in the beginning readers usually consists of a few word families and a few sight vocabulary words. Matrices can be developed that depict the single-syllable words that can be generated when given a specific vowel sound (see Table 4.1). Word families can then be de-

FIGURE 4.6   *Selected Linguistic Reading Programs*

Let's Read. (1965). Detroit: Wayne State University Press.
The Linguistic Readers. (1971). New York: Benziger.
Merrill Linguistic Readers. (1986). Columbus, Ohio: Merrill.
Miami Linguistic Readers. (1970). Lexington, Mass.: D. C. Heath.
Sullivan Associates Programmed Reading. (1968). New York: Sullivan Press, Webster Division, McGraw-Hill.

veloped by grouping together all the words in a column. Appendix A provides a chart that demonstrates the variety of word families or phonograms that can be taught.

In using this approach the words are often introduced before the students read. Words are introduced by using a word family format, with the students taking turns reading the words (e.g., *an: fan, can, ran, tan, pan*). When students cannot identify a word in the list, they are encouraged to look at another known word in the list and make the sound substitution or to think of the family and then add the beginning sound. Sight words are kept to a minimum and are introduced as whole words. When reading, students are cued to look for the family when they come to words they cannot identify. Families are introduced systematically, generally with short-vowel sound families (e.g., *-at, -an, -ot, -et, -en, -and, -ap, -it*) presented before long-vowel sound families (e.g., *-ade, -ake, -oat*).

▬ Comments: The linguistic approach has demonstrated its usefulness with students who are having difficulty developing sight vocabulary and learning phonic generalizations. Because of its highly controlled vocabulary, students are frequently able to experience success. Two cautions should be mentioned, however. First, this approach concentrates on giving the students the skills to "crack the code." Due to this emphasis and such highly controlled text, little stress can be placed on comprehension or

the use of context clues. To demonstrate this point, reread the text given in Figure 4.7 and then try to generate eight comprehension questions, making sure that several are inferential. Second, some words introduced in a family may represent unfamiliar or abstract concepts. For example, when learning the *og* family, a student may be asked to read about "the fog in the bog."

Reading Mastery and Corrective Reading

Reading Mastery (Englemann, Bruner, Hanner, Osborn, Osborn, and Zoref, 1983–84), formerly Distar Reading (Engelmann and Bruner, 1973–75), and *Corrective Reading* (Engelmann, 1988) are highly structured reading programs that utilize a direct instruction model for teaching (Carnine, Silbert and Kameenui, 1990) and a synthetic method for teaching phonic and structural analysis. These programs stress the synthetic method by directly teaching individual sound-symbol relationships and teaching the students to build these elements into words. The

FIGURE 4.7   *Sample Passage from Merrill Linguistic Reader*

Nat and Rags

Nat sits on Sam's lap.
Sam pats the cat.

Rags can see Nat on Sam's lap.
She is sad.
Can Rags fit on Sam's lap?
She can.

Rags and Nat nap.

Source: R. G. Wilson and M. K. Rudolph, *Merrill Linguistic Readers, Dig In* (Columbus, Ohio: Charles E. Merrill, 1986), p. 7. Copyright 1986 by Merrill Publishing Company. Reprinted by permission of the publisher.

TABLE 4.1 *Short "a" Word Family Matrix*

	b	c	d	g	l	m	n	p	s	t
b			bad	bag			ban			bat
c	cab		cad		cam	can	cap			cat
d	dab		dad		dam	Dan				
f	Fab		fad			fan				fat
g	gab			gag	gal			gap	gas	
h			had	hag	Hal	ham			has	hat
j	jab			jag		jam		jap		
k										
l			lad	lag				lap	lass	
m		Mac	mad	Mag		Mam	man	map		mat
n	nab			nag			Nan	nap		nat
p			pad		pal	Pam	pan		pass	pat
r				rag		ram	ran	rap		rat
s			sad	sag	Sal	Sam		sap		sat
t	tab		Tad	tag		Tam	tan	tap		
v							van			vat
w				wag						
y										

programs also include components in comprehension. Whereas *Reading Mastery* is designed for elementary-level students, *Corrective Reading* is designed for students in grades four through twelve who are having difficulty reading. Both programs are designed to be taught in small to medium-sized groups.

— *Procedures: Reading Mastery* and *Corrective Reading* are built on the following principles:

1. Explicitly teach rules.
2. Provide extensive practice with the rules.
3. Provide practice in a variety of contexts, including words both in isolation and in text.
4. Provide corrective feedback.
5. Require active and frequent participation on the part of the learner.
6. Teach skills in a cumulative manner.
7. Provide a reinforcement system, including a point system within the program.
8. Provide a monitoring system.

When the students and the teacher are learning individual words, the students are cued, "Do it with me. Sound it out. Get ready." The teacher points to each letter while the students say each sound without pausing in between sounds (e.g., *mmmmmmeeeeee*). When the students can sound the word successfully they are then cued, "Say it fast. What is the word?" The teacher points to the word and the students respond with the word (e.g., *me*).

In both programs the teacher is given specific procedures to follow, including scripted lessons. These scripted lessons specify what the teacher is to say and do, including tone of voice and hand movements. Part of Lesson 4 from *Corrective Reading*, Decoding—Level A, is presented in Figure 4.8. Lessons are designed to last from thirty to fifty minutes with time provided for direct teaching, group reading, individual reading practice, and monitoring of progress. Both *Reading Mastery* and *Corrective Reading* teach skills in word identification and comprehension.

FIGURE 4.8   *Excerpt from* Corrective Reading *Lesson*

Lesson 4

Decoding—Level A

Core skills are being introduced in this lesson. The following skills are being learned and practiced.

- Pronouncing orally presented words so that all the sounds are audible
- Identifying the middle sound in words such as **seed** that are presented orally
- Identifying the eight sounds that have been introduced (exercise 3)
- Reading word parts and two-sound words (exercise 4)
- Reading three-sound words (exercise 5)
- Rhyming, in which specified sounds precede specified endings (exercise 6)
  The worksheet includes the following activities.
- Writing sounds dictated by the teacher
- Sounding out word parts and words
- Matching sounds
- Matching and copying sounds
- Scanning a display of letters for a specific letter that appears repeatedly in the display
- Individual checkout on reading worksheet words

Remember, you can earn 4 points if everybody in the group responds on signal, follows along when somebody else is reading, and tries hard.

EXERCISE 1   Pronunciations

Task A

1. **Listen. He was mad.**
   Pause. **Mad. Say it.** Signal. *Mad.*
2. **Next word. Listen. They wrestled on a mat.**
   Pause. **Mat. Say it.** Signal. *Mat.*
3. **Next word: ram. Say it.** Signal. *Ram.*
4. Repeat step 3 for **sat, reem, seem.**
5. Repeat all the words until firm.

Task B   Sit, rim, fin

1. **I'll say words that have sound m̄. What sound?**
   Signal. *m̄.* **Yes, m̄.**
2. Repeat step 1 until firm.
3. **Listen: sit, rim, fin.**
   Your turn: sit. Say it. Signal. *Sit.*
   Yes, sit.
4. **Next word: rim. Say it.** Signal. *Rim.*
   Yes, rim.

5. **Next word: fin. Say it.** Signal. *Fin.*
   Yes, fin.
6. Repeat steps 3–5 until firm.
7. **What's the middle sound in the word rrrīīīmmm?**
   Signal. *m̄.* **Yes, m̄.**
8. Repeat step 7 until firm.

EXERCISE 2   Say the sounds

1. **Listen: sssēēē.** Clap for each sound.
2. **Say the sounds in sssēēē. Get ready.**
   Clap for each sound. *sssēēē.* Repeat until the students say the sounds without pausing.
3. **Say it fast.** Signal. *See.*
4. **What word?** Signal. *See.* **Yes, see.**
5. Repeat steps 1–4 for **sad, mad, mat, me, seed, in, if, sat, rat, ran.**

i d e
d r t
s a m

EXERCISE 3   Sound introduction.

1. Point to **i. One sound this letter makes is m̄. What sound?** Touch. *m̄.*
2. Point to **d. This letter makes the sound d. What sound?** Touch. *d.*
3. **Say each sound when I touch it.**
4. Point to **i. What sound?** Touch under **i.** *m̄*
5. Repeat step 4 for **d, ē, d, r, t, s, ā, m.**
   To correct:
   a. Say the sound loudly as soon as you hear an error.
   b. Point to the sound. **This sound is _____ .**
      What sound? Touch.
   c. Repeat the series of letters until all the students can correctly identify all the sounds in order.

Individual test

I'll call on different students to say all the sounds. If everybody I call on can say all the sounds without making a mistake, we'll go on to the next exercise.
Call on two or three students. Touch under each sound. Each student says all the sounds.

Source: From *Corrective Reading: Series Guide* by Siegfried Engelmann, Wesley C. Becker, Susan Hanner, and Gary Johnson. Copyright © Science Research Associates, Inc. 1983, 1974, 1969. Reprinted by permission.

In its beginning lessons, *Reading Mastery* uses modified letters so as to reflect some letter sounds. For example, the letters *th* are written in a connected fashion to denote one sound. The silent *e* at the end of a word is written smaller than the rest of the letters (see Figure 4.9).

▬ *Comments:* Research suggests that these programs are effective in improving reading skills of students with reading difficulties and students from disadvantaged backgrounds (Becker, 1977; Becker and Gersten, 1982; Lloyd, Epstein, and Cullinan, 1981; Polloway, Epstein, Polloway, and Ball, 1986). These results may be related to the fact that both *Reading Mastery* and *Corrective Reading* are well-designed for systematic skill development and monitoring of that development. Much of the teaching of phonic analysis skills is conducted in an explicit manner, which may also be advantageous for a student with learning and behavior programs. Several cautions, however, should be noted. First, there is a strong emphasis on phonic and structural analysis skills, the use of passages that have a "low probability" for the use of context clues, and the absence of illustrations and picture clues. Use of literature and trade books should provide students with additional opportunities to build meaning-based strategies. Second, these programs rely heavily on oral presentation by the teacher and oral responses and reading by the students. Third, the programs are difficult to modify to meet individual needs, since detailed scope and sequences of skill development are not provided, but only detailed scripted lessons.

Phonic Remedial Reading Lessons

The *Phonic Remedial Reading Lessons* (Kirk, Kirk, and Minskoff, 1985) were originally developed in the 1930s to teach phonic analysis skills to high-functioning mentally retarded students. The lessons follow principles of systematic programmed instruction in that they utilize such principles as minimal change, one response to one symbol, progress from easy to hard, frequent review and overlearning, corrective feedback, verbal mediation, and multisensory learning. The lessons are designed as an intensive phonics program to be used individually or in groups of no more than two to three students. They are not recommended as a general technique for teaching beginning reading, but rather as a technique for students who have not yet learned an efficient method of identifying unknown words (Kirk, Kirk, and Minskoff, 1985).

▬ *Procedures:* The program begins by developing the readiness level for the lessons. These readiness skills include auditory discrimination and auditory sound blending. Figure 4.10 presents a simple procedure for teaching sound blending. Developing readiness also includes learning the sound-symbol associations for the short *a* sound and eleven consonants.

Once these skills have been learned, the first lesson is introduced (see Figure 4.11). For each lesson, students sound out each word in each line, one letter at a time, and then give the complete word. Each lesson is organized into four parts and is based on the principle of minimal change. In the first part, only the initial consonant changes in each sequence; in the second part, only the final consonant changes; in the third part, both the initial and final consonants change; and in the fourth part, the words are spaced normally.

In addition to these drill lessons, high-frequency sight words are introduced and highly controlled stories are interspersed throughout the program. Frequent review lessons are also provided.

▬ *Comments:* This program provides for a systematic and intensive approach to teaching phonic analysis skills to beginning readers. However, the approach places little emphasis on comprehension and reading for meaning. The authors suggest using other books to provide students with the opportunity to try both their word identification and comprehension skills in other reading materials.

FIGURE 4.9 *Sample Text from* Reading Mastery: Distar Reading 1

the bug bus

a little bug sat on the back of a big

dog. "get down," said the dog. "I am not

a bus."

the bug did not get down. shē went to

slēēp. the dog said, "I am not a bed."

the dog ran to the pond and went in.

the bug got wet. the bug said, "I am

not a fish. tāke mē back to the sand."

"nō," the dog said.

sō the bug said, "I will get mōre bugs

on this dog." ten bugs cāme and got on

the dog.

the dog said, "I fēēl līke a bug bus."

and the dog went back to the sand with

the bugs.

Source: From *Reading Mastery: Distar® Reading 1, Storybook 2* by Siegfried Engelmann and Elaine C. Bruner. Copyright © Science Research Associates, Inc. 1983, 1974, 1969. Reprinted by permission.

FIGURE 4.10   *Procedure for Teaching Sound Blending*

To train a child in sound blending, use the following procedure.

Teacher: "Say shoe."
Child: "Shoe."
Teacher: "Now, what am I saying? /**sh-sh-sh/ oo-oo-oo/**." (Say it with prolonged sounds, but no break between the sounds.) If the child responds correctly, say: "Good. Now what am I saying?" (Give a little break between the sounds.) "/**Sh/oe/**." Then say (with the child), "Shoe. Now what am I saying?" (Give a quarter-second break between the sounds.) "/**Sh/oe/**."
Child: "Shoe."
Teacher: "Shoe. Good. What am I saying now?" (with a half-second break between the sounds) "/**Sh/oe/**."
Child: "Shoe."
Teacher: "Now what am I saying?" (give a one-second break between the sounds) "/**Sh/oe/**."

At each step, if the child does not respond with "shoe," repeat the previous step and then again stretch out the sounds, confirming or prompting at each step. Proceed by increasing the duration until the child can say "shoe" in response to the sounds with approximately one second between them.

Repeat this experience with the word "me."

The main task for the teacher is to give a word with two sounds, increasing the duration of time between them until the child gets the idea of putting the sounds together. Then the child is presented with three-sound words such as /**f/a/t/**, and then with four-sound words such as /**s/a/n/d/**. It is important to recognize that the number of sounds in a word may not correspond to the number of letters in a word. For example, the word "shoe" has four letters, but only two sounds. The teacher must be careful to present the sounds correctly and use the correct timing.

Source: S. A. Kirk, W. D. Kirk, and E. H. Minskoff, *Phonic Remedial Reading Lessons* (Novato, Calif.: Academic Therapy Publications, 1985), pp. 12–13. Reprinted by permission.

Gillingham-Stillman Method

The Gillingham-Stillman method (Gillingham and Stillman, 1973) can be classified as a synthetic method of teaching reading that incorporates a multisensory (VAK: visual-auditory-kinesthetic) approach. Like the Fernald technique, it is designed for children who are unable to learn to read by traditional school methods, specifically those with learning disabilities and dyslexia. This method involves repeated associations between how a letter or word looks, how it sounds, and how the speech mechanism or hand feels when producing it. It is designed for third- through sixth-grade students of average or above average ability and normal sensory acuity. With some adaptations it can be modified to work with both older and younger students.

▬ *Procedures:* This method is designed to teach students how to identify words by teaching phonic generalizations and how to apply these generalizations in reading and spelling. It is to be used as the exclusive method for teaching reading, spelling, and penmanship for a minimum of a two-year period. Initially students who use this method should read only materials that are designed to conform with the method. Other written information such as content area textbooks should be read to the students.

The method is introduced by discussing the importance of reading and writing, how some children have difficulty learning to read and spell using whole-word methods, and how this method has helped other students. Thereafter, a sequence of lessons is completed, beginning

FIGURE 4.11   *First Lesson from* Phonic Remedial Reading Lessons

a

at	sat	mat	hat	fat
am	ham	Sam	Pam	tam
sad	mad	had	lad	dad
wag	sag	tag	lag	hag

sat	sap	Sam	sad
map	mam	mad	mat
hag	ham	hat	had
cat	cap	cad	cam

sat	am	sad	pat	mad
had	mat	tag	fat	ham
lag	ham	wag	hat	sap
sad	tap	cap	dad	at

map	hag	cat	sat	ham	tap
sap	map	hat	sad	tag	am
Pam	mat	had	tap	hat	dad
fat	mad	at	wag	cap	sag

Source: S. A. Kirk, W. D. Kirk, and E. H. Minskoff, *Phonic Remedial Reading Lessons* (Novato, Calif.: Academic Therapy Publication, 1985), p. 22. Reprinted by permission.

with learning the names of the letters and the letter sounds, learning words through blending sounds, and reading sentences and stories.

Teaching Letters and Sounds: The teaching of letter names and letter sounds employs associations between visual, auditory, and kinesthetic inputs. Each new sound-symbol relationship or phonogram is taught by having the students make three associations.

1. *Association I (Reading).* The students are taught to associate the written letter with the letter name and then with the letter sound. The teacher shows the students the letter name. The students repeat the name. The letter sound is learned using the same procedure.

2. *Association II (Oral Spelling).* The students are taught to associate the oral sound with the name of the letter. To do this the teacher says the sound and asks the students to give its corresponding letter.

3. *Association III (Written Spelling).* The students learn to write the letter through the teacher modeling, tracing, copying, and writing the letter from memory. The students then associate the letter sound with the written letter by the teacher directing them to write the letter that has the _____ sound.

When teaching these associations:

1. Cursive writing is preferred and suggested over manuscript.

2. Letters are always introduced by a key word.

3. Vowels and consonants are differentiated by different colored drill cards (i.e., white for consonants, salmon for vowels).

4. The first letters introduced (i.e., *a, b, f, h, i, j, k, m, p,* and *t*) represent clear sounds and nonreversible letter forms.

5. Drill cards are used to introduce each letter and to provide practice in sound and letter identification.

6. The writing procedure is applied to learning all new letters. The procedure for writing is:
   a. The teacher makes the letter.
   b. The students trace the letter.
   c. The students copy it.
   d. The students write it from memory.

Teaching Words: After the first ten letters and sounds have been learned using the Associations, then begin blending them together into words. Words that can be made from the ten letters are written on yellow word cards and kept in student word boxes (jewel cases). Students are taught to read and spell words.

To teach blending and reading, the letter Drill Cards that form a word (e.g., *b - a - t*) are laid out on the table or put in a pocket chart. The students are asked to give the sounds of the letters in succession, repeating the series of sounds again and again with increasing speed and smoothness until they are saying the word. This procedure is used to learn new words. Drill and timed drill activities are used to give the students practice reading the words.

To teach spelling, the analysis of words into their component sound should begin a few days after blending is started. To teach this method of spelling the teacher pronounces a word the students can read, first quickly and then slowly. The teacher then asks the students, ''What sound did you hear first?'' and then asks, ''What letter says /b/?'' The students then find the *b* card. When all cards have been found, the students write the word. Gillingham and Stillman (1973) stress the importance of using this procedure for spelling. After the teacher pronounces /bat/:

Child repeats /b/	Child names letters b-a-t	Child writes, naming each letter while forming it b-a-t	Child reads /bat/

This procedure is referred to as Simultaneous Oral Spelling, or SOS. Gillingham and Stillman comment that after a few days of practice in blending and SOS, it should be an almost invariable routine to have the students check their own errors. When a word is read wrong, the student should be asked to spell what he or she has just said, and match it against the original word. When a word is misspelled orally the teacher may write the offered spelling and say, ''Read this (e.g., *bit*)." The student would respond, "Bit." The teacher would say, "Correct, but I dictated the word /bat/."

As the students continue to learn and practice new words, they also continue to learn new sound-symbol associations or phonograms. As new phonograms are introduced, more and more words are practiced and added to the word boxes. An example of a daily lesson that lasts from forty-five to sixty minutes might be:

> Practice Association I with learned phonograms
> Practice Association II with learned phonograms
> Practice Association III with learned phonograms
> Drill words for reading
> Drill words for spelling and writing

Sentences and Stories: When the students can read and write three-lettered phonetic words, sentence and story reading is begun. This begins with reading simple, highly structured stories, called "Little Stories." These stories are first practiced silently until the students think they can read them perfectly. They can ask the teacher for assistance. The teacher pronounces nonphonetic words and cues the student to sound out phonetically regular words. Then the students read the sentence or story orally. The story is to be read perfectly with proper inflection. Later, the stories are dictated to the student. An example of a story is:

> Sam hit Ann.
> Then Ann hit Sam.
> Sam ran and Ann ran.
> Ann had a tan mitten.
> This is Ann's tan mitten.
> Ann lost it.
> Sam got the mitten.
> Sam sent the mitten to Ann.

▬ Comments: The Gillingham-Stillman method incorporates multisensory techniques into a synthetic approach for phonics. Slingerland adapted this method in developing a teacher's guide and a set of auxiliary teaching materials, *Multi-Sensory Approach to Language Arts for Specific Language Disability Children* (1974). Traub and Bloom (1970) have also modified the method in their program, *Recipe for Reading*. Although the Gillingham-Stillman method does provide a systematic means of teaching phonics, several cautions are relevant. First, the method requires students to learn both letter names and letter sounds. Letter sounds are used when reading but letter names are repeated when the students are spelling words. Learning two associations and when to use letter names and when to use letter sounds may be confusing. Second, the reading material has been criticized by some as being uninteresting and so highly structured that transference to "natural" text is sometimes difficult, hence students are given a distorted view of the reading process. Third, this method requires a substantial commitment on the part of the teacher and the students: a minimum of two years with five sessions per week is suggested.

Techniques for Building Sight Words

Some children who experience difficulties with developing automatic recognition of printed words need additional opportunities to practice recognizing and remembering the words they are leaning. This section presents several activities that teachers and students can use to assist students in remembering words. In addition, a number of games can be used as well as computer-assisted instruction. These activities are not approaches to reading and should not be used in isolation but as reinforcement activities used in conjunction with the meaning-emphasis and code-emphasis strategies and approaches discussed in the previous two sections.

Sight Word Association Procedure

The sight word association procedure uses corrective feedback and drill and practice to assist students in associating spoken words with written form. Unlike the previous approaches, which are designed to teach initial reading and word identification, the sight word association procedure (SWAP) is best used as a supplemental activity for the acquisition of sight vocabulary. By using visual configuration to identify words, it teaches sight vocabulary to an automatic level. SWAP can be used in conjunction with approaches and materials such as patterned language and predictable reading materials, language experience approach, basal reading series, or fluency building techniques. The procedure is appropriate to use with students who are beginning to learn to identify words across various contexts or texts, or with students who require more practice of new sight vocabulary than the amount provided in the current reading program. It is designed to be used individually or with small groups.

— **Procedures:** Begin by selecting words from the text that the students consistently miscall or do not identify at an automatic level. Write each word on a word card. The procedure for teaching these words (usually five to ten words at a time) is:

1. Discuss the words with the students to assure that they understand the meanings of the words as the words are being used in the text.

2. Present the words to the students one word at a time. Each word is exposed for five seconds, with the teacher saying the word twice.

3. Shuffle the cards and ask the students to identify the word on each card. Provide corrective feedback by verifying the correctly identified words, giving the correct word for any word miscalled, and saying the word if the students do not respond in five seconds.

4. Present all the words again, using the same format given in step 2.

5. Have the students identify each word, using the same format given in step 3. Repeat this step at least two more times or until the students can automatically recognize all the words.

If students continue to have difficulty recognizing a word after the seventh exposure to the word, switch from a recall task to a recognition task. To do this, place several word cards on the table and have the learners point to each word as you say it. If the students still continue to have difficulty learning the words, use a different technique to teach the words, such as picture association techniques, sentence/word association techniques, or a cloze procedure. A record sheet for keeping track of individual student responses is presented in Figure 4.12.

After teaching the words on the initial day, the words should be reviewed for several days to determine if the words are being retained.

— **Comments:** This procedure provides a technique for systematically teaching and practicing sight words. It utilizes principles of corrective feedback and mass and distributed practice to teach individual sight words. However, there are several important cautions regarding sight word association. First, this is only a supplemental technique and it needs to be used in conjunction with an approach to reading that stresses reading text and utilizing other word identification strategies such as context clues. Second, students should understand the meanings of the words being taught. Third, in addition to the isolated word practice provided by this technique, students should be given ample opportunity to read these words in context.

Picture Association Technique

When identifying a word, using a picture to aid in identifying the word can sometimes be beneficial, particularly if the picture is well matched to the text. It allows the readers to associate the word with a visual image. It is on this premise that picture association techniques use pictures to help students associate a spoken word with its written form. Like SWAP, the picture association technique is designed to assist students in developing sight words. It is meant to be used in conjunction with a reading approach that stresses reading words in text. When reading text, stu-

FIGURE 4.12   *Sight Word Association Procedure Record Sheet*

Words	Initial Teaching					Retention			Comments
	1	2	3	4	5	1	2	3	

✔ Correct
0 Incorrect

dents should be encouraged not only to think of their picture association, but also of a "word that makes sense."

— *Procedures:* Select words that the students are having difficulty identifying when reading. At first, choose words that are easily imaged such as nouns, verbs, and adjectives. Write each word on a card (usually five to ten words are taught at the same time). On a separate card, draw a simple picture or find a picture and attach it to the card. In some cases, the students may want to draw their own pictures. Use the following procedure to teach the picture-word association:

1. Place each picture in front of the student, labeling each one as you present it. Have the students practice repeating the names of the pictures.

2. Place next to each picture the word it represents, again saying the name of the word (see Figure 4.13). Have the students practice saying the names of the words.

3. Tell the students to match the words to the pictures and to say the name of the word while matching it. Repeat this process until the students easily match the pictures and words.

4. Place the words in front of the students and have them identify the words as you say them. If they cannot identify the correct word, have them think of the picture to aid in their recognition. If they still cannot point to the word, show them the picture that goes with the word.

FIGURE 4.13 *Picture Word Association Cards*

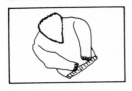

sweater

needle

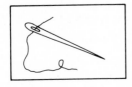

sewing

this procedure should be used only as a supplemental procedure. The students should be given ample opportunities to read the words in text and they should understand the meanings of the words they are learning.

Picture associations have been used in beginning reading programs such as the Peabody Rebus Reading Program (Woodcock, Clark, and Davies, 1969). Using the rebus method, concrete symbols or pictures are substituted for words (see Figure 4.14). Student learn to read these symbols and then transfer their skills to traditional print by making picture/word association.

Sentence/Word Association Technique

The sentence/word association technique encourages students to associate an unknown word with a familiar spoken sentence or word to aid in recognizing the word when reading. This technique, which is designed to be used individually or in small groups, relies on the students' abilities to associate old information with new information.

5. Have the students recall the words by showing the word cards one at a time. Again, if the student cannot recall a word, have them think of the picture. If they still cannot think of the word, tell them to look at the picture that goes with the word.

6. Continue this procedure until the students can identify all the words at an automatic level. The same record sheet as the one used for SWAP (Figure 4.12) can be used for this procedure.

7. Have the students review the words on subsequent days and, most importantly, give the students plenty of opportunities to read the words in context. When a student is reading and cannot identify a word, encourage him or her to think of the picture and to think of a word that makes sense.

— *Comments:* This picture association technique assists students in forming visual images that may facilitate their identification of words. As with the sight word association procedure,

— *Procedures:* Select from five to ten words that the students are consistently having difficulty recognizing. Discuss the words with the students and ask them to find the words in the text and read them in a sentence. Tell the students to decide on a key word or a sentence that will help them remember the word. For example, for the word *was* a sentence might be "Today he is, yesterday he _____ ." For the word *there* the sentence might be "Are you _____ ?" Put the words to be taught on word cards and put the associated key word or sentence on separate cards. Teach the associations between the key sentence or word and the unknown word, using the same procedures described for the picture association technique. The key in teaching is to have the students associate the new unknown word with a familiar sentence or word. After teaching, when a student is reading and comes to one of the new words and cannot recognize it, have the student think of the associated word or sentence.

FIGURE 4.14   *Sample of Rebus Vocabulary and Passage*

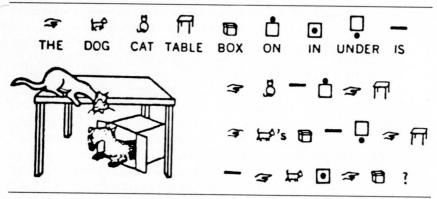

If the student cannot think of the associated clue orally, tell him or her.

— Comments: We have used this technique with reading-disabled students who frequently cannot remember or confuse such words as *was, were, there, they, that, them, this, these, those, when, what, where,* and *who.* After using sentence/word association, these students will see the unknown word, remember their associated key word or sentence, say the associated clue aloud, and then remember the word. As soon as the associated clue is no longer needed, the students seem to quit using it. As with the previous two techniques, this is only a supplemental procedure. Students should be given ample opportunities to practice their newly learned sight words in context.

Cloze Word Identification Procedure

The cloze word identification procedure encourages students to use semantic and syntactic clues to assist in identifying unknown words when reading. Sometimes beginning readers who are having difficulty utilizing word identification strategies will not use the strategies related to their oral language. They will rely primarily on visual configuration or phonic analysis. The cloze procedure incourages students to use semantic and syntactic clues by omitting words, thereby making it impossible for the students to use configuration clues or phonic analysis.

The cloze procedure has not only been used as an instructional technique but also as a technique for assessing if a text is at an appropriate reading level for a student (Taylor, 1953) and as a measure of reading comprehension (Woodcock, 1987; Woodcock and Johnson, 1977). Traditionally, the cloze procedure has also been viewed as a method of teaching reading comprehension (Bloomer, 1962; Guice, 1969; Jongsma, 1971, 1980). However, lately its relationship to reading comprehension has been questioned (Shanahan, Kamil, and Tobin, 1982; Shanahan and Kamil, 1983). Consequently, as the technique is described here it can be considered a word identification technique since its purpose is to teach the reader to use semantic and syntactic clues more effectively when identifying unknown words.

— Procedures: The cloze procedure consists of designing and using materials that follow a progression from providing grapho-phonic clues to requiring the students to rely solely on semantic and syntactic clues. The reading material should consist of short paragraphs or sentences that are written at the students' approximate instructional level. The progression suggested is adapted from the progression suggested by Tierney, Readence, and Dishner (1985).

1. Begin with sentences or short paragraphs in which one word is deleted per sentence and the student is given the first letter or phoneme in the word. For example, "We saw a ch _____ during our trip to the farm."

2. Use the same format as in Progression 1 but do not give the first letter of phoneme. For example, "We saw a _____ on our trip to the farm."

As you use these cloze materials, encourage the students to "think of a word that makes sense." When first teaching this skill, have the student generate a list of words and then try each word and judge if it makes sense. Have them talk about why the words make sense; in other words, that it is the same kind of word or part of speech (syntactic clue) and that it makes sense (semantic clue). Schell (1972) suggests that nouns should be deleted initially, later deleting verbs, adjectives, adverbs, and function words (e.g., prepositions, connectives).

▬ Comments: It may be necessary to provide some students with more grapho-phonic clues. This can be done by increasing the number of letters provided or by switching to a multiple-choice task. For example, "We saw a _____ (chicken, cheese, cheating) during our trip to the farm." This has been referred to as the *maze technique* (Guthrie, Burnham, Caplan, and Seifert, 1974) in assessment of reading. Like many other word identification techniques, the skills taught in this technique will not generalize unless the students are given ample opportunity to use the skill in

text. When first generalizing to typical text, the students will probably need to be cued to "think of a word that makes sense."

Teaching a Word Identification Strategy

What would you say if a junior-high student asked you, "What do you do when you are reading and come to a word you don't recognize?" You might say that at first you decide if you need to identify the word. If the decision is yes, then you use the appearance of the word and the context to try to figure it out. If that doesn't work, you look for any prefixes, suffixes, or endings, and separate them from the root word. Then you try to say each part and figure it out. If that doesn't work, you try to break the word into syllables and then sound it out. If that still doesn't work, you look it up in the dictionary. What you have reported to the student is a strategy for applying the word identification skills you already have.

Based on the Learning Strategy Model (see Chapter Two), Deshler and his colleagues (Lenz, Schumaker, Deshler, and Beals, 1984) developed and researched the effectiveness of teaching a word identification strategy to learning-disabled students. Using the strategy with twelve junior-high learning-disabled students, they found that after instruction the students made fewer word recognition errors than before instruction (Lenz and Hughes, 1990). However, the increases in word recognition did not automatically result in gains in reading comprehension for all students.

The acquisition and generalization steps from the Learning Strategy Model are used to teach this word identification strategy. The teaching procedure for this strategy entails pretesting the skill, obtaining a commitment from the students, and then describing and modeling the strategy. Then the students rehearse the steps in the strategy, practice and master the strategy in instructional level materials, and eventually practice and master the strategy in grade-appropriate material. Finally, the strategy is posttested, and the students work to generalize the strategy to a variety of reading situations.

The steps the students use to identify the unknown words are:

1. *Discover the word's context.*

2. *Isolate the prefix.* To isolate the prefix of a difficult word, students must look at the beginning of the word to see if the initial letters of the word match any of the prefixes they know. If they do recognize a prefix, they should isolate it. For example, *ex/claim.* If students do not recognize a prefix, they should proceed to step 3.

3. *Separate the suffix.* To separate the suffix, students must look at the end of the word to see if the last letters match any of the suffixes they know. If they do recognize a suffix, they should separate it; if not, they should go to the next step.

4. *Say the stem.* The stem is what is left after the students isolate the prefix and separate the suffix. If they can immediately say the stem, that means they can say the prefix, stem, and suffix together, which means saying the whole word. Once the students can say the whole word, they should read the entire sentence again and make sure they understand what it means. Reading can then be continued. If students cannot say the stem, they should proceed to step 5.

5. *Examine the stem.* When examining the stem, students need to dissect it into easy-to-pronounce parts. To do this, they will need to apply the Rules of Twos and Threes (see Figure 4.15). Once they have examined the stem and can pronounce the whole word, students should go back and reread the whole sentence to check their understanding. If they still cannot figure out the word after examining the stem, they need to go to step 6.

6. *Check with someone.*

7. *Try the dictionary.* If students cannot find someone to ask or if the person doesn't know, then they should try the dictionary. This step can

FIGURE 4.15   *Word Identification Strategy Rules for Examining the Stem of a Word*

RULES OF TWOS AND THREES

Rule 1

If a stem or part of the stem begins with:

- A vowel, divide off the first two letters.
- A consonant, divide off the first three letters.

Rule 2

If you can't make sense of the stem after using Rule 1, take off the first letter of the stem and use Rule 1 again.

Rule 3

When two different vowels are together, try making both of the vowel sounds (diet).

If this does not work, try pronouncing them together using only one of the vowel sounds (believe).

Source: B. K. Lenz, J. B. Schumaker, D. D. Deshler, and V. L. Beals, *Learning Strategies Curriculum: The Word Identification Strategy* (Lawrence: The University of Kansas, 1984), p. 71. Copyright 1984 by University of Kansas. Reprinted by permission and with the recommendation that training be obtained from the Institute for Research in Learning Disabilities, University of Kansas, Lawrence, Kansas 66045.

also be used if students have dissected a word and they do not know what it means.

The mnemonic for the steps in this strategy is DISSECT the first letter in each step. Specifics for teaching the word identification strategy, including scripted lessons, cue cards for learning and generalizing the strategy, and worksheets and passages for practice, are presented in the instructor's guide, *The Word Identification Strategy* (Learning Strategies Curriculum) (Lenz et al., 1984).

This program provides an example of how metacognitive skills can be taught to students. However, it is important to remember that such a strategy requires that the students already have developed basic word identification strategies (i.e., context clues, phonic analysis, structural analysis and syllabication).

Instructional Activities

Appendix B provides instructional activities that are related to word identification. Some of the activities teach new skills; others are best suited for practice and reinforcement of already acquired skills. For each activity, the objective, materials, and teaching procedures are described.

Summary

Reading is a strategic thinking process in which readers use their prior knowledge to interact with the text in order to construct meaning. A number of factors may be related to students' difficulty in becoming effective readers, including poor teaching and limited opportunities to read and write, delays in oral language or language differences, and inefficient cognitive, metacognitive, and/or metalinguistic processing.

Many students with learning and behavior problems experience difficulties in learning to read, particularly in learning and applying word identification strategies. There are a variety of reasons why they have difficulties identifying unknown words and learning to read. Some children have not been provided with methods and materials that build on the natural pattern and flow of language. For these students, approaches such as the modified language experience approach, patterned language books, or Reading Recovery may assist them in learning to read. These instructional approaches, which are meaning-oriented, emphasize the use of semantic, syntactic, and visual configuration clues.

In contrast, other students may profit from code-emphasis strategies that emphasize how to analyze a word into parts (e.g., sounds, syllables, structural units). Many of these programs, such as linguistic reading programs, *Corrective Reading,* and *Phonic Remedial Reading Drills,* explicitly teach word parts and incorporate them into highly controlled reading materials. Students who have not succeeded in using traditional and meaning-oriented approaches may need these highly structured programs for success.

Students with severe reading problems often profit from approaches that incorporate the kinesthetic and tactile input modes into their programs. Whereas the Fernald (VAKT) approach incorporates these modes into a meaning-emphasis approach to initial teaching, the Gillingham-Stillman method incorporates these modes into a code-emphasis approach.

Other students may not have received the necessary opportunities to practice identifying words and therefore do not recognize them at an automatic level. For these students, the addition of supplementary teaching activities such as the sight word association procedure, the picture association or sentence/word association procedures, or the cloze procedure may provide the additional practice.

Some students have the necessary basic word identification skills but fail to apply them in a systematic manner. Teaching students a consistent method for identifying words can be quite helpful.

As teachers, we need to determine the most effective and efficient ways for students with learning and behavior problems to develop and utilize word identification strategies. By taking into account the characteristics of the learners and their past and current reading program, we can make "educated guesses" concerning which approaches might be the most advantageous. As teachers, it is important to know a variety of teaching strategies and approaches so that we might meet the differing needs of these students.

APPENDIX 4.1 _____

Predictable and Patterned Language Books

Adams, Pam. *This Old Man*. New York: Grossett and Dunlap, 1974.

Alain. *One, Two, Three, Going to Sea*. New York: Scholastic Press, 1964.

Aliki. *Go Tell Aunt Rhody*. New York: Macmillan, 1974.

Aliki. *Hush Little Baby*. Englewood Cliffs, N.J.: Prentice-Hall, 1968.

Aliki. *My Five Senses*. New York: Thomas Y. Crowell, 1962.

Asch, Frank. *Monkey Face*. New York: Parents' Magazine Press, 1977.

Balian, Lorna. *The Animal*. Nashville: Abingdon, 1972.

Balian, Lorna. *Where in the World is Henry?* Scarsdale, N.Y.: Bradbury Press, 1972.

Barohas, Sarah E. *I Was Walking Down the Road*. New York: Scholastic Press, 1975.

Barrett, Judi. *Animals Should Definitely Not Wear Clothes*. New York: Atheneum, 1970.

Barton, Byron. *Buzz, Buzz, Buzz*. New York: Scholastic Press, 1973.

Baskin, Leonard. *Hosie's Alphabet*. New York: The Viking Press, 1972.

Battaglia, Aurelius. *Ole Mother Hubbard*. Racine, Wis.: Golden Press, 1972.

Becker, John. *Seven Little Rabbits*. New York: Scholastic Press, 1973.

Beckman, Kaj. *Lisa Cannot Sleep*. New York: Franklin Watts, 1969.

Bellah, Melanie. *A First Book of Sounds*. Racine, Wis.: Golden Press, 1963.

Berenstain, Stanley, and Berenstain, Janice. *The B Book*. New York: Random House, 1971.

Bonne, Rose. *I Know an Old Lady*. New York: Scholastic Press, 1961.

Brandenberg, Franz. *I Once Knew a Man*. New York: Macmillan, 1970.

Brooke, Leslie. *Johnny Crow's Garden*. New York: Frederick Warne, 1968.

Brown, Marcia. *The Three Billy Goats Gruff*. New York: Harcourt Brace Jovanovich, 1957.

Brown, Margaret Wise. *Four Fur Feet*. New York: William R. Scott, 1961.

Brown, Margaret Wise. *Goodnight Moon*. New York: Harper & Row, 1947.

Brown, Margaret Wise. *Home for a Bunny*. Racine, Wis.: Golden Press, 1956.

Brown, Margaret Wise. *Where Have You Been?* New York: Scholastic Press, 1952.

Burningham, John. *Mr. Gumpy's Outing*. New York: Scholastic Press. 1970.

The Bus Ride. Glenview, Ill.: Scott, Foresman, 1971.

Cameron, Polly. *I Can't Said the Ant*. New York: Coward, McCann, and Geoghegan, 1961.

Carle, Eric. *The Grouchy Ladybug*. New York: Thomas Y. Crowell, 1977.

Carle, Eric. *The Mixed Up Chameleon*. New York: Thomas Y. Crowell, 1975.

Carle, Eric. *The Very Hungry Caterpillar*. Cleveland, Ohio: Collins World, 1969.

Charlip, Remy. *Fortunately*. New York: Parents' Magazine Press, 1971.

Charlip, Remy. *What Good Luck, What Bad Luck*. New York: Scholastic Press, 1964.

Considine, Kate, and Schuler, Ruby. *One, Two, Three, Four*. New York: Holt, Rinehart & Winston, 1965.

Cook, Bernadine. *The Little Fish that Got Away*. Reading Mass.: Addison-Wesley, 1976.

Crews, Donald. *Freight Train*. New York: Greenwillow, 1978. (Incorporates position words and follows as sequence.)

de Regniers, Beatrice Schenk. *Catch a Little Fox*. New York: Seabury Press, 1970.

de Regniers, Beatrice Schenk. *The Day Everybody Cried*. New York: The Viking Press, 1967.

de Regniers, Beatrice Schenk. *The Little Book*. New York: Henry Z. Walck, 1961.

de Regniers, Beatrice Schenk. *Willy O'Dwyer Jumped in the Fire*. New York: Atheneum, 1968.

Domanska, Janina. *If All the Seas Were One Sea*. New York: Macmillan, 1971.

Duff, Maggie. *Johnny and His Drum*. New York: Henry Z. Walck, 1972.

Duff, Maggie. *Rum Pum Pum*. New York: Macmillan, 1978.

Einsel, Walter. *Did You Ever See?* New York: Scholastic Press, 1962.

Emberly, Barbara. *Drummer Hoff*. Englewood Cliffs, N.J.: Prentice-Hall, 1967.

Emberly, Barbara. *Simon's Song*. Englewood Cliffs, N.J.: Prentice-Hall, 1969.

Emberly, Ed. *Klippity Klop*. Boston: Little, Brown, 1974.

Ets, Marie Hall. *Elephant in a Well*. New York: Viking, 1972.

Flack, Marjorie. *Ask Mr. Bear*. New York: Macmillan, 1932.

Florian, Douglas. *A Bird Can Fly*. New York: Greenwillow, 1980. (Pattern: Three pages state what an animal or bird can do, a fourth what it cannot do, and introduces another that can.)

Galdone, Paul. *Henny Penny*. New York: Scholastic Press. 1968.

Galdone, Paul. *The Little Red Hen.* New York: Scholastic Press, 1973.

Galdone, Paul. *The Three Bears.* New York: Scholastic Press, 1972.

Galdone, Paul. *The Three Little Pigs,* New York: Seabury Press, 1970.

Greenberg, Polly. *Oh Lord, I Wish I Was a Buzzard.* New York: Macmillan, 1972.

Guilfoile, Elizabeth. *Nobody Listens to Andrew.* New York: Scholastic Press, 1957.

Higgins, Doin. *Papa's Going to Buy Me a Mockingbird.* New York: Seabury Press, 1968.

Hoban, Tana. *Count and See.* New York: Macmillan, 1972.

Hoffman, Hilde. *The Green Grass Grows All Around.* New York: Macmillan, 1968.

Hutchins, Pat. *Good-Night Owl.* New York: Macmillan, 1972.

Hutchins, Pat. *Rosie's Walk.* New York: Macmillan, 1968.

Hutchins, Pat. *Titch.* New York: Collier Books, 1971.

Joslin, Sesyle. *What Do You Say Dear?* New York: Scholastic Press, 1958.

Kalan, Robert. *Rain.* New York: Greenwillow, 1978.

Keats, Ezra Jack. *Over in the Meadow.* New York: Scholastic Press, 1971.

Kent, Jack. *The Fat Cat.* New York: Scholastic Press, 1971.

Kesselman, Wendy. Illustrated by Tony Chen. *There's a Train Going by My Window.* Garden City: Doubleday, 1982. (Rhythmic verse and refrain.)

Klein, Leonore. *Brave Daniel.* New York: Scholastic Press, 1958.

Kraus, Robert. *Good Night Little ABC.* New York: Scholastic Press, 1972.

Kraus, Robert. *Whose Mouse Are You?* New York: Collier Books, 1970.

Krauss, Ruth. *Bears.* New York: Scholastic Press, 1948.

Langstaff, John. *Gather My Gold Together: Four Songs for Four Seasons.* Garden City: Doubleday, 1971.

Langstaff, John. *Oh, A-Hunting We Will Go.* New York: Antheneum, 1974.

Laurence, Ester. *We're off to Catch a Dragon.* Nashville: Abingdon, 1969.

Le Tora, Bijow. *Nice and Cozy.* New York: Four Winds, 1980. (Rhyming text and refrain.)

Lexau, Joan. *Crocodile and Hen.* New York: Harper and Row, 1969.

Lobel, Anita. *King Rooster, Queen Hen.* New York: Greenwillow, 1975.

Lobel, Arnold. *A Treeful of Pigs.* New York: Greenwillow, 1979.

Mack, Stan. *10 Bears in My Bed.* New York: Pantheon, 1974.

Mars, W. T. *The Old Woman and Her Pig.* Racine, Wis.: Western Publishing Company, 1964.

Martin, Bill. *Brown Bear, Brown Bear, What Do You See?* New York: Holt, Rinehart & Winston. 1967.

Martin, Bill. *Fire! Fire! Said Mrs. McGuire.* New York: Holt, Rinehart & Winston, 1970.

Martin, Bill. *Freedom Books.* Los Angeles: Bowmar, 1965.

Martin, Bill. *A Ghost Story.* New York: Holt, Rinehart & Winston, 1970.

Martin, Bill. *The Haunted House.* New York: Holt, Rinehart & Winston, 1970.

Martin, Bill. *Instant Readers.* New York: Holt, Rinehart & Winston, 1970.

Martin, Bill. *Little Owl Series.* New York: Holt, Rinehart & Winston, 1965.

Martin, Bill. *Monday, Monday, I Like Monday.* New York: Holt, Rinehart & Winston, 1970.

Martin, Bill. *Spoiled Tomatoes.* Los Angeles: Bowmar, 1967.

Martin, Bill. *Sounds of Language.* Allen, Tex.: DLM, 1990.

Martin, Bill. *Wise Owl Series,* New York: Holt, Rinehart & Winston, 1967.

Mayer, Mercer. *If I Had . . .* New York: Dial, 1968.

Mayer, Mercer. *Just for You.* Racine, Wis.: Golden Press, 1975.

McGovern, Ann. *Too Much Noise.* New York: Scholastic Press, 1967.

Memling, Carl. *Riddles, Riddles from A to Z.* Racine, Wis.: Golden Press, 1972.

Memling, Carl. *Ten Little Animals.* Racine, Wis.: Golden Press, 1961.

Moffett, Martha. *A Flower Pot Is Not a Hat.* New York: E. P. Dutton, 1972.

O'Neill, Mary. *Hailstones and Halibut Bones.* Garden City: Doubleday, 1961.

Palmer, Janet. *Ten Days of School.* New York: Bank Street College of Education, Macmillan, 1969.

Patrick, Gloria. *A Bug in a Jug.* New York: Scholastic Press, 1970.

Peek, Merle. *Roll Over!* Boston: Houghton Mifflin, 1981.

Petersham, Maud, and Petersham, Miska. *The Rooster Crows: A Book of American Rhymes and Jingles.* New York: Scholastic Press, 1971.

Polushkin, Maria. *Mother, Mother, I Want Another.* New York: Crown, 1978.

Preston, Edna M. *The Temper Tantrum Book.* New York: Viking, 1969.

Preston, Edna Mitchell. *Where Did My Mother Go?* New York: Four Winds, 1978.

Quackenbush, Robert M. *Poems for Counting.* New York: Holt, Rinehart & Winston, 1965.

Quackenbush, Robert. *She'll Be Comin' Round the Mountain.* Philadelphia: Lippincott, 1973.

(continued)

APPENDIX 4.1   *continued*

Quackenbush, Robert. *Skip to My Lou*. Philadelphia Lippincott, 1975.

Rokoff, Sandra. *Here is a Cat*. Singapore: Hallmark Children's Editions, no date.

Rossetti, Christina. *What is Pink?* New York: Holt, Rinehart & Winston, 1965.

Scheer, Jullian, and Bileck, Marvin. *Rain Makes Applesauce*. New York: Holiday House, 1964.

Scheer, Jullian, and Bileck, Marvin. *Upside Down Day*. New York: Holiday House, 1968.

Sendak, Maurice. *Chicken Soup with Rice*. New York: Scholastic Press, 1962.

Sendak, Maurice. *Where the Wild Things Are*. New York: Scholastic Press, 1963.

Dr. Seuss. *Dr. Seuss's ABC*. New York: Random House, 1963.

Shaw, Charles B. *It Looked Like Spilt Milk*. New York: Harper & Row, 1947.

Skaar, Grace. *What Do the Animals Say?* New York: Scholastic Press, 1972.

Sooneborn, Ruth A. *Someone Is Eating the Sun*. New York: Random House, 1974.

Spier, Peter. *The Fox Went Out on a Chilly Night*. Garden City: Doubleday, 1961.

Stover, JoAnn. *If Everybody Did*. New York: David McKay, 1960.

Thomas, Patricia. Illustrated by Mordicai Gerstein. *"There are Rocks in My Socks!" Said the Ox to the Fox*. New York: Lothrop, 1979. (Repetition and rhyme.)

Tolstoy, Alexei. *The Great Big Enormous Turnip*. New York: Franklin Watts, 1968.

Wahl, Jan. *Drakestail*. Illustrated by Byron Barton. New York: Greenwillow, 1978. (Refrain and cumulative plot.)

Watson, Clyde. *Father Ox's Pennyrhymes*. New York: Scholastic Press, 1971.

Welber, Robert. *Goodbye, Hello*. New York: Pantheon, 1974.

Westcott, Nadine Bernard. *I Know an Old Lady Who Swallowed a Fly*. Boston: Little, Brown, 1980.

Wildsmith, Brian. *The Twelve Days of Christmas*. New York: Franklin Watts, 1972.

Withers, Carl. *A Rocket in My Pocket*. New York: Scholastic Press, 1967.

Wolkstein, Diane. *The Visit*. New York: Knopf, 1977.

Wright, H. R. *A Maker of Boxes*. New York: Holt, Rinehart & Winston, 1965.

Zaid, Barry. *Chicken Little*. New York: Random House, no date.

Zemach, Margot. *Hush, Little Baby*. New York: E. P. Dutton, 1976.

Zemach, Margot. *The Teeny Tiny Woman*. New York: Scholastic Press, 1965.

Adapted from: R. J. Tierney, J. E. Readence, and E. K. Dishner, *Reading Strategies and Practices: A Compendium,* 2nd ed. (Boston: Allyn and Bacon, 1985), pp. 248–254. Reprinted with permission.

APPENDIX 4.2

Sample Books for Use with Reading Recovery

Author or Series	Book	Publisher
Level 1		
Nancy Tafuri	*Have You Seen My Duckling?*	Puffin
Ann Jonas	*Now We Can Go*	Greenwillow
Picture Puffin	*Weather*	Puffin
Brian Wildsmith	*Cat on the Mat*	Oxford
Level 2		
Joy Cowley	*Huggles Goes Away*	Write Group
Harriet Ziefert	*Where Is my Dinner?*	Grosset & Dunlap
Joy Cowley	*Yuk Soup*	Wright Group
Level 3		
Manipulative Series	*Little, Big, Bigger*	Bowmar
Brian Wildsmith	*All Fall Down*	Oxford
Reading Rigby	*The Flea*	Rigby

Author or Series	Book	Publisher

Level 4

Bill Martin	*Brown Bear, Brown Bear*	Holt, Rinehart and Winston
Merle Peek	*Roll Over*	Clarion
Talk-a-Rounders	*Under and Over*	Children's

Level 5

Story Box	*Horace*	Shortland
Oxford Reading Tree	*Nobody Wanted to Play*	Oxford
William Stobbs	*One, Two, Buckle My Shoe*	Bodley

Level 6

Barbro Lindgren	*Sam's Ball*	Morrow
Barbro Lindgren	*Sam's Teddy Bear*	Morrow
First Reader Stories	*On a Cold, Cold Day*	Golden Press
Merle Peek	*Mary Wore Her Red Dress*	Clarion

Level 7

Charles Shaw	*It Looked like Spilt Milk*	Harper & Row
Rookie Reader	*Ice Is . . .*	Children's Press
Story Box	*Danger*	Shortland
Read-a-Lot Book	*I Love My Dog*	Oxford

Level 8

Eric Hill	*Where's Spot?*	Putnam
First Reader Stories	*Bill's Baby*	Golden Press
Reading Rigby	*Five Cars*	Rigby
John Langstaff	*Oh, A-Hunting We Will Go*	Atheneum
Rod Campbell	*Henry's Busy Day*	Viking

Level 9

Pat Hutchins	*Rosie's Walk*	Macmillan
Ron Maris	*Is Anyone Home?*	Greenwillow
Colin West	*Have You Seen the Crocodile?*	Harper & Row
Colin West	*"Pardon?" Said the Giraffe*	Harper & Row
Just-Beginning-To-Read	*The Cookie House*	Follett
Rookie Reader	*Too Many Balloons*	Children's Press

Level 10

First Reader Stories	*Excuses, Excuses*	Golden Press
Anne Rockwell	*Cars*	Dutton
Cindy Wheeler	*Marmalade's Nap*	Knopf
Cindy Wheeler	*Rose*	Knopf
Beatrice de Regniers	*Going for a Walk*	Harper & Row
Story Box	*Grumpy Elephant*	Shortland

Level 11

Picture Puffin	*I'm the King of the Castle*	Penguin
Fuzz Buzz	*The Garden*	Oxford
Robert Kraus	*Whose Mouse Are You?*	Macmillan
John Stadler	*Snail Save the Day*	Harper & Row

(continued)

APPENDIX 4.2   *continued*

Author or Series	Book	Publisher

Level 12

John Burningham	*The Cupboard*	Crowell
Pat Hutchins	*Titch*	Crown
Ruth Krauss	*The Carrot Seed*	Macmillan
Erlene Long	*Gone Fishing*	Scholastic
Byron Barton	*Buzz Buzz Buzz*	Penguin
	More Spaghetti I Say	Scholastic

Level 13

Ann Jonas	*Two Bear Cubs*	Greenwillow
Maryann Kovakski	*The Wheels on the Bus*	Little, Brown
Alexei Tolstoy	*The Great Big Enormous Turnip*	Macmillan
	Rapid Robert Roadrunner	Children's Press

Level 14

Pam Adams	*There Was an Old Lady Who Swallowed a Fly*	Scholastic
Pat Hutchins	*You'll Soon Grow into Them, Titch*	Greenwillow
Robert Kraus	*Where Are You Going, Little Mouse?*	Greenwillow
Story Box	*Obadiah*	Shortland

Level 15

Suzy Kline	*Don't Touch!*	Penguin
Audrey Wood	*The Napping House*	HBJ
M. Friskey	*Indian Two Feet and His Horse*	Children's Press
	Ten Sleepy Sheep	Scholastic

Level 16

Pat Hutchins	*Goodnight Owl*	Penguin
Robert Kraus	*Leo the Late Bloomer*	Windmill
Mercer Mayer	*There's a Nightmare in*	Dial
Martha Alexander	*We're in Big Trouble, Blackboard Bear*	Dial
I Can Read Book	*Albert the Albatross*	Heinemann
Else Minarick	*A Kiss for Little Bear*	Harper & Row

Level 17

Paul Galdone	*The Little Red Hen*	Scholastic
Pat Hutchins	*The Doorbell Rang*	Greenwillow
Arnold Lobel	*Mouse Soup*	Harper & Row
Jellybeans	*Ten Loopy Caterpillars*	Shortland
I Can Read Book	*This Is the House Where Jack Lives*	Heineman

Level 18

Eric Carle	*The Very Hungry Caterpillar*	Penguin
Arnold Lobel	*Owl at Home*	Harper & Row

Author or Series	Book	Publisher

Level 18 (continued)

Maurice Sendak	Where the Wild Things Are	Harper & Row
	There Is a Carrot in My Ear	Scholastic
	The Man Who Didn't Do His Dishes	Scholastic

Level 19

John Burningham	Mr. Gumby's Outing	Penguin
Pat Hutchins	The Surprise Party	Penguin
Arnold Lobel	Frog and Toad Are Friends	Harper & Row
Jellybeans	Earthquake	Shortland
City Kids	When Tony Got Lost at the Zoo	Nelson

Level 20

Pam Allen	Who Sank the Boat?	Coward
Maurice Sendak	Chicken Soup with Rice	Scholastic
Paul Galdone	The Three Little Pigs	Scholastic
Story Chest	The Three Wishes	Shortland

Source: Adapted from G. S. Pinnell, D. E. DeFord, and C. A. Lyons (1988), *Reading Recovery: Early intervention for at-risk first graders.* Arlington, Va.: Educational Research Service and from M. Clay and B. Watson (1987), Reading Recovery Book List, Auckland, New Zealand: University of Auckland.

Chapter Five

Reading: Fluency and Comprehension

Chapter Questions

- *Describe several reasons why a student might have difficulty with fluency or reading comprehension.*
- *Why is it important to read aloud to a student who is having difficulty learning to read?*
- *Describe the framework for reading comprehension presented in this chapter. After reading a piece of text, write several questions/answers of each of the following types: textually explicit, textually implicit, and scriptually implicit.*
- *Select an informational text that you plan or might plan to read with students. Describe how you would use brainstorming, Pre Reading Plan, or K-W-L to assist students in activating background knowledge.*
- *Describe how a ''think-aloud'' would be used with a paraphrasing or retelling strategy. Select a passage and a strategy (e.g., RAP, SPOT) and do a think-aloud by describing what you are thinking as you carry out the steps in the strategy.*
- *Compare and contrast the Directed Reading Activity and the Directed Reading-Thinking Activity.*
- *What four comprehension and comprehension monitoring strategies are highlighted in reciprocal teaching?*
- *Describe how you would set up a special education classroom using a whole language or literature-based reading program.*

Reading provides a window for learning in schools and in later life. Research indicates that a key to becoming a good reader is to have opportunities to read. As teachers our goal is to provide students with a wide choice of literature and other reading materials, with opportunities to read and discuss what is being read and with instruction in strategies that allow students to actively comprehend and critically think about what they are reading. Whereas the last chapter focused on strategies for word identification, this chapter presents strategies oriented toward fluency and comprehension.

Teaching Fluency

Although Jeff can recognize most of the words in his second-grade reader, he continues to sound out the words rather than rely on the visual configuration of the word, context clues, and his memory. Consequently, his reading, whether oral or silent, is very slow. He expends so much effort on identifying the words that he frequently misses the main points of the passage.

Diane, a fourth grader, had great difficulty learning to read. After several years of failure, she finally learned to identify words readily by using a linguistic approach. However, Diane's rate of reading is slow and she is experiencing some difficulties in comprehension. When asked to define reading, she places emphasis on "reading the word correctly" rather than on understanding what she reads. Though Jeff and Diane have developed a system for identifying words, they are having difficulties reading fluently (quickly and easily).

The purpose of fluency instruction is to increase both word recognition and rate of reading. According to the theory of automaticity (LaBerge and Samuels, 1974; Samuels, 1987), fluent readers automatically process information at the visual and phonological levels, and are therefore able to focus most of their attention on the meaning codes in the text and integrate this information with their background knowledge.

Let's look at several strategies for helping students develop fluency in their reading.

Reading and Reading Aloud

Students develop reading fluency through reading and through listening and watching others read aloud. For example, Anderson, Wilson, and Fielding (1988) found that one of the better predictors of reading achievement was the amount of time fifth-grade children spent reading books out of school. Within the last decade, a growing emphasis has been placed on the importance of reading aloud to children as a means for developing not only an enjoyment of literature and books, but also as an avenue for learning to read and building fluency (Kimmel and Segal, 1988; Trelease, 1989a).

Reading aloud to students with learning and behavior problems is not a remedial strategy. It is, however, an activity that teachers often do not find the time to do with students who have reading problems because it is perceived that they need to be reading themselves instead of listening to someone else. Reading aloud promotes the development of reading and fluency in a number of ways.

First, it allows the teacher to model fluent reading. When reading aloud to a group of students just learning to read, the use of big books can be helpful because it allows the teacher to point to the words as she or he reads. It also allows the teacher the opportunity to discuss the pictures with the students. If the teacher or parent or volunteer is reading aloud to one child, then sitting next to the child or having the child sit on the teacher's lap (depending on the age of the child), makes it easy for the child to interact with the print, the pictures, and the teacher. When reading aloud, it is fun and helpful to read with expression and to have the character take on different voices. This allows the child to see how conversations are represented in print.

Second, reading aloud allows the students to listen to and discuss books that are above their current reading level. Many students with learning and behavior problems have listening comprehension that is several years more advanced than their reading comprehension. Reading a book aloud affords the students the opportunity to talk about literature that is at the more advanced level.

Third, reading aloud provides background knowledge for the students reading the book themselves. Once children have listened to a book, they are more likely to select it as a book they want to read. In a study of kindergartners, Martinez and Teale (1988) found that children chose very familiar books (read repeatedly by the teacher) to read during freetime three times more frequently than unfamiliar books (unread). Since students have already listened to and talked about the book, they will have a wealth of knowledge about the book to assist them in reading.

Fourth, reading aloud can be orchestrated so that older less adept readers can read books to young children. This provides the opportunity for the older students to read aloud and to serve in the role model of a "good reader," an opportunity not often available in the regular or resource classroom.

Jim Trelease, author of *The New Read-Aloud Handbook* (1989b), suggests that reading aloud

- provides a positive reading role model
- furnishes new information
- demonstrates the pleasures of reading
- develops vocabulary
- provides examples of good sentences and good story grammar
- enables students to be exposed to a book they might not otherwise be exposed to
- provides opportunity for discussions concerning the content of the book (Trelease, 1989a)

Repeated Reading

Have you noticed how young children thoroughly enjoy having the same story read to them many, many times? As you sit with them and read a familiar book, they automatically begin to read along with you. At first, they join in on some of the words and phrases. Eventually, they are reading with you for most of the book. With repeated reading of a story, the children are becoming so familiar with the text that their memory becomes a great aid to them. Repeated reading is based on the notion that as students repeatedly read text, they become fluent and confident in their reading (Samuels, 1979). And because they are exposed to the same story numerous times, they have the opportunity to practice identifying unknown words while relying on their memory of the language flow to assist them.

▬ *Procedures:* Repeated reading consists of rereading short, meaningful passages several times until a satisfactory level of fluency is reached. The procedure is then repeated with a new passage. The general format for this reading procedure is to have the student repeatedly read passages that range from 50 to 200 words in length, until they reach a more fluent reading rate (e.g., 85 words per minute) and with an adequate word recognition level (e.g., 90 percent word recognition accuracy). When a student reads under the direct supervision of a teacher, the words a student does not recognize are pronounced by the teacher. To foster comprehension, discussion of the book follows reading.

Carbo (1978) and Chomsky (1976) have used tape-recorded books for this procedure. Using taped books, the students listen to the stories and follow along with the written text. They listen to and read the same story until they can "read the book by themselves." The teacher then listens to students individually read the story and discusses the story with the students. Guidelines for tape-recording books and keeping records of students' reading are presented in Figure 5.1.

▬ *Comments:* Students reading below grade level who have used repeated reading have consistently demonstrated gains in both fluency and reading comprehension (Carbo, 1978;

FIGURE 5.1 *Guidelines for Using Taped Books for Repeated Reading*

Selecting Books

Select books that are of interest to the students.

Have the students select the books.

Record books and stories that the students write.

Patterned language books are a good source for students just learning to read (see Appendix 4.1).

The Read-Aloud Handbook by Jim Trelease (1985, New York: Penguin Books) is another good source for books.

Tape Recording the Books

Recording Books with Pauses so That the Students Can Reread

Read the book and decide where to break the text for repeated reading. Mark these spots in the text. For younger students you may want to use a picture of a stop sign.

Get ready to record by gathering the book, a good quality tape and tape recorder with a counter, and a signal (e.g., bell, beeper, rattle) to signal the places to stop.

Record the book, using a natural rate of reading and expression. When you come to a spot where you are suppose to stop, signal the stop. Wait at least five seconds before you continue. When you continue say the page number first and then continue.

Write the counter number next to the signal in the book. In this way the students will know how far to rewind if they want to go back and reread with the tape.

Recording Books Without Pauses So That the Student Can Read Along

Use the same procedure except only signal the turning of pages.

Purchase prerecorded taped books.

Have parent volunteers record the books.

Kirk (1986) suggests forming student committees to select and record the books. Have the students practice reading the books before recording them.

Storing the Taped Books

Store the books on a shelf. Glue or tape a library pocket on the back of the book and place the tape in the pocket.

In the inside cover place a Reading Record Sheet. On this sheet have the students record their name and the date they first read the book. In this way you and the rest of the students know who has read a book. These students can then get together to discuss the book.

Keeping Student Records

Have each student make a reading folder. Staple forms inside the folder on which the student can record the name of the book, the author, the date, how he or she read the book, and with whom he or she discussed the book. In this way, both the teacher and the student have a record of the student's reading.

Name of Book	Author	Dates	Read with				Discussed with	
			Self	Tape	Student	Teacher	Student	Teacher

Chomsky, 1976; Herman, 1985; Koskinen and Blum, 1985). Using tape-recorded stories, Carbo presented three variations of the repeated readings method to students reading two to four years below grade level. For the first three-month period students reread entire books. In the second variation, students listened to smaller amounts of text during each session, with the reading material more closely related to the students' language comprehension level. In the third variation, the material consisted of a set of high-interest paperback books arranged in order of difficulty. Average gains by the students were three, eight, and six months, respectively, indicating that rereading smaller segments of text may be helpful. Computers can also be utilized with repeated reading (Rashotte and Torgesen, 1985; Torgesen, 1986). Using Apple Super-PILOT (1985), 100-word passages were placed on the computer so the entire passage was in view simultaneously. The students repeatedly read the practice passages. Rashotte and Torgesen also varied the number of times the same words were repeated within and across passages. Implications from their study indicated that the computer can be an effective tool for implementing this procedure and that frequent repetition of words helps students increase their fluency.

Given this information, we suggest that combining the patterned language approach (discussed in Chapter Four) with repeated reading could be a powerful strategy for building fluency in those students who have limited reading skills. Repetition of patterned language passages would give poor readers the needed extra practice in using linguistic clues such as syntax and semantics, as well as in extracting the grapho-phonemic word structure.

Choral Repeated Reading

Choral repeated reading is a strategy that combines ideas and procedures from repeated reading and choral reading. It was developed by one of the authors (Bos, 1982), because of her concern that fluency-building strategies for less adept readers tend to ignore the teaching of either word identification skills or comprehension (e.g., neurological impress). We have used the approach almost exclusively with students who have significant reading difficulties in word identification and reading rate.

■ *Procedures:* Choral repeated reading is designed for students who are able to comprehend material read to them but, due to difficulties in word identification and reading rate, are unable to read material commensurate with their listening comprehension level. Students should have a sight vocabulary of at least twenty-five words. We suggest the following procedure:

1. Explain the technique to the student.

2. With the student, select a book of interest that is one to two levels above his or her current instructional reading level and that has frequent repetition of words. At times, we have used books from the patterned language book list shown in Chapter Appendix 4.1. Have the student read a short passage from the book to check word recognition. It should range from 75 to 85 percent. If it is much lower, a different book should be selected.

3. Establish a purpose for reading by perusing the book and making predictions. Read the book with the student, using the following three-step process:

   a. *Teacher reads.* Start at the beginning of the book and read a piece of text to the student, ranging from several sentences to a paragraph. (The length of each section should be short enough that the student can rely on his or her short-term memory as an aid for reading.) Read at a normal rate and move your finger smoothly along underneath the words as the student watches, making sure that your reading matches your movement from word to word.

   b. *Teacher and student read.* Read the same section together with the student. Continue to point to the words. The two of you may read the section once or several times, rereading until the student feels comfortable reading the section independently. **c.** *Student reads:* Have the student read the section independently. Pronounce any unknown words and note words the student consistently has difficulty recognizing.

4. After reading each section, discuss how it related to your predictions and what you have learned. New predictions and purposes for reading can be set.

5. Repeat the three-step process throughout the book. The length of each section usually increases as the book is read, and the number of times you and the student read together usually decreases. For some students the first step is discontinued.

6. Write on word cards the words the student consistently has difficulty identifying automatically. Use a variety of activities to give him or her more experience with these words. For example, discuss the word meanings or locate the words in the text and reread the sentences. Use the supplemental whole-word activities discussed in Chapter Four such as the sight word association procedure, the sentence/word association procedure, or the cloze procedure. You can also have the student use some of the word identification instructional activities described in Appendix B.

7. Have the student keep records of his or her progress. Using bar or other types of graphs can be particularly reinforcing for students as they gain fluency, because the increases are so clearly depicted (Figure 5.2). Word recognition and reading rate can be checked easily by having the student read 100 to 300 words of the book they are currently reading. Have the student record his or her results on the graph or chart. Check progress at least every third day when initially using the procedure.

In this method, reading sessions usually last fifteen to twenty minutes, with most of the time focusing on oral reading. As the student becomes more confident in reading ability, use repeated readings with tape-recorded books or stories as independent reading activities. Spelling words can be selected from words in the books and words can be organized to teach phonic and structural analysis skills (see Chapter Four).

▬ Comments: We have used this procedure with a number of students who have severe word identification and/or fluency problems. Because this procedure allows the teacher and student to attend to word identification skills and comprehension as well as fluency, it is a more comprehensive reading procedure than either neurological impress or repeated readings. Using the three-step process also allows the student to read more difficult books. We have found this particularly rewarding for older nonreaders in that it quickly gives them success in reading books.

Cautions Regarding Fluency Techniques

It is suggested that when teaching fluency, techniques for improving word identification skills and comprehension should be taught. As presented in the repeated choral reading technique, word recognition and word extension activities can be developed naturally from the text. For example, the same activities that are recommended for the word cards generated from language experience stories (see Figure 4.3) can be used with word cards generated from these fluency techniques. Although improving fluency can provide students with more attention to allocate toward comprehension, not all students will automatically acquire the skills associated with effective comprehension. The next section discusses methods of teaching comprehension.

Teaching Comprehension

Comprehension is the ultimate goal of the reading process. It is constructing meaning by integrating the information provided by the author with the reader's background knowledge. It re-

FIGURE 5.2   *Form for Recording Reading Fluency*

Name: _____

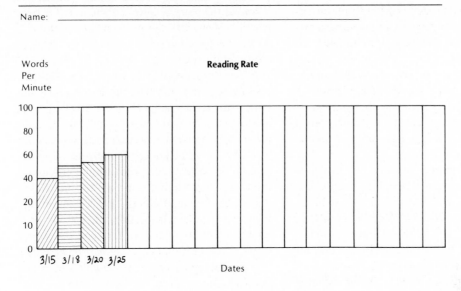

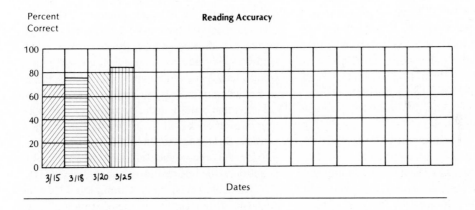

quires that the reader interacts with the text to construct meaning. There are many reasons why students may have difficulty comprehending what they read.

As a fourth grader reading on second-grade level, Amanda would probably better comprehend what she reads if she did not have to allocate so much attention to word identification. On the other hand, Scott is a word caller. He thinks reading is "reading the words correctly." Even though he is able to read fluently, he does not attend to the meaning of the passage. He frequently has difficulty recalling both the gist and details of a story. Carrie is diagnosed as language-disabled, with difficulties in syntax and semantics. These low oral language skills affect her comprehension of what she reads.

Sam can remember what he reads but does not relate it to what he already knows about the topic (schema). Therefore, he has particular difficulty answering questions that require him to use his background knowledge. Ron, on the other hand, relies too heavily on his background knowledge. This is adversely affecting his reading comprehension.

Kim fails to monitor her comprehension as she reads. She often reports that everything makes sense and she understands what she is reading. Yet when her teacher asks questions it becomes obvious that Kim has achieved limited comprehension.

All these students are having difficulty with reading comprehension although their problems are very different. For students such as Amanda, word identification difficulties get in the way of comprehension. Focusing on building word identification skills is probably appropriate for her. However, comprehension skills should not be ignored. This may mean building listening comprehension at her current grade level as well as working on reading comprehension at her current reading level. For Amanda, it is making sure that reading is perceived as understanding and interacting with the text to construct meaning, and not just reading the words correctly. Although word identification skill development may consume part of reading instruction time, teaching comprehension still needs to be an important part of instruction.

For Scott, the major portion of reading instruction should focus on comprehension. The teacher needs to assist Scott in changing his definition of the reading process. Helping Scott set comprehension-oriented purposes for reading and teaching him how to ask questions as he reads should assist him in changing his definition of reading.

Carrie's problems relate to a language problem that affects her reading comprehension as well as her receptive language. For students such as Carrie instruction in reading comprehension often parallels instruction in receptive language. Both reading and listening comprehension can be improved simultaneously. For example, when Carrie either listens to or reads a story she needs to learn to ask and answer such questions as, "Who is the story about?" "Where did it happen?" "What was the problem in the story?" "What happened to solve the problem?" "How did the story end?"

Some students fail to relate what they are reading to what they already know about the topic. This is the case with Sam. Other students have limited background knowledge to bring to the reading process. Research in schema theory has shown that the knowledge one brings to the reading task affects comprehension, particularly inferential comprehension (Anderson, Reynolds, Schallert, and Goetz, 1977; Hansen and Pearson, 1983; Pearson, Hansen, and Gordon, 1979). Teaching strategies that encourage students to activate their knowledge, or activities that provide opportunities for students to enrich the backgrounds prior to reading, can facilitate comprehension.

Although some students do not rely enough on background knowledge, other students may rely too much on background knowledge, as is the case with Ron. Often these are the same students who tend to overrely on context clues when identifying unknown words. When these students begin reading informational and technical texts that require accurate recall of information, comprehension problems become more evident. Strategies that encourage self-questioning can encourage such students to pay closer attention to the information presented in the text.

Kim, like many other learning-disabled students, has difficulty with the metacognitive skill of comprehension monitoring (Bos and Filip, 1984; Palincsar and Brown, 1987; Wong, 1979, 1987). Strategies that teach students to ask questions about their comprehension and that require them to paraphrase and summarize what they read should help them develop metacognitive skills.

Within the last ten years, increasing emphasis has been placed on reading comprehension and techniques for improving reading comprehension. First, we will look at a framework for reading comprehension to better understand the scope and sequence of comprehension. Then we will focus on instructional strategies for improving reading comprehension. Finally, we will discuss four approaches used for teaching reading and reading comprehension.

A Framework for Reading Comprehension

One way of guiding reading comprehension instruction is to determine the different reasoning and information processing skills that are required by readers in order to construct meaning from what they read. Read the passage in Apply the Concept 5.1.

Now answer each of the following questions and think about the processes that were needed for you to arrive at an answer.

1. What did Pat do first to get help?
2. Where did you find the information to answer the question?

Was it available from the text? The answer, of course, is yes. If information is found in the text, then we say that the information is *textually explicit* or *literal* (i.e., taken directly from the text) or we are *reading the lines* (Dale, 1966).

3. What time of day was it in the story?
4. Where did you find that information?

You may have automatically answered question 3 as "early in the morning" or "in the morning" without looking back at the text. If you did this, now go back and read to see if that information is in the text. It is not. Instead, you will find in the first paragraph that "Pat watched the sun come up over the mountains." You may have automatically integrated that information with your background knowledge to conclude, "It was in the morning." When information is not in the text but requires you to activate your background knowledge to generate the answer, then we say the information is *implicit* or *inferential* (e.g., not stated directly in the text). Can we be more specific about this kind of implicit information? Pearson and Johnson (1978) refer to this kind of relationship between the question and the answer as *scriptally implicit*. It requires

Apply the Concept 5.1

THE DRIVE TO BIG LAKE

Pat and her father were driving to Big Lake in the Blue Mountains. They were going to Big Lake to go fishing. As they drove Pat watched her father talk on the C.B. radio and watched the sun come up over the mountains.

When Pat and her father were near Big Lake it became very foggy. Pat's father drove slowly but did not see a sharp bend in the road. The car ran off the road and into a ditch. Pat was OK, but she knew that she needed to get help for her father.

She climbed out of the car and went to the road. She thought maybe a car would come by, but none did.

She walked down the road. She was looking for a house. As she walked, she yelled for help.

The she remembered the C.B. radio that was in the car. She ran back to the car. She had never used the C.B., but she tried to call for help on it. A fisherman at Big Lake was listening to his C.B. Pat told him where she and her father were. Fifteen minutes later help came.

By this time Pat's father had opened his eyes and was OK. The police helped Pat and her father get the car out of the ditch and back on the road. Everyone was proud of Pat.

Source: C. S. Bos, *Inferential Operations in the Reading Comprehension of Educable Mentally Retarded and Average Students.* Doctoral dissertation, University of Arizona, Tucson, 1979, p. 164.

you to use your schema or *script* about "morning" to generate the answer. Dale (1966) has referred to this as *reading beyond the lines*.

5. Was Pat successful in using the C.B. radio?
6. Where did you find that information?

It was in the text, but not nearly so clearly as in the case of the first question. In this case you had to read several sentences and piece the information together. The information was *implicit* in that it was not directly stated in the text, but it did not require you to use your background knowledge in the same way that question 4 did. Pearson and Johnson (1978) refer to this kind of implicit information as *textually implicit*. The relationship between the question and the answer required you to get the information from the text, but the relationship is not clearly *(explicitly)* stated. You had to use your knowledge about language and how ideas related to answer the question. Dale (1966) has referred to this relationship as *reading between the lines*.

Therefore, when teaching reading comprehension, we can divide comprehension into types of reasoning according to how readers have to activate their background knowledge to construct the meaning. These three arbitrary categories are:

- *Textually explicit:* Information is derived directly from the text with minimal input from the readers' background knowledge.
- *Textually implicit:* Information is derived from the text but readers are required to use their background knowledge to put together the ideas presented in the text.
- *Scriptally implicit:* Information is not stated in the text. Readers have to activate and use their background knowledge to obtain the information.

We can also categorize comprehension by the type of information or relationship it represents. For example, the first question, "What did Pat do first to get help?" requires the reader to focus on the sequence of the events in the story.

Therefore, it requires a sequencing or temporal relationship. The question "Why was everyone proud of Pat?" requires a causal relationship. Barrett (1976) has identified a number of types of information or relationships that can be represented in text (e.g., details, main ideas, sequence, cause and effect) as part of his taxonomy of reading. We can combine types of information with processes required (i.e., textually explicit, textually implicit, and scriptally implicit) to form a matrix for reading comprehension (Table 5.1).

This matrix can be used in planning comprehension instruction, such as planning activities that will encourage students to engage in all the different facets of comprehension (cells in the matrix). For example, to work on sequencing of ideas, students could retell a story by having each student in the group tell one episode from the story; copy a story onto sentence strips and discuss how to arrange the sentences in a logical order; read an explanation of how to do something and write a list of the steps in order; ask each other sequence questions about a description of how to make something; and write a description of how to make something and then have the other students in the group read the description and make the object. Whereas all of these activities focus on sequencing, both explicit and implicit comprehension are required to complete the various activities.

A matrix rather than a taxonomy is used to depict the various aspects of comprehension because comprehension should not necessarily be thought of as a set of hierarchical skills. The comprehension process entails ongoing interactions between the text and the reader's background knowledge. To generalize that one can carry out implicit processing only after he or she can do explicit processing, is not to take into consideration the important role that prior knowledge plays in the comprehension process (Simon, 1971).

In addition to the various facets of reading comprehension depicted in the matrix, we also read to reflect on the quality of the information or content presented and on the quality or the

TABLE 5.1   *Matrix for Reading Comprehension*

| | Type of Reasoning Based on Background Knowledge | | |
| | *Textually* | *Textually* | *Scriptally* |
Type of Information	*Explicit*	*Implicit*	*Implicit*
Detail	x	x	x
Main idea/Summary	x	x	x
Sequence	x	x	x
Comparative relationship	x	x	x
Cause/Effect relationship	x	x	x
Conditional relationship	x	x	x
Vocabulary definition	x	x	x
Vocabulary application	x	x	x
Figurative language definition	x	x	x
Figurative language application	x	x	x
Conclusion	x	x	x
Application	x	x	x

manner in which the piece is written (literary style). Barrett (1976) has referred to the first area of reading comprehension as *evaluation* and the second area as *appreciation*. Others have referred to the evaluation of the information as *critical reading* and to the appreciation and evaluation of literary style as *aesthetic* reading (Rosenblatt, 1978).

Both critical reading and aesthetic reading require readers to reflect and make comments and judgments about what they have read and believe. For example, after Mrs. Gomez's intermediate-level special education class finished reading about Pat and her father (Apply the Concept 5.1), Mrs. Gomez encouraged the students to comment on the quality of the piece by starting the discussion. She commented, "I liked the story, but I thought the author could have told us more information about how Pat got help." Figure 5.3 lists sample areas of critical and aesthetic reading and sample comments teachers might use to encourage critical and aesthetic reading.

Guidelines for Improving Comprehension

In many classrooms, instruction in reading comprehension consists of the teacher asking stu-

dents questions and monitoring their responses. Teachers generally provide minimal substantive information concerning what reading comprehension is, why it would be useful, or how to do it (Anderson, Brubaker, Alleman-Brooks, and Duffy, 1986; Duffy and McIntyre, 1982; Durkin, 1978-79). Furthermore, teachers provide a steady diet of literal comprehension questions, a ratio of 4:1 literal to inferential, with lower reading groups getting asked even more literal questions than higher-level groups (Guszak, 1972).

As teachers of students with learning and behavior problems, we have to provide instructional strategies that will demonstrate to students how to interact with the text in such a way as to construct meaning. Asking questions after reading will not provide this instruction. Therefore, our instruction in reading comprehension should incorporate many of the aspects of cognitive behavior modification and the sociocultural theory of learning (see Chapter Two), including the modeling and "think aloud" procedures. Based on notions from information processing and schema theories, our instruction should also assist students in activating their prior knowledge about the topic before they read so that it will be easier for them to apply this knowledge during reading and after they read. Our instruction

FIGURE 5.3   *Critical and Aesthetic Reading*

Critical Reading

Critical reading is when the reader reflects upon and makes judgments about the content or information in the piece.

Sample Areas of Reflection or Judgment	Sample Comments
Reality or Fantasy	I don't think the author expected us to think this could really happen.
Fact or Opinion	You really get the idea they are pushing their point of view.
Adequacy and Validity	Some of this information just isn't right.
Worth	This piece really helped me write my report. I think this article could hurt his political campaign.

Aesthetic Reading

Aesthetic reading is when the reader reflects upon and makes judgments about the literacy style of a piece.

Sample Areas of Reflection or Judgment	Sample Comments
Plot	I like the way the author always kept me interested in what was happening.
Characters	I didn't know enough about the witch to really understand why she did it.
Imagery	I could just picture myself being there.
Language	When the author said, "That was one frightened man," it sounded great.

should also demonstrate to students the importance of predicting and questioning as they read.

For each technique presented in this section, begin by giving the students shorter selections at their independent to instructional reading levels. When students are using the comprehension strategy or skill effectively, gradually introduce longer and more difficult passages. Comprehension instruction should encourage students to engage actively in the comprehension process. This can be prompted by the following activities:

1. *Before reading* activate the students' background knowledge for the selected passage and/or provide experiences to enrich their backgrounds. Assist students in setting purposes for reading by predicting and asking questions about what they are going to read.

2. *During reading* encourage students to self-question and monitor their comprehension as they read.

3. *After reading* use follow-up activities such as:

   a. Discussions that focus on the content of the reading as well as evaluation of the content and the writing style

   b. Discussions that encourage students to generate more questions and ideas for further reading and investigation

   c. Retellings that assist students in summarizing and organizing what they have read

Activating Student Background Knowledge

What activities can the teacher use that will help to activate relevant background knowledge (schema) prior to reading? Four such activities are discussed: brainstorming, the Pre Reading Plan (Langer, 1981), K-W-L (Ogle, 1986), and a schema activation strategy (Hansen, 1981). While the first activity is more general, the next two activities are easier to use when the text is more informational *(expository);* the fourth technique works well when the text tells a story *(narrative)*.

Brainstorming

Brainstorming is a teaching strategy that activates the students' relevant prior knowledge, aids the teacher in determining the extent of the students' prior knowledge, and stimulates interest in the topic.

▬ *Procedures:* Brainstorming works best with groups of students reading the same or related selections. Prior to beginning the activity, determine the major topic or concept presented in the selection(s). Next, decide what to use as a stimulus to represent that topic. It might be a single word or phrase, a picture, a poem, or a short excerpt from the reading passage. Prior to reading, conduct the brainstorming session.

1. Present the stimulus to the students.
2. Ask the students to list as many words or phrases as they can associate with the stimulus. Encourage them to think about everything they know about the topic or concept. Allow several minutes for the students to think, write their lists, and get ready to report their ideas.
3. Record their associations on the chalkboard. Ask for other associations and add them to the list. Do not make any judgments concerning the appropriateness of any of the associations.

4. With the students, categorize the associations. Clarify the ideas and discuss what titles to use for the categories.

You may also want to organize the ideas into a map. Strategies for organizing story maps are discussed later in this chapter and strategies for developing content maps are discussed in Chapter Seven.

Although the brainstorming activity usually ends before reading begins, we recommend that you encourage students to continue to add to their list of associations as they read. After the students have completed the reading assignment, review the list and add any new associations.

▬ *Comments:* Brainstorming is a quick and simple procedure for activating background knowledge. It usually takes five to ten minutes to complete. However, for some student and topic combinations, simple associations without further discussion may not provide enough input to activate and build the students' prior knowledge. The next procedure provides additional activities for further activating relevant schema.

Pre Reading Plan

The Pre Reading Plan (PReP) is a three-phase instructional/assessment strategy that builds on the instructional activity of brainstorming. Designed by Langer (1981), it assists students in accessing knowledge related to the major concepts presented in a reading selection.

▬ *Procedures:* Brainstorming works best with groups of students reading the same or related selections. Prior to beginning the activity, phrase, or picture to stimulate group discussion about a key concept in the text. For example, if a science selection was about the types and characteristics of mammals, *mammals* might serve as the stimulus word. After introducing the topic, conduct the following three-phase process:

1. *Initial association with the concept.* Cue the students by saying, "Say anything that comes to mind when . . . (e.g., you hear the word *mammals*)." Have the students free associate, writing a list of their associations. Record the associations on the board, noting the student's name by each association.

2. *Reflections on initial associations.* Now ask the students, "What made you think . . . (the responses given by each of the students during Phase 1)?" This phase requires the students to bring to the conscious level their prior knowledge and how it relates to the key concept. It also allows the students to listen to each other's responses. Langer states, "Through this procedure they [students] gain the insight which permits them to evaluate the utility of these ideas in the reading experience" (1981, p. 154).

3. *Reformation of knowledge.* After each student has had an opportunity to think and tell about what triggered his or her ideas, ask the students, "Based on our discussion, have you any new ideas about . . . (e.g., mammals)?" This phase gives the students the opportunity to discuss how they have elaborated or changed their ideas based on the previous discussion. Because the students have the opportunity to listen to other students, new links between prior knowledge and the key concept are also formed.

Based on the information gathered during this three-phase procedure, Langer presents a means of assessing prior knowledge into levels to determine if further concept building will need to be completed prior to reading (see Figure 5.4). In a study with Nicholich (Langer and Nicholich,

FIGURE 5.4   *Pre Reading Plan: Levels of Prior Knowledge*

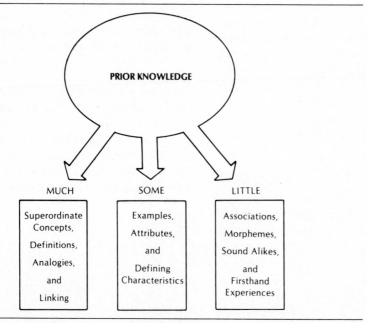

Source: Judith A. Langer. "Facilitating Text Processing: The Elaboration of Prior Knowledge," in J. A. Langer and M. T. Smith-Burke (eds.). *Reader Meets Author/Bridging the Gap* (Newark, Del.: International Reading Association, 1982), p. 156. Reprinted by permission of Judith A. Langer and the International Reading Association.

1981), Langer found this assessment method a better predictor of reading comprehension for a particular passage than either IQ or standardized reading scores. The three levels and their instructional implications are:

1. *Much knowledge.* Students whose free associations reflect superordinate concepts, definitions, analogies, or a linking of the key concept to other relevant concepts demonstrate *much* integration of the key concept with concepts already in accessible memory. Comprehension for these students should be adequate.

2. *Some knowledge.* Students whose free associations are primarily examples, attributes, or defining characteristics have *some* knowledge concerning the concepts being taught. Comprehension should be adequate, but some instructional activities that assist the students in making the critical links between existing and new knowledge may be necessary.

3. *Little knowledge.* Students whose free associations reflect morphemes (prefixes, suffixes, root words), rhyming words, or unelaborated or unrelated firsthand experiences demonstrate *little* knowledge of the concept. These students need concept instruction before reading commences, with the reported firsthand experiences serving as a reference point for starting instruction.

■ *Comments:* The Pre Reading Plan provides a direct means of activating the students' background knowledge. The authors have frequently used both brainstorming and PReP, particularly with upper elementary and secondary learning-disabled and emotionally handicapped students. We find that taking the extra time to conduct the Pre Reading Plan is worthwhile since it requires the students to bring to the conscious level why they made their associations and it gives them the opportunity to reflect on what they have learned through the discussion. Similar to brainstorming, PReP does not include any activities to apply during or after reading.

However, we would again encourage that you have students add to and adjust their lists during reading and after they read.

K-W-L

K-W-L is another strategy designed to activate students' background knowledge and to assist students in setting purposes for reading expository text. This strategy is based on research that highlights the importance of background knowledge in constructing meaning during reading (e.g., Anderson, 1977; Anderson, Reynolds, Schallert, and Goetz, 1977).

■ *Procedures:* The K-W-L strategy consists of three basic steps representative of the cognitive/metacognitive steps employed by the students as they utilize the strategy:

accessing what I <u>K</u>now
determining what I <u>W</u>ant to Learn
recalling what I did <u>L</u>earn

To assist the students in using the strategy, Ogle developed a simple worksheet for the students to complete during the thinking-reading process (see Figure 5.5).

During the *Know* step the teacher and students engage in a discussion designed to assist students in thinking about what they already know about the topic of the text. For this step the teacher starts by using a *brainstorm* procedure (see section on Brainstorming). As in the Pre Reading Plan, students are encouraged to discuss where or how they learned the information so as to provide information concerning the source and substantiveness of their ideas. After brainstorming, the teachers and students discuss the general *categories of information* likely to be encountered when they read and how their brainstormed ideas could help them determine the categories. "For example, the teacher might say 'I see three different pieces of information about how turtles look. Description of looks is certainly one category of information I would

FIGURE 5.5   *K-W-L Strategy Sheet*

K-W-L Strategy Sheet		
1. K—What we know	W—What we want to find out	L—What we learned and still need to learn

2. Categories of information we expect to use
   A.   E.
   B.   F.
   C.   G.
   D.

Source: D. M. Ogle, "K-W-L: A teaching model that develops active reading of expository text," *The Reading Teacher, 39* (1986):565.

expect this article to include' '' (Ogle, 1986, p. 566).

During the *Want to Learn* step, the teacher and students discuss what they want to learn from reading the article. While most of the W step utilizes group discussion, before students begin to read, they each write down the specific questions in which they are most interested.

During the *What I Learned* step, the students write what they learned from reading. They should also check the questions that they generated in the *Want to Learn* step to see if they were addressed in the article.

▬ *Comments:* K-W-L represents a strategy for assisting students in actively engaging in the reading process and for assisting teachers in teaching reading using an interactive model of reading. Informal evaluation of the strategy indicates that students recalled more information in articles when they used K-W-L and that they enjoyed using the strategy and used it

independently (Carr and Ogle, 1987; Ogle, 1986).

Schema Activation Strategy

Hansen (1981) developed a technique designed to get students to think about and apply what they already know (schemas) to stories. The technique encourages students to discuss, prior to reading, something they have done that is similiar to the event in the story and to hypothesize what will happen in the story. In this way they are encouraged to activate and integrate schema-based inferences.

▬ *Procedures:* Although Hansen (1981) used instructional-level basal readers, high-interest/low-vocabulary stories or library books could be used. Prior to working with the students, preview the story and select three important events or ideas and/or three events or ideas the students might have difficulty understanding. For each idea think of one question that requires the students to think about something that happened to them that is similar to what happened in the story, and one question to help them predict what they think will happen in the story.

The technique consists of two structured discussion periods, one prior to reading and one after reading.

1. *Prereading discussion.* The purpose of this discussion is to get the students to see the importance of activating prior knowledge and to get them to make predictions about the passage based on their prior experiences. This period begins with a discussion about the importance of comparing their own lives to situations in a text. For example:

Teacher:	What is it that we have been doing before we read each story?
Focus of responses:	We talk about our lives and how we might have experiences similar to the story.
Teacher:	Why do we make these comparisons?
Focus of responses:	These comparisons will help us understand the stories.
Teacher:	Last week I asked you to think what it would be like to live in another country. Today, pretend that you are going on a trip with your Dad and he gets hurt. Have you ever been around someone else when he or she got hurt?
Gist of responses:	Students relate personal experiences and explain how the experiences relate to the text.

Next introduce the three main ideas from the story. First, ask the students to relate a previous experience to the main idea. Second, have the students predict something similar that might happen in the story. For example:

Important idea:	Pat has to stay calm and get help.
Previous experience:	Tell us about a time when you had to get help.
Hypothesis question:	In our next story, Pat and her dad are going on a trip. Pat's dad gets hurt and she has to get help. How do you think Pat will get help?

The students discuss and write the answers on a piece of paper. When Hansen (1981) used this technique with second graders, the answers were written on strips of paper (gray for the prior knowledge in the brain and colored for the new knowledge). The strips of paper were woven by the students to represent the weaving of new information into old information that already exists in one's brain.

This prereading discussion period takes from fifteen to twenty minutes, after which the students read the story silently.

2. *Postreading discussions.* After reading, discuss the story and ask at least ten scriptally implicit questions. Ask the students to support their answers by either referring to the text or their prior knowledge. Discuss the questions and answers that were made prior to reading.

– Comments: Hansen originally used this strategy with second graders. Later, Hansen and her colleagues (Hansen and Hubbard, 1984; Hansen and Pearson, 1983) used the strategy with other readers, including good and poor readers. They found the poor readers benefited substantially from the instruction, whereas the good readers did not benefit as much since they already seemed to activate appropriate schema automatically. After training, the poor readers not only correctly answered more scriptally implicit (inference) questions, but also more explicit questions.

Questioning Strategies

As discussed earlier, asking questions is a major tool for checking reading comprehension. Workbooks, reading kits, and teachers' manuals are filled with questions. Content area textbooks have lists of questions to be answered at the end of each chapter. However, simply asking questions does not ensure that students will develop questioning strategies. In many ways, the problems with questions is the manner in which they are currently used—they are used for assessment purposes rather than for encouraging active comprehension (Durkin, 1983). Questioning, when taught as comprehension and comprehension monitoring strategies, plays an important role in the comprehension process. As already demonstrated, teacher and student questioning prior to reading helps to activate prior knowledge and to set purposes for reading. Self-questioning during reading (e.g., "Does this make sense?" "Am I understanding what I am reading?" "What will happen next?") assist students in comprehension and monitoring comprehension (one of the metacognitive activities discussed in Chapter Two).

This section presents four techniques for teaching questioning strategies. These techniques require teachers to model comprehension questions and comprehension monitoring questions, to teach students to recognize types of questions, and to encourage students to self-question before, during, and after they read. Teaching questioning strategies to students with learning and behavior problems seems particularly important since these students do not spontaneously self-question or monitor their comprehension (Bos and Filip, 1984; Wong, 1979).

ReQuest on Reciprocal Questioning

The ReQuest procedure is a reciprocal questioning technique designed to assist students in formulating their own questions about what they read. The procedure was developed by Manzo (1969), who stressed the importance of students setting their own purposes for reading and asking their own questions as they read.

■ *Procedures:* This procedure relies heavily on modeling, which is a major premise of cogni-

tive behavior modification and sociocultural theory of learning (Chapter Two). To use this procedure, select materials at the students' instructional to independent reading levels. You and the students read a sentence or section of the passage and then take turns asking each other questions. Your role is to model "good" questioning and to provide feedback to students about their questions. In modeling, include questions that require you to use scriptally and textually implicit information and that require critical and aesthetic reading.

Manzo suggests that this procedure first be introduced on an individual basis and then used in small groups. He suggests that you use the following explanation when beginning a ReQuest session:

> The purpose of this lesson is to improve your understanding of what you read. We will each read silently the first sentence [section]. Then we will take turns asking questions about the sentence [section] and what it means. You will ask questions first, then I will ask questions. Try to ask the kinds of questions a teacher might ask in the way a teacher might ask them.
>
> You may ask me as many questions as you wish. When you are asking me questions, I will close my book (or pass the book to you if there is only one between us). When I ask questions, you close your book (Manzo, 1969, p. 124).

The rules are: (1) the answer "I don't know" is not allowed; (2) unclear questions are to be restated; and (3) uncertain answers are to be justified by reference to the text or other source material if necessary. In addition, you and the students may need to discuss unfamiliar vocabulary.

The procedure itself consists of the following steps:

1. *Silent reading.* You and the students read the sentence or section silently.

2. *Student questioning.* Close your book while the students ask questions. Model appropriate answers and reinforce appropriate questioning behavior. The students ask as many questions as possible.

3. *Teacher questioning.* The students close their books and you ask questions. The Matrix for Reading Comprehension (Table 5.1) is an excellent guide to use in forming the type of questions to ask. Don't forget to ask some critical and aesthetic reading questions.

4. *Integration of the text.* After completing the procedure with the first sentence or section, repeat the process with subsequent sentences or sections. Integrate the new section with previous sections by asking questions that relate to new and old sections.

5. *Predictive questioning.* When the students have read enough to make a prediction about the rest of the passage, terminate reciprocal questioning and ask predictive questions (e.g., ''What do you think will happen?'' ''Why do you think so?''). If the predictions and verification are reasonable, you and the students move to the next step.

6. *Silent reading.* You and the students read to the end of the passage to verify your predictions. Discuss your predictions.

▬ *Comments:* One important aspect of this strategy is the questions that the teacher models. Manzo and Manzo (1990) suggest that teachers employ a variety of questions including:

- ▬ *predictable questions*—the typical *who, what, when, where, why,* and *how* questions
- ▬ *mind-opening questions*—designed to help the students understand how written and oral language is used to communicate ideas
- ▬ *introspective questions*—metacognitive questions oriented to self-monitoring and self-evaluation
- ▬ *ponderable questions*—questions which stimulate discussion and for which no right or wrong answer is apparent
- ▬ *elaborative knowledge questions*—questions which require the students to integrate

their background knowledge with the information given in the text.

The ReQuest procedure builds on the principles of modeling and feedback to assist students in developing appropriate questions. We have used several variations of these procedures. For instance, we have introduced the ReQuest procedure as a game. The students and teacher takes turns asking questions and keeping score of appropriate answers. Legenza (1974) has adapted this procedure by having kindergarten children ask questions about a picture rather than a text.

One major concern regarding ReQuest is how to get this questioning attitude to generalize to other reading situations. Students may need to be cued to remember to stop while reading and ask themselves questions like the type asked during the ReQuest procedure. Or students may need to be taught a self-questioning strategy.

Question-Answering Strategy

The question-answering strategy (Raphael, 1982, 1984, 1986) is designed to assist students in labeling the type of questions being asked and to use this information to help guide them as they develop an answer. This strategy was developed by Raphael and Pearson (1982) to facilitate correct responses to questions. The strategy is based on question/answer relationships developed by Pearson and Johnson (1978) (e.g., *textually explicit, textually implicit,* and *scriptally implicit*), discussed earlier in this chapter. It helps students realize they need to consider both the text and their prior knowledge when answering questions and to use strategic behavior to adjust the use of each of these sources.

▬ *Procedures:* The questioning strategy was originally taught by Raphael (1984), using the three categories of information suggested in the Matrix for Reading Comprehension (Table 5.1). The three categories were renamed for use with students.

1. *Right There.* Words used to create the question and words used for the answer are in the same sentence (textually explicit).
2. *Think and Search.* The answer is in the text, but words used to create the question and those used for an appropriate answer would not be in the same sentence (textually implicit).
3. *On My Own.* The answer is not found in the text but in one's head (scriptally implicit).

Based on input from teachers, Raphael (1986) modified these strategies to include two major categories *(In the Book* and *In My Head).* She then further divided these categories, as shown in Figure 5.6.

Teaching the question-answer relationships (QARs) consists of first having students learn to differentiate between the two major categories and then between the subcategories. The students also learn how to apply knowledge of the question-answer relationships as a strategy for improving reading comprehension. A cue card, which labels and explains the four types of question-answer relationships, is used during instruction (Figure 5.7).

Raphael suggests the following procedure for introducing the strategy. The first day, introduce the students to the concept of question-answer relationships (QARs), using the two major categories. Use several short passages (from two to five sentences) to demonstrate the relation-

ships. Provide practice by asking students to identify the type of QAR, the answer to the question, and the strategy they used for finding the answer. The progression for teaching should be from highly supportive to independent:

1. Provide the text, questions, answers, QAR label for each question, and reason for why the label was appropriate.
2. Provide the text, questions, answers, and QAR label for each question. Have the students supply the reason for the label.
3. Provide the text, questions, and answers, and have the students supply the QAR labels and reasons for the labels.
4. Provide the text and questions, and have the students supply the answers, QAR labels, and the reasons for the labels.

When the students have a clear picture of the difference between *In My Head* and *In the Book,* teach the next level of differentiation for each one of the major categories. First, work on *In the Book,* then go to *In My Head.* The key distinction between the two subcategories under *In My Head* (i.e., *Author and You* and *On My Own*) is "whether or not the reader needs to read the text for the questions to make sense" (Raphael, 1986, p. 519). When the information must come from the reader, but in connection with the information presented by the author, then the QAR is *Author and You.* For example, in the story about

FIGURE 5.6   *Relationship Among the Four Types of Question-Answer Relationships*

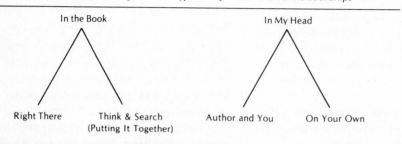

In the Book

Right There   Think & Search
                   (Putting It Together)

In My Head

Author and You   On Your Own

Source: Adapted from T. E. Raphael, "Teaching Question-Answer Relationships, Revisited," *The Reading Teacher,* 39(6) (1986):517.

FIGURE 5.7   *Illustrations Explaining Question-Answer Relationships (QARs) to Students*

In the Book QARs	**In My Head QARs**

Right There
The answer is in the text, usually easy to find. The words used to make up the question and words used to answer the question are **Right There** in the same sentence.

Author and You
The answer is *not* in the story. You need to think about what you already know, what the author tells you in the text, and how it fits together.

**Think and Search
(Putting It Together)**
The answer is in the story, but you need to put together different story parts to find it. Words for the question and words for the answer are not found in the same sentence. They come from different parts of the text.

On My Own
The answer is not in the story. You can even answer the question without reading the story. You need to use your own experience.

Source: T. E. Raphael, "Teaching Question-Answer Relationships, Revisited," *The Reading Teacher, 39*(6) (1986):519.

Pat and her father (Apply the Concept 5.1), the question "How did the fisherman alert the police?" requires the reader to use his or her background knowledge but relate it to the information in the text. In comparison, the question "What would you have done if you were in Pat's shoes?" is an example of an *On My Own* QAR.

Once the students are effectively using the QAR strategy in short passages, gradually increase the length of the passages and the variety of reading materials. Review the strategy and model its use on the first question. Have the students then use the strategy to complete the rest of the questions.

▬ Comments: After teaching this strategy using the original three categories, Raphael (1984) found that groups of low-, average-, and high-achieving, fourth-grade students had higher performance on a comprehension test and gave evidence that the question-answering strategy transferred to reading improvement in the content areas. Whereas this strategy facilitated lower-achieving students with the ability to answer all three types of questions, for high-achieving students it facilitated only the answering of scriptally implicit questions. Raphael notes that a sixth-grade good reader offered a probable reason for this increase, "Someone should have told me about QARs long ago. I have a lot of information in my head—I just didn't know I was allowed to use it!" (1984, p. 306). In contrast, a low-achieving reader explained, "I know this is an *On My Own* question, and I went to my head, but there was nothing there!" (p. 306). For the low-achieving students, strategy training particularly improved their performance on textually explicit and implicit questions.

Dixon (1983) used a similar procedure with learning-disabled fourth through six graders and also found positive results. Labeling the types of questions and then using that information to assist in answering questions appears to be an effective strategy for students and one that encourages active involvement in the comprehension process.

Self-Questioning Strategies

Several techniques for teaching students to use self-questioning spontaneously as they read have been developed. One strategy, developed by Wong and Jones (1982), focuses primarily on asking questions related to the main idea.

When investigating the reading comprehension skills of upper elementary learning-disabled students, Wong (1979) found that in text without inserted questions, learning-disabled students had poorer recall of the thematically important ideas than average readers. She hypothesized that learning-disabled students do not self-question when they read. To demonstrate this point, she inserted questions in the text for a second group of learning-disabled and average students, and she no longer found significant differences between the recall of the average and learning-disabled readers. Whereas the inserted questions resulted in significantly better recall for the learning-disabled students, no such effect was evident with average readers, indicating that the learning-disabled students were not as effective at self-questioning.

Based on this research, Wong and Jones (1982) developed a self-questioning technique to determine if junior-high-level learning-disabled students could be taught to self-question as they read.

— *Procedures:* First, teach the students the concept of a main idea. During this stage, teach the students how to identify the main idea(s) in paragraphs. For Wong and her colleagues, this took up to three one-hour sessions.

During the next stage, teach the students the steps in self-questioning strategy:

1. What are you studying this passage for? (So you can answer some questions you will be given later.)
2. Find the main idea(s) in the paragraph and underline it (them).
3. Think of a question about the main idea you have underlined. Remember what a good question should be like. ("Good questions" are those that directly focus on important textual elements. Write the question in the margin.)
4. Learn the answer to your question. (Write the answer in the margin.)
5. Always look back at the previous questions and answers to see how each successive question and answer provide you with more information.

In teaching, model the strategy and then have the students study the steps in the strategy. Next, have the students practice using this strategy on individual paragraphs and provide them with immediate corrective feedback. Have the students use a cue card to assist them in remembering the steps in the strategy. When the students are successful, switch to multiple paragraph passages and gradually fade the use of the cue card. Give corrective feedback at the end of each passage. At the end of each lesson, discuss the students' progress and the usefulness of the self-questioning strategy.

– *Comments:* Results from the Wong and Jones (1982) study indicate the learning-disabled students trained in the self-questioning strategy performed significantly higher on comprehension tests than the untrained students. Wong and Jones state, "The performance gap between trained and untrained learning disabled students in predicting/identifying important textual elements clearly indicates that self-questioning training is essential in maintaining learning-disabled students' awareness of and comprehension of important textual elements" (1982, p. 238).

Another self-questioning strategy was developed at the Kansas University Institute for Research in Learning Disabilities (Clark et al., 1984; Nolan, Alley, and Clark, 1980). It was used to assist secondary-level learning-disabled students in comprehending and remembering the important information presented in content area textbooks. Students read the title of a section and then ask questions regarding *who, what, when, where, why,* and/or *how.* They then read the section to answer their question(s).

Both of these self-questioning strategies proved effective in increasing learning-disabled students' reading comprehension. This may be related to the development of comprehension monitoring, which both of these techniques encourage.

Paraphrasing and Retelling Strategies

Giving the gist, main idea(s), or summary of a paragraph, a narrative, or an expository piece is a skill that many students with learning and behavior problems have difficulty developing (Brown and Palincsar, 1982; Graves, 1986; Wong, 1979). A number of strategies have been developed to improve a student's ability to understand the main idea.

Paraphrasing Strategy

This learning strategy, developed and validated at the Kansas University Institute of Research in Learning Disabilities (Schumaker, Denton, and Deshler, 1984), instructs students in recalling the main ideas and specific facts of materials they read.

– *Procedures:* To teach the strategy you would use the teaching acquisition and generalization steps presented in Apply the Concept 2.4.

The steps in the learning strategy that the students learn are as follows:

1. *Read a paragraph.* Read the paragraph silently. As you read, be sure to think about what the words mean.

2. *Ask yourself, "What were the main ideas and details of this paragraph?"* After reading the paragraph, ask yourself, "What were the main ideas and details?" This question helps you to think about what you just read. To help you, you may need to look quickly back over the paragraph and find the main idea and the details that are related to the main idea.

3. *Put the main idea and details in your own words.* Now put the main idea and details into your own words. When you put the information into your own words, it helps you remember the information. Try to give at least two details related to the main idea.

The acronym for the steps in the strategy is RAP. (Paraphrasing is like rapping or talking to yourself.) Students are also given rules for finding the main idea. They are:

1. Look for it in the first sentence of the paragraph.
2. Look for repetitions of the same word or words in the whole paragraph (Schumaker, Denton, and Deshler, 1984, p. 59).

Figure 5.8 lists the criteria used when generating a paraphrase. Specifics for teaching the strategy, including a scripted lesson, cue cards for learning and generalizing the strategy, record and worksheets, and suggested materials for practicing the strategy, are presented in the instructors'

FIGURE 5.8   *Paraphrasing Strategy: Requirements for a Paraphrase*

Requirements for a Paraphrase

1. Must contain a complete thought
   - subject
   - verb
2. Must be totally accurate
3. Must have new information
4. Must make sense
5. Must contain useful information
6. Must be in your own words
7. Only one general statement per paragraph is allowed

Source: J. B. Schumaker, P. H. Denton, and D. D. Deshler, *The Paraphrasing Strategy* (Lawrence: University of Kansas, 1984), p. 60. Copyright 1984 by the University of Kansas. Reprinted by permission and with the recommendation that training be obtained from the Institute for Research in Learning Disabilities, University of Kansas, Lawrence, Kansas 66045.

guide, *The Paraphrasing Strategy* (Learning Strategies Curriculum) (Schumaker, Denton, and Deshler, 1984).

▬ Comments: Learning-disabled students who learned and used the paraphrasing strategy increased their ability to answer comprehension questions about materials written at their grade level from 48 percent to 84 percent (Schumaker, Denton, and Deshler, 1984). This strategy provides an example of how metacognitive skills can be taught to students. Although the research was conducted with high-school learning-disabled students, we have used the strategy with upper elementary students and found it successful. The simplicity of the strategy and the basic nature of the skill being taught make it appropriate to use with elementary as well as secondary students.

When using this strategy, the students orally repeat the paraphrases into a tape recorder rather than writing them. This approach seems particularly advantageous for students with learning and behavior problems, since many of them also experience writing problems. However, once the

students have mastered the skill, it may be helpful for students to sometimes write their paraphrases. These can then serve as an overview from which the students can integrate the information across the entire passage. This procedure helps to alleviate a concern for this strategy. The strategy does not encourage the students to summarize at a level higher than the paragraph level.

You and the students may also want to vary the size of the unit that the students paraphrase. For example, in some books it may be more advantageous to paraphrase each section or subsection rather than each paragraph.

Story Mapping and Retelling Strategies

Whereas teaching students to paraphrase can assist them in determining the main idea and related details for the materials they read, more specific techniques can be used when students are attempting to understand and recall narratives. Story retelling strategies provide the students with a framework for retelling the key points of narrative texts. The strategies can be combined with story maps, which provide the students with a visual guide to understanding and retelling stories.

Both story mapping and story retelling strategies are based on the notion that narratives are composed of a fairly predictable set of components and that narratives have an overall text structure or grammar that is unique to them. In general, narrative texts can be organized into components such as the setting, the problem statement, the goals, event sequences or episodes, and the ending (Mandler and Johnson, 1977; Stein and Glenn, 1979; Warren, Nicholas, and Trabasso, 1979). The event sequences can be further broken down into initiating events, reactions, and outcomes. Using this grammar, visual displays of a story or story maps can be generated that show the story components and their relationship one to another. Figure 5.9 shows the visual framework for a simple story.

Using these grammars, educators have taught students how to utilize simplified story maps and story strategies to aid in comprehend-

FIGURE 5.9 *Simple Story Map*

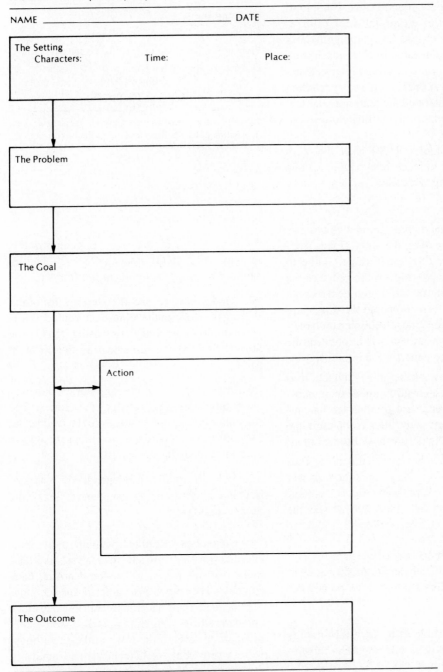

NAME _____ DATE _____

The Setting
    Characters: Time: Place:

The Problem

The Goal

Action

The Outcome

Source: From *Journal of Learning Disabilities, 20*(4), p. 199. By L. Idol Group. Story Mapping: A Comprehension Strategy for Both Skilled and Unskilled Readers. Copyright 1987 by Pro-Ed. Reprinted by permission.

ing and retelling stories (Beck and McKeown, 1981; Box, 1987; Fowler and Davis, 1985; Idol, 1987a, 1987b). For example, Idol (1987a, 1987b) used a model-lead-test paradigm (Carnine, Silbert, and Kameenui, 1990) to teach story mapping to five learning-disabled intermediate-grade students. Bos (1987) used a story retelling strategy to assist intermediate learning- and language-disabled students in retelling stories.

▬ Procedures: Idol (1987b) used the story map in Figure 5.9 to teach story mapping. She used the following procedure to teach story mapping:

1. During the *model* phase, model how to use the story map by reading the story aloud, stopping at points where information pertaining to one of the story components is presented. Ask the students to label the part and then demonstrate how to write the information onto the story map. Have the students copy the information onto their own maps. If the information is implicit in the story, model how to generate the inference.

2. During the *lead* phase, have students read the story independently and complete their maps, prompting when necessary. Encourage the students to review their maps after completing the story, adding details that may have been omitted.

3. During the *text* phase, ask students to read a story, generate their map, and then answer questions such as: Who were the characters? Where did the story take place? What was the main character trying to accomplish?

One of the authors (Bos, 1987) used principles based on cognitive behavior modification to teach a story retelling strategy. The procedures are:

1. Motivate the students to learn the strategy by demonstrating how it will help them remember what they have read.

2. Describe the components in a story and the steps used to identify and remember the different

FIGURE 5.10   *Story Retelling Strategy*

SPOT the Story

Setting—Who, What, When, Where

Problem—What is the problem to be solved?

Order of Action—What happened to solve the
              problem? (correct/logical order)

Tail End—What happened in the end?

Source: C. S. Bos, *Promoting Story Comprehension Using a Story Retelling Strategy.* Paper presented at the Teachers Applying Whole Language Conference, Tucson, Az., October 1987.

components (see Figure 5.10). Explain how this strategy will help the students "SPOT" and remember the important parts of the story.

3. Model how to use the strategy by orally reading the story and labeling each component as you read. Then retell the story using "SPOT the Story" as a cue for remembering the different parts.

4. Practice together reading stories, labeling the components, and retelling the stories. The students can retell their stories to the teacher, to each other, tape record their retellings, or answer questions about the stories.

5. Have the students independently read stories and retell them by using the "SPOT the Story" strategy.

▬ Comments: Results from both studies indicate that students were able to recall substantially more relevant information after learning each strategy. They were also able to answer more explicit and implicit comprehension questions about the stories. Students were also more likely to label the parts of the story in their retellings, thereby providing the listener with a framework for listening. These same strategies have also been adapted and used to help students plan and write stories.

Comprehensive Approaches for Teaching Reading Comprehension

So far we have talked about strategies to facilitate the use of specific comprehension skills such as activating prior knowledge, assisting students in asking and answering questions, and helping students paraphrase and recall what they have read. In this section we will look at approaches to teaching reading and reading comprehension. These approaches are more comprehensive in that they incorporate a variety of comprehension and, in some cases, word identification skills. The first approach, the Directed Reading Activity (Betts, 1946), has been the standard framework used for teaching reading in basal readers. The Direct Reading-Thinking Activity (Stauffer, 1969, 1970) is an adaptation of this approach which encourages active participation on the part of the reader. Reciprocal teaching (Palincsar and Brown, 1984) combines four reading comprehension strategies: *predicting, clarifying, summarizing,* and *questioning,* to present a framework for teaching reading comprehension that reflects the more recent research in schema theory and metacognition. The fourth orientation, the whole language (Goodman, 1986) and literature-based approach to reading (Cullinan, 1987; Holdaway, 1979), emphasizes the use of literature as the major medium for teaching reading and stresses reading comprehension and meaning-emphasis strategies for teaching word identification.

Directed Reading Activity
The Directed Reading Activity (DRA), developed by Betts (1946), is the general framework or lesson plan used in many basal readers. The DRA is a systematic method for providing instruction in reading, including procedures for teaching word identification as well as comprehension.

■ *Procedures:* This general method for teaching reading is designed to be used with students reading at any level who are reading the same selection. Betts describes the DRA procedures:

> First, the group should be prepared, oriented, or made ready, for the reading of a story or selection. Second, the first reading should be guided silent reading. Third, word-recognition skills and comprehension should be developed during the silent reading. Fourth, the rereading—silent or oral, depending upon the needs of the pupil—should be done for purposes different from those served by the first, or silent, reading. Fifth, the follow-up on the "reading lesson" should be differentiated in terms of pupil needs (1946, p. 492).

The following outline presents the stages usually found in a DRA (Betts, 1946).

1. Readiness
   a. Developing conceptual background
   b. Creating interest
   c. Introducing new vocabulary
   d. Establishing purposes for reading
2. Directed silent reading
3. Comprehension check and discussion
4. Rereading
5. Follow-up activities
   a. Extending skill development
   b. Enriching and generalizing

■ *Comments:* Although the DRA is suggested as a framework for teaching in many basal readers, modifications will probably be necessary for students who experience reading difficulties. These students may need more direct instruction of comprehension strategies than is provided in the DRA format and more prereading activities that focus on activating background knowledge. For example, the Pre Reading Plan or the schema activation strategy could be added to the readiness stage of the DRA to activate and build prior knowledge.

Another caution concerning the DRA is that it is teacher-dominated and, therefore, may not facilitate the development of independent reading skills. Encouraging the students to set their own purposes for reading, to self-question as they read, and to generate their own questions and follow-up activities will help alleviate this teacher-dominated emphasis. The next technique, the Directed Reading-Thinking Activity, builds on this notion of self-directedness.

Directed Reading-Thinking Activity

The Directed Reading-Thinking Activity (DR-TA) was developed by Stauffer (1969, 1970, 1976) as a framework for teaching reading, which stresses students' abilities to read reflectively and to use prediction. The purpose of the DR-TA is to provide readers with the ability to:

- Determine purposes for reading
- Extract, comprehend, and assimilate information
- Use prediction while reading
- Suspend judgments
- Make decisions based on evidence gained from reading

It is based on the notion that reading is a thinking process that requires the students to relate their experiences to the author's ideas, and thereby construct meaning from the text.

In using this approach, the construction of meaning starts by setting purposes for reading and generating hypotheses about meaning. It continues as the students acquire more information and confirm or disconfirm hypotheses and establish new hypotheses. It ends when the hypotheses have been confirmed and the purposes for reading have been met.

Stauffer (1969) describes a number of distinguishing features about group DR-TA activities:

1. Pupils of approximately the same reading level are grouped together.

2. The group size ranges from two to ten students to promote interaction and participation.

3. All students in a group read the same material at the same time. This permits each member to compare and contrast predictions, paths to answer, and evaluations with those of his or her peers.

4. Purposes for reading are declared by the *student*. The art of asking insightful questions is probably the best mark of a scholar. Each pupil learns how to raise questions in order to become a reading-thinking scholar.

5. Answers to questions are validated. Proof is found in the text and tested, with the group judging whether or not the offered proof is trustworthy.

6. Immediate *feedback* helps develop integrity and a regard for authenticity.

7. The teacher serves as a facilitator or moderator and asks provocative questions that require the students to interpret and make inferences from what they have read. The teacher serves as a directing catalyst.

The DR-TA can be used with reading materials written at any level and having either narrative or expository structures. Stauffer (1969) suggests that beginning basal readers (primer and preprimer materials) that have limited plots will not lend themselves to this procedure.

- *Procedures:* An outline for guiding a DR-TA is presented in Figure 5.11. The processing entailed in a DR-TA is summarized as follows:

1. Pupil actions
   a. Predict (set purposes)
   b. Read (process ideas)
   c. Prove (test answers)
2. Teacher actions
   a. What do you think? (activate thought)
   b. Why do you think so? (agitate thought)
   c. Prove it! (require evidence) (Stauffer, 1969)

FIGURE 5.11   *Directed Reading-Thinking Activity Outline*

I. Identifying purposes of reading
   A. Individual pupil purposes delimited by
      1. Pupil experience, intelligence and language facility
      2. Pupil interests, needs, and goals
      3. Group interests, needs, and goals
      4. Influence of the teacher
      5. Influence of the content
         a. nature and difficulty of the material
         b. title and subtitles
         c. pictures, maps, graphs, charts
         d. linguistics clues
   B. Group purposes determined by the
      1. Experiences, language facility, and intelligence of each member of the group
      2. Interests, needs, and goals of each member of the group
      3. Concensus of the group and/or of subgroups
      4. Influence of the teacher
      5. Influence of the content
II. Adjusting rate of reading to the purposes declared and to the nature and difficulty of the material. This adjustment is made to
   A. Survey: to overview a selection or text
   B. Skim: to read swiftly and lightly for single points
   C. Scan: to read carefully from point to point
   D. Read critically: to read, to reread, and to reflect so as to pass judgment
III. Observing the reading
   A. Noting abilities to adjust rate to purpose and material
   B. Recognizing comprehension needs and providing help by clarifying
      1. Purposes
      2. Concepts
      3. Need for rereading
   C. Acknowledging requests for help with word recognition needs by providing immediate help in the use of
      1. Context clues: meaning clues
      2. Phonetic clues: sound clues
      3. Structural clues: sight clues
      4. Glossary clues: meaning, sound, and sight clues
IV. Developing comprehension
   A. Checking on individual and group purposes
   B. Staying with or redefining purposes
   C. Recognizing the need for other source material
   D. Developing concepts
V. Fundamental skill training activities: discussion, further reading, additional study, writing
   A. Increasing powers of observation (directed attention)
   B. Increasing powers of reflection by
      1. Abstracting: reorganizing old ideas, conceiving new ideas, distinguishing between ideas, generalizing about ideas, and making inductions and analyses
      2. Judgment: formulating propositions and asserting them
      3. Reasoning: inferring and demonstrating, and systematizing knowledge deductively
   C. Mastering the skills of word recognition: picture and language context analysis, phonetic and structural analysis, and dictionary usage

(continued)

FIGURE 5.11   *continued*

D. Developing vocabulary: pronunciations; word meanings; semantic dimensions; analogous words, contrasted words; word histories; new words
E. Developing adeptness in conceptualization and cognitive functioning: making and testing inferences; particulars, classes, and categories; reversibility, mobile equilibrium and conservation
F. Mastering the skills of oral reading: voice enunciation, and expression; reading to prove a point or to present information; reading to entertain (prose and poetry); choral reading.

Source: R. G. Stauffer, *Directing Reading Maturity as a Cognitive Process* (New York: Harper & Row, 1969), pp. 41–42.

Adapt the following specific procedures when using a DR-TA:

1. After each student receives a copy of the material, direct the students to identify a purpose for reading by studying the title, subtitles, pictures, and so on, to develop a hypothesis about what the passage is about. Questions you might ask to stimulate hypothesis settings are:

a. What do you think a story with this title might be about?

b. What do you think might happen in this story?

Have students share these hypotheses, discussing how they arrived at them. Encourage students to make several different suggestions and to discuss agreements or disagreements with one another's suggestions. Have students use information from their prior knowledge to substantiate their predictions.

2. Once each student has stated his or her hypothesis, encourage the students to adjust their rate of silent reading to their purpose for reading.

3. Teach or remind the students of the strategy they are to use when they come to a word they cannot identify:

a. Read to the end of the sentence.

b. Use picture clues, if available.

c. Sound out the word.

d. Ask the teacher or a friend for help.

4. Select a logical segment of the passage and direct the students to read it to themselves to check on their predictions. Be responsible for ensuring that students read for meaning by observing reading performance and helping those who request help with words.

5. When the students have finished reading, have them discuss their predictions. Target questions to ask are:

a. Were you correct?

b. What do you think now?

Have students reread orally the sections of the text that confirm or contradict their hypotheses. Assist the students in determining if other source materials may be necessary to clarify meaning, and have the students discuss concepts and vocabulary that are critical to the comprehension process.

6. Repeat the procedure (hypothesis setting, silent reading to validate, oral reading to prove, and discussion) with subsequent segments of the text.

7. Once the passage is completed, use skill activities to teach "skill training" (Stauffer, 1969). This entails rereading the story, reexamining selected words, phrases, pictures, and/or diagrams for the purpose of concurrently developing the students' reading-thinking abilities with the other reading-related skills (Tierney, Readence, and Dishner, 1985). These might include word attack skills and concept clarification and development.

Stauffer (1969) suggests that once the students are comfortable with the DR-TA process they should be encouraged to use an individualized DR-TA. In other words, the students should use this systematic, predictive process as they read individually. Figure 5.12 presents a sample worksheet that students might use to guide them as they complete individual DR-TAs.

▬ *Comments:* The DR-TA provides the teacher with a procedure for teaching students to become active thinkers as they read. This is particularly relevant for students with learning and behavior problems since it requires the students to assume responsibility for the reading-learning process. In comparison to the DRA, where the teacher sets the purpose for reading and preteaches vocabulary, the DR-TA encourages the students to set their own purposes and decide which vocabulary warrants further development. However, two cautions seem relevant to the DR-TA. First, it requires a great deal of self-directiveness on the part of the students, particularly the individualized DR-TA. Second, it does not teach word identification skills in a systematic manner, which may be necessary for students who have word identification difficulties.

Reciprocal Teaching

Reciprocal teaching (Palincsar and Brown, 1984, 1986) is another more comprehensive approach to teaching reading comprehension. This technique is built on notions associated with metacognition, schema theory, and a sociocultural theory of learning. From metacognition comes the strong emphasis on comprehension monitoring activities (e.g., checking to see if understanding is adequate, given the purposes for reading). From schema theory, reciprocal teaching incorporates activities that encourage students to activate and use relevant background knowledge to aid in comprehension and learning. From a sociocultural theory of learning comes the notion of scaffolded instruction in which the teacher and students take turns assuming the leader role.

Reciprocal teaching is built on the notion that successful comprehension and learning is based on six activities:

1. Clarifying the purpose of reading (i.e., understanding the task demands, both explicit and implicit)
2. Activating relevant background knowledge
3. Allocating attention so that concentration can be focused on the major content at the expense of trivia
4. Critical evaluation of content for internal consistency and compatibility with prior knowledge and common sense
5. Monitoring ongoing activities to see if comprehension is occurring, by engaging in such activities as periodic review and self-interrogation
6. Drawing and testing inferences of many kinds, including interpretations, predictions, and conclusions (Brown, Palincsar, and Armbruster, 1984, p. 263)

In the initial research, Palincsar and Brown (Palincsar, 1982; Palincsar and Brown, 1984) selected four comprehension strategies to teach seventh-grade students who had average decoding skills but were seriously deficient in comprehension skills. The four strategies were *summarizing* (self-review), *questioning, clarifying,* and *predicting.* They utilized an interactive mode of teaching that emphasized modeling, feedback, and scaffolded instruction. This was conducted in the context of a dialogue between the students and teacher as they participated in the process of reading with the goal of deriving meaning from the text.

▬ *Procedures:* The procedure used to teach the four strategies was *reciprocal teaching,* a technique in which the teacher and students took turns leading a dialogue that covered sections of the text. The procedure is similar to, but more extensive than, the reciprocal questioning-ReQuest procedure (Manzo, 1969), a comprehension technique discussed in the section on

FIGURE 5.12 *Directed Reading-Thinking Activity Individual Prediction Sheet*

Name:

Passage/Book:

Pages	Prediction	Outcome

Summary:

questioning. Palincsar and Brown (1984) described the teaching procedure as follows:

> The basic procedure was that an adult teacher, working individually with a seventh-grade poor reader, assigned a segment of the passage to be read and either indicated that it was her turn to be the teacher or assigned the student to teach the segment. The adult teacher and the student then read the assigned segment silently. After reading the text, the teacher (student or adult) for that segment asked a question that a teacher or test might ask on the segment, summarized the content, discussed and clarified any difficulties, and finally made a prediction about future content. All of these activities were embedded in as natural a dialogue as possible, with the teacher and student giving feedback to each other.
>
> Initially, the adult teacher modeled the activities, but the students had great difficulty assuming the role of dialogue leader when their turn came. The adult teacher was sometimes forced to construct paraphrases and questions for the students to mimic. . . . Gradually, the students became much more capable of assuming their role as dialogue leader and . . . were providing paraphrases and questions of some sophistication (Palincsar and Brown, 1984, pp. 124–125).

In providing feedback, the adult teacher used:

Prompting. "What question do you think might be on a test?"

Instruction. "Remember, a summary is a short version—it doesn't include details."

Modifying the activity. "If you can't think of a question right now, go ahead and summarize and then see if you can think of one."

Praise. "That was a clear question, because I knew what you wanted." "Excellent prediction — let's see if you're right."

Corrective feedback. "That was interesting information. It was information I would call a detail. Can you find the most important information?"

Modeling. "A question I would have asked would be. . . . "

The following reciprocal teaching dialogue (Palincsar, 1988) illustrates how a teacher working with at-risk first graders who have listened to a passage about aquanauts used the four comprehension strategies and the reciprocal teaching techniques.

Student 1:	My question is, what does the aquanaut need when he goes under water?
Student 2:	A watch.
Student 3:	Flippers.
Student 4:	A belt.
Student 1:	Those are all good answers.
Teacher:	Nice job. I have a question too. Why does the aquanaut wear a belt, what is so special about it?
Student 3:	It's a heavy belt and keeps him from floating up to the top again.
Teacher:	Good for you.
Student 1:	For my summary now. . . . This paragraph was about what the aquanauts need to take when they go under the water.
Student 5:	And also about why they need those things.
Student 6:	That's the special things they need.
Teacher:	Another word for gear in this story might be *equipment,* the equipment that makes it easier for the aquanauts to do their job.
Student 1:	I don't think I have a prediction to make.
Teacher:	Well, in the story they tell us that there are "many strange and wonderful creatures" that the aquanauts see as they do their work. My prediction is that they will describe some of these creatures. What are some of the strange creatures that you already know about that live in the ocean.

Student 6:   Octopuses.
Student 3:   Whales.
Student 5:   Sharkes!
 Teacher: Let's listen and find out! Who will
               be our teacher?

Palincsar (1988) suggests that to introduce reciprocal teaching, it is logical to start with a discussion regarding why text may be difficult to understand, why it is important to have a strategic approach to reading and studying, and how reciprocal teaching will help students understand and monitor their understanding. The students are given an overall description emphasizing the use of interactive dialogues or discussions and of a rotating leader. To ensure a level of competency, each strategy is introduced in a functional manner (e.g., summarize a television show or movie) and opportunities provided for the students to practice using the strategy. Palincsar (1988) provides a number of suggestions regarding each comprehension strategy:

Questioning

- Encourage students to ask "teacherlike" questions.
- Fill-in-the-blank questions should be discouraged.
- If the students cannot think of a question, have the students summarize first.
- Provide prompts if needed (e.g., identify the topic, provide a question word).

Summarizing

- Encourage students to identify the "main idea" and an example of supportive information.
- Encourage students to attempt their summaries without looking at the passage.
- Remind students of the rules for generating summaries:
  Look for a topic sentence.
  Make up a topic sentence if one is not available.
  Give a name to a list of items.
  Delete what is unimportant or redundant.

Predicting

- Begin a new passage by having students predict based on the title.
- Encourage students to share information they already know about the topic.
- Refer to their predictions and background knowledge as you read, interweaving the text with them.
- Use headings to help students make predictions.
- Use other opportunities to predict such as when the author asks questions or gives information about what will be covered next.
- Predictions should be used in an opportunistic and flexible manner.

Clarifying

- Opportunities for clarifying generally occur when:
  Referents (e.g., *you, he, it*) are unclear.
  Difficult or unfamiliar vocabulary is presented.
  Text is disorganized or information incomplete.
  Unusual, idiomatic, or metaphorical expressions are used.
- Clarifying will not always be necessary.
- It may be helpful if students are asked to point out something that might be unclear to a younger student.

- **Comments:** Palincsar and Brown studied the effectiveness of reciprocal teaching by using the technique with poor comprehending seventh-grade students who were taught individually or in groups of four to seven students (Brown, Palincsar, and Armbruster, 1984; Palincsar, 1986; Palincsar and Brown, 1984). After instructing approximately thirty minutes over a number of weeks, they found the effects of this instruction to be substantial, reliable, durable over time, and generalizable to classroom settings. Even substantial improvements in standardized reading comprehension scores were reported for the majority of students. This technique combines many of the principles of teaching and learning discussed in Chapter Two and it explicitly teaches students several general strategies for comprehending text.

Whole Language and Literature-Based Reading Programs

As discussed in Chapter Four, a growing emphasis is being placed on literacy programs that stress whole language (integration of reading, writing, and oral language) and the use of literature and "real books" rather than traditional basal reading materials (e.g., basal readers, workbooks, and worksheets). This emphasis is reflected in such educational trends as the 1986 California Reading Initiative which describes a comprehensive plan for using literature-based reading programs in California public schools (Alexander, 1987). It is also reflected in the new editions of several basal reading programs which have shifted from basal readers toward the use of anthologies and literature sets.

Whole language and, to varying degrees, literature-based reading programs are derived from a psycholinguistic model of reading as articulated by Smith (1988) and Goodman (1984). The philosophy is evident in the following statements:

> . . . a psycholinguistic approach" to reading would be the very antithesis of a set of instructional materials. . . . The child learning to read seems to need the opportunity to examine a large sample of language, to generate hypotheses about the regularity underlying it, and to test and modify these hypotheses on the basis of feedback that is appropriate to the unspoken rules that he happens to be testing.
>
> None of this can, to our mind, be formalized in a prescribed sequence of behaviorally stated objectives embalmed in a set of instructional materials, programmed or otherwise. The child is already programmed to learn to read. He needs written language that is both interesting and comprehensible and teachers who understand language-learning and appreciate his competence as a language-learner (Smith and Goodman, 1971, pp. 179–180).

As Goodman and Goodman (1982) state:

> In this method there are no prereading skills, no formalizing reading readiness. Instead, learning is expected to program *from whole to part,* from general to specific, from familiar to unfamiliar, from vague to precise, from gross to fine, from highly contextualized to more abstract. Children are expected to read, first, familiar meaningful wholes—easily predictable materials that draw on concepts and experiences they already have. These may be signs, cereal boxes, or books. . . . By carefully building on what children already know, we assure their readiness (p. 127).

▬ Procedures: The focal points of whole language and literature-based reading programs center on: (1) involving students in lots of reading and writing; (2) creating an environment that accepts and encourages risk-taking; (3) maintaining a focus on meaning (Goodman and Goodman, 1982). A teacher using a whole language approach would draw heavily on the principles associated with a sociocultural theory of learning (see Chapter Two). As Watson and Crowley (1988) explain:

> In their own unique ways all whole-language teachers facilitate certain activities and procedures:
>
> 1. They find out about students' interests, abilities, and needs. And then they go an important step further—they use that information in planning curriculum.
> 2. They read to students or tell them stories every day.
> 3. They see to it that students have an opportunity to participate in authentic writing every day.
> 4. They see to it that students have an opportunity to read real literature every day.

5. They initiate discussions in which students consider the processes of reading and writing.
6. They know that kids can help other kids many times and in many ways that no one else can; therefore, they take advantage of the social nature of literacy (reading and writing) in order to promote it (p. 235).

Strategies for comprehension are taught within the context of books with the teacher and students discussing not only the content but the processes used in constructing meaning from text. Writing is tied to reading in a reciprocal manner so that the students have opportunities to work in the roles of both reader and author. Process writing (see Chapter Six) and conferencing about books and written pieces allows the teacher to facilitate the students' understanding of the processes associated with language learning.

Literature for reading and topics for writing are oftentimes self-selected, giving the students the opportunity to explore topics of interest to them. Students are also encouraged to learn about the authors and illustrators of the books they are reading. With this approach, the librarian and annotated bibliographies of children's literature become invaluable resources. Figure 5.13 provides a list of resource books containing annotated bibliographies and information on children's literature. Chapter Appendix 4.1 also provides a list of predictable and patterned language books that could be used when using a literature-based reading program.

▬ *Comments:* This orientation to teaching literacy reflects a philosophy to language learning that is highly child-centered. For students with learning and behavior problems, such a child-centered approach should be advantageous particularly when ample opportunities are provided for teaching literacy strategies during reading and writing. Research investigating the use of literature-based reading programs and whole language with students who are experiencing reading difficulties is limited both in scope and rigor, but there is some evidence that such approaches improve students' attitude toward reading and reading achievement (Roser, Hoffman, and Farest, 1990; Tunnell and Jacobs, 1989).

FIGURE 5.13   *Selected Books and Bibliographies on Children's Literature*

Cullinan, B. E. (Ed.) *Children's Literature in the Reading Program.* Newark, Del.: International Reading Association, 1987.

Davis, J. E., & Davis, H. K. (Eds). *Your Reading: A Booklist for Junior High and Middle School Students* (7th ed.). Urbana, Ill.: National Council of Teachers of English, 1988.

Freeman, J. (1984). *Books Kids Will Sit Still For.* Hagerstown, Md.: Alleyside Press.

Huck, C. S., Helper, S., and Hickman, J. (1987). *Children's Literature* in *The Elementary School* (4th ed.). Fort Worth: Holt, Rinehart and Winston.

Monson, D. L. (1985). *Adventures with Books: A Booklist for Pre-K through Grade 6* (new ed.). Urbana, Ill.: National Council of Teachers of English.

Moss, J. F. (1984). *Focus Units in Literature: A Handbook for Elementary School Teachers.* Urbana, Ill.: National Council of Teachers of English.

Norton, D. E. (1987). *Through the Eyes of a Child: An Introduction to Children's Literature* (2nd ed.). Columbus, Ohio: Merrill.

Oppenheim, J., Brenner, B., and Doegenhold, B. D. (1986). *Choosing Books for Kids: Choosing the Right Book for the Right Child at the Right Time.* New York: Ballantine Books.

Reed, A. J. S. (1988). *Comics to Classics: A Parent's Guide to Books for Teens and Preteens.* Newark, Del.: International Reading Association.

Trelease, J. (1989). *The New Read-Aloud Handbook.* New York: Penguin.

Instructional Activities

Appendix B provides instructional activities that are related to reading comprehension and fluency. Some of the activities teach new skills; others are best suited for practice and reinforcement of already acquired skills. For each activity, the objective, materials, and teaching procedures are described.

Summary

Many students with learning and behavior problems struggle with learning word identification skills. We, as special education teachers, spend a considerable amount of our instructional time focusing on these basic skills, assuming that fluency and comprehension will follow. What we have found is that these students also experience difficulties in reading fluently and in integrating their background knowledge with the text in order to construct meaning and comprehend the text. Consequently, we need to systematically plan and implement fluency and comprehension instruction.

Strategies for fluency instruction first focus on providing students frequent opportunities to listen to literature being read aloud and on having students read familiar books. In addition, the strategies of repeated reading and repeated choral reading are stressed because they provide students with additional instructional support when developing fluent reading patterns.

Much of what teachers refer to as instruction in reading comprehension is, in fact, better described as the assessment of students' comprehension after they have read. So as to draw attention away from teacher questioning, this chapter presented a framework for reading comprehension that was not tied to level of reading comprehension questions. Instead, it was tied to the reasoning processes required (i.e., textually explicit, textually implicit, or scriptally implicit) and the types of information or relationships represented. We can use this matrix in planning instruction in that we can implement techniques and strategies that will assure many different facets of comprehension are tapped.

In discussing methods for teaching reading comprehension, emphasis is placed on the importance of planning activities before the students read that will help them activate their background knowledge or schemas. Techniques such as brainstorming, the Pre Reading Plan, K-W-L, and a schema activation strategy can facilitate this process. In the area of questions, emphasis is placed on helping students learn to predict and ask their own questions rather than just respond to the questions of the teacher.

Teaching students strategies for activating prior knowledge and for predicting, self-questioning, and comprehension monitoring (e.g., story retelling, paraphrasing, self-questioning, directed reading-thinking, reciprocal teaching) is the key to teaching comprehension. A steady diet of strategies for effective comprehension rather than a steady diet of answering literal comprehension questions should not only teach students how to understand what they read but also how to be strategic thinkers. This strategic thinking orientation toward teaching reading and reading comprehension is represented in such comprehensive approaches as directed reading-thinking activities, reciprocal teaching, and whole language and literature-based reading programs.

Chapter Six

Written Expression

Chapter Questions

- *What are the elements of the writing process approach to instruction?*
- *What is a writing conference and how can it be used with students with learning and behavior problems?*
- *What are several critical aspects to establishing a writing program for students with learning and behavior problems?*
- *How do you conduct and apply error analysis to the spelling errors of students with learning problems?*
- *What are the key principles for teaching spelling to students with learning problems?*
- *Can you describe several methods of teaching spelling to students with learning and behavior problems?*
- *Can you describe several methods of teaching handwriting to students with learning and behavior problems?*

A high-school teacher of learning-disabled students reports, "The adolescents in my program do not want to write. They do not even want to answer questions in writing. Writing a theme for a class is torture."

Most young children love to scribble. They enjoy writing and drawing on paper, sidewalks, chalkboards, and, unfortunately, even on walls. On the first day of school when first graders are asked if they know how to write, most of them say yes. What happens to the interest and joy in writing from age three to age thirteen?

Many researchers in the field feel that students do not spend enough time on writing as a craft and are given too little choice about what they write. Writing has many negative associations for students because it is often used as a form of punishment and when their writing is returned to them it is filled with corrections. This chapter is about what happens in writing when students are given choices in topics and time and encouragement to write. The chapter presents background and instructional procedures for using the writing process approach to instruction. Getting started in writing, the writing process, and establishing a writing community are discussed. (See Apply the Concept 6.1.) In addition, this chapter presents approaches to teaching spelling and handwriting to students who have learning difficulties. A rationale for why manuscript and cursive are taught is provided in Table 6.1.

Teaching the Writing Process

Several years ago Marynell Schlegel, a resource room teacher who works with students who have learning and emotional handicaps, decided she disliked teaching writing almost as much as the students hated learning it. An interview with these students on the characteristics of good writing revealed that they perceived good writing as spelling words correctly, writing "correct" sentences, and having good handwriting—the very skills these students often have the most difficulty developing. None of the children included a purpose for writing in their description of good writing. Writing was not perceived by them as a means of conveying a message, which is considered by experts to be the most important element in writing (Murray, 1984, 1985).

During the summer Marynell decided to read about writing and to change her writing instruction. After reading Graves (1983), she decided to implement the writing process approach to written expression.

The Writing Process for Students with Learning and Behavior Problems

After spending the summer preparing for the changes in her instructional approach to writing, Marynell Schlegel decided she was ready to begin. She arranged for students with writing problems to come to the resource room for four

Apply the Concept 6.1 _____

LEARNING-DISABLED STUDENTS' KNOWLEDGE OF WRITING STRATEGIES

Students identified as learning-disabled differ from low-achieving and high-achieving students in their knowledge of strategies related to writing. They are less aware of steps in the writing process and ideas and procedures for organizing their written text. Students with learning disabilities are also more dependent upon external cues such as how much to write, teacher feedback, and mechanical presentation of the paper (Englert, Raphael, Fear, and Anderson, 1988).

TABLE 6.1   *Manuscript vs. Cursive*

Manuscript	*Cursive*
1. It more closely resembles print and facilitates learning to read.	1. Many students want to learn to write cursive.
2. It is easier for young children to learn.	2. Many students write cursive faster.
3. Manuscript is more legible than cursive.	3. Many adults object to students using manuscript beyond the primary grades.
4. Many students write manuscript at the same rate as cursive and this rate can be significantly influenced through direct instruction.	
5. It is better for LD students to learn one writing process well than to attempt to learn two.	

fifty-minute periods a week. During this time they were to write. Writing included selecting topics of their choice and, within each written piece, focusing first on the message and only later on the mechanics of writing. Skills such as organizing ideas and editing for capitalization, punctuation, and spelling would be taught based on the students' individual needs and within the context of their written pieces rather than through the familiar drill and practice activities. Marynell initiated the program with many reservations. She was concerned that this writer-centered format for teaching writing would require her to have a built-in scope and sequence for the development of written expression. She had taught reading and math for a number of years and had developed a scope and sequence of the skills required at each grade level, but written expression was much less developed in her mind and in the various teachers' guides she consulted. Marynell knew that one way to develop a better understanding of what to teach and when to teach it was to observe students as they learn to become writers. Getting ready to implement the writing process approach to instruction involves considerations in several areas, including setting, scheduling and preparing materials, teaching skills, and the teachers' role as a writer.

Setting.   Marynell decided that the environment would be one of the most important components to ensure a successful writing program for her students who had already experienced failure in writing. According to Graves (1983), the setting should create a working atmosphere similar to a studio, which promotes independence and in which students can easily interact. Figure 6.1 depicts how Marynell arranged her room to create such an atmosphere. Materials and supplies for writing, and the students' individual writing folders were stored in specific locations in the room. Students knew where materials could be found, so they did not have to rely on the teacher to get them started at the beginning of the writing period. The room was arranged so students could work together or individually. Conferencing between small groups of students, teacher and student, and student and student were facilitated with the room arrangement.

Scheduling and Preparing Materials.   Marynell set up individual writing folders. In the daily writing folders, illustrated in Figure 6.2, students kept all their unfinished writing, a list of possible writing topics, a list of all writing pieces they had completed, a list of writing skills they had mastered, a list of skills and topics in which they had expertise, and dates when con-

FIGURE 6.1   *Setting the Stage*

1. Create a working atmosphere that is similar to a studio.
2. Create an atmosphere where students can interact easily.
3. Create an atmosphere that encourges independence.

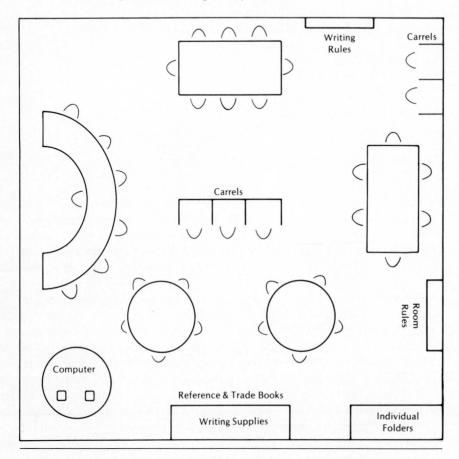

ferences with the teacher were held. A list of the words an individual student was learning to spell, along with a procedure for learning the words and measuring mastery, was also included in the folder (see Figure 6.3). In addition to the current writing folder, students had access to their permanent writing folder, which included all of the writing they had completed.

In setting up the writing program Marynell also made a substantial time commitment. Her previous written language instruction had focused on short periods of time several days a week—just enough time for the student to complete a skill activity or a piece of writing on an assigned topic. Her research convinced her that students need an extended period of time on a daily basis if they are to develop as writers. So, coordinating with the regular classroom teachers, Marynell scheduled fifty minutes per day, four days per week, for writing.

FIGURE 6.2 *Individual Writing Folder*

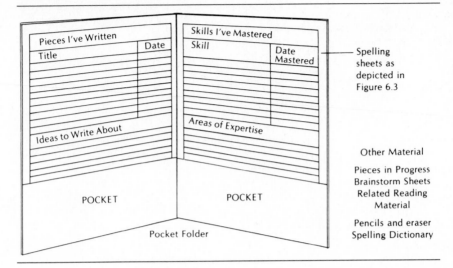

Pocket Folder

She scheduled approximately eight to ten students to come to the resource room during the writing period. These students included behaviorally disordered, learning-disabled, and low-achieving students who were experiencing difficulties in written expression.

Teaching Skills. What was scheduled within each writing period varied depending on the students' needs. Most of the time was devoted to individual writing and conferences with classmates and the teacher. Time for sharing ideas and drafts was often scheduled near the end of the period.

Marynell conducted short (five to fifteen minutes) skill lessons with individual or small groups of students. The topics and groupings for these lessons were based on the students' needs. Skill lessons were decided based on observations of student writing, requests for help, and data collected from conferences. Students were selected to participate in the skill lessons contingent upon their abilities and needs. The same topic with different activities was usually covered for four lessons to help provide sufficient practice. To help promote generalization, Marynell and students would use conferences to discuss how the skill was working in the writing process.

Teachers as Writers. Writing with the students was also an important part of Marynell's writing program. She planned her schedule so that she was writing when the students entered the room at the beginning of the period. She found that this set the tone and facilitated getting the students to start writing. Joan Gervasi, a teacher of emotionally disturbed adolescents, thinks that a teacher's writing is the most important ingredient to success with the students. Joan frequently writes with her students and shares her writing with them. Because she writes, she feels she can better understand their writing difficulties and can speak with them author to author.

Setting the tone for writing requires the teacher to write, to share his or her writing, to be genuinely interested in what the students say in their writing, to listen carefully, and to confer and provide feedback. According to Graves

FIGURE 6.3 *Sample Spelling Form for the Individual Spelling Folder*

Student: _____

Words I'm Learning to Spell

Date	Word	Written on Card	Practiced Using Strategy	Learned for Test	Learned in Writing	Date Mastered
3/12	1. mystery	✓	✓	✓		
	2. chasing	✓	✓	✓		
	3. haunted	✓	✓	✓		
	4. wouldn't	✓	✓			
	5. elsewhere	✓	✓	✓		
	6. whatever	✓	✓	✓		
	7. their	✓	✓	✓		
	8. there	✓	✓	✓		
	9.					
	10.					
	11.					
	12.					
	13.					
	14.					
	15.					
	16.					
	17.					
	18.					
	19.					
	20.					

(1983), the tone for writing is set by what the teacher does.

Elements of the Writing Process

The elements of the writing process include prewriting, composing, revising, editing, and publishing. Authors do not pass through these elements as stages in the order they are listed. In fact, many authors circle back through previous elements and jump ahead to later ones while they are writing their drafts. For example, Steven realized after he read his draft to his friend Jacob that he needed to have more information about what submarines look like on the inside. He returned to the prewriting stage and checked out several books on submarines so he could complete his story.

Some elements of the writing process are not used at all. For example, Sheryl decided she was going to write about her first date with Jerry, and she used little of what we describe as prewriting as she began her writing. Mark discussed an idea for writing with his teacher and then, after writing a draft and reading it to a friend, decided he was unhappy with the topic and left it. These elements are not stages that a writer passes through but merely processes that are often used in writing.

In prewriting, a writer collects information about a topic through observing, remembering, interviewing, and reading. In composing, the author attempts to get ideas on paper in the form of a draft. This process tells the author what he or she knows and does not know. During revising, points are explored further, ideas are elaborated, and further connections are made. When the author is satisfied with the content, he or she edits the piece, reviewing it line by line to determine that each word is necessary. Punctuation, spelling, and other mechanical processes are checked. The final element is publication. If the piece is a good one for the author, it is published. Obviously, not all pieces are published.

Stires (1983), who has used the writing process approach with learning-disabled students, concludes that disabled writers are different from nondisabled writers in the degree to which components of the writing process are difficult for them. Many learning-disabled students experience significant problems in editing and writing final copies because they have difficulty with mechanical skills such as spelling, punctuation, and handwriting. These students often produce well-developed stories but they are hard to read because of the mechanical errors. Other students with learning disabilities have difficulty organizing their first drafts and need to rethink sequencing and order during their revisions.

Prewriting: Getting Started. The first hurdle in starting the writing process approach with your students is topic selection.

Selecting topics. ''The most important thing children can learn is what they know and how they know it'' (Graves, 1985, p. 39). This is the essence of topic choice. Once students can identify what they know and talk about it, they have completed the first step in topic selection.

Give each student and yourself a piece of paper. Say to them, ''You know lots of things about yourself, about your family, and about your friends. You have hobbies and activities that you like to do. You have stories about things that have happened to you and/or to others you know. You have lots of things to share with others. I want you to make a list of things you would like to share with others through writing. Do not put them in any specific order—just write them as you think of them. You will not have to write on all of these topics. The purpose of this exercise is to think of as many topics as you can. I will give you about ten minutes. Begin.'' Model the process for the students by writing as many topics as you can think of during the assigned time. When time is up, tell the students to pick a partner and share their topics with him or her. They may add any new topics they think of at this time. When they finish sharing their topics with their partner, share your list with the entire group and comment on topics you are looking forward to writing about as well as the topics you feel you may never write about. Ask for volunteer students to read their topic list to the entire group. Now ask the students to select the three topics they are most interested in writing about and to write them at the top of the list and then place their topic list in their writing folder. Explain that this list can be consulted later for possible topics. Also, if the students think of new topics they want to write about, they may add them to the list. Finally, ask the students to select a topic and begin writing.

Topic selection is decided by the student. It is not decided by the teacher through story starters, picture cues, or other stimuli. Every student knows things and has stories to tell. We need to have confidence in them and give them an opportunity to discover what they know.

Problems in topic selection. There are two common problems in topic selection: difficulty in finding a topic and persistence in writing about the same topic.

Maintaining a supply of writing topics is difficult for some students and rarely a problem for others. When students tell you stories, ask them if the story generates a topic they want to write about. When students are reading or you are reading to them, ask if the reading has given them ideas for their own writing. If they were going to write the ending of this story, how would they do it? If they were going to continue this story, what would happen? If they were going to add characters to the story, what type of characters would they add? Would they change the setting?

You can also facilitate topic selection by presenting a range of writing styles including stories, factual descriptions, mysteries, and observations. Students often begin writing by telling personal experiences. Through your writing and the writing of other authors, the students can be introduced to a wide range of categories that can provide alternative topics. One teacher sent student reporters to other classrooms to interview students about what topics they think would be interesting to write about.

Marynell's resource room contained a list of suggestions for what the students should do when they are stuck about a topic for writing (see Figure 6.4). A good example of how a friend can help was observed in Marynell's classroom.

Ruth Ann, a student in Marynell's classroom, was stuck for a topic. "What can I write about?" she asked as Marynell observed during writing period.

"Check on the poster, check in your folder, or ask a friend," Marynell suggested.

Ruth Ann got up and went over to another table where Cary was working on the first draft of a piece about a talking dishwasher. "Can you help me?" Ruth Ann asked. "I don't know what to write about."

"Let me find my idea sheet so I can help you out," replied Cary. "And go get a piece of paper

FIGURE 6.4   *Up in the Air for a Topic?*

- Check your folder and reread your idea list.

- Ask a friend to help you brainstorm ideas.

- Listen to other's ideas.

- Write about what you know: your experiences.

- Write a make-believe story.

- Write about a special interest or hobby.

- Write about how to do something.

- Think about how you got your last idea.

Apply the Concept 6.2

A FRIEND HELPS WITH TOPIC SELECTION

Ruth Ann returned with a piece of blank paper, which she handed to Cary. Cary wrote Ruth Ann's name on the paper and underlined it. Then she conducted a rather sophisticated interview.

"Think of three ideas. Want to write about your first day of school?"

"I can't remember. That was five years ago," answered Ruth Ann.

"How about the first day in the learning lab?" continued Cary.

"I don't remember that either. It was over a year ago."

Looking at her idea sheet, Cary commented, "I'm writing about a talking dishwasher. Do you want to write about that?"

"Not really," replied Ruth Ann.

"Where do you go on vacations?" asked Cary.

"To Iowa, but I've already written about that."

"Well, have you ever been to a circus?" Cary pursued.

"No."

"How about a zoo?"

"The Los Angeles zoo," Ruth Ann answered.

"Do you want to write about that?" asked Cary.

"Yeah," remarked Ruth Ann, "that's a good idea."

Cary wrote the number 1 on the paper she had labeled with Ruth Ann's name, and wrote, "las angels zoo" beside it. She remarked, "I don't know how to spell Los Angeles."

"Don't worry," Ruth Ann commented. "I can find that out when I start writing about it."

"OK, let's think up another idea. Have you ever ridden a horse?" asked Cary as she continued the interview.

"No," replied Ruth Ann.

"Do you have any pets?" asked Cary.

"Yea, I have a cat named Pierre."

"Do you want to write about him?" continued Cary.

"Yes, I could do that," replied Ruth Ann enthusiastically.

Cary wrote the number 2 on the paper and beside it wrote, "writing about your cat."

The interview continued, with Cary explaining that it is helpful to think up three ideas so that you have some choice when you decide what to write about. After more questioning, Ruth Ann decided it would be okay to write about a talking shoe, so Cary wrote down Ruth Ann's third idea. Then Cary helped Ruth Ann decide that she was first going to write about her cat. Cary wrote this idea at the bottom of the page and starred it to note that Ruth Ann had selected this topic. Cary ended the interview with the request, "Put this paper in your writing folder so that the next time you have to select a topic we'll already have two ideas thought up."

---

while I finish this." The rest of the interview between Cary and Ruth Ann is described in Apply the Concept 6.2.

In addition to difficulty in thinking of a topic, students often repeat the same topic. Many children with learning and behavior problems find security in repeating the same topic or theme in their writing. They like the control they have over the language, spelling, and content. Look carefully at their work and determine whether or not the stories are changing through vocabulary development, concept development, story development, or character development. It could be that the student is learning a great deal about writing even though the story content is changing very little. Continue to confer and ask questions about the student's writing. If you feel the student is not moving forward, then suggest a change in topic.

Another problem that may concern some teachers is when one student selects a topic and other students copy the idea. For example, Scott wrote a story about a talking dictionary that was stolen and how Scott endangered his life to recover the dictionary. The idea had special meaning for him since he generally misspelled about 50 percent of the words he used in his writing. Once the story was shared with his classmates, over half of the other children wrote about talking objects, including dishwashers, brooms, and shoes. These stories written by other students (repeating Scott's theme) served as a vehicle for several students to write better developed stories than they had written previously, and for one rather good storyteller, Cary, to expand the story format into a traditional murder mystery for her next story. Of course, when she shared her story, many students followed by copying the theme.

Brainstorming. Many students with learning and behavior problems begin writing without much planning about what they are going to write. They find that when they read their drafts aloud, others have difficulty understanding the story or following the sequence. Sometimes we need to teach students prewriting skills so the writing and rewriting stages are easier.

Learning-disabled students are limited in text organization skills because they have difficulty categorizing ideas related to a specific topic, providing advanced organizers for the topic, and relating and extending ideas about the topic (Englert and Raphael, 1988).

In teaching the thinking that goes into a piece, teachers need to model their thinking as they move from topic selection to writing a first draft. Some teachers have found it helpful to teach this thinking process by writing their ideas in an organized structure (Bos, 1990; Thompkins and Friend, 1986). In Marynell's classroom this was referred to as brainstorm sheets; however, they have also been called structured organizers (Pehrsson and Robinson, 1985), semantic maps (Pearson and Johnson, 1978), and story frames or maps (Fowler and Davis, 1985). Although these visual organization devices have been used as aids to reading comprehension, they also serve

Apply the Concept 6.3 _____

SAMPLE BRAINSTORMING SHEET

Name: Mrs. Turk

Date: 2/17

Working Title: Horseback Ride

Setting:

Where: Mt. Graham

start at trash dump

When: When I was ten years old

Who: Dad and I, also mom and brother

Action:
Dad and I were riding on trail.
Trail got bad.
Dad's horse stumbled on rock.
Dad fell off + hurt his arm.
Finally he got on horse. I helped.
Rode to top of mt.
Mom met us. So did brother.
Went to hospital.

Ending: Dad was OK.

to facilitate the writing process (Pehrsson and Robinson, 1985). Mary Beth Turk, a resource teacher who works with Marynell, used a "think-aloud" technique to model how to use the brainstorm sheet presented in Apply the Concept 6.3. She drew a large brainstorm sheet on the board and then introduced the brainstorming technique to the students.

Mary Beth began, "I want to write a story about a time when I was really scared. So I decided to write about the time when I was about ten years old and my dad and I went for a horse-back ride. He got hurt and I wasn't sure we'd get back to the car. There is so much to remember about this story that I am going to jot down a few ideas so that when I begin to write my story, I can remember them all and put them in order. To

help me organize my ideas, I'm going to use a Brainstorm Sheet."

At this point, Mary Beth explained the brainstorm sheet and the parts of a story. Through class discussion, the students identified a story they had written recently and each part in their story.

Mary Beth continued modeling, using the brainstorm sheet. "I am going to call my story the 'Horseback Ride' for now. I may want to change the name later since it's easier for me to think of a title after I write the story. Well, it happened when we were on a trip to Mount

FIGURE 6.5 *Brainstorm Sheet*

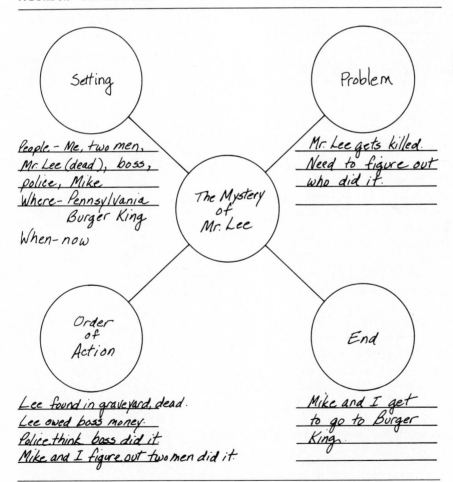

Graham. So I'm going to write 'Mt. Graham' by 'Where.' I'm not sure how to spell Mt. Graham, but it doesn't matter that I spell it correctly now. I can find out later. Also, since the brainstorm sheet is for me, I don't have to write sentences—just ideas that will help me remember when I'm writing my first draft of the story.'' Mary Beth continued to think aloud as she completed the sheet.

Mary Beth demonstrated that the students did not have to fill in the brainstorm sheet in a linear fashion. Sometimes it is easier to fill out the ending first. She also demonstrated how, after she listed all the ideas under the action section, she could go back and number them in the order that made the most sense.

In subsequent lessons Mary Beth demonstrated how to write a story from the brainstorm sheet. She also worked individually with students to write brainstorm sheets and to use them in their writing.

During the year several different brainstorm sheets were used in Mary Beth's classroom. Figure 6.5 shows a brainstorm sheet that was developed for expository writing (writing that describes the facts or information about a subject

FIGURE 6.6 *Cary's Brainstorm Sheet*

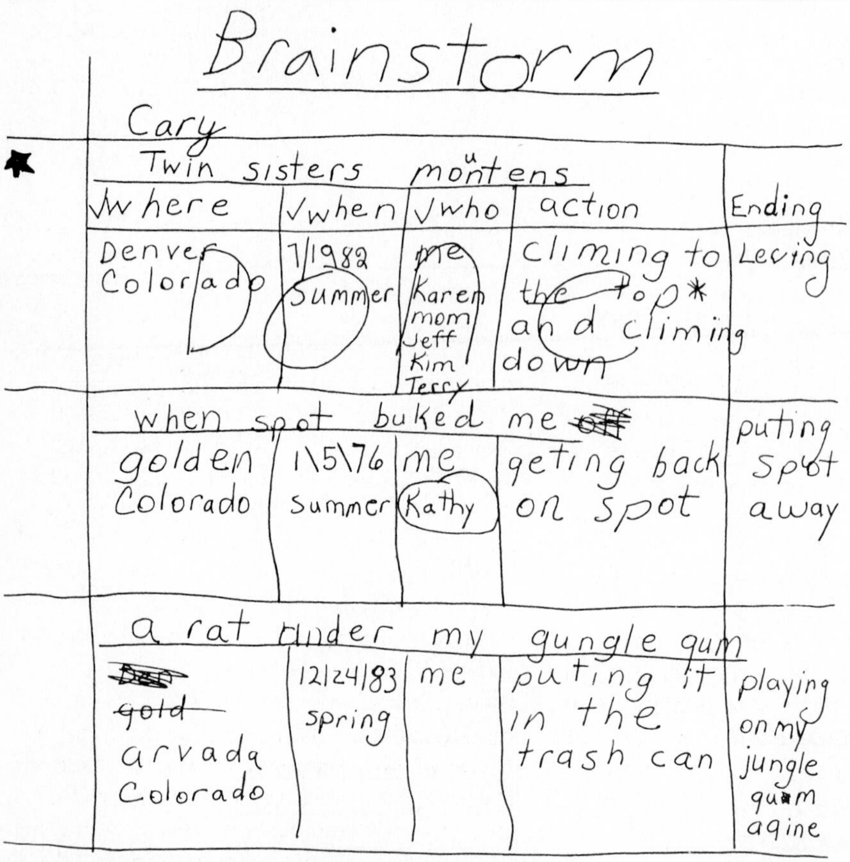

Permission granted by author and her parents.

Apply the Concept 6.4

THE BIG PICTURE

"The most difficult thing for me to teach my students," said Mrs. Zaragoza, "is to think about the ideas in their writing, not about whether or not they can spell the words correctly. My students thought good writing and good spelling were the same thing."

A common problem with poor writers is that they are overly concerned with the surface structure of their writing—the spelling, grammar, and punctuation. Many students with learning problems do not focus on thinking about their story. Their stories are often poorly organized and their ideas are disconnected and/or missing. These same students can *tell* you about the story, but have a hard time getting all of the ideas about the story in writing.

Following is the description of a procedure developed by Kucer (1986) to help poor writers focus on the "big picture" of writing:

1. Give students notecards and allow them to write possible topics on the cards (one topic per card).

Students then share ideas about topics and make additions on their topic cards.

2. Students select a writing topic about which they would like to write.

3. Major ideas related to the writing topic are written on notecards. The major ideas may come from the student's knowledge and experience, or, if the writing is in a content area, the student may need to seek the assistance of class notes, books, and magazines. Major ideas are written as key concepts or thoughts rather than complete sentences.

4. Students share their major ideas about the topic with each other. They make any additions or comments about the ideas they feel will be helpful in writing about the topic.

5. Once major ideas are selected, they are organized in a meaningful sequence.

6. With their cards as a guide, students write their piece.

---

area; often associated with social studies and science). However, the students also used this brainstorm sheet for stories. They wrote the title in the center circle, and information related to the setting, problem, action, and ending in the four other circles and their accompanying lines. Students also developed their own brainstorming sheets. For example, Cary combined topic selection and brainstorming together and developed the brainstorm sheet presented in Figure 6.6. Her rationale was, "You really need to pretty well think through a piece before you decide if you want to write about it."

Teaching students to think about what they are going to say before they write is generally a helpful technique. However, completing a visual representation prior to writing may not facilitate writing for all students (see Apply the Concept 6.4).

Composing. Many students with learning and behavior problems begin the writing process here. They think of a topic and, without much planning, begin writing. Often the prewriting skills described in the previous section must be taught to enhance the writing process.

Once children begin composing, sharing their work with others plays an important role. Children need time to read and discuss their pieces with individual students, small groups of students, and the teacher. The author's chair (Graves and Hansen, 1983) is a formal opportunity to share writing. Leila, a behaviorally disturbed fifth grader, signed up for "author's chair" early during the week. She thought her story about a dog who could fly was pretty good and she looked forward to reading it to the entire class. During "author's chair," she sat in a special chair in a circle, which included all students and the teacher. She enjoyed the attention from the group while she prepared to read. During her reading she could tell the story was going over well because the students were laughing and listening carefully. After the reading she asked them if they had any comments or questions. She called on several students who commented on sections of the story they liked and other students who asked questions. Mike wanted to know more about what the wings on the dog looked like. Rhonda wondered why the story ended the way it did. Leila answered the questions with the ownership of a professional author and made some decisions about parts she would change and how she would add more description about what the dog looked like. Sharing, as Leila did in the ''author's chair,'' motivates her to keep writing and will help her with rewriting.

Teachers often need to set rules about students' behavior when a classmate is sharing their work in the author's chair. These rules may include: raise your hand, ask a question or make a positive comment, give feedback when asked.

Revising.   Revising is a difficult task for all authors, especially beginning writers. Getting the entire message down on paper the first time is difficult enough; making changes so the piece is its best and can be understood by others is a most formidable task. Many authors need to go back to prewriting and obtain more information, or they spend time conferring with others to find out what parts of the piece are going over well and what parts need additional work. It is also at this stage that some authors abandon the piece. They feel it can never be really good, and so they start again with a new idea.

Most students with learning and behavior problems have difficulty revising. Many would like to move straight to publication, with little or no revision. Teachers often find it is best to allow students initially to move to publication without much revision, and then, through conferencing and reading the work of others, encourage students to see the benefits of revision. Joan Gervasi suggests modeling and patience. From her experience in using the writing process approach with students, she finds they will eventually revise their pieces, but it usually takes time.

FIGURE 6.7   *Sample Poem Written by Student*

Shyness

My Shyness is like the color white
It is wanting to tell a girl how you feel
Shyness is girls who look up with a smile
Then walk away from me
Shyness is wishing I could disappear
From a crowd

At first, their writing is more like a journal—a chance to write about how they feel and what is happening in their relationships. It is an intimate exchange between them and the teacher, and eventually between them and selected students, and finally between them and a larger audience. This progression does not happen quickly, nor in this order. For some students, it takes the entire school year. Joan helps students with revising by demonstrating how she rewrites pieces. She even brings in letters she is writing to ex-students and discusses the revision process she uses. Joan writes a lot of poetry and shares her poetry with her students. Figure 6.7 shows a drawing and a poem written by an adolescent in response to a poem written by his teacher.

It is important during revising to focus on the message and content rather than mechanics. Hansen (1985) discusses the importance of not

FIGURE 6.8 *Editing Rules*

Ⓒircle misspelled words.

Put a box around punctuation.

Underline writing that doesn't sound so good.

Add a ∧ to insert a word or phrase.

Add a ⊕ with a number to insert a sentence.

focusing on spelling until the student is finished with composing: ''If writers think they should spell correctly on early drafts, they interfere with the main goal of their own writing: produce an interesting message (p. 185).'' Hansen continues, ''Further, if they think the spelling in every piece of writing must be corrected, they interfere with their own progress because the time they spend fixing the spelling on a deadend piece of writing would be better spent on a piece of writing that may turn out to be significant'' (p. 185). Thus, whereas correcting mechanical errors such as spelling and punctuation may occur during the composing and revising process, it is not focused on until the next stage—editing.

In addition to editing their own work, students serve as editors for the work of their peers. This can work several ways. One way is to have students edit their own work first and then to ask a friend to edit it. Another possibility is to establish a class editor. The responsibility of the class editor is to read the material and search for mechanical errors. The role of the class editor could rotate so that every student has an opportunity to serve in that capacity.

Editing. Whereas revision focuses mainly on content, editing focuses mainly on mechanics. After the student and teacher are happy with the content, it is time to make corrections for spelling, capitalizing, punctuation, and language. Students are expected to circle words they are unsure how to spell, put boxes in places where they are unsure of the punctuation, and underline the sentences where they feel the language may not be correct. Students are not expected to correct all errors but are expected to correct known errors. Figure 6.8 provides a poster that can be used in a classroom to remind students of the editing rules. Figure 6.9 depicts a form that can be included inside the students' folders to remind them of editing skills they know how to use.

Although many spelling, punctuation, and language modifications are made during writing and revising, when students edit they focus solely on mechanical errors. Often they need to read the text for each type of error. First, they read the text, looking for spelling difficulties; next, they read the text, looking for punctuation and capitalization difficulties; and finally, they read the text, looking for language problems such as noun-verb agreement. Young students may not know what noun-verb agreement is, so they should simply look for sentences that do not ''sound right'' when they read them aloud.

FIGURE 6.9 *Editing Skills I Know*

Spelling
1. done
2. was
3. from
4. come
5. girl
6. because
7. what
8. where
9. children
10. playground

Punctuation
1. Put a period at the end of sentence.
2. Put a question mark at the end of asking sentence.

Capitalization
1. Capitalize the first letter of sentence.
2. Capitalize the first letter of a person's name.
3. Capitalize the name of a town.

Publishing. Not all writing is published; often only one in five or six pieces is published. What does it mean to have a piece published? A piece is prepared in some way that it can be read and shared by others. Often this is in the form of books that have cardboard binding decorated with contact paper or scraps of wallpaper. Sometimes these books include a picture of the author, a description of the author, and a list of books published by the author.

Young children who are writing shorter pieces may be publishing every two weeks, whereas older students who spend more time composing and revising would publish less frequently. Why publish? Publishing is a way of confirming a student's hard work and sharing the piece with others. Writing requires an audience, and periodically we need to share what we write. It is important for *all* students to publish—not just the best authors. Publishing is a way of involving others in school and home with the students' writing.

Apply the Concept 6.5

SAMPLE STUDENT WRITING

"My best football game"

Football is my favrite game I like to play it even when I was little I played for a good team the bandits and one game we played against Macarther school and it started off with us 0 and them 7 and then the game was tied 7 to 7 and then it was time for me to sit on the bench and the score was 7-14 we was winning soon they told me to go back into the game it was getting close to the end and we wanted to win they said it was my turn to run a play and so I ran fast down the feild after the ball was Mike and I look back and see the ball coming right at me and I thoght I was going to miss it but I kept looking at it and after I watched it I reached up and pulled the ball down and I kept on running and we won the game 7 to 21.

Apply the Concept 6.6

CONFERENCING WITH THE AUTHOR OF
"MY BEST FOOTBALL GAME"

Teacher: "Mark, this football game was a special one for you. I bet you have a lot of feelings about this game. What are some of your feelings about this game?"

Mark: "I felt good."

Teacher: "Did you feel good like when you remember your homework or was it stronger than that?"

Mark: "It was stronger. I felt great. Like I was a hero or something."

Teacher: "Like a hero?"

Mark: "Yeah, like in the movies I really saved the game. Well, I guess not really saved the game because we were already winning. But it was, like, cause I made the last touchdown it really said something."

Teacher: "What do you think it said?"

Mark: "It said, hey, watch out cause I'm good. Also, that we won and I scored the final points. It was great."

Teacher: "What could you do so the reader of your piece would know all of the things you just told me?"

Mark: "I guess I could include more about how I felt and all."

Teacher: "How could you do that? Where would it go?"

The teacher decided it was too early to focus on mechanical errors such as spelling and punctuation. Besides being discouraging to Mark, focusing too early on mechanical errors sidetracks the writer from the story. After the author's story is complete, then working on mechanical errors can begin.

Aspects of the Writing Process

The Writing Conference. Conferring, which occurs throughout the writing process, is the heart of the writing procedure. The student comes to the writing conference prepared to read his or her piece, to describe problem areas, and to be asked questions. When students confer with the teacher, they know they will be listened to and responded to. The teacher's nonverbal and verbal interactions communicate to them that they want to listen and help.

Students also know that they will be asked challenging questions about their work. Questions are not asked in a rapid-fire sequence with little time for the student to formulate answers. Instead, questions should be carefully selected and enough time should be allowed for the student to respond. Conferences need to focus on specific areas and should not cover all parts of the writing. During the conference with the author of "My best football game" (see Apply the Concept 6.5), the teacher realized there were many problems with the piece of writing. She was aware of grammatical, spelling, and punctuation errors. She was also aware the story rambled, did not provide sufficient details, and lacked the voice of the author. However, she was ecstatic that this fourteen-year-old student had produced a piece of writing that he was excited about. Apply the Concept 6.6 presents the conference the teacher had with the student.

Some key points about conferring with students are:

1. Follow the lead of the child during the conference. Do not attempt to get the writer to write about a topic because it is of interest to you or to write the story the way you would write it.
2. Listen and accept what the child says. You are being too directive during conferences when you talk more than the writer.
3. Ask questions the student can answer.

Apply the Concept 6.7 _____

CONFERENCING: FOLLOWING THE LEAD OF THE STUDENT

During conferences, the teacher listens to what students say, follows the lead of the students, and asks questions that teach.

> *Teacher:* "How's it going, Karin?"
> *Karin:* "Not very good. I don't know what to write about."
> *Teacher:* "You are having trouble with a topic?"
> *Karin:* "I was going to write about how I want to go and live with my real mom again but I don't know what to say. All I do is write that I want to live with my real mom and then the story is over."

> *Teacher:* "It's hard to think of what else might go in the story?"
> *Karin:* "Well, yeah. I guess I could tell why, but I don't know why, I just want to."
> *Teacher:* "Would it be any easier to get started if you told the story as though it were about someone else?"
> *Karin:* "Like I could tell about a kid who wanted to go and live with her real mom. Then I could tell it like a story."
> *Teacher:* "What are some of the things you might write if you told the story this way?"

4. Ask questions that teach. (Apply the Concept 6.7 illustrates a conference in which the teacher asks questions that teach.)
5. Conferences should be frequent and brief. Although conferences can range from thirty seconds to ten minutes, most of them last only two to three minutes.

During conferences we listen to what students have written and we tell them what we hear. We and other students make comments and suggestions based on what we have learned from writing. As Nancy Atwell (1985) suggests, we can only offer—writers may reject our advice.

Establishing a Writing Community. Writing requires trust. For students to write well within their classroom, an environment of mutual trust and respect is essential. The writer must also be able to depend on the predictability of the classroom structure. Establishing a writing community requires the following:

1. *Write every day for at least thirty minutes.* Students need time to think, write, discuss, re-write, confer, revise, talk, read, and write some more. Good writing takes time.

2. *Encourage students to develop areas of expertise.* At first, students will write broadly about what they know. However, with encouragement, they can become class experts in a particular area, subject, or writing form. It will take them time and inducement before they discover their own writing "turf."

3. *Keep students' writing in folders.* Folders should include all writing as documentation of what each student knows and has accomplished. This means students' work stays with them during the year. Work can be referred to for illustration of gains made, to indicate skills learned, and to demonstrate range of topic. Selected pieces from the year should be with the student for the next year.

4. *The teacher writes.* Teachers write outside of the classroom and with the students in the classroom. Using an overhead or easel, teachers may share with the students how they compose. Just as students share their writing with each other, the teacher shares his or her writing with the students.

Apply the Concept 6.8

TEN POINTERS FOR TEACHING WRITING TO SPECIAL EDUCATION STUDENTS

1. *Allocate adequate time for writing.* Adequate time is a necessary but not sufficient criteria for improving the writing skills of special learners. Students who merely spend ten to fifteen minutes a day practicing the craft of writing are not spending adequate time to improve their skills. Students need a minimum of thirty minutes of time for writing everyday.

2. *Provide a range of writing tasks.* Writing about what students know best—self-selected topics—is the first step in writing. After students' skills improve, the range of writing tasks should broaden to include problem solving, writing games, and a variety of writing tasks.

3. *Create a social climate that promotes and encourages writing.* Teachers set the tone through an accepting, encouraging manner. Conferences between students, students and teachers, and students and other persons in the school are encouraged to provide constructive feedback on their writing and to provide an audience to share what is written.

4. *Integrate writing with other academic subjects.* Writing can be integrated with almost every subject that is taught. This includes using writing as a means of expression in content area subjects such as social studies and science as well as part of an instructional activity with reading and language arts.

5. *Focus on the processes central to writing.* These processes include prewriting activities, writing, and rewriting activities.

6. *During the writing phase focus on the "higher order" task of composing and attend to the basic elements of spelling and punctuation after the writing is complete.* With some students, their mechanics of writing are so poor that it interferes with their ability to successfully get ideas down on paper. With these students, focus first on some of the basic elements so that the writing process can be facilitated.

7. *Teach explicit knowledge about characteristics of good writing.* The implicit knowledge about writing needs to be made explicit. For example, different genres and their characteristics need to be discussed and practiced.

8. *Teach skills that aid "higher level" composing.* These skills include conferencing with teachers and peers, and strategy instruction. Strategy instruction may provide guidelines for brainstorming, sentence composition, or evaluating the effectiveness of the written piece.

9. *Ask students to identify goals for improving their writing.* Students can set realistic goals regarding their progress in writing. These goals can focus on prewriting, writing, and/or rewriting. Both the students and the teacher can provide feedback as to how successful the students have been in realizing their goals.

10. *Do not use instructional practices that are not associated with improved writing for students.* There are several examples of instructional practice that are not associated with improved writing including: grammar instruction, diagramming sentences, and overemphasis on students' errors.

Source: S. Graham and K. R. Harris (1988). Instructional recommendations for teaching writing to exceptional students, *Exceptional Children, 54*(6):506–512.

5. *Share writing.* Conclude the writing time with an opportunity for students to read their writing to others and to exchange comments and questions.

6. *Read to the students.* Share and discuss books, poems, and other readings. There is a strong connection between reading and writing.

7. *Expand the writing community outside of the classroom.* Place published books in the library for use by other students and allow students to share their writing with other classes. Encourage authors from other classrooms to visit and read their writings.

8. *Develop children's capacity to evaluate their own work.* Students need to develop their own goals and document their progress toward them. By conferring with the teacher, they will learn methods for evaluating their own work.

9. *Slow the pace.* Don Graves (1985) says, "Teachers need to slow down so kids can hurry up." Teachers need to be patient when they ask questions, allowing the students time to answer.

The writing process approach to instruction with children who have special needs requires time—time to set up the classroom, follow the progress of students, confer with students, and teach skills. More importantly, it requires time each day for the students to write. (See Apply the Concept 6.8.) Suzanne, a teacher of emotionally disturbed adolescents who has used the writing process approach for the first time this year, comments, "Yes, it takes a great deal of time but it is worth it. The students want to write. They have even started their own school newsletter. Best of all, they are seeing the connection between reading and writing. I feel it is worth the time."

Teaching Skills

The writing process approach is a good technique for improving content and structure of writing as well as increasing the students' perception of themselves as writers. Often this is not enough, however. Most students with learning and behavior disorders need specific instruction in the mechanics of writing, such as spelling and handwriting. This section of the chapter will discuss approaches to teaching spelling and handwriting and provide a scope and sequence chart for written expression.

Spelling

Manuel hates spelling and finds it the most frustrating part of writing. He is an eighth-grade student who is adjusting to the transition from a self-contained classroom for emotionally disturbed students to a resource room in a junior-high setting. He has been involved in the writing process approach for the past two years and has learned to use writing to express his feelings,

convey information, and create stories. Manuel is proud of the way his writing has improved and he often shares his stories with others. But his spelling skills are lacking. Manuel has learned to use inventive spelling (spelling words the way they sound or the way he thinks they are spelled) to aid in getting his ideas on paper but he has difficulty editing because he is unable to detect or correct most of his spelling errors. Manuel, like many students with learning and behavior disorders, needs specialized instruction in spelling in order to be a successful writer.

Spelling is an important tool in our society. Many people measure one's intelligence or education by the ability to spell. Spelling is particularly difficult in the English language because there is no one-to-one correspondence between spoken words and written words. We learn to spell many words by remembering the unique combination or order of letters that produce the correct spelling of that word. Spelling facilitates the writing process by freeing the writer to concentrate on content. Although the majority of learning-disabled students have spelling difficulties (Johnson and Myklebust, 1967), spelling is often difficult even for those without a learning disability. Most beginning writers identify spelling as the key problem they need to solve in writing (Graves, 1983). Many good readers are poor spellers, and almost all poor readers are poor spellers (Carpenter and Miller 1982; Frith, 1980).

Students who have a very difficult time learning to read perform worse than average readers on tasks of phonological awareness (e.g., Vellutino and Scanlon, 1987). Ehri (1989) suggests that they have phonological difficulties because they have not learned to read and spell. Thus, their lack of phonological awareness is due to this deficit in their learning and is not a cause of their reading and spelling difficulties.

This section will focus on teaching spelling to students who have learning difficulties. Techniques for analyzing students' spelling errors will be discussed first, followed by a discussion of principles to be applied in developing spelling programs and approaches to teaching spelling.

Spelling Instruction

The first step in developing an appropriate spelling program is to determine the type and pattern of the students' spelling errors. After completing an error analysis, a spelling approach based on students' needs can be implemented.

Error Analysis. Error analysis should be done by using both dictated spelling tests and a student's written work. Random errors do not occur in the spelling of most learning-disabled students. They are consistent in the types of misspellings to which they are prone (DeMaster, Crossland, and Hasselbring, 1986).

When Manuel and his teacher, Mr. Larkin, attempted to develop Manuel's spelling program, they began by selecting samples of Manuel's written work, which included writing he created and work written from dictation. Mr. Larkin examined these pieces to determine if there was a pattern to Manuel's spelling errors. He asked himself the following questions about Manuel's spelling:

1. Is he applying mistaken rules?
2. Is he applying rules that assist him in remembering spellings?
3. Is he making careless errors of words he can spell?
4. Is he spelling words correctly in isolation but not in context?
5. Are there frequently used words that he is consistently misspelling?

After examining Manuel's work and answering these questions, Mr. Larkin discovered:

1. Manuel did not apply the "ing" rule appropriately. For example, *run* became *runing*.
2. Manuel did not use the spelling rule "*i* before *e* except after *c*." For example, he spelled *believe* as *beleive* and *piece* as *peice*.
3. He was inconsistent in spelling words. He would spell them correctly in one piece of written work but not in another.

4. He spelled several words correctly on spelling tests but not in context.
5. He misspelled many frequently used words, such as *there, was, because, somewhere, very,* and *would.*

After answering the questions, Mr. Larkin examined Manuel's work to look for the following error patterns, suggested by Edgington (1967).

1. Additions of unneeded letters (e.g., *boxxes*)
2. Omissions of letters (e.g., *som*)
3. Reflections of mispronunciations (e.g., *ruf* for *roof*)
4. Reflections of dialect (e.g., *sodar* for *soda*)
5. Reversals of whole words (e.g., *eno* for *one*)
6. Reversals of consonant order (e.g., *cobm* for *comb*)
7. Reversals of consonant or vowel directionality (e.g., *Thrusday* for *Thursday*)
8. Phonetic spellings of nonphonetic word parts (e.g., *site* for *sight*)
9. Neographisms, which are spellings that don't resemble the word (e.g., *sumfin* for *something*)
10. Combinations of error patterns

In addition to examining Manuel's work, Mr. Larkin interviewed and observed Manuel to determine what strategies he used when he was unable to spell a word and whether he used any corrective or proofreading strategies after he wrote. Mr. Larkin observed Manuel's writing and then asked him the following questions:

1. When you finish writing a piece, what do you do? (Mr. Larkin was attempting to determine if Manuel rereads for spelling errors.)

2. If you are writing and do not know how to spell a word, what do you do? (Mr. Larkin was attempting to determine what, if any, strategies Manuel used. Did he use invented spelling to facilitate the writing process and underline the

word so he could check the spelling later? Did he stop and try to visualize the word or look for how it was spelled in another location? Did he continue writing and go back later to check the spelling?)

Mr. Larkin discovered that Manuel used few strategies to check or recall spelling when he was writing. In addition to teaching and rehearsing spelling rules, Manuel needed to learn and apply strategies for improving his spelling. After error analysis, intervention included discussing with Manuel the types of errors he was making, teaching him proofreading skills, teaching him techniques for remembering the correct spelling of words, and teaching him one of the spelling approaches (discussed in a later section of this chapter, Spelling Approaches). Before looking at specialized approaches to teaching spelling to students with learning and behavior disorders, we will first examine traditional approaches to spelling instruction.

Traditional Spelling Instruction. Spelling is taught in most classrooms through the use of spelling basal programs. Typical spelling basals included a prescribed list of weekly words to be mastered by all students. The usual procedure is that a pretest occurs on Monday, followed on Tuesday by a description of the spelling theme (e.g., long *e* words, homophones, *au* words, etc.). Wednesday and Thursday are usually assignments from the text that students work on independently. These assignments usually include dictionary activities, sentence or paragraph writing using the spelling words, writing the words a designated number of times, using the words in sentences, stories, or crossword puzzles, and so on. Friday is usually designated for the posttest in spelling. Although variations on this format occur, such as the teacher who attempts to individualize the spelling program, most classrooms follow a procedure similar to this.

How effective is this procedure for teaching spelling to learning-disabled students? What other procedures might need to be considered to develop effective spelling strategies for students with learning problems? Spelling practices used in most classrooms are based more on tradition than they are on research (Gettinger, 1984). For students with learning difficulties, the introduction of all the words at once, often words that are not in the learning-disabled students' reading vocabularies, and the lack of systematic practice and specific feedback make spelling difficult if not impossible for most. Before discussing specific strategies for teaching spelling to learning-disabled students, the following section will discuss the role of phonics rules in teaching spelling.

Phonics Rules for Spelling. How much emphasis should be given to teaching phonics rules to improve spelling? There is probably no area of the language arts curriculum that has been more carefully reviewed, researched, and debated than spelling. At the heart of many of the debates is the efficacy of using a phonics approach to teaching spelling. Some researchers suggest that a phonics approach increases spelling ability (Baker, 1977; Gold, 1976; Thompson, 1977), whereas others argue that students learn the rules without direct instruction in phonics (Schwartz and Doehring, 1977), and still others insist that intensive phonics instruction is not necessary (Grottenthaler, 1970; Personkee and Yee, 1971; Warren, 1970). Since there is a lack of consistency with phonics rules, primary emphasis should be given to basic spelling vocabulary with supplemented instruction in basic phonics rules (Graham and Miller, 1979). According to Graham and Miller (1979), the phonetic skills that should be taught include base words, prefixes, suffixes, consonants, consonant blends, digraphs, and vowel sound-symbol associations.

The important relationship between rhyming and spelling is illustrated in Apply the Concept 6.9.

Principles for Teaching Spelling to Students with Learning Difficulties. There are several principles that should be included in any spelling

Apply the Concept 6.9 _____

RELATIONSHIP BETWEEN RHYMING AND SPELLING

Rhyming and alliteration are positively and significantly related to progress in spelling (Bradley and Bryant, 1985). A possible explanation is that rhyming teaches students to identify phonological segments and it demonstrates how words can be grouped together according to common sounds. Students' participation at an early age, prior to school, in rhyming games and activities may be an important prerequisite to spelling success.

approach used with students who have learning problems.

Teach in small units. Teach three words a day rather than four or five a day (or fifteen at the beginning of the week). In a study (Bryant, Drabin, and Gettinger, 1981) in which the number of spelling words allocated each day to learning-disabled students was controlled, higher performance and less distractibility and less variance in overall performance were obtained from the learning-disabled group assigned three words a day, when compared with groups assigned four and five words a day.

Provide sufficient practice and feedback. Give students opportunities to practice the words each day with feedback. Many teachers provide this by having students work with spelling partners who ask them their words and provide immediate feedback. The following methods can be used for self-correction and practice. Fold a paper into five columns. Write the correctly spelled words in the first column. The student studies one word, folds the column back, and writes the word in the second column. The student then checks his or her spelling with the correctly spelled word in column one. Folding the column back, the student writes the word in the third column. The student continues writing the word until it is spelled correctly three times. The student then moves to the next word. He or she continues until the word is spelled correctly three times in a row. This procedure should not be confused with spelling assignments that require the student to write the assigned spelling words a designated number of times. These procedures are often ineffective because the student does not attend to the details of the spelling word as a whole, the student often writes the word in segments, and he or she usually copies rather than writes from memory. The student also fails to check words after each writing, sometimes resulting in words being practiced incorrectly.

Select appropriate words. The most important strategy for teaching spelling is that the students should be able to read the word and know its meaning. Spelling should not focus on teaching the students to read and know the meaning of the word. Selection of spelling words should be based on the students' reading and meaning vocabularies.

Teach spelling through direct instruction. Incidental learning in spelling is primarily reserved for good spellers. Spelling words can be selected from the students' reading or written words or can be part of a programmed text, such as lists provided in basal readers. Direct instruction includes mastery of specific words each day, individualized instruction, and continual review. Words should be presented in a list rather than in context so the students can focus on the assigned word.

Maintain previously learned words. Maintenance of spelling words requires previously

Apply the Concept 6.10

PEER TUTORING AND SPELLING

Use of *peer tutors* to teach spelling can be helpful in improving spelling for the tutors and the tutees. When a peer tutoring system was used with a mainstreamed LD student and a good speller from the classroom, the LD student's spelling performance improved and both students rated the peer tutoring system favorably (Mandoli, Mandoli, and McLaughlin, 1982). To increase effectiveness, peer tutors should be trained to implement the spelling approach most suitable for the target student.

---

learned words to be assigned as review words, interspersed with the learning of new spelling words. Previously learned words need to be frequently reviewed to be maintained. Gettinger, Bryant, and Fayne (1982) conducted a study with learning-disabled students to determine the efficacy of a spelling procedure designed to practice the principles of teaching smaller units, sufficient and distributed practice, and maintenance of words learned. Experimental group learning-disabled students were able to reach an 80 percent criterion on more of the spelling words and were able to spell 75 percent of the transfer words when compared with a control group of learning-disabled students involved in a spelling program that did not emphasize these principles.

Teach for transfer of learning. After spelling words have been mastered, provide opportunities for students to see and use spelling words in context.

Motivate students to spell correctly. Using games and activities, selecting meaningful words, and providing examples of the use and need for correct spelling are strategies that help motivate students and give them a positive attitude about spelling (Graham and Miller, 1979).

Include dictionary training. As part of the spelling program, dictionary training should be developed, which includes alphabetization, identifying target words, and locating the correct definition when several are provided.

Spelling Approaches. There are many approaches to teaching spelling. No one approach has been proven to be superior to others with all learning-disabled students. Some students learn effectively with a multisensory approach, such as the Fernald method, and others learn best with a combination of several approaches. The following are several approaches to teaching spelling, all of which make use of the principles discussed in the previous section. Apply the Concept 6.10 describes the effects of peer tutoring as a procedure for teaching spelling.

The test-study-test method. This method of learning spelling words is superior to the study-test method (Fitzsimmons and Loomer, 1980; Yee, 1969). In using the test-study-test method, students are first tested on a list of words and then instructed to study the missed words. Strategies for recalling the correct spelling of these words are taught. These strategies often include verbal mediation—saying the word while writing it or spelling it aloud to a partner. After instruction and study, students are then retested over the words. Using this process, students then correct their own spelling test, which is an important factor in learning to spell.

A description of several word study techniques that can be applied when using the test-study-test method are presented in Figure 6.10.

FIGURE 6.10 *Word Study Techniques*

Fitzgerald Method (Fitzgerald, 1951a)

1. Look at the word carefully.
2. Say the word.
3. With eyes closed, visualize the word.
4. Cover the word and then write it.
5. Check the spelling.
6. If the word is misspelled, repeat steps 1–5.

Horn Method 1 (E. Horn, 1919)

1. Look at the word and say it to yourself.
2. Close your eyes and visualize the word.
3. Check to see if you were right. (If not, begin at step 1).
4. Cover the word and write it.
5. Check to see if you were right. (If not, begin at step 1).
6. Repeat steps 4 and 5 two more times.

Horn Method 2 (E. Horn, 1954c)

1. Pronounce each word carefully.
2. Look carefully at each part of the word as you pronounce it.
3. Say the letters in sequence.
4. Attempt to recall how the word looks, then spell the word.
5. Check this attempt to recall.
6. Write the word.
7. Check this spelling attempt.
8. Repeat the above steps if necessary.

Visual-Vocal Method (Westerman, 1971)

1. Say word.
2. Spell word orally.
3. Say word again.
4. Spell word from memory four times correctly.

Gilstrap Method (Gilstrap, 1962)

1. Look at the word and say it softly. If it has more than one part, say it again, part by part, looking at each part as you say it.
2. Look at the letters and say each one. If the word has more than one part, say the letters part by part.
3. Write the word without looking at the book.

Fernald Method Modified

1. Make a model of the word with a crayon, grease pencil, or magic marker, saying the word as you write it.
2. Check the accuracy of the model.
3. Trace over the model with your index finger, saying the word at the same time.
4. Repeat step 3 five times.
5. Copy the word three times correctly.
6. Copy the word three times from memory correctly.

Cover-and-Write Method

1. Look at word. Say it.
2. Write word two times.
3. Cover and write one time.
4. Check work.
5. Write word two times.
6. Cover and write one time.
7. Check work.
8. Write word three times.
9. Cover and write one time.
10. Check work.

Source: S. Graham and L. Miller, "Spelling Research and Practice: A Unified Approach," *Focus on Exceptional Children, 12*(2) (1979): 11. Reprinted with permission.

The visualization approach. This approach to spelling teaches students to visualize the correct spelling as a means to recall. The visualization approach uses the following procedures:

1. The teacher writes a word that the child can read but cannot spell on the board or on a piece of paper.
2. The student reads the word aloud.
3. The student reads the letters in the word.
4. The student writes the word on paper.
5. The teacher asks the student to look at the word and "take a picture of it" as if his or her eyes were a camera.
6. The teacher asks the student to close his or her eyes and spell the word aloud, visualizing the letters while spelling it.

7. The teacher asks the student to write the word and check the model for accuracy.

The five-step word-study strategy. This strategy requires the student to learn and rehearse the following five steps and practice them with the teacher and then alone. The steps are (1) say the word, (2) write and say the word, (3) check the word, (4) trace and say the word, (5) write the word from memory and check, and (6) repeat the five steps. When the student learns this technique the teacher models the procedure, then the student practices the procedure with assistance from the teacher, and finally the student demonstrates proficiency in the application of the procedure without teacher assistance. This procedure has been effectively used with elementary learning-disabled students (Graham and Freeman, 1985).

The Johnson and Myklebust technique. Johnson and Myklebust (1967) suggest working from recognition to partial recall to total recall when teaching new spelling words. Recognition can be taught by showing the students a word and then writing the word with several unrelated words, asking the students to circle the word they previously saw. The task can gradually be made more difficult by writing distracting words that more closely resemble the target word. In teaching partial recall, the correct word can be written with missing spaces for completing the spelling under it. For example.

with
w __ th
wit __
__ ith
wi __ __
w __ __ __
__ __ __ __

Total recall requires the students to write the word after it is pronounced by another or write the word in a sentence. This approach gives repeated practice and focuses the students on the relevant details of the word. Many learning-disabled students are more efficient in writing spelling words than spelling them orally. Johnson and Myklebust (1967) also suggest that when initial spelling tests are given, the teacher may need to say the word very slowly, emphasizing each syllable. As students learn to spell the words correctly, the test is given in a normal voice and rate.

The cloze spelling approach. This is referred to as the cloze spelling approach because the student needs systematically to supply missing letters in much the same way the students supply words in the cloze reading procedure. The cloze spelling approach uses a four-step process for teaching students to spell words.

1. *Look study.* The student is shown the word on a card. He or she looks at the word and studies the letters and their order.

2. *Write missing vowels.* The student is shown the same word on a card with blanks where the vowels usually appear. The student writes the entire word, supplying the missing vowel(s).

3. *Write missing consonants.* The student is shown the word with blanks where the consonants usually appear. The student writes the entire word, supplying the missing consonant(s).

4. *Write the word.* The student writes the word without the model.

The Fernald method. Fernald (1943) felt that most spelling approaches were useful for the extremely visual student but not for those students who need auditory and kinesthetic input for learning. Because poor spellers are characterized by poor visual imagery, many may need to be taught through multisensory approaches such as the Fernald method.

According to Fernald (1943), specific school techniques that tend to produce *poor* spellers include:

1. Formal spelling periods in which children move through a series of practice lessons, writing, and taking dictation with little time to think about how the word is spelled before writing it.

2. Focus on misspellings and spelling errors because it builds a negative attitude toward spelling.

A brief description of the Fernald approach to teaching spelling includes the following procedures:

1. The teacher writes the word to be learned on the chalkboard or paper. The word can be selected from the spelling book or by the child.

2. The teacher pronounces the word clearly. The student repeats the pronunciation of the word while looking at the word. This is repeated several times.

3. The teacher allows time for the student to study the word for later recall. If the student is a kinesthetic learner, the teacher writes the word in crayon and has the student trace the letters of the word with his or her finger. Fernald found that tracing is necessary in learning to spell only when the spelling difficulty is coupled with a reading disability.

4. Remove the word and have the student write it from memory.

5. The student turns the paper over and writes the word a second time.

6. The teacher creates opportunities for the student to use the word in his or her written expression.

7. The teacher gives written, not oral, spelling drills.

In contrast with Fernald's approach, which recommends not focusing on the student's errors and suggests blocking out errors immediately, other researchers have found some support for a spelling strategy that emphasizes imitation of students' errors plus modeling (Kauffman,

Hallahan, Haas, Brame, and Boren, 1978; Nulman and Gerber, 1984). Using the imitation plus model strategy, the teacher erases the misspelled word and imitates the child's error by writing it on the board. The teacher then writes it correctly with the student and asks the student to compare what he or she wrote with the correct spelling of the word.

The Gillingham and Stillman approach. According to Gillingham and Stillman (1973), "spelling is the translation of sounds into letter names (oral spelling) or into letter forms (written spelling)" (p. 52). Spelling is taught by using the following procedure:

1. The teacher says the word very slowly and distinctly and the student repeats the word after the teacher. This is referred to as *echo speech*.

2. The student is asked what sound is heard first. This process continues with all of the letters in the words. This is referred to as oral *spelling*.

3. The student is asked to locate the letter card with the first letter of the word on it and then write the letter. The student continues with this process until the cards for each letter are found, placed in order, and written. This is referred to as *written spelling*.

4. The student reads the word.

When writing the word, the student orally spells the word letter by letter. This establishes visual auditory-kinesthetic association.

Correctional procedures in the Gillingham and Stillman approach include:

1. The student checks his or her own written word and finds errors.

2. If a word is read incorrectly, the student should spell what he or she said and match it with the original word.

3. If a word is misspelled orally, the teacher writes what the student spelled and asks him or her to read it, or the teacher may repeat the pronunciation of the original word.

The Constant Time Delay Procedure. The time delay procedure is a method designed to reduce error in instruction. Stevens and Schuster (1987) applied the procedure this way:

1. The verbal cue, ''Spell _____ (target word)'', is immediately followed with a printed model of the target word to be copied by the student.

2. After several trials in which there is no time delay between asking a child to spell a word and providing a model of the word, a five-second delay is introduced. This allows the child to write the word, or part of the word, if they know it, but does not require them to wait very long if they are unable to correctly write the word.

3. The amount of time between the request to spell the word and the presentation of the model can be increased after several more trials.

The time delay procedure has been effective with a learning-disabled student and has several advantages as a spelling instructional method. It is a simple procedure that is easy to implement. It is fun for the student because it provides for nearly errorless instruction.

Self-Questioning Strategy for Teaching Spelling. Wong (1986) has developed the following self-questioning strategy for teaching spelling.

1. Do I know this word? *(location)*
2. How many syllables do I hear in this word? (3)
3. Write the word the way you think it is spelled.
4. Do you have the right number of syllables?
5. Underline any part of the word that you are not sure how to spell.
6. Check to see if it is correct. If it is not correct, underline the part of the word that is not correct and write it again.

7. When you have finished, tell yourself you have been a good worker.

Handwriting

Often described as the most poorly taught subject in elementary curriculum, handwriting is usually thought of as the least important. Unfortunately, handwriting difficulties provide barriers to efficient work production and influence grades received from teachers (Briggs, 1970; Markham, 1976). Many students dislike the entire writing process because they find the actual motor skill involved in handwriting so laborious.

Despite the use of word processors, typewriters, and other devices that can facilitate the writing process, handwriting is still an important skill. Taking notes in class, filling out forms, and success on the job often require legible, fluent writing.

Manuscript and Cursive Writing

Traditionally, most students learn manuscript writing first and then, in about second or third grade, make the transition to cursive writing. Although this procedure seems to be effective for most students, many learning-disabled students have difficulty with the transition from one writing form to another. Many learning-disabled specialists advocate the use of instruction in only one form of handwriting, either manuscript or cursive. Some argue that manuscript is easier to learn, is more like book print, is more legible, requires less difficulty in making movement (Johnson and Myklebust, 1967), and should be the only writing form taught. Others feel cursive is faster, is continuous and connected, is more difficult to reverse letters, teaches the student to perceive whole words, and is easier to write. They feel cursive should be taught first as the only writing form. (See Table 6.1 for a summary of manuscript vs. cursive.) The greater bulk of evidence appears to be in the direction of teaching learning-disabled students to use manuscript effectively and neatly, with the exception of learning to write their name in cursive. For most learning-disabled students with hand-writing difficulties, manuscript should be taught in the early years and maintained throughout the educational program. Some learning-disabled students can and want to make the transition to cursive and benefit from its instruction. On some occasions, students who have struggled with manuscript writing feel learning cursive is "grown up" and thus respond well to the introduction of a new writing form.

Reversals

When five-year-old Abe signed his name on notes to his grandmother, he often reversed the direction of the *b* in his name. When writing other letters he would often write them backwards or upside down. His mother was very concerned because she worried that it might be an indication that Abe was dyslexic or having reading problems. Many parents are concerned when their children make reversals and often their alarmed response frightens their children. Most children, age five and younger, make reversals when writing letters and numbers. Reversals made by students before the age of six or seven are not an indication that the student is learning-disabled or dyslexic and are rarely cause for concern.

Information teachers should have about reversals includes:

1. Reversals are common before the age of six or seven. Teachers should provide correctional procedures for school-age students who are reversing letters and numbers but should not become overly concerned.

2. A few students after the age of seven continue to reverse numbers and letters and may need direct intervention techniques.

For those students who persist in reversing letters and numbers, the following direct instructional techniques may be helpful.

1. The teacher traces the letter and talks aloud about the characteristics of the letter, asking the students to model the teacher's procedure. For example, while tracing the letter *d* the teacher says, "First I make a stick starting at the top of the page and going down, and then I put a ball in front of the stick." The student is asked to follow the same procedure and to talk aloud while tracing the letter. Next, the student is asked to do the same procedure, this time drawing the letter. Finally, the student is asked to draw the letter and say the process to himself or herself.

Tracing letters is a frequently used method of improving legibility; however, there is little research that suggests tracing is an effective method of teaching letter formation. Hirsch and Niedermeyer (1973) found that copying is a more effective technique for teaching letter formation than tracing.

2. The teacher and the student can develop a mnemonic picture device that helps the student recall the direction of the letter. For example, with a student who is reversing the direction of the letter *p,* the teacher might say, "What letter does the word *pie* begin with? That's right, *pie* begins with the letter *p*. Now watch me draw *p*. Drawing the straight line, the teacher says, "This is my straight line before I eat pie, then after I eat pie my stomach swells in front of me. Whenever you make *p* you can think of pie and how your stomach gets big after you eat it, and that will help you make a *p* the right way." This procedure can be repeated several times, with the student drawing the letter and talking through the mnemonic device. Different mnemonic devices can be developed to correspond with the specific letter or number reversal(s) of the child.

The next section focuses on teaching handwriting, including discussions on posture, pencil grip, position of the paper, and legibility and fluency in writing. Specific instructional techniques such as the Hanover approach and Hagin's Write Right-or-Left are also discussed.

FIGURE 6.11 *Letter Formation Strategies*

Fauke Approach (Fauke et al., 1973)

1. The teacher writes the letter, and the student and teacher discuss the formational act.
2. The student names the letter.
3. The student traces the letter with a finger, pencil, and magic marker.
4. The student's finger traces a letter form made of yarn.
5. The student copies the letter.
6. The student writes the letter from memory.
7. The teacher rewards the student for correctly writing the letter.

Progressive Approximation Approach (Hofmeister, 1973)

1. The student copies the letter using a pencil.
2. The teacher examines the letter and, if necessary, corrects by overmarking with a highlighter.
3. The student erases incorrect portions of the letter and traces over the teacher's highlighter marking.
4. The student repeats steps 1–3 until the letter is written correctly.

Furner Approach (Furner, 1969a, 1969b, 1970)

1. The student and teacher establish a purpose for the lesson.
2. The teacher provides the student with many guided exposures to the letter.
3. The student describes the process while writing the letter and tries to write or visualize the letter as another child describes it.

4. The teacher uses multisensory stimulation to teach the letter form.
5. The student compares his or her written response to a model.

VAKT Approach

1. The teacher writes the letter with crayon while the student observes the process.
2. The teacher and student both say the name of the letter.
3. The student traces the letter with the index finger, simultaneously saying the name of the letter. This is done successfully five times.
4. The student copies and names the letter successfully three times.
5. Without a visual aid, the student writes and names the letter correctly three times.

Niedermeyer Approach (Niedermeyer, 1973)

1. The student traces a dotted representation of the letter 12 times.
2. The student copies the letter 12 times.
3. The student writes the letter as the teacher pronounces it.

Handwriting with Write and See (Skinner & Krakower, 1968)

The student traces a letter within a tolerance model on specially prepared paper. If the student forms the letter correctly, the pen writes gray; if it is incorrect, the pen writes yellow.

Source: S. Graham and L. Miller, "Handwriting Research and Practice: A Unified Approach," *Focus on Exceptional Children* (1980):11. Reprinted with permission.

Teaching Handwriting

Teaching handwriting requires the teacher to assess, model, and teach letter formation, spacing, and fluency as well as posture, pencil grip, and position of the paper. A brief description follows of these important components to an effective handwriting program.

Legibility. Legibility is the most important goal of handwriting instruction, and incorrect letter formation the most frequent interference. The following four letters account for about 50 percent of all malformed letters at any grade level: *a, e, r,* and *t* (Newland, 1932). Spacing between letters, words, and margins, connecting lines, and closing and crossing of letters (e.g., *t, x*) also influence legibility (Kirk and Chalfant, 1984).

The following remedial procedures for teaching letter formation are suggested by Graham and Miller (1980):

1. Modeling
2. Noting critical attributes (comparing and contrasting letters)

3. Physical prompts and cues (physically moving the student's hand or using cues such as arrows or colored dots)
4. Reinforcement (providing specific reinforcement for letters or parts of letters formed correctly, and corrective feedback for letters that need work)
5. Self-verbalization (saying aloud the letter formation and then verbalizing it to self while writing)
6. Writing from memory
7. Repetition

A summary of approaches to teaching letter formation is presented in Figure 6.11.

Fluency. Nine-year-old Marta's handwriting has improved considerably during the past year. She and her teacher have identified letters that were not formed correctly and Marta has learned to write these letters so they are legible. Now that her handwriting is easier to read, the teacher realizes Marta has another handwriting problem. In the regular classroom Marta has difficulty taking notes and writing down assignments that are given orally, because she is a very slow writer. She needs to learn writing fluency, which is the ability to write quickly and with ease without undue attention to letter formation. Marta's teacher decides to teach fluency by gradually increasing expectations about the speed at which letter formation occurs. Marta selects two paragraphs and is told to write them as quickly as she can while still maintaining good letter formation. The teacher times her in this procedure. They decide to keep a graph of her progress by indicating the time it takes her each day to write the two paragraphs legibly. Marta found the graphing of her progress very reinforcing (see Figure 6.12 and Apply the Concept 6.11). Since Marta's fluency problems were not just for copying but also for writing from dictation, her teacher implemented the same program, this time requiring Marta to time herself on oral dictations.

Posture, Pencil Grip, and Position of the Paper. Many students have handwriting problems because they do not correctly perform three important components of the handwriting process.

Posture. The hips should touch the back of the chair and the feet should rest on the floor. The torso leans forward slightly, in a straight line, with both forearms resting on the desk and elbows slightly extended.

Pencil grip. The pencil should be held lightly between the thumb and first two fingers, about one inch above the point. The first finger rests on top of the pencil. The back of the pencil points in the direction of the shoulder and rests near the large knuckle of the middle finger.

Position of the paper. When writing manuscript, the paper should be in front of the student. For a righthander, the left hand holds the paper in place, moving it when necessary. In writing cursive, the paper is slanted counterclockwise for a righthander and clockwise for a lefthander.

Instructional Principles. The following instructional principles are suggested for any effective handwriting program.

1. Direct instruction.
2. Individualized instruction.
3. A variety of techniques and methods are used, matching the students' individual needs.
4. Handwriting is taught frequently, several times a week.
5. Short handwriting lessons are taught within the context of the students' writing.
6. Handwriting skills are overlearned in isolation and then applied in context and periodically checked.
7. Students evaluate their own handwriting and, when appropriate, the handwriting of others.

FIGURE 6.12   *Marta's Fluency*

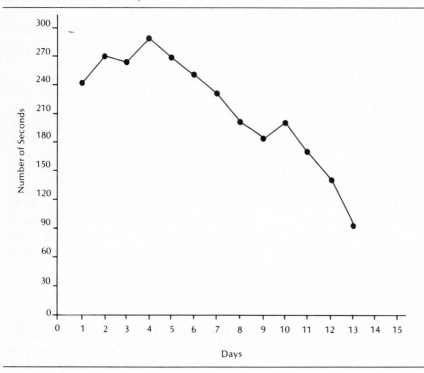

8. The teacher's handwriting is a model for the students to follow.
9. Teach handwriting not just as a visual or a motor task, but as both (Hagin, 1983).

Self-instructional strategies can be taught to students to improve their handwriting (Graham, 1983; Kosiewicz, Hallahan, Lloyd, and Graves, 1982). The self-instructional procedure that was used in the Graham (1983) study was based on a cognitive-behavioral model. The six-step procedure follows:

Step 1: The teacher models the writing of the target letter and describes the formation of the letter. The student then describes the formation of the letter. This step is repeated three times.

Step 2: The teacher writes the letter while describing the process. This continues until the student can recite the process for writing the letter.

Step 3: The student traces the letter and the teacher and the student recite the process of the letter formation together.

Step 4: The teacher writes the letter, traces it, and then verbally discusses the process, including corrections (e.g., "My letter is too slanted.") then provides self-reinforcement (e.g., "Now, that looks a lot better."). The procedure continues with and without errors, until the student can model the process.

Step 5: The teacher writes the letter and the student copies it while defining the process and providing self-correction. The

Apply the Concept 6.11

OBTAINING A FLUENCY SAMPLE

The following procedures can be used to obtain a fluency sample:

1. The student becomes familiar with the test sentence.
2. The teacher tells the student to write the test sentence·a designated number of times at his or her usual rate (two-to three-minute sample).

3. After relaxing, have the student write the sentence as well and as neatly as he or she can.
4. After relaxing, have the student write the sentence as quickly and as many times as he or she can in three minutes.
5. After relaxing, the student and the teacher repeat this process with the dictated sentence.

---

student needs to complete this process successfully three times before moving to step 6.

Step 6: The student writes the letter from memory.

Following are several methods devised for teaching students who have handwriting difficulties.

Write Right-or-Left. Hagin (1983) suggests a process for teaching cursive that is based on manuscript and the vertical stroke learned in manuscript. In Hagin's *Write Right-or-Left* approach, the student learns cursive writing in the following manner:

1. The student learns motifs, which form the foundation for later letter formation. These motifs are taught and practiced on the chalkboard. See Figure 6.13 for an illustration of the motifs and the letters that correspond with them.

2. After the motifs are learned at the chalkboard, the student learns and practices the letters associated with each of the motifs at the chalkboard.

3. At the desk, the student traces the letters while verbal cues as to letter direction and formation are given by the teacher.

4. In this step the student writes the letters without a model.

5. Through matching, the student compares the model with the product produced in step 4. Both the teacher and the student give feedback and determine whether additional practice is needed before the next step.

6. The student writes a permanent record of the letters that have been mastered.

The Hanover Method. Hanover's method (1983) of teaching cursive writing is founded on a single principle—the grouping of letters based on similar strokes into letter families. The letter families include:

b, o, v, w	This family has a handle to which the next letter is attached.
n, s, y	This family is grouped together to emphasize the correct formation of hump-shaped letters.
e, l, h, f, b, k	This is the *e* family and is taught first.
c, a, d, o, q, g	This is the *c* family.
n, m, v, y, x	This is the hump family.
f, q	This family has tails in the back.
g, p, y, z	This family has tails in the front.

Some letters are included in more than one group. According to this approach, cursive let-

FIGURE 6.13   *Write Right-or-Left: Learning Motifs*

Ferry boats

Teaches smooth movements across the page.

Waves

Foundation for the letters a, c, d, g, and q

Pearls

Foundation for the letters e, i, h, j, m, n, u, y, and z

Wheels

Foundation for the letters o, v, b, w, and x

Arrows

Foundation for the letters k, l, t, r, and f

Source: Adapted from R. A. Hagin, ''Write Right or Left: A Practical Approach to Handwriting,'' *Journal of Learning Disabilities,* 16(5) (1983):266–271.

ters are learned faster and easier when they are taught in their grouped families because of the similar strokes within the groups.

Teaching Handwriting at the High-School Level. Handwriting often becomes important in the junior-high and high-school period because of the emphasis on taking notes and submitting written assignments. Many students have found that although the content of their assignment is correct they have lost points or were given a lower grade because their handwriting is difficult to read. Teaching handwriting to older students

is difficult because the immediate needs of most older students are content-related and it is often difficult for the teacher to justify instructional time for handwriting, and because most materials for handwriting instruction are developed for younger students and are insulting to high-school students. The teacher needs to evaluate carefully the handwriting problems of the students to determine if handwriting instruction could be helpful in a relatively short period of time, or if the students should learn compensatory methods such as typing or word processing. The two most important criteria for evaluating handwriting at the high-school level are legibility and fluency.

In selecting curriculum for older students, specific attention should be given to the students' letter formation and fluency within context. Corrective feedback, short trace and copy exercises, and content exercises that require little thinking and allow the students to concentrate on letter formation and fluency should be emphasized when teaching handwriting to older students (Ruedy, 1983).

Instructional Activities

Appendix B provides instructional activities that are related to written expression, including spelling and handwriting. Some of the activities teach new skills; others are best suited for practice and reinforcement of already acquired skills. For each activity, the objective, materials, and teaching procedures are described.

Summary

Students start school feeling confident they know how to write. It is not uncommon to see young children writing notes to grandparents and other significant persons, making up letters and words as they go along, assured they are able to communicate in print. Most of these same students later find expressing themselves in writing one of the most difficult tasks required of them in school. The chapter described a process approach to writing instruction and discussed how to teach spelling and handwriting skills as aids to written expression. The assumption underlying the writing process approach presented in this chapter is that all children know something, and writing gives them the opportunity to share what they know. This approach has potential with students who have learning and behavior problems, as it focuses on writing from their own experiences and feelings, allowing them a systematic process for interacting with peers and teachers and providing consistent opportunities to write and receive feedback.

This chapter presented procedures for starting the writing process approach, including a description of materials needed, skills taught through the process approach, and the teacher as writer, modeling through writing and sharing with students. The elements of the writing process approach, which include prewriting, composing, revising, editing, and publishing were defined, and examples were presented of how they are taught and integrated into the writing process approach with students who have learning and behavior problems. Guidelines for conducting effective writing conferences, the key to successful writing, were described, and examples of students conferring with each other as well as with the teacher were provided.

In addition to describing the writing process as an approach to written expression, this chapter discussed how to teach spelling and handwriting skills to students with learning and behavior problems. Most of those students need direct instruction in spelling and handwriting, and this chapter provided specific instructional techniques that have been successful. Since effective spelling instruction begins with understanding the types of spelling errors the student makes, how to conduct an error analysis in spelling was presented. Principles for teaching spelling to students with learning difficulties were discussed and spelling approaches were presented.

The handwriting section of the chapter discussed the advantages and disadvantages of teaching manuscript and/or cursive, as well as information all teachers should know about reversals. Approaches to teaching handwriting were also presented.

Chapter Seven

Content Area Learning and Study Skills

Chapter Questions

- *Why is it difficult for students with learning problems to succeed in content area classes in secondary schools?*
- *What is a content analysis? Select a chapter from a content area text and complete a content analysis.*
- *What is "considerate" text? Using the ideas in the section on "Evaluating the Considerateness of Instructional Materials," select a text and evaluate it for considerateness and appropriateness for your students.*
- *Explain the difference between a concept diagram, a semantic map, and a relationship chart. Select a chapter and develop each of these instructional aids for the chapter. Compare the differences and similarities.*
- *What should you include in a unit on self-management? Plan the unit for a group of students with learning and behavior problems.*
- *What are the characteristics of listener-friendly lectures? Plan a lecture that is listener-friendly.*
- *What should teachers keep in mind when they are adapting a textbook? Select a chapter from a text and adapt it for students with learning and behavior problems.*

When Ms. Chou moved from her elementary resource room job to a high-school resource position, her experience and education in teaching learning strategies and writing process served her well for part of the school day. However, in addition to the two English periods she teaches daily, she is also expected to teach sections of American history and American government to students with learning and behavior problems. Although she minored in political science and history in college, she feels as if her content knowledge is rusty in these areas and her techniques for teaching content information are limited. She has also been asked to teach a section of general science, but she has chosen to team-teach the class with a science teacher, because of her limited content knowledge.

When Desmond entered Bailey Junior High School, he had been receiving help in a special education resource room since second grade. For the past three years Mrs. Jackson, the resource room teacher, has been working with Desmond on word identification and basic comprehension skills as well as spelling and writing compositions. In elementary school, Desmond went to the resource room for forty-five minutes every afternoon. For the last three years he consistently missed either social studies or science in the regular classroom while he was receiving special assistance in the resource room.

Desmond is not prepared for the demands of junior high. He attends resource English and reading but has social studies, science, and home economics classes in the mainstream with regular education students. All of these classes require him to listen to lectures in class and take notes, read chapters filled with technical vocabulary and answer the questions at the end of each section, take timed tests, write reports, and keep track of assignments and turn them in on time. By the end of the first nine weeks, Desmond is receiving failing slips in all three classes. He is frustrated by his classes and is becoming disruptive.

Doreen worked hard in high school and, despite her reading and writing disabilities, graduated with a high enough grade point average to enter college. However, as a freshman in a large university, she is finding herself overwhelmed by the demands of her classes. She is barely passing freshman English and classical literature and is even struggling in her math and science courses—areas that were her strengths in high school. Doreen can't seem to get organized. She has difficulty estimating how long it will take her to complete an assignment, and she is unable to keep up with the reading assignments in literature class. Doreen is a bright student with good potential to succeed as an architect or engineer, but she may never get through the basic liberal arts courses required for her degree.

Both Desmond and Doreen need strategies to assist them in being more effective learners. They need study skills in managing their time, organizing their notebooks, taking notes, studying for tests, taking tests, reading textbooks, learning new vocabulary, and writing reports and essays. Desmond and Doreen have mastered many of the basic reading and writing skills, but they are having difficulty applying these skills in content area classes.

Ms. Chou, Desmond, and Doreen are experiencing difficulties functioning in the secondary and postsecondary school environments. In these environments the task demands for teachers and students change dramatically. The special education teacher often teaches content subjects or needs to provide content area teachers with learning and teaching strategies to facilitate learning content area information. The students are asked to apply learning strategies and study skills as well as basic skills in listening, reading, writing, and math, in order to learn content area subjects such as biology, American history, welding, wood shop, and home economics (Schumaker and Deshler, 1984).

Link (1980) surveyed 133 secondary and upper elementary teachers and administrators

FIGURE 7.1 *Academic Skills Rated as Most Essential for Adequate Classroom Performance*

1. Follow oral and written directions.
2. Make logical deductions.
3. Read at grade level.
4. Recall information for tests.
5. Locate answers to questions.
6. Turn in assignments on time.
7. Ask relevant questions.
8. Clearly express ideas in writing.
9. Locate information in textbooks.
10. Participate in discussions.

Source: Adapted from D. Link, *Essential Learning Skills and the Low Achieving Student at the Secondary Level: A Rating of the Importance of 24 Academic Abilities.* Unpublished master's thesis, University of Kansas, Lawrence, Kansas, 1980.

and asked them to rank twenty-four academic skills on a 1–7 Likert scale. The top ten skills are presented in Figure 7.1. These skills reflect study skills rather than basic skills in reading and writing. Students with learning and behavior problems often need instruction in such study skills.

This chapter focuses on strategies for teaching content area subjects and study skills. The chapter is divided into two sections. First, we will look at teaching techniques and strategies a teacher might use to assist low-achieving students learning content area information, particularly the wealth of new concepts and related vocabulary associated with classes in social studies, science, and vocational education. Next, we will examine methods of teaching students to be more effective and efficient learners.

Although the focus of this chapter is on teaching and learning strategies for secondary and postsecondary level students, many of the techniques presented are appropriate for upper elementary students. Both students and teachers alike have commented that using such techniques in upper elementary grades would greatly facilitate low-achieving students in secondary settings.

Teaching Content Area Information

If you are going to teach content, whether it be in courses of home economics, history, auto mechanics, biology, or government, then one of your major tasks is to teach the important concepts and their relationships. *Concepts* are general ideas that are associated with smaller but related ideas (Anders and Bos, 1984).

The following concept might be used in a science course:

> "Bacteria are very small living things that help people, other animals, and plants; however, bacteria also do things that hurt people, other animals, and plants" (Anders and Bos, 1984, p. 54).

This generalization encompasses several related ideas. For example:

> Bacteria are tiny; you use a microscope to see them; bacteria multiply; bacteria can make you ill; bacteria can spoil food.

The vocabulary associated with the general concept and its related concepts is the *conceptual vocabulary.* They are the words that are necessary for understanding the general idea and are associated with it. Examples of the conceptual vocabulary for the bacteria concept are: *bacteria, microscope, colony, multiply, reproduce,* and *decay.* These words and their meanings facilitate understanding of the overall, general concept.

A Process for Teaching Concepts

A six-step process can be used to teach concepts and their labels. The first step in teaching content area information is deciding what concepts and related conceptual vocabulary to teach. Admittedly, some concepts and vocabulary are more important than others. Deciding what concepts

FIGURE 7.2   *A Process for Teaching Concepts*

A six-step process can be used to teach concepts and their labels:

1. Decide what concepts and related conceptual vocabulary to teach.
2. Evaluate the instructional materials to be used for "considerateness."
3. Assess the students' background knowledge for these concepts and related vocabulary.
4. Utilize prelearning or prereading activities to facilitate learning.
5. Conduct the learning or reading activity.
6. Provide postlearning activities that further reinforce the concepts and information learned.

and labels to teach is a crucial part of content area teaching. The six-step process is presented in Figure 7.2 and discussed in more detail in the following sections.

Step One: Selecting the Concepts and Related Vocabulary

The first step in getting ready to teach content information is selecting the major concepts and related vocabulary to be taught, and generating a framework for facilitating understanding of the ideas to be learned. Schema theory would suggest that teaching content area information is teaching the scaffolding or relationships between the concepts as well as teaching the slots or concepts themselves.

Selecting the major concepts and related vocabulary to be taught in a unit, a chapter, a section of a book, or a lecture needs to be completed prior to having the students interact with the material (Bos and Anders, 1990; Lenz, Bulgren, and Hudson, 1990). As the teacher, you need to determine the conceptual framework for the unit so that the information might be presented in an organized fashion based on this framework.

The process a teacher uses for determining the major concepts depends on his or her expertise and knowledge in the content area. A teacher who has specialized in a given content area can

probably generate concepts from personal knowledge and experiences. Such a teacher could use the assigned textbook as the primary resource for verifying the appropriateness of those concepts. A teacher with limited background knowledge could use a variety of resources for determining the concepts, such as the assigned textbooks, trade books, state or local curriculum guides, and other teachers or experts in the field. Some texts—especially those written for students with reading problems—tend to include too much detail and fail to explain the overall concept or to relate the concepts (Anders and Mitchell, 1980; Armbruster and Anderson, 1988; Scanlon and Anders, 1988).

Generally, a concept is best understood by the students when it is articulated to the point that it can be stated in a complete sentence. Some examples of content area concepts from an eighth-grade social studies unit are:

1. The culture found in the Southwest has roots in the cultures of Spain and Mexico.
2. The Spanish conquered Mexico because they wanted the riches they thought would be found there.
3. The priests were, in part, responsible for changing the lifestyle of the Indians (Estes and Vaughn, 1978, p. 419).

After articulating the major concepts to be learned, you next generate and organize the related vocabulary. To do this, study the assigned text and instructional materials and compile a list of relevant related words and phrases from the text. As you read, you may realize that some important vocabulary is missing from the text; if so, add it to the list.

To organize the list of vocabulary, group words that are related together. Then create a semantic or content map to visually represent the relationships among these terms. Figure 7.3 depicts a map developed with the conceptual vocabulary a teacher generated from a chapter in a biology text. The map highlights the critical vocabulary and the organization and relationships

FIGURE 7.3   *A Content Map of a Biology Chapter on Mollusks*

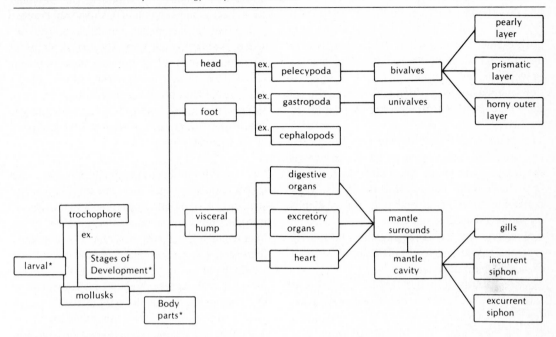

*Note: There seem to be two concepts being developed (apologies to the biologists among us):
   1 When classifying animals biologists look for relationships between animals during the various stages of development from birth to adulthood.
   2 Biologists describe the body parts of animals and the functions of each part.

Source: P. L. Anders and C. S. Bos, "In the Beginning: Vocabulary Instruction in Content Classes," *Topics in Learning and Learning Disabilities,* 3(4) (1984):56. Reprinted with permission of Pro-Ed.

of the concepts (Anders and Bos, 1984; Lenz and Bulgren, in press). The most important or encompassing concept should appear nearest the concept statement in the map. These concepts are likely to be the most important information to cover to assure understanding, and should be taught unless they are already known by the students.

The map helps to solve an all too common problem that confronts content area teachers: deciding what concepts and related vocabulary to teach in a content lesson. So many possibilities exist for any given concept that there simply is not enough time to teach every word associated with a concept. McKeown and Beck (1988) suggest that in addition to using the criterion of

importance in relation to understanding the major concepts, the teacher may also want to consider general utility, relationship to other lessons and classroom events, and relationship to the specific domain of knowledge.

Step Two: Evaluating the Considerateness of the Instructional Materials

Before teaching the concepts and related vocabulary, teachers need to evaluate the instructional materials they intend to use in teaching the unit. Within the last decade educators have become much more interested in the characteristics of instructional materials. They have concentrated on textbooks, because textbooks still continue to be the predominant medium of instruction (Goodlad, 1976; Muther, 1985). How concepts are presented in a text will affect how easily they are comprehended by the students. The manner in which the text is organized (e.g., use of headings and subheadings, highlighted words, marginal notes) will also affect comprehensibility of the text.

Traditionally, emphasis in evaluating content area texts was placed on the readability of the text as determined by readability formulas (e.g., Dale and Chall, 1948; Fry, 1977). Most readability formulas, including the Fry readability formula presented in Figure 7.4, are based on two factors: sentence complexity as measured by sentence length and word difficulty as indexed by word length or frequency.

Readability formulas should be used cautiously and as only one aspect of evaluating a text for several reasons. First, the typical standard error of measurement for readability formulas is plus or minus approximately 1.5 grade levels (Singer and Donlan, 1989). Consequently, a text whose readability formula is predicted as 7.5 by chance can range from 6.0 to 9.0. Second, readability formulas do not take into account many characteristics of *text* that are important in comprehension and learning. For example, to reduce readability as measured by readability formulas, textbooks and, particularly, adapted textbooks that are designed for students with learning and behavior problems are written using short sentences. Oftentimes this means that important relational words such as *and, or, because,* and *if...then* have been eliminated to shorten the length of the sentences, and consequently reduce the readability level as predicted by the formula. However, it is these relational words that signal the reader to the relationships among the concepts (Davison, 1984). Consequently, although the readability according to the formula may be reduced, the text is actually more difficult to understand. Third, readability formulas neglect to consider the characteristics of the *reader* that

affect comprehension, including interest, purpose, background knowledge, and perseverance.

What characteristics should be considered when evaluating the considerateness or user-friendliness of text? Armbruster and Anderson (1988) have conducted a program of research to develop salient criteria for determining the considerate text. Their criteria fall into three broad categories: structure, coherence, and audience appropriateness.

1. *Structure* refers to the manner in which the text is organized and how the text signals its structure. Use of titles, headings, subheadings, introductions, and summary statements, informative and relevant pictures, charts, and graphs, highlighted key concepts, marginal notes, and signaling words (e.g., *first, second, then, therefore*) can facilitate comprehension. In evaluating the text, it is important not only to check if such structural features are used, but if they match the content. For example, sometimes headings will not relate well to the text contained under the headings. In this case, the structural features may serve more as a source of confusion than as an aide. Also, check to see if the highlighted words in the text represent the important concepts or simply the words that are difficult to decode. In the latter case, using these words as signals for understanding would not necessarily facilitate comprehension.

Also, consider how the text that you are evaluating is situated in the textbook. Do the format and the Table of Contents assist the reader in drawing relationships between the various chapters by using such devices as sections and subsections? Do introductions to each section or chapter encourage the reader to draw connections between previous ideas and concepts already discussed and the new ideas to be presented?

2. *Coherence* refers to how well "the ideas in a text stick together" (Armbruster and Anderson, 1984, p. 48). With coherent text the relationships among concepts are clear. For

FIGURE 7.4 *Fry Readability Graph. Graph for Estimating Readability—Extended*

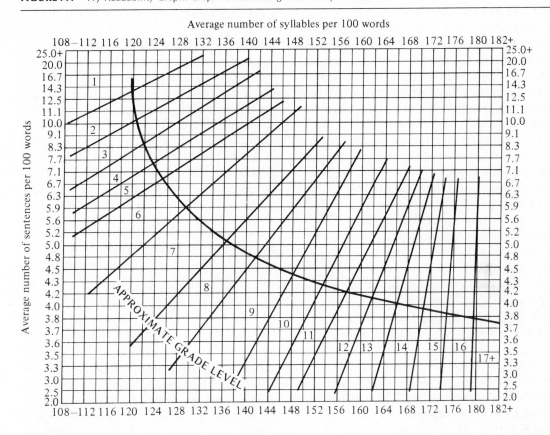

1. Randomly select three text samples of exactly 100 words, beginning with the beginning of a sentence. Count proper nouns, numerals, and initializations as words.
2. Count the number of sentences in each 100-word sample, estimating the length of the last sentence to the nearest one-tenth.
3. Count the total number of syllables in each 100-word sample. Count one syllable for each numeral or initial or symbol; for example, 1990 is one word and four syllables, LD is one word and two syllables, and "&" is one word and one syllable.
4. Average the number of sentences and number of syllables across the three samples.
5. Enter the average sentence length and average number of syllables on the graph. Plot a dot where the two lines intersect. The area in which the dot is plotted will give you an approximate estimated readability level.
6. If there is a great deal of variability in the syllable or sentence count across the three samples, more samples can be added.

Source: Edward Fry, "Fry's readability graph: clarifications, validity, and extension to level 17." *Journal of Reading, 21* (1977):242–252. Reproduction permitted—no copyright.

example, when Herman, Anderson, Pearson and Nagy (1987) rewrote text about the circulatory system and made explicit the connections between motive and action, form and function, and cause and effect, student learning improved. Coherence is also facilitated by using different kinds of *cohesive ties*—linguistic forms that help convey meaning across phrase, clause, and sentence boundaries (Halliday and Hassan, 1976). Examples of cohesive ties are *conjunctions* and *connectives, pronoun referents* (using a pronoun to refer to a previously mentioned noun), and *substitutions* (using a word to replace a previously used noun or verb phrase). Textbooks that use list-like formats such as some of those found in vocational education courses do not fare well in terms of coherence (Scanlon and Anders, 1988).

3. *Audience appropriateness* refers to how well the textbook is suited to the readers' content knowledge and reading and study skills. The text needs to provide enough explanation, attributes, examples, and analogies to provide readers with adequate information to relate to their background knowledge. Superficial mentioning of new topics for which the reader has limited background knowledge does little to build understanding. On the other hand, too many or too technical supporting details can obscure the important concepts.

Another area to consider with relation to the audience is the explicitness of main ideas. As was discussed in the chapters on reading (Chapters 4 and 5), many students with learning and behavior problems have difficulty identifying and comprehending the main ideas of a text. Therefore, text in which the main ideas are explicit and regularly placed at the beginning of paragraphs and sections should facilitate learning. However, Baumann and Serra (1984) in examining social studies textbooks designed for the second, fourth, sixth, and eighth grades found that only 27 percent of the short passages contained explicitly stated main ideas, only 44 per-

cent of the paragraphs contained them, and only 27 percent of the paragraphs began with them.

Part of the process of preparing to teach content knowledge is evaluating the instructional materials to be used. By considering the criteria of structure, cohesion, and audience appropriateness in evaluating text or other types of instructional materials (e.g., films, lectures, demonstrations), the teacher develops a good idea of the ''considerateness'' or ''user-friendliness'' of the materials. Based on this evaluation, the teacher may decide to modify, augment, or adapt the instructional materials.

Step Three: Assessing Students' Prior Knowledge of Concepts and Vocabulary

Before content area teachers assign a specific chapter to read or present a lecture on a topic, they need to assess the students' background knowledge for the concepts and related vocabulary to be covered. In special education we often spend a substantial amount of time assessing the skill level of students in reading, writing, and math. However, we spend much less time assessing students' knowledge of a topic. Research in schema theory indicates that prior knowledge plays a critical role in determining how effectively students will comprehend the information and vocabulary to be presented (Anderson, Reynolds, Schallert, and Goetz, 1977; Stahl, Jacobson, Davis, and Davis, 1989). One technique for assessing prior knowledge is using the prereading plan with which you are familiar (see Chapter Five). The prereading plan not only assesses students' knowledge, but also serves to activate this knowledge, thus facilitating comprehension.

A second procedure that can be used to assess and activate students' background knowledge is semantic mapping (Johnson, Pittelman, and Heimlich, 1986; Pearson and Johnson, 1978). Like PReP, this technique uses free association as a stimulus activity to generate a list of words and phrases related to the key concept. The teacher and students take the associations given by the students and relate them to the key concept, developing a network that notes the various relations (e.g., class, example, property). A semantic map for the concept of ''desert'' was developed with a group of fifth-grade learning-disabled students preparing to study deserts, using the free associations they gave. The map, shown in Figure 7.5, indicates that the students can give examples and properties or characteristics of a desert. However, the students did not produce any superordinate class relations, for example ''type of geographical region.'' Additionally, the property and example relations that were generated lacked technical vocabulary despite further probing on the part of the teacher. The semantic map in Figure 7.5 serves not only as a visual representation for the students' current understanding of the concept of deserts, but the map also functions as a blueprint for teaching. Further development of the map can guide the teacher and students in organizing information about deserts and other types of geographical regions (Anders and Bos, 1984).

Based on assessment information from such procedures as PReP or semantic mapping, decisions can be made as to the necessity of providing further prelearning activities.

Step Four: Utilizing Prelearning Activities

Limited background knowledge signals the teacher that students need more instruction to learn the information that will be presented in the text or lecture. This section discusses several prelearning activities—advance organizers, semantic feature analysis, semantic mapping, and concept diagrams—that students can use before reading an assigned text or listening to a lecture.

Advance Organizers

The concept of advance organizers was introduced by Ausubel in the 1960s. He defined an advance organizer as information that is presented ''in advance of and at a higher level of generality, inclusiveness, and abstraction than

FIGURE 7.5   *Semantic Map of Learning-Disabled Student's Concept of Deserts*

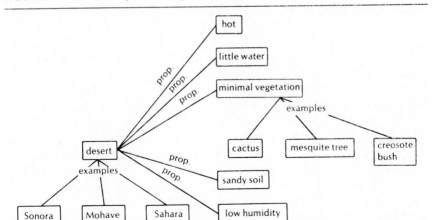

Source: P. L. Anders and C. S. Bos, ''In the Beginning: Vocabulary Instruction in Content Classes,'' *Topics in Learning Disabilities*, 3(4) (1984):59. Reprinted by permission of Pro-Ed.

the learning task itself'' (Ausubel and Robinson, 1969, p. 606).

The purpose of an advance organizer is to facilitate learning information. It is based on schema theory and the notion that some students need to have a framework provided for the material to be learned so as to help them assimilate the new information into their current schemas or cognitive structure. Mayer (1979) reviewed the studies that have tested the effectiveness of advance organizers on learning and drew the following conclusions:

1. There is consistent advantage for the advance organizer groups over control groups. This advantage diminishes when material is familiar, when learners have an extensive background of knowledge about the area, when learners have high IQs, and when tests fail to measure the breadth of transfer ability.

2. Advance organizers particularly aid students of lower ability and/or limited background knowledge.

3. Advance organizers are more effective when presented prior to a learning task rather than after the task.

Using this information, Lenz (1983; Lenz, Alley, and Schumaker, 1987) demonstrated that both the quality and quantity of learning for learning-disabled adolescents could be significantly improved by using advance organizers. He found that regular content area teachers are able to implement advance organizers with minimal teacher training (forty-five minutes). The teachers who utilized the advance organizers expressed satisfaction with the learning-disabled students' response to the instruction as well as the improvement in the overall quality of their own instruction. However, Lenz did find that teacher use of an advance organizer alone was not enough to facilitate student learning. ''Learning disabled students had to be made aware that advance organizers were being presented and then had to be trained in the types of

information presented in the advance organizer and ways in which that information could be made useful'' (Lenz, 1983, p. 12).

▬ *Procedures:* Lenz identified ten steps in using an advance organizer (see Figure 7.6). The resource teacher trained the learning-disabled students to utilize advance organizers by giving the student a worksheet with each of the ten steps as headings. The students then practiced listening to advance organizers given by the resource teacher and completing the worksheets. Next, the students used the advance organizer worksheet in content area classes, with the resource teacher and students meeting to discuss the success of the worksheets. The resource teacher and the students later met and discussed how the advance organizer information can be used to organize notes and how the worksheet can be modified to assist the students to cue in on the most common organizing principles used by particular teachers.

In giving an advance organizer, the teacher provides an organizational framework for the information to be learned (see Figure 7.6, Step 3). This framework might be an outline, a diagram, or picture in which the parts are labeled, or a content map, as discussed earlier. Townsend and Clarihew (1989) found that a pictorial component in a verbal advance organizer was necessary to improve the comprehension of eight-year-old students with limited background knowledge. The use of visual representations or pictures may be particularly salient for students with learning and behavior problems. The next teaching strategy, semantic feature analysis, provides another way in which the major concepts to be learned can be organized and discussed prior to reading a text or listening to a lecture.

Semantic Feature Analysis

Like an advance organizer, semantic feature analysis (SFA) is a prelearning activity that serves to organize the major concepts and related vocabulary to be taught in a unit, chapter, or lecture. This activity aids students in seeing the

FIGURE 7.6 *Steps in Using an Advance Organizer*

Step 1: Inform students of advance organizers
    a. Announce advance organizer
    b. State benefits of advance organizer
    c. Suggest that students take notes on the advance organizer

Step 2: Identify topics of tasks
    a. Identify major topics or activities
    b. Identify subtopics or component activities

Step 3: Provide an organizational framework
    a. Present an outline, list, or narrative of the lesson's content

Step 4: Clarify action to be taken
    a. State teachers' actions
    b. State students' actions

Step 5: Provide background information
    a. Relate topic to the course or previous lesson
    b. Relate topic to new information

Step 6: State the concepts to be learned
    a. State specific concepts/ideas from the lesson
    b. State general concepts/ideas broader than the lesson's content

Step 7: Clarify the concepts to be learned
    a. Clarify by examples or analogies
    b. Clarify by nonexamples
    c. Caution students of possible misunderstandings

Step 8: Motivate student to learn
    a. Point out relevance to students
    b. Be specific, short-term, personalized, and believable

Step 9: Introduce vocabulary
    a. Identify the new terms and define
    b. Repeat difficult terms and define

Step 10: State the general outcome desired
    a. State objectives of instruction/learning
    b. Relate outcomes to test performance

Source: B. K. Lenz, "Promoting Active Learning Through Effective Instruction," *Pointer, 27*(2) (1983):12. Copyright 1983 by Heldref Publications. Reprinted by permission.

relationships between the major concepts, the related vocabulary, and their current knowledge of the topic.

The theoretical foundation for the SFA teaching strategy is schema theory (Rumelhart, 1980), the closely related knowledge hypothesis (Anderson and Freebody, 1981), and concept attainment theory (Klausmeier and Sipple, 1980). These theories suggest that knowledge is hierarchically organized, that relating the new concepts to students' prior knowledge will help students learn these new concepts, and that teaching attributes of a concept as well as teaching examples and nonexamples are important to concept learning.

— ***Procedures:*** The first step in preparing for the SFA activity is to develop a relationship chart. This chart is based on the notion that ideas or concepts are related to one another in terms of a hierarchy of abstractness. The most inclusive or abstract ideas are called *superordinate concepts* and the most concrete or narrow ideas are identified as *subordinate concepts*. Ideas or concepts that fall in between the superordinate and subordinate concepts are referred to as *coordinate concepts* (Frayer, Frederick, and Klausmeier, 1969). These ideas are then organized into a relationship chart, and the students and teacher discuss the relationship between the various levels of concepts and their own background knowledge. This SFA activity was originally developed for use in teaching isolated vocabulary (Johnson and Pearson, 1984). In their interactive teaching research, Anders and Bos have adapted this strategy to text (Anders and Bos, 1986; Bos and Anders, 1987, 1990).

When Ms. Chou used this technique in her American government class, she first read the assigned American government chapter on contracts. As she read, she listed the important concepts or vocabulary and then arranged them according to superordinate, coordinate, and subordinate concepts. She used words as well as relevant phrases.

Contracts	Counteroffer
Promise	Holding Good
Contracting Parties	Conditions
Buyer	Acceptance
Seller	Consideration
Written Contracts	Statute of Frauds
Verbal Contracts	Legal Obligation
Contractual Offer	Legal Action

Next, she organized the vocabulary into a relationship chart (see Figure 7.7). The superordinate concept "Contracts" is used as the name for the chart. The five coordinate concepts (main ideas in the text) serve as the column headings and are listed as the important or major ideas. The related vocabulary or subordinate concepts are listed down the side of the chart. Notice that Ms. Chou decided not to

include Buyer and Seller because she decided that the students would already be knowledgeable concerning the definitions and their relationship to contracts. Notice also that Ms. Chou left blank spaces for adding important ideas and important vocabulary to the chart. In this way students during discussion would be encouraged to add relevant information from their background knowledge.

The relationship chart became Ms. Chou's instructional tool. She duplicated it and she made a transparency to project on the screen at the front of the class. She used the relationship chart as her prelearning activity to assist students in seeing relationships among the important ideas and the related vocabulary. To do this, Ms. Chou gave each student a copy of the relationship chart and, using the model relationship chart projected on the screen, she introduced the topic (superordinate concept) of the assignment and the students discussed what they already knew about contracts. Next, she introduced each coordinate concept (important idea) by assisting the students in generating meanings. During this introduction and throughout the activity, she encouraged students to add their personal experiences or understandings of the terms. For example, when Ms. Chou presented the major idea of "contract," Joe inquired if a contract had to be written to be legal. This led to Anne's conveying a firsthand experience of her dad making a verbal contract and having the contract honored in court even though it was not written. The discussion ended with one purpose for reading being the clarification of what was needed for a verbal contract to be considered legal.

Following the discussion of the coordinate concepts, Ms. Chou introduced each subordinate concept. Again, Ms. Chou and her students predicted what the meanings would be in relation to the topic of "contracts." For the more technical vocabulary (e.g., *contractual offer, Statute of Frauds*), sometimes Ms. Chou provided the meaning or the students decided to read to clarify the concept. After introducing each concept, she and the students discussed the relationship be-

FIGURE 7.7   *Relationship Chart: Contracts*

CONTRACTS   Name _____

Period _____

Important Ideas

	Contract	Promise	Written Contracts	Verbal Contracts	Conditions		
Legal Action							
Consideration							
Legal Obligation							
Holding Good							
Contractual Offer							
Counteroffer							
Acceptance							
Statute of Frauds							
Contracting Parties							

Important Vocabulary

+ = positive relationship
− = negative relationship
0 = no relationship
? = unknown relationship

tween each coordinate concept or phrase and each subordinate term or phrase. They used the following symbols to signify each of the relationships: a plus sign (+) represented a positive relationship, a minus sign (–) represented a negative relationship, a zero (0) signified no relationship, and a question mark (?) represented that no consensus could be reached without further information. Using this system, the students and Ms. Chou filled in the relationship chart by discussing and attempting to reach consensus on the relationship between each of the coordinate and subordinate terms.

Ms. Chou found that student involvement during the discussion was important to the success of the SFA strategy. One key to a successful discussion was to encourage students to ask each other why they reached a certain relationship rating. This seemed to encourage students to use their prior knowledge regarding the topic, and in turn, seemed to encourage other students to activate what they already knew about the vocabulary. When trying to justify a positive and negative relationship between "holding good" and "promise," several of Ms. Chou's students discussed the relationship of moral obligation to legal obligation, using first-hand experiences and episodes from several specific TV programs as their rationale for deciding on their choice.

After completing the relationship chart, Ms. Chou guided the students in setting purposes for reading. These purposes, for the most part, focused on the chart, reading the assignment to confirm their predictions and to determine the relationships between the terms for which no agreement could be reached. After completing the reading, Ms. Chou and the students reviewed the relationship chart, using discussion. They changed any of the relationships if necessary and reached consensus on those previously unknown.

Sometimes when Ms. Chou and her students used a relationship chart, they found that some information was still unclear after reading the text. Then, they checked other sources such as experts in the field, technical and trade books, and other media. Ms. Chou also taught the students how to use the relationship chart to study for chapter tests. The students learned to ask each other questions based on the meanings of the concepts and vocabulary and on their relationships (e.g., What is a contractual offer? What are the conditions necessary to have a contract?) She even demonstrated how the chart could be used to write a report about the concepts.

▬ *Comments:* One of the authors and her colleagues have conducted a series of intervention studies with learning-disabled secondary students using the SFA teaching strategy. Whether comparing it to the more traditional activity of looking the words up in the dictionary (Bos, Anders, Filip, and Jaffe, 1985, 1989) or the direct instruction of word meanings (Anders, Bos, Jaffe, and Filip, 1986; Bos, Allen, and Scanlon, 1989; Bos and Anders, 1990), they found that when teachers and researchers used this strategy, students consistently learned more vocabulary and had better comprehension of the chapters they read. Bos and her colleagues feel that one of the most important questions asked during discussion is "Why?" (e.g., "Why is *evidence* positively related to *evidence in court?*"). Students need to justify their reasoning and the reasoning of others. By answering "Why?" questions, students think through concepts, reaching a deeper understanding and more effectively relating new information to old.

Semantic Mapping, Graphic Organizers, and Structured Overviews

Semantic mapping (Pearson and Johnson, 1978), graphic organizers (Barron, 1969), and structured overviews (Barron and Earle, 1973) are three similar ways of visually representing the concepts and important vocabulary to be taught (see Figure 7.5). Semantic mapping, graphic organizers, and structured overviews can be used as prelearning activities that assist students in activating their prior knowledge and in seeing the relationships between new concepts and related vocabulary.

▬ *Procedures:* In using maps, organizers, or overviews, the teacher can begin by putting the major concept for the lecture or text on the board and then having the students generate a list of related vocabulary from their background knowledge, as was described in the section on brainstorming (see Chapter 5). However, when presenting more technical vocabulary, the teacher could begin by writing on the board the list of important vocabulary he or she generated in reviewing the text chapter or developing the lecture. After the words have been listed, discuss the meanings of the words, using a procedure similar to the one presented in the section on semantic feature analysis. Next, arrange and rearrange the vocabulary with the students until you have a map that shows the relationships that exist among the ideas. For example, when presenting the following words for a chapter on "Fossils," the students and teacher first grouped the animals together.

trilobites	small horses
crinoids	winged insects
ferns	geography of the
dinosaurs	present
lakes	land masses

bodies of water	brachiopods
animals	saber-tooth tigers
geography of	guide fossils
the past	rivers
trees	plants
oceans	continents

Next, they grouped the plants together. In the case of guide fossils and several other types of fossils with which the students were not familiar (e.g., crinoids, trilobites), they decided to wait until they had done some reading to place the concepts on the map. Finally, they grouped together the geography terms. After the map is completed, instruct the students to refer to the map while reading and/or listening to the lecture.

Like the relationship chart of semantic feature analysis, the semantic map can provide a framework for setting purposes for reading. The students read to confirm and clarify their understanding in relation to the map and make changes in it during discussions held as they read or after completing a chapter. The map can also serve as a blueprint for studying and for writing reports.

▬ *Comments:* Recently, a number of researchers have investigated the use of semantic mapping or graphic organizers with learning-disabled and low-achieving students. In some cases the students generated the maps as described above (Bos, Allen, and Scanlon, 1989; Bos and Anders, 1990), while in other studies the framework for the map or organizer was already generated and the students filled in the information (Horton, Lovitt, and Bergerud, 1990; Idol, 1987). In other studies, the map or visual spatial display (see Figure 7.8) is presented to the students in completed form and systematic Direct Instruction (Carnine, 1989) is used to assist the students in learning the information contained in the display (Bergerud, Lovitt, and Horton, 1988; Darch and Carnine, 1986). Consistently the research has been encouraging in this area with the use of semantic maps or visual representa-tions of information increasing the learning performance of students with learning and behavior problems.

Concept Diagrams
Concept diagrams (Bulgren, Schumaker, and Deshler, 1988) provide another means for teaching concepts presented in text or lectures. Building upon the work in concept development, the diagram (see Figure 7.9) assists students in determining the characteristic, examples and non-examples, and a content-related definition of a concept.

▬ *Procedures:* When using a concept diagram, the first step is to prepare the diagram. First, the teacher identifies major concept(s) and related concepts of which the students need a deeper or more technical understanding. In a science chapter on fossils, Mr. Thomas felt that it was important that the students develop a more technical understanding of the concept of fossils, so this became the concept to diagram. Second, Mr. Thomas used the instructional materials and his knowledge to list important characteristics of fossils. He also thought about whether or not each characteristic is "always present," "sometimes present," or "never present." Third, he located examples and nonexamples of the concepts in the instructional materials. He found in reviewing the chapter that nonexamples were not provided, so he decided to show the students fossils and nonfossils to help them to start thinking about examples and nonexamples. Finally, Mr. Thomas constructed a definition. Lenz and Bulgren (in press) specify a concept definition as the "naming of the superordinate concept which includes the concept under consideration, a listing of the characteristics which must always be present in the concept, and a specification of the relationships among those characteristics" (p. 33).

After preparing the concept diagram, the next step is using it with the students to develop their understanding of the concept. The teaching sequence includes:

FIGURE 7.8 *Visual Spatial Display*

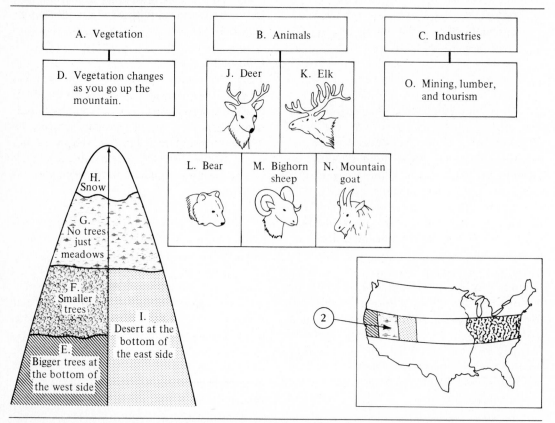

Source: C. Darch and D. Carnine, "Teaching content area material to learning disabled students," *Exceptional Children, 53* (1986):243. Copyright 1986 by The Council for Exceptional Children. Reprinted with permission.

1. Give an advance organizer.
2. Elicit a key word list or list of ideas related to the major concept.
3. Explain or review the symbols of the concept diagram.
4. Name and define the concept. (This may be completed after the students have discussed characteristics and examples/nonexamples if a teaching method oriented more toward discovery is being used.)
5. Discuss the characteristics always present, sometimes present, and never present.
6. Discuss examples and nonexamples of the concept.
7. Link the examples and nonexamples to the characteristics.
8. Give a post organizer.

This teaching sequence or concept teaching routine (Bulgren, Schumaker, and Deshler, 1988) should employ interactive discussions which encourage the students to fine-tune and deepen their understanding of the concept being studied.

━ Comments: When Bulgren and her colleagues worked with content area high-school teachers in whose classes learning-disabled students were mainstreamed, they found that when the teachers used the concept diagrams and the concept teaching routine the learning performance of both the learning-disabled and other students in the class improved.

Steps Five and Six: Reinforcing Concept Learning During and After Reading or Lecturing

In a typical "learning from reading" or "learning from lecturing" assignment, the teacher has three opportunities to enhance the learning of concepts and the related vocabulary: *before* the reading or listening, *during* the actual reading or lecture, and *after* the assignment has been read or heard (Anders and Bos, 1984; Manzo and Manzo, 1990). The previous section discussed three prelearning activities that can be used to facilitate concept learning. These activities, as with most prelearning activities, are generally extended to serve as "during" and "after" learning activities.

Whether using an advance organizer, semantic feature analysis, semantic map, or

FIGURE 7.9

CONCEPT DIAGRAM

Concept Name: fossils

Definitions: Fossils are remains or prints of plants or animals who lived thousands of years ago which have been preserved in the earth.

Characteristics Present in the Concept:

Always	Sometimes	Never
remains or prints	frozen in ice	still alive
plants or animals	trapped in tar	still decaying
thousands of years old	crushed by water	
preserved in the earth	in volcanic ash	

Example:

- tigers in La Brea tar pits
- Siberian mammoth
- petrified forest in Arizona
- fish skeleton in limestone layers

Nonexample:

- your pet cat
- elephant in Africa today
- tree limbs and leaves in your yard
- fish in supermarket

concept diagram, these frameworks can be used to guide students as they read the text or listen to the lecture and as they react to their learning. For example, when using semantic feature analysis, the teacher encourages the students to read or listen to clarify relationships for which there was no consensus during the prelearning activity. After reading or listening, the students and teacher discuss these relationships based on the new information they have gathered. Continued lack of consensus might encourage students to seek other sources such as resource and trade books or an expert in the field. The list of major ideas obtained from the advance organizer can serve as the framework in which students can take notes when listening to a lecture. After the lecture, students can meet in small groups and share their notes to create one overview that can serve as a study guide for the test. Students can be instructed on how to develop questions based on a concept diagram or semantic map. These questions can serve as self-questions to be asked when reading and when studying for a test. After reading, the teacher and students should review, modify, or further develop a structure overview based on the information gleaned from reading.

In addition to effective teaching, students with learning and behavior problems need a cadre of study skills to succeed in these classes. Let's look at some strategies for teaching study skills.

Study Skills

In addition to learning content area information, students with learning and behavior problems also need to develop study skills and habits so that they can take advantage of the teaching-learning situation. They need to develop effective metacognitive strategies. Particularly as students move into secondary and postsecondary settings, the task demands require more emphasis on such skills as time management, self-monitoring and feedback, listening and notetaking, studying from textbooks, and test-taking skills.

Surveys and observational studies conducted in secondary settings show: (1) a heavy reliance on written products as a means of evaluating performance, (2) the need to listen to lectures containing few advance organizers and limited opportunities for interactions, and (3) a limited amount of individual help and teacher feedback (Devine, 1978; Moran, 1980; Schumaker, Wildgen, and Sherman, 1982).

Study skills can be defined as those competencies associated with acquiring, recording, organizing, synthesizing, remembering, and using information and ideas (Devine, 1987). Study skills are the key to independent learning, and they help students gain and use information effectively. Lock (1981) divides study skills into three areas:

1. *Personal development skills:* personal discipline, management and organizational skills, self-monitoring and reinforcement, and positive attitude toward studying

2. *Process skills:* technical methods of studying such as notetaking, outlining, learning information from a text, and library reference skills

3. *Expression skills:* retrieval skills, test-taking skills, and using oral and/or written expression to demonstrate understanding

As would be expected, these are the skills that students with learning and behavior problems have difficulty developing. One reason for this may be that most study skills are not directly and systematically taught in the same manner in which reading and math skills are taught (Devine, 1987).

Personal Development Skills

Personal development skills include personal discipline, management and organizational skills, self-monitoring and reinforcement, and positive attitude toward studying. Many of the personal management and organizational skills related to school focus on time management and scheduling, self-monitoring and reinforcement, and notebook organization.

Time Management and Scheduling

Jon's mom is concerned because Jon, her learning-disabled son, falls asleep while trying to finish book reports the night before they are due. Even if she gets him up early in the morning, there is little chance Jon will have time to finish—and then there would only be a first draft. This just seems to be the way that Jon works. Even though Jon knows about the assignments for three weeks he waits until two nights before they're due to start reading, despite her queries about homework. The last time Jon had a report due, he decided that he wouldn't have time to finish the book but would try to write the report on what he had read. By 10 P.M., he was asleep, with about two-thirds of a first draft completed. Either he would have to get a time extension or receive another failing grade in English. Granted, it takes Jon longer than the other students to select, read, and report on a book, but Ms. Brice, his teacher, had given him enough time by giving him the assignment early. He has the skills to get a B or C on the assignment if he would just start earlier. He fails to use that extra time effectively, and again he is "stuck behind the eight ball."

Many parents and teachers can identify with this scenario. Jon has the skills to complete the assignment successfully, he just lacks the personal management skills, particularly time management. The need to develop and use time management skills is routinely discussed in books dealing with study skills. *Time management* is simply organizing and monitoring time so that tasks can be scheduled and completed in an efficient and timely manner. The following ideas can be used to teach students how to schedule and manage their time.

Rationale. The first step in getting students to schedule and manage their time is to build a rationale for its importance to success in school and later life. Bragstad and Stumpf (1982) suggest nine reasons (as presented in Figure 7.10) why time management is worth the investment.

Determining How the Time Is Spent. Before students can decide how to schedule their time they need to determine how they are currently spending it. Using a schedule, such as the one presented in Figure 7.11, have students keep track of their activities for one or two weeks. Also have them list the school assignments they have for the time period and if they have "too little," "enough," or "too much" time to complete them. At the end of the one or two weeks, have them summarize their results by figuring the percent of time that is spent on major activities such as sleeping, eating, studying, class time, leisure time, working, commuting, and miscellaneous activities.

Estimating Time. Before students can accurately schedule, they need to have a good idea of how long it takes to complete various tasks. As part of the time management process, have students determine how long it takes them to complete regularly scheduled tasks such as meals, commuting, reading assignments in their various textbooks, writing a paragraph on a topic, completing a ten-problem math assignment, answering five questions over a chapter, and so on. Although there will probably be considerable variability in the time taken to complete a task, most students with learning and behavior problems underestimate the time it takes. Having students get an idea of the time required can be helpful when planning a schedule.

Scheduling. If students feel that they do not have enough time to get their tasks completed or if they do not have regular times for studying, encourage them to set up a schedule. Some suggestions that students might want to use when setting up their schedules are:

1. Plan regular study times.

2. Plan at least one-hour blocks of time in which to study.

3. Plan which assignments you are going to work on during the study time.

4. Take the first five minutes of each study activity to review what you have done already and what you have already learned, and to plan what you are going to accomplish today. This helps promote long-term learning and a sense of accomplishment.

5. When studying longer than one hour, plan breaks and stick to the time allowed for the breaks.

6. Use daytime or early evening for study if possible. Most people are less efficient at night.

7. Work on your most difficult subjects when you are most alert.

8. Distribute your studying for a test rather than cram.

9. Balance your time between studying and other activities. Allow time for recreational activities.

10. Reward yourself by marking through your schedule each time you meet a scheduled commitment and by crossing off items you complete on your "to do" list.

Not only should regular times for studying be listed on the schedule, but due dates for assignments and dates for other events should be noted so that the schedule also serves as a calendar.

Students should also be encouraged to set aside some time they can use as they please, if they accomplish their tasks on schedule during the day or week. This type of self-determined reinforcer may serve as an extra motivation for some students.

Monitoring. Setting up a schedule will do little good unless students follow and monitor their schedules. Provide students with a weekly schedule and have them fill in those activities

FIGURE 7.10 *Why Bother with a Time Schedule?*

Each year in school, assignments seem to become longer and more difficult. If you want to be a successful student, scheduling your time will be helpful. Here are some of the advantages of scheduling time that other high-school students have discovered:

1. Parents will "get off your back" when they see that you have planned your study time. As they observe you becoming responsible, they may gradually stop checking on what you are doing.
2. Writing down what you must do each day relieves your mind. Then when you study, you can focus and think more effectively. Get into the habit of having a daily "to-do list" to free your mind.
3. You are less likely to procrastinate, that is, to put off your work, if you have a set time to begin.
4. When you set a certain amount of time to do each assignment, your concentration improves so that you work better. This saves time. You may even beat the clock as you become more efficient.

5. With a schedule, you are less likely to let a ten-minute break extend into the rest of the evening. Gradually, you learn to discipline yourself to get the work finished so that you can really relax.
6. You experience a feeling of satisfaction when you are in control of your life, knowing *what* you want to do *when*. You feel better about yourself.
7. Organizing your time helps you come to class prepared; you learn more because the class presentation or activity has more meaning. As a result, your grades improve.
8. When you assume control of your time, you feel relaxed and ready to have fun when you have some free time because your work is up-to-date. You get rid of that feeling of anxiety or pressure.
9. Scheduling your use of time is the intelligent way to operate if you want to learn, to achieve, and to have more time for fun with your friends.

Source: B. J. Bragstad and S. M. Stumpf, *A Guidebook for Teaching Study Skills and Motivation* (Boston: Allyn and Bacon, 1982), p. 200. Reprinted with permission.

FIGURE 7.11 Weekly Schedule And Activity Summary

NAME: Jon

WEEK OF: Sept. 25

Time	MON.	TUES.	WED.	THURS.	FRI.	SAT.	SUN.
6:00 a.m.							
7:00	get up & eat →				↑	sleep	sleep
8:00	ride bus / History	ride bus	ride bus	ride bus	ride bus		
9:00	English						
10:00							go to Church
11:00	P.E.					do yard work	eat lunch
12:00	Welding					work	
1:00 p.m.	Lunch					go to the	read mags
2:00	Algebra	*same every day*				gym	
3:00	General Science / ride bus						play video games
4:00	ride bus					→	
5:00	watch TV	play video games	work on report	gym	goof off with friends		games
6:00	eat dinner	eat dinner	eat dinner	eat dinner		eat dinner	eat
7:00	watch TV	watch TV	go to library to work on report	watch movie on VCR	with friends	date	watch TV
8:00	study	sleep →	sleep →	sleep →			study
9:00	study						→
10:00	sleep						
11:00	sleep		sleep	sleep	sleep	sleep	sleep
12:00							
1:00							
2:00 a.m.							

ACTIVITY SUMMARY

Activity	Number of hours per week
Sleep	51
Meals	14
Job	3
Transportation	5
Class Time	30
Talking on phone	2
Watching TV	9
Other Recreation	19
Study	8

COMMENTS: Had report due Thurs. for history. Didn't have enough time to get it done well. Just an OK job.

they feel are important to monitor. Figure 7.12 presents a schedule for Jon. His study time, time spent working out, time spent on his after-school job, and TV time were the most important tasks for him to monitor, so he scheduled them in each week. He also noted when the next book report was due and he assigned time to begin reading the book on a daily basis so that the last night "impossible job" would not continue to plague him.

Jon developed a contract with himself. If he studied at least 80 percent of the time he had scheduled during the week, then he could work out at the gym two extra hours on Saturday. In this way Jon is not only monitoring his schedule but setting goals and providing rewards for meeting his goals. Although Jon realizes that schedules need to be flexible, he has found that planning, even when plans change, helps him get more accomplished in a timely manner.

Using a "To Do" List. If we don't keep a list of things we need to buy at the grocery store, invariably we forget at least one item. If we don't write ourselves a reminder to pick up the cleaning, we get all the way home from work before we remember. Using a "to do" list simply takes the burden of remembering off the mind by writing it down. Notice how the schedule that Jon uses integrates a "to do" list with the weekly schedule (see Figure 7.12). Jon's resource teacher taught him an additional way to use his "to do" list and schedule. She showed him how to break a difficult assignment into several smaller tasks and then add each task to the "to do" list so that he is not trying to complete the entire task in one night. She also showed him how to cross off completed tasks, something that gives him a real sense of accomplishment. Hence, the "not enough time" scenario described earlier is becoming less and less frequent. This is important for Jon since he plans to attend a community college and study electronics next year.

Self-Monitoring and Reinforcement

"By the end of the month I want to lose five pounds. If I reach my goal, I'm going to buy a new pair of jeans." How many times have you set a goal and then promised yourself some kind of reinforcement if you reach that goal? Then you probably start weighing yourself every day or so to see how you are progressing toward that goal. You might even put a chart on the wall next to the scale and keep track of the number of pounds you are losing. If you go to this trouble, then your chances of reaching your goal are increased significantly, for you are self-monitoring your progress and using a contingent reinforcer.

In the case of students with learning and behavior problems there is much research to support the notion that they have difficulty self-monitoring, whether it be in the areas of attention and memory, reading comprehension, or personal and management skills (Bos and Filip, 1984; Palincsar and Brown, 1987; Torgesen and Licht, 1983; Wong, 1979).

Van Reusen and Bos (in press) developed a strategy that students can use to assist them in setting goals and keeping track of their progress. The strategy requires the students to make a list of goals and prioritize them. Next, the students determine a plan for reaching their goals. In this step of the strategy, students develop a plan of action and predict how successful they think it will be. Then, the students carry out the plan. They keep records of their progress by using a simple monitoring form and adjusting their plan of action if necessary. Finally, when students reach their goals, they reward themselves. We have used this strategy with junior-high and high-school students who have learning and behavior problems. They found the training and goal regulation strategy to be helpful in increasing the number of goals accomplished. It also gave the students a better perspective of what their educational, vocational, and personal goals were.

FIGURE 7.12 *Weekly Schedule and "To Do" List*

NAME: Jon

WEEK OF: Oct 14

	MON.	TUES.	WED.	THURS.	FRI.	SAT.	SUN.	
6:00 a.m.	get up and eat ———————→							6:00 a.m.
7:00	ride					sleep	sleep	7:00
8:00	bus							8:00
9:00	History					house &		9:00
10:00	English	*same every day*				yard	go to	10:00
11:00	PE					chores	church	11:00
12:00	Welding						eat	12:00
1:00 p.m.	Lunch					eat	read	1:00 p.m.
2:00	Algebra					go	for fun	2:00
3:00	General Science					to gym	goof	3:00
4:00	ride bus						off and eat	4:00
5:00	recreational activity			study		eat and		5:00
6:00	eat ————————→				eat have fun	have fun		6:00
7:00	study	study	study	study			study	7:00
8:00								8:00
9:00								9:00
10:00	sleep ————→					sleep	10:00
11:00					sleep →			11:00

TO DO LIST						
history paper due math assign finish book	math assign	math assign book report due	math assign welding project due	science test math test	chores mow grass pull weeds fix cooler	start English paper

Notebook Organization

Although Susan shows up on time for each of her high-school classes, the only things she regularly remembers are her comb and make-up. Her notebook, pencils, assignments, and textbooks show up on an irregular basis. When she does bring her notebook, it is so disorganized that it proves to be of little assistance to her. Susan is not unlike other students with learning and behavior problems. Their difficulty in organizing materials is frequently observed by teachers and parents. Teachers of these students and other low-achieving students have found it helpful to take the time to conduct a unit on notebook organization, providing information about the type of notebook materials that facilitate both flexibility and organization.

You may want to start the year in a resource or self-contained secondary program by conducting a unit on notebook organization and time management. In fact, if you know the previous spring who your students are going to be, you may want to send home a suggested list of materials that students and parents should purchase. Figure 7.13 presents an adapted list of those materials Scheuneman and Lambourne (1981) suggest for a "guaranteed successful notebook system." A three-ring binder is advantageous over other types of notebooks because it allows one to add and delete materials easily and to file materials according to classes.

The weekly schedule and the "to do" list that were presented earlier in this chapter can be used in this notebook. Most students also find it helpful to have a monthly or semester calendar in the front of their notebook to keep track of long-term projects and activities.

Under each class section, place class syllabi and assignments at the beginning of the section. Use the extra notebook paper for taking notes and then place the dated notes in chronological order under the appropriate section. Handouts from class can also be integrated into the notes or kept at the beginning or end of the class section. Some students have found it useful to keep an assignment sheet at the beginning of each class

FIGURE 7.13   *List of Notebook Materials*

1 large three-ring notebook
1 school supply pouch
   4 pens (2 black, 2 blue)
   2 pencils
   1 eraser for pencil and ink
   1 first aid kit
      2 bandaids
      2 aspirins
      2 quarters for phone call
   1 small hole punch
   1 small calculator
   1 small package file cards
13 dividers with tabs marked as follows:
   schedule and calendar
   1st period (name of class)
   2nd period (name of class)
   etc.
   reference information
   dictionary (if available)
   personal word list
   extra notebook paper
   extra graph paper
   1 twelve-inch metric and inch ruler
   1 notebook dictionary (if available)
   2 assignments per class
   1 notebook calendar
   8 weekly schedule sheets
   1 personal word list (of commonly misspelled words)
Any relevant reference information
Notebook paper
Graph paper

Source: Adapted from R. S. Scheuneman and J. Lambourne, *Study Skills for School Success* (Tucson, Ariz.: Study Skills for School Success, 1981). Reprinted with permission.

section using the headings of Assignment, Date Due, Progress Update, Completed, and Grade. This allows a student to keep track of his or her progress and grades for the various assignments in a class.

The personal word list can be used to keep an alphabetical list of words the student uses frequently and often misspells. For some students it may be advantageous to purchase the *Bad Speller's Dictionary* (Kreviski and Linfield, 1974) or the *Misspeller's Dictionary* (1983). These dictionaries alphabetically list words by their common misspelling. After each misspelling the correct spelling is given.

Process Skills

Process skills include the technical methods of studying such as notetaking, outlining, learning information from text, and research and library skills.

Taking Notes on Lectures

People spend more time listening than reading, speaking, or writing. Listening is central to learning, and it is generally considered to develop before speaking, reading, and writing (Lundsteen, 1979). On the average, 55 percent of the time in an elementary classroom is spent with children listening (Wilt, 1958); this amount increases in secondary settings. By the time students reach secondary level, the information load in lectures is so great that notetaking becomes necessary to help alleviate the memory load.

Think back for a minute to your educational experiences. When did you learn how to listen to lectures and take notes? Was it your eighth-grade English teacher who covered this topic and had you practice taking notes, or was it your tenth-grade history teacher? Although listening and notetaking play an important role in secondary and postsecondary learning, surveys of classroom practices show that direct instruction is neglected. Carrier and Newell (1983) found that less than 2 percent of undergraduate students reported that they had received any instruction on how to take notes, and more than half indicated they would like to take a course to improve their skills. Textbooks for both students and teachers tend to ignore listening and notetaking instruction (Devine, 1978). Given the attentional, listening, and writing problems that many students with learning and behavior problems experience, it is critical that they receive direct instruction in learning to take notes from lectures.

Developing Listener-Friendly Lectures. Let us digress for a moment with an analogy. Since the popularity of personal computers, people have discussed software programs in terms of their "user friendliness." In other words, is the program easy to understand? Does the program use familiar language or at least define unfamiliar terms? Does the program give you cue words to signal the important ideas and processes? If you don't understand something, does the program allow you to ask questions? Does the program have more than one way to explain a difficult concept or process? If the program has these features, then one might consider it "user friendly."

Now take a minute to go back and reread the previous paragraph but substitute the word *lecture* for the word *program* (hence the term *listener-friendly lecture*). One of the most important aspects of teaching notetaking is to begin by using listener-friendly lectures. Just as using "considerate" or "user friendly" text assists students in learning the critical information, a well-organized lecture makes the students' work easier in that it assists them in seeing relationships among concepts and in distinguishing important from supplementary information. It also helps them relate new information to old. Well-designed lectures seem particularly beneficial to listeners with relatively low language skills and little prior knowledge of the content because of the reduced processing burdens (Cronbach and Snow, 1977; Tobias, 1978). Figure 7.14 presents some ideas to use when developing lectures that facilitate notetaking, and Table 7.1 adapts Gagne and Briggs's (1979) scheme for "events of instructions" into a useful framework for organizing lectures (Carrier, 1983). Once students can take notes on lectures that utilize advance organizers, listening guides, cue words, and background activating teaching strategies, they can begin to generalize their skills to less friendly lectures.

Teaching Students to Take Notes. Research supports the notion that students who take lecture

FIGURE 7.14   *Ideas for Creating Listener-Friendly Lectures*

1. Use advance organizers.
2. Use cue words or phrases (e.g., "It is important that you know," "In summary," "Let's focus," "The conclusion we can draw") to let students know that an important concept is going to be presented.
3. Repeat important ideas or key phrases so that students realize their importance and have time to write them down.
4. Vary your voice tone and quality to stress important ideas.
5. Number ideas or points you are making or use ordinal numbers or temporal cues such as *first, next, then,* and *finally*.
6. Write important ideas on the board.
7. Write technical words and words that are difficult to spell on the board so that students are not having to allocate too much of their attention to spelling rather than listening.
8. Better yet, provide students with a listening guide that lists the major concepts to be presented in such a manner that students need only to fill in the supportive information.
9. Use pictures and diagrams to show relationships among ideas. For example, use a timeline to present temporal relationships in history, and use directional arrows to show cause-effect relationships.
10. Base your lecture on a semantic map, concept diagram or semantic feature analysis (see section on "Teaching Content Information") that was developed as a prelecturing or prereading activity.
11. Provide examples and nonexamples of the concepts you are presenting.
12. Ask questions during the lecture that require students to relate this new information to old information you have already presented or to their background knowledge.
13. Encourage students to ask questions during the lecture.
14. Use the pause procedure (Hudson, 1987) where at a natural break in a lecture students work in small groups and discuss and ask comprehension questions regarding the concepts just presented.
15. Allow a few minutes at the end of a lecture for students to look over their notes so that they can summarize to themselves and ask any questions.

notes appear to learn more than those who just listen (Carrier, 1983; Ladas, 1980). Furthermore, students tend to learn more if they record and review their *own* notes (Fisher and Harris, 1973; Thomas, 1978).

Formats for Notetaking. Numerous formats for notetaking have been suggested (Bragstad and Stumpf, 1982; Langan, 1982; Manzo and Manzo, 1990; Palmatier, 1971, 1973; Pauk, 1974). One aspect that these systems have in common is the focus on making notetaking and reviewing an interactive learning process (Aaronson, 1975). To facilitate this interactive process, two- or three-column notetaking sys-

tems have been developed. Figure 7.15 gives an example of each. Students take class notes in the far right-hand column in both systems, using only the front side of the paper. Modified outlining is the format that is most often suggested for taking these notes. In the two-column system, students note the key concepts in the left-hand column. Devine (1987) refers to these concepts as *triggers* since they are meant to "trigger" the ideas noted in the other column. Later, in reviewing, students should be able to cover the right column and use their personal triggers to help them remember the ideas covered in the class notes. Palmatier (1971), in his Notetaking System for Learning procedure, suggests that imme-

TABLE 7.1 *Notetaking and the Events of Instruction*

Instructional Event	A Lecturer Might Operationalize This Event in the Following Ways:	Which Encourages Notetakers to:
1. Gaining attention	*Physical movement*-e.g., Move to podium. Arrange lecture notes. Switch on overhead projector *Verbal interaction*-Good morning. Let's begin. Overview the lecture content	Prepare to listen Locate place to take notes
2. Informing learner of objective	Suggest how the information will be useful	Formulate a rationale why material should be noted
3. Stimulating recall of prerequisite learning	Review terminology Summarize main points from previous lecture Ask questions to determine if students recall key terminology, concepts, principles Provide 5 minutes for students to review notes from an earlier session	Retrieve critical information from long-term memory to working memory Search for past associations Review earlier notes
4. Presenting the stimulus material	Speak at a comfortable pace Provide salient organization of lecture points Pause to allow for questions, clarification	Alternate between own words and lecturer's words
5. Providing "learning guidance"	Use verbal cues such as "Note the following," "This is important to remember," "Record this in your notes" Use blackboard, overhead transparencies judiciously to highlight major points Raise questions to test comprehension of an idea Provide an outline	Discriminate between essential and nonessential information Uses mnemonics
6. Eliciting performance	During lecture, provide sample questions/problems similar to those which will be presented on an examination	Practice performance by overtly or covertly responding to questions/ problems Highlight notes material relevant to responses
7. Providing feedback about performance correctness	Request other students to respond to student answers Models responses to questions/ responses	Correct inaccuracies Attend to essential information
8. Assessing the performance	Encourage distributed and massed review of lecture content	Rehearse notes content in preparation for examination
9. Enhancing retention and transfer	Present divergent examples, nonexamples, and problem situations during lectures Explicitly link information from previous lecturer with current lecture	Integrate new information into existing notes

Source: Reprinted from C. A. Carrier, "Notetaking Research: Implications for the Classrooms," *Journal of Instructional Development,* 6(3) (1983):25. Reprinted by permission of the Association for Educational Communications and Technology. Copyright 1983 by AECT.

FIGURE 7.15 *Formats for Notetaking*

Sample Two-Column System

Topic: _____
Date: _____

Triggers or Key Concepts	*Class Notes*

Sample Three-Column System

Topic: _____
Date: _____

Triggers or Key Concepts	*Class Notes*	*Text Notes*

diately after notetaking (or as soon as possible) students should write down labels in the left column. These labels should tell what sort of information is found in the right column. He also suggests filling in any gaps in the notes while rereading and labeling. In three-column systems, the additional column generally serves as a space to write textbook notes so that they can be integrated with class notes. This is most helpful when the teacher's lectures make frequent, direct ties to the textbook. The following list gives several hints for helping students develop efficient notetaking skills.

1. Take notes using either a two- or three-column system.
2. Take notes on only one side of the paper.
3. Date and label the topic of the notes.
4. Generally use a modified outline format, indenting subordinate ideas and numbering ideas when possible.
5. Skip lines to note changes in ideas.
6. Write ideas or key phrases, not complete sentences.
8. Use pictures and diagrams to relate ideas.
9. Use consistent abbreviations (e.g., w/ = with, & = and).

10. Underline or asterisk information the lecturer stresses as important.

11. Write down information that the lecturer writes on the board or transparency.

12. If you miss an idea you want to include, draw a blank _____ so that you can go back and fill it in.

13. If you cannot automatically remember how to spell a word, spell it the way it sounds or the way you think it looks.

14. If possible, review the previous sessions' notes right before the lecture.

15. If the lecture is about an assigned reading topic, read the information before listening to the lecture.

16. As soon as possible after the lecture, go over your notes, filling in the key concept column and listing any questions you still have.

17. After going over your notes, try to summarize the major points presented during the lecture.

18. Listen actively! In other words, think about what you already know about the topic being presented and how it relates.

19. Review your notes before a test!

Direct Instruction of Notetaking. For many students with learning and behavior problems, just telling them how to take notes is insufficient. Teachers may want to develop and conduct a unit on listening and notetaking. The following is a list of teaching ideas for developing such a unit:

1. *Have students evaluate the effectiveness of their current notetaking skills and determine if they will profit from instruction.* Generally, this can be assessed in two ways. First, have the students bring to class current examples of notes and have them evaluate them for completeness, format, ease of use for review, and legibility. Second, present a simulated ten- to fifteen-minute lecture and ask the students to take notes. Give a test covering the information on the following day. Have the students again evaluate their notes and their test results.

2. *Use videotaped or audiotaped lectures when teaching students to listen effectively and to take notes.* The use of videotaped or audiotaped lectures is particularly helpful because it allows the students to replay the tape so that they can watch or listen for main ideas. For example, you may be teaching students to watch and listen for cues the lecturer gives to note the important information. After listening to a short segment of videotape, have the students list the cues and then discuss why they are important. Then replay the segment so that students can verify their list of cues and add other cues they may have missed.

3. *Control the difficulty of the lectures.* When first introducing new listening or notetaking skills such as listening for cues or using a two-column system, begin with short, well-organized lectures with ample use of advance organizers and visual aids, covering fairly simple, relatively familiar materials. As students reach proficiency, gradually increase the length of the lectures, reduce the use of organizers and visual aids, and increase the difficulty and novelty levels of the materials.

4. *Have students learn how to review their notes for tests.* Although students may learn to take more effective notes, they may fail to use them to study for tests. Teach students how to review their notes and ask themselves questions, using the "triggers" column to develop questions over the "notes" column.

5. *Have students monitor the use and effectiveness of notetaking in other classes.* To increase the probability that students will generalize the notetaking skills to other classes, have them discuss in which classes the skills would be helpful and then have them monitor and discuss their effectiveness in those classes.

6. *Have students determine the effects that notetaking has on learning.* Students need to know there is a payoff for their increased effort. Have students rate how well they feel they have taken notes over a unit or lecture and have them monitor their performance on tests over the material. This will aid them in determining if better notetaking leads to better learning.

Learning from Text

Probably the best-known technique for learning information from text is SQ3R, developed by Robinson (1946). This acronym stands for the five steps in this study skill: Survey, Question, Read, Recite, Review. The purpose of this technique is to provide students with a systematic approach to studying text. The following is a brief description of each one of the five steps in the process.

Survey: Read through the headings quickly to learn what is to be studied.

Question: Change each heading into a question (to have in mind what is to be learned from the reading).

Read: Read to answer the question.

Recite: At the end of each heading, either write brief notes about the highlights of the reading or engage in self-recitation.

Review: After completing the above steps on the entire selection, review the main points of the notes by self-recitation and check to see if the information is correct. (Adapted from F. P. Robinson, *Effective Study* [New York: Harper and Brothers], 1946.)

Although SQ3R seems well based in information processing theory, research has yet to support its effectiveness (Adams, Carnine, and Gersten, 1982; Johns and McNamara, 1980). One of the major difficulties associated with the SQ3R method is the complexity of the process, particularly for students who are experiencing reading problems. In content area classes, these students are often attempting to read and learn information from textbooks written above their instructional reading levels.

Multipass. Schumaker, Deshler, Alley, Warner, and Denton (1982) have developed a strategy based on SQ3R. It incorporates the learning acquisition and generalization stages from the Learning Strategy Model (see Chapter 2) and it is designed for students who experience problems learning information from textbooks. This strategy is referred to as *Multipass* because the students make three passes through the text while carrying out the process. Each pass through the text (i.e., Survey, Size-up, and Sort-out) entails the use of a different substrategy. Because each substrategy represents a fairly complex set of behaviors, each of the substrategies is taught as a unit, with the students reaching proficiency in the first substrategy before they learn the next substrategy. Prerequisite skills include the ability to paraphrase and a reading level of fourth grade or above. Research conducted with eight learning-disabled high-school students indicated that the students were able to master the strategy in instructional level materials and were able to use the strategy in grade-level materials without further training or practice. The students' grade on content tests improved—from barely passing to grades of C or better.

Survey: During the Survey Pass, students become familiar with the main ideas and organization of the chapter. In completing the Survey Pass, students are directed to do the following:

1. *Title.* Read the chapter title and think about how it fits with what you have already studied. Predict what the chapter is going to be about.

2. *Introduction.* Read the introduction and make a statement about the main idea of the chapter. If there is no introduction, read the first paragraph, which is generally the introduction.

3. *Summary.* Turn to the last page of the chapter, read the summary, and make a summary statement. If there is no summary, check the last paragraph to see if it is a summary. If it is not a summary, make a mental note so that you can summarize later.

4. *Organization.* Look through the chapter to see how the chapter is organized. Use the major headings to make a written outline. Paraphrase each heading.

5. *Pictures, maps, charts.* Look at the illustrations. Think about why they might have been included.

6. *Table of Contents.* Find out how this chapter fits in with the other information in the book by perusing the table of contents. Decide what relationships this chapter has with the others, especially the chapters immediately preceding and following. For example, in a history book, chapters are often related because of chronological sequence. Chapters might also have a causal relationship (e.g., Chapter 6 talks about the causes of the Depression; Chapter 7 talks about its effects). Other types of frequently occurring relationships include: general/specific, compare/contrast, and related concepts.

After completing this process, close the book and think about what the chapter is going to be about and what you already know about the topic.

Using the Learning Strategies Model, the teacher first describes and then models this survey process. The students should practice with guidance and feedback in materials at their reading instructional level until they are effective and efficient at surveying a chapter.

Size-up. During the Size-up Pass, students gain more specific information from the chapter without reading the chapter from beginning to end. Whereas the Survey Pass provides a general framework for the chapter, the Size-up Pass allows the students to look for the information that fits into that general framework using *textual cues.* In learning the Size-up Pass, students do the following:

1. *Illustrations.* Again, look over the pictures, maps, and charts and read the captions. Think about why they are included.

2. *Questions.* Read the questions, including those found at the beginning or interspersed in the chapter. If you can already answer a study question, put a check by it.

3. *Words.* Read over the vocabulary words, including any vocabulary list and words highlighted in the chapter.

4. *Headings.* *Read* the heading. *Ask* yourself a question that you think will be answered in the section. *Scan* for the answer. When you find the answer, *paraphrase* it orally or state something you have learned from the information under the heading. *Note* on your outline what information you have learned from the section.

Like the Survey Pass, the teacher will need to model the Size-up process and the students should practice in instructional level material until they are proficient.

Sort-out. During this third and final pass, the students test themselves on the material in the chapter. This pass assists them in determining what they have learned and on what information they should still concentrate. In the final pass, the students read and answer each question at the end of the chapter, using the following process.

1. *Read.* Read the study question at the end of the chapter or each question provided by the teacher.

2. *Answer.* Answer the question if you can.

3. *Mark.* If you can answer a question, put a check by it; if you cannot, put a box in front of it. If you do not know the answer, scan the headings on your outline to determine in which section it most likely will be answered. When you find the likely section, look for the answer. If you find the answer, paraphrase it and check the box. If you do not find the answer, scan the headings a second time for another likely place to find the answer. Again, look for the answer and paraphrase it if you find it. If you do not find the answer after trying twice, circle the box so you know you need to come back to it later and possibly get help.

Like the other two steps, the students should practice in instructional materials until they are effective and efficient at answering questions over the material presented in the chapter.

▬ *Comments:* From the description of Multipass, it should be clear that when students use this strategy they do not have to read the text in its entirety. Instead, they study the text to determine the main ideas, its overall framework and related details, and to answer the study questions. In this way students can use this strategy in textbooks that are written above their instructional level. However, several cautionary notes are in order. First, remember to have the students reach proficiency on the Survey Pass before they begin learning the Size-up Pass, and to reach proficiency on the Size-up Pass before they learn the Sort-out Pass. This way, a complex study skill is broken down into more learnable processes for the students. Second, when the difference between the students' instructional reading level and reading level of the textbook is greater than one to two years, students will have difficulty moving from instructional-level materials to grade-level materials. Teachers will generally need to provide graduated instructional materials. (For example, Hector's instructional reading level is fifth grade and he is a ninth grader. Rather than moving from fifth-grade reading material directly to ninth-grade material, Hector will probably need to practice using the strategy in seventh-grade material as an intermediary step.) Third, do not expect students with learning and behavior problems to transfer this study strategy automatically to various content area textbooks. You will need to instruct for generalization (e.g., have students use the strategy in current textbooks, and try the strategy in regular content area classes).

Adapting Textbooks. Teachers may also find it necessary to adapt textbooks for students whose reading instructional level is well below the reading level of the textbook and who have not learned such study skills as Multipass. One of the most common ways in which texts are adapted is to put the text on audiotape so students can listen as they follow along in the text or simply listen to the tape. However, due to the listening and attentional deficits of many students with behavior and learning problems, this technique has not been shown to be as successful as anticipated. Figure 7.16 presents some ideas for adapting textbooks that require more than simply taping the next.

Expression Skills

Expression skills include memory, retrieval, and test-taking skills, as well as other oral and/or written expression skills used to demonstrate understanding and application of knowledge.

Remembering Information

Have you ever found yourself at the grocery store with your grocery list still on the kitchen table? There you are, trying to remember what was on the list. What are the strategies you utilize to help you get home from the store with what you need? Perhaps you first try to remember how many items were on the list. Then you might try going up and down the aisles, looking at the various items and trying to remember if they were on the list. Or you might visualize (picture in your mind) your kitchen. First you think of the refrigerator and try to remember what was missing. Next you think of each cabinet to remind you of the items that might have been on your list. Or you might try to remember the list, particularly if it is relatively short and you can remember the number of items on it.

In some ways, remembering information for a test is not unlike remembering the items on a grocery list. Often we are asked to remember a list of things (e.g., the major exports of England, the different kinds of flour and their uses, the names of the cranial nerves). During tests we may be asked to take this informaton and apply

FIGURE 7.16 *Ideas for Adapting Textbooks*

1. Select compatible reading materials that cover similar content but have a lower estimated readability.
2. Provide an outline of the text that the students can complete as they read. This serves to guide the students' reading.
3. Underline key points and use margin notes to highlight important information.
4. Develop a question guide in which the reader is asked to answer several relevant questions for each section.
5. Tape record the text. When tape recording, incorporate the following suggestions:
   - Rather than recording an entire chapter, verbatim, read the key sections and paraphrase the less important sections.
   - Code the text so the reader or listener will know if the person on the tape is reading or paraphrasing.
   - Provide a short advanced organizer on the tape to assist the student in getting ready to read and listen.
   - Insert questions that the reader or listener can stop and think about.
   - Remind the reader or listener to stop and periodically think about what he or she has read.
   - Use a natural tone of voice and a comfortable rate.
   - Have students experiment with taped texts to see if they comprehend better with or without the text.

it to specific situations (e.g., to support why England's economy is struggling), but we still need to remember the basic information.

Information processing and schema theory stress the importance of helping students develop strong relationships among the new concepts being presented and between the new information and prior knowledge. Many content area learning strategies such as semantic mapping, advance organizers, and semantic feature analysis can be thought of as teaching procedures that facilitate memory. In addition to these kinds of activities, a number of formal schemes have been deliberately designed to improve memory. These are often referred to as *mnemonic devices* (Devine, 1987). For mnemonic devices, the information to be learned needs to be distilled so that the students are learning conceptual lists or frameworks. It is this information that is then operated on when using mnemonics. Mnemonic devices can be grouped into three types: organization and association, visualization or mental imagery, and rehearsal.

Organization and Association. Organizing and associating information refers to arranging the information or associating it with other information in such a way that it is easier to remember. Study the list of terms below in order to remember them:

Democracy	Mammals
Socket Wrench	Judiciary
Biology	Anatomy
Photosynthesis	Drill Press
Lathe	Blow Torch
Freedom of Speech	Constitution

Chances are that you categorized the words according to three superordinate categories, possibly labeled *tools, science concepts*, and *social studies concepts*. Now, instead of learning twelve unrelated words you are learning three sets of four related words. Research would show that the second task is considerably easier. Research and practice have also demonstrated that although most normally achieving school-aged children spontaneously categorize or associate items, students experiencing learning problems do not tend to make these associations spontaneously. Therefore, one mnemonic device to teach students when trying to remember lists of information is to associate or categorize related ideas.

Another type of association is the use of acronyms. Do you remember learning the names of the spaces on the treble clef as the word *FACE* and the names of the lines as *"Every Good Boy Does Fine"*? These are types of acronyms. In the first type, the first letter in each word or phrase of the list is used to form a word. If needed, extra letters can be inserted, or the letters can be rearranged. Schumaker, Denton, and Deshler (1984) used this strategy when developing the paraphrasing strategy RAP (*R*ead, *A*sk yourself, *P*araphrase).

The second type of acronym is one in which the first letter of each item of the list is used to make a sentence or saying. For example, using the sentence, *"Kings play cards on fine green sofas"* can aid memory of the biological classification system:

Kingdom	Family
Phylum	Genus
Class	Species
Order	

One of the strategies in the Learning Strategies Curriculum teaches students how to make lists of important information, develop an acronym, and memorize the list (Nagel, Schumaker, and Deshler, 1986). After the students have made their lists they design a mnemonic device using the following steps:

Form a word.
Insert a letter(s).
Rearrange the letters.
Shape a sentence.
Try combinations.

Hence, the name of the strategy is *The FIRST-Letter Mnemonic Strategy.*

Visualization. Another technique that can be helpful in remembering is the use of visualization. Visualization is simply seeing in your mind's eye what you are trying to remember. You may have used visualization when trying to remember what was on your grocery list by trying to "picture" the list. Visualization plays an important role in spelling. Another related mnemonic device is the use of *mental imagery*. With mental imagery the person usually formulates a picture or sequence of pictures that helps him or her remember the items. Often the pictures are absurd or novel.

One method that capitalizes on this mental imagery and has been intensively researched with learning-disabled students is *reconstructive elaborations* and the *keyword method* (Pressley, Levin, and Delaney, 1982; Scruggs and Mastropieri, 1989a). This method has been particularly successful in improving the ability of students with learning disabilities and language disorders to remember vocabulary words and their meanings in content area texts (e.g., Mastropieri, Scruggs, and Mushinski Fulk, 1990; Mastropieri, Scruggs, McLoone, and Levin, 1985; Scruggs and Mastropieri, 1989b). To help students remember critical information from units or chapters in social studies, science, or other content areas, reconstructive elaborations are used to make the information more familiar and concrete and to demonstrate relationships in an interactive picture or image (Mastropieri and Scruggs, 1989). An example will demonstrate how this method works: In studying mythology, it may be important to remember that *Zeus* was the *king* of the gods. To learn this information using the *keyword* method, the learner first *recodes* the stimulus, *Zeus*, into a familiar, easily pictured, similar-sounding keyword. *Zoo* is a good keyword here because it is easily pictured and sounds much like *Zeus*. In the *relating* stage, the learner relates the transformed stimulus, *Zoo*, to the to-be-associated response, *king*, via an interactive picture. In this case, a king could be pictured in a zoo (see Figure 7.17). With the final *retrieving* component, when the

FIGURE 7.17   *Mnemonic Representation for Zeus (king of gods)*

KING of Gods   Zeus (zoo)

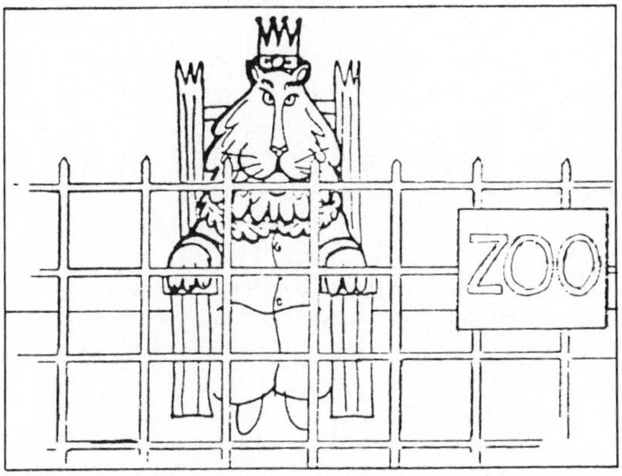

Source: M. A. Mastropieri, T. E. Scruggs, B. McLoone, and J. R. Levin, "Facilitating Learning Disabled Students' Acquisition of Science Classification," *Learning Disability Quarterly, 8*(4) (1985):300. Reprinted by permission from the Council for Learning Disabilities.

learner is asked about *Zeus,* he is reminded of the keyword *Zoo,* which leads to the picture of the zoo with a king in it which, in turn, produces the appropriate response, *king.* (Mastropieri et al., 1985, pp. 299-300).

Mastropieri and Scruggs (1989) suggest three rules that help a teacher decide the type of reconstructive elaboration that might work best:

> *Rule A:* If the stimulus-response information is already concrete and meaningful to the learners, simply provide an interactive elaboration between the stimulus and response. Use of picture or mental images is particularly helpful.
> *Rule B:* If the information is familiar but abstract, reconstruct that stimulus into something more concrete and more meaningful for the learners, and then provide an interactive illustration or image for the learners with the reconstructed stimulus and the response. This may be accomplished by concretizing abstract concepts like "justice" or "liberty" with symbolic representations, such as scales, or Uncle Sam as a symbolic representation of United States policy.
> *Rule C:* If the information is unfamiliar, such as with unfamiliar names, places, and vocabulary words, reconstruct the item into something more concrete and familiar for the learner by means of the keyword method, and then depict that more concrete and familiar response in an interactive elaborative picture or image (p. 76).

Rehearsal. Rehearsing or saying aloud or to yourself the information over and over again can help facilitate memory, particularly short-term memory. One caution should be mentioned, however: Rehearsal is most effective if there is not a great deal of interference between the time of the rehearsal and the time of recall, and if the number of items to be remembered is limited. An example of interference would be if students were asked to learn the major exports of five Western European countries and used the technique of verbal rehearsal starting with France and then learning England, Spain, Germany, and Switzerland. By the time they learned the exports for Germany and Switzerland, this information will probably be interfering with their memory for the exports of France.

General Memory Strategies. Often several mnemonic devices are used simultaneously. For example, after you categorized the words listed on page 245 you could use acronyms within each category to help you remember the specific words, and then use rehearsal to practice, review, and test your memory. Teaching students with learning and behavior problems which devices to use for which types of information and how to combine strategies will generally be necessary.

In addition to teaching students how to use the various memory strategies, it is also important to teach students to use periodic review to minimize forgetting. Bragstad and Stumpf (1982) integrate the concept of regular review into their memory tips (see Apply the Concept 7.1).

Apply the Concept 7.1 _____

MEMORY TIPS

Jot your personal comments on the suggestions under the "headings" in the left-hand column.

1. What's your attitude?

What is your very favorite thing in life—a person? baseball? music? reading? How tough is remembering new information about that particular thing? That answer reveals your "memory potential." Are you impressed? You should be! (One student knows the batting averages of all the best players in the baseball leagues.)

"But," you say, "math is no fun." Keep telling yourself that and it never will be fun. Your prejudices affect your learning. Instead, give some *extra time* to the subjects you dislike. Research indicates that the more you know about any subject, the more interested you become. Positive achievement is likely to follow.

Don't be victimized by your own biases. You more readily forget what you don't agree with, so you'll reap remembering dividends by keeping an open mind!

2. Do you intend to remember?

Or do you just want to get the assignment out of the way? Without a conscious decision to remember, you probably won't, and no one remembers what she or he has never really learned in the first place.

Have high expectations of yourself! Focus on how good you'll feel after reading, when you know the material instead of just the three songs that played on the radio while you "studied."

Also, studying subjects that are different, rather than similar, one after another (for example, history, then math rather than political science), guards against interference and forgetting.

3. Do you personalize the material?

Have you ever forgotten a friend's comments on why you're special? Or a compliment paid you by someone you truly admire? Probably not. This shows the power of your memory if you are personally involved. As much as you can, follow this same principle in studying. For example, while reading, ask yourself, "How am I affected by this?"

4. Do you "chunk" the learning?

Right now, list three major ideas from the last reading assignment you completed. If you can't do it, then you're choosing to operate at a handicap. When you've finished studying a chapter and can recall seven or so major points, you've got those "key thoughts" that trigger your recall of the related significant details. A prime contributor to comprehension and memory, then, is to categorize ideas.

5. Do you "handle" the material?

The more means you use to learn new material, the greater the likelihood you'll remember it. *Draw* pictures to illustrate points. *Talk* over assignments with friends. *Recite* information to yourself. *Write* notes on important points. Each one of these aids will increase your chance of recalling information the next time you need it. "Handling" the new ideas results in their moving from short-term to long-term memory.

Remember—if you don't use it, you will lose it!

6. Do you recite and review regularly?

Without any special study approach, you will forget 80 percent of what you learn within two weeks! But you can reverse that trend if you recite (speak aloud) immediately after studying. Thereafter, review the content about once a week. When you feel that you've mastered the content, review it again— *overlearn* it—just to be sure.

Taking Tests

One of the major means teachers use to determine if students have learned new concepts and their application is through testing. There are several techniques students can use when preparing for taking different types of tests.

Preparing for Tests. There are several strategies to employ when preparing for tests.

1. *Manage study time.* Time management plays an important part in test preparation. Scheduling time to keep up with assigned material and to review the material will make the need to cram for a test considerably less, and it will reduce test anxiety.

2. *Find out about the test.* The more information students have concerning the format, type, and time allotment for a test, the more effectively they can study. Encourage students to find out the type of questions to be asked, the content to be covered, the level of detail expected, and the time allotment for the test. Demonstrate to students the importance of knowing this information by showing them how to study differently,

depending on the type of questions to be asked and the level of information required.

3. *Predict questions.* Demonstrate to students how they can predict the questions that will be asked. Have students use what they know about the teacher's testing style, their notes, including their "trigger words," their semantic maps or relationship charts, their frameworks developed from Multipass, or other study guides to predict questions. Encourage students to work in small groups and share information and predictions and to discuss answers to their predicted questions.

4. *Think general to specific.* Have students first paraphrase the major concepts or generalizations and then identify the specifics. Assist them in understanding how they can use notes and other organizing activities they have completed to help them determine the general and specific information.

5. *Think positive.* Students with learning and behavior problems have low self-concepts in regard to academic achievement and they are often test-anxious (Bryan, Sonnefeld, and Grabowski, 1983). Teachers can help to alleviate test anxiety by directly teaching students test-taking skills and having them monitor their effects on test results.

General Strategies for Taking a Test. The following general strategies for taking tests are suggested (Bragstad and Stumpf, 1982; Langan, 1982; Carman and Adams, 1972; Deese and Deese, 1979):

1. Bring the necessary materials.

2. Be on time and sit where you will not be disturbed.

3. Survey the test.

4. Schedule your time.

5. Be sure you understand the scoring rules.

6. Read carefully, including the directions. Look for clue words. This will vary for different types of tests.

7. If you have memorized a specific list of information for questions or a specific outline for an essay question, write that information before you forget it.

8. When answering questions, place a mark in the margin for those questions that are more difficult or those to which you want to return. After finishing the easier questions, then return to the more difficult one.

9. Place the questions in the context. Ask yourself how this question should be answered in light of the textbook or what has been said in class.

10. Review your answers.

Many of these general strategies for test taking have been incorporated in the Test-Taking Strategy (Hughes, Schumaker, Deshler, and Mercer, 1988), which is based on the Learning Strategies model. This strategy teaches students to prepare to succeed by first reviewing the test to gauge the time it will take and to get in a mindset to do well. Second, students inspect the instructions, underlining what to do and where to

respond and noticing special requirements. Third, students read each question, remember what they have studied in relation to it, and reduce their answer choices. Fourth, students decide to answer or abandon each question. Fifth, students use test-wiseness information to estimate their answers if they are not sure. Finally, students survey or review the test to ensure all questions have been answered and to review any problematic questions. While using such a strategy may not increase student performance dramatically, it can make the difference between receiving a D or C and a B.

Answering Specific Types of Questions. In addition to these general test strategies, additional ideas can be used, depending on the type of test. Apply the Concept 7.2 presents information that is helpful when answering objective-type questions (e.g., true-false, multiple-choice, matching, and completion) and essay questions. It is important to demonstrate the differences between the instructional words found in essay questions (see Figure 7.18 for instructional words and their definitions). One group activity that demonstrates these differences is to have students study the same information. Then ask the students to respond to questions using the various instructional words and to discuss how varying the instructional word varies the answer given. For example, ask students to define *democracy* and to describe it. Then compare the responses.

Instructional Activities

Appendix B provides instructional activities that are related to content area learning and study skills. Some of the activities teach new skills; others are best suited for practice and reinforcement of already acquired skills. For each activity, the objective, materials, and teaching procedures are described.

Apply the Concept 7.2

HINTS FOR TAKING OBJECTIVE AND ESSAY TESTS

To study for objective tests be sure to learn and review key terms, their definitions, and examples that clarify the meaning of these terms. Also study lists of items found in the textbook or in lecture notes.

Find out whether you will lose points for guessing incorrectly.

Specific Hints for Answering True-False Questions

1. Remember everything has to be true if a statement is to be marked true, but if it is to be marked false, only one detail needs to be false.
2. Analyze qualifiers. Read each question carefully, looking for qualifying words that tend to make statements false (e.g., *all, always, everyone, everybody, never, no, none, no one, only*). Several examples of false statements are:

   all: It was necessary for *all* the states to ratify the Constitution before it went into effect.

   always: In modern history, depressions have *always* followed wars.

   none: *None* of the Tudor kings was a Roman Catholic.

   only: In 1900, Britain and Germany were the *only* industrial states in the world.

3. Analyze qualifiers by looking for qualifying words that tend to make statements true (e.g., *certain, generally, most, often, probably, some, sometimes, usually*). Several examples of true statements are:

   some: *Some* colonists remained British subjects in preference to declaring independence.

   usually: Periods of prosperity *usually* produce great art.

   most: *Most* of the voting population in 1936 approved of the New Deal.

   certain: *Certain* types of personalities seem to make popular presidents.

4. Pick out key words. There will usually be a word or group of words upon which the truth or falsity of the statement depends.
5. Simplify questions with double negative by crossing out both negatives and then determining if the statement is true or false.

You won't be unprepared for essay exams if you anticipate several questions and prepare your answers.

Changes to:
You will be prepared for essay exams if you anticipate several questions and prepare your answers.

6. Usually your first impression is correct. Don't change unless you have a good reason.

Specific Hints for Answering Matching Questions

1. Read the directions carefully. Determine if there are an equal number of items in each column and if items can be used more than once.
2. Don't start matching items until you have read both columns and gotten a sense of the alternatives.
3. Start with the easiest items. One by one, focus on each item in one column and look for its match in the other column.
4. If you are allowed to use items only once, cross out items as you use them.

Specific Hints for Answering Multiple-Choice Questions

1. Answer the questions you know, checking or circling the numbers of the ones you want to come back to later.
2. Remember that you may not always be given a perfect answer to a question. In such cases, you must choose the best answer.
3. Use the process of elimination, crossing out the answers you know are wrong.
4. Be sure to read all the possible answers to a question, even though you are pretty sure an early answer is correct. Other options that could be correct are answers such as:

   c. A and B
   d. All of the above

5. Look for the key words in the stem and use those key words to help you eliminate answers.

   The American philosopher most influential in the philosophy of education is:

(continued)

Apply the Concept 7.2   *continued*

a. William James
b. Bertrand Russell
c. John Dewey
d. Nathaniel Hawthorne

Key words are *American, philosopher,* and *education.*

6. Minimize the risk of guessing by reading the stem and then the first possible answer. Next, read the stem with each separate answer. Breaking the items down this way will often help you identify the option that most logically fits the stem.
7. When you have no idea of the answer and must guess, use the following signals to help you determine the correct answer:
   a. The longest answer is often correct.
   b. The most complete and inclusive answer is often correct.
   c. The first time "all of the above" or "none of the above" is used, it is usually correct.
   d. An answer in the middle, especially one with the most words, is often correct.
   e. If two answers have the opposite meaning, one of them is probably correct.
   f. Answers with qualifiers such as *generally, probably, sometimes,* and *usually* are frequently correct.

Specific Hints for Answering Completion Questions

1. Read the question to yourself so you can hear what is being asked.
2. If more than one response comes to mind, write them down and then reread the question using each response to see which one fits best.
3. Make sure the answer you provide fits grammatically and logically into the blank.

An _____ lists ideas in a sequence. You know this answer must be a noun that starts with a vowel (i.e., *enumeration*).

4. If the instructor does not use a standard length for the blank, use this as a clue.
5. Some completion questions can require more than one word in the blank.

Hints for Taking Essay Tests

1. Read over the entire exam before you begin. If you have memorized information related to specific questions, jot down that information before you start answering individual questions.
2. Look for key instructional words in the question to help you determine how to structure your answer and determine what information to include. For example, you would include different information and use a different structure if you were asked to *list* the reasons for the American Revolution versus *discuss* them.
3. Organize your answers. A rule of thumb in answering essay questions is that you should spend at least one-fourth of your time planning what you are going to write. An outline or semantic map can be most helpful in planning.
4. Leave time to proofread your answers for clarity, legibility, spelling, and grammar.
5. When writing an answer, leave margins and do not write on the back of the paper. If your writing is large, write on every other line. This will make the exam easier for the instructor to grade.
6. If you do not have time to write an answer you may want to write your outline for the answer. Often teachers will give you a substantial amount of credit if they can see that you knew the information and simply didn't have time to write the answer.

Selected ideas adapted from J. Langan, *Reading and Study Skills,* 2nd ed. (New York: McGraw-Hill, 1982).

Summary

For secondary and postsecondary settings as well as the upper elementary grades, the success with which students with learning and behavior prob- lems are mainstreamed is dependent on the teaching effectiveness of the content area teacher and the study skills of the student. This chapter focused on both those topics, capitalizing on the relationship between the teacher and the learner.

FIGURE 7.18 *Instructional Words for Essay Questions*

Apply
  Take the principles and discuss how they would apply to the novel situation.

Compare
  Look for differences and similarities.

Contrast
  Look for differences and similarities, stressing the differences.

Define
  Provide a clear, concise statement that explains the concept.

Diagram
  Provide a drawing.

Discuss
  Provide an in-depth explanation. Be analytical.

Explain
  Give the reasons or the causes. Present a logical development that discusses the reasons.

Illustrate
  Use examples or, when appropriate, provide a diagram or picture.

Interpret
  Explain and share your own judgment about it.

Justify
  Provide reasons for your statements or conclusions.

List
  Provide a numbered list of items.

Outline
  Organize your answer into main points and supporting details. If appropriate, use outline form.

Prove
  Provide factual evidence to support your logical argument.

Relate
  Show the connectedness between the ideas.

Review
  Provide a critical summary in which you not only summarize but also present your comments about it.

Summarize
  Provide a synopsis without providing your comments.

Trace
  Describe the development or progress of it.

Utilizing teaching strategies that assist students to organize and relate information has been shown to increase their ability to learn from text and from lectures. Therefore, it behooves us to be listener-friendly lecturers and to use such instructional techniques as advance organizers, semantic feature analysis, concept diagrams, and semantic mapping.

At the same time, we can work with students to teach them effective methods of studying. This includes time management and notebook organization skills, strategies for learning from lectures and texts (e.g., Multipass), and strategies for remembering and retrieving information and for taking tests.

If we can provide students with sound content area instruction while at the same time teaching them study skills, then we have facilitated their success in secondary school settings.

Chapter Eight

Mathematics

Chapter Questions

- *What factors and learning difficulties might interfere with mathematics learning for students with learning and behavior problems?*
- *What are five important teaching perspectives that should be considered when designing a math intervention program for students with learning and behavior disorders?*
- *What are the mathematics skills that need to be taught so that students will have an adequate knowledge of numeration and place value?*
- *What are the strategies that can be taught to students who are having difficulty with basic math facts?*
- *How would you convince a fellow teacher that the use of calculators can be helpful when learning mathematics?*
- *What factors affect successful problem solving and what problem-solving strategy might be effective to assist students in becoming better math problem solvers?*

Esteban, a third-grade student who spends most of his day in a special classroom for behavior-disordered students, goes to the regular third-grade classroom each day for mathematics. He is in the top math group and is proud of this achievement. His special education teacher is pleased that he is fulfilling his behavior contract and has not had any serious disturbances in the first step to more involvement in the regular classroom.

Claudia, a seventh-grade student who spends part of her day in a classroom for students with learning disabilities, is not nearly so successful in math. In fact, when asked what her favorite academic time is during the day, she quickly answers, "I love to write. In fact, I think I will be an author. I have already written several books for the classroom and one was even selected for the library." When asked what she thinks of math, she looks away and says, "No way—Don't even mention it. I can't do math. We don't get along."

Claudia has had difficulty with mathematics since she was in the primary grades. Her first-grade teacher just thought she wasn't very interested in math, and asked her parents to obtain special tutoring help during the summer. Her parents found that the special help did little good, and when Claudia continued to have serious difficulty with math in second grade, the teacher referred her for assessment for possible learning disabilities. The assessment results suggested she had difficulty with spatial relations and using memory to recall rote math facts. She has received special help in math for the past four years, and though she seems to make progress, her math skills are still her weakest academic area.

Some students with learning and behavior problems have difficulty with language arts (reading, writing, and spelling), some have difficulty with mathematics, and some have difficulty with both. However, despite the number of students who have math problems, reading has received by far the most attention from researchers, writers, and even clinicians. Reading is often viewed as an essential skill for survival in our society, whereas math is often considered less important. With an increased need for students to understand problem solving for success in the workplace, the inferior status of mathematics instruction may need to change. Presently, learning-disabled resource room teachers spend approximately one-third of their time teaching mathematics (Carpenter, 1985).

This chapter's purpose is to increase your understanding of how to teach mathematics to students who have difficulty learning. The chapter begins by discussing factors and characteristics that interfere with math performance and then presents teaching perspectives that provide general guidelines for teaching math. The chapter follows with teaching suggestions for pre-number skills, followed by numbers and place value, computation, fractions, and measurement. The chapter ends by discussing strategies for teaching problem solving and approaches to increasing math performance.

Factors Influencing Math Ability

Kosc (1981) identifies the following four variables as significant influences on mathematics ability:

1. *Psychological factors* such as intelligence/cognitive ability and cognitive learning strategies
2. *Education factors* such as the quality and amount of instructional intervention across the range of areas of mathematics (e.g., computation, measurement, time, and problem solving
3. *Personality factors* such as persistence, self-concept, and attitudes toward mathematics
4. *Neuropsychological patterns* such as perception and neurological trauma

In examining these four factors it is not surprising that many students with learning and behavior problems have difficulty in math. Whereas most students with learning difficulties have average or above intelligence, they have been identified as inactive learners and as less likely to utilize cognitive strategies. Because much of their educational intervention has focused on computation, they often have limited exposure to other elements of math, including measurement, time, and practical problem solving. They are unable to apply the computation skills to everyday math problems. Many of these students have lowered self-concepts and lack persistence, which are characteristics that may interfere with learning math skills. The fourth factor identified, unique neuropsychological patterns, certainly characterizes many students with learning and behavior problems.

Homan (1970) suggests that the following difficulties may interfere with a learning-disabled student's performance in mathematics.

1. *Perceptual skills.* Because learning-disabled students often have difficulty with spatial relationships, distances, size relationships, and sequencing, these difficulties will interfere with such math skills as measurement, estimation, problem solving, and geometry. Students with perceptual skills difficulties will need practice in estimating size and distance and then in verifying estimates with direct measurement.

2. *Perseveration.* Some students may have difficulty mentally shifting from one task or operation to the next. This may interfere with a student's performance on problems that require multiple operations or on applied mathematics problems that often require several steps. The teacher can provide cues to illustrate the number of steps involved in each operation. After the skills for two operations have been mastered (e.g., addition and subtraction), the teacher can provide worksheets that include both types of problems.

3. *Language.* The student may have difficulty understanding such mathematical concepts as first, last, next, greater than, less than, and so on. When teaching arithmetic, the teacher's instructions should be precise. Presenting unnecessary concepts and rules is interfering and confusing to the students and distracts them from concentrating on the concept being presented. The teacher should demonstrate as well as provide instruction. Concrete objects should be used to illustrate abstract concepts. Give plenty of examples and allow students to provide examples to demonstrate understanding of concepts.

4. *Reasoning.* Reasoning is often difficult because it requires a great deal of abstract thinking. Teachers should use concrete materials and real-life application whenever possible. After students understand the mathematical concept at an automatic level, introduce tasks that ask students to think through the process, explain the rationale, and apply reason.

5. *Memory.* Many students with learning and behavior problems have difficulty remembering information that was presented to them. Teachers can assist students with memory problems by reducing the amount of new information the students are required to learn, increasing the number of exposures to the new materials, and giving the students opportunities to verbalize and demonstrate the new material.

These variables partially explain why students with learning and behavior problems have difficulty with mathematics. Students with learning disabilities often have difficulty applying learning strategies and are frequently characterized as having perceptual and neurological complications. Students with emotional disturbances may have greater difficulties with mathematics than other areas because it requires persistence and concentration.

Teaching Perspectives

When developing math programs for students with special needs there are several teaching perspectives that need to be considered for all ages and programs. These teaching perspectives include:

1. *Comprehensive programming.* Mr. Noppe was not happy with his math program. He taught a varying exceptionalities classroom (a special education classroom that serves all mildly handicapped students) at an elementary school, and 90 percent of his math program consisted of teaching math computation. In discussing his math program with a co-teacher, he said, "I know I need to include more than just computation, but I'm not sure what else I should be teaching. I guess I should ask the students to apply some of their math computation. Next year, I want to concentrate on my math program and make it more comprehensive."

Students need to be taught and involved in a full range of mathematics skills, including basic facts, operations, word problems, mathematical reasoning, time, measurement, fractions, and math application. Teachers should not focus their entire mathematics remediation on math facts and the four basic operations: addition, subtraction, multiplication, and division. The National Council of Supervisors of Mathematics (1977) described ten basic skill areas that should be part of a math program: problem solving; applying mathematics to everyday situations; alertness to the reasonableness of results; estimation and approximation; appropriate computational skills; geometry; measurements; reading and interpreting tables, charts, and graphs; using mathematics to predict; and computer literacy.

2. *Individualization.* Esteban and Claudia, the two students described in the beginning of this chapter, have very different needs in math. Students with learning difficulties are different from each other in their math abilities and disabilities. Individualized programs that respond to the needs of each student are necessary. Individualization in math programming refers not just to the task but also to the way the task is learned. Some students learn math facts through rote drill, whereas other students learn math facts by associating them with known facts. We often assume that an individualized program means the student works alone. However, individualization means the program is designed to meet the individual needs of the student, thus it is often beneficial for the student to work in small groups to learn new skills and rehearse and practice problems. In addition, small groups that focus on solving the same problem can include students of different abilities, particularly when the teacher creates a cooperative environment for solving the problems and allowing the students to learn from each other.

3. *Correction and feedback.* Receiving immediate feedback about performance is particularly important in math. If students are performing an operation incorrectly, they should be told what parts are correct and what parts are incorrect. Showing students patterns in their errors is an important source of feedback. Students also need to learn to check their own work and monitor their own errors. Remember, feedback includes noticing improvements as well as monitoring needed changes.

Students in Ms. Wong's math class were given a worksheet to practice their new skill of using dollar signs and decimal points in their subtraction problems. Ms. Wong told the students to do only the first problem. After they completed the first problem they were to check it and make any necessary changes. If they felt problem one was correct they should write a small "c" next to the answer. If they felt it was incorrect they should mark a small "i" next to the answer. They were also to indicate with a checkmark (✓) where they felt they had made a mistake. Ms. Wong moved quickly from student to student, checking their first problem. Students who had the first problem correct were given encouragement and directions for the rest of the problems. "Good for you. You got the first problem correct and you had the confidence, after checking it, to call it correct. I see you remembered to use both a decimal point and a dollar sign. After you finish the first row, including checking your problems, meet with another student to see how your answers compare. Do you know what to do if there is a discrepancy in your answers? That's right. You'll need to check each other's problem to locate the error." When Ms. Wong locates a student who incorrectly solved the problem, she says, "Talk aloud how you did this. Start from the beginning and as you think of what you're doing, say it aloud so I can follow." Ms. Wong finds that students often notice their own errors, or she will identify some faulty thinking on the part of the students that keeps them from correctly solving the problem.

4. *Alternative approaches to instruction.* If a student is not succeeding with one approach or program, make a change. Despite years of research there has been no single method of mathematics instruction that has been proven to be significantly better than others. This includes using a range of formats such as textbooks, workbooks, math stations, manipulatives, and so on.

5. *Applied mathematics.* Concrete materials and real-life applications of math problems make math real and increase the likelihood that students will transfer skills to applied settings such as home and work. Students continue to make progress in math throughout their school years. Emphasis needs to be on problem solving rather than rote drill and practice activities (Cawley and Miller, 1989).

After Ms. Wong's students were successfully able to use dollar signs and decimals in subtraction, she gave each of them a mock checkbook, which included checks and a ledger for keeping their balance. In each of their checkbooks was written the amount $100.00. During math class for the rest of the month she gave students "money" for the checkbook when their assignments were completed and their behavior was appropriate. She asked them to write her

checks when they wanted supplies (pencils, erasers, chalk) or privileges (going to the bathroom, free time, meeting briefly with a friend). Students were asked to maintain their balance in their checkbooks. Students were penalized $5.00 for each mistake the "bank" located in the checkbook ledgers at the end of the week.

6. *Generalization.* Generalization or transfer of learning needs to be taught. As most experienced teachers know, students can often perform skills in the special education room and are unable to perform them in the regular classroom. In order to facilitate the transfer of learning between settings, teachers must provide opportunities to practice skills by using a wide range of materials such as textbooks, workbooks, manipulatives, and word problems. Teachers also need to systematically reduce the amount of help they provide students in solving problems. When students are first learning a math concept or operation, teachers provide a lot of assistance to students in performing it correctly. As students become more skillful, less assistance is needed.

After Ms. Wong's students were able to apply subtraction with dollars and decimals to their checkbooks, she obtained the math textbook that was used in the regular classroom. She wrote the assignment on the board, just as it would be done in the regular classroom. Students were asked to copy the problems from the book and complete the assignment with very little teacher assistance. Ms. Wong was attempting to see how well their skills would transfer to tasks assigned in a way similar to the way they would be assigned in the regular classroom. Ms. Wong realized that before she could say the students had mastered the skill, they needed to perform the skill outside of her classroom and without her assistance.

7. *Allow students to participate in setting their own goals for mathematics.* Participation during goal selection is likely to increase the individual's commitment to the goal. Students who selected their own math goals improved their performance on math tasks over time more than did those students whose math goals were assigned to them by a teacher (Fuchs, Bahr, and Rieth, 1989). Even very young children can participate in selecting their overall math goals and keep progress charts on how well they are performing.

The National Research Council (NRC) has conducted an examination of U.S. mathematics education from kindergarten through graduate study (National Research Council, 1989). This joint activity was conducted by the Mathematical Sciences Education Board, Board on Mathematical Sciences, Committee on the Mathematical Sciences in the Year 2000, and National Research Council. The extensive report resulting from the work of these committees not only outlines problems in mathematics education but charts a course for remedying them. The suggestions that relate to students with learning and behavior problems follow:

- Do not alter curricular goals to differentiate students; change the type and speed of instruction.
- Make mathematics education student-centered, not an authoritarian model that is teacher-focused.
- Encourage students to explore, verbalize ideas, and understand that mathematics is part of their life.
- Provide daily opportunities for students to apply mathematics and to work problems that are related to their daily lives. Instill in them the importance and need for mathematics.
- Teach mathematics so that students understand when an exact answer is necessary and when an estimate is sufficient.
- Teach problem solving, computer application, and use of calculators to all students.
- Teach students to understand probability, data analysis and statistics as they relate to daily decision making, model building, operations research, and applications of computers.
- Shift from primarily performing paper-and-pencil activities to use of calculators, computers, and other applied materials.

The National Research Council (1989) reports that mathematics is "the invisible culture of our age" and emphasizes that mathematics is embedded in our lives in many ways:

Practical—mathematical knowledge can be put to immediate use. This includes figuring unit prices, comparing interest rates on loans, appreciating the effects of inflation, calculating the effects of a salary increase, and calculating risks.

Civic—mathematical concepts relate to public policy. This includes understanding taxation, inferences drawn from statistics on crime, health issues, and other related public issues, and reading charts and graphs depicting change in spending.

Professional—mathematics is a tool for success on the job. This includes all knowledge of basic and theoretical mathematics that is necessary for success in the workplace.

Recreational—mathematics can be a source of recreation and relaxation. This includes participating in games of strategy, puzzles, lotteries, and other related activities.

Cultural—mathematics is the appreciation of mathematics for its beauty and power to solve problems. Like language, art, and music, mathematics is an important part of our human culture.

As a teacher, you may want to be sure your curriculum includes all five dimensions of mathematics: practical, civic, professional, recreational, and cultural.

Prenumber Skills

Many students come to school with few experiences that allow them to develop important prenumber skills, such as one-to-one correspondence, classification, and seriation. The following section focuses on these important prenumber skills.

One-to-One Correspondence

Matching one object with another is a core skill in any mathematics curriculum. It eventually leads the student to a better understanding of numeration and representation. Early man used one-to-one correspondence when he kept track of how many bags of grain he borrowed from a neighbor by placing a rock in a bucket to represent each one. One-to-one correspondence is used today when we set the table, one place setting for each person; go to the theater, one ticket and seat for each person; and distribute paper in the classroom, one piece for each child. A sample of activities for teaching one-to-one correspondence include:

1. Use every opportunity to teach students the relationship between number words (e.g., *one, two, three, four*) and objects. For example, "Here are two scissors, one for you and one for Margo." "There are five students in our group and we need one chair for each student."

2. Use familiar objects such as small cars or blocks and give a designated number (e.g., three) to each student. Ask the student to place one block next to each of the objects pointing to the objects. "You have one block here and you placed one block next to it. You have a second block here and you placed a block next to it. And you have a third block here and you placed a block next to it."

3. Give the student a set of cards with numbers the student recognizes. Ask the student to put the correct number of blocks on top of each number card. Reverse the task by giving objects to the student and asking him or her to put the correct number card next to the objects.

Classification

Classification is the ability to group or sort objects based on one or more common property. For example, classification can occur by size, color, shape, texture, or design, Classification is an important prenumber skill because it focuses the student on common properties of objects and requires the student to reduce large numbers of objects to smaller groups. Most students are naturally interested in sorting, ordering, and classifying. A sample of activities for teaching classification include:

1. Ask students to sort articles into groups. Ask them which rule they used for sorting their articles.

2. Give students an empty egg carton and a box of small articles. Ask the students to sort the articles according to one property (e.g., color). Now ask them to think of another way they can sort them (e.g., size, texture).

3. Using an assortment of articles, ask students to classify several of the articles into one group. Other students then try to guess the property(ies) that qualifies the articles for the group.

4. Students can use pictures for sorting tasks. Animals, foods, plants, toys, and people can all be sorted by different properties.

5. Board games and bingo games can be played by sorting or classifying shapes, colors, or pictures.

Seriation

Seriation is similar to classification in that it depends on the recognition of common attributes of objects. With seriation, ordering depends on the degree to which the object possesses the attribute. For example, seriation can occur by length, height, color, or weight. A sample of activities for teaching seriation include:

1. Give students some objects of varied length and ask them to put them in order from shortest to longest.
2. Ask students of varied heights to put themselves in order from shortest to tallest.
3. Using a peg with varied sizes of rings, put the rings on the peg from largest to smallest.
4. Fill the same size jars with varied amounts of sand or water and ask students to put them in order.

Numeration and Place Value

Teachers and parents often assume that children understand numerals because they can count or name them. Understanding numerals is a very important and basic concept; many children who have trouble with computation and word problems are missing numeral concepts. For example, Michael's beginning experiences with math were positive. He had learned to read and write numerals and even to perform basic addition and subtraction facts. However, when Michael was asked to perform problems that involved addition with regrouping, he demonstrated he had very little knowledge of numerals and their meaning (as shown here), and thus quickly fell behind his peers in math.

$$
\begin{array}{ccc}
48 & 37 & 68 \\
+26 & +55 & +17 \\
\hline
614 & 812 & 115
\end{array}
$$

Understanding numeration and place value is necessary for:

1. *Progress in computation.* Like Michael, many students fail to make adequate progress in math because they lack understanding of numerals and place value.
2. *Estimation* (e.g., "number sense"). Many students with learning difficulties in math do not have a sense of how much $1.00 is, what it means

to have 35 eggs, or "about" how much 24 and 35 equals. They cannot check their answers by looking at problems and determining which answers could not be correct because the answer doesn't make "sense."

3. *Reducing conceptual errors.* Students who understand the meaning of the numerals 43 and 25 would be less likely to make the following error:

$$
\begin{array}{c}
43 \\
-25 \\
\hline
22
\end{array}
$$

4. *Understanding place value.* Students who know the meaning of the numeral 28 are going to have far less difficulty understanding the value of the "2 place" and the "8 place." Students need to understand the 2 in 28 represents two tens and the 8 represents eight ones.

5. *Understanding regrouping.* Regrouping errors, such as those below, are less likely to occur if a student understands numeration.

$$
\begin{array}{ccc}
39 & 56 & 41 \\
+27 & -18 & -24 \\
\hline
516 & 42 & 23
\end{array}
$$

6. *Application of math computation to everyday problems.* Students who do not understand the real meaning of numerals have difficulty applying computation to everyday problems.

7. *Understanding zero.* Students need to understand that 0 (zero) has more meaning than just "nothing." For example, in the number 40, students need to understand the meaning of the 0 as a place holder.

Readiness for Numeration

Engelhardt, Ashlock, and Wiebe (1984) identified seventeen numeration readiness concepts that can be assessed through paper-and-pencil assessment and interview. A list of the behaviors that correspond with each concept, along with examples of how it can be assessed, follows.

Concept 1

Cardinality—The face value of each of the ten digits (0 through 9) tells how many.

1. Identify sets with like numerousness (1–9). Circle the groups with the same number of "x's".

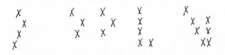

2. Identify, write, and name the numeral that corresponds to the numerousness of a set (1–9). Circle the numeral showing how many mice there are.

How many mice are there?

3   2   6   4   9

3. Construct sets with a given numerousness (1–9). Draw 5 dots.

4. Recognize sets of one to five without counting. Place from one to five objects behind a book. Say to the students, "As soon as I move this book I want you to tell me how many objects there are." Without counting, the students should tell you how many objects are in the group.

5. Represent and name the numerousness of the empty set (zero). The box has 2 hats in it. Make 0 hats in the circle.

Concept 2

Grouping Pattern—When representing quantity, objects are grouped into sets of a specified size (base) and sets of sets.

1. Form sets of ten from a random set of objects or marks. Circle the x's to make as many groups of ten as possible.

XXXXXXXXXXXXX   XXXXX   XXXXXX

XXXXXXXXXXXXX   XXXXX   XXXXXX

2. Construct appropriate groups to show how many. Give students about 125 popsicle sticks and rubberbands. Say, "Bundle these sticks so it will be easy to tell how many there are."

Concept 3

Place Value—The position of a digit in a multi-digit numeral determines its value (places are assigned values).

1. Given two multidigit numerals with the same digits but in different orders, identify the position of the digits as distinguishing the two numerals. How are 145 and 154 alike? Different?

2. Explain that the value of a digit in a multi-digit number is dependent on its position. Using the number 5, place it in each column and ask, "How does the number change?" "How much is it worth?"

100s	10s	1s

Concept 4

Place Value (base 10)—A power of ten is assigned to each position or place (the place values).

1. Identify, name, and show the values for each place in a multidigit numeral. Show the number 1,829 and say, "What is the name of the 8's place?"
2. Select the place having a given value. Show the number 6,243 and say, "Circle or point to the number in the thousands place."

Concept 5

One Digit per Place—Only one digit is written in a position or place.

1. Identify and name which numerals (digits) can be assigned to a place. Say to the students, "Tell me the numbers that can be written in the tens place."
2. State that no more than one digit should be written in a place or position. Then ask, "What's wrong with these problems?"

$$\begin{array}{ccc} 85 & 27 & 13 \\ +39 & +35 & +48 \\ \hline 1114 & 512 & 511 \end{array}$$

3. Rewrite or restate a nonstandard multidigit numeral (or its representation) as a numeral with only one digit in each place or position. Say to the students, "Write the number for this:"

$$\begin{array}{cc} 10s & 1s \\ \hline 5 & 4 \end{array}$$

Concept 6

Places–Linear/Ordered—The places (and their values) in a multidigit (whole number) numeral are linearly arranged and ordered from right to left.

1. Identify the smaller-to-larger ordering of place values in a multidigit numeral. Show the number 6,666 to the students and say, "Underline the 6 that is worth the most and put an X through the 6 that is worth the least."

2. Describe how the place values are ordered. Show the number 8,888 to the students and ask, "How can you tell which 8 is worth more?"
3. State or demonstrate that the places in a multidigit numeral are linearly arranged. Say to the students, "Rewrite this problem correctly."

$$\begin{array}{cccc} 7 & & 1 & \\ & 2 & & 4 \\ & 6 & 3 & 8 \\ + & & & 0 \\ \hline \end{array}$$

Concept 7

Decimal Point—The decimal point in a decimal fraction indicates the location of the units (ones) and tenths places.

1. Given a decimal fraction, identify the digit in the units (ones) place. Show the number 29.04 to the students and say, "Circle the number in the ones place."
2. Given juxtaposed digits and a digit's value, identify and place the decimal point to show the appropriate multidigit numeral. Show the number 284 to the students and say, "Place the decimal in the correct place to show 4 tenths, 2 tens, and 8 ones."
3. State the meaning (function) of the decimal point.

Concept 8

Place Relation/Regrouping—Each place in a multidigit numeral has a value ten times greater than the place to its right and one-tenth the value of the place to its left (place relationships and regrouping).

1. Describe the relationships between the values of two adjacent places in a multidigit number. Show the number 222 to the students and say, "How does the first 2 in the number compare with the second 2?"

2. Express the value of a multidigit numeral in several ways. Give the following problem to the students: 1 hundred, 8 tens, and 6 ones can also be expressed as ___ tens and ___ ones.

Concept 9

Implied Zeros—All numerals have an infinite number of juxtaposed places, each occupied by an expressed or implied digit. In places to the left of nonzero digits in numerals for whole numbers, zeros are understood; in places to the right of nonzero digits and the decimal point in decimal fractions, zeros are understood.

1. Name the digit in any given place for any multidigit numeral. Tell the students to rewrite each numeral and show a digit in each place.

	1000s	100s	10s	1s
683				
27				
79				

2. Rewrite a given numeral with as few digits as needed. Tell the students to X out the zeros that are not needed.

0301   004
1010   105

3. State a rule for writing zeros in a multidigit numeral. Ask the students, "When do we need to write zeros in a number?"

Concept 10

Face Times Place—The value of any digit in a multidigit numeral is determined by the product of its face and place values (implied multiplication).

1. Show, name, and identify the value of a specified digit within a multidigit numeral. Show the number 1468 to the students and ask, "How much is the 6 worth: 0, 6, 10, 60, or 16?"

2. Name and identify the operation used to determine the value of a digit in a multidigit numeral. Ask the students, "In 1468 we find 6 is worth 60 when we: add, subtract, multiply, or divide?"

3. State a rule for finding the value of a specified digit in a multidigit numeral. Ask the students, "How do you know 6 is worth 60 in the number 1468?"

Concept 11

Implied Addition—The value of a multidigit numeral is determined by the sum of the values of each digit (implied addition).

1. Express any multidigit numeral as the sum of the values of each digit.

294 = ___ ones + ___ tens + ___ hundreds

2. Express the sum of digit values as a multidigit numeral. Ask the students to write the numeral for:

4 ones + 3 tens + 6 hundreds = _____

3. Identify the operation used to determine the value of a multidigit numeral. Ask the students, "To know the value of 287, do we add, subtract, multiply, or divide the value of each numeral?"

Concept 12

Order—Multidigit numerals are ordered:

1. Order multidigit numerals. Say to the students, "Put these numbers in the correct order from smallest to largest: 1689, 1001, 421, 1421."

2. Describe a procedure for determining which of two unequal multidigit numerals is larger. Show the numbers 984 and 849 to the students and ask, "How do you know which is larger?"

Concept 13

Verbal Names (0–9)—In English, the verbal names for the numbers zero through nine are unique.

1. Identify the oral/written names of the ten digits. Ask the students to write the name next to each digit:

   0 _____ 4 _____ 8 _____
   1 _____ 5 _____ 9 _____
   2 _____ 6 _____
   3 _____ 7 _____

2. State the name for the ten digits.

Concept 14

Verbal Names with Places—In English, the verbal names for multidigit numbers (except ten through twelve) are closely associated with the written numerals (i.e., combining face and place names).

1. Give a multidigit numeral, identify the verbal name for one of the digits that includes both a face and place name. Show the number 2,847 and ask the students, "How is the 8 read?"

   a. eight   c. eighty
   b. eight hundred   d. eighteen

2. Identify the digit in a multidigit numeral that is stated first when giving the verbal name. Say to the students, "Write the number that is said first when reading the number."

   44 _____   6,186 _____
   284 _____   37 _____

3. Select two-digit numerals whose naming pattern is different from most. Ask the students to circle the numbers that when read aloud are different from the others: 17, 43, 126, 11, 281.

Concept 15

Periods and Names—Beginning with the ones place, clusters of three (whole numbers) adjacent places are called periods and are named by the place value of the right-most member of the number triad (e.g., ones, thousands, millions, etc.)

1. Given a multidigit numeral, insert commas to form "periods." Ask the students to put commas in the correct places: 28146   682   7810   192642
2. Name the periods of a given multidigit numeral. Ask the students, "Which number represents the periods?"

284,000,163 _____ .

ones, tens, hundreds, thousands, millions

Concept 16

Naming in Ones Period—Numerals in the ones period are named by stating, from left to right, each digit's name (except zero) followed by its place name (ones being omitted). (Special rules exist for naming tens.)

1. Name three-digit numerals (tens digit not 1). Tell the students to write the name for 683.
2. Name three-digit numerals (tens digit of 1). Tell the students to write the name for 718.

Concept 17

When naming a multidigit numeral, the digits in each period are read as if they were in the ones period, followed by the period name (ones period name being omitted).

1. Name multidigit numerals up to six digits. Tell the students to write the name for 284,163.
2. Name multidigit numerals over six digits. Ask the students to read the following

numbers: 1,846,283   27,219,143
103,600,101   3,078,420*

Teaching Place Value

Place value is directly related to the students' understanding of numeration. Students need to be able to:

1. *Group by ones and tens.* Using manipulatives, pictures, and then the numerals, students need practice and instruction in grouping by ones and tens. Students can sort manipulatives such as buttons or sticks in groups of tens. Students can also use a table grid to record their answers.

Tens	Ones	Numeral
2	3	23
6	2	62
4	7	47

Use "ten blocks" and "single blocks" to represent numerals. For example, 24 can be represented as:

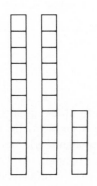

Flannel boards can also be used to group tens and ones.

2. *Naming tens.* Teach students to identify numerals by the number of tens. For example,

six tens is 60, four tens is 40, eight tens is 80, and so on. Give students opportunities to count by tens and then name the number. For example, "Count by tens three times." "Ten, twenty, thirty." "Counting by tens seven times." "Ten, twenty, thirty, forty, fifty, sixty, seventy." Also give students opportunities to draw picture diagrams that represent the place values of tens and ones and to identify the number from diagrams.

3. *Place value beyond two digits.* Once students can accurately group and identify numbers at the two-digit level, introduce them to three- and four-digit numbers. It is a good idea to be certain students have overlearned the concept of two-digit place value before introducing numerals and place value greater than two digits. Many of the principles students have learned with two-digit place value will generalize to three digits and beyond. Give students plenty of opportunity to group, orally name, and sequence three- and four-digit place values.

4. *Place value with older students.* Since place value is a skill that is taught in the math developmental sequence during the primary grades, students who have not adequately learned the skill will likely have problems with computation and word problems, and yet may have little opportunity to learn place value. Many of the games and activities designed to teach place value focus on young children and are less appropriate for older students. The following are some ideas that may be useful for teaching place value to older students:

a. An odometer

b. Numbers from students' science or social studies texts

c. Numbers from the population of the school (e.g., number of freshmen, sophomores, juniors, seniors, etc.)

d. Population data from the town, county, state, or country

e. The financial data page from the newspaper

*Source: From Helping Children Understand and Use Numerals (pp. 89–149) by J. M. Engelhardt, R. B. Ashlock, and J. H. G. Wiebe, 1984, Boston: Allyn and Bacon. Copyright 1984 by Allyn and Bacon. Adapted by permission.

Computation: Addition, Subtraction, Multiplication, Division

Most of students' time in math is spent on computation. Memorizing facts and practicing addition, subtraction, multiplication, and division problems are the major parts of many math programs. Students spend lots of time completing math sheets, workbook pages, and problems copied from a book that require the continued practice and application of math computation principles. It is probably for this reason that many students find math boring and not applicable. Computing math problems is much easier for students if they understand numeration and place value and if they are given frequent practical application of the math problems.

When students are having difficulty performing math computation, it may be because they:

1. Do not have an understanding of numeration and/or place value
2. Do not understand the operation they are performing
3. Do not know basic math facts and their application to more complicated computation.

Understanding Numeration and/or Place Value

The preceding section of this chapter focused on understanding numeration and place value. The material on understanding numeration presented guidelines for identifying and teaching students who have difficulty with numeration and place value.

Understanding the Operation

Ask the students to demonstrate their understanding of the operation by drawing picture diagrams and illustrating with manipulatives. For example, Sylvia was able to write the correct answer to the multiplication fact 3 x 2 = 6. However, when asked to draw a picture to represent the problem, she drew three flowers and two flowers. She seemed totally undisturbed that the number of flowers she drew was different from the answer she wrote. When asked why she drew the number of flowers she did, Sylvia said, "I drew three flowers for the 3 and two flowers for the 2." When the teacher questioned her further, she discovered that Sylvia had no understanding of multiplication. She had rotely memorized the answers to some of the elementary multiplication facts. The teacher used manipulatives such as chips and buttons to illustrate multiplication.

The following activities can be helpful in teaching students to understand the operation.

1. The following drawing illustrates how chips in rows can be used to illustrate multiplication. For example, ask, "How many fours make twenty?" "Fours are placed on the board _____ times."

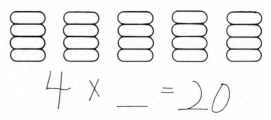

2. Have students "talk aloud" what is involved in solving a problem. Do not let them merely *read* the problem; ask them to *explain* what it means. For example, "63 − 27 means that someone had 63 pieces of gum and gave 27 pieces to a friend."

3. Have students explain the process to another student by using block manipulatives. For example, "24 + 31 is the same as adding 4 one-block pieces to 1 one-block piece with 2 ten-block pieces to 3 ten-block pieces."

4. Have students close their eyes and use noises to illustrate operations. For example, to illustrate multiplication, the teacher can tap in groups of six. "How many times did I tap a group of 6?"

tap-tap-tap-tap-tap-tap
tap-tap-tap-tap-tap-tap
tap-tap-tap-tap-tap-tap

"Yes, I tapped a group of 6 three times. Now I am going to tap a group of 6 three times again and I want you to tell me how many taps there are altogether." "Yes, when you tap a group of 6 three times there are 18 total taps." This same process can be used for addition and subtraction (Bley and Thornton, 1981).

Knowing Basic Math Facts

Two of the reasons students may have difficulty with computation have been discussed: (1) they do not understand numeration and/or place value, and (2) they do not understand the computation process. A third reason students may have difficulty with computation is they do not know the basic math facts. A common instructional misconception is that if students learn basic arithmetic facts they will no longer have difficulties with other arithmetic operations and problems. Arithmetic facts do not help the student in analyzing or understanding the application of arithmetic operations; however, they do aid in the acquisition and speed of performing arithmetic operations. Students who do not know the basic math facts are going to be considerably slower and less accurate in math computation. It is difficult for them to understand the math process because so much of their attention is focused on computing one small segment of the problem.

Using thinking strategies assists in the acquisition and retention of basic math facts (Thornton and Toohey, 1985). Without direct instruction, learning-disabled students often do not discover and use these strategies and relationships for learning and retaining math facts (Thornton, 1978).

Some of the thinking strategies used by students who are successful at solving basic math facts (Thornton and Toohey, 1985; Thornton, Tucker, Dossey, and Bazik, 1983) can be taught to students who are having difficulties.

1. *Using doubles.* Students can learn to use doubles to solve basic math facts. If the student knows 6 + 6 = 12, then the student can easily compute 6 + 7. Apply the Concept 8.1 illustrates picture devices to associate with learning doubles.

2. *Counting-on.* Students do not need to resort to counting from one to solve math facts. They can learn to count on from the largest numeral in an addition fact. For example:

Apply the Concept 8.1 _____

USING DOUBLES

Double	Visual Cue	Auditory Cue
2 + 2	(car picture)	The car fact (2 front tires, 2 back tires)
3 + 3	(grasshopper picture)	The grasshopper fact (3 legs on each side)
4 + 4	(spider picture)	The spider fact (4 legs on each side)
5 + 5	(hands picture)	The hands fact (10 fingers)
6 + 6	(egg carton picture)	The egg carton fact (6 in each row)
7 + 7	(crayon pack picture)	The crayon pack (7 in each row)

Source: N. S. Bley and C. A. Thornton, *Teaching Mathematics to the Learning Disabled* (Rockville, Md.: Aspen, 1981), p. 163. Reprinted with permission of PRO-ED, Inc.

$$7 + 2 = \underline{\qquad}$$

The student counts on two more from 7: "seven, eight, nine." Students can use this same principle when subtracting, only they count backwards. For example:

$$7 - 2 = \underline{\qquad}$$

The student counts backwards two from 7: "seven, six, five." Counting-on can be taught to students before operations are taught, and then they will only need to learn to apply the principle.

3. *Using the commutative idea.* The commutative property means that adding or multiplying any two numbers always yields the same answer regardless of their order. Students can be taught that with addition and multiplication, if they know it one way they know it the other. For example:

$$3 + 5 = 8$$
$$5 + 3 = 8$$

$$2 \times 9 = 18$$
$$9 \times 2 = 18$$

4. *Thinking one more or less than a known fact.* Yvette knew several basic math facts but had trouble with the more difficult ones. When her teacher taught her how to use the math facts she knew to solve the more difficult ones, her math performance improved. For example, Yvette knew $5 + 5 = 10$, but when she was presented with $5 + 6$, she began counting on her fingers. Her teacher taught her to think of $5 + 6$ as one more than $5 + 5$, and $5 + 4$ as one less than $5 + 5$. Pictures such as the following can help to illustrate the principle:

$$5 + 5 = 10 \qquad \vdots \ + \ \vdots \ =$$

$$5 + 6 = \qquad \vdots \ + \ \vdots \ =$$

$$5 + 4 = \qquad \vdots \ + \ \vdots \ =$$

5. *Using tens.* Students can learn that 10 + any single-digit number merely changes the 0 in the 10 to the number they are adding to it.

6. *Using nines.* There are two strategies students can apply to addition facts that involve nines. First, they can think of the 9 as a 10 and then subtract 1 from the answer. As illustrated here, the student is taught to "think" of the 9 as a 10.

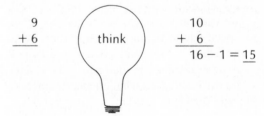

$$\begin{array}{c} 9 \\ + 6 \\ \hline \end{array} \qquad \text{think} \qquad \begin{array}{c} 10 \\ + 6 \\ \hline 16 - 1 = \underline{15} \end{array}$$

Second, students can think whenever there is a 9 in an addition problem the answer is always one less than the number they are adding to the 9. For example:

$$\begin{array}{c} 9 \\ +4 \\ \hline 13 \end{array} \qquad \begin{array}{c} 8 \\ +9 \\ \hline 17 \end{array} \qquad \begin{array}{c} 9 \\ +6 \\ \hline 15 \end{array}$$

7. *Counting by twos, threes, fours, fives, and tens.* Beginning with 10, teach students to count by the number. This may be done with individual students or with a small group. It is sometimes helpful to develop a rhythm to the counting sequence:

10—20—30—40—50—60—70—80—90—100

After students can count by tens to 100, ask them to count aloud by ten from two points other than 10 and 100. For example, "Count aloud from 20 to 80." After students have learned to count by tens, they should be taught to count by fives and then by twos, threes, and fours. Being able to count by multiples helps in addition, multiplication, and division. Multiplication facts can be taught by interpreting 3 x 4 as counting by threes four times. Division facts, such as $8 \div 2$ can be interpreted as, "How many times do you count by twos before you reach 8?"

8. *Relationship between addition and subtraction; multiplication and division.* After students learn addition facts, they can be shown the relationship between the addition fact and subtraction. For example, if a student knows $7 + 6 = 13$, students can learn the relationships between the known addition fact and the subtraction fact, $13 - 7 = $ _____ . Whenever possible, reinforce this principle as students are working, "You know $8 + 4 = 12$, so $12 - 4 = $ must be _____ ." Give students known addition facts and ask them to form subtraction problems. These sample relationships can be used to teach multiplication and division facts (see Figure 8.1).

If you think these strategies for assisting students in learning math facts seem logical and automatic, you are right. They are for most students. However, students with learning difficulties in math do not use these strategies automatically and it prevents them from acquiring the needed math facts for accurate and speedy computation.

When these strategies are directly taught, students' math performance improves. When Mrs. Zaragoza taught math strategies to students who were having difficulty in math she used the math strategies summarized in Apply the Concept 8.2, and she used other students who were performing the math skill accurately

to help her. She interviewed students who knew how to perform the skill and asked them to "talk aloud" while they solved the problems so she could learn what strategies they used. She then taught these strategies to students who were having problems.

Touch Math

Touch math (Bullock, Pierce, Strand, and Branine, 1981) is a procedure for teaching addition, subtraction, multiplication, and division to students with learning problems.

Many teachers comment on the effectiveness of using touch math, yet others are concerned about the long-range consequences (Flexer and Rosenberger, 1987). Concerns include: concepts of addition, subtraction, multiplication, and division are not really taught; number concepts are lost; counting backward is confusing to children; and it leaves students unprepared to do computational problem solving.

In *addition,* the student touches the dots on the numerals and counts forward. A circle around a dot means that the student counts it twice.

FIGURE 8.1 *Relationships Between Addition and Subtraction; Multiplication and Division*

Known Addition Facts	Made-up Subtraction Facts
$5 + 5 = 10$	$10 - 5 = 5$
$3 + 2 = 5$	_____
$8 + 8 = 16$	_____
$6 + 4 = 10$	_____

Known Multiplication Facts	Made-up Division Facts
$7 \times 4 = 28$	$28 \div 4 = 7$
$8 \times 8 = 64$	_____
$5 \times 9 = 45$	_____
$5 \times 10 = 50$	_____

The student touches the dots and says, "One, two, three, four, five, six, seven, eight, nine."

In *subtraction,* the student learns to count backwards.

The student says, "Eight," and then touches the dots on the three and says, "Seven, six, five "

Multiplication is taught by skip counting.

Apply the Concept 8.2

STRATEGIES FOR TEACHING ADDITION FACTS

Addition Facts Groups by Strategy for Recall

	Fact Group	Examples	Most Popular Strategy for Working Out Unknown Answers
	Count Ons	(+1, +2, +3, facts)	"Feel" the count
	Zero facts	(6 + 0, 0 + 4)	Show it
	Doubles	(4 + 4, 7 + 7)	Use pictures (e.g., 7 + 7 is the 2-week fact; 7 + 7 = 14)
No fingers needed!	10 sums	(especially 6 + 4)	Use 10-frame
	9's	(4 + 9, 9 + 6)	Use pattern
	Near Doubles	(4 + 5, 7 + 8)	Relate to doubles (via pictures)
	4 last facts	(7 + 5, 8 + 4, 8 + 5, 8 + 6)	Make 10, add extra

Note: Turn-arounds (commutatives of facts within each group) would be learned before moving to a different group of facts.

Verbal Prompts Used in the Addition Program

Fact Group	Sample Facts		Sentence Patterns (Verbal Prompts)
Count Ons	8 +2	3 +7	Start BIG and count on.
Zeroes	6 +0	0 +3	Plus zero stays the same.
Doubles	5 +5	7 +7	Think of the picture.
Near Doubles	5 +6	7 +8	Think doubles to help.
9's	4 +9	9 +6	What's the pattern?
Near Tens	7 +5	6 +8	Use 10 to help.

Source: C. A. Thornton and M. A. Toohey, "Basic Math Facts: Guidelines for Teaching and Learning," *Learning Disabilities Focus 1* (1) (1985): 50, 51. Reprinted with permission of the Division for Learning Disabilities.

$3 \times \cancel{4} = 12$ | The student counts by threes, touching a dot on the 4 with each count, saying, "Three, six, nine, twelve."

Division is taught by skip counting.

$24 \div 6 = 4$
/ / / / | The student is taught to skip count by six until he or she reaches 24. The student puts a slash on the paper with each count, saying, "Six, twelve, eighteen, twenty-four."

Math Computation Errors

How could students make the errors in Figure 8.2? It appears as though all the students did was guess. Yet each of the students who computed the problems can tell you what they did to get the answer. Most errors that students make are rule governed. Although the rule they are applying may not always be obvious, they are using some rule to tell them how to compute a problem. In Figure 8.2 problem (A), Erika said, "I took 1 away from 7 to get 6, and 0 away from 5 to get 5." In problem (B), Jeff added across, adding the 3 and 1 to get 4, and 2 and 3 to get 5. In problem (C), Yolanda said, "I knew this wasn't right but it was the best I knew how to do. I multiplied 3 x 4 to get 12, and then 6 x 4 to get 24." In problem (D), Shawn knew that 7 plus 7 plus 7 was 21, but he was operating under the faulty rule that you always carry the smaller

FIGURE 8.2

(A)	15		(B)	31		(C)	63
	− 7			+ 23			× 24
	65			45			2412

	(D)	37		(E)	13
		27			+ 4
		17			53
		72			

number, so he wrote the 2 in the ones column and carried the 1. Paulette, in problem (E), said, "I added 4 plus 1 because it was easier than adding 4 plus 3." When given several similar problems, she had no concerns about placing the number in the ones or tens column depending upon where it was easier for her to add. All of these students applied faulty rules for how they performed math computations. Once the teacher discovered the faulty rule they were applying, she was able to teach them the underlying concept and the correct rule for completing computations.

Teachers can learn a great deal about students' thinking in mathematics through an oral diagnostic interview (Lankford, 1974). Such an interview will provide information about what each student is doing and why he or she is doing it that way. For the diagnostic interview to yield accurate, helpful information, the teacher must ask the student questions about math computation in a nonthreatening way. For example, "I am interested in learning what you say to yourself while you do this problem. Say aloud what you are thinking." It is often most effective to use a different problem than the one the student has performed incorrectly. The assumption behind this interview is that there is an underlying reason behind the mistakes, and understanding why a student is making errors provides valuable diagnostic information which leads directly to instruction. Roberts (1968) identified four common "failure strategies" in computation. These are summarized in Apply the Concept 8.3.

Language of Math Computation

"What do you mean by 'find the difference'? Am I supposed to add or subtract? Why don't you just say it in plain English?" Many students with learning and behavior problems have difficulty with the language of computation. Yet understanding the vocabulary is important for success in the regular classroom, application to math story problems, and communication with others. Understanding the terminology of the four basic operations as well as the symbols associated with

Apply the Concept 8.3

ERRORS IN COMPUTATION

1. *Wrong operation.* The pupil attempts to solve the problem by using the wrong process. In this example the student subtracted instead of added.

$$\begin{array}{r} 24 \\ +\ 11 \\ \hline 13 \end{array}$$

2. *Computational error.* The student uses the correct operation but makes an error recalling a basic number fact.

$$\begin{array}{r} 24 \\ +\ 35 \\ \hline 58 \end{array}$$

3. *Defective algorithm.* The pupil attempts to use the correct operation but uses a wrong procedure for solving the problem. The error is not due to computation.

$$\begin{array}{r} 24 \\ -\ 17 \\ \hline 13 \end{array}$$

4. *Random response.* The student has little or no idea how to solve the problem, and writes numbers randomly.

$$\begin{array}{r} 304 \\ -\ 196 \\ \hline 396 \end{array}$$

Source: Adapted from G. H. Roberts, "The Failure Strategies of Third Grade Arithmetic Pupils," *The Arithmetic Teacher, 15* (1968): 442–446.

the processes is important. Students also need to understand the vocabulary that is associated with the answer that is derived from each of these processes. Table 8.1 shows a chart that can be used to illustrate the relationship between the process, symbol, answer, and problem.

After teaching the information on the chart, the following activities can be employed:

1. Cover one column (e.g., the symbols) and ask the student to write the answer.

2. Place each of the symbols, answers, and problems on a separate index card and ask the student to sort them by process.

TABLE 8.1 *Relationship of Process, Symbol, Answer, and Problem*

Process	Symbol	Answer	Problem
Addition	+	Sum	6 + 4 =
Subtraction	−	Difference	5 − 3 =
Multiplication	×	Product	8 × 5 =
Division	÷	Quotient	12 ÷ 6 =

3. Play concentration with two columns. Two columns of index cards (e.g., the symbol cards and answer cards) are laid answer down and each student takes turns searching for matching pairs by selecting two cards. When the student picks up a matching pair, he or she keeps the pair and takes another turn.

Use of Calculators

Many students with learning and behavior problems let computation interfere with their ability to learn problem solving. They spend so much time learning to compute the problem accurately that they miss the more important aspects of mathematics such as concept development and practical application.

In 1974, the National Council of Teachers of Mathematics issued a statement that urged teachers to use calculators in mathematics instruction (NCTM, 1974). Teachers did not adequately respond to this plea, with fewer than 20 percent of elementary teachers using calculators as part of their instructional program (Suydam, 1982). Many teachers did not use calculators because they felt the use of calculators threatened the acquisition of basic skills. Mr. Coffland, a third-grade teacher, put it this way: "If I let my students use calculators to solve problems, they will not have adequate practice in basic skills. They will become too dependent on using the calculator." Research suggests that Mr. Coffland has little to fear. The results of a summary of seventy-nine studies (Hembree, 1986) on the use of calculators suggest:

1. The use of calculators does not interfere with basic mathematics skill acquisition. In fact, calculator use can increase skill acquisition.

2. Only in grade 4 does sustained calculator use interfere with skill development.

3. The use of calculators in testing situations results in much higher achievement scores, particularly when students are low in problem-solving ability.

4. Using calculators improves students' attitudes towards mathematics.

In summary, as long as students are involved in basic skills instruction, the use of calculators is a positive aid to mathematics instruction. There are several ways calculators can be used with students who are having difficulty with mathematics instruction.

1. *Develop a positive attitude.* Using a calculator removes the drudgery associated with solving computations and makes problem solving fun.

2. *Increase self-concept.* Being able to compute extremely complex problems on the calculator gives students confidence in their mathematics abilities.

3. *Improve practice in problem solving.* Students are willing to tackle difficult problem-solving tasks when they have the assistance of the calculator in solving the problem. Students still have to decide what numbers are used, what operation is used, and whether ad-

ditional operations are necessary. Using the calculator can free students from the burden of computation and allow more focus on thinking about the problem.

4. *Develop their own problems.* Using the calculator lets students develop their own problems. They can then exchange their problems with each other, and use their calculators to solve them.

Fractions

Because of the availability of calculators, there is less emphasis on being able to compute fractions and greater emphasis on understanding the meaning and use of fractions.

The *concept* of a fraction can be introduced before the actual fractions are even discussed. For example, Figure 8.3 shows the relationship between common fractional terminology and its represented unit.

Children as young as ages three, four, and five are introduced to the concept of fractions as they help cook. "We use 1 cup of milk and 1/2

FIGURE 8.3 *Unit Representation of Fractions*

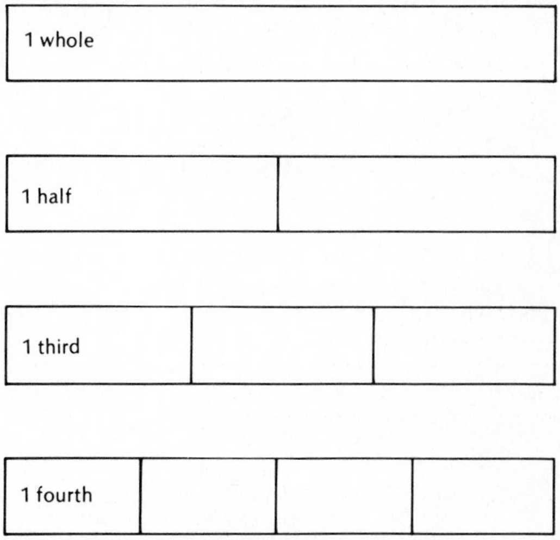

cup of flour." "You'll need to share the cookie with your brother. You each may have one-half of a cookie." Teachers often use cooking activities to enhance students' understanding of fractions.

There are many manipulative aids that can be used to teach fractions: colored rods, cardboard strips and squares, blocks, fractional circle wheels, cooking utensils such as measuring cups, and any unit dividers such as egg cartons and muffin pans.

Teaching fractions, as in teaching most concepts, proceeds from concrete to abstract. Apply the Concept 8.4 demonstrates the teaching sequence.

Measurement

Measurement includes weight, distance, quantity, length, money, and time. Measurement can be taught almost entirely with applied problems. For example, students learn time by using the clock in the classroom or by manipulating a toy clock; they learn money by making purchases with real or toy money; and they learn measures like cup, pint, and teaspoon through following recipes. With each measurement unit taught (e.g., weight, distance, money), the students need to learn the vocabulary and concepts for that

unit. Only after students understand the terminology and concepts and have had experience applying the concepts in real measurement problems, should they be exposed to measurement instruction through the use of less applied procedures such as textbooks and worksheets. Lerner (1985) refers to this as the "concrete-to-abstract progression" (p. 364). Lerner states that the teacher should plan three instructional states: (1) concrete or applied; (2) representational (e.g., toy money); and (3) abstract (e.g., workbook page with money problems). It is particularly important when teaching measurement to have overlearning occur at the concrete or applied stage. This section will focus on two forms of measurement: time and money.

Time

Even before coming to school, most children can tell time by the hour or know when the clock says it's time to go to bed or time for dinner. The following teaching sequence assists students in understanding time.

1. Teach students to sequence events. Younger students can sequence the normal routine of the school day. For instance, "First we have a group story, then reading, then we go to recess." Additional practice in sequencing events can

Apply the Concept 8.4 _____

SEQUENCE FOR TEACHING FRACTIONAL CONCEPTS

The student

1. Manipulates concrete models (e.g., manipulating fractional blocks and pegs)
2. Matches fractional models (e.g., matching halves, thirds, fourths)
3. Points to fractional model when name is stated by another (e.g., the teacher says "half" and the student selects a model of "half" from several distractors)
4. Names fractional units when selected by another (e.g., the teacher points to a fractional unit such as a "fourth" and the student names it)

5. Draws diagrams or uses manipulatives to represent fractional units (e.g., the teacher says or writes fractional units such as "whole," "half," and "third," and the student uses manipulatives or drawings to represent these units)
6. Writes fraction names when given fractional drawings (e.g., next to ▬▬▭ the student writes "half")
7. Uses fractions to solve problems (e.g., place 1½ cups of sugar in a bowl)

occur with story cards, events that occur at home, field trips, and so on.

2. Ask students to identify which events take longer. Name two events (e.g., math time and lining up for recess) and ask the student to identify which event takes longer. name several events and ask students to put them in order from the event that takes the longest to the one that is quickest to complete.

3. Incorporate calendar activities into the daily schedule. On each day discuss the special activities that will occur. For example, "Today is Monday. What special activity do we have on Monday? Yes, on Monday we go to P.E. Do we go to P.E. in the morning or in the afternoon?" When planning classroom activities use the calendar to discuss the day and date. Mr. Kyle developed a monthly class calendar and gave a copy to each student. He frequently refers to the calendar when discussing assignments, special events, holidays, or school business.

4. Introduce students to the concept of minute, half-hour, and hour by timing activities. For example, ask students to close their eyes for one minute. Ask them how many minutes it takes them to eat lunch, or how many minutes they spend working on their math.

5. Introduce the hands of the clock only after students understand the passage of time and about how long common events take. Introduce the hour hand first, without introducing the minute hand. When students can accurately tell time by the hour, introduce the minute hand.

6. Teach students to count by fives, then introduce the minute hand by asking them to count off by five. For example, after looking at the long hand of the clock on the 3, students count by fives three times. They conclude that it is 7:15.

7. Teach students to match, recognize, and identify the time on a clock, with the time written in digit form, and with the time written out. For example:

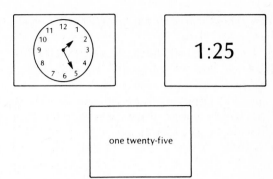

A scope and sequence of skills for teaching time is presented in Figure 8.4.

Money

Students with learning disabilities often have difficulty applying money concepts because they have not mastered many of the earlier concepts such as the value of coins, how coins compare (e.g., a quarter is more than two times as much as a dime), and how the value of the coins relates to what can be purchased. One parent reported that her child was frequently taken advantage of because he would trade coins of high value for coins of less value. Students with learning difficulties often do not know the price of common goods. Although they may not need to know the exact price of a loaf of bread or a television set,

FIGURE 8.4 *Time*

- Tells time to the hour
- Tells time to the half hour
- Knows the days of the week
- Knows the names of the months
- Tells time to the quarter hour
- Knows the number of days in a week
- Knows the number of months in a year
- Can use a calendar to answer questions about the date, the day, and the month
- Writes time to the hour
- Writes time to the half hour
- Writes time to the quarter hour
- Can solve simple story problems using time

they should have an estimate of what these items cost.

When initially teaching students to identify money, start with real coins. After they learn to recognize real coins, switch to play money, and then to representations of money on workbook pages. The following sequence is useful when teaching money identification:

1. First teach students to match the same coins. Give students several different coins and ask them to place all of the same coins in the same group.

2. Ask students to point to the coin when you name it. Depending on the students' skill level you may want to start with two coins (e.g., a penny and a nickel) and then progress to three and four. At this point the students do not need to be able to tell the name of the coin but merely to locate it when it is named.

3. Students name the coin. At this level the students tell the name of the coin.

After students are able to identify accurately the name of the coins, the value of the coins is discussed. Coins and dollars are discussed, both in terms of their purchase power and how they relate to each other. Activities and problems that require students to use money and make change assure students that they can apply what they've learned about money. For example, students can learn to use a cash register and to balance and keep a checkbook.

A scope and sequence for teaching money is presented in Figure 8.5.

Problem Solving

"I can read the arithmetic all right; I just can't read the writing" (Barney, 1973, p. 57). Many students with learning problems have trouble with traditional story problems in mathematics because their difficulty in reading makes understanding the math problem almost impossible. In

FIGURE 8.5 *Money*

- Identifies correctly penny, nickel, and dime
- Knows how many cents are in a penny, nickel, and dime
- When shown combinations of pennies, nickels, and dimes, can add to the correct amount
- Can describe items that can be purchased with combinations of pennies, nickels, and dimes
- Can solve simple word math problems involving pennies, nickels, and dimes
- Identifies correctly quarter, dollar, five dollar, ten dollar, and twenty dollar
- Knows the value of combination of quarters and dollars
- Can solve verbal math problems with quarters and dollars

---

addition, students with learning problems often have difficulty with logical reasoning, which is the basis of many story problems. It is also common that their mathematics education has focused primarily on the operation and not on understanding the why of doing it, or even a thorough understanding of the numbers involved in the operation. So, because of their difficulties with reading and logical reasoning, and perhaps because of insufficient instruction in mathematics, students with learning problems often find problem solving the most difficult part of mathematics.

Despite its difficulties, teaching problem solving may be the most important skill we teach students who have learning and behavior problems. Whereas most other students are able to apply the operations they learn to real-life problems with little direct instruction, students with learning problems will be less able to apply these skills without instruction, rehearsal, and practice. Learning-disabled students lack metacognitive knowledge about strategies for math problem solving. Poor math performance is not solely a function of math computation difficulties (Montague and Bos, in press).

Students need to know when and how to add, subtract, multiply, and divide. Knowing *when* involves understanding the operation and applying it in the appropriate situation. Knowing *how* is the accurate performance of the operation. Most students are better at *how* than at *when;* problem solving gives students practice at these skills.

Factors Affecting Successful Verbal Problem Solving

The factors that affect successful verbal problem solving or story problems (Goodstein, 1981) need to be considered by teachers when writing and selecting story problems and instrucing students.

1. *Cue words.* The presence or absence of cue words can significantly affect students' ability to solve verbal word problems. The cue word, *altogether,* is illustrated in the following example: "Mary has 4 erasers. Joe has 7 erasers. How many erasers do they have *altogether*?" The cue word, *left,* is illustrated in the following example: "Jackie has 9 pieces of candy. She gave 3 pieces to Tom. How many does she have *left*?" Students need to be taught to look for cue words that will guide them in solving problems.

2. *Reasoning.* Ask students to think about the idea behind the story problem. Does it appear the person in the problem will get more or less? Why? What operation will help solve this? What numbers in the story do we have to use? Are there numbers we do not have and need to compute?

3. *Syntactic complexity.* The sentence structure within the story problem needs to be kept simple. Learner performance can be significantly impaired when the sentence contains a complex interrogative sentence structure (Larsen, Parker, and Trenholme, 1978). The sentence length and vocabulary may also affect verbal problem solving.

4. *Extraneous information.* Extraneous information in word problems causes difficulties because the majority of students attempt to use all of the information in solving the problem. For example: "Mary's mother baked 10 cookies.

Mary's sister baked 8 cookies. Mary's brother baked 3 cupcakes. How many *cookies* were baked?" The information regarding Mary's brother baking three cupcakes is extraneous, yet many students will use the information in attempting to solve the problem. Extraneous information introduced into story problems is associated with decreases in accuracy and computation speed with students. Blankenship and Lovitt (1976) explain students' difficulties with extraneous information by suggesting that the difficulties are based not on reading the entire story problem but merely on knowing which numbers are needed to solve the problem. Students will construct the problem using the numbers available in the story problem, disregarding the question and the content available in the story problem. After students are successfully able to complete story problems without extraneous information, teach them to complete story problems with extraneous information.

5. *Content load.* The content load refers to the number of ideas contained within a story problem. The story problem should not be overloaded with concepts (West, 1978) and, if it is, the students need to be taught to discriminate between relevant and irrelevant concepts.

6. *Suitable content.* The story problems should contain content that is interesting and appealing to the students and relevant to the types of real problems the students have or will encounter.

Methods of Teaching Story Problem Solving

There are two important steps in preparing students for success in solving story problems: (a) provide story problems in an appropriate sequence, and (b) make students aware of the types of errors that are commonly made. Students also need to learn specific strategies that will assist them in using a successful process for mastering story problems in class and applying those principles to the mathematics of everyday life.

Apply the Concept 8.5 _____

STEPS FOR TEACHING STUDENTS TO SOLVE STORY PROBLEMS

Story Problem: Mark had $1.47 to spend. He spent
.34 on gum. How much money does he have left?

I. Read the Problem
   A. Find unknown words
   B. Find "cue words" (e.g., *left*)

II. Reread the Problem
   A. Identify what is given
     1. Is renaming needed?
     2. Are there unit changes?

B. Decide what is asked for
   1. What process is needed?
   2. What unit or category is asked for? (e.g.,
      seconds, pounds, money)

III. Use Objects to Show the Problem
   A. Decide what operation to use

IV. Write the Problem

V. Work the Problem

A step-by-step strategy for teaching sixth-grade students to solve story problems is illustrated in Apply the Concept 8.5 (Smith and Alley, 1981). Students need first to learn the strategies, practice them with support from a teacher, and then practice them independently until they can apply the principles with success. After continued success, students make adaptations in or condense the steps they use. The section on cognitive behavior modification in Chapter Two discusses how to teach students learning strategies.

Fleischner, Nuzum, and Marzola (1987, p. 216) devised the following instructional program to teach arithmetic problem solving to students with learning disabilities:

READ	What is the question?
REREAD	What is the necessary information?
THINK	Putting together = addition
	Taking apart = subtraction
	Do I need all the information?
	Is it a two-step problem?
SOLVE	Write the equation
CHECK	Recalculate
	Label
	Compare

Montague and Bos (1986a, 1986b) demonstrated the efficacy of the learning strategy approach, described in Apply the Concept 8.6, with high-school learning-disabled adolescents.

In summary, when teaching story problems to students with learning and behavior problems, keep the following guidelines in mind:

1. Be certain the students can perform the arithmetic computation before introducing the computation in story problems.

2. Develop a range of story problems that contain the type of problem you want the student to learn to solve.

3. Instruct with one type of problem until mastery is attained.

4. Teach the students to read through the word problem and visualize the situation. Ask them to read the story aloud and tell what it is about.

5. Ask the students to reread the story—this time to get the facts.

6. Identify the key question. In the beginning stages of problem solving, the students should write the key question so it can be referred to when the computation is complete.

7. Identify extraneous information.

8. Reread the story problem and attempt to state the situation in a mathematical sentence. The teacher plays an important role in this step

Apply the Concept 8.6

TEACHING ADOLESCENTS TO SOLVE STORY PROBLEMS

The eight steps in the verbal math problem solving strategy are described below:

1. *Read the problem aloud.* Ask the teacher to pronounce or define any word you do not know. (The teacher will pronounce and provide meanings for any words if the student asks.)

   Example: In a high school there are 2,878 male and 1,943 female students enrolled. By how many students must the enrollment increase to make the enrollment 5,000?

2. *Paraphrase the problem aloud.* State important information giving close attention to the numbers in the problem. Repeat the question part aloud. A self-questioning technique such as What is asked? or What am I looking for? is used to provide focus on the outcome.

   Example: Altogether there are a certain number of kids in high school. There are 2,878 boys and 1,943 girls. The question is by how many students must the enrollment increase to make the total enrollment 5,000. What is asked? How many more students are needed to total 5,000 in the school?

3. *Visualize.* Graphically display the information. Draw a representation of the problem.

   Example:

4. *State the problem.* Complete the following statements aloud. I have . . . I want to find . . . Underline the important information in the problem.

Example: I have the number of boys and the number of girls who go to the school now. I want to find how many more kids are needed to total 5,000.

5. *Hypothesize.* Complete the following statements aloud. If I . . . Then . . . how many steps will I use to find the answer? Write the operation signs.

   Example: If I add 2,878 boys and 1,943 girls, I'll get the number of kids now. Then I must subtract that number from 5,000 to find out how many more must enroll. First add, then subtract. + − This is a two-step problem.

6. *Estimate.* Write the estimate. My answer should be around . . . or about . . . (The skills of rounding and estimating answers should be reinforced at this step.) Underline the estimate.

   Example: 2,800 and 2,000 are 4,800. 4,800 from 5,000 is 200. My answer should be around *200*.

7. *Calculate.* Show the calculation and label the answer. Circle the answer. Use a self-questioning technique such as, Is this answer in the correct form? (Change from cent sign to dollar sign and decimal point should be reinforced when solving money problems.) Correct labels for the problems should be reinforced.

   Example:
   $$\begin{array}{r} 2,878 \\ +\,1,943 \\ \hline 4,821 \end{array} \qquad \begin{array}{r} 5,000 \\ -\,4,821 \\ \hline 179 \text{ students} \end{array}$$

8. *Self-check.* Refer to the problem and check every step to determine accuracy of operation(s) selected and correctness of response and solution. Check computation for accuracy. (Checking skills will be reinforced at this step.) Use the self-questioning technique by asking if the answer makes sense.

Source: From "The eight steps in the verbal math problem solving strategy" by M. Montague and C. S. Bos, (1986), *Journal of Learning Disabilities, 19*:27–28. Copyright 1986 by PRO-ED, Inc. Reprinted by permission.

by asking the students questions and guiding them in formulating the arithmetic problem.

9. Tell the students to write the arithmetic problem and compute the answer. (Some problems can be computed by the students in their heads without completing this step.)

10. Tell the students to reread the key question and be sure they have completed the problem correctly.

11. Ask the students if their answer is likely, based on their estimate.

Teaching math story problems does not have to be limited to the content area of math. Cawley (1984) discusses how story problems can be integrated with instruction in reading so that reading level does not interfere with understanding the math story problem. At the same time, story problems can enhance and support what the student is doing in reading. For example, a story about a mother duck and her babies was part of a student's reading lesson. During mathematics, the teacher makes minor changes in the story and uses it for instruction in story problems in mathematics (see Figure 8.6).

This same procedure can be used with junior high and high-school students' content area textbooks. Math story problems can be taken from social studies and science tests; Cawley and Miller (1986) refer to these as knowledge-based problems. Usually these problems require specific knowledge in the content area. Cawley (1984) identifies the integration of math into other content areas as an important means of promoting generalization of math concepts.

Goldstein (1981) recommends the use of pictures to facilitate processing information in solving mathematic word problems. For example, using Figure 8.7, the teacher could say, ''The small monkeys have four bananas and the large monkeys have six bananas. How many bananas would they have if they put them all together?''

FIGURE 8.7 *Pictures Help Solve Math Story Problems*

Approaches to Increasing Math Performance

Cognitive Approaches

Cognitive behavior modification (CBM) can be used with instructional procedures in mathematics. Cognitive behavior modification often takes the form of self-instruction, which relies on using internalized language to facilitate the problem-solving process. Based largely on the work of Meichenbaum and his associates (Meichenbaum, 1977, 1985; Meichenbaum and Goodman, 1971), CBM is receiving attention as an alternative strategy for teaching arithmetic to students with learning difficulties. Lovitt and Curtiss (1968) found that when students verbalize the answer before writing it, as opposed to just writing the answer, they make fewer computational errors. It could be that the process of verbalization focuses the students on the answer and gives them a second opportunity to check whether the answer makes sense and is correct. When verbalizations are added to the arithmetic process, either by naming the sign before proceeding (Parsons, 1972) or verbalizing the steps in the arithmetic process while solving the problem (Grimm, Bijou, and Parsons, 1973), there is

FIGURE 8.6

The mother duck went to the pond with her *8* babies. They looked for their new friend. *Two* more baby ducks joined them. How many baby ducks were there?

a significant improvement in performance. Leon and Pepe (1983) taught a five-step self-instructional sequence to special education teachers. Students participating in arithmetic instruction from these teachers who were trained in the sequence improved greatly in both arithmetic computation and in generalizing skills acquired.

The following sequence for using self-instruction in mathematics is a modification of the approach used by Leon and Pepe (1983).

1. *Modeling.* The teacher demonstrates how to compute the problem by using overt self-instruction. This overt self-instruction, or talking aloud of the process, assists students who have learning problems in knowing what they should say to themselves and what questions they should ask to keep them focused on the process.

2. *Co-participation.* Both teacher and students compute the problem together by using overt self-instruction. This step helps the students put the procedure in their own words and yet supplies the support of the teacher while they are still learning the process.

3. *Student demonstration.* The students compute the problem alone by using overt self-instruction and the teacher monitors the students' performance. The students are more independent in this step; however, the teacher is still available to give correction and feedback.

4. *Fading overt self-instruction.* The students continue to demonstrate the computation of the problem with internal self-instruction. Often students have a check sheet of symbols or key words to cue them to the key points.

5. *Feedback* The students complete the problem independently by using covert self-instruction and providing self-reinforcement for a job well done.

Operant Approaches

Operant techniques can be used to increase students' math performance. As you know, stimulus cues precede responses and often control or provide information to control responses. In arithmetic instruction, the teacher needs to identify the relevant cues and determine whether the students are aware of these cues and are using them appropriately. In Figure 8.8 three different problems are presented; there are many different cues a students must understand and attend to before accurately performing these problems. For example, in problem 1 of Figure 8.8 the student must know what " + " means, what the numbers represent, and what procedure to follow to perform the problem. In problem 2 the student must know what the picture represents, the difference between the short and long hands of the clock, and what each of the numbers represents. Problem 3 requires the student's understanding of the cue *long,* and what type of tool is needed to address the problem. Math provides many stimulus cues and the teacher needs to be certain that the students recognize and understand the cues and attend to them.

Teachers can also provide cues to assist students in learning new skills. For example, the following illustrates cues a teacher provided when students were first learning long division.

÷	(divide)	$6\overline{)478}$ $8\overline{)521}$
×	(multiply)	
−	(subtract)	
↓	(bring down)	

FIGURE 8.8

(1)   37
           24
       +89

(2) *(clock face showing a time)*

What time is it? _____

(3)   How long is this line? _____

Providing corrective feedback reinforces students' performance. Corrective feedback involves telling the students what they are doing well, including procedures, accuracy of responses, and work style. It also involves identifying in what area a student needs further assistance. Corrective feedback should be given frequently. Do not wait until students have completed tasks; give feedback while they are working on the task. Be precise with feedback; rather than saying, "You are doing a good job," say, "You remembered to carry. All of the answers in the first row are correct. Good job."

Task analysis is a process of specifying the behaviors needed for a particular task that can help shape student responses. The student is taught behaviors from the simple to the more complex until he or she can perform the target behavior. For example, the teacher's goal may be for a student to complete two-place addition with carrying by solving a verbal math problem. The student's present level of performance is knowledge of math facts when adding numbers between 0 and 9. Through task analysis, the teacher identifies the many behaviors that need to be shaped before the student is performing the target behavior.

For example, the teacher identifed the skills needed between knowing math facts between 0 and 9 and being able to solve a verbal math problem with two-place addition.

1. Number concepts
   0–9
2. Number concepts
   10–100
3. Place value
4. Simple word   Answers require
   problems (oral) 0–9   addition facts
5. Simple word   Answers require
   problems (written)   addition facts
   0–9
6. Two-place addition
   problems

7. Word problems   Answers require
   (oral) addition   two-place addition
   computation
8. Word problems   Answers require
   (written) addition   two-place addition
   computation

The teacher decided that it would take approximately three months to reach the goal. She knew that her mathematics program would focus on other skills during that period (e.g., time, measurements, and graphs) and it would take approximately three months for the target students to meet the goal.

Focus on Real-World Mathematics

Many students with learning and behavior problems manage to graduate with only a minimum understanding of mathematics skills. Many, relieved to escape formal education in mathematics, have the unfortunate misconception that they are finished with mathemtics. Unfortunately, they are sadly mistaken and they soon find that functioning as an adult requires applying mathematic concepts. Managing money, checkbooks, interest on loans, and credit cards is only the beginning. Adults must file taxes, complete employment forms for deductions, and use basic math skills in their jobs. The mathematics skills all students need to acquire because they are essential for survival in the real world are listed in Figure 8.9. To function completely in society, all students should be able to demonstrate applied knowledge and understanding of these skills.

Functional Math

Halpern (1981) suggests that mathematics instruction for learning-disabled students focus on teaching functional skills necessary for independent living. Many of the skills most important for learning-disabled students are not contained in

FIGURE 8.9 *Mathematical Concepts for the Everyday World*

More and more science and technology are permeating our society and with this the need for more mathematics to understand the scientific and technological concepts is increasing. The new level of mathematical competencies, skills, and attitudes toward mathematics required of modern citizenry is much higher than what was expected 25 years ago. The following represent the skills and competencies considered necessary for adults to participate effectively in contemporary society:

1. Numbers and Numerals
   - Express a rational number using a decimal notation.
   - List the first ten multiples of 2 through 12.
   - Use the whole numbers (four basic operations) in problem solving.
   - Recognize the digit, its place value, and the number represented through billions.
   - Describe a given positive rational number using decimal, percent, or fractional notation.
   - Convert to Roman numerals from decimal numerals and conversely (e.g., data translation).
   - Represent very large and very small numbers using scientific notation.

2. Operations and Properties
   - Write equivalent fractions for given fractions such as 1/2, 2/3, 3/4, and 7/8.
   - Use the standard algorithms for the operations of arithmetic of positive rational numbers.
   - Solve addition, subtraction, multiplication, and division problems involving fractions.
   - Sovle problems involving percent.
   - Perform arithmetic operations with measures.
   - Estimate results.
   - Judge the reasonableness of answers to computational problems.

3. Mathematical Sentences
   - Construct a mathematical sentence from a given verbal problem.
   - Solve simple equations.

4. Geometry and Measurement
   - Recognize horizontal lines, vertical lines, parallel lines, perpendicular lines, and intersecting lines.
   - Recognize different shapes.
   - Compute areas, surfaces, volumes, densities.
   - Understand similarities and congruence.
   - Use measurement devices.

5. Relations and Functions
   - Interpret information from a graphical representation.
   - Understand and apply ratio and proportion.
   - Construct scales.

6. Probability and Statistics
   - Determine mean, average, mode, median.
   - Understand simple probability.

7. Mathematical Reasoning
   - Produce counter examples to test invalidity of a statement.
   - Detect and describe flaws and fallacies in advertising and propaganda where statistical data and inferences are employed.
   - Gather and present data to support an inference or argument.

8. General Skills
   - Maintain personal bank records.
   - Plan a budget and keep personal records.
   - Apply simple interest formula to calculate interest.
   - Estimate the real cost of an item.
   - Compute taxes and investment returns.
   - Appraise insurance and retirement benefits.

Source: M. C. Sharma, "Mathematics in the Real World." In J. F. Cawley (Ed.), *Developmental Teaching of Mathematics for LD* (Rockville, Md.: Aspen, 1984), pp. 224–225. Reprinted with permission of PRO-ED, Inc.

mathematics curricula because they do not need to be taught through direct instruction to non-learning-disabled students. Halpern suggests learning-disabled students learn (1) the realistic prices of products, (2) how to estimate, and (3) how to tell time and estimate time intervals. According to Halpern (1981), most arithmetic done in the real world is done orally, and yet arithmetic done in classrooms is done with pencil and paper. More attention to oral practice in the classroom is needed.

Schwartz and Budd (1981) recommend math curricula for mildly handicapped students be based on the functional math skills they need. Figure 8.10 presents an outline of content for teaching functional math.

Schwartz and Budd (1981) recommend an eight-step functional math teaching sequence useful for initiating teaching strategies for a functional math curriculum. This approach appears to be particularly useful with junior-high and high-school students.

1. *Become motivated.* Students need to feel there is a valid reason for learning to solve mathematics problems. This may include identifying how math is used at home and on the job. Students can interview their parents to determine all of the ways they use functional math. Ask former students or speakers to discuss the need for math as they join the work world.

2. *Choose the operation.* When students are able to identify the question being asked, it is much easier for them to identify the appropriate operation for resolving the question. Students must understand how the operation is performed before they use the operation in functional mathematics.

3. *Understand the problem.* Students need to understand the type of question being asked in verbal problem solving. They need to understand such terminology as *fewer, greater, more, all together, in addition to,* and so on, in order to be successful at functional math. Present realistic problem situations and discuss the questions

FIGURE 8.10   *Content for Teaching Functional Math*

Consumer Skills
  Making change
  Determining cost of sale items utilizing percentages
    (e.g., "25% off")
  Determining tax amounts
  Doing cost comparisons
  Buying on "time"
  Balancing a checkbook
  Determining total cost of purchases

Homemaking Skills
  Measuring ingredients
  Budgeting for household expenses
  Calculating length of cooking and baking time
    when there are options (e.g., for a cake using two
    9" round pans vs. two 8" round pans)
  Measuring material for clothing construction
  Doing cost comparisons

Health Care
  Weighing oneself and others
  Calculating caloric intake
  Determining when to take medication

Auto Care
  Calculating cost of auto parts
  Measuring spark plug gaps
  Determining if tire pressure is correct
  Figuring gas mileage

Home Care
  Determining amount of supplies (paint, rug
    shampoo) to buy
  Determining time needed to do projects
  Measuring rods and drapes
  Finding cost of supplies
  Finding cost of repairs

Vocational Needs
  Calculating payroll deductions
  Determining money owed
  Knowing when to be at work
  Doing actual math for various jobs

Source: S. E. Schwartz and D. Budd, "Mathematics for Handicapped Learners: A Functional Approach for Adolescents," *Focus on Exceptional Children 13* (7) (1981): 7–8. Reprinted with permission from Love Publishing, Denver, Colorado.

being asked. Ask students to focus on key words and discuss their meaning. Assist students in identifying unnecessary information.

4. *Estimate the answer.* This step encourages students to check to determine if their selected operation is reasonable. For example, give the following problem: "How much money will John have left after he lends half of his total savings of $8.40 to his sister?" The student selects multiplication as the operation for solving the problem. The student estimates the answer and has a second opportunity to check whether the correct operation was chosen. Questions such as the following should be asked of the student. "After multiplying, will John have more money or less?" "When we lend money to people do we usually have more money or less?" "Is multiplying the correct operation?"

5. *Do the operation.* The students should be able to perform the operation, but a review of skills may be necessary.

6. *Check the answer.* The student checks to be sure the numbers were copied correctly and the problem was performed correctly. Students are encouraged to answer the question, "Is this a reasonable answer to the problem?"

7. *Understand the answer.* After determining the answer, the student should be able to interpret it. The teacher may ask additional questions that allow the student to more fully demonstrate understanding of the answer and the problem.

8. *Apply the skill.* Students are encouraged to counter. The application of the first seven steps is discussed relative to generated problems by the students and the teacher.

Curriculum and Materials

Traditional math curricula have provided problems for students with learning disabilities. These problems have been summarized by Blankenship (1984).

1. The reading vocabulary is difficult and the reading level is too high.

2. The sequencing of material presented is poor, with multiple concepts being introduced and skipping from one concept to another.

3. There are insufficient problems covering each concept.

4. There are insufficient opportunities and problems focusing on application.

5. There is too much variance in the formatting of the pages.

6. Students often do not have the prerequisite skills that the text assumes they possess.

Teachers who attempt to use traditional curricula with students who have learning difficulties will need to control for these factors in their teaching.

Recently a number of curricula have been developed that focus on teaching math skills to students with learning difficulties.

Project Math

Project Math (Cawley, Fitzmaurice, Sedlak, and Althaus, 1976) is a well-recognized math curriculum designed specifically for mildly handicapped students. The program includes work on sets, patterns, numbers, operations, fractions, geometry, measurement, and lab activities. It is both a developmental and remedial program and it has eliminated many of the problems associated with traditional arithmetic programs. Project Math reduces the reading level, provides a direct link between assessment and instruction, teaches to mastery, and provides procedures for individualizing instruction. It appears to be a very useful program for teaching mathematics to students with learning difficulties.

DISTAR Arithmetic

The DISTAR arithmetic program (Englemann and Carnine, 1972, 1975, 1976) stresses direct instruction through a highly sequenced format that provides immediate feedback to the student. The DISTAR Arithmetic Kits come complete with a detailed teacher's guide, workbooks, teaching book, and take-homes. The teacher's guide tells the teacher exactly what to say and do—even such directions as, "Say 'Good'." The materials are designed to be fast-paced with lots of oral drill. The DISTAR Arithmetic programs have been effectively used in teaching skills to economically disadvantaged children (Abt Associates, 1976; Becker and Englemann, 1976; Stallings and Kaskowitz, 1974).

Additional Sources of Curriculum and Materials

There are many other sources of curriculum suitable for teaching mathematics to students who have learning problems.

1. The *Computational Arithmetic Program,* developed by Smith and Lovitt (1982), provides 314 worksheets to teach basic math skills from grades one through six.

2. The *Corrective Mathematics Program,* by Englemann and Carnine (1982), provides remedial basic math for students in grades three through twelve.

3. *Structural Arithmetic* by Stern (1965) involves students in kindergarten through third grade making discovering and learning math concepts and facts.

4. *Cuisenaire Rods,* by M. Georges Cuisenaire, to give conceptual knowledge of the basic structure of mathematics.

5. *Milliken Wordmath,* developed by Coffland and Baldwin (1985), uses computer programs to teach problem solving within the mathematics curriculum to children in fourth grade and up who are unable to apply their computational knowledge to the solving of everday problems.

Instructional Activities

Appendix B provides instructional activities related to mathematics. Some of the activities teach new skills; others are best suited for practice and reinforcement of already acquired skills. For each activity, the objective, materials, and teaching procedures are described.

Summary

Developing appropriate mathematics instruction for students with learning and behavior problems involves comprehensive programming with an emphasis on its application to daily living skills. Special attention is given to factors that might influence the math learning abilities of special students. Psychological factors, educational factors, neuropsychological factors, perceptual skills, language skills, and reasoning need to be considered when developing a student's instructional program.

When developing comprehensive programming it is necessary to consider all facets of math instruction including: numeration, place value, facts, computation, time, money, fractions, and verbal problem solving. Success in teaching math is directly related to the student's ability to apply the concepts to math problems that occur in daily living.

Traditional math curricula have provided problems for students with learning and behavior problems. Often the reading level is difficult, the material is not sequenced, and there are not enough problems covering each concept so mastery can be assured before the next concept is introduced. These students need math problems to be directly linked to their real-world application.

Teaching math to students with learning and behavior problems is a challenge—potentially, a very rewarding challenge. Students with learning difficulties have evidenced greater gains through appropriate instruction in math than in most other content areas. Although students have access to computers and calculators, which can assist them in solving math problems they understand, they must know what problems they want to solve, the operation needed, and the procedures for computing the answers before they can fully use these instruments to assist in solving problems. Because of the increased need to use mathematics at the workplace, students need to understand mathematics now more than ever before.

Chapter Nine _____

Socialization

Chapter Questions

- *What is social competence?*
- *What are the characteristics of students with social disabilities?*
- *What are two types of social interventions used with students with learning and behavior problems? What are the procedures for implementing these social interventions?*
- *What are several principles for teaching social skills to students with learning and behavior problems?*

As Donna Douglas listened to her son, Jeff, playing with a classmate in his room, she closed her eyes and clinched as she heard him say, "That's not how you do it. I know how to do it, give it to me." She hoped the classmate would understand Jeff and not find his difficulty interacting with others so disagreeable that he would not return. Donna knew her son was not mean or cruel, but he had a difficult time communicating interpersonally with others. He had trouble making and maintaining friends. He didn't seem to know how to listen and respond to others, and often he expressed himself harshly and inconsiderately.

Mark's special education teacher's first comment to the school counselor was, "I feel let down. Mark and I had an agreement that I would give him free time at the end of the day if he brought a signed note from his regular classroom teachers that indicated his behavior was appropriate in class. After three days of signed notes and free time, I checked with his regular classroom teachers only to find out that Mark had his friends forge the teacher's initials. The teachers had not seen the note. Though this experience is discouraging, I comfort myself with the thought that two years ago Mark was incapable of spending even thirty minutes in a regular classroom without creating havoc. He has improved and he even has a friend in the regular classroom. It is comforting to know that despite periodic setbacks his social skills have gradually improved."

Jeff and Mark both have social skill deficits. Many students with learning and behavior problems have difficulties in school, home, and at work because of their interaction with others. This chapter will help you understand the social characteristics of students who have learning and behavior problems. How these students are perceived by others and how they respond to others will be discussed. In addition, interventions you might use to improve the social behaviors of your students will be presented, along with programs and activities

that may assist in teaching interpersonal social skills. The first issue to be discussed is social competence.

Social Competence and Social Difficulties

Social difficulties are frequently a characteristic of students with behavior problems, but what about students with learning disabilities? The Interagency Committee on Learning Disabilities offers the following changes to the definition by the National Joint Committee for Learning Disabilities (NJCLD). Changes made to the NJCLD definition are italicized.

> Learning disabilities is a generic term that refers to a heterogeneous group of disorders manifested by significant difficulties in the acquisition and use of listening, speaking, reading, writing, reasoning, or mathematical abilities, *or of social skills.* These disorders are intrinsic to the individual and presumed to be due to central nervous *system* dysfunction. Even though a learning disability may occur concomitantly with other handicapping conditions (e.g., sensory impairment, mental retardation, social and emotional disturbance), *with socio*environmental influences (e.g., cultural differences, insufficient or inappropriate instruction, psychogenic factors), *and especially with attention deficit disorder, all of which may cause a learning problem, a learning disability* is not the direct result of those conditions or influences (Kavanagh and Truss, 1988, 550–551).

Understanding the social difficulties of students with learning and behavior problems begins with an understanding of social competence and the characteristics associated with it. This section will also discuss the social characteristics of these students, along with a description of the social problems associated with adolescents.

Definition of Social Competence

We have all met people who seem to know what to say and what to do no matter who they are with or what situation they are in. Sometimes we watch with envy as they move from person to person, group to group, sometimes listening, sometimes talking, but always seemingly at ease. We often refer to these people as *socially competent*.

In an attempt to better understand social competence, a panel of experts met under the auspices of the Office of Child Development (Anderson and Messick, 1974). The result was twenty-nine statements describing social competence, ranging from self-concept to self-care to perceptual skills (see Figure 9.1).

According to Foster and Ritchey (1979), *social competence* is defined as ". . . those responses, which within a given situation, prove effective, or in other words, maximize the probability of producing, maintaining, or enhancing positive effects for the interactor" (p. 626), and, it should be added, without harm to the other. Social skills are not a specific skill to be acquired, but rather a set of skills that allows one

FIGURE 9.1   *Facets of Social Competency*

1. Differentiates self-concept and consolidation of identity.
2. Perceives self as an initiator and controller.
3. Meets common standards for personal maintenance and care.
4. Realistic appraisal of self and positive feelings of self worth.
5. Knows and understands the implications of feeling in self and others.
6. Sensitive and understanding in social relationships.
7. Develops positive and affectionate relationships.
8. Perceives and appreciates the range or roles assumed by self and others.
9. Appropriate regulation of antisocial behavior.
10. Exhibits prosocial behavior and is aware of the moral reasons for it.
11. Curious and exploratory about environment.
12. Direction, duration, and intensity of attention is controlled by the child.
13. Appropriate perceptual skills.
14. Appropriate fine motor skills.
15. Appropriate gross motor skills.
16. Appropriate perceptual-motor skills.
17. Appropriate language skills.
18. Appropriate categorizing skills.
19. Appropriate memory skills.
20. Uses critical thinking skills and is able to appraise own capabilities and resources in problem situations.
21. Uses creative thinking skills to generate a wide range of responses and conceptions to situations.
22. Uses problem-solving skills to generate solutions and make decisions.
23. Flexibility in the application of information-processing strategies.
24. Demonstrates age appropriate levels of concept attainment, understanding, and skills.
25. Demonstrates age appropriate general knowledge.
26. Demonstrates motivation to improve and become competent.
27. Uses external resources (e.g., adults, children, library, civil servants) to obtain assistance and learning.
28. Demonstrates some positive attitudes towards learning and school experiences.
29. Demonstrates appropriate involvement in humor, play, and fantasy.

Source: Adapted from S. Anderson and S. Messick, "Social Competency in Young Children," *Developmental Psychology, 10*(2) (1974).

to adapt and respond to the expectations of society. Social competence is a process that begins at birth and continues throughout our life span. The process of social competence begins within the confines of our immediate family and expands to include extended family, friends, neighbors, and social institutions.

Vaughn and Hogan (1990) have described a model of social competence that is analogous to intelligence in that it describes social competence as a higher-order, global construct that is made up of many components. Their model of social competence includes the following four components:

1. *Positive relations with others.* This includes the ability to make and maintain positive relations with a range of people including classmates, teachers, parents, and at later ages, intimate relations. With students the focus is usually on peer, parent, and teacher relations.

2. *Accurate/age-appropriate social cognition.* This component includes how the child thinks about self and others, as well as the extent to which the child understands and interprets social situations. This component includes social problem solving, attributions, locus of control, empathy and social judgment.

3. *Absence of maladaptive behaviors.* This component focuses on the absences of behavior problems that interfere with social functioning such as disruptive behaviors, anxiety, attention problems, and lack of self-control.

4. *Effective social behaviors.* This includes the range of social behaviors that are often included in social skills intervention programs. These social behaviors include initiating contact with others, responding cooperatively to requests, and giving and receiving feedback.

The most discriminating characteristic of students with behavior problems is their lack of social competence. These students are referred for special education because of severe difficulty in adapting to society and interacting successfully with others. Whereas the common characteristic of students with learning disabilities is problems in learning, many learning-disabled students are perceived by their peers and others as having social difficulties. Thus all students with behavior problems and many students with learning disabilities have difficulties with social skills.

Perceptions of Students with Social Disabilities

The social interaction of behavior-disordered students is often described as having two dimensions: externalizing and internalizing (Achenback and Edelbrock, 1978). Behaviors that are extremely disturbing and intolerable to others are referred to as *externalizing,* and behaviors that appear to be more disturbed than disturbing are referred to as *internalizing.* Figure 9.2 lists characteristics of internalizing and externalizing behaviors.

Behavior-disordered students who exhibit externalizing behaviors appear to be experts at identifying and performing behaviors that are most disturbing to others. Donald, in the following example, is a student who exhibits externalizing behaviors.

When Mr. Kline discovered Donald was to be placed in his fourth-grade class next year, his stomach did a flip flop. "Any student but Don-

FIGURE 9.2 *Characteristics of Internalizing and Externalizing Behaviors*

Internalizing	Externalizing
1. Social Withdrawal	1. Delinquent
2. Depressed	2. Aggressive
3. Immature	3. Hyperactive
4. Somatic Complaints	4. Cruel
5. Uncommunicative	5. Sex Problems
6. Obsessive-Compulsive	
7. Anxious-Obsessive	

Source: T. M. Achenbach, "Current Status of the Child Behavior Checklist and Related Materials." October 1984. Department of Psychiatry, University of Vermont, Burlington, Vermont, 05401.

ald,'' thought Mr. Kline, ''he's the terror of the school.'' Every teacher who had Donald in class had come to the teacher's lounge at the end of the day exhausted and discouraged. The real catastrophe was the effect he seemed to have on the rest of the class. Students who were only mild behavior problems seemed to blossom with Donald's encouragement. Donald's hot temper and foul language left him continually fighting with other students. This year he had socked his teacher in the chest when she tried to prevent him from running out of the classroom. While escaping, he shouted, ''I'll sue you if you touch me.'' As he was thinking of next year's plight, Mr. Kline saw Donald running full speed down the hall, knocking over students along the way, screeching as though he were putting on brakes as he turned into his classroom. Mr. Kline knew it was going to be a difficult year.

Students like Donald are frequently avoided by more socially competent students in class and are disliked and feared by other members. They are either loners, who move from one group to the next after alienating its members, or they develop friendships with other students whose behavior is also disturbing to others. These students are extremely difficult classroom management problems.

Behavior-disordered students who exhibit internalizing behaviors are often less disturbing to others but frequently concern others because of their bizarre behavior. Elisa, in the following example, is a student who exhibits internalizing behaviors.

Elisa, a fifth grader, was brought to the school office by her mother. Elisa's parents had just moved to the area and her mother brought Elisa to register for school but refused to speak with the school secretary. She demanded to register Elisa with the school principal. In meeting with the school principal, Elisa's mother told him Elisa would sometimes act ''funny.'' She told the principal Elisa only acted that way to get attention and she should be told to ''stop'' as soon as she tried it. The principal noted that Elisa had not said one word. In fact, she had sat in a chair next to her mother looking down and rocking gently. Elisa's mother said she had been receiving special education services during part of the day and was in a regular classroom most of the day. In the regular classroom, Elisa was a loner. She spoke to no one. When another student approached her, she reared back and scratched into the air with her long nails, imitating a cat. If other children said something to her, she would ''hiss'' at them. She would sit in the room, usually completing her assignments and, whenever possible, practicing scrolling cursive letters with her multicolored pen. She spent most of the day rocking. She even rocked while she worked.

Problems like Elisa's are usually thought of as being internal and related to their own pathology. Other classmates, recognizing that these children are very different, may make attempts to be compatible, but they are usually rebuked. Students with internalizing behaviors are easy victims for students whose behaviors are more externalizing.

Externalizing and internalizing behaviors are more frequently characteristics of students with behavior problems rather than students with learning disabilities. Learning-disabled students typically display less severe emotional and behavior difficulties. However, many students with learning disabilities have difficulties making and maintaining positive interpersonal relationships with others.

When compared with their non-learning-disabled peers, learning-disabled students are:

1. Less accepted and more frequently rejected (Bryan, 1974; Bryan, 1976)
2. Less popular (Bruininks, 1978; Bryan and Bryan, 1978)
3. Less frequently selected to play (Hutton and Palo, 1976)
4. Perceived as having lower social status (Stone and LaGreca, 1990)
5. Less accepted by peers even prior to being identified as learning-disabled (Vaughn, Hogan, Kouzekanani, and Shapiro, 1990)

6. More willing to conform to peer pressure to engage in antisocial activities (Bryan, Pearl, and Fallon, 1989)
7. More prone to behavioral difficulties such as withdrawal, attention problems, and other personality problems (Bender, 1989; Epstein, Cullinan, and Nieminen, 1984)
8. Lower levels of social interaction and participation in activities (McConaughy and Ritter, 1986)
9. Recipients of lower sociometric ratings from peers (Hutton and Palo, 1976)
10. Perceived negatively by peers and rejected by peers, even when integrated into a new setting (Bryan, 1976).

Unfortunately, the lowered social status of learning-disabled students reflects not only the perceptions of peers but of their teachers as well. Teachers perceive learning-disabled students as less desirable to have in the classroom (Garrett and Crump, 1980; Keogh, Tchir, Windeguth-Behn, 1974). One possible interpretation of the lowered social status of learning-disabled students is that it is a reflection of how the teacher feels about them. The teacher's negative perception of a learning-disabled student is conveyed to other students in the classroom, thus lowering the child's social status and how the child is perceived and responded to by peers. Some research suggests this may not completely explain the lowered social status of learning-disabled students, since strangers, after viewing a few minutes of students' social interaction on videotapes, perceive learning-disabled students more negatively than their non-learning-disabled peers (Bryan, Bryan, and Sonnefeld, 1982; Bryan and Perlmutter, 1979; Bryan and Sherman, 1980). Additionally, students who are later identified as learning-disabled, as early as two months into their kindergarten year, are already more highly rejected and less frequently chosen as best friends than other students in the kindergarten class (Vaughn, Hogan, Kouzekanani, and Shapiro, 1990). Whereas teachers view learning-disabled students more negatively than their non-

learning-disabled peers, they are more favorably disposed towards having learning-disabled students in their classroom than they are emotionally handicapped or mentally retarded (Abroms and Kodera, 1979; Moore and Fine, 1978). Teachers regard emotionally handicapped students as the most disruptive and the most difficult students to effectively work with in the regular classroom.

When discussing the social skills of learning-disabled students and how they are perceived by others, it is important to realize we are talking about learning-disabled students as a group. Not all learning-disabled students have social difficulties. Whereas students with behavior disorders are characterized by deficits in social skills, many learning-disabled students are socially competent, making and maintaining friends and struggling to please their teachers and parents. Many learning-disabled adults who are participating in postsecondary education programs identify their social skills as their strengths.

Characteristics of Students with Social Disabilities

We expect students with behavior disorders to have difficulty in successfully interacting with others. Students with behavior disorders are identified and placed in special programs because their social problems are so interfering that they are unable to adequately function with only those services provided by the regular classroom. Why is it that many learning-disabled students have difficulty developing and maintaining relationships with others? Research is just at the beginning stages of identifying how learning-disabled students interact differently from their non-learning-disabled peers.

Social Interaction
Learning-disabled students do not interact less frequently with teachers and peers than do non-learning-disabled students, but the quality of

these interactions is different. Learning-disabled students are more likely to approach the teacher and ask questions (Dorval, McKinney, and Feagans, 1982; McKinney, McClure, and Feagans, 1982). Teachers interact almost four times as often with learning-disabled students as with their peers; however, 63 percent of teachers' initiations towards learning-disabled students involve managing their behavior (Dorval, McKinney, and Feagans, 1982). The interactions learning-disabled students have with their teachers are often not appropriate to the situation. They attempt to display impulsively their knowledge, request more time to complete assignments, and request time to speak individually with the teacher to ask questions. Teachers report that questions from learning-disabled students are inappropriate, as they often ask questions when the answer to the question was just stated. Although classroom teachers spend more time with learning-disabled students, the nature of the involvement during that time is not viewed positively by the teachers (Siperstein and Goding, 1985). One teacher describes it this way: "When Carlos raises his hand, I dread it. He usually asks me what he is supposed to do. I find myself trying to reexplain a thirty-minute lesson in five minutes. I'm sure he can tell I'm frustrated."

Communication Difficulties

Being able to express our ideas and feelings and to understand the ideas and feelings of others is an integral part of socialization. Adults and children with good social skills are able to communicate effectively with others, whereas students with learning and behavior problems frequently have trouble in this area. Torgeson (1982) describes the learning style of learning-disabled students as inactive. An inactive learner is one who is passively involved in the learning process, does not attempt to integrate new information with previously learned information, and does not self-question or rehearse. It appears learning-disabled students also demonstrate an inactive style during the communication pro-

cess. While communicating with others, learning-disabled students are less likely to make adaptations in their communication to accommodate the listener. When most of us speak with a young child, we make modifications in how we speak to them, such as using simpler words and asking questions to be sure they understand us. Many learning-disabled students fail to make these modifications (Bryan and Pflaum, 1978; Soenksen, Flagg, and Schmits, 1981). When discussing the reading difficulties of learning-disabled students, we talked about their difficulty in responding to ambiguous information in print. In much the same way, learning-disabled students do not request more information when given ambiguous information through oral communication (Donahue, Pearl, and Bryan, 1980). The learning-disabled student is often a difficult communication partner who makes few adaptations to his audience, does not question inappropriate verbal statements, and does not "code switch," that is, pick up on what was said by the other. For example, learning-disabled and normal-achieving boys were involved in a task in which they were asked to give essential information about a game of checkers (Knight-Arest, 1984). The adult they were supposed to give the information to claimed not to know how to play the game. As found in other studies, the communication skills of learning-disabled students were less effective than those of normal-achieving students. Learning-disabled students:

1. Talked more
2. Provided less information
3. Were more likely to use gestures and demonstrations
4. Were less able to respond to the needs of the listener

If the listener appeared confused, they were more likely to repeat the message without reformulating it. It is interesting to note that familiarity with one's partner positively affects the performance on communications tasks of learning-disabled students, but has no impact for non-learning-disabled children (Mathinos, 1987). Perhaps knowledge of one's partners serves as a motivator for learning-disabled students to use the communication skills they have.

The communication style of students with learning disabilities appears to be egocentric. That is, they do not appear to be interested in the responses of their partner and they demonstrate less shared responsibility for maintaining a social conversation (LaGreca, 1982; Mathinos, 1987). In a study of the friendship-making and conversation skills of learning-disabled and non-learning-disabled boys, LaGreca (1982) reports that learning-disabled and non-learning-disabled boys did not differ in how to handle social situations (positive and negative), nor did they differ in their knowledge of how to make friends. Naive observers identified the boys with learning disabilities as less skillful in social skills including more egocentric and lacking in reciprocity in their conversations. The impression is that many students with learning disabilities display communication styles that suggest they are just waiting for the speaker to stop rather than interested in what the speaker is saying.

Since learning-disabled students are frequently rejected by peers, it could be that this communication pattern is sufficiently frustrating to others that they find the learning-disabled student an undesirable social partner.

Stone and LaGreca (1984) compared learning-disabled and non-learning-disabled students on their ability to comprehend nonverbal communication. Their findings indicated that when attention is controlled for with learning-disabled students by reinforcing them for attending to the social cues given, they perform as well as their non-learning-disabled peers. These authors suggest the attention problems of learning-disabled students often appear as poor social skills.

Aggression

Many children with severe behavior disorders are characterized by aggressive behavior. *Aggressive behaviors* include assaultiveness, fighting, temper tantrums, quarrelsomeness, ignoring the rights of others, negative tone of voice, threatening, and demands for immediate compliance. Aggression does not go away without treatment and is related to such negative outcomes as alcoholism, unpopularity, aggressive responses from others, academic failure, and adult antisocial behaviors. Specific skills for teaching students to deal more effectively with their aggressive responses is an important component of social skill programs for behavior-disordered students.

Appearance

Appearance may be a more important factor influencing the social status of students with learning difficulties than was previously thought. In a study evaluating the social status, academic ability, athletic ability, and appearance of learning-disabled students (Siperstein, Bopp, and Bak, 1978), researchers found that whereas academic and athletic ability were significantly related to peer popularity, the correlation between physical appearance and peer popularity was twice as great as the other two.

Two children from a study (Vaughn, Lancelotta, and Minnis, 1987) illustrate this point. Chris was a fourth-grade learning-disabled student who worked as a model for children's clothing in a large department store. Her position gave her access to the latest children's fashions and she was well recognized by both girls and boys in her class as attractive. She ranked first when sociometric data asking peers to rate the extent to which they liked others in the classroom were analyzed. Her best friend, Carmen, who was also identified as learning-disabled, ranked second from the bottom by her classmates on the same sociometric test. In looking at the tests of social skills administered to these students, there was little difference between the scores of Chris and Carmen.

In another study, 35 percent of junior-high learning-disabled students exhibit some problem in grooming, neatness of clothing, posture, and general attractiveness, as compared with 6 percent of the non-learning-disabled junior-high students (Schumaker, Wildgen, and Sherman, 1982). Bickett and Milich (1987) found learning-disabled boys to rate as less attractive than non-learning-disabled boys. Since appearance is highly related to popularity, it could be helpful to give feedback and pointers to students who display problems with appearance. Many students with behavior disorders display atypical appearance as a means of demonstrating identification with a group or gang. These students may wear their hair or clothing in nonconforming ways in order to let others know their allegiance. This style may be highly accepted by a particular group and highly rejected by others. These nonconforming appearances often become stylish, as have styles of the punk-rock movement in the late seventies and early eighties.

Hyperactivity

Hyperactivity is a trait of many children with learning and behavior disorders. Hyperactive children are characterized by distractibility, excitability, restlessness, impulsivity, inattention, and overactivity. Strauss, one of the founders of the learning disabilities movement, gave specific directions for how the learning environment was to be arranged to reduce hyperactivity and distraction. Although many of these directives, such as wearing dark clothing, no jewelry, and keeping hair tied back, seem unnecessary now, they were initial attempts to reduce a significant problem—distractibility.

Medication is frequently used in an attempt to modify hyperactivity. These medications typically involve stimulants such as methylphenidate hydrochloride (Ritalin), dextroamphetamine sulfate (Dexedrine), and Pemoline (Cylert). As many as 85 percent of children identified as hyperactive may be on medication for at least six months. What is particularly shocking is that no one seems to know how many children are receiving medication to control inappropriate behavior. Although drugs may be helpful in reducing movements, verbalizations, disruptive noises, and inappropriate behaviors with some hyperactive children, they have less positive outcomes for other children. Some children respond with unpleasant physical symptoms, and are affected by the drugs in some settings but not others. Most children receiving medication for hyperactivity are under the care of a physician whom they see infrequently. Thus the monitoring of the effectiveness of the drug is often the responsibility of parents and teachers. Perhaps the most effective technique for monitoring the effects of the drug is through behavior management. The teacher identifies and defines specific behaviors that are indicative of hyperactivity and then charts the occurrence of these behaviors. Whereas medication may be necessary for some children, attempts to treat the student's learning disability through changing their hyperactivity have not been very successful (Routh, 1979).

A learning characteristic frequently associated with hyperactivity is *selective attention,* which is the ability to attend to relevant information and ignore irrelevant information (Hallahan, Tarver, Kauffman, and Graybeal, 1978). This characteristic occurs in learning-disabled children about two years later than in normal children (Tarver, Hallahan, Kauffman, and Ball, 1976; Tarver, Hallahan, Cohen, and Kauffman, 1977). The delayed development of selective attention with learning-disabled populations may be related to the conceptual tempo of learning-disabled students, which is more impulsive than reflective. A more reflective conceptual tempo is associated with success in academic subjects such as reading and math, whereas a more impulsive tempo is associated with learning difficulties. One characteristic of impulsive responders is they do not stop and think before responding.

Self-Concept

What we think of ourselves and how we view ourselves is highly related to our comparison group, thus it is not surprising that students with learning and behavior difficulties have poor self-concepts. These students are very aware of how their learning difficulties compare with others.

There is some evidence that students with learning difficulties make higher gains in self-esteem and perception of their abilities when they are placed in special education classes (Battle and Blowers, 1982; Ribner, 1978), whereas other research suggests the special education placement has not significantly affected either self-concept or peer acceptance (Sheare, 1978). Learning-disabled students with reading difficulties view themselves more negatively than do learning-disabled students with normal reading scores (Black, 1974) and older learning-disabled students view themselves more negatively than do younger learning-disabled students. In an attempt to interpret the sometimes conflicting results of studies, Morrison (1985) demonstrated that there are two factors that significantly influence self-perception with learning-disabled students: type of classroom placement (e.g., self-contained, regular classroom) and what aspect of self-perception is being evaluated (e.g., academic, social, behavioral, or anxiety-laden). When achievement is controlled, for example, there are no differences in self-perception measures between learning-disabled students in resource rooms and self-contained settings (Yauman, 1980).

The self-perceptions of students with learning disabilities have been surprisingly accurate. In general they rate themselves as low on academic ability (Chapman and Boersman, 1980) and like other children on overall feelings of self-worth (Bryan, 1986; Cooley and Ayres, 1988). They identify reading and spelling as the academic areas in which they are lower than other children and yet perceive themselves as being relatively intelligent (Renik, 1987). A longitudinal study of students with learning disabilities suggests that they may differ from low-achieving students in that they do not become more negative about themselves as they grow older (Kistner and Osborne, 1987).

Teachers and parents need to be aware of the effects of learning and behavior difficulties on self-concept and provide opportunities for students to demonstrate and recognize their abilities. Teachers and parents can provide opportunities for students to demonstrate what they do well and encouragement in their areas of difficulty. One parent described it this way: "The best thing that happened to my son is swimming. We knew from the time Kevin was an infant that he was different from our other two children. We were not surprised when he had difficulties in school and was later identified as learning-disabled. His visual motor problems made it difficult for him to play ball sports so we encouraged his interest in swimming. He joined a swim team when he was six and all his friends know he has won many swimming awards. No matter how discouraged he feels about school, he has one area in which he is successful."

Teachers may want to discuss with students the nature of their learning and behavior difficulty and how it affects their performance in specific situations. Assisting students in identifying and predicting how they might respond in situations allows them to prepare for the situation and develop strategies for more successfully dealing with it.

Role Taking

The ability to take on the role of another, frequently referred to as *role taking,* decentering, and empathy, is a critical social skill influencing the child's ability to make and maintain positive relationships with others. *Egocentricity* is the opposite of role taking; children who are unable to understand the feelings and positions of others are often thought to exhibit egocentric behavior. Students who are egocentric do not understand the position and feelings of others and therefore are perceived less positively by others. Research with learning-disabled populations has demonstrated they are less able to display interpersonal decentering (Horowitz, 1981) and less able to take on an alternative viewpoint (Wong and Wong, 1980). We know from the communication skills of learning-disabled populations they are less likely to make adjustments in their communication with others. It could be their difficulty taking on the role of the other influences, both their social relationships with others and their ability to communicate successfully with others.

Locus of Control

Persons with an *internal locus of control* view events as controlled largely by their own efforts, whereas persons with an *external locus of control* interpret the outcome of events as due largely to luck, chance, fate, or other events outside of their own influence. Locus of control proceeds along a continuum, with learning- and behavior-disordered children frequently having a high external locus of control, unable to view the cause of events as related to their own behavior. For this reason, they are not motivated to change events that are undesirable to them because they feel there is little they can do to improve the situation.

Mrs. Mulkowsky, a junior-high learning-disabled teacher, said, ''My students act as though there is nothing they can do to improve their grades in their regular classes. They feel they are unable to succeed in most of these classes and they give up. They come to my class, sit down, and expect me to tutor them in their regular classes. They act as though it is *my* responsibility. These students are actually the ones who are still working; others have given up entirely and expect little from themselves and little from me.''

When learning-disabled students were compared with two other groups of non-learning-disabled students, learning-disabled students were more likely to interpret positive results as luck than were either of the other two groups (Sobol, Earn, Bennett, and Humphries, 1983). This suggests that when learning-disabled students perform well, they are less likely to attribute it to their own effort and therefore may be less likely to maintain the effort that produced the positive outcome. In contrast, learning-disabled students do attribute their failures to being within their own control and not to external factors outside of their control (Dudley-Marling, Snider, and Tarver, 1982). When learning-disabled students are

compared with behavior-disordered students and students who are both learning-disabled and behavior-disordered on three dimensions of locus of control: intellectual, social, and physical (Morgan, 1986), learning-disabled students had higher internal locus of control on all three dimensions than did the other two groups. The learning-disabled/behavior-disordered students had the most external scores on all three dimensions of locus of control.

It could be that learning-disabled students have difficulties in social situations because they fail to realize that successful interaction with others can be influenced by their behavior. To assist students in developing an internal locus of control, teachers need to show students the relationships between what they do and its effect on others and reciprocally on themselves. Giving students ownership for their tasks and behavior and teaching them to set their own goals are first steps toward increasing their internal locus of control (Cohen, 1986). Also, teachers may want to interview children to learn more about their locus of orientation (Lewis and Lawrence-Patterson, 1989). Borkowski and colleagues (Borkowski, Weyhing, and Carr, 1988; Borkowski, Weyhing, and Turner, 1986) have used attributional training paired with specific strategy training (for example, in the area of reading) to influence students' use and generalization of strategies. Attributional training helps the student see the role of effort in academic success or strategy use. Reasons for not doing well that do not relate to controllable factors are discouraged. Students are encouraged to see the relationship between strategy use and success, ''I tried hard, used the strategy, and did well'' (Borkowski, Weyhing, and Carr, 1988, p. 49).

Learned Helplessness

The concept of *learned helplessness* was introduced by Seligman (1975) to explain the response animals and humans have when exposed to a number of trials in which they are unable to influence the outcome. When subjects learn there is no relationship between what they do and their ability to impact the environment or reach their goal, they give up and respond passively. Although learned helplessness, or the perceived inability to influence a situation, may be situation-specific, it often generalizes to other learning situations. For example, when a learning-disabled student with severe reading problems approaches a reading task, the student is frequently unable to reach his or her goal—being able to read the passage successfully. Whereas the student may initially be very persistent in attempting to read, the student who meets with continued failure learns his or her attempts are useless and there is nothing he or she can do to impact the situation, thus the individual responds as though he or she is "helpless." Unfortunately, the idea of being "unable" as a learner may generalize across other tasks; hence the student perceives himself or herself as helpless in all academic tasks. Thus a student who may have the potential to succeed in particular academic tasks does not appear to be trying because the student perceives that he or she is helpless as a learner. Many students with learning problems act like they are learned helpless (Thomas, 1979).

Learned helplessness leads to lowered self-concept, lethargy, reduction in persistence, and reduced levels of performance. There is a remarkable resemblance between the descriptions of learned helplessness and the observations of special education teachers about learning-disabled and behavior-disordered students. "Learning-disabled children have been portrayed as no longer able to believe that they can learn" (Thomas, 1979, p. 209).

The concepts *learned helplessness* and *locus of control* are highly related. Students who have a feeling of learned helplessness toward a particular academic task perceive there is nothing they can do to impact their ability to perform the task successfully. It is also likely they view results from their "work" on that task as "external" and not related to what they do. Thus there is a high correlation between learned help-

lessness and external locus of control. Apply the Concept 9.1 describes what teachers might be able to do to affect learned helplessness and locus of control.

Social Difficulties Prevalent During Adolescence

In addition to the characteristics of students with learning and behavior disorders discussed above, there are three difficulties prevalent during adolescence that may affect students with special needs. These are suicide, anorexia nervosa, and drug and alcohol abuse.

Suicide

Two Leominster, Massachusetts, teenagers died in a shotgun suicide pact next to an empty bottle of champagne, after writing farewell notes that included "I love to die I'd be happier I know it! So please let me go. No hard feelings" (*The Boston Herald,* November 10, 1984, p. 1). Although the autopsy showed high levels of alcohol in the girls' bloodstreams, there were no indications that either girl was involved with drugs or was pregnant. It appeared as though both girls willingly participated in the suicide act. In another note left by one of the girls, she said, "I know it was for the best. I can't handle this sucky world any longer" (*The Boston Herald,* November 10, 1984, p. 7). The cause of the suicide pact is unknown.

Suicide of a child or adolescent is a shocking event. Childhood suicide occurs between the ages of birth and fifteen and adolescent suicide between the ages of fifteen and nineteen. Many deaths of adolescents are viewed as accidents and not reported as suicide; therefore, the statistics on adolescent suicide are meaningless (Toolan, 1981). However, suicide is one of the top three causes of death for persons under twenty-four years of age. There is agreement, however, that the rate of adolescent suicide is on the rise (Hawton, 1982; Toolan, 1981; Wicks-Nelson and Israel, 1984), and female attempts at suicide

Apply the Concept 9.1

*HOW TEACHERS MIGHT AFFECT LEARNED HELPLESSNESS
AND LOCUS OF CONTROL*

In order to reduce the impact of learned helplessness and external locus of control on students' behavior, teachers may want to:

1. Reduce the amount of external reinforcement and focus on reinforcing student performance. Rather than saying, "Good work" or "Excellent job," focus on the behaviors, such as, "You really concentrated and finished this biology assignment. You needed to ask for help but you got it done. How do you feel about it?"
2. Link students' behaviors to outcomes. "You spent ten minutes working hard on this worksheet and you finished it."
3. Provide encouragement. Because they experience continued failure, many students are discouraged from attempting tasks they are capable of performing.
4. Discuss academic tasks and social activities in which the student experiences success.
5. Discuss your own failures or difficulties and express what you do to cope with these. Be sure to provide examples of when you persist and examples of when you give up.

6. Encourage students to take responsibility for their successes. "You received a 'B' on your biology test. How do you think you got such a good grade?" Encourage students to describe what they did (e.g., how they studied). Discourage students from saying, "I was lucky," or "It was an easy test."
7. Encourage students to take responsibility for their failures. For example, in response to the question, "Why do you think you are staying after school?", encourage students to take responsibility for what got them there. "Yes, I am sure Billy's behavior was hard to ignore. I am aware that you did some things to get you here. What did you do?"
8. Structure learning and social activities to reduce failure.
9. Teach students strategies for how to learn information and demonstrate their control of their learning task.
10. Teach students to use procedures and techniques to monitor their own gains in academic areas.

---

greatly outnumber male (Hawton, 1982); however, male attempts are more frequently successful.

The suicide attempts of adolescents can frequently be explained by one or more of the following factors:

1. Relief from stress or from stressful situations
2. A demonstration to others of how desperate they are
3. An attempt to hurt or get back at others
4. An attempt to get others to change (Wicks-Nelson and Israel, 1984)

Suicide attempts most frequently occur following interpersonal problems with boy- or girlfriends, parents, or teachers. Often these re-

lationships have had prolonged difficulties. Disturbed peer relationships are a large contributing factor to suicide attempts. Adolescents feel unique, as if there are no solutions to their problems. "Life is a chronic problem. There appears no way out. Solutions previously tried have failed. To end the chronic problem, death appears to be the only way left" (Teicher, 1973, p. 137 in Sheras, 1983).

"Suicidal patients are often very difficult because they so frequently deny the seriousness of their attempts" (Toolan, 1981, p. 320). They often make comments such as, "It was all a mistake. I am much better now." Even though they may attempt to discount the attempt, it should be treated with extreme seriousness.

Sheras (1983) discusses the following general considerations when dealing with adolescent suicide attempts.

1. All suicide attempts must be taken seriously. Do not interpret the behavior as merely a plea for "attention." Do not try to decide whether the attempt is real or not.
2. Develop or reestablish communication with the person. Suicide is a form of communication from a person who feels he or she has no other way to communicate.
3. Reestablish emotional or interpersonal support. Suicide is an expression of alienation and the person needs to be reconnected with significant others.
4. Involve the adolescent in individual and/or family therapy. Often the adolescent feels unable to establish communication with a significant person (e.g., a parent) and needs assistance from another to do so.

Rourke and colleagues (Rourke, Young and Leenaars, 1989) identify a specific subtype of learning disabilities as being at risk for depression and suicide. This subtype is referred to as nonverbal learning disability and includes such characteristics as: bilateral tactile-perceptual deficits, bilateral psychomotor coordination problems, severe difficulties in visual-spatial-organizational abilities, difficulty with nonverbal problem solving, good rote verbal capacities, and difficulty adapting to novel and complex situations. Fletcher (1989) urges that students with nonverbal learning disability be identified early and treated. Since verbal skills are highly valued, particularly in school settings, it is likely that many students with nonverbal learning disabilities go unnoticed.

Anorexia Nervosa
"Anorexia nervosa refers to a persistent refusal to eat, which appears to be motivated by the pursuit of extreme thinness and a fear of gaining weight rather than genuine lack of hunger" (Wicks-Nelson and Israel, 1984, p. 120). Anorexia nervosa is largely a female disease, with only about 5 to 15 percent of reported cases being male. The highest incidence is in females between the ages of fifteen to twenty-four, and it occurs most frequently in higher socioeconomic levels (Jones, Fox, Haroutun, Babigian, and Hutton, 1980). "The most obvious thing about anorexia is the persistence of the sufferer's food refusal. She desperately wants to be thin and she transforms her body dramatically to this end" (Orback, 1986, p. 13). Characteristics associated with anorexia include:

1. Loss of menstrual cycle
2. Sensitivity to cold
3. Sleep disturbance

Because our society places a premium on thinness, exercise, and dieting, the symptoms of anorexia are not recognized soon enough to prevent it. The target person insists on remaining thin and does not perceive that she or he has a problem.

Why someone would deliberately starve themselves is puzzling. In attempting to unravel the mystery of anorexia nervosa, researchers have examined several factors that may contribute to the disease, including biological factors, such as malfunctioning of the hypothalamus; psychodynamic factors, such as an enmeshed family which makes it difficult for the adolescent to express individual identity; thus the adolescent's refusal to eat becomes a form of rebellion. There is little doubt that a combination of these biological and psychological factors contributes to anorexia nervosa.

Adolescent Drug and Alcohol Abuse
There is probably nothing parents fear more than the possibility their child will abuse drugs. With an increase in drug availability and use in the early to mid-1960s, parents became aware of the numbers of adolescents using drugs. There is a great deal of media attention focusing on the consequences of drug use. Stories of youngsters from stereotypically "normal" famliies becoming addicted to drugs and committing crimes to maintain their habits are featured in magazines and newspapers across the country.

There seems to be strong support for parental concerns about the availability and use of drugs among adolescents. According to a summary by Wicks-Nelson and Israel (1984) of reports from the Department of Justice (1980) and the FBI (1980), 90 percent of a sample of high-school seniors reported that marijuana was very easy or fairly easy to get. Some 59 percent said the same thing about amphetamines and 49.8 about barbiturates. Availability and use of drugs is not the only concern. Some 88 percent of high-school seniors reported using alcohol in the last twelve months, and 71.8 percent in the last thirty days. The number of children between the ages of twelve and seventeen indicating they consume alcohol has increased significantly. Cocaine abuse among teenagers is growing faster than any other substance abuse. The number of high-school students who have tried cocaine has increased in the past decade from 9 percent to 17 percent.

The pattern of drug and alcohol consumption is the most important issue. Typically the pattern is conceptualized along five points: non-users, experimenters, recreational users, problem users, and addicts (Krug, 1983). In the senior class of 1980, 9.1 percent reported daily use of marijuana, and 6 percent reported consuming alcohol daily.

Since daily marijuana use is second only to cigarette use, teachers need to be familiar with some of the outcomes of marijuana use so they can identify and counsel users.

Reported psychological effects of marijuana use include (Krug, 1983):

1. Inner satisfaction
2. Sense of contentment
3. Tranquilization/relaxation
4. Heightened awareness of sound and colors
5. Giddiness
6. Alteration in time and space perception
7. Euphoria

Users may have these adverse psychological effects:

1. Occasional anxiety and suspiciousness
2. Impairment of immediate memory recall
3. Severely impaired memory
4. Loss of goal-related drive
5. Inability to think and speak clearly
6. Decrease in testosterone production

It is quite difficult to use characteristics from checklists to identify drug users. Many drug users are aware of the behavioral and physiological consequences of drug use and use disguises such as eyedrops and sun glasses to hide the "red eyes." They have also learned to control their behavior to avoid calling undue attention to themselves. Teachers most often rely on identifying drug abusers through the abusers' self-disclosures or disclosures by concerned others.

Understanding the difference between drug and alcohol use and abuse is difficult. As Zinberg (1984) explains, what would be drug abuse for one person is manageable use for another. Zinberg interviewered many drug users who were functioning well in society and used drugs on a daily basis. This pattern is unusual, however; the majority of daily users have a difficult time functioning in society.

Elementary, junior-high, and high-school programs are preparing materials and disseminating information about drug and alcohol use. Teachers, particularly at the junior-high and high-school levels, should be aware of drug and alcohol terminology, characteristics of users, and consequences. Familiarity with local referral agencies providing guidance and assistance to students involved with drugs and alcohol is important for all teachers.

Now that we understand social competence and how students with behavior and learning difficulties feel about themselves, are perceived by others, and interact socially with others, let us focus on intervention theory and specific programs and activities for teaching social skills.

Intervention Strategies

Understanding and using different interventions when attempting to affect the social skills of learning-disabled and behavior-disordered students is extremely important. The wide variety of social difficulties exhibited by students with learning and behavior disorders is great; using a particular intervention may be very effective with one student, yet be considerably less effective with another student or another problem. By understanding many approaches, we increase the likelihood of success with all students. The real challenge to teachers is knowing when to use which approach with which child under which condition.

Whereas there is a range of intervention strategies to assist in teaching appropriate social skills to learning-disabled and behavior-disordered students, effective social skills training programs share the same goals. The purpose of social skills training is to teach the students a complex response set that allows them to adapt to the numerous problems that occur in social situations. Common goals of social skills training programs include:

1. The ability to solve problems and to make decisions quickly
2. The ability to adapt to situations that are new or unexpected
3. The ability to utilize coping strategies for responding to emotional upsets
4. The ability to communicate effectively with others
5. The ability to make and maintain friends

A scope and sequence list of the hierarchy of social skills is presented in Appendix A.

Following is a brief description of four intervention approaches used to teach appropriate social behaviors. These include intervention by prescription, interpersonal problem solving, behavioral therapy, and ASSET: A Social Skills Program for Adolescents. This section will also describe curricula that have been developed to assist teachers in teaching social skills in their classrooms.

Intervention by Prescription Model

Intervention by Prescription (IBP) is a developmentally based model within a problem-solving framework. This model provides a developmental framework for assessing student behavior and then assists the teacher in determining the type of intervention that would best meet the needs of the student. The purpose of the model is to bridge developmental theory to application so it can be used by practitioners. This model was based on the developmental theories of Loevinger, Erikson, Piaget, Kohlberg, and Selman (Rezmierski, 1984). There is no specific type of intervention strategy advocated; for example, the model does not rely solely on a behavioral approach nor solely on a cognitive approach. Within this model the teacher selects the approach based on how the student is performing. Thus some students will be operating primarily according to a behavioral approach and other students may be partially involved in a behavioral approach, partially involved in a problem-solving approach, and partially involved in a cognitive-behavioral approach.

Impulse Management

As can be seen in Figure 9.3, impulse management develops along a continuum, with students performing at stage 1 having a high external locus of control. A list of corresponding needs is provided that relates to each stage. For example, a student operating at level 4 manages impulses by anticipating short-term rewards or punishments from another who is present. A student operating on level 4 needs consistent and predictable reinforcement, cause and effect interpretations, and self-talk. By knowing how the student manages impulses, we can identify what the student needs to learn and what intervention is most effective in meeting those needs. Thus the IBP model does not subscribe to one mode of inter-

FIGURE 9.3 *How Are Impulses Managed?*

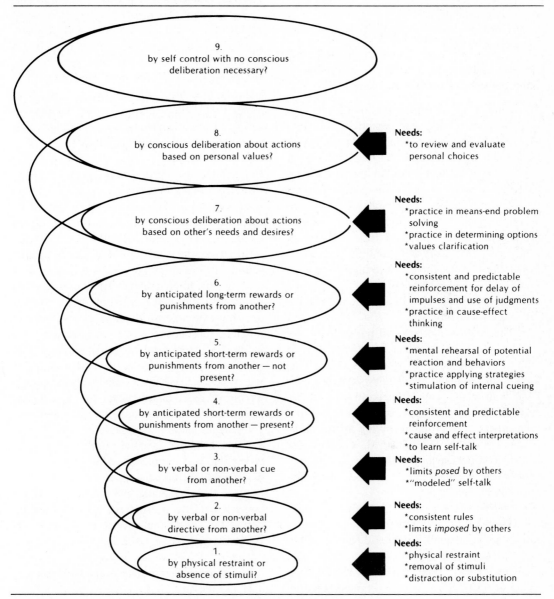

9.
by self control with no conscious deliberation necessary?

8.
by conscious deliberation about actions based on personal values?

Needs:
*to review and evaluate personal choices

7.
by conscious deliberation about actions based on other's needs and desires?

Needs:
*practice in means-end problem solving
*practice in determining options
*values clarification

6.
by anticipated long-term rewards or punishments from another?

Needs:
*consistent and predictable reinforcement for delay of impulses and use of judgments
*practice in cause-effect thinking

5.
by anticipated short-term rewards or punishments from another — not present?

Needs:
*mental rehearsal of potential reaction and behaviors
*practice applying strategies
*stimulation of internal cueing

4.
by anticipated short-term rewards or punishments from another — present?

Needs:
*consistent and predictable reinforcement
*cause and effect interpretations
*to learn self-talk

3.
by verbal or non-verbal cue from another?

Needs:
*limits *posed* by others
*"modeled" self-talk

2.
by verbal or non-verbal directive from another?

Needs:
*consistent rules
*limits *imposed* by others

1.
by physical restraint or absence of stimuli?

Needs:
*physical restraint
*removal of stimuli
*distraction or substitution

Source: © 1982 The Regents of The University of Michigan. Written and developed by Virginia Rezmierski, Assistant to the Vice-Provost for Information Technology and Adjunct Associate Professor of Education. Reprinted with the permission of the above university.

vention but allows the teacher to select from many modes, depending on the stage in which the student is operating and the student's needs. For example, students operating at stages 1 through 4 will need a systematic behavioral approach to intervention, along with initial instruction in cognitive self-monitoring strategies. Interventions with students in stages 5 through 9 will be largely cognitive and may include problem solving and group therapy approaches. For more thorough description of the IBP model, see Rezmierski (1984).

Interpersonal Problem Solving

We spend an extraordinary amount of time preventing and solving interpersonal problems. Whether we are concerned about what to say to our neighbor whose dog barks long and loud in the middle of the night, how to handle the irate customer at work or our relationships with our parents and siblings, interpersonal problems are an ongoing part of life. Some people seem to acquire the skills necessary for interpersonal problem solving easily and with little or no direct instructions, yet others, particularly students with learning and behavior disorders, need more direct instruction in how to prevent and resolve difficulties with others.

The goal of interpersonal problem-solving training programs is to teach students how to employ a wide range of strategies that allows them to develop and maintain positive relationships with others, cope effectively with others, solve their own problems, and resolve conflict with others. The problem-solving approach attempts to provide the child with a process for solving conflicts, with the ultimate goal being a positive change in the child's interpersonal problem-solving behavior.

Interpersonal problem solving has been used successfully with a wide range of populations, including adult psychiatric patients (Platt and Spivack, 1972), preschoolers (Ridley and Vaughn, 1982), kindergartners (Shure and Spivack, 1978), mentally retarded chldren (Vaughn, Ridley, and Cox, 1983), children with learning disabilities (Vaughn, Levine, and Ridley, 1986), and aggressive children (Vaughn, Ridley, and Bullock, 1984). Spivack, Platt and Shure (1976), along with their colleagues at the Hahnemann Medical College, have conducted the most comprehensive examination of the rela-

tionship between interpersonal problem solving and adjustment. Their research has led them to explore the effects of interpersonal problem-solving training programs with emotionally disturbed adolescents, disadvantaged preschoolers, and impulsive kindergartners (Spivack, Platt, and Shure, 1976; Shure and Spivack, 1978, 1979, 1980). Based on their work, adaptations and extensions of teaching interpersonal problem solving to special populations have evolved.

Components of Interpersonal Problem-Solving Programs

Four skills appear to be particularly important for successful problem resolution (D'Zurilla and Goldfired, 1971; Spivack, Platt, and Shure, 1976). First, the student must be able to identify and define the problem. Second, the student must be able to generate a variety of alternative solutions to any given problem. Third, the student must be able to identify and evaluate the possible consequences of each alternative. Finally, the student must be able to implement the solution. This may require rehearsal and modeling. Whereas these four components are characteristic of most interpersonal problem-solving programs, many programs include additional components and procedures.

For example, a social problem-solving intervention was conducted with fifty seriously emotionally disturbed students (Amish, Gesten, Smith, Clark, and Stark, 1988). The intervention consisted of fifteen structured lessons which occurred for forty minutes once each week. The following problem-solving steps were taught:

1. Say what the problem is and how you feel.
2. Decide on a goal.
3. Stop and think before you decide what to do.
4. Think of many possible solutions to the problem.
5. Think about what will happen next after each possible solution.
6. When you find a good solution, try it.

The results of the intervention indicated that seriously emotionally disturbed students who participated in the intervention improved their social problem-solving skills and were able to generate more alternatives to interviewing and role-playing measures.

Following are descriptions of several interpersonal problem-solving (IPS) programs that have been developed, implemented, and evaluated with learning- and behavior-disordered students.

FAST

FAST is a strategy taught as part of an IPS program to second-, third-, and fourth-grade learning-disabled students identified as having social skills problems (Vaughn, Lancelotta, and Minnis, 1988). The purpose of FAST is to teach students to consider problems carefully before responding to them and to consider alternatives and their consequences. Figure 9.4 presents the FAST strategy. In step one, Freeze and Think, students are taught to identify the problem. In step two, Alternatives, students are taught to consider possible ways of solving the problem.

FIGURE 9.4 *FAST: An Interpersonal Problem-Solving Strategy*

FAST

FREEZE AND THINK!
What is the problem?

ALTERNATIVES?
What are my possible solutions?

SOLUTION EVALUATION
Choose the best solution:
   safe?
   fair?

TRY IT!
Slowly and carefully

Does it work?

In step three, Solution Evaluation, students are asked to prepare a solution or course of action for solving the problem that is both safe and fair. The idea is to get students to consider solutions that will be effective in the long run. The fourth step, Try It, asks students to rehearse and implement the solution. If they are unsuccessful at implementing the solution, students are taught to go back to alternatives. Learning-disabled students practiced this strategy by using real problems generated by themselves and their peers.

▬ *Procedures:*

1. In each classroom ask peers to rate all same-sex classmates on the extent to which they would like to be friends with them. Students who receive few friendship votes and many "no friendship" votes are identified as rejected. Students who receive many friendship votes and few "no friendship" votes are identified as popular. See Coie, Dodge, and Coppotelli (1982) for exact procedures in assessing popular and rejected students.

2. Rejected, learning-disabled students are paired with same-sex popular classmates and identified as the social skills trainers for the class. The school principal announces to the school and to parents through a newsletter who the social skills trainers are for the school.

3. Children selected as social skills trainers are involved in learning social skills strategies and are removed from the classroom two to three times a week for approximately thirty minutes each session.

4. Social skills training includes learning the FAST strategy as well as other social skills such as accepting negative feedback, receiving positive feedback, and making friendship overtures.

5. At the same time period that social skills trainers are learning social skills strategies, their classmates are recording problems they have at home and at school and placing their lists in the classroom problem-solving box (a decorated shoe box). The purpose of the problem-solving box is for students to ask questions about problems they have. Problems from the problem-solving box are used by trainers as they learn the strategies outside of class, as well as for in-class discussion which occurs later and is led by the social skills trainers.

6. After the social skills trainers have learned a strategy, for example, FAST, they teach the strategy to the entire class with backup and support from the researcher and classroom teacher.

7. During subsequent weeks, social skills trainers leave the room for only one session per week and practice the FAST strategy as well as other strategies with classmates at least one time per week. These reviews include large group explanations and small-group problem-solving exercises.

8. Social skills trainers are recognized by their teacher and administrator for their special skills.

Other students are asked to consult the social skills trainer when they have difficulties.

— *Comments:* The above approach to teaching social skills and increasing peer acceptance has been successfully applied in two studies with learning-disabled youngsters (Vaughn, Lance-lotta, and Minnis, 1988; Vaughn, McIntosh, and Spencer-Rowe, in press) but has not been evaluated for behavior-disordered students or adolescents.

Apply the Concept 9.2 shows an activity sheet used as part of a homework assignment for students participating in the training.

TLC: Teaching, Learning and Caring

Teaching, Learning and Caring (Vaughn, Cohen, Fournier, Gervasi, Levasseur, and Newton, 1984; Vaughn, 1987) is an interpersonal problem-solving skills training program based

Apply the Concept 9.2 _____

ACTIVITY SHEET

This activity sheet can be used to give children written practice in using the FAST strategy.

You are in the cafeteria. Another student keeps bugging you. He hits you, pokes you, tries to steal your food, and will not stop bullying you. You start to get angry. What would you do? Use FAST to help you solve the problem.

1. *Freeze and think.* What is the problem?

_____

_____

2. *Alternatives.* What are your possible solutions?

_____

_____

_____

3. *Solution evaluation.* Choose the best one. Remember: safe and fair; works in the long run.

_____

_____

4. *Try it.* Do you think this will work?

_____

A friend of yours is upset. She is teased a lot, especially by a boy named Kenny. She told you that she wants to run away from school. What could you tell your friend to help her solve the problem? Use FAST to help you.

1. _____

_____

_____

2. _____

_____

_____

3. _____

_____

_____

4. _____

_____

_____

FIGURE 9.5 *Overview of the TLC Model*

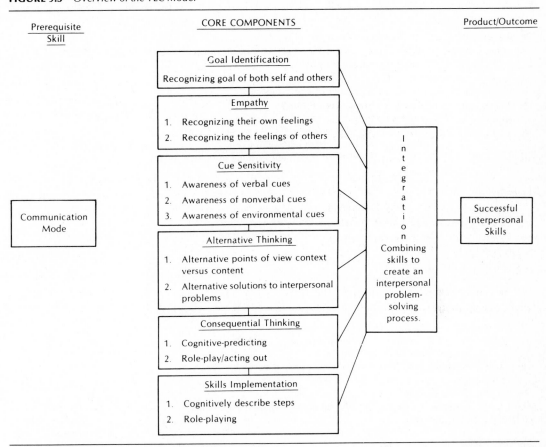

Prerequisite Skill

CORE COMPONENTS

Product/Outcome

Communication Mode

Goal Identification
Recognizing goal of both self and others

Empathy
1. Recognizing their own feelings
2. Recognizing the feelings of others

Cue Sensitivity
1. Awareness of verbal cues
2. Awareness of nonverbal cues
3. Awareness of environmental cues

Alternative Thinking
1. Alternative points of view context versus content
2. Alternative solutions to interpersonal problems

Consequential Thinking
1. Cognitive-predicting
2. Role-play/acting out

Skills Implementation
1. Cognitively describe steps
2. Role-playing

Integration
Combining skills to create an interpersonal problem-solving process.

Successful Interpersonal Skills

on the work of Vaughn and Ridley (e.g., Vaughn, Ridley, and Bullock, 1984).

Teaching, Learning and Caring (TLC) is a program developed to teach specific social problem-solving strategies to severely emotionally handicapped and learning-disabled adolescents. The program was developed and initiated within a self-contained classroom for severely learning- and behavior-disordered students.

The TLC curriculum includes six major components: goal identification, cue sensitivity, empathy, alternative thinking, consequential thinking, and skills implementation. In addition to these core components, a communication mode was identified as a process for listening, responding, and addressing the needs of others, which would facilitate the acquisition of all program components. Figure 9.5 provides a model diagram of the core components of the curriculum.

Communication mode enhances the core components and is summarized in Figure 9.6. Although the core components of the program are taught directly during class, they are also reinforced by teachers and students throughout the day.

Goal Identification

The purpose of *goal identification* is to teach students to identify what they and others want

FIGURE 9.6 *TLC Skills*

Communication Mode

1. Repeating the content of another's message,
2. Identifying the main idea of the content of another's message,
3. Identifying the stated feelings in another's message,
4. Identifying the underlying feelings in another's message,
5. Identifying the main idea of the content of one's message,
6. Identifying the underlying feeling in one's message,
7. Using self-disclosure appropriately,
8. Using open and closed questions appropriately,
9. Listening to the problems of another without discounting, and
10. Listening to the problems of another and hypothetical situations which influence behavior.

Empathy

1. Identifying words which convey emotions, e.g. jealous, hurt, angry, hostile, shy, afraid, furious,
2. Matching past situations and the feelings associated with the situation,
3. Discussing the relationship between identifying emotional states as the first step in responding appropriately to them,
4. Identifying how you would feel in hypothetical situations,
5. Identifying the feelings of others in pictures, films, and hypothetical situations.

Goal Identification

1. Defining own goal(s) when in a problem situation,
2. Defining the goal(s) of another when in a problem situation,
3. Identifying immediate and long term goals,
4. Sharing identified goals with the student group and accepting feedback,
5. Listing the steps to reaching identified goals,
6. Charting progress towards reaching goals, and
7. Identifying and describing the needs and goals of others.

Cue Sensitivity

1. Identify environmental cues in pictures and responding by asking questions and summarizing content and feelings.
2. Identify environmental cues in real situations which influence behavior,
3. Identify the personal cues people use and what they mean in role plays and films,
4. Identify the personal cues used by others in real situations,
5. Identify own cues when interacting with others and what they mean,
6. Identify several cues you want to include in your repertoire, and
7. Identify cues of others, your typical response to them, and possible alternative responses.

Alternative Thinking

1. Identifying likely alternatives to solving hypothetical problems,
2. Identifying likely alternatives to solving real problems,
3. Identifying nonaggressive alternatives to solving hypothetical problems, and
4. Identifying nonaggressive alternatives to solving real problems.

Skills Implementation

1. Identifying the best procedure for implementing the selected alternative,
2. Identifying a person who implements the alternative well and describing what they do,

3. Describing the step-by-step process for implementing the selected alternative,
4. Role play, practice, and rehearse the selected alternative,
5. Use feedback from self and others to make changes in the procedure,
6. Implement selected alternative, and
7. Evaluate the outcome and the procedure.

Consequential Thinking

1. Predicting the likely consequences to a series of events not involving them,
2. Predicting the likely consequences to hypothetical stories and role play situations,
3. Predicting the likely consequences to interpersonal interactions of others,
4. Identifying short run and long run solutions to solving hypothetical problems,
5. Identifying problems in the long run when implementing short run solutions to hypothetical situations,
6. Identifying the consequences of selected behaviors in interpersonal situations involving others,
7. Identifying the consequences of selected behaviors in interpersonal situations involving self, and
8. Implementing a "stop and think" approach to solving interpersonal difficulties.

Integration

1. Observing models (counselors, teachers, and peers) integrate the problem solving process in solving hypothetical problems,
2. Observing models (counselors, teachers, and peers) integrate the problem solving process in solving real problems,
3. Integrating the problem solving process in solving group problems,
4. Integrating the problem solving process in solving hypothetical problems, and
5. Integrating the problem solving process in solving real problems.

Source: S. Vaughn, "TLC-Teaching, Learning, and Caring: Teaching Interpersonal Problem-Solving Skills to Behaviorally Disordered Adolescents," *The Pointer, 31*(2) (1987): 25–30. Reprinted with permission of the Helen Dwight Reid Educational Foundation. Published by Heldref Publications, 4000 Albemarle St. N.W., Washington, D.C. 20016. Copyright © 1987.

when in a problem situation. In addition, goal identification teaches students to identify both long- and short-range goals. Students are also taught to differentiate goals from needs. The rationale for goal identification is that as students become more skillful in recognizing what they want, they become more adept at planning and reaching the desired goal. Many students with social difficulties respond impulsively to problems without stopping to think about what they want or the needs of another.

In addition to identifying immediate goals, students learn to identify long-range goals and to plot the procedure for reaching the goal. Many students with behavior problems have a difficult time projecting themselves into the future to determine what they might be able to do now to make the future like they want it. Many of these students are so bombarded with what it takes for

them to function in daily life they give little thought to tomorrow, much less next month, next year, or when they leave school.

Mrs. Louise Fournier, a teacher of emotionally disturbed adolescents, used the following guidelines for teaching goal identification to her students.

1. In a small group, she asked students to identify academic subjects in which they would like to be doing better.

2. She then asked students to identify one thing they might be able to do that week that would improve their performance in each of the academic subjects they listed.

3. After students wrote the answers to items 1 and 2, they each took turns reading them aloud to the group. The students in the group listened to the identified areas and gave constructive feedback. For example, Danny said, "My main area of difficulty is math. I hate it and so there is nothing I can do to do better in it." The members of the group gave feedback to Danny. Roland, the first student to reply, said, "You haven't really set a goal. Unless you take one small step you'll never do any better in math." Malcolm suggested Danny start by doing the Thursday night math assignment with a friend to help him understand it. Each student in the group gave Danny feedback. Danny was then asked to re-write his weekly goal. Although Mrs. Fournier said this process was time-consuming at first, it eventually paid off as the students were able to write several academic goals at the beginning of each week and the group increased their ability to give feedback.

4. As students were able to make and reach weekly goals, Mrs. Fournier taught the students to use a similar process for setting monthly goals and goals for their future academic learning.

5. Mrs. Fournier suggested starting with academic goals and then moving toward personal growth goals. Academic goals are less threatening and it is easier for students to give and receive feedback about academic goals.

6. Students eventually wrote weekly academic and personal growth goals each Monday and then on Friday wrote next to each goal the extent to which they met it. Monthly and yearly goals were also written and evaluated.

The skills taught in goal identification are summarized in Figure 9.6.

Cue Sensitivity

Cue sensitivity is the ability to interpret one's environment accurately and to understand both verbal and nonverbal messages consistently. When we speak to people we give them many cues that enhance our ability to communicate with them successfully. We smile approvingly, furrow our brow to represent confusion, step away to indicate we need to get going, touch to create intimacy, and roll our eyes to let a friend know how we feel about the person they are discussing. These are just a few of the more obvious nonverbal cues we use. As important as learning to *send* these cues is the need to learn to *interpret* them when they are sent by another. Many students with social difficulties are unable to give and interpret social cues successfully; therefore, they miss information, misinterpret information, and do not provide necessary information for others to adequately understand and respond to them.

Teaching cue sensitivity begins with focusing students' attention on relevant cues that are given. Students are also taught to identify relevant cues from pictures. How a person dresses, how she stands, and the look on her face are discussed as means to obtain information. Students identify the cues their parents, friends, and members of the group use to communicate. Students learn that the more information we are able to obtain about another and the more accurately we are able to give information to others, the more successful we will be in interacting with them. Skills taught in cue sensitivity are summarized in Figure 9.6.

Empathy

Empathy is taking on the emotional state of another to such an extent that we not only feel as the other feels, we may exhibit the nonverbal behaviors of another. Empathy is the opposite of egocentrism. It is the single skill that has been most systematically associated with success in developing and maintaining positive relationships across the life span (Clark, 1980; Feshbach, 1975; Guerney, 1977). Two levels of empathic responding are taught: cognitive and affective (Ridley, Vaughn, and Wittman, 1982). Students are first taught to recognize their own feelings, then the feelings of others, and finally to respond appropriately to their own feelings and the feelings of others.

Empathy is taught sequentially. First, the students learn the vocabulary necessary to identify feeling states in self and others. Students are taught the meanings and applications of such feeling words as *frustrated, disgusted, jealous, perturbed, disappointed, delighted, concerned, furious, outraged,* and *embarrassed.* In the process of teaching a range of emotive words, the students not only learn the meaning of the word but link the feelings to specific situations in which they or others felt that way. Through the group process, students and teachers disclose experiences in which their feelings match the one discussed (e.g., jealous). Students learn that we all share common emotional responses and that our ability to identify those feeling states is the first step in being able to respond appropriately to them.

Second, students learn to identify the feeling state of others and self through pictures and hypothetical stories. Teachers use filmstrips, movies, pictures, and stories to demonstrate a range of emotions. Students are also asked to link feeling states to behaviors. For example, "I could tell he felt jealous because when he saw his girlfriend with another guy, he instantly got upset rather than waiting to find out why she might have been talking to him."

Third, students are asked to identify their own feeling states. Students are asked to identify how they felt in situations they have recently experienced. They are also asked to predict how they would feel in hypothetical situations and, finally, to identify their feelings as they are involved in situations.

Fourth, students are taught to respond appropriately to the feelings of others. After learning to identify the feelings of others and self, students are taught to respond to these feelings appropriately by discussing the possible consequences of a range of responses. For example, Mike is aware that Charlie is upset with him because he was talking to Charlie's girlfriend, Angela. Mike is asked to list the ways he could respond to Charlie and the consequences of each response. The goal is that Mike will select a response that is beneficial to both Mike and Charlie. Being able to identify Charlie's feelings should provide both motivation and direction for responding appropriately. Skills taught in empathy are summarized in Figure 9.6.

Alternative Thinking

The purpose of teaching *alternative thinking* is to teach students to generate a variety of potential solutions for solving a problem situation rather than responding impulsively to the problem. The rationale is that as the students' range of alternatives for solving problems increases, so does the likelihood that the problem will be resolved successfully. Most students with social difficulties have a very limited response repertoire to problems. They either strike back aggressively or withdraw. These strategies are rarely effective and have other negative side effects.

Alternative thinking is directly linked to goal identification and empathy in that students must be able to identify their feelings about the problem and persons involved and how it is perceived by others. The students then learn to generate a number of different potential solutions to the problem. Initially this process occurs with the entire group so that the suggestions from others can be used to generate alternatives. After the students receive a wider range of solutions from the group, the students are asked to generate alternatives with just one other student or teacher. Finally, the students are asked to use alternative thinking in real problem situations. Skills taught in alternative thinking are summarized in Figure 9.6.

Consequential Thinking

Consequential thinking is the ability to anticipate the possible consequences of a behavior before implementing the behavior. The rationale is that by anticipating the possible consequences, the students are better able to select an effective alternative. Consequential thinking requires the students to ask, "What might happen next if I do . . . (the selected alternative)?" and "What will happen in the long run if I do . . .?'' The purpose is to teach students to stop and think before implementing solutions and to evaluate the long-range effects of selected behaviors. Many students respond impulsively without considering how these reactions will affect them. Skills taught in consequential thinking are summarized in Figure 9.6.

Skills Implementation

The purpose of *skills implementation* is to teach students the skills or strategies necessary to implement the selected alternative. For example if Mike solves the anticipated problem he would have with his friend Charlie by selecting the alternative, ''Explain to Charlie that I was only speaking with his girlfriend Angela because she wanted to know what information she had missed the day she was absent from class,'' Mike needs to have the skills to explain adequately to Charlie. The specific skills needed for implementing this alternative would be discussed, modeled, rehearsed, and feedback provided. Sometimes students already have the skills in their repertoire and just need to decide when to use them. Other students need to learn the skills in order to implement successfully the selected alternative. Skills taught in implementation are summarized in Figure 9.6.

Social Decision-Making Skills (Elias and Clabby, 1989) is a curriculum based on cognitive interpersonal problem solving and designed for both regular and special education elementary-age students. The curriculum provides for readiness areas and steps for social decision making and problem solving. The teacher's guide is very complete and includes sample worksheets, tips for teaching the skills, and directions for how to structure role plays.

Behavior Therapy

Behavior Therapy, or Applied Behavior Analysis (ABA), is based primarily on operant learning principles. The application of these principles to change maladaptive behaviors is referred to as behavioral therapy.

The major components of ABA include:

1. *Target behaviors are defined operationally.* For example, a teacher described the behaviorally disturbed child in her classroom as ''emotional.'' Although most of us know what *emotional* means, it is likely that each of us imagines a somewhat different behavioral repertoire when we think of a student as behaving in an emotional way. In the same way, if we were asked to chart the emotional behavior of a student, it is unlikely that any two observers would get the same results. For this reason, the teacher is asked to describe the behaviors she observes when the student is acting emotional. Identifying the specific behaviors the student exhibits assists the teacher in clarifying what is disturbing to her, and it also assists in the second step, measurement.

2. *Target behaviors are measured.* To determine the student's present level of functioning and to determine if the selected intervention is effective, target behaviors must be measured before and during intervention. Some behaviors are easy to identify and measure. For example, the number of times John completes his arithmetic assignment is relatively easy to tabulate. However, behaviors such as ''out of seat'' and ''off task'' require more elaborate measurement procedures.

The three types of measurement procedures most frequently used are event, duration, and interval time sampling. *Event sampling* measures the number of times a behavior occurs in a designated amount of time. Sample behaviors include the number of times the bus driver reports misconduct regarding a student, the number of times a student is late for class, or the number of times a student does not turn in a homework assignment. *Duration sampling* measures the length of time a behavior occurs. Sample behaviors include the amount of time a student is ''out of seat,'' how long a student cries, or the amount of time a student is ''on task.'' You can see that it is possible to use event and duration samplings for the same behavior. You may want to measure the behavior both ways or select the measurement procedure that will give you the most information about the behavior. *Interval sampling* designates whether or not a behavior occurs during a specific interval of time. For example, a teacher may record whether a student is reported for fighting during recess periods. Interval sampling is used when it is difficult to tell when a behavior begins or ends and also when a behavior occurs very frequently.

In addition to the measurement of the target behavior, it is helpful to identify the antecedents and consequences of the target behavior. A listing of what occurs before the behavior and what occurs immediately after gives important information that assists in developing an intervention procedure. If every time the student cries, the teacher talks to the student for a few minutes, it could be the teacher's attention is maintaining the behavior. The listing of antecedents may provide information about the environment, events, or people who trigger the target behavior. An analysis of antecedents and consequences facilitates the establishment of a successful intervention procedure.

3. *Goals and treatment intervention are established.* Based on observation and measurement data and an analysis of antecedents and consequences, goals for changing behavior and intervention strategies are established. The purpose of establishing goals is to determine the desired frequency or duration of the behavior. Goal setting is most effective when the person exhibiting the target behavior is involved in establishing the goals. For example, Dukas is aware he gets into too many fights and wants to reduce his fighting behavior. After the target behavior is identified and measured, the teacher and student examine the data and identify that the only time he gets into fights is during the lunch-time recess. They set up a contract in which the teacher agrees to give Dukas ten minutes of free time at the end of each day in which he does not get into a fight. The student agrees with the contract. The teacher

continues to measure the student's behavior to determine if the suggested treatment plan is effective.

There are many treatment strategies in behavior therapy that can be used by the teacher to effect change. For example, the teacher may use reinforcers to shape new behaviors, reinforce incompatible behaviors, or maintain or increase desired behavior. The teacher may use extinction, punishment, or time-out to eliminate undesired behaviors. The teacher may use contracts or token economies to change behavior. These strategies are discussed in Chapter Two, in the section on operant learning theory. With these intervention strategies, consequences are controlled by another (e.g., the teacher). Self-management is a procedure in which the consequences are controlled by the target person. These procedures are particularly effective with older children, adolescents, and adults because the control and responsiblity for change is placed in their hands. With assistance from a teacher, counselor, or other influential adult, the adolescent implements a self-management program by following three processes.

1. Identify the behavior he or she wants to change (e.g., late for school).

2. Identify the antecedents and consequences associated with the behavior (e.g., Doreen says, "When the alarm rings I continue to lie in bed. I also wait until the last minute to run to the bus stop and I frequently miss the bus").

3. Develop a plan that alters the antecedents and provides consequences that will maintain the desired behavior. Doreen decides to get up as soon as the alarm rings and to leave for the bus stop without waiting until the last minute. Doreen arranges with her parents to have the car every Friday night of the week in which she has arrived at school on time every day. An obvious disadvantage of a self-control behavior change model is that it relies on the motivation of the student for success. Students who are not interested in changing behaviors and who are not willing to analyze antecedents and consequences and develop potentially successful intervention strategies will be unsuccessful with self-determined behavior change plans.

ASSET: A Social Skills Program for Adolescents

The purpose of ASSET is to teach adolescents the social skills they need to interact successfully with peers and adults (Hazel, Schumaker, Sherman, and Sheldon-Wildgen, 1981). The eight social skills considered fundamental to successful relationships are listed below.

1. *Giving positive feedback.* This skill teaches students how to thank someone and how to give a compliment.
2. *Giving negative feedback.* This skill teaches students to give correction and feedback in a way that is not threatening.
3. *Accepting negative feedback.* This skill teaches students the all-important ability to receive negative feedback without walking away, showing hostility, or other inappropriate emotional reactions.
4. *Resisting peer pressure.* This teaches students to refuse their friends who are trying to seduce them into some form of delinquent behavior.
5. *Problem solving.* This teaches students a process for solving their own interpersonal difficulties.
6. *Negotiation.* This teaches students to use their problem-solving skills with another person to come to a mutually acceptable resolution.
7. *Following instructions.* This teaches students to listen and respond to instructions.
8. *Conversation.* This teaches students to initiate and maintain a conversation.

The Leader's Guide (Hazel, Schumaker, Sherman, and Sheldon-Wildgen, 1981) that comes with the ASSET program provides instructions for running the groups and teaching the skills. There are eight teaching sessions provided on videotapes that demonstrate the skills. Program materials include skill sheets, home notes, and criterion checklists.

▬ *Procedures:* Each lesson is taught to a small group of adolescents. There are nine basic steps to each lesson: (1) review homework and previously learned social skills; (2) explain the new skill for the day's lesson; (3) explain why the skill is important and should be learned and practiced; (4) give a realistic and specific example to illustrate the use of the skill; (5) examine each of the skill steps that are necessary to carry out the new social skill; (6) model the skill and provide opportunities for students and others to demonstrate correct and incorrect use of the skills; (7) use verbal rehearsal to familiarize the students with the sequence of steps in each social skill and provide a procedure for students to be automatic with their knowledge of the skill steps; (8) use behavioral rehearsal to allow each student to practice and demonstrate the skill steps until they reach criterion; (9) assign homework providing opportunities for the students to practice the skills in other settings. These nine steps are followed for each of the eight specific social skills listed above.

▬ *Comments:* The ASSET program has been evaluated with eight learning-disabled students (Hazel, Schumaker, Sherman, and Sheldon, 1982) and demonstrated that the learning-disabled students involved in the intervention increased in the use of social skills in role-play settings. The curriculum guide provides specific teaching procedures and is particularly relevant to teachers working with adolescents.

Mutual Interest Discovery

Rather than specifically teaching social skills, *Mutual Interest Discovery* is an approach to increasing peer acceptance which has been used with learning-disabled students (Fox, 1989). The rationale is that people are attracted to persons with whom they share similar attitudes. The more we know about someone the more likely it is that we will like them. Structured activities are provided for non-learning-disabled and learning-disabled students to get to know each other with greater acceptance being the outcome.

■ *Procedures:* The overall goal of mutual interest discovery is to participate in structured activities with a partner (learning-disabled and non-learning-disabled paired) to identify things you have in common and to get to know your partner better.

1. All students in the class are paired with learning-disabled students who are paired with non-learning-disabled classmates.

2. Students interact on preassigned topics for approximately forty minutes once each week for several weeks. Preassigned topics include interviewing each other on such things as sports, entertainment preferences, hobbies, and other topics appropriate for the specific age group with which you are working.

3. After the structured activity each member of the pair writes three things they have in common or three things they learned about the other person.

4. Partners complete a brief art activity related to what they learned about their partner and place it in a mutual art book to which they contribute each week.

5. At the bottom of the art exercise each partner writes two sentences about something new they learned about their partner. If there is time, art activities and sentences are shared with members of the class.

■ *Comments:* Partners who participated in the mutual interest discovery intervention demonstrated higher ratings of their partners over time than did a control group of students. This intervention is not designed to teach specific social skills but to increase the acceptance and likability of learning-disabled students in the regular classroom. It is likely that this intervention paired with social skills training has promise for success with learning-disabled students.

Principles for Teaching Social Skills

There are several points teachers need to consider, no matter what social skills program they utilize. These include:

1. *Develop cooperative learning.* Classrooms can be structured so there is a win-lose atmosphere in which children compete with each other for grades and teacher attention, or classrooms can be structured so children work on their own with little interaction between classmates, or classrooms can be structured for cooperative learning so children work alone, with pairs, and with groups, helping each other master the assigned material. Cooperative learning techniques in the classroom result in increases in self-esteem, social skills, and learning (Johnson and Johnson, 1986). Teachers can structure learning activities so they involve cooperative learning and teach students techniques for working with pairs or in a group. The following four elements need to be present for cooperative leraning to occur in small groups (Johnson and Johnson, 1986):

    a. Students must perceive they cannot succeed at the required task unless all members of the group succeed. This may require appropriate division of labor and giving a single grade for the entire group's performance.

    b. Assure individual accountability so each member of the group is assessed and realizes his or her performance is critical for group success.

    c. Teach students the necessary collaborative skills so they are able to function effectively in a group. This may include managing conflicts, active listening, leadership skill, and problem solving.

d. Allow time for group process. This may include discussing how well the group is performing, developing a plan of action, and identifying what needs to happen.

2. *Involve peers in the training program for low-social-status students.* An important function of social skills training is to alter the way peers perceive students identified as low in social status. Including popular peers in the social skills training program increases the likelihood that they will have opportunities to observe the changes in target students and to cue and reinforce appropriate behavior in the classroom. For example, in a study conducted by Vaughn, McIntosh, and Spencer-Rowe (1988), they found popular students involved in the social skills training with low-social-status students were more likely to increase the social-status ratings of the low-social-status students than were popular students not involved in the training.

Even when a social skills program is effective in producing the desired child change with target students, it does not always alter the way these students are perceived by their peers (Bierman and Furman, 1984). Involving students with high social status with those with lower social status will increase the way the low-social-status students are perceived by others.

3. *Use principles of effective instruction.* Many teachers claim they do not know how to teach social skills. Considering the social skills difficulties of special education students, methods of teaching social skills to students may need to become part of our teacher training programs (Vaughn, 1985).

Teaching social skills requires implementing principles of effective instruction. These have been used and explained throughout this text and include: obtain student commitment, identify target behavior, pretest, teach, model, rehearse, role play, provide feedback, practice in controlled settings, practice in other settings, posttest and follow-up. A listing of social skills that learning- and behavior-disordered students frequently need to be taught follows:

a. *Body language.* This includes how the student walks, where he or she stands during a conversation, what his or her body "says," gestures, eye contact, and appropriate facial reactions.

b. *Greetings.* This may include expanding the student's repertoire of greetings, selecting appropriate greetings for different people, and interpreting and responding to the greetings of others.

c. *Initiating and maintaining a conversation.* This includes a wide range of behaviors such as knowing when to approach someone; knowing how to ask inviting, open questions; knowing how to respond to comments made by others; and maintaining a conversation with a range of persons, including those who are too talkative and those who volunteer little conversation.

d. *Giving positive feedback.* Knowing how and when to give sincere, genuine, positive feedback and comments.

e. *Accepting positive feedback.* Knowing how to accept positive feedback from others.

f. *Giving negative feedback.* Knowing how and when to give specific negative feedback.

g. *Accepting negative feedback.* Knowing how to accept negative feedback from others.

h. *Identifying feelings in self and others.* Being able to recognize feelings both in self and others. It is also how the student is able to predict how he or she will feel in a given situation and preparing appropriately for it. Responding appropriately to own and others' feelings.

i. *Problem solving and conflict resolution.* Knowing and using problem-solving skills to prevent and solve difficulties.

4. *Teach needed skills.* According to Perlmutter (1986), many social skills training programs fail because youngsters are trained to do things they already know how to do. For example, in a social skills training group with learning-disabled students, the trainer was teaching the students to initiate conversations with others. Through role playing, the trainer soon learned that the students already know how to initiate conversations but they did not know how to sustain them. In addition to being taught appropriate skills, students need to learn when and with whom to use the skills. One student put it this way: "I would never try problem solving like this with my father, but I know it would work with my mom."

5. *Teach for transfer of learning.* Many programs for teaching social skills effectively increase students' performance in social areas during the skills training or within a particular context, but the skills do not generalize to other settings (Berler, Gross, and Drabman, 1982). In order for social skills to generalize to other settings, the program must require the rehearsal and implementation of target skills across settings. Social skills training programs need to assure learned skills are systematically demonstrated in the classroom, on the playground, and at home.

6. *Empower students.* Many students with learning difficulties feel discouraged and unable to influence their learning. They turn the responsibility for learning over to the teacher and become "passive" learners. How can we empower students?

    a. *Choice.* Students need to feel they are actively involved in their learning.

    b. *Consequences.* Students will learn from the natural and logical consequences of their choices.

    c. *Document progress.* In addition to teacher documentation of progress made, students need to learn procedures for monitoring and assessing their progress.

    d. *Control.* Students need to feel as though they can exercise control over what happens to them. Some students feel as

though their learning is in someone else's hands and therefore is someone else's responsibility.

Instructional Activities

Appendix B provides instructional activities related to developing socialization skills. Some of the activities teach new skills; others are best suited for practice and reinforcement of already acquired skills. For each activity, the objective, materials, and teaching procedures are described.

Summary

This chapter described the social behaviors of students with learning and behavior disorders. Students identified as behavior-disordered display behaviors that are inappropriate and/or harmful to self or others. Many behavior-disordered students have appropriate social skills but do not use them or do not know when and with whom to use them. Other students do not have the skills and need to be taught them.

Students with learning disabilities are frequently identified as having social difficulties. As a group, they are more frequently rejected by their peers and teachers. They have been characterized as having social interaction difficulties, communication difficulties, low role-taking skills, and low self-concepts.

Four interventions to increase appropriate social behavior and decrease inappropriate social behavior were presented: intervention by prescription, interpersonal problem solving, behavior therapy, and ASSET. Intervention by prescription is a model that focuses on the student's impulse management. Appropriate intervention procedures are applied according to the student's need for external control or ability to utilize internal control. Behavioral approaches are utilized when the student has low impulse control and needs external controls; more cognitively oriented interventions are used as the student demonstrates more internal impulse control. Interpersonal problem solving teaches students strategies for communicating effectively with others and solving and preventing interpersonal conflicts with others. Behavioral therapy is based on the principles of applied behavior analysis for increasing and decreasing behaviors.

There are a number of intervention approaches that have been effectively implemented to increase appropriate social behaviors. Four of these approaches were discussed in this chapter and provide effective techniques for developing appropriate social behaviors.

Chapter Ten

Computer-Assisted Instruction
by Nancy Mather, Ph.D.

Chapter Questions

- *What are the four major types of instructional software?*
- *Describe each major type of software by giving its characteristics and the purpose for which it is most useful.*
- *If you were planning to buy a computer for your resource room, what peripherals would you want to purchase and why?*
- *Describe how you would integrate a computer and computer software into your writing program.*
- *For what other purposes could you use a computer in the classroom other than for instructional purposes?*
- *In evaluating instructional software, what are the important criteria to keep in mind?*

Microcomputers are being used by teachers in a variety of ways: to assist in grading, to help score standardized tests, to prepare individual educational programs, and to monitor student progress. Many teachers are presently employing microcomputers with students experiencing learning and behavior problems to provide assistance in academic instruction. Some special education teachers have been able to set up computer stations within their classrooms and adapt instruction to meet individual needs.

Although microcomputer instruction has been deemed highly motivating, one concern has been that teachers spend little time with students working on the microcomputer (Cosden, Gerber, Semmel, Goldman, and Semmel, 1987). Contrary to the norm, some teachers are quite involved. With careful instructional planning, the microcomputer can help a busy resource teacher individualize instruction. In many ways, integrating computer-based instruction into the resource room is similar to instructional planning without a computer: a teacher must determine objectives and an individual plan for each student (Farrell and Kaczka, 1988). This plan takes into account a learner's characteristics and needs.

When entering the classroom of Miriam Furst, a computer specialist and resource teacher, an observer notes students busy at work. Ms. Furst describes the various activities of the students:

> *Charlie is working hard on a drill and practice program. His scores in basic math computations have increased by six months in the last three months. He is anxious to see if he can make even more progress in the next three months.*
>
> *Alice, Pete, and Richard are writing notes as they play a mystery adventure game. At this moment, they are rereading their notes and discussing strategies for finding the hidden treasure and the thief who stole it. They have compiled a long list of words that they need to know how to spell to play the game.*
>
> *Miles and Mary are using the computer to practice their spelling words. Each spelling word flashes on the screen and then they try to type in the word from memory. Miles and Mary have learned how to enter the words they want to practice. Their weekly spelling scores reflect their hard work on the microcomputer.*
>
> *Sara and Carlos are using an authoring system to write a simulation program of a playground fight. When they are finished, the players will be allowed to react to a situation in a variety of ways and discover the consequences of their behavior. A player will have to make thoughtful choices or risk ending up in the principal's office.*
>
> *Bill is using the same authoring system to write a quiz about the science unit his class is studying. By the time the quiz is written, the class will have moved on to the next unit, but that's okay because his quiz will be used for class review.*

As demonstrated by the activities of the students in this resource room, computers can provide many types of instruction. This type of instruction is often referred to as computer-assisted instruction (CAI), or learning accomplished through the use of the computer. These electronic tools may be used in the classroom to enhance traditional methodology. Microcomputers can help learning-disabled students acquire, practice, and improve both cognitive and academic skills. In addition to a brief description of the microcomputer, this chapter provides an introduction to instructional software, general application software, authoring systems, computer languages, peripherals, and software evaluation.

The Microcomputer

A microcomputer is an electronic machine capable of storing both instructions and data in its memory and then executing those instructions in logical order. The actual equipment is called hardware. Examples of hardware include the keyboard, screen, disk drives, and ports for connecting external devices to the system. The computer system may be stationary or portable. Many varieties of laptop computers exist which are light-weight and may be carried from classroom to classroom.

In most instances, instructions and information are entered into a microcomputer (input) by typing on a keyboard. The central processing unit (CPU), often described as the brains of the microcomputer, works on the information and then displays the results (output). Before the CPU can function, software or instructions are necessary. Software includes commercial programs, available on cassette tapes and disks, as well as programs that are written by the user in special computer languages.

Programs are loaded into a microcomputer's memory by using cassette recorders, or more commonly, disk drives. A microcomputer may have a hard drive and/or floppy disk drives for storage and retrieval of information. Hard disks are located inside the computer, whereas floppy disks are inserted into external drives by the user. Inside a disk drive is a magnetic read/write head, similar to that in a cassette tape player, that is capable of reading any data stored on the disk or writing any new data on the disk. When a program is loaded into the computer's memory, changes can be made without altering the copy stored on the disk. Programs may also be saved or stored on disks for future access. In addition, most computers are capable of producing sound and colorful graphic illustrations. The availability and quality of software are prime determinants in the successful integration of the microcomputer into the classroom. Pres-

ently, a variety of educational software is available.

Instructional Software

The general purpose of instructional software is to provide students with interactive experiences that promote or supplement learning. Several different types of instructional programs exist: (1) drill and practice, (2) instructional games, (3) tutorial, and (4) simulation.

Drill and Practice

Brad works daily for ten minutes on a drill and practice program on multiplication facts. Each day he records his performance on a chart that shows the amount of progress he has made in the last month. Brad needs this daily repetition to memorize the multiplication facts. The microcomputer is a patient teacher.

Drill and practice programs provide repetition of previously learned concepts. Typically, in this type of software, the computer displays a problem, the student enters a response, then the computer evaluates the response and provides appropriate and immediate feedback. Like an electronic worksheet, drill and practice software is used to supplement instruction; the emphasis is on improving skills that require rote memory rather than on developing conceptual understanding.

With drill and practice software, the computer initiates and directs the person-machine interaction (Pogrow, 1983). Some educators feel that drill and practice software is of minor importance because it continues traditional methods of instruction and that the computer's capacity for conceptual teaching is more important (Hofmeister, 1982; Maddux and Johnson, 1983; Papert, 1980). Others believe that since many learning-disabled children evidence problems in processing efficiency rather than conceptual understanding, drill and practice activities may be considered the first priority for computer-assisted instruction with learning-disabled children (Torgesen and Young, 1983).

The most important function of drill and practice software is to aid in developing skills to an automatic level. This automaticity results from overlearning. Patterson and Smith (1986) state:

> Properly constructed drill and practice programs should enhance cognitive processing by requiring students to increase speed in retrieving information and in carrying out skill activities to the point where these activities become automatic. This automatic processing, in turn, should assist higher-order thinking by reducing certain cognitive demands on students when they are faced with a problem-solving situation (p. 92).

Hasselbring, Goin, and Bransford (1988) advised that drill and practice programs are most effective when students have developed a skill, such as finger counting for addition facts, but lack response speed on the automatic recall of facts from memory.

Teachers rarely have enough time to provide children with a sufficient amount of drill, and many students with learning and behavior problems require greater amounts of drill and practice than other students for mastery of facts (Schiffman, Tobin, and Buchanan, 1982; Torgesen and Young, 1983). Evidence suggests that microcomputers can enhance the reading decoding skills of learning-disabled children (Jones, Torgesen, and Sexton, 1987; Torgesen, 1986). Effective practice can be organized and sequenced to remediate reading skill deficits. This computer-aided practice in decoding is integrated with the total reading program. To ensure the effectiveness of CAI, previous research indicates that teachers must carefully attend to their total program of instruction (Torgesen, 1986). See Apply the Concept 10.1.

Extended practice on the microcomputer has been most successful with two basic skill areas: word recognition and elementary mathematics. Research results indicate that students with learning problems become more automatic and efficient in assessing information stored in memory (Goldman and Pellegrino, 1987).

Consequently, drill and practice programs may be especially beneficial to a student with memory problems because the microcomputer is patient and repetitive, showing no displeasure with the student who takes excessive time to memorize (Taber, 1983). Since performance feedback is immediate, the chances for retention are increased (Hagen, 1984). Also, the computer can deliver continual practice. Results from a recent study indicated that without this repetition, second- and third-grade learning-disabled children forgot about 30 percent of the sight words learned within a month's time (Waters and Torgesen, 1985). Other experimental research

Apply the Concept 10.1 _____

USING MICROCOMPUTERS TO TEACH BASIC DECODING SKILLS

Results from several evaluation studies indicate that the computer can provide effective practice to learning-disabled children on specific component skills in reading (Torgesen, 1986; Jones, Torgesen, and Sexton, 1987). Since many of these children have problems decoding individual words in text, this type of intensive, speed-oriented practice on the microcomputer is effective for enhancing basic reading skills. Children in the experimental groups improved in speed and accuracy for both context-free word reading and oral reading of connected text (Jones, Torgesen, and Sexton, 1987). Torgesen states: "If this practice is organized and sequenced effectively, and if deficits in decoding skills are really an important factor underlying poor reading comprehension, then it is likely that CAI can contribute to the effective remediation of the reading difficulties of LD children" (p. 80).

Apply the Concept 10.2

MAXIMIZING GAINS WITH DRILL AND PRACTICE SOFTWARE

Initial gains made by learning-disabled students on drill and practice mathematics programs are likely the result of the novelty of the computer and are not maintained over time (Howell, Sidorenko, and Jurica, 1987). In examining the effects of an intervention strategy for teaching multiplication facts to a learning-disabled student, Howell et al. found that the intervention was much more effective when the teacher worked with the student at the computer. By observing the student's

methods, the teacher was able to discover and change the inadequate strategies used by the student to solve the problems. The combination of specific teacher intervention with drill and practice software proved to be a highly beneficial treatment that is more likely to produce lasting benefits. Combining teacher intervention with selected software is an effective instructional strategy.

indicates that hyperactive children were more motivated by drill and practice on the microcomputer than by pencil and paper (Kleiman, Humphrey, and Lindsay, 1981). Findings of this nature, however, may be more the result of the novelty of the computer than the superiority of microcomputer instruction.

As with workbooks and worksheets, drill and practice exercises on the microcomputer must be carefully monitored or the activity can evolve into mere busy work. Unfortunately, some drill and practice programs are boring after one use (Bitter, 1984). Too much drill is unproductive. Ten to fifteen minutes a day is likely to provide sufficient practice time for most students. Prior to drill and practice microcomputer instruction, a teacher must determine the rationale for the drill, select an appropriate presentation style, set a criterion level for performance, and then carefully document student progress. Investigations by Howell, Sidorenko, and Jurica (1987) suggest that specific teacher intervention is necessary to maintain gains made with drill and practice software. See Apply the Concept 10.2.

One major criticism of microcomputer application has been an overreliance on drill and practice software. Although drill and practice activities should not be the sole application of microcomputers in a classroom, they are appropriate for certain types of students and certain

types of instruction, such as mastery of sight word vocabulary and basic math facts. When combined with teacher insight, a superior teaching exercise may not exist (Williams and Williams, 1984).

Instructional Games

Instructional games, available in all subject areas, attempt to combine video arcade-style graphics and audio effects with scholastic objectives. For example, the object may be to destroy enemy spaceships and save the planet Earth by solving basic addition or multiplication problems. Some games may be played by several people; the computer keeps track of whose turn it is and provides a score at the end of each round. Playing these games often requires considerable hand-eye coordination and manual dexterity. In many programs, the game and academic skill level can be adjusted to student ability by regulating the presentation rate, the response time, and the number of problems per round.

The main intent of this type of software is to motivate students to practice and improve basic skills. Many students enjoy drill in a game format; others do not. As with drill and practice software, a game may quickly lose its appeal. The interactive nature and motivational appeal of some games, however, make them particularly valuable as a reinforcement activity or as a supplement to classroom instruction. Several features of educational video arcade-type games are useful for motivating reluctant students to master educational objectives: (1) feedback (immediate determination of whether or not a response is correct); (2) improvement (ability to change in performance and increase skill); (3) a fast pace that demands high response rates; and (4) unlimited ceilings on performance, allowing successive increases in difficulty level (Chaffin, Maxwell, and Thompson, 1982).

Tutorial

Tutorial programs are designed to review concepts and/or present new material in small sequential steps. In this type of program, instructional problems are presented that evaluate the student's comprehension of the materials at varied levels of ability. Patterson and Smith (1986) differentiate between content tutorial and heuristic tutorial software. *Content tutorial* software teaches new facts to students and provides sufficient groundwork to prepare a student for more complex problems. *Heuristic tutorial* provides practice in the use of problem-solving strategies in structured, make-believe settings of gamelike environments. Both types of software may be successful in enhancing problem-solving skills.

Tutorial software often contains *branching,* defined as a set of alternatives for the next operation (Williams and Williams, 1984). The presentation routes the student to preset sequences. Depending on a student's response, the program moves to a higher level with more difficult material, or a lower level with less difficult material that reviews prerequisite skills or concepts.

Although tutorial programs in general attempt to individualize instruction, program branching does not guarantee individualization or adequate instruction because children fail items for different reasons (Senf, 1983). Consequently, further drill or simpler problems may not be what a child needs to master or understand the presented concepts. The computer only provides logical distinctions (yes/no) (Bitter, 1984);

the teacher must analyze student performance and determine appropriate instruction. In discussing the teaching of new content in relation to prior student knowledge, Patterson and Smith (1986) state:

> Here the computer is at a distinct disadvantage when compared to a human teacher; not even the most powerful electronic brain comes close to the capacity of the human brain to make judgments about students' previous experience and to tailor information to meet special group and individual needs (p. 94).

Simulation

A *simulation* is defined as a model of some aspect of reality that is usually simplified to focus on points of interest (MacArthur, 1984). Simulation software is designed to replicate real-life and imaginary situations so that students can experience a given set of conditions (Bitter, 1984). Simulations could include such scenarios as fighting historic battles, landing spaceships, performing a science experiment, or driving a car through city streets (Taber, 1983). For example, a program may simulate flying an airplane. The navigator uses instrument controls to monitor the plane position. Simulations involve students as active learners as they must participate in the decision making and problem solving. This type of software can introduce students to subject matter that was previously out of the scope of the school curriculum. Although the availability of this type of software is somewhat limited, the educational potential is most promising (Bitter, 1984; Maddux, 1984).

One variety of simulation software is the adventure game. The primary advantage of these text and graphic adventures is the motivational power of fantasy (MacArthur, 1984). In a typical adventure game, the player is placed in a perilous environment with a specific mission to accomplish, such as slaying a dragon, discovering hidden treasures, or exploring a haunted house. A command line on the screen will query: What shall I do now? The player directs the course of action by entering various commands that can range from two-word, noun-verb combinations to complete sentences. The software includes a parser that recognizes certain syntax and vocabulary; some parsers recognize adjectives, prepositions, and pronouns as well as noun-verb combinations.

Many adventure games are difficult to solve. A typical game can take up to forty hours of playing time. Often elaborate maps are required, as an environment can contain as many as one hundred rooms and locations. Fortunately, games can be saved at any time; an adventurer quickly learns to save a game before attempting something risky like jumping from a ledge or entering a strange cave.

Because of the time-consuming nature of adventure games, a teacher may have some difficulty integrating this type of software into the classroom. Despite time limitations, these motivating games do, however, seem to promote problem-solving and language skills. Both logic and memory are necessary; the player must be able to organize and analyze a myriad of clues. Also, playing a game requires many of the basic skills: reading, writing, spelling, and typing. Several software companies have produced adventures designed specifically for children. Other software programs exist that allow children to create their own adventure games just by entering the text descriptions, then the software does the programming. Interactive novels are also available; here, a student reads the text and makes critical decisions that affect the story outcome. The author and others (Mather, 1986; Patterson and Smith, 1986) have observed students with severe reading and writing problems working diligently on adventure games with only a text format. The motivational effectiveness of these games, the sustained cognitive activity, and the opportunity to control the environment make adventure games a powerful teaching device (Patterson and Smith, 1986).

A recent innovation in the application of the computer is *export systems* technology. In those applications, the computer simulates a consultation with a human expert. The system gathers information by asking the user questions. Hofmeister and Lubke (1988) discuss the potential applications of export systems for the diagnosis and treatment of learning disabilities.

Table 10.1 provides a brief overview of some potential advantages and disadvantages of drill and practice, instructional games, tutorial, and simulation software. Although these generalizations summarize some of the features of a particular type of instructional software, it is important to remember that factors that are negative for one individual may be positive for another. For example, one student may enjoy a high-paced competitive game, whereas another may become frustrated. One student may enjoy the routine of drill and practice software, whereas another may lose interest after a few problems. As with all carefully selected instructional materials, the choice of software is guided by instructional intent, student needs, and knowledge of an individual's learning style.

General Application Software

General application programs simplify or organize various paperwork tasks. These programs have functions that enable a user to complete specific jobs. For example, many standardized tests provide computerized scoring programs to simplify the scoring process. These programs save the user time and increase accuracy. Several types of application software exist: word processing, data base management, and electronic spreadsheets.

Word Processing

Although Alicia has extreme difficulty with spelling, she loves to write creative stories. Working on a word processor allows Alicia to develop a story and return and edit the story before she prints a draft. She has also learned to

TABLE 10.1   *Advantages and Disadvantages of Instructional Software*

	Advantages	Disadvantages
Drill and Practice	Develops skill to automatic level of responding	Reduced cognitive demands
	Provides for overlearning and repetition	No guarantee of conceptual understanding
	Provides immediate feedback	May be monotonous, workbook format
Instructional Games	Requires hand-eye coordination, manual dexterity, and quick reaction time	Required motor skills may frustrate some students
	Immediate feedback, provides competition and successive increases in difficulty level	Emphasis on reaction time
	Highly motivating, good reinforcement activity, stimulating graphics	Video arcade format may be disruptive to classroom atmosphere
	Learning in a game format	May tire of format, may not coincide with educational objectives
Tutorial	Presents instruction in small sequential steps	Effectiveness depends on prior knowledge
	Instruction in problem solving	Problem may not be relevant to student's instructional needs
	May work independently	Must be motivated to work independently
	Provides varied levels of difficulty	Branching doesn't guarantee adequate instruction
	Provides review of concepts	Review may not be sufficient
Simulation	Replicates real life	May be difficult to integrate with academic curriculum
	Involves students as active learners	May require considerable teacher assistance
	Promotes problem solving and/or language skills	Time consuming

use a spelling checker, which helps her detect many of her misspellings independently. After she edits her first draft, she prints a copy for her teacher to edit. When the draft is returned, Alicia enters the corrections, rewrites a few sections, and then prints the final draft. With the help of a word processing program, Alicia is able to develop her ideas in writing without becoming frustrated by her low spelling skills.

A word processor is useful for writing stories, poems, articles, or reports. This special computer program allows writers to input text into the computer's memory and then save the text for future retrieval. Data files are saved and stored on a hard disk or floppy disk for future use. A hard copy, or paper copy, of what is written is reproduced through a printer that is attached to the computer.

All word processing programs contain text editors that allow the user to change, insert, and delete words or sentences by using simple keyboard commands. Consequently, editing and correcting papers do not involve retyping or recopying, as the writer corrects only the elements in the original text that need revision. Once revisions are made, a new copy can be printed.

Many word processing packages include spelling checkers that will help the user identify and correct typing and spelling mistakes. The text is matched against the computer's dictionary, then the user is advised of any misspellings. In many programs, the user is prompted with the correct spelling. To obtain the correct spelling, however, the student's representation of the word must be close enough for the computer to recognize it. Punctuation, capitalization, usage, and style checkers are also available for some systems. A computerized thesaurus can also be used to assist the writer in word choice. In addition, word processors can be supported with synthesized speech output.

Word processing programs vary in complexity and in the number of features. Simple word processors developed for children often present the commands and instructions on the top lines of the screen. Most students can begin to write and edit text after a brief twenty minutes of instruction. More sophisticated word processors demand intensive study, but they provide the user with complete control over the format of the printed page, including such features as line justification, centering, margin settings, and underlining. Some word processors allow the user to combine graphic and text output by splitting a text block and inserting a picture. Although many secondary students will select a more powerful word processing system, program choice depends entirely on an individual's capabilities and needs. See Apply the Concept 10.3. Messerer and Lerner (1989) described three word processing programs that have useful features for students with learning disabilities. They also described a variety of instructional applications and strategies for using word processing.

Although the commands of a simple word processing system are easy to master, adequate typing skills are a prerequisite for efficient use. If students will be using word processing software in the classroom, some time should be spent on the acquisition of keyboard and typing skills. A concern at the elementary level has been when and how to teach these touch typing skills. Many elementary teachers do not have the time or background to teach children how to type. One solution is to introduce beginning typing skills into the elementary curriculum. Another is to acquire typing tutor software that can be used to help children develop keyboard skills. With five or ten minutes of daily practice, children can develop typing skills with little teacher assistance. Some educators feel that microcomputer typing should be introduced to learning-disabled children as soon as their fingers can span the keyboard (Hagen, 1984).

Many authors have strongly recommended the use of word processing software with learning-disabled students (Hagen, 1984; Hummel and Balcom, 1984; Messerer and Lerner, 1989; Rosegrant, 1985). Hagen states: "The alternative provided by a microcomputer and word pro-

Apply the Concept 10.3

LEARNING TO USE A WORD PROCESSOR

In observing learning-disabled students learning to use a word processor, MacArthur and Schneiderman (1986) noted that the students had a slow rate of typing and had difficulty mastering the editing features. The students tended to use the simplest procedures rather than the most efficient. Several principles for evaluating word processors for learning-disabled students emerged from this study: (1) the structure and program organization should be simple and logical enough that the user can form a mental map; (2) the procedures for saving and loading documents should be clear and the system should verify the user's request before data are erased; (3) the vocabulary should be easily understood; and (4) little-used options, such as setting margins, should be accessed only on user request and not each time a document is printed.

cessing programs for learning disabled children is equal to the reinvention of written language, designed specifically for their needs. Strong words? Yes, but strong medicine needs strong words'' (p.38).

Throughout her school career, Sandy had difficulty developing legible handwriting. Severe visual-motor problems were diagnosed in second grade. In fourth grade, Sandy learned to type. Now in secondary school, Sandy uses a laptop computer and word processing program for all her writing assignments. She carries her computer from class to class and even uses it for taking lecture notes and examinations. Use of a computer allows Sandy to circumvent her difficulty with handwriting.

Word processing allows students with learning problems to circumvent a messy paper and to take pride in the product. Ease of revision frees the student to concentrate on content rather than mechanics. Once an idea is developed, the student can edit the text for organization, sentence structure, and spelling and grammatical mistakes. Proofreading is no longer an aversive task. Writing becomes a cyclic process of creating, evaluating, and revising. Prompting programs may also be used to aid in the revision process. Students are asked a set of questions about their text and then, based upon the responses, are offered suggestions for improvement. Word processing assists in removing the pencil and paper blockade of many learning-disabled students (Hagen, 1984). It is not, however, a panacea for all writing problems. This software does not assist with the creative aspect of writing (Hummel and Balcom, 1984). It facilitates the writing process but it does not teach students how to write (Bos, 1983). In general, research involving the effectiveness of word processing on the written expression of learning disabled students has produced mixed results (Keefe and Candler, 1989). The word processing environment, however, is unique because of the accessibility a teacher has to a student's writing; a teacher may observe the writing strategies of the student, both in the planning and composing stages. The computer supports the cognitive processes employed in planning, writing, and revising (MacArthur, 1988). Because of the visibility of the writing process, working on a word processor provides opportunities for collaboration and increased communication between a student and teacher.

Data Base Management

Data base management systems have many uses. For example, students in a biology class may want to catalog the lab results of all class members, or students in an English class may want to establish a data base on paperback books. In a typical secondary school computer lab, individuals often devise their own customized data bases. Henry uses the computer to keep track of the performance statistics of the members of his favorite baseball team. Martha keeps a record of all the activities of students in the Debate Club. Sheila maintains a class budget. Bill established a system to record student schedules and can print backup copies whenever a person needs to contact or locate a student. Each of these students has selected a different way to manage and store pertinent data.

Data base management programs have been described as electronic filing cabinets. This type of software is designed to help the user manage information and maintain records more efficiently. To create the data base, information is entered onto single data files, much like an individual file folder. Individual data records can then be modified, added, or deleted at any time. Once records are entered, they can be sorted and catalogued in a variety of ways.

Many different problem-solving applications of data bases exist: (1) discovering similarities and differences among groups, (2) analyzing relationships, (3) exploring trends in data, (4) testing hypotheses, (5) organizing and sharing information, (6) maintaining current lists, and (7) arranging information in meaningful ways (Hunter, 1985). As with word processing, this type of computer application may enhance the performance of students with learning and behavior problems, particularly at the secondary level. Both data base management and word processing programs involve the student as an active planner and communicator who directs the computer to a prescribed outcome (Hummel and Balcom, 1984).

Teachers may also use data base management programs as record keepers. These programs may be used for recording scores, computing grades, and printing grades quickly and accurately. Additionally, many computerized versions for creating Individual Education Programs (IEPs) are available. Many teachers find that these applications decrease the paper workload and increase their time for teaching.

Electronic Spreadsheets

Spreadsheets are computational tools that involve columns and rows of figures. Arithmetic relationships are established between the individual cells that contain the sums of the column or row. With some programs, numbers can be taken from a spreadsheet and converted into charts and graphs to illustrate the data. These electronic worksheets are most useful for jobs that require repetitive calculations. Consequently, spreadsheets are commonly employed in office, business, and administrative applications. Some secondary students, however, may enjoy learning to perform calculations by using spreadsheets.

Authoring Tools

Many software programs assist teachers in creating instructional materials. Some programs enable the teacher to develop his or her own word search games, matching games, and crossword puzzles. Others assist in designing specific classroom lessons and quizzes. With minimal programming knowledge, teachers and students can create their own programs by using an authoring system. The teacher supplies the presentation information, the questions and answers, and

the feedback for correct and incorrect responses (Taber, 1983). In many of these programs, the teacher follows a series of menus and prompts that specify what information should be entered into the computer.

Authoring systems can be separated into two categories: mini-authoring systems and major authoring systems (Hagen, 1984). Mini-authoring systems have a fixed framework and are useful in creating drill and practice lessons, usually in a multiple choice or question and answer format. An example of a mini-authoring system would be a generic program called Shell Games. These skeletons allow the teacher to add material to a basic question-and-answer format. Programming knowledge is not necessary; the teacher simply enters the quiz problems into the program structure. Question sets can be deleted, modified, or altered at any time. Graphics and sound may be added to enrich the instruction.

Major authoring systems are more flexible than mini-authoring systems but they also require more expertise. Programs developed using this type of authoring tool tend to be more tutorial in nature. An example of a major authoring system or an authoring language is PILOT, an acronym for Programmed Inquiry, Learning or Teaching. An authoring language like PILOT can assist the teacher in creating interactive courseware that allows the entry of narrative descriptions. This language works with basic core commands, called instructions, that enable the user to create a sequence of questions and answers. Using these instructions, the teacher or student creates a program that will ask questions about a specific subject.

Instructions are placed at the beginning of the program line, using letter codes. For example, the command "TYPE" tells the computer to display what is written on the screen, and "MATCH" tells the computer to check student response. If the response is incorrect, further explanation can be provided. The command "JUMP" tells the computer to branch to another part of the program where an explanation or

FIGURE 10.1   *A Sample CAI Program Using PILOT*

Commands	Example
T: (TYPE) Entered text is displayed on screen	T: Hello. What is your name?
A: (ACCEPT) Waits for and stores student response	A: $Name
	T: Hi, $Name (prints student's name). We are going to practice states and their capitals.
Named "Question #1"	T: What is the capital of Arizona?
M: (MATCH) Checks student response. The "Ph" allows the answer to be counted correct if the first two letters are correct.	M: Phoenix, Ph
TY: (Yes): Prints what follows the colon if a match was made.	TY: Yes, you are correct. Phoenix is the capital of Arizona.
TN: (NO): Prints what follows the colon if a match was not made.	TN: No, it is the largest city in Arizona.
J: (JUMP) Sends computer to different part of the program. Repeats Question 1.	J: Question 1.

reinforcement is provided. Color, graphic effects, and musical accompaniment can be added to enrich the program. Figure 10.1 provides a simple illustration of a PILOT program.

A language like PILOT allows teachers to create their own structure or lesson framework with relative ease. Most teachers can start creating interactive instruction after studying PILOT for only a few hours. The easiest part of using PILOT is the programming; the most difficult part is the planning (Tyre, 1984). Before programming, a teacher must establish a goal, provide the strategy and the outline, and determine the program content. PILOT may be used to create individual exams for students of varying abilities or to provide reviews of factual information for a test.

Students can also create lessons. Tyre suggests that this may be PILOT'S best application: "By having to know enough to specify the subject matter as well as plan how to present it, students wind up learning more" (p. 54). An authoring language like PILOT can be an effective instructional tool, particularly for content area instruction. With careful planning, teachers can adapt lessons to individual needs. Criticisms of PILOT include lack of flexibility and limited capabilities (Taber, 1983). Maddux and Cummings (1985) reiterate that PILOT is designed for ready use and that its strength lies in its interactive capabilities, or in the power of the "MATCH" command to evaluate student response.

Before purchasing an authoring tool, a teacher may want to examine provision for the following capabilities: (1) answer matching, (2) feedback, (3) flexible branching, (4) record keeping, (5) screen display features, and (6) variable time for responses (Pattison, 1985).

Computer Languages

Computer languages are used to create programs. These languages are specific sets of instructions that tell the computer what to do. Unless personally motivated, teachers do not need to learn advanced programming skills to use the microcomputer effectively in the classroom. General familarity with the programming process, however, is helpful as a teacher may provide beginning instruction to interested students. Two computer languages, Logo and BASIC, have particular application to school-age children. For some students, learning to program the computer is a highly motivating experience.

Miriam Furst, the computer specialist and resource teacher who was introduced at the begining of this chapter, describes a young girl's experience of learning to program in BASIC: "In fifth grade, Jessie would cry as she tried to read the simplest words in books or other written materials. She became frustrated and angry during reading lessons. By the end of sixth grade, Jessie was standing proudly in front of an audience of teachers at a district conference. She had written a quiz about the life and times of the artist Winslow Homer. In designing and writing her program, Jessie not only learned to read every word but also mastered many BASIC commands. This successful experience altered Jessie's attitude toward reading instruction; she became highly motivated to learn."

Ms. Furst believes that three factors were responsible for Jessie's change of attitude. First, Jessie had not failed at the computer; it was a new medium for her that was not associated with the endless stream of books and worksheets that represented years of frustration and defeat. Second, Jessie was in control of the computer. She was in charge of the total content and design of the program, which is a powerful experience for a child who previously felt incapable of having a positive impact on her environment. Third, Jessie had a good reason for working hard. She knew her programs were going to be shared with others and that they might help other children learn the information that had been so difficult for her to acquire.

Logo

Logo, a programming language primarily for elementary-age students, was developed at the Massachusetts Institute of Technology by Seymour Papert. Papert (1980) attempted to create a computer language based on Piagetian learning principles that would help children formulate an intuitive sense of mathematical relationships. Papert envisioned the computer as an instrument of explanation that allows children to explore and discover thinking processes. One unique quality of this educational software is that development was based on educational theory (Maddux, 1984).

Many versions of this language are available, including a revised version of the original Logo (Papert, 1986). In the most well-known Logo application, a child creates pictures and designs on the monitor by typing simple English word commands. These commands direct a small triangle, called a turtle, in four different direction: forward, back, right, and left. For example, LEFT 60, rotates the pointer on the turtle 60 degrees to the left. Distance is controlled by adding a numeric value, such as FORWARD 30.

Through experimentation, a child may soon realize that a series of 90-degree turns results in a square. Commands that are combined or used in a series to produce a specific design are called a *procedure*. The following illustrates a simple Logo procedure that will teach the computer to draw a square on the screen.

```
? TO SQUARE
> REPEAT 4 [FD 40 RT 90]
> END
SQUARE DEFINED
```

Once a definition is completed, the instructions may be saved. The next time the computer sees the command SQUARE, it will find a copy of the instructions and then produce the drawing. These procedures can be combined with other commands to build more colorful geometric drawings or graphics that can be saved on disk.

In addition to graphic applications, Logo can be used to create and handle specific word processing tasks, perform numeric manipulations, or control voice synthesizers and robots (Papert, 1986). Students may create greeting cards or video games with words and music. The next section illustrates a simple quiz written in Logo.

```
TO QUIZ
PRINT [WHAT DAY COMES AFTER MONDAY?]
TEST READLIST = [TUESDAY]
IFTRUE[PRINT[THAT'S RIGHT.]STOP]
PRINT [NO, TRY AGAIN.]
QUIZ
```

A major advantage of Logo is that the child is in control of the microcomputer, rather than the computer being in control of the child. This makes the learning process both active and self-directed and allows children flexibility for expressing their individual learning styles (Papert, 1980; Papert, 1986). Papert (1986) states that Logo capitalizes on a basic Piagetian principle: "The knowledge you have is something you make." Hagen (1984) feels that using Logo stimulates a child's thought processes and logical sequencing, allowing the child to use the microcomputer as a learning tool. She indicates that the strongest feature of Logo is freedom from imposed constraints of the mind. Logo allows children to concentrate on experimentation.

This language has been used with many different age groups, including preschool children. Despite certain conceptual difficulties in understanding the Logo commands, these children appear to learn intuitive math concepts, linguistic skills, letters and numbers, and logical sequencing (Vaidya and McKeeby, 1984). One study indicated that fourth- and fifth-grade learning-disabled students were able to learn to program with Logo as well as their non-learning-disabled peers (Chiang, Thorpe, and Lubke, 1984). Bradley (1985) examined the relationship among information-processing styles, Logo programming, academic achievement, and cogni-

tive abilities. One conclusion of this research was that Logo achievement has a positive relationship with the ability to conceptualize the structure of a task.

In general, little empirical evidence exists regarding the possible outcomes of learning Logo (Ginther and Williamson, 1985). Ginther and Williamson suggested that the most significant outcomes of learning Logo may be in the personal-social sphere rather than the logical-analytical dimension. In observing children learning Logo, they noted the following outcomes: (1) persistence in response to frustration, (2) articulate communication, (3) cooperation and sharing of ideas, (4) attention to details, (5) ability to follow directions, and (6) recognition of the need for assistance balanced with appropriate independence.

Summaries of recent research indicate that Logo (1) is an effective tool for facilitating pro-social interactions, communication, positive attitudes toward learning, and independent work habits; (2) can raise scores on tests of metacognition, originality, and creativity; (3) seems to have little direct impact on acquired knowledge or what children know; and (4) has potential for applications with special populations (Clements, 1985, 1986; Howell, 1985).

Presently, many issues regarding the efficacy of programs designed to teach discovery learning are unresolved (Goldman and Pellegrino, 1987; Howell, 1985). It is difficult for researchers to document Logo's effects on problem-solving strategies, or to locate a sample of children with similar Logo experiences (Maddux, 1984). Controlled, systematic, and sensitive research studies that address the cognitive impact and the effects of materials and teachers on learning Logo remain priority areas (Howell, 1985). Logo does seem to hold promise for combining "the abstract and mathematical with the concrete and aesthetic" (Clements, 1985, p. 69). Hopefully, future research will help clarify the accrued and long-term benefits derived from Logo programming.

FIGURE 10.2 *A Sample BASIC Program*

```
10   REM Demonstration Program

20   PRINT "What is your first name?";

30   INPUT N$

40   PRINT "What is 5 + 5";

50   INPUT A

60   If A = 10 then 90

70   PRINT "Sorry, "N$", Try again"

80   GOTO 40

90   PRINT "Great Job", "N$";

100  PRINT "See you later."
```

BASIC

BASIC, an acronym for Beginner's All-purpose Symbolic Instruction Code, is another computer language that is composed of English words, abbreviations, and mathematical symbols. As with Logo, several versions exist. Teachers and students may use this language to develop simple drill programs. Figure 10.2 presents an example of a simple program.

Additional commands such as random numbers, loops, subroutines, and arrays can be added as programming expertise develops. Some teachers may feel that BASIC is too complicated for their students, and prefer to use Logo (Hagen, 1984). The simple rudiments of BASIC programming, however, can be mastered and applied with relative ease.

For example, if a teacher has access to several microcomputers, creating text programs can be used as an alternative to a writing assignment. Some students will enjoy creating mini-adventures, modeled after the branching adventure stories. This type of program is possible by using four simple commands: PRINT, which displays text on the screen; INPUT, which accepts a user's response; IF-THEN, which analyzes the response; and GOTO, which tells the computer to execute the following line number. A short example of a mini-adventure is provided in Figure 10.3.

Programs can continue to branch and become more complex. For example, the programmer can provide the user with several possible responses, all with varying consequences. Before writing a program of this nature, students can outline on paper the story paths and program lines. Students who want to create more complex subroutines may refer to the step-by-step process for developing adventure games outlined in *Basic Fun with Adventure Games* (Lipscomb and Zuanich, 1984).

Maddux and Cummings (1985) provide a more in-depth description of BASIC, Logo, and PILOT, with the intention of helping educators choose a language to teach children. Some secondary students with advanced programming skills may prefer to use or explore other programming languages, like PASCAL or FORTRAN, that have greater power than BASIC. Choosing the most appropriate computer language for a classroom will be determined by specific educational and programming needs.

FIGURE 10.3 *Adventure Program in BASIC*

```
10   PRINT "You have entered a haunted house that
     contains a hidden treasure."

20   PRINT "Suddenly a ghost appears."

30   PRINT "Do you want to run or talk to the
     ghost?"

40   INPUT A$

50   If A$ = "Run" then GOTO 80

60   If A$ = "Talk to ghost" then GOTO 90

70   GOTO 30

80   PRINT "As you run from the house, you fall
     down the stairs and disappear into the eerie
     darkness!"; END

90   PRINT "The ghost tells you to climb the stairs
     and you will find the hidden treasure."; END
```

Peripheral Hardware to Facilitate Learning

Additional hardware, or peripherals, may be added to microcomputers to enhance learning. A device called an *interface* allows the computer to work with the external attachment. Common peripherals include printers, disk drives, joysticks, speech synthesizers, modems, light pens, graphics tablets, and tape recorders.

Printers

Printers are used to produce hard copy or printouts of information entered into the computer. Some printers produce letter-quality type, identical to that of an office typewriter; others produce dot-matrix type, where letters are formed by rows of pins that hit the ribbon to create letter shapes. Printers vary in cost, capabilities, and print quality. Most classrooms can manage with a relatively inexpensive, but durable, model.

Speech Synthesizers

A speech synthesizer is capable of producing artificial speech. Synthesizers use phonetic pronunciations to form understandable speech. The quality of voice output ranges from robotic speech with unlimited pronunciation capabilities to natural speech with more limited pronunciation capabilities.

A speech synthesizer may be useful in spelling and reading instruction. Words or sentences to be pronounced may be typed by the teacher or student. Since the computer reads sounds to produce speech, a student will quickly grasp phonetic principles to obtain the best pronunciation from the computer. Fisher (1983) noted that several learning-disabled adults were able to make faster progress in spelling by using a speech synthesizer than by using more conventional methods.

Many software programs have been designed to work with speech synthesizers. These audible programs combine text, graphics, and speech to optimize instruction. For example, students can use a light pen to trace around letters on the screen while the synthesizer produces the letter sound or name. Also, a speech synthesizer can be interfaced with a word processor for use as a basic writing and reading tool (Rosegrant, 1985, 1986). By using simple commands, the text typed on the keyboard can be read and rewritten with ease.

Rosegrant (1985) describes software, called the Talking Screen Textwriter, that provides auditory visual, and motor support to learning-disabled children. Children using the talking textwriter made significant improvements in both reading and writing. Various talking programs are of great benefit to some learning-disabled children, particularly nonreaders or poor readers who are likely to benefit from the auditory feedback (Pommer, Mark, and Hayden, 1983). Multiple presentation formats, such as auditory, verbal, and pictorial, enhance memory (Jay, 1983).

Cassette Control Devices

A cassette control device permits the teacher to synchronize a tape recorder with a text. This device allows for simultaneous visual and auditory presentation of material. The tape recorder is controlled by the computer so that the teacher-recorded instructions are played at the appropriate time. This type of peripheral is less frequently used, but can be effective for tasks such as reading lists of words.

Modems

A modem, an abreviation for modulator/demodulator, allows people to link computers together for sharing information by converting computer codes into signals that can be carried over telephone lines. Using a modem, a person can receive information from many electronic data bases or send information to other computers. In a classroom with a telephone line, modems can be used to access an encyclopedia, share programs, or send electronic mail to pen pals. Some schools currently have these resources. Many students enjoy using a modem on home computers.

Other Enhancements

Joysticks, paddles, or a mouse are often used for video arcade-style games to move objects around the screen. Joysticks often have a fire button that releases missiles. With a joystick an object can be moved in any direction, whereas paddles are used to move an object up, down, left, or right. A mouse may be used to select a choice from a menu or to move the cursor around the screen.

Light pens allow the user to trace or draw pictures, letters, or words directly on the screen. The screen lights up as it is touched by the pen. Drawings may also be created by using a graphics tablet. This type of tablet has a pressure-sensitive surface on a grid. As the user presses down on the surface of the tablet with a special pen, the tablet tells the computer the coordinates to light so that the picture on the tablet is displayed on the screen. A graphics plotter will produce good-quality graphs, charts, and pictures on paper.

Software Evaluation

This year Ms. Downing received two microcomputers to use in her resource program. Although she was excited about the equipment, she had no idea where to begin. Having never touched a computer before, she was somewhat frightened and mystified by this new instructional technology. She was filled with questions: How would she ever learn something so complicated? Where would she find software for her students? Would she ever find programs that could be adapted to different levels?

Ms. Downing was fortunate. She called her district office for assistance and the informed her of a group of teachers who met weekly to discuss software application and availability. After three

or four meetings, Ms. Downing selected several programs from the media center that would be appropriate for the special students in her program. Although she knew she would discover new software programs each week, Ms. Downing had dispelled her initial apprehension and was eager to switch on the microcomputer.

Two problems in evaluating educational software are the shortage of programs designed for children and the lack of research to support the effectiveness of programs (Spencer and Baskin, 1986). As knowledge about instructional software increases, the effectiveness of microcomputer usage with mildly handicapped students will improve (Goldman, Semmel, Cosden, Gerber, and Semmel, 1987). When evaluating software, a teacher should consider the particular needs of the students enrolled in the class. Some software that is extremely relevant and appropriate for one individual is useless for another. Some students respond well to game format for learning multiplication tables or typing skills; others are distracted by the graphics and frustrated by the fast pace. Instead of judging whether a particular program is good or bad, the evaluator should consider its utility with particular types of students (Hofmann, 1985).

Jay (1983) considers the implications of cognitive research on computer courseware guidelines or the relationship of information processing theory to courseware design. He presents five human information processing abilities that must be considered in the development of good courseware: (1) memory and attention, (2) language or text characteristics, (3) graphics and visual processing, (4) cognitive characteristics of a user, and (5) user feedback. Within each area, basic principles from cognitive theory are suggested and then translated into strategies for instructional design. In addition to software development, the information processing principles are relevant to software evaluation for students with learning and behavior problems.

In selecting and adapting software, a teacher should consider several aspects of a student's learning characteristics (Taymans and

Malouf, 1984). First, a teacher should estimate the required reading level necessary to operate the program, as the text demands should be matched to the learner's instructional level. Second, the teacher should consider the perceptual, motor, and memory demands of the software. A student with slow motor response is likely to need software with an adjustable presentation rate. A student with a severe deficit in visual perception may have difficulty making discriminations or viewing a screen with numerous symbols. A hyperactive student may become overstimulated by busy graphics and audio effects. Third, as with any teaching materials, the instructor must determine whether or not the content and demands of the software match the student's capabilities and comprehension level. In most cases, it is more appropriate to determine the student's developmental level and then to locate the software that matches the child's instructional needs. Finally, the teacher must consider the motivational value of the software; program appeal is best determined by student evaluation.

Ability to modify software is a major determinant of continued classroom utility. Many programs allow a teacher to alter content with ease or to adapt presentation style to individual needs. With little effort, the user can modify such aspects as presentation speed, response mode, criterion, screen presentation, and/or reading level. These types of modifications enable a teacher to accommodate individual learning styles. Another important consideration is a random factor where a new situation is presented each time a program is used (Behrmann and Levy, 1986). A random factor and adaptable content maximize program longevity.

Various software evaluation forms and review criteria are available in several publications (Cohen, 1983; Hummel and Senf, 1985; Sanders and Sanders, 1983; Spencer and Baskin, 1986; Taber, 1983; Test, 1985). Pogrow (1983) provides a list of characteristics of desirable software. These checklists, rating scales, and evaluative criteria provide a format for assessing the technical adequacy, instructional design, and instructional content of a program. Although checklists can be useful, reading complete courseware reviews in journals often imparts a sense of quality beyond mere checklist procedures (Jay, 1983).

Pommer, Mark, and Hayden (1983) present specific evaluative criteria for using computer software to instruct learning-disabled students. Several educators have used or recommended a software field review process where a student is observed using the software and the teacher evaluates program effectiveness (Anderson and Senf, 1982; Hummel, Mather, and Senf, 1985). The software field review form presented in Chapter Appendix 10.1 (included in Hummel and Senf [1985]), was used to evaluate software for learning-disabled students (Hummel, Mather, and Senf, 1985).

Many school districts or groups of teachers will want to create their own criteria. Once a form has been created or adopted, teachers will want to share evaluations to assist in software selection and acquistion. Teachers may gather together for a swap session where they demonstrate and acquaint one another with their favorite new software programs (Spencer and Baskin, 1986). Perhaps, the biggest challenge today is successful integration of educational software into the curriculum.

In an observation of three teachers with limited computer instruction, Sapona, Lloyd, and Wissick (1985/86) found that the teachers were able to integrate software into learning disability resource rooms and devise interesting uses of the microcomputer to enhance instruction. To further the successful implementation of microcomputers, these authors encourage educators to disseminate examples of applications of microcomputer use in special education settings.

Many exciting, educational applications of the microcomputer exist. Future technological advances and new software will expand these applications. Although only a tool, when used appropriately, the microcomputer can extend the abilities of both teacher and learner (Stallard,

1982) and assist in providing individualized instruction and monitoring educational progress. Students enjoy working with computers. The level of student motivation and engagement with the computer is significantly higher than that found for other types of instructional activities (Cosden, Gerber, Semmel, Goldman, and Semmel, 1987). Subsequently, the microcomputer may prove most beneficial for learning-disabled students and unmotivated students who have failed in school (Budoff, Thormann, and Gras, 1984). Unlike many instructional materials, computer instruction may be adapted to each individual's level of comprehension (Jay, 1983). The ability of the learner and the teacher to control the instructional sequence make the microcomputer unique. As with all instructional materials, selected software should provide a valuable learning experience to the student and be consistent with student goals. Careful evaluation, selection, and application of educational software will enhance educational success and opportunity for all students. The teacher, the learner, and the microcomputer can be envisioned as a three-component system where goals may be pursued in a carefully constructed, active fashion (Goldman and Pellegrino, 1987).

Summary

Microcomputers can be used to provide many different types of instruction. Programs range from simple drill and practice activities that promote automaticity, to more complex simulation games that require problem-solving abilities. Application programs, such as word processing and data base management, allow a student to be an active planner and communicator. Authoring systems permit teachers and students to prepare individualized lessons and exams. Several computer languages, such as Logo and BASIC, may be learned and applied in the regular or special classroom.

Careful evaluation, selection, and application of educational software are critical factors for student progress. In developing an instructional program, the choice of software will depend entirely on an individual's identified needs. With successful software application, students with learning problems may acquire, practice, and improve both cognitive and academic skills. The unique capabilities of the microcomputer provide a teacher and learner with many exciting educational opportunities.

APPENDIX 10.1

Software Evaluation Form

Name of Software: _____

Date of Review: _____

Courseware
Evaluator   Name _____
                Position _____
                District _____
                Address _____
                Phone _____
                Computer Experience _____
                Teaching Experience _____
How much and how was courseware used during the evaluation period _____
Student
User   Please describe the number and grade level(s) of the students who tested this program. If the students have any special characteristics please briefly indicate what they are.
     #of Students   Grade   Special Characteristics

PACKAGING
1. The packaging of the program and documentation is convenient to use.
(e.g. parts do not fall on the floor when the package is opened.)
Yes _____
No _____ If no please describe the problem
_____

DOCUMENTATION
2. The instructions for operating the program are easy to carry out and follow (e.g. no jargon, clear sentences).
Yes _____
No _____ If no please describe why they weren't
_____

3. The instructions for operating the program are accurate (i.e. does the program work when you follow the instructions?).
Yes _____
No _____ If no please describe the problem.
_____

4. Please give us any suggestions you may have for improving the documentation.
_____

INSTRUCTIONS TO STUDENT USER
(That is, the instructions which appear on the screen·when a student uses the program.)
If you have tested the program with students at different grade levels please be sure to specify which students did not have difficulties with the program. If the grade level is not specified it will be assumed that all students reacted in a similar way.
5. Did the students have difficulty with language used in the instructions? (e.g. level of language too difficult for the suggested user)
No _____
Yes _____ If yes, please describe what the problem was and where in the program it occurred _____
_____

6. Did the students have any difficulty using the keyboard to operate the program? (e.g. the amount of keyboard use interfered with smooth progress through the program)
   No _____
   Yes _____ If yes, please describe the problem _____
7. Did the students have any difficulty understanding the instructions? (because of format and graphics rather than level of languge)
   No _____
   Yes _____ If yes, please describe the problem _____
8. Did the program work when the student followed instructions?
   Yes _____
   No _____ If no, please describe the problem _____
9. Though the program did work, were there any inaccuracies in the instructions? (e.g., misspelled words, incorrect punctuation or grammar, too difficult syntax, etc.).
   No _____
   Yes _____ If yes, please describe what they were and where they are in the program _____
10. Were there any places in the program where more instructions are needed? (i.e. times when the student didn't know what to do next and there was no explanation)
    No _____
    Yes _____ If yes, please describe where in the program _____
11. If a "help file" was available did the students use it?
    None available _____   Some students did _____
    Most students did _____   No students did _____
    Many students did _____
    Was the "help file" useful?
    Yes _____
    No _____If not, please describe the problems _____
12. What teacher assistance was necessary to get the students *started* with the program? _____
13. What teacher assistance was necessary for the student to *complete* the program? _____
14. Please give us any suggestions for improving the instructions to the student user. _____

PROGRAM
15. Was the content of the program consistent with the stated purpose of the program?
    Yes _____
    No _____ If not, please describe why not _____
16. Were there any inaccuracies in the content?
    No _____
    Yes _____ If yes, please describe them _____
17. If the program had graphics, how did the students react to them? _____
18. If the program had sound effects how did the students react to them? _____
19. If the program had animation how did the students react to it? _____
20. If you felt there were problems with the graphics, sound effects or animation please describe them. _____
21. Does the program provide rewards for correct responses?
    No _____
    Yes _____ If yes, how did students react to them? _____
    Did you feel they were appropriate? (too much, too little, type appropriate to age level of students) _____

(continued)

APPENDIX 10.1   *continued*

22. Does the program provide answers to incorrect responses?
    No ——
    Yes —— If yes, a) How many incorrect responses may be made before the answer is given? ——
                    b) Was this number right for your students? Explain ——————————
23. Does the program provide explanations when the student gives wrong answers?
    No ——
    Yes —— If yes, a) Does the explanation come too quickly? ——————————
                    b) Does the explanation not come quickly enough? ——————
                    c) Did the students understand the explanation? ——————
                    d) Did you feel the explanation was useful? ——————————
24. Was there a scoreboard of correct/incorrect responses?
    No ——
    Yes —— If yes, was it helpful for your students? ——————————————
25. Were any students bored or frustrated with the program?
    No ——
    Yes —— Please describe ——————————————————
26. If the student can exit the program at any time, what were the positive or negative aspects of this ability. ——————————————————————
27. Is there a system in the program for storing information on student performance or progress?
    No ——
    Yes —— If yes:

    a) Was it easy to use?   b) Was the stored information useful?
        Yes ——   Yes ——
        No —— Describe why not: No —— Describe why not:
        ———————————   ———————————

    c) Was there information it could have stored   d) Did you experience any problems with
        but didn't which would have been useful?   accessing this information? (e.g.
        No ——   unauthorized users obtaining it)
        Yes —— If yes, what?   No ——
        ———————————   Yes —— If yes, please describe:
                                             ———————————

    e) Any other comments about the data storage capability: ——————————
28. Did the program crash at any point, i.e., simply stop working?
    No ——
    Yes —— If yes, please describe where ——————————————
29. Can students get the program to crash?
    No ——
    Yes —— If yes, please describe how ——————————————
30. Was there any part of the program that you or your students found conflicted with your values?
    (sexist or racist material, encouragement of inappropriate behavior, etc.
    No ——
    Yes —— If yes, please describe ——————————————
31. Did you feel:
    a) The material has educational significance?
        Yes ——
        No —— If no, describe ——————————————
    b) The program is worth the cost?
        Yes ——
        No ——

32. Were there particular students for whom this program was most and least useful?
    Most _____
    Least _____
33. If you modified any program parameters or otherwise altered the program or its use for students with special needs, please describe what their needs were and what changes you made. (e.g. rate of presentation) _____
34. If you were going to make changes in this program to make it maximally useful for your students, what would you change? _____
35. Do you have any other comments about the program?

Chapter Eleven

The Special Education Teacher: Consultant, Collaborator, and Manager

Chapter Questions

- *Why is effective management and communication important for success as a special education teacher?*
- *What variables should you keep in mind when making decisions regarding the instruction and physical arrangement of the educational environment?*
- *What special considerations should a special education teacher keep in mind when planning a schedule for a secondary-level program?*
- *Describe your philosophy regarding classroom management. Based on your philosophy write the rules you would want to use in your classroom. Compare your philosophy and rules to those of Ms. Schiller.*
- *Compare and contrast the models of Teacher Assistance Teams and Collaboration in the Schools.*

If you ask people in business to list the critical elements for a successful business, they will undoubtedly include *communication and sound management*. Although the product, service, and marketing are important, communication and management of the business are the cornerstone. It is the ability of the manager or the management team to make sound decisions regarding product development and research, marketing, service, fiscal policies, and personnel that makes the difference between success and failure. It is also the ability to effectively communicate when making decisions and disseminating them that determines how effectively and efficiently the business operates.

In the same way that management and communication are the cornerstone of business, so are they the cornerstone of effective teaching. Whether serving as a consultant, resource, or self-contained teacher, the special education teacher makes thousands of management decisions each day regarding the teaching-learning process and the instructional cycle. It is the ability of the teacher to develop a teaching-learning context that facilitates communication and learning; to set learning and instructional goals and market those goals to others, including the students; and to establish sound classroom and instructional policies, routines, and procedures that makes the difference between success and failure. Management and communication are central to the task of teaching (Berliner, 1983; Doyle, 1979, 1986). This chapter deals with the issue of the special education teacher as a manager, communicator, and collaborator.

Getting Started

"I'm really looking forward to next year," commented Ms. Downing as she completed her first year of teaching as a junior-high resource teacher. "The first year of teaching has to be the hardest. There is so much to get organized at the beginning of the year, so many decisions to be made, and so many new routines and procedures

to learn. You have to figure out what your resources are as well as the students' needs. You also have to decide what type of instructional program you want. Based on this, you need to determine how to arrange the room to facilitate learning, what materials to select or develop, and how to organize the materials so that the students can find them easily. You must decide how to group the students and how to schedule the students into the room. In comparison to this year, next year should be a breeze. I'll be able to spend much more time refining my teaching skills, focusing on the students, and strengthening the program."

In many ways, Ms. Downing is a manager. At the beginning of the year, management decisions are required at a fast and furious pace. We will explore some of the decisions that teachers have to consider in getting started and look at some options they might consider in making those decisions.

Arranging the Environment

In Chapter One, we discussed how the teaching-learning process takes place within a context. Making this context or environment pleasant and conducive to learning can facilitate the teaching-learning process. As teachers, we want to consider both the instructional arrangement and the physical arrangement of that context.

Instructional Arrangement

Instructional arrangement refers to the manner in which the teacher groups the students and selects the format for learning. Generally, there are six instructional arrangements: (1) large group instruction, (2) small group instruction, (3) one-to-one instruction, (4) independent learning, (5) collaborative learning, and (6) peer teaching (Mercer and Mercer, 1989). Whether teaching in a resource room where students attend in small- to medium-sized groups for relative short periods of time each day, or in a self-contained classroom where students spend the majority of their school day, most teachers want to have the flexibility to provide for several different instructional arrangements within their classrooms.

Large Group Instruction. Large group instruction usually consists of the teacher lecturing or engaging in discussions with a group of six or more students. It is appropriate to use when the content of instruction is similar for all students. Teachers often employ this type of instructional arrangement when teaching social skills and content area subjects such as social studies, science, health, and career education. This arrangement can be used both for didactic instruction (i.e., instruction where one person, usually the teacher, is providing information) and for interactive instruction (i.e., where the students and teachers are discussing and sharing information). In large group instruction students usually get less opportunity to receive feedback concerning their performance and less opportunity to receive corrective feedback. Since large group instruction is the most frequently used arrangement in regular education classrooms, particularly in secondary settings, it is helpful to provide students with experiences in large groups as they make the transition from a self-contained special education classroom to regular education classrooms.

Small Group Instruction. Small group instruction usually consists of groups of two to five students and is employed when the teacher wants to be in closer proximity to the students and provide more feedback. This instructional arrangement is often used for teaching specific academic skills, since students are often grouped by skill level when learning basic skills in reading, writing, oral language, and math. When a teacher is using small group instruction he or she usually involves one group of students while the remaining students participate in independent learning, cooperative learning, or peer tutoring. Sometimes teachers who work in resource rooms schedule students so that only two to five students come at one time, so that all the students can participate in small group instruction at once. Many teachers prefer using a horseshoe

table for small group instruction, since it allows them to reach the materials in front of each student in the group easily.

One-to One Instruction. One-to-one instruction is when the teacher works individually with a student. This instructional arrangement allows the teacher to provide intensive instruction, closely monitoring student progress and modifying and adapting procedures to match the student's learning patterns. The Fernald (VAKT) method of teaching word identification and Reading Recovery, as discussed in Chapter Four, are examples where one-to-one instruction is the recommended instructional arrangement. At least some one-to-one instruction is recommended for students with learning and behavior problems, since it provides the students with some time each day to ask questions and receive assistance from the teacher (Archer and Edgar, 1976). The major drawback of one-to-one instruction is that while one student is working with the teacher, the remaining students need to be actively engaged in learning. To accomplish this, independent learning, collaborative learning, or peer tutoring is frequently used.

Independent Learning. Independent learning is one format for providing students practice with a skill for which they have already received instruction and have acquired some proficiency (Stephens, 1977; Wallace and Kauffman, 1986). We frequently associate independent learning with individual worksheets, but computer activities, various audiovisual assignments such as listening to a taped book, writing a story, reading a library book, or making a map for a social studies unit can also be independent learning activities.

The key to effective use of independent learning activities is selecting activities that the student can complete with minimal assistance. For example, when Samantha selects library books, Ms. Martino asks Samantha to read approximately the first hundred words to her and then she asks Samantha several questions. If

Samantha misses five words or less and can answer the questions easily, then Ms. Martino encourages her to read the book on her own. If Samantha misses five to ten words, then Ms. Martino arranges for her to read the book using collaborative learning or peer tutoring. If Samantha misses more than ten words and struggles to answer the questions, then Ms. Martino may encourage her to select another book. In fact, Ms. Martino has even taught Samantha and the rest of the students in her self-contained classroom for students with behavior disorders the "Five-Finger Rule."

> **Five-Finger Rule.** If in reading the first couple of pages of a book, you know the words except for about five and you can ask yourself and answer five questions about what you have read, then this book is probably a good book for you to read.

Collaborative/Cooperative Learning. Collaborative or cooperative learning is when students work together and use each other as a source for learning. Four basic elements need to be included for small group learning to be cooperative: interdependence, individual accountability, collaborative skills, and group processing (Johnson and Johnson, 1986; Slavin, 1987). Interdependence is facilitated by creating a learning environment where the students perceive that the goal of the group is that *all* members learn, that rewards are based on group performance, that materials needed to complete the task are distributed across the members of the group, and that students are given complementary roles that foster the division of labor. Group processing refers to giving the students the opportunity to discuss how well they are achieving their goals and working together (Johnson and Johnson, 1984a).

Two basic formats for cooperative learning are oftentimes used in regular or special education classrooms. With a *group project* students pool their knowledge and skills to create a project or complete an assignment. The students in the group are included in all the decisions and tasks that ensure completion of the project. Using the *jigsaw format,* each student in a group is assigned a task that must be completed for the group to reach its goal. For example, in completing a fact finding sheet on fossils, each student might be assigned to read a different source to obtain information for the different facts required on the sheet.

Johnson and Johnson (1975) suggest the following guidelines for working cooperatively:

1. Each group produces one product.
2. Group members assist each other.
3. Group members seek assistance from other group members.
4. Group members will change their ideas only when logically persuaded to do so by the other members.
5. Group members take responsibility for the product.

Collaborative learning can be used to complete group projects in content area subjects. In Chapter Six, the process approach to teaching writing employed aspects of collaborative learning. For example, students shared their written pieces with each other to get ideas and feedback about their writing, and in some cases they wrote pieces together. Slavin and his colleagues (Slavin, Stevens, and Madden, 1988) have developed a program, *Cooperative Integrated Reading and Composition,* which utilizes a process approach for teaching composition as well as basal-related activities, and direct instruction in reading comprehension. Using heterogeneous cooperative learning groups in regular elementary classroom, the researchers found that this type of program paired with cooperative learning facilitates the learning of most mainstreamed special education and remedial reading students.

Providing opportunities to participate in cooperative learning experiences is particularly important for students with behavior and learning problems because it assists these students in developing social skills as well as the targeted academic skill. It assists them in developing positive interactions with peers and in developing strategies for supporting others. These skills are particularly important when students are being mainstreamed into regular classrooms where cooperative learning is employed (Johnson and Johnson, 1984b, 1986).

In orchestrating collaborative learning, it is important to provide the students with enough directions that they know the purpose of the activity and the general rules for working in groups. Initially, the teacher may want to participate as a collaborator, modeling such collaborative behaviors as: (1) asking what the other people think, (2) not ridiculing other collaborators for what they think, and (3) helping other collaborators and accepting help from others. As the students become comfortable in collaborating, they can collaborate independently without the teacher's input.

Peer Teaching.   In this instructional arrangement, one student who has learned the skills assists another student in learning the skills. This teaching takes place under the supervision of the teacher. One advantage of peer teaching is that it increases opportunity for the student learning the skills to respond (Delquadri, Greenwood, Whorton, Carta, and Hall, 1986). Peer teaching achieves this by allowing peers to supervise their classmate's responses. When using peer teaching the teacher needs to plan the instruction and demonstrate the task to the pair. The tutor then works with the learner, providing assistance and feedback.

One important aspect of peer teaching is training the students to serve as peer tutors (Fowler, 1986). They need to learn basic instructional procedures for providing reinforcement and corrective feedback and for knowing when to ask the teacher for assistance. Research focusing on peer tutoring with special education students has most frequently been used to teach or monitor basic skills such as oral reading, answering reading comprehension questions, and practicing spelling words, math facts, and new sight word vocabulary (Gerber and Kauffman, 1981; Scruggs and Richter, 1985).

Physical Arrangement
The physical arrangement of the classroom should provide for the different types of instructional arrangements that will be used in the classroom. In addition, it should reflect a pleasant atmosphere that facilitates efficient learning. Figures 11.1 and 11.2 present two room arrangements. Both rooms contain a teaching area, an individual learning area, an audiovisual/computer area, and a recreational area. The second room arrangement also incorporates learning centers and a time-out area.

As dicussed in Chapter Two, a time-out area is an area in which students do not have the opportunity to receive reinforcement. It is usually used as a means for reducing inappropriate behavior. A learning center is an area where instructional materials focus on one curriculum area or topic of study and are arranged in such a manner that students can work in the area individually or cooperatively to accomplish a task. For example, Ms. Marks currently has a social studies learning center in her junior-high resource room. In this center she has arranged maps, source books, and trade books on a bookshelf and put a small table with four chairs in the center. Every two to four weeks she introduces the students to a new cooperative learning project for the center (e.g., writing a governing constitution for the classroom, drawing a map of the surrounding neighborhood and locating everyone's home). The first semester, Ms. Marks used the learning center as a writing skills center, utilizing an individual learning model, but this semester she switched to a cooperative learning model.

The room arrangement should be flexible enough so that different instructional arrangements can be utilized. For example, the individual learning area can be reorganized into a large group instructional area by rearranging the desks. The small group instructional area can also be used for a cooperative learning project.

FIGURE 11.1   *Sample Room Arrangement*

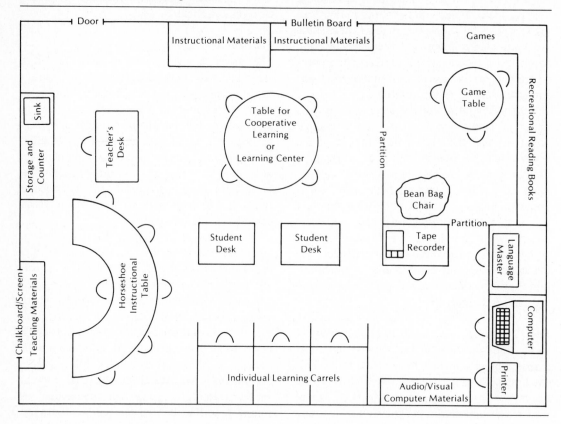

Several ideas to keep in mind when developing the room arrangement are:

1. To the extent possible, place the recreational and audiovisual/computer areas away from the teaching area. These areas will naturally be somewhat noisier than the other areas.

2. Place student materials in a place where students can easily access the materials without bothering other students or the teacher.

3. Place your teaching materials directly behind where you teach so that you may access materials without having to leave the instructional area.

4. If used, place the time-out area out of the direct line of traffic. Also, use partitions that keep a student in the area from having visual contact with other students. (See Chapter Two for principles governing the use of time-out.)

5. Make the recreational area comfortable with a carpet, comfortable reading chairs, and a small game table if possible.

6. Place all the materials needed for a learning center in the learning center area. In this way students will not be moving around the room to collect needed materials.

Instructional Materials and Equipment

Selecting, developing, and organizing the instructional materials and equipment is an important aspect of getting a program organized. The instructional materials and the equipment used by the teacher have a major influence on what and how information and skills are taught (Wilson, 1982; Wallace and Kauffman, 1986).

One decision a teacher has to make is whether to purchase materials already available or develop the materials. Some teachers tend to select published materials for their main instructional materials (e.g., sets of literature books based on different themes or units, several reading programs each representing a different approach to reading such as linguistic and phonic approaches), and then they develop instructional aids and games to supplement the program (e.g., flash cards, sentence strips, tape recordings of the stories, board games).

Whether selecting or developing materials, there are several factors to consider:

1. What curricular areas (e.g., reading, English, math, social skills) will I be responsible for teaching?
2. What are the academic levels of the students I will be teaching?
3. In what instructional arrangement(s) do I plan to teach each curricular area?
4. How can the materials be used across the stages of learning (i.e., acquisition, proficiency, maintenance, generalization, and application)?
5. Will the materials provide a means for measuring learning?

FIGURE 11.2   *Sample Room Arrangement*

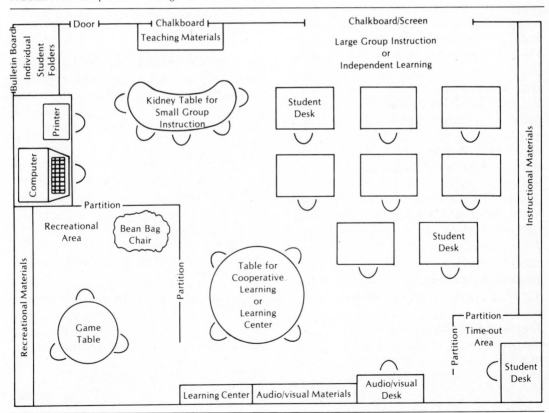

Selecting Published Materials

Besides considering the factors just mentioned, it is also important to think of the cost, durability, consumability, and quality of the published materials. Before purchasing materials it is advantageous to evaluate them. Sample materials can generally be obtained from the publisher or found at educational conferences or district-wide instructional libraries. If possible, talk with other teachers who use the materials and borrow the materials and have the students try them and evaluate them. Chapter Appendix 11.1 presents a form a teacher can use in evaluating published materials. It focuses not only on general information but on how the material will fit into the teacher's program. Chapter Appendix 11.2 presents a form the students can use in evaluating the materials.

Most teachers have restricted budgets for purchasing instructional materials. Once the instructional materials are selected, it is helpful to prioritize them according to need. Before eliminating materials from that list, determine if they can be obtained through means other than the teaching budget. For example, school districts often have an instructional materials library that allows teachers in the district to check out materials for a relatively long period of time. You may be able to borrow the materials from the library rather than purchase them. Librarians are often interested in additional materials to order; it might be possible to request that they order the materials for the library. Publishers are often interested in how their materials work with low-achieving students and students with learning and behavior problems. They may be willing to provide a set of materials if the teacher is willing to evaluate the materials and provide feedback regarding how they work with the students.

Selecting and Utilizing Instructional Equipment

In addition to selecting instructional materials, the teacher will also want to choose some equipment to facilitate learning. Chapter Ten specific-ally deals with computers, including the selecting of computers, peripherals, and computer software. This equipment, along with various software programs, is becoming an increasingly important part of the tools a teacher has available. In addition to a computer in the classroom and/or the use of a computer lab in the school, there is other equipment that will facilitate learning.

Tape Recorder.   Tape recorders are relatively inexpensive equipment that can be used in a variety of ways in the classroom. In selecting a tape recorder, select one of good quality that is easy to operate. Also select a recorder that has a counter. This allows a student to quickly find a particular section in a tape rather than having to hunt for it. Headphones to accompany the tape recorder allow students to listen to the tape recorder without disturbing others. Following are some instructional applications for the tape recorder.

1. Tape record reading books so that students can follow along during recreational reading or for using with repeated reading or the pattern language approach. Figure 5.1 (page 142) provides guidelines for tape recording books and stories.

2. One way to adapt textbooks is to tape record them. Figure 7.16 (page 245) presents some suggestions for tape recording textbooks.

3. For some students it is helpful for them to record what they want to write before they write their first drafts. They can tape record their ideas and then listen to them as they write the first drafts.

4. So that the students can hear their progress in reading, have them tape record their reading every two to four weeks. Each student should have his or her own tape that serves as a record of progress. After a student records his or her reading, it is important that the teacher and the student discuss the reading, identifying strengths

and areas that need improvement. This tape recording can also be shared with parents to demonstrate progress and continuing needs.

5. Spelling tests can be tape recorded so that students can take them independently. First, record the words to be tested, allowing time for the students to spell the words. After the test is recorded, spell each word so the student can self-check.

6. At the secondary level, class lectures can be taped and then listened to so that the student can review the material and complete unfinished notes.

7. Have students practice taking notes by listening to tape recordings of lectures. By using tape recordings, students can regulate the rate at which the material is presented.

8. Oral directions for independent learning activities can be tape recorded so that students can listen to them. This may prove to be particularly helpful if the teacher is trying to conduct small group or one-to-one instruction while these students are working on independent learning activities.

9. When working on specific social or pragmatic language skills (e.g., answering the telephone, asking for directions, introducing someone), tape record the students so that they can listen to and evaluate themselves.

10. Many instructional materials utilize prerecorded tapes.

Language Master. The language master is an adaptation of a tape recorder. It is a machine that tape records and plays cards that have a piece of recording tape attached along the bottom (see Figure 11.3). The cards are four inches high and range in length from several inches to over a foot. Depending on the length of the card, words, phrases, or sentences can be recorded. The words and sentences are recorded by inserting the card into the card slot on the top of the machine, and gently pushing the card to start it moving over

FIGURE 11.3 *Language Master and Language Master Card*

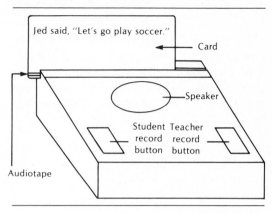

the recording head. As the card moves over the head, the record button is pressed for recording. Listening to the recorded cards is accomplished by the same action, except the record button is not pushed. There are two recording tracks on the tape—one designated for the teacher and one designated for the student. Therefore, the student can listen to the tape to hear what the teacher says, and then pass the card through the machine again to record his or her response. Visual cues (e.g., words, phrases, math problems) can be written directly on the cards. The cards can be made reusable by laminating them or covering them with clear contact paper so that the visual cues can be erased. Teachers can purchase blank cards as well as prerecorded cards. Before purchasing a language master or cards, see if they are available from the district instructional library. The following are suggestions for how a teacher might use the language master in the classroom.

1. Record the word cards, phrase cards, and/or sentence cards for the stories that the students are to read. Students can independently listen to these words prior to reading and/or after reading to provide practice in identifying words. Organize the cards by stories so that students can easily locate the correct words to listen to.

2. Record the math facts, cutting a notch in the tape so that the student hears the fact, the card stops, and when the student is ready he or she engages the card again to hear the answer. Write the fact on the front of the card and the answer on the back.

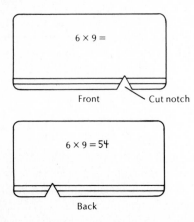

Front   Cut notch

Back

3. Spelling words can be presented orally on the card and the correct spelling written on the back. The student then listens to the word, writes his or her answer, and then turns the card over to check the answer.

4. Record math word problems. The problem can be written on the front and the answer on the back.

5. Record a word family (e.g., *cat, fat, rat, bat*), cutting a notch in the card so that the student hears the words, the card stops, and when the student is ready he or she engages the card again to hear the name of the family. Write the family words on the front of the card and the answer on the back.

6. Record a cloze sentence (e.g., "The little girl is smiling because she is —— ."), cutting a notch in the card so that the student hears the sentence, the card stops, and when the student has filled in the blank, he or she engages the card

again to hear the answer. Write the sentence on the front of the card and the answer on the back.

7. Have the students write riddles and then put them on language master cards so that the other students can listen. The author may want to sign his or her riddle.

8. Record three to four examples of a specific category (e.g., red, yellow, purple, orange—colors; happy, sad, angry—ways you feel). Cut a notch in the card so that the student hears the examples, the card stops, and when the student has said the category, he or she engages the card again to hear the name of the category. Write the examples on the front and the name of the category on the back.

Overhead Projector. The overhead projector is an excellent teaching tool. It allows the user to display on a screen or blank wall the images from a transparency. Transparencies are generally teacher-made, although some are available with published instructional materials. The overhead projector allows the teacher to model a skill and to highlight, write, color in, and/or point to important information. For example, a teacher may use an overhead projector to demonstrate how to add quotation marks to a story, or a student may use it to demonstrate how he or she worked a long division problem.

In preparing transparencies, write in large, bold writing. Two types of markers are available for making transparencies—permanent markers and nonpermanent markers. Transparencies are also available that can be used in copying machines so that the original is copied onto a transparency rather than a piece of paper.

When using an overhead projector keep the following suggestions in mind:

1. Using an overhead can be easier than a chalkboard for presenting a lecture or leading a discussion since it does not require the teacher to turn around to write.

2. Keep the amount of information presented on the overhead relatively limited.

3. Use a different colored pen to highlight important points.

4. Keep extra markers available when using the overhead.

5. By laying a piece of paper over the transparency, each part of a transparency can be revealed as it is being discussed, thereby helping to focus the students' attention.

6. Use the overhead projector to develop language experience stories.

7. Use the overhead projector to demonstrate editing and revisions in writing.

8. Use the overhead projector along with a "think aloud" procedure to demonstrate math procedures such as how to work long division.

Other Small Equipment. Several other pieces of small equipment should be considered when selecting equipment for either a resource room or a self-contained classroom.

A *stopwatch* can serve as an instructional tool and a motivator. For some tasks it is important that students learn to respond at an automatic level (e.g., sight words, math facts). Students can use a stopwatch to time themselves or their classmates. These times can then be easily recorded on a time chart (see Figure 11.4). Using these charts, students can set goals, record their times, and try to beat previous times.

A *individual writing board* is a excellent tool for obtaining indiviual written responses during small group and large group discussion. Mr. Howell uses these boards during review sessions in his resource high-school history class. During the review sessions he asks students questions and they write their answers on the writing boards. He then asks them to display their boards. In this way each student responds to each question in writing instead of one student orally responding to each questions. Mr. Howell and the students feel that this is a better way to review since it requires them to think about and answer every question

and to write the answers. Writing is important since it is generally required when the students take tests. Although small chalkboards can be used as individual writing boards, white erasable writing surface boards and special felt markers are now available.

A *flannel board* and a *magnetic board* are particularly useful in elementary classrooms. These can be used in teaching and learning centers for such activities as depicting stories, spelling words, and working simple math problems.

As discussed in the math chapter, Chapter Eight, *calculators* are an invaluable tool for students when learning and for teachers when completing many of the routine activities associated with assessment and evaluation.

Developing Instructional Materials
In addition to published materials and equipment, most teachers find the need to develop their own instructional materials. Many of these materials can be used to supplement commercial materials. For example, sentence strips containing the sentences from each story in beginning readers can be made. Many teachers develop materials to provide students with additional practice in skills they are learning. Therefore, developing self-correcting materials and/or materials in a game format can be advantageous.

Self-Correcting Materials. Self-correcting materials provide students with immediate feedback. Students with learning and behavior problems frequently have a history of failure and are reluctant to take risks when others are watching or listening. Self-correcting materials allow them to check themselves without sharing the information with others. Many computer programs and electronic learning games incorporate self-correction into their programs. Several of the suggestions for the language master provide for self-correction (see pages 357–358). Figure 11.5 presents an example of a self-correcting activity that teachers can easily make.

FIGURE 11.4   *Timing Chart*

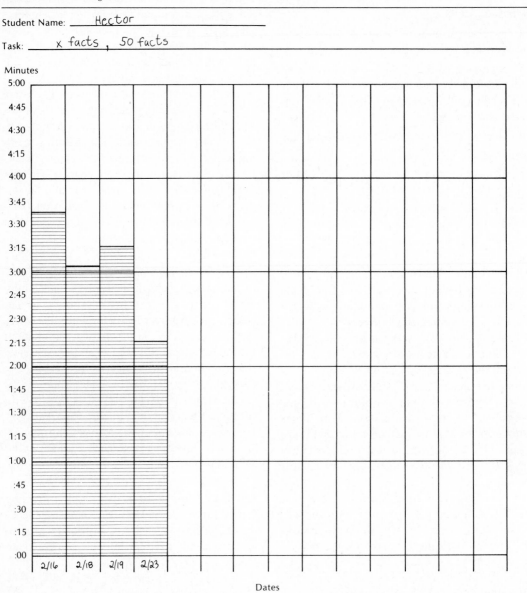

Student Name: ___Hector___

Task: ___x facts , 50 facts___

One key to self-correcting materials is immediate feedback (Mercer, Mercer, and Bott, 1984). The materials should be simple enough so that students can learn to use the materials easily and to check their answers quickly. The materi-als should be varied so that the interest and novelty level remain relatively high.

Another key to developing self-correcting materials is to make them durable so that they can be used and reused. Laminating and covering the

FIGURE 11.5   *Self-Correcting Activity*

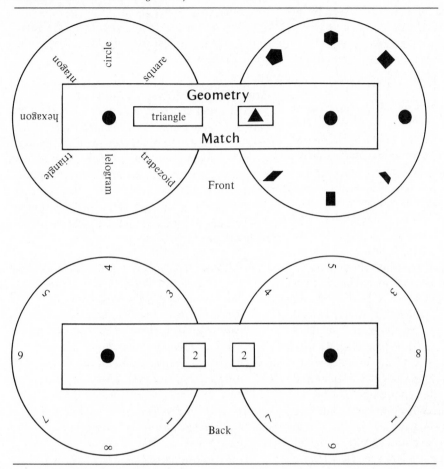

materials with clear contact paper are good ways to make materials more durable. Special marking pens or grease pencils can then be used. Using heavy cardboard can also increase the durability of materials.

Instructional Games.   Students with learning and behavior problems frequently require numerous opportunities to practice an academic skill. Instructional games can provide this practice in a format that is interesting to the students.

The first step in designing an instructional game is to determine the purpose of the game. For example, the purpose might be to provide practice in:

1. Forming word families (e.g., *-at, fat, sat, cat, rat*)
2. Identifying sight words associated with a specific piece of reading materials being used in the classroom

3. Using semantic and syntactic clues by using the cloze procedure (e.g., For dessert Brian wanted an ice _____ cone.)
4. Recalling multiplication facts
5. Reviewing information (e.g., identifying the parts of a flower)

The second step is to select and adapt a game in which to practice a skill or review knowledge. For example, commercial games such as Monopoly, Chutes and Ladders, Candyland, Clue, Sorry, and Parcheesi can be adapted. A generic game board can also be used (see Figure 11.6). Generic game boards can be purchased from some publishing companies. The key in selecting and adapting a game is to require the students to complete the instructional task as part of the turn-taking procedure. For example, when adapting Candyland to practice sight words, students would select a sight word card and a Candyland card. If they can correctly read the sight word then they can use their Candyland card to move as indicated. When adapting Monopoly for math facts, students would have to first select and answer the math fact. If answered correctly, they earn the opportunity to throw the dice and take a turn. When the same skills are practiced by many students in the class, the teacher may want to develop a specific game for the skill. Math Marathon is a specific game in which students move forward on a game board, depicting a marathon race by answering math word problems. Different sets of math word problem game cards can be developed, depending on the math problem-solving levels of the students.

The third step is to write the directions and develop the materials. MacWilliams (1978) recommends making a rough draft of the game and testing it. Posterboard glued to cardboard or manila folders make good game boards. With manila folders the name of the game can be written on the tab and the board can be stored so that the students can scan the tabs to find the game. The materials for the game can be kept in an envelope inside the folder. The directions for the game and a list of materials that should be found inside may be written on the envelope.

The fourth step is to demonstrate the game to the students so that they can learn to play the games independently.

Organizing and Managing Materials

Selecting and developing materials is only one part of effective materials management. These materials need to be organized in the classroom in such a manner that the teacher and students have easy access to the materials without bothering other students. Let's see what suggestions Ms. Wilcox, an elementary resource teacher, has for developing a materials management system.

It has taken me about three years to really organize the management system for this classroom. One of the most important aspects of this system is that it is color-coded and labeled so that students who can't read well can find and use materials. I have placed all the instructional materials along one wall of my classroom and organized it into sections by academic and content areas. For each academic and content area I have put my teaching materials that I am not currently using on the top shelves. The materials I am currently using I put on a shelf behind the horseshoe table. That way, I can get to them easily. On the middle shelves I put the small group and independent learning activities. The bottom shelves I have reserved for instructional games. One section of the shelf has general instructional materials. This includes generic game boards, different kinds of paper and writing instruments, scissors, glue, and so on.

I have color-coded all the textual materials by approximate reading level. I have also color-coded the recreational reading books that are found in the free-time area.

FIGURE 11.6 *Generic Board Game*

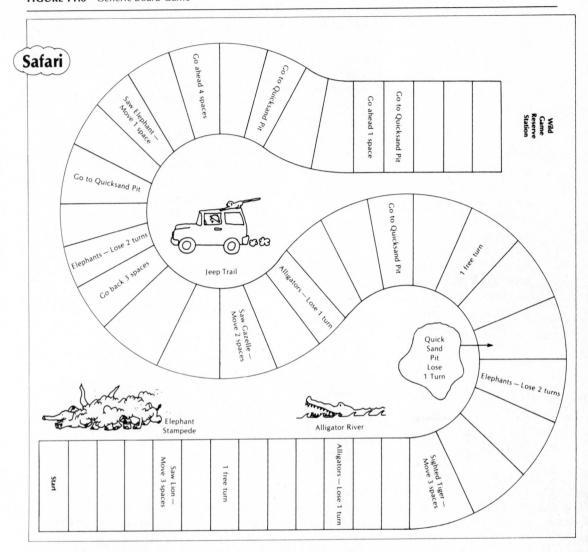

1. You are on a safari, trying to get to the Wild Game Reserve Station.
2. Begin at Start.
3. Each player rolls a die. The player with the highest number goes first.
4. Roll the die and draw a Game Card. If you answer the Game Card correctly, move the number shown on the die. If you do not answer the Game Card correctly, do not take a turn.
5. The first player to get to the Wild Game Reserve Station wins.

Since I have a limited budget I haven't been able to purchase many practice-type workbooks. One way to make those consumables into nonconsumables is to cover each page with clear contact paper or have the students place an acetate page over them. I staple each page in a file folder and label the tab with the book name and page number, then place all the pages in a box so that the tabs are easily read. I label the box with the name of the skill or workbook. Then the students simply go to the box, pull the assigned page, and complete it. Sometimes I have made answer keys for each page or purchased a copy of the teacher's edition. I place these at the back of the box. The students know that if they are to self-check, they get the answer key or teacher's workbook after finishing the work and then check it.

It took me a while to set up this system but I think it is well worth the time for several reasons. First, it is easy to expand. I keep an inventory list of all my materials on the computer, and I simply add to the list whenever I get new materials and then add the materials to the shelves. (Figure 11.7 contains a sample format for an inventory list.) This way I'm not always redoing the system. Second, I often have six to eight students in my room at once. I want to be able to provide small group and one-to-one instruction. To do this I need a system where students can retrieve the materials they need to use when doing independent and collaborative learning tasks without having to ask me for help. This system does a pretty good job of accomplishing that.

Oh, by the way, there is one other important piece of information. So that the students know how to use the different materials, at the beginning of the year and each time we get new materials the

FIGURE 11.7   *Partial Outline for Materials Inventory List*

Reading (R)
- R.1   Patterned Language Books
- R.2   Language Experience Materials and Activities
- R.3   Basal Reading Books and Materials
- R.4   Linguistic Readers and Materials
- R.5   Phonic Books, Materials, and Activities
- R.6   Structural Analysis Materials and Activities
- R.7   Cloze Materials and Activities
- R.8   Syllabication Materials and Activities
- R.9   Comprehension Materials and Activities
- R.10   Vocabulary Materials and Activities
- R.11   Other Reading Materials and Activities

Mathematics (M)
- M.1   Place Value Materials and Manipulatives
- M.2   Readiness Materials and Activities
- M.3   Addition Materials and Activities
- M.4   Subtraction Materials and Activities
- M.5   Multiplication Materials and Activities
- M.6   Division Materials and Activities
- M.7   Fraction Materials and Activities
- M.8   Percentages Materials and Activities
- M.9   Word Problem Materials and Activities
- M.10   Money Materials and Activities
- M.11   Measurement Materials and Activities
- M.12   Time Materials and Activities
- M.13   Geometry Materials and Activities
- M.14   Math Series
- M.15   Other Math Materials and Activities

(Other curricular areas include: language, writing, social skills, study skills, social studies, science, health, and career/vocation education.)

students will be using, we spend the first few minutes of the session demonstrating the materials and talking about how to use them. Then I make sure each student has the opportunity to use them within the next several days. In this way, I don't have to explain how to use the same materials to each student individually.

Scheduling

When teachers talk about the most difficult aspects of their jobs, they often mention scheduling. Elementary resource teachers generally work with fifteen or more regular classroom teachers to schedule the students who attend the resource program. Special education teachers also work closely with counselors and teachers at the secondary level to see that students are placed in classes that will help them reach the goals and objectives developed on the individual education program (IEP) as well as meet graduation requirements. Special education teachers working in self-contained classrooms are responsible for their students' entire curriculum. They face decisions regarding how to provide instruction in the various curricular areas (e.g., reading, math, writing, English, social studies, science, art, music), while still providing the students with adequate one-to-one and small group instruction so that the students might reach the educational goals targeted in the academic areas of concern.

Scheduling within the Classroom

Whether teaching in a resource or self-contained classroom, it is important to use the time students spend in the classroom efficiently. Ms. Wilcox highlighted her concern for scheduling when she discussed the need to provide one-to-one or small group instruction. Mr. Wolf explains his dilemma in scheduling when he discusses his self-contained intermediate-level class for learning-disabled students.

I am responsible for the educational programs for fourteen learning-disabled fifth- and sixth-grade students. They are in my classroom throughout the day except for twice a week, once when they attend music and once when they attend art. Seven of the students attend regular classes for some subjects: three for social studies, two for science, and two for math. I'm lucky because I have a great teacher aide. My concern in scheduling is that these students have so many needs. All of them are at least two to three grade levels below in reading and writing. We could easily spend the whole day just on

reading, writing, and math. By the time my aide and I work with each student individually or in small groups in reading, most of the morning is over. I could easily spend the rest of the day on writing and math. But that would be unfair to the students. They need to learn social studies, health, science, and career concepts.

There are no easy answers to scheduling. However, the following list presents some guidelines to use when developing a schedule for the classroom, whether it be a resource or self-contained class.

- Schedule time to communicate with regular classroom teachers. The amount of time you schedule will be dependent on the time your students spend in the regular classroom. Generally speaking, consultant teachers should schedule more time than resource teachers, and resource teachers should schedule more time than self-contained teachers. This time should prove invaluable in assisting students to be successful in regular classrooms.
- Schedule time to observe in the regular classrooms in which your students are placed or are going to be placed. This alerts you to the class demands and schedules of the classroom and will help you in planning for your students' learning in that classroom.
- Schedule time to meet with other professionals (e.g., speech/language pathologist, school psychologist).
- Schedule so that you alternate instructional arrangements. For example, do not schedule a student to participate in independent learning activities for more than forty-five minutes at a time.
- Plan for time to provide the students with advance organizers and feedback and evaluation. In this way students will know what is going to happen, and they will have the

FIGURE 11.8   *Schedule for Fourth- through Sixth-Grade Students While Attending the Resource Room*

Date: 4/15

Time	José	Amelia	Scott	Todd	Carmen	Frank
10:00	Small Group Instruction Reading ↓	Language Master Inferential Comprehension Computer Activity ↓	Small Group Instruction Reading ↓	Social Studies Text using Request Procedure with Carmen ↓	Social Studies Text with Request Procedure with Todd ↓	Small Group Instruction Reading ↓
10:20	Inferential Comprehension Activity on Computer	Small Group Instruction Reading ↓	Social Studies Text with Self-Questioning ↓	Small Group Instruction Reading ↓	Small Group Instruction Reading ↓	Language Master Word Drill Social Studies Text with Self Questioning
10:40	Writing Process ↓ Spelling	Writing Process ↓ Spelling	Writing Process (Computer) Spelling	Writing Process ↓ Spelling	Writing Process ↓ Spelling	Writing Process Computer Spelling
11:15	Practice Computer	Practice Game	Practice Game	Practice Tape Recorder Test	Practice Game	Practice Game

opportunity to think about what they have accomplished.

- Plan time for direct instruction. Sometimes we have students spend the majority of their time in independent learning activities, which results in little time for them to receive direct instruction from the teacher, aide, or tutor.
- Alternate preferred and less preferred activities or make preferred activities contingent upon less preferred activities.
- Let students know when the time for an activity is just about over. This gives students time to reach closure on the one activity and get ready for the next activity or to ask for a time extension.
- Be consistent in scheduling yet flexible and ready for change.

Figures 11.8 and 11.9 present sample schedules for a resource and self-contained classroom. For the resource room, the schedule for one group of students is presented, while the entire day's schedule is presented for the self-contained class.

Developing an Overall Schedule for a Resource Consultant Program

Scheduling students' time while in the special education classroom is one issue, but the overall schedule for a resource room often presents other issues and requires that the teacher work closely with teachers and other professionals in the school. Teachers who assume roles as resource teachers must first clarify and decide what their job responsibilities will be. Generally these responsibilities can be divided into four general areas:

1. Directly provide instruction to the students
2. Indirectly provide instruction to the students by consulting with regular classroom teachers
3. Assess current and referred students
4. Serve as an instructional resource for other teachers within the school

The time a teacher spends in each one of these roles will directly influence the schedule the teacher develops. For example, if the major roles of the teacher are to provide instructional services indirectly to students, to assess current and referred students, and to serve as an instructional resource, then little time will be spent scheduling groups of students into the resource room. In-

stead, the teacher will serve primarily in the role of a consultant to others. A sample schedule for a consulting teacher is presented in Figure 11.10.

On the other hand, Ms. Wilcox provides direct instruction to most of the students she serves for an average of sixty minutes per day, four days per week. Since she serves twenty-two students, she has developed a schedule that allows her some time to consult with regular classroom teachers, but she has also allocated time to teach and assess current and referred students. To facilitate her scheduling, she grouped students according to grade level for the most part, with the older students attending in the morning and the younger students in the afternoon.

She explains her schedule as follows:

I have arranged for the older students to come in the morning because I feel that I

FIGURE 11.9   *Sample Schedule for Intermediate Level Self-Contained Class*

| Time | Activity | | | |
	Group 1	Group 2	Group 3	Group 4
8:15	Writing Process Students working on reports			
9:15	Reading: Small-group instruction (teacher)	Reading: Independent learning activities	Learning center: Map reading	Reading: Small-group instruction (aide)
9:45	Reading: Independent learning activities	Reading: Small-group instruction (aide)	Reading: Small-group instruction (teacher)	Learning center: Map reading
10:15	Announcements			
10:20	Recess			
10:45	Math: Group instruction (teacher)		Computer lab for Math practice (aide)	
11:15	Computer lab (aide)		Group instruction (teacher)	
11:50	Lunch			
12:40	Recreational Reading/Writing			
1:00	Social Studies: Large-group instruction			
1:45	Science: Cooperative learning activities			
2:15	Recess			
2:40	Health—Mon./Art—Tues./P.E.—Wed./Special Activity—Thurs., Fri. (Current: Producing a play)			
3:10	Earned "fun time" or time to complete work			
3:30	Dismissal			

FIGURE 11.10   *Consultant Teacher Schedule*

Week of: <u>April 15th</u>

Time	Monday	Tuesday	Wednesday	Thursday	Friday
7:30	IEP meeting	Instructional Review Meeting (2nd grade)	Child Study Team Meeting	IEP Meeting	Instructional Review Meeting (4th grade)
8:15	Work with 5th grade low reading group ⟶				⟶
9:00	Observe and assist LD/EH students in classroom (1st grade)	Assessment	Observe and assist (2nd grade, kindergarten)	3rd grade 4th grade	5th grade 6th grade
11:30	Meet with individual teachers	Planning and material development ⟶	⟶	Meet with individual teachers	Planning and material development
12:30	Lunch ⟶				⟶
1:00	Work with 2nd grade low reading group ⟶				⟶
1:30	Conduct study skills class for selected 4th–6th graders	Conduct social skills class for group of EH students	Conduct study skills class	Conduct social skills class	Conduct study skills class
2:00	Work with Ms. Jones on implementing writing process ⟶		⟶	Work with Mr. Peterson on using semantic feature analysis for teaching vocabulary	Assessment
2:30	Provide direct instruction in reading to 5 LD students ⟶			⟶	
3:30	Dismissal (check with teachers as needed) ⟶				⟶
3:45	End of day				

can take over the resposibility for teaching these students reading and writing—the content that is usually taught in the morning in many regular classrooms. I have developed a strong program in teaching reading comprehension, and I am using a process approach to teaching writing (see Figure 11.8). Currently I am using content area textbooks, trade books, and literature for teaching reading comprehension, and the students are working on writing reports, *literature critiques, and short stories on topics of their choice. Since I am responsible for these students' reading and writing, I am accountable for grading these students in these areas. Using this schedule, these students for the most part are in the regular classroom for content area subjects and math. I feel that this is important. When they go to junior high, they will probably be taking regular math, science, social studies, and other content area classes. If they have been missing these classes in the regular classroom during the fourth through sixth grades, they will really have trouble catching up. It's hard enough for these students—we want to give them every advantage possible.*

I have the younger students come after lunch, because I feel many of these students need two doses of reading, writing, and math. These students get instruction in these areas in the morning in the regular classroom and then I give them additional instruction in the afternoon. With this arrangement it is important that I communicate with the regular classroom teachers so we each know what the other is doing. We don't want to confuse the students by giving them conflicting information or approaches to reading.

I also have one day a week that I use for assessment, consulting with classroom teachers and checking on the students in the regular classroom. I feel that this time is very important. All of my students spend most of the school day in the regular classroom. If they are really struggling in those settings, I need to know so that I can provide additional support.

There are always some exceptions to the general guidelines I use for scheduling. I have three students who I

only monitor in the regular classroom. These students see me as a group on my assessment/consulting day. We talk about how it is going and discuss what is working for them and what frustrates them. I feel this time is critical for their successful mainstreaming. I also have two fifth-grade students who have good oral language skills but are reading on the first-grade level. They come for an additional thirty minutes late in the day, and we use the Fernald (VAKT) method to learn sight words.

Special Considerations for Scheduling in Secondary Settings

Scheduling in resource and consultant programs in secondary settings generally is less flexible than in elementary-level programs. Teachers must work within the confines of the instructional periods and the curricular units that students must complete for high-school graduation. One of the major responsibilities for resource/consultant teachers in secondary settings is to determine in which subject areas the students need special classes and those subjects in which they can succeed in regular or special materials classes with or without instructional support. These decisions about scheduling must be made on an individual basis and should be made with the involvement and commitment of the student as well as the teachers involved.

With the greater use of learning and study strategies curricula in secondary special education programs, secondary special education teachers may want to consider their role as that of learning specialists (Schumaker and Deshler, 1988). For the most part, they teach classes in learning and study strategies that provide students with the necessary skills and strategies to function in regular content classes. These learning specialists may also spend part of their day consulting with the content area teachers/specialists and in some cases may co-teach.

Classroom Management

When someone mentions classroom mangement, most teachers think of discipline and classroom management rules. Duke and Meckel (1980) refer to classroom management as the procedures needed to establish and maintain an environment in which instruction and learning can occur. Classroom rules, routines, and order play an important part in classroom management (Doyle, 1986). Students need to have expectations for the behaviors and routines of the classroom.

Early in the year it is important to establish processes and procedures that sustain order (Doyle, 1979; Emmer, Evertson, and Anderson, 1980). One way to inform students of the classroom rules is to discuss the rules with them. As new children enter the class during the year, assigning a ''veteran'' student as a guide or mentor can help the new student understand the rule system of the classroom.

The purpose of some classroom rules is to regulate student behaviors that are likely to disrupt learning and teaching activities or cause damage or injury to property or others. In addition to explicit conduct rules, most classrooms also have a set of implicit rules under which they function (Erickson and Shultz, 1981). Sharing the explicit conduct rules and demonstrating the rewards of working within the rule system is particularly important for students with behavior problems. Making rewards contingent upon full class participation can also assist a teacher because students will encourage each other to work within the rule system.

Ms. Schiller works with junior-high emotionally handicapped students in a self-contained setting. Establishing conduct rules early in the year and setting up a reward system for ''good behavior'' is an important part of her program. Ms. Schiller comments:

> *As far as I know, all of the students in this class are here primarily because they cannot cope with the rule systems in regular classrooms. This is due to a variety of reasons, and as a part of our social skills program we discuss some of the reasons and how to cope with them. But the majority of the day is focused on academic learning. To accomplish effective learning, we have to have a set of written and unwritten rules that the students and I are willing to operate under. We establish these rules at the beginning of the year during class meetings. In these meetings we talk about how the school operates and the rules it operates under, and then we decide what rules we want the classroom to function under. Usually it takes several days to establish these rules. The rules we generally decide on are:*
>
> > *During discussions, one person talks at a time.*
> > *When a person is talking, it is the responsibility of the rest of us to listen.*
> > *Work quietly so you won't bother other people.*
> > *No hitting, shoving, kicking, etc.*
> > *No screaming.*
> > *Do not take other people's possessions without asking.*
> > *When outside the classroom, follow the rules of the school or those established by the supervisor.*
>
> *Each day when we have a class meeting, we discuss the rules, our success with using these rules, and how the rules have operated. Sometimes we add new rules based on our discussions. I involve the students in this evaluation and decision making. Eventually we begin to decide when the rules can be made more flexible. In this way I hope that I am helping the students assume more responsibility for their own behavior, while at the same time maintaining a learning environment that is conducive to academic as well as social growth.*

I think there are three main reasons this rule system works in my classroom. First, the students feel like they own the system and have a responsibility to make it work. We have opportunities to discuss the system and to make changes. Second, we also establish a token system (see Chapter Two) for appropriate behavior and learning. Third, I communicate regularly with the parents, letting them know how their child is performing.

The classroom rules a teacher establishes are dependent on the social context of the school and the classroom, and the teaching-learning process as described in Chapter One. Some guidelines to use in developing and implementing classroom rules and management systems follow.

- Have the students help in selecting rules for the classroom.
- Select the fewest number of rules possible.
- Check with the principal or appropriate administrative personnel to determine if the rules are within the guidelines of the school.
- Select rules that are enforceable.
- Select rules that are reasonable.
- Determine consistent consequences for rule infractions.
- Have students evaluate their behavior in relation to the rules.
- Modify rules only when necessary.

The section on behavioral theory in Chapter Two also provides further ideas in terms of establishing reinforcement and token systems within the classroom.

Strategies for Mainstreaming and Consultation

As discussed in the first chapter, mainstreaming is the concept of educating handicapped students in classes with nonhandicapped students. The consultation service delivery model administers to the student in the regular classroom either through the coordinated teaching of the regular and special education teachers or by the classroom teacher, with the special education teacher serving as a consultant/collaborator.

Most students with emotional and learning handicaps spend at least some of their school day in regular classrooms with their nonhandicapped peers. Although the concept of mainstreaming was not specifically presented in PL 94-142, a related concept, least restrictive environment, was embraced by the law. With the recent emphasis on moving even more students with special needs into full-time placement in the regular classroom with the special education teacher serving as a consultant/collaborator (sometimes referred to as the Regular Education Initiative), the emphasis on mainstreaming and consultation/collaborative models has grown (e.g., January 1988 issue of *Journal of Learning Disabilities,* Fall 1988 issue of *Learning Disabilities Focus,* April 1990 issue of *Exceptional Children,* and November/December issue of *Remedial and Special Education*).

There are several reasons why mainstreaming is important for students with learning and behavior problems. First, the research has not clearly demonstrated either the academic or social benefits of placing students in segregated special education classrooms in comparison to regular classrooms. Second, students may be likely to be viewed as socially and academically more acceptable when they remain in the regular classroom. Third, court decisions have encouraged placement of handicapped students in the regular classroom to the extent possible. (Gottlieb, Alter, and Gottlieb, 1983; Hallahan, Keller, McKinney, Lloyd, and Bryan, 1988; McKinney and Hocutt, 1988; Prillaman, 1981; Schultz and Turnbull, 1984.)

If students with learning and behavior problems are to be successful in the mainstream, then special education and regular education teachers need to work together so that the students can make both academic and social progress. Following are some strategies to incorporate into an instructional program whose objective is to assist students in the regular classroom.

- Work closely with the regular classroom teacher.
- Observe in the regular classroom to determine the academic and social demands.
- Simulate the academic and social demands of the regular classroom in the special education classroom.
- Involve the student in the mainstreaming process by setting successful mainstreaming as a shared goal.
- Have the student observe in the regular classroom before being mainstreamed.
- Assist the regular teacher in adapting materials, instruction, and the instructional environment to facilitate the student's needs.
- Monitor the student once he or she is mainstreamed.
- At first, meet regularly with the mainstreamed student to discuss progress and concerns.
- At first, communicate frequently with the regular classroom teacher to discuss progress and concerns.
- Suggest that the regular classroom teacher use a "buddy" system in which the mainstreamed student is paired with a "veteran" to help the mainstreamed student learn the rules, procedures, and routines of the classroom.

Ms. Peress demonstrates many of these strategies as she mainstreams the intermediate-level, learning-disabled students from her self-contained classroom to regular classrooms. Ms. Peress describes her mainstreaming strategy as follows: "I am convinced that these students need to be in regular classrooms if at all possible. However, I've learned that we need to prepare them both socially and academically. Much of what we do in special education classrooms does not prepare them for regular education. They are used to individual and small group instruction, receiving lots of feedback, lots of reinforcement, and being relatively free to ask and receive assistance. This does not reflect what happens in the regular classrooms in this school. Although the teachers are great, they have twenty-eight to thirty-two students in each class. Large group instruction and cooperative and independent learning are the most frequently used instructional arrangements." Ms. Peress continues:

The first key to making mainstreaming work is to cooperate with the regular classroom teacher and to observe that classroom to determine the learning and social demands.

The second key is to gain a commitment from the student. He or she has to want to work toward the goal. I always describe the classroom demands to the student and sometimes he or she goes to observe. Then we plan how we're going to get ready for "going to Mrs. Fetter's class for math."

The third key is to begin simulating those learning and social demands in my classroom. I start gradually. Usually I start by decreasing the feedback and reinforcement. Next I focus on the academic demands. I get the lessons and textbooks from the classroom teacher and I begin to assign the lessons. At first the rate of learning is matched to the student's learning rate. But once the student is succeeding with the assignments, I begin to increase the rate until it matches that of the regular classroom. As this procedure continues, I continue to reduce the amount of reinforcement and feedback and to work with the student to become a more independent learner.

The fourth key is to wait to begin mainstreaming until the student is working on the same materials and at the same rate as the regular classroom. Then when he or she moves to the classroom the student only has to cope with a new teacher and setting and not with new materials.

The fifth key is to monitor the student and to continue to work with the classroom teacher to modify and adapt materials, methods, and the teaching-learning environment as needed.

I have developed this strategy through experience. Many times I have found that my test scores, informal assessments, and student progress data indicate that the student is reading at grade level. In the past I would jump to the conclusion that the student was ready to return to the regular classroom. Yet too often I would find the student back in my class within three weeks, after failing in the regular classroom. I was really setting the students up for failure. I had only attended to their reading level, not to the social and academic demands.

I've been very successful with this strategy. It's February and already I have all but four of my fourteen students mainstreamed for at least one academic subject (e.g., reading, math, writing, social studies, science).

Ms. Peress's discussion of how she mainstreams her students into the regular classroom demonstrates that she has a philosophy that places importance on communication, collaboration, and consultation with the regular classroom teachers. A number of models for consultation and collaboration between regular educators and special educators have been developed.

Teacher Assistance Teams

Teacher Assistance Teams (TAT) (Chalfant, Pysh, and Moultrie, 1979; Chalfant and Pysh,

1989, in press) is a within-building problem-solving model designed to provide a teacher support system for classroom teachers. Chalfant and Pysh identified five reasons for which schools may struggle with meeting the needs of all students including mainstreamed handicapped students in the regular classroom. First, with more special needs students remaining in the classroom and the general school population growing in terms of the number of at-risk students, the demands on classroom teachers have increased. Second, sufficient funds are not available to provide direct supportive services to all the children who need individulized assistance within our schools. Third, the classroom teacher may lack the time or preparation to plan and individualize instruction for these students. Fourth, because of the necessary assessment and placement safeguards built into the special education support system, this system is oftentimes not responsive to the immediate needs of teachers. Fifth, in some cases the teachers perceived need for help has led to the overreferral of students for special education assessment and placement (Chalfant, 1987; 1989; Chalfant, Pysh, and Moultrie, 1979).

The teacher assistance team is a school-based problem-solving unit designed to assist teachers in generating intervention strategies. The TAT model provides a forum whereby classroom teachers can meet and engage in a collaborative problem-solving process. The model is based on four assumptions related to teacher empowerment:

1. Considerable knowledge and talent exists among classroom teachers.

2. Classroom teachers can and do help many students with learning and behavior problems. Every effort should be made in the regular classroom before a referral for special education services is made.

3. Teachers can resolve more problems by working together than by working alone.

4. Teachers learn best by doing; the best way to increase teachers' knowledge and skills is by helping them solve immediate classroom problems (Chalfant and Pysh, 1989; Chalfant, Pysh, and Moultrie, 1979).

▬ *Procedures:* The core team is generally composed of three elected members (primarily classroom rather than special education teachers) with the requesting teacher also participating as a team member. The team may ask other teachers, specialists, or the principal to join the team as they deem necessary or to serve as permanent members. One person serves as coordinator and is charged with such responsibilities as alerting the team members to the time and place for the meetings and distributing information prior to the meeting so that the members have read the information prior to the problem-solving meeting.

When teachers refer classroom problems to the team, they complete a request for assistance in which they address four areas:

1. Describe what you would like the student *to be able to do* that he/she does not presently do.
2. Describe what the student *does (assets)* and what he/she *does not do (deficits)*.
3. Describe what you have done to help the student cope with his/her problems.
4. Provide background information and/or previous assessment data relevant to the problem (Chalfant and Pysh, 1981; Chalfant, Pysh and Moultrie, 1979).

Once a request for assistance is received, the person on the team responsible for that case reviews the information obtained from the request for assistance, observes in the classroom if necessary, interviews the teacher to clarify information, and constructs a problem-interaction diagram that visually represents and summarizes the concerns (Chalfant and Pysh, in press). This information is distributed to the team members prior to the meeting.

At the TAT meeting, the team members complete a thirty-minute problem-solving process for each request consisting of:

1. Reviewing the summary information, providing the opportunity for the teacher to clarify or provide additional information, and reaching consensus on what the problem is
2. Identifying the primary concern and establishing an objective for solving the problem
3. Brainstorming ideas for solving the problem and reaching the objective
4. Having the teacher requesting assistance select intervention strategies, which the teacher and team refine into a classroom intervention plan
5. Developing a means of measuring the success of the intervention plan
6. Establishing a date and time for a fifteen-minute follow-up meeting

Using this type of format, a teacher assistance team generally handles two new requests during a one-hour meeting or one new request and two follow-ups.

▬ *Comments:* The TAT model has been used widely through the United States and Canada. This model has been shown to be effective in assisting teachers in coping with the learning and behavior problems of students in the general school population. It is also particularly effective in reducing the number of students inappropriately referred for special education (Chalfant and Pysh, 1989). Its success in reducing the number of inappropriate referrals to special education has resulted in the TAT model being identified in the literature as a pre-referral intervention. However, the original intent of the process was to serve as a building resource for all students. This process has also been used with students already identified as handicapped with the children's special education and regular education teachers serving as team members and participating in the problem-solving process.

Several factors seem particularly relevant to the success of this model within a school. First, it is important that the school administration support such a program by providing teachers with the time for meetings and some type of support or incentive for serving as team members. Second, school-wide training in effective and efficient problem-solving strategies and the TAT process facilitates the success of the model (Chalfant and Pysh, 1989).

Collaboration in the Schools

Collaboration in the Schools (West, Idol, and Cannon, 1989) is one of a number of consultation models that focuses on the special education teacher consulting directly with regular classroom teachers to assist them in the successful mainstreaming of students with learning and behavior problems. This consultation model is based on the concept of collaborative consultation which Idol and West and their colleagues define as "an interactive process that enables people with diverse expertise to generate creative solutions to mutually defined problems.... The major outcome of collaborative consultation is to provide comprehensive and effective programs for students with special needs within the most appropriate context, thereby enabling them to achieve maximum constructive interaction with their nonhandicapped peers" (Idol, Paolucci-Whitcomb, and Nevin, 1986, p.1).

Like TAT, this model grew out of a need to provide more effective and coordinated services for students with special needs. West and Idol (1990) cite three reasons for using consultation models for special-needs students within the schools. One reason is based on the expense of assessing and placing students with learning and behavior problems in special education, approximately $1,270 per assessment (U.S. Department of Education, 1985-86). They suggest that collaborative problem solving can serve as a preventative model. The second reason is evi-

dence from research on effective schools (see Purkey and Smith, 1985, for a review), which indicates that collaborative planning and collegial relationships are two key process variables that are present in effective schools. A third reason is based on a professional development needs survey of the members of the Council for Exceptional Children, the major professional organization for special educators. The results indicate that the three top-ranked items focused on collaboration, communication, and consultation between special and regular educators (Council for Exceptional Children, 1989).

The purposes for collaborative consultation are to prevent learning and behavior problems, remediate learning and behavior problems, and coordinate instructional programs (West et al., 1989). The model is based on a set of forty-seven collaborative consultation skills which were validated by experts in the field (West and Cannon, 1988) and are grouped into the following areas:

- Consultation theory/models
- Research on consultation theory, training, and practice
- Personal characteristics
- Interactive communication
- Collaborative problem solving
- Systems change
- Equity issues and values/belief systems
- Evaluation of consultation effectiveness

- *Procedures:* The model is based on a six-stage collaborative consultation process completed by a collaborative team:

> *Stage 1: Goal/Entry.* Roles, objectives, responsibilities, and expectations are negotiated.
> *Stage 2: Problem Identification.* Nature and parameters of the presenting problem are defined.
> *Stage 3: Intervention Recommendations.* Potential interventions are generated and effects predicted. Recommendations are prioritized and selected. Objectives are

developed to specify the intervention details, the procedures, and the means for determining if the problem has been solved.

Stage 4: Implementation Recommendations. Procedures and plan of action are implemented.

Stage 5: Evaluation. Evaluation of the intervention is completed, including its impact on the child, the consultant and consultee, and the system or context in which the intervention is occurring.

Stage 6: Redesign. Intervention is continued, redesigned, or discontinued based on the evaluation (West and Idol, 1990).

Chapter Appendix 11.3 presents a problem-solving worksheet to use in conjunction with this consultation process. Collaborative consultation may occur at varying levels of teacher and school involvement. For example, a resource and regular English classroom teacher in a middle school or high school may use collaborative consulation to assist learning-disabled students who are being mainstreamed into regular English classes. Or an intermediate resource teacher and the speech/language pathologist may work with the intermediate teachers in an elementary school to develop strategies for facilitating concept and language development in the content areas. Or an elementary school may adopt collaborative consultation at the building level with the consultation be used in the prereferral process as well as for a means of coordinating the special and regular education programs for special-needs students.

➖ *Comments:*   Like TAT, collaborative consultation has been used in a number of schools and districts throughout the United States. West and Idol (1990) suggest that a number of factors need to be considered in implementing collaborative consultation. These parallel those relevant to TAT, including systematic and ongoing staff development, administrative support, and scheduling.

Summary

Effective and efficient management and communication are key aspects of "good" teaching, particularly when designing and implementing educational programs for students with learning and behavior problems. This chapter provides information concerning the management and communication responsibilites of special education teachers. Specifically it focuses on strategies and ideas for setting up different types of special education programs, utilizing equipment, designing and arranging instructional materials, scheduling, and consulting and collaborating with regular classroom teachers. Because management and communication vary depending on the setting, we encourage you to arrange to visit several special education programs and speak with the teachers if you are not familiar with different programs and settings for students with learning and behavior problems. This should help you envision how the information presented in this chapter can be used in school settings.

APPENDIX 11.1 ——————————————————————————————

Materials Evaluation Form

General Information

Name: Schoolhouse: A Word Attack Skills Kit
Author(s): M. Clarke and F. Marsden
Publisher: Science Research Associates

Copyright Date: 1973
Cost: $220

Description of the Materials

Purpose of Materials: Provide practice with phonic and structural word analysis skills
Instructional Level(s) of Materials:
  1st–3rd grades
Content of Materials:
  Plastic overlays and markers, 170 exercise cards (2 copies) and answer keys represent
  10 color-coded areas (e.g., initial consonants, vowels), progress sheets
Target Age:
  Could be used with students ages 6–12
Theoretical Approach to Learning:
  Behavior approach in that it assumes skills can be taught in isolation
Type of Instructional Arrangement (Individual, Cooperative Learning, etc.):
  Individual
Teacher Involvement Requirements: Demonstrating mechanics of programs. Checking
  student understanding of directions and pictures. Spot checking of student self-checks.
  Evaluating progress.
Time Requirements:
  10–15 minutes per exercise card.
Space Requirements:
  Materials come in 12″ × 12″ × 24″ box.
Equipment Requirements:
  None

Evaluation	*Poor*	*Fair*	*Good*
1. Materials sequentially organized	1	2	③
Progress from easy to hard			
Use pictures in early exercises			
2. Materials organized for easy retrieval	1	2	③
Students should be able to find exercise card			
without assistance			
3. Directions clear	1	2	③
Yes and written with a low readability level			
4. Provides adequate examples	1	②	3
Most of the time			
5. Provides for adequate practice	①	2	3
Would like to see more cards covering each			
phonic or structural element			
6. Conducive to providing feedback	1	2	③
Student can self-check and could plot progress			
7. Allows for checking/self-checking	1	2	③

(continued)

APPENDIX 11.1 *continued*

Evaluation	Poor	Fair	Good
8. Provides suggestions for adapting the materials	①	2	3
No			
9. Provides suggestions for generalization	①	2	3
No, this is a major concern.			
10. Interest Level	1	②	3
Although pictures are fairly easy to interpret, there is a limited number. Format repetitive.			

Description of Role in Instructional Program

How would this material fit into my instructional program?

Only as a reinforcement activity. Need to discuss with students how this practice will help them when they read (generalization).

APPENDIX 11.2

Student Materials Evaluation Form

Student Name: Jason

Date of Evaluation: March 15

Name of Materials: Criminal Justice (textbook)

Evaluation	Poor	Fair	Good
1. Directions are clear.	1	2	③
I understand the activities at the end of the chapter.			
2. Materials are interesting.	1	2	③
Yes. I like the personal stories.			
3. There are enough examples so that I know what to do.	1	②	3
Pretty much			
4. I get enough practice so that I learn the information or the skill.	1	②	3
Only if we discuss it in class			
5. It is easy to determine if I am doing the tasks correctly.	①	2	3
Not really			
6. I like using these materials.	1	2	③

7. I think that these materials teach:
   About how our government works
8. The thing(s) I like best about these materials is:
   They're interesting
9. The thing(s) I don't like about these materials is:
   Sometimes it doesn't tell enough and I have to read other places.
10. I would recommend using these materials for:
    Government classes

APPENDIX 11.3 _____

Problem-Solving Worksheet

Resource Teacher _____

Classroom/Content Teacher_____

Date _____

Problem: ┌───┐

Details: _____

_____

_____

_____

Alternative Solutions	Possible Consequences	Priority
1.		
2.		
3.		
4.		
5.		
6.		
7.		
8.		

Solution to Be Tried First:

_____

Adapted from: Ann Knackendoffel, Institute for Research in Learning Disabilities, University of Kansas.

(continued)

APPENDIX 11.3 *continued*

Implementation Steps	*When*	*Who*
_____	_____	____
_____	_____	____
_____	_____	____
_____	_____	____
_____	_____	____
_____	_____	____
_____	_____	____
_____	_____	____
_____	_____	____

How Will the Plan Be Monitored?

_____

_____

_____

_____

How Will Progress Be Evaluated?

_____

_____

_____

_____

Date and Time of Next Appointment

_____

_____

Source: J. R. West, L. Idol, and G. Cannon, *Collaboration in the schools: An inservice and preservice curriculum for teachers, support staff, and administrators* (Austin, Tex: PRO-ED, 1989), pp. 187–188. Reprinted by permission of PRO-ED, Inc.

Chapter Twelve

Communicating with Parents and Professionals

Chapter Questions

- *What are the principles of communication that facilitate the communication process with parents, teachers, and other professionals?*
- *What are the steps for conducting an effective interview?*
- *What are some of the needs of parents of children with learning disabilities and behavior problems? How might these needs be met?*

Mrs. Babson works in a hospital emergency room, so she is accustomed to talking to people who are grieving. Mrs. Babson states:

> *I often speak to parents about the recovery of their children. Fortunately, most of the children have injuries or illnesses in which they will recover completely. I've been trained in the importance of telling the parents as quickly and completely as possible all we know about their child's condition. The only reason I'm telling you this is that I want you to understand that I am accustomed to dealing with difficulties. But I was unprepared for the inconsistent information I would receive about our son.*
>
> *When our third child, Chad, was born, my husband and I couldn't have been happier. Our first two children were girls, who we enjoy immensely, but both of us were hoping for a boy. Chad walked and talked later than the girls, but I knew boys are often developmentally slower than girls so we were not concerned. Even when he was a preschooler, we knew Chad was different. He often had difficulty thinking of the right word for an object and he was clumsier than other children his age. When we spoke with his pediatrician he informed us that this was not uncommon.*
>
> *When Chad entered kindergarten he did not know all of his colors and showed little ability to remember the names of the alphabet. His kindergarten teacher said she had seen a number of students like Chad, often boys, and suggested we keep Chad in kindergarten another year. Our neighbor, who is a teacher, thought this might not be a good idea since Chad was already large for his age. We spoke with the principal, who seemed very busy and thought we should take the advice of the kindergarten teacher. We retained Chad. Spending another year in kindergarten*

> *seemed to do little good, however. Chad was still unable to identify letters, though he was very popular because of his size and knowledge of the kindergarten routine.*
>
> *First grade was worse yet. Chad showed no signs of reading and was confusing letters. His writing resembled that of a much younger child. By now we were very concerned and made several appointments with his first-grade teacher. She was very responsive and suggested that we have Chad tutored during the summer. The tutor said Chad had an attention problem and was having trouble with letter and word reversals. She suggested we have him tested for learning disabilities. The school psychologist agreed to do the testing and it was late in the fall before we were called and given the results.*
>
> *Though both my husband and I are professionals, we felt somewhat intimidated by the number of school personnel at the meeting. On our way home, as we tried to reconstruct what we heard, we realized that we had misunderstood and missed a lot of information. I heard the school personnel say Chad's intelligence was normal, but my husband thought that it couldn't be normal because his verbal intelligence was low. We decided to make a list of questions to ask at our next meeting. We felt we had made a major stride forward since Chad would now be receiving special instruction one hour each day from a learning disabilities specialist, however, we still felt we understood very little about his problems. I only wished we had been told more completely and quickly about Chad's problem.*

Many parents have had similar experiences. They have noticed that their child is different in some areas from other children the child's age.

These parents seek advice from friends, medical professionals, and school professionals, and often feel confused and frustrated. When the child is identified as learning-disabled or emotionally handicapped, many parents feel relieved at first, hoping this identification will lead to solutions that will eliminate the child's learning or behavior problem. The difficult adjustments are that the child will probably always have learning or behavior problems and the special education teacher will be unable to provide any magic cures and certainly no quick solutions.

Learning disabilities and emotional handicaps are complex phenomena and knowledge of all the factors they involve is incomplete. Special education teachers must be sensitive to parental concerns about identification and intervention, and yet speak honestly about what they know and don't know. They provide parents with encouragement yet do not give false hopes.

This chapter focuses on the teacher as a communicator. This communication occurs between teacher and parent and between special education teacher and other school-related professionals. The first part of the chapter focuses on principles of communication that can be used with parents and professionals. Effective communication skills are the basic needs in working effectively with parents and other professionals. The second part of the chapter focuses on teachers' roles with parents, parental needs, and how to facilitate an interactive relationship between school and home that will allow parents and professionals to exchange information. The third part of the chapter discusses special education teachers' roles with other professionals.

Communication Skills

In addition to assessment, intervention, curriculum development, and classroom management, a major role for the teacher of students with learning and behavior problems is communication. Effective special education teachers communicate regularly with parents, other special and regular education teachers, school administrators, and other educational and psychological professionals such as the school psychologist, speech and language therapist, and so on. Ability to communicate effectively is a skill that significantly affects an exceptional educator's job success. Despite the importance of this skill, most people finish school with no formal training in communication.

Principles of Communication

Some teachers communicate effectively with parents and other teachers with little effort. They seem to be naturals at making other people feel at ease and willing to disclose information. However, most teachers can benefit from specific skills training that teaches them effective communication skills. The following are some basic principles designed to facilitate the communication process with parents, teachers, and other professionals.

Acceptance

People know if you do not accept them or do not value what they have to say. Parents are aware when teachers do not really want to see them during conferences but are merely fulfilling a responsibility. Lack of acceptance interferes with parental and professional participation in a child's program. Other teachers seem to know how to extend their acceptance and interest. Ms. Skruggs has been teaching special education for twelve years. She has worked with a range of parents and professionals during her career—some easier to work with than others. Despite expected frustrations and disappointments, she communicates her care and concern to the parents and professionals with whom she interacts and always manages to find the few minutes necessary to meet with them. Ms. Skruggs claims, ''Parents have a great deal to teach me. They have spent a lot of time with their child and have seen patterns of behavior that can assist me in teaching.''

Effective Listening

Effective listening is more than waiting politely for the person to finish. It requires hearing the message the person is sending. Often this requires restating the message to assure understanding. Effective listeners listen for the "real content" of the message as well as listen for the "feelings" in the message. Without using phony or overused statements or parroting what was said, they restate the message and allow the speaker an opportunity to confirm and/or correct. In summary, effective listening involves:

1. Listening for the "real content" in the message
2. Listening for the "feelings" in the message
3. Restating or summarizing content and feelings (but not after every statement!)
4. Allowing the speaker to confirm or correct the perception

Mrs. Garcia, the mother of twelve-year-old Felipe, telephoned his special education resource room teacher, Mr. Sanchez.

Mrs. Garcia:	Felipe has been complaining for the past couple of weeks that he has too much work to do in his biology and math classes and that he is falling behind. He says he is flunking biology.
Mr. Sanchez:	How much would you say he is studying each night?
Mrs. Garcia:	Well it's hard to say. He stays out with his friends until dinner and then after dinner he starts talking about all his homework. Sometimes he sits in front of the TV with his books and sometimes he goes to his room.
Mr. Sanchez:	He has mentioned how much work he has to do in my class. I wonder if he is feeling a lot of pressure from different teachers, including me?
Mrs. Garcia:	Well, he has said he thinks you are working him too hard. I know sometimes he is lazy but maybe you could talk to him.
Mr. Sanchez:	Felipe works very hard in my class and I expect a great deal from him. I will talk with him after school and arrange a meeting with his other teachers as well.
Mrs. Garcia:	Thank you, and please do not tell Felipe I called. He would be very upset with me.

Effective Questioning

Knowing what type of question to ask will often help individuals in obtaining the information we need. Questions can be discussed in terms of open or closed. An open question is a question that allows the respondent a full range of responses and discourages the respondent from short, yes or no answers. Open questions may begin with *How, What, Tell me about,* and so forth. Following are several open questions.

- What do you think might be happening?
- What do you know about ___ ?
- How do you interpret it?
- What do you suggest?
- How might you describe it?
- How does this relate to his behavior at home?

Mrs. Gilmore suspected Matt, one of her students, was staying up very late at night. He was coming to school very tired and seemed to drag all day. He was also resting his head in the afternoon on his desk. She decided to call Matt's father to discuss the problem. She started the conversation by giving Matt's father some information about a meeting of parents that was going to be held in the school district that she thought would be of particular interest to him. She then proceeded to describe Matt's behavior in class. Finally, Mrs. Gilmore asked, "What do you think might be happening?'' Matt's father began to confide that he was not paying much attention to Matt's bedtime and he was staying up late watching movies on the new VCR. Mrs. Gilmore's question gave Matt's father the opportunity to explain what he thought was happening. Rather than posing several possibilities, or telling Matt's father that Matt was staying up too late at night, Mrs. Gilmore asked an open question, which allowed Matt's father to interpret the situation.

Involving people in identifying the problem increases the likelihood that they will not feel threatened by you, and they will be willing to make the necessary changes.

Provide Encouragement

Begin and end with something positive but genuine. With every student, even ones who have serious learning and behavior problems, teachers can find something positive to say. Perhaps the child is improving in some area, perhaps he contributed some interesting information to a class discussion, perhaps she said or did something that was humorous. In addition to hearing positive reports about their children, parents and professionals need encouragement about what they are doing. Since special education teachers often have meetings with parents and professionals to discuss problems, it is important to begin and end these meetings on a positive note.

Stay Directed

Follow the lead of parents and professionals whenever they are talking about a student. A skillful consultant is able to respond to others and still keep the discussion focused. It is not uncommon when speaking with parents about their child that they initiate other related home factors that may be influencing their child's progress in school. These may include marital difficulties, financial problems, or other personal problems. When others begin discussing serious problems that are beyond our reach as educators, we need to assist them in finding other resources to help them with their problems.

Develop a Working Alliance

It is important that, in every way possible, teachers communicate to parents and professionals that all of you share a common goal—developing the best program for the child. Whenever possible share information about changes in a child that would be of interest. Let parents know when the student is making exceptional progress. Let other professionals know when their intervention is paying off.

Developing Interviewing Skills

Special education teachers often work as consultants to regular classroom teachers, to other educational and psychological specialists, and to parents. Consultants need interviewing skills in order to identify problems fully and to implement appropriate interventions. These interviewing skills involve the need to ask questions that inform and to follow up appropriately on information provided. There are five steps to a good interview:

1. *Ask open questions.* As discussed in the previous section, an open question permits respondents a full range of answers, which allows them to bring up a topic or problem they have on their mind. Open questions are generally followed by questions that require more specificity. Mr. Schwab, the special education resource room teacher, began his interview with Mrs. Francosa, the fourth-grade teacher, by asking an open question: "How is John's behavior lately?"

2. *Obtain specificity.* This requires asking questions or making restatements that identify or document the problem. After Mrs. Francosa describes John's behavior in the regular classroom, Mr. Schwab attempts to identify key points and to obtain specificity in describing the behavior: "You said John's behavior is better in the classroom but worse on the playground. Can you identify which behaviors in the classroom are better and which behaviors on the playground are

worse?'' Without drilling the interviewee, an attempt is made to identify the problem and provide documentation for its occurrence so that an appropriate intervention can be constructed.

3. *Identify the problem.* This is done by the consultant based on information obtained, or it can be done by the person being interviewed, often in the process of answering questions: ''It seems like there is good progress in terms of completing classroom work. Let's figure out a way of reinforcing that behavior. There's a problem with his responding to teasing on the playground. His response has been to fight, which is getting him in more trouble. Any thoughts about how we might change that behavior?''

4. *Problem-solve.* Suggestions for solving identified problems and implementing the solutions are generated. Both the professional being interviewed as well as the consultant contribute suggestions to solving the problem. Often other professionals are included in the suggestions: ''Perhaps we could discuss John's problem with his counselor and ask her to teach him some strategies for coping with teasing. It's also possible to identify the students who are teasing him and reinforce them for not teasing.''

5. *Summary and feedback.* Summarize the problem and the plan of action. Be sure to indicate who is responsible for what. Whenever possible, establish a timeline for completing the tasks: ''You will send home notes to his parents, informing them of his progress in seatwork in the classroom. I will meet with the counselor regarding his problem on the playground, and you will talk with his peers and arrange a system for reinforcing them for not teasing. I'll check back with you during lunch this week to see how things are going. I'm very pleased with this progress and I am sure much of it is due to your hard work and follow-up.'' Figure 12.1 provides a summary of the interview process.

Effective consultants listen openly without a defensive posture. They stay focused and re-

FIGURE 12.1 *Steps to a Successful Interview*

Step 1: Open Question or Statement:
"Tell me about John's behavior."

Step 2: Obtain Specificity:
"How do the other children respond when John gets angry?"

Step 3: Identify the Problem:
"Sounds like fighting is occurring during noon recess most frequently after being teased."

Step 4: Problem Solving:
"Lets start by seeing how John perceives the problem and developing an intervention that includes his peers. What might be reinforcing to John and/or his peers?"

Step 5: Summary and Feedback:
"You'll meet with John and his peers tomorrow. I'll speak with the counselor and we'll schedule a team meeting for Wednesday."

member the needs of the student. They look for alternatives that can be implemented and they seek the advice of other professionals. When plans for solving problems are developed, they determine who is responsible for what tasks and provide feedback on performance. Interviews are the key to open communication and effective intervention.

Working with Parents

This section of the chapter will highlight the teacher's role with parents. Family adjustment to a child with learning and behavior problems is discussed first. Within this section, parent adjustment, sibling adjustment, and the problems of constructing an effective summer program will be described. Parent involvement with the schools and their role in the planning of the child's educational program will be presented.

Family Adjustment

There has been a great deal written on parental response to having a handicapped child. Most of what is written focuses on parents of the mentally retarded and physically handicapped. This literature may provide little insight into the adjustment of parents who have children identified by the schools as learning- or behavior-disordered. Most parents of children with learning and behavior problems do not receive a ''diagnosis'' until the child is in school. Though they may have identified the child's behavior as different from their other children and peers, most parents are unsure of what the problem is. Often they seek advice from their family physician who either makes referrals to other professionals or suggests they wait until the child enters school. Although many parents are aware their child is different long before diagnosis, they still continue to hope that their observations are incorrect and that the child will outgrow the problem.

From a systems perspective, the family is an important force in the child's learning and development. For this reason, many mental health professionals recommend an integrated approach to working with learning-disabled and behavior-disordered students who are troubled. This integrated approach typically involves all or part of the family in the program. This may include an initial meeting with the entire family, involvement of selected family members, or ongoing clinical help that may involve the family at certain times. Not all families who have children with learning and behavior problems need therapeutic assistance.

Because of concern over their child, mothers of learning-disabled children often expect less of them than the children expect of themselves. Teachers need to be aware of when parents are expecting too little of their children and assist them in readjusting their expectations. Many parents' and teachers' misconceptions about children teach them that they are unable and so the child acts as though he or she is unable. Many learning-disabled children leave school unprepared for work, postsecondary education, and life expectations. Often they leave school with fewer skills than the mentally retarded (Cummings and Maddux, 1985). Teachers can help parents by reminding them to communicate the importance of education to their child; for example, sharing their successes and failures when they were in school, and emphasizing that even when they did not do well they continued to do the best they could.

Simpson (1982) suggests that the needs of parents of exceptional children fall into five general categories:

1. *Information exchange.* Parents need conferences, program and classroom information, progress reports, interpretations of their child's academic and social needs, and informal feedback about their child.

2. *Consumer and advocacy training.* Parents need information about their rights and responsibilities, procedures for interacting during conferences, resources available through the school and community, and assertiveness training.

3. *Home/community program implementation.* Parents need procedures for assisting their child academically and behaviorally at home, including procedures for tutoring and classroom management.

4. *Counseling, therapy, and consultation.* Parents need support groups, consultation, referrals for conflict resolution, problem solving, and therapy.

5. *Parent-coordinated service programs.* Parents need to be in a position to provide and receive services to and from other parents through advisory councils, parent-to-parent participation, advocacy, and other options.

In a study reported by Simpson (1988), the most widely requested services by parents of children with learning and behavior problems were program information and informal feed-back.

Adjusting to a child with learning and be-havior disorders is difficult. Understanding how parents are adjusting and interacting with the child based on their interpretation of the child's needs is an important role for the special educa-tion teacher.

Siblings

In addition to how parents respond to a child with learning or behavior problems, the response by other siblings is also important. Many parents are concerned because their learning-disabled or be-havior-disordered child takes more time and con-sideration than do their other children. Siblings may feel as though the child with special needs is getting all of the attention and special privi-leges. It is important for parents to develop schedules so they will have assigned special time for all of their children. A sibling of a learning-disabled child commented:

Everything always seems to center around Scott. He always seems to be the focus of the conversation and whom my parents are concerned about. I do pretty well in school and don't seem to have many problems, so sometimes I feel left out. It really meant a lot to me when my mother and father both scheduled time during the week for me to be alone with them. Usually my dad and I would go to the park and sometimes we would go on an errand. Often my mom and I would work together in the kitchen, making my favorite dessert, chocolate chip cookies. The best part was that it was just me and them. I really think it helped me be more understanding of Scott. Somehow, I just didn't resent him so much anymore.

Summers

Summers seem to be particularly difficult for children with learning and behavior problems.

They often have too much unstructured time and too many opportunities to discover trouble. The summer is an extended time without exposure to structured learning experiences, and often what was done during the school year is undone during the three months without school. Parents often have a very difficult time with summers because of the additional pressure to find an appropriate educational or social experience. Billy's mother describes it this way:

My son, Billy, needs a special summer program so he can learn to play with other kids. . . . My ex-husband, Arthur, thinks I bug Billy too much and that we should leave him alone. That's what happened last summer, and it didn't work. I don't know how to convince him or where to begin to find a good camp. I'm exhausted. I'm doing all I can manage. Last week, the school people reminded me that it was time to plan for the summer. And then they told me how much trouble Billy was having playing with the other children. Maybe I misinterpreted it, but I felt they were saying I should be helping him even more (The Exceptional Parent, 1984, p. 43).

Teachers can assist parents during the sum-mer by developing a list of community resources that provide structured programs for children and adolescents. Each community has a range of such programs, some of which include:

1. *Public library.* The public library offers many programs that focus on literacy, including authors reading their books, books on tapes and records, and other special programs.

2. *Children's museums.* Many towns and cit-ies have developed children's museums that offer a range of special programs for children.

3. *Theater groups.* Often local theater groups offer summer programs on acting, cinema, and stage design.

4. *Museums.* Check with local art museums, historic museums, and science museums to determine what types of programs they will be offering during the summer.

5. *Parks and recreation.* Parks offer arts and crafts as well as organized recreational activities during the summer that are often free or very inexpensive.

6. *YMCA, YWCA.* These organizations offer many special summer programs, including day camps, swimming lessons, and arts and crafts.

7. *Universities, colleges, and community colleges.* Often these organizations offer special programs for children in the summer.

Preparing a list of activities available in the community as well as a list of tutors available during the summer helps parents and children with a smooth transition from school to summer, and may help teachers with the transition next fall from summer to school.

Parents as Tutors

Parental responsibility is to "insure that the home is a relaxed and pleasant place, a source of strength to the child" (Kronik, 1977, p. 327). Often parents want so much to help that they get overly involved in the child's homework or tutoring. Although spending time with their child in relaxing activities such as reading to the child, going for walks, sitting and talking, going to the zoo, and so on, are recommended by all educational and psychological specialists, few recommend direct instructional tutoring in the home. Home tutoring by the parent usually creates more problems than it solves. Often children need help with homework assignments; this is not the equivalent of home tutoring. Home tutoring is the supplementing of the child's educational program by the parent in the home. If parents insist on home tutoring, ask them to comply with the following suggestions adapted from Cummings and Maddux (1985).

1. Have specific, realistic goals developed with the special education or classroom teacher.

2. Begin and end each tutoring session with an activity that is fun and in which the child is successful.

3. Keep the tutoring session brief—not more than fifteen minutes for children up to grade six and not more than thirty minutes for older students.

4. Work on small segments of material at a time.

5. Use creative and novel ways of reviewing and teaching new material.

6. Prevent the student from making mistakes. If the student does not know the answer, give it.

7. Keep a tutoring log in which you record a couple of sentences about what you did and how the child performed.

8. Provide encouragement and support.

9. Practice the activities in ways that reduce boredom.

10. Work should be challenging but not too difficult.

11. Tutor at the same time and in the same place so the child has an expectation set for what will happen.

12. If you are getting frustrated or your interactions with your child are strained or stressful during the tutoring, stop. Your relationship with your child is much more important than what you can teach him or her during the tutoring session.

Parent Involvement with Schools

By the time children reach school, parents have already spent five years observing them. Many parents are aware from the day their child enters school that the child is different from other children. Often the child spends two to three difficult years in school before the child is referred for learning disabilities or behavior disorders. Dur-

Apply the Concept 12.1

WHAT PARENTS OF LD STUDENTS WANT FROM PROFESSIONALS

In a survey of over 200 parents of learning-disabled children, parents indicated what they really wanted from professionals (Dembinski and Mauser, 1977). A summary of the findings follows.

1. Parents want professionals to communicate without the use of jargon. When technical terms are necessary, they would like to have them explained so they can understand.
2. Whenever possible, they would like conferences to be held so both parents can attend.
3. They would like to receive written materials that provide information that will assist them in understanding their child's problem.
4. They would like to receive a copy of a written report about their child.
5. Parents would like specific advice on how to manage specific behavior problems of their children or how to teach them needed skills.
6. Parents would like information on their child's social as well as academic behavior.

ing this time, many parents have spent hours communicating with school counselors, psychologists, and teachers. In a study in which parents of learning-disabled students were interviewed following the initial placement of their child, parents reported having an average of six contacts with the school before their child was identified (Vaughn, Bos, Harrell, and Laskey, 1988). Some of these contacts were initiated by the parent. Often parents feel frustrated and alone. They are unsure what to do and because of the complexity of their child's condition, professionals are often unable to provide the precise answers parents need. See Apply the Concept 12.1.

Parental Involvement in Planning and Placement Conferences

Turnbull, Turnbull, and Wheat (1982) consider the provisions of PL 94-142 radical because of the extent of parent participation guaranteed. Parents provide consent for evaluation, participate in the program and educational plan, and are kept involved in all decisions regarding the child's educational program. The rationale for extensive parent involvement is twofold. First, it assures a cooperative role between home and school. Parents can provide information about the child the schools may not have access to, and parents can follow up on educational goals in the

home. Second, it assures that parents will have access to information regarding student evaluations and records and can better monitor appropriate placement and programming for the school. One of the greatest potential benefits to the child and family is to involve the parents in the planning and placement conference for the child. The information obtained about the child's learning and behavior problems can increase parental understanding, which leads to changes in parent behavior toward the child. In addition, parents learn about the focus of the child's program at school and can follow up on those learning and behavior programs in the home. Unfortunately, this is more often a description of the ideal than the real. Despite the best intentions of school personnel and parents, cooperative and extensive involvement in the placement and planning process is minimal.

There are many explanations for lack of parent involvement in the educational planning. One is that school personnel do not have adequate time to meet with parents and fully explain the child's program. Often parent meetings must be held early in the morning before parents go to work, or late at night on their way home. These times usually conflict with school personnel schedules and require school personnel to meet with parents outside of their required work time. Because of their dedication and interest in the child, professionals are often willing to meet at these times, but they are not motivated to meet for extended periods of time.

A second explanation is that many parents feel professionals will make the best decisions in their child's interest and do not want to be coparticipants in their child's educational program. This may not indicate a lack of interest in the child's program but merely less confidence in participating in this way. To assume that all parents want to be actively involved in planning their child's educational program may not be accurate. Winton and Turnbull (1981) found that when they interviewed parents of preschool handicapped children, 65 percent of the parents identified informal contact with teachers as the activity they most preferred, followed by 13 percent who chose parent training opportunities, and 10 percent identified to help others understand the child. It is interesting to note that a common theme in studies evaluating parent satisfaction with the placement and IEP conference is that parents state that they feel satisfied with the conference even though data indicate they played relatively passive roles (Lynch and Stein, 1982; Vaughn, Bos, Harrell, and Laskey, 1988). Some 25 percent of the parents of learning-disabled students who participated in placement and planning conferences did not recall the IEP document itself, and of those who did recall it, few had any knowledge of its content (McKinney and Hocutt, 1982).

It could be that parents would like to be more involved but feel intimidated by the number of professionals and the uncommon terminology.

> *No matter how well we might know our own children, we are not prepared to talk to teachers, principals, psychologists, or counselors, much less participate in the educational decision making process. Although parents do have a lot of information, it is not the "right" kind. When we go to speak to administrators at school we hear about IEP's, MA's,*

> *criteria, auditory processing, regulations, and sometimes, due process. At first, there seems to be no correspondence between what we know and what the people in schools are talking about (Exceptional Parent, March, 1984, p. 41).*

Special education teachers need to be sensitive to the parents' feelings and needs during conferences and serve as advocates for the parents. Often the teacher can "act as if" he or she is the parent and ask questions that he or she feels the parent may have wanted to ask but did not.

Public Law 99-457 and Parent Involvement

Public Law 99-457, The Education of the Handicapped Act Amendments, passed in 1986, provides guidelines for a free, appropriate public education for all handicapped children from birth to age three. The law provides for early intervention services that meet the developmental needs of the youngster and his/her family including: physical development, cognition, language, social, and self-help skills. The parents and family play an important role and an individualized program plan must be designed to meet their needs. This program plan, called the individualized family service plan (IFSP), should provide a coordinated array of services, including:

- screening and assessment
- psychological assessment and intervention
- occupational and physical therapy
- speech, language, and audiology
- family involvement, training, and home visits
- specialized instruction for parents and the target youngster
- case management
- health services that are needed to allow the child to benefit from the intervention service

What Are the Criteria for Establishing an IFSP?

The IFSP is a family-oriented approach to designing an effective management plan for the handicapped youngster. The IFSP must be developed by a multidisciplinary team and should include:

- A description of the child's level of functioning across the developmental areas: cognitive, speech and language, social, motor, and self-help
- An assessment of the family, including a description of the family's strengths and needs as the relate to enhancing the opportunities for the handicapped child
- A description of the major goals or outcomes expected for the handicapped child and the family (as they relate to providing opportunities for the handicapped child)
- Procedures for measuring progress including timeline, objectives, and evaluation procedures
- A description of the intervention services needed to provide an appropriate intervention for the handicapped child and family
- Specifically when the specialized intervention will begin and how long it will last
- An appointed case manager
- A specific transition plan from the birth-to-three program into the preschool program

Parent Education Programs

In a review of parent involvement programs for parents of learning-disabled children, the two types of programs most frequently provided for parents were counseling and tutoring (Shapero and Forbes, 1981). Overall findings indicated parent involvement programs can have positive effects on the academic performance of learning-disabled children. Providing organized parental programs may be helpful to some parents of children with learning and behavior problems. These programs need to be interactive and take advantage of the knowledge and needs of the participants.

A procedure for involving parents in their child's education is described in Apply the Concept 12.2.

There are a number of variables that influence the success of learning-disabled adults, including parental factors. The educational and economic levels of the parents significantly influence the likelihood that children with learning disabilities will have good jobs that pay well (O'Connor and Spreen, 1988).

Waggoner and Wilgosh (1990) interviewed eight different families regarding their experiences and concerns of having a child with learning disabilities. The results of these interviews elucidated several common themes including: parent involvement in the child's education, parents' relationship with the school, support for the parents, social concerns for the child, concerns about the child's future, emotional strains

Apply the Concept 12.2 ———————————————————

PAIRING TEACHER PRAISE NOTES WITH PARENT PRAISE

Imber, Imber, and Rothstein (1979) found that pairing teacher praise notes with parent praise regarding the note was effective in producing improvement in the academic performance of their children. After praise notes from the teacher were sent home, parents were asked to:

1. Read the note and praise the child as soon as possible.
2. Praise the child in front of others in the family.
3. Place the note where others can see it.
4. Express to the child that they hope the child will receive another one.

of parenting, and the effects on the family. The interviews indicated that parents needed to be willing to help the child at home with school work and to interact frequently with the school to serve as an advocate for their child. While all of the parents reported at least one positive experience with teachers and the schools, seven out of eight of the parents also reported negative experiences. These negative experiences revolved around teachers not feeling as though the child had a "real" problem and was just not performing as well as he or she could.

Working with Professionals

Consulting and communicating with professionals is an important role for teachers of students with learning and behavior problems. Teachers need to develop and maintain contact with the school psychologist, counselor, speech and language therapist, physical therapist, PE teacher, principal, and other related professionals. Since 90 percent of all students with learning and behavior disorders are mainstreamed for all or part of the day, a positive, cooperative working relationship with the regular classroom teacher may be most important of all.

Special Education Teacher as Consultant

Since most students with learning and behavior problems spend part of their day in the regular classroom, coordination and consultation is the key to a successful program. Consultation is important because the special education teacher is often the only resource that regular classroom teachers have to discuss programming for special students in the regular classroom. Since regular classroom teachers have less experience with exceptional learners, most of them expect special education teachers to provide suggestions for developing specialized programs. Unfortunately, research suggests that although regular

classroom teachers desire assistance and special education teachers would like to spend more time consulting (Friend, 1984), consultation between special and regular teachers is not occurring at a very high rate. As little as 8.5 percent of resource teachers' time is spent consulting with other teachers (Sargent, 1981). Evans (1980) found there was a significant difference between the actual and ideal amounts of time resource room teachers spent consulting. Of the resource room teachers participating in the study, 80 percent stated that consulting time was inadequate and consumed 5 percent or less of their time.

A successful exceptional education specialist is a consultant, a teacher, a diagnostician, and an advocate. As a consultant, the specialist does much more than just disseminate information. The consultant listens and suggests manageable ways of solving problems. Peters and Austin (1985) describe the characteristics of a leader and a nonleader. Many of these characteristics are important for special education teachers as they often serve as team leaders looking to develop the best programs for exceptional students. Table 12.1 lists these characteristics.

Role of the Special Education Teacher in Mainstreaming

When a student with special needs is being considered for placement in the regular classroom, there are several steps the special education teacher can take to initiate contact and communication with the regular classroom teacher. These steps include:

1. Describe the type of learning or behavior problem the child has and some general guidelines for how to deal with it in the regular classroom.

2. Give a copy of the child's IEP to the classroom teacher and discuss the goals, objectives, special materials, and procedures needed.

TABLE 12.1 *Characteristics of a Leader and a Nonleader*

Leader	Nonleader
Appeals to the best in each person.	Gives orders to staff— expects them to be carried out.
Thinks of ways to make people more successful. Looks for ways to reinforce them.	Thinks of personal rewards or how she or he looks to others.
Schedules frequent, short meetings to "touch base."	Meets infrequently with coworkers.
Good listener.	Good talker.
Notices what's going well and improving.	Only notices what's going wrong.
Available.	Hard to reach.
Persistent.	Gives up.
Gives credit to others.	Takes credit.
Consistent and credible.	Unpredictable.
Never divulges a confidence.	Cannot be trusted with confidences.
Makes tough decisions.	Avoids difficult decisions.
Treats teachers and students with respect.	Treats others as if they don't matter.

Source: Adapted from T. Peters and N. Austin, *A Passion for Excellence* (New York: Random House, 1985).

3. Describe the progress reports you will be sending to the classroom and home.

4. Develop a schedule for regular meetings and discuss other times that both the classroom teacher and special teacher are available for meetings.

4. Ask the classroom teacher how you can help and what special accommodations are needed.

5. Ask the classroom teacher how you can help and what special accommodations are needed.

In addition to communicating and consulting with teachers, there are a number of other roles that the exceptional education teacher can play to facilitate mainstreaming. These roles include providing inservice education on special education procedures or methods, bringing in guest speakers to discuss relevant topics, writing newsletters, and developing teacher assistance teams. The special education teacher's role in the teacher assistance team is further discussed in a later section within this chapter.

Even when special education teachers develop and maintain an effective communication and consultation program with regular education teachers, there are still a number of potential barriers to successful mainstreaming.

1. *The regular classroom teacher may feel unable to meet the needs of the mainstreamed student.* Ms. Clements has been teaching second grade for two years. When she was informed that Samuel, a student identified as emotionally disturbed, was going to be mainstreamed into her regular classroom for several hours each morning, she panicked. She explained to the principal that she had not taken any coursework in special education and was unable to meet the needs of the new student. The special education teacher met with Ms. Clements. She described Samuel's behavior and explained the progress he was making. She assured Ms. Clements that Samuel would be carefully monitored and that she would check with Samuel and her daily and then less frequently as he adapted to the new setting and schedule. She asked Ms. Clements to explain what types of activities usually occurred during the time Samuel would be in her room and she identified ways to be successful. The special education teacher took careful notes and asked many questions about Ms. Clements' expectations so she could prepare Samuel before his transition to the regular classroom. In this situation, consultation that provides specific information about the student's learning problems and what the classroom teacher can do to assure a successful learning environment is most helpful. In addition, the special education teacher obtained expectations about the regular classroom so she could best prepare the student for the transition.

2. *The regular classroom teacher may not want to work with the mainstreamed student.* Mr. Caruffe, a seventh-grade science teacher, expected all students to perform the same work at the same time, with no exceptions. He was particularly opposed to having special education students mainstreamed into his classroom because he felt they needed modifications from his core program. His philosophy was, "If students need modifications they don't belong in the regular classroom, they belong in special education." Teachers like Mr. Caruffe can be particularly challenging for the special education teacher. Despite continuous attempts to work out a collaborative effort, educational philosophies can be sufficiently different that the special education teacher feels it is hopeless to attempt mainstreaming in certain classrooms. The problem is when alternative classrooms are not available without reducing the content areas available to special students. If there are multiple teachers for each content area, students may be mainstreamed into classes where teachers are more accepting. Principals can be helpful by setting school policy that rewards teachers for working appropriately with mainstreamed pupils.

3. *Finding time to meet regularly with all classroom teachers is difficult.* At the elementary level the exceptional educational teacher meets regularly with all classroom teachers who have students mainstreamed for all or part of the day. This consultation includes discussing student progress, planning the student's program, adapting instruction in the regular classroom, and solving immediate academic and social problems with the student. It is better to meet weekly with classroom teachers for a short period of time (ten to fifteen minutes) than to meet less often for longer periods of time. When classroom teachers and their students perceive the special education room as a resource, rather than a closed room for special students, they have positive perceptions of the teacher and the students who attend (Vaughn and Bos, 1987).

At the secondary level continued involvement with all classroom teachers is a challenge. In large schools the exceptional students' regular classroom teachers vary within content area and

by year. It is possible for exceptional education teachers to have over twenty-five teachers with whom they consult. Special education teachers manage this by meeting with teachers in small groups. Sometimes they organize these groups by content area to discuss successful adaptations made within a common content. Sometimes meetings are organized to focus on the needs of a particular student and all teachers who work with this student meet at the same time. Finding time and maintaining contact with regular education teachers requires creativity and persistence.

4. *Students may not be accepted socially by peers in the regular classroom.* This problem occurs not just with students who have behavior problems but also with students who have learning disabilities. Because students are placed in classrooms where their peers are displaying appropriate social behaviors does not mean that students with learning and behavior disorders will model these appropriate behaviors (Gresham, 1982). According to both regular and special classroom teachers, the skills most essential to success in the regular classroom are interacting positively with others, following class rules, and exhibiting proper work habits (Salend and Lutz, 1984). Following is a list of behaviors considered important by both regular and special educators for success in the mainstream.

- Follows directions
- Asks for help when it's appropriate
- Begins an assignment after teacher gives assignment to the class
- Demonstrates adequate attention
- Obeys class rules
- Tries to complete task before giving up
- Doesn't speak when others are talking
- Works well with others
- Respects feelings of others
- Refrains from cursing and swearing
- Avoids getting in fights with other students
- Plays cooperatively with others

- Respects property of others
- Shares materials and property with others
- Refrains from stealing property of others
- Tells the truth*

Special education teachers may want to focus on teaching these behaviors before and during mainstreaming.

Working with Paraprofessionals

Many exceptional education specialists work closely with paraprofessionals as teaching assistants. Although teaching assistants never have complete responsibility for planning, implementing, or evaluating a student's program, they often participate in all of these roles. It is important for paraprofessionals not to be assigned to certain students who the teacher then spends little time seeing. Paraprofessionals need to have their teaching responsibilities rotated among many students so that the teacher spends frequent intervals teaching and evaluating all students. Since paraprofessionals are often responsible for implementing class rules, they need to be completely familiar with class and school rules and their consequences. Many paraprofessionals comment that they are successful in their roles when they have confidence in understanding what is expected of them.

Working with Administrators

The principal is the instructional and administrative leader of the school. The principal's perceptions and interactions with special education will be conveyed to classroom teachers and will be reflected in the procedures established to handle students with special needs. A supportive princi-

pal is the key to a supportive staff. When building principals find special education nothing but a headache or more paper work, this message is conveyed to the staff. When principals find special education an opportunity to provide necessary services to deserving students, this message is also conveyed. An effective relationship between the principal and the special education teacher will promote better programs for students and overall job satisfaction (Cheek and Lindsey, 1986).

Often the principal serves as the leader and coordinator of services between regular and special education. There are five activities principals can perform to facilitate the role of special education in the school (Chalfant and Pysh, 1979, 1986).

1. *Set the tone.* The principal sets a tone that establishes the importance of developing effective and responsive programs for students with learning and behavior problems. Too few teachers view administrators as support personnel. Many special education teachers feel they have to do as much as they can for students with little administrative support. In fact, many teachers state they just wish administrators wouldn't get in the way—they have long since given up on support. Many special education teachers have found that a positive tone about special education can be obtained from building-level principals through informing and involving principals in special education achievements, not just problems; providing feedback about how special education is demonstrating child gains; soliciting parent and community support; and developing good intervention programs that get school and district recognition.

2. *Reinforce teachers for developing programs that respond to the individual needs of students.* Principals can be effective agents for encouraging classroom teachers to develop programs that respond to the individual needs of the special students in their classroom.

3. *Provide consultation time.* Principals can arrange schedules of their support staff to serve as consultants to regular classroom teachers, providing programs for students with learning and behavior problems. The services of the school psychologist, speech and language therapist, physical therapist, counselor, special education teacher, and other support staff can be made available to regular classroom teachers.

4. *Provide inservice activities to staff.* This includes the provision of workshops, consultants, or lectures, focusing on the needs of staff to provide adequate service to students with learning and behavior disorders.

5. *Organize school-based assistance teams.* School-based assistance teams focus on the development of teams to assist classroom teachers with all students having learning and behavior problems, not just students identified to receive special education services. In fact, the school-based assistance teams (Chalfant and Pysh, 1979, 1983) were originally developed to assist in reducing unnecessary referrals for special education. The next section describes the role of school-based assistance teams.

School-Based Assistance Teams

The purpose of school-based assistance teams is to develop a team of professionals to work cooperatively with classroom teachers to develop successful programs and strategies in the regular classroom for students with learning and behavior problems. Often these teams are established to eliminate unnecessary testing and referral for special education. Whereas the original purpose was to work with students who have learning and behavior problems who were presently not placed in special education, it is possible to establish teams that focus on students identified as special education.

Who serves on the team? The membership can include the building principal, two regular classroom teachers, the teacher seeking assistance, and other persons as needed, such as a parent, the student, or a member of the special education staff. Team members can be selected by the staff or appointed by the principal.

How is the team contacted for assistance? When a classroom teacher seeks assistance in solving a student's learning or behavior problem in the classroom, the teacher seeks help from the school-based assistance team. Chalfant and Pysh (1979, 1983) suggest assistance be requested by answering four questions:

1. What do you want the student to do that he or she is not presently doing?
2. What does the student do (assets) and not do (deficits)?
3. What have you done to help the student cope with his or her problem?
4. What other background information and/or test data are relevant to the problem?

What does the team do? The team often responds to a problem identified by the classroom teacher. Frequently the teacher identifies the problem and selects a member of the team to observe the student and/or the teacher. In addition, informal assessment may be conducted. The team generates instructional alternatives and may assist in the implementation of these alternatives. It also establishes policies for monitoring progress and providing feedback.

School-based assistance teams have successfully decreased the number of referrals for special education. They also provide the necessary support needed by classroom teachers to cope effectively with students who have learning and behavior disorders.

Summary

This chapter focused on an important role for the special education teacher: communicating with parents and professionals. Although most of the chapters in this book discuss strategies for increasing teachers' skills in working directly with students who have learning and behavior disorders, this chapter is about communicating with the key people who interact with the student.

The first part of the chapter discussed the communication skills necessary for interacting with parents and professionals. These skills include acceptance, effective listening, effective questioning, providing encouragement, keeping the focus of the conversation directed, and developing a working alliance. In addition to these communication skills, acquiring interviewing skills such as asking open questions, obtaining specificity, identifying the problem, solving the problem, and providing feedback are discussed.

The second part of the chapter centered on understanding the needs of parents and communicating with them. Parents play a critical role in the successful delivery of services to students with special needs. They are involved in the identification, assessment, and educational planning of their child. Parents who are aware of academic and social goals for the child are more likely to follow up on these goals at home. Unlike other handicapping conditions (e.g., mental retardation and sensory impairment), learning and behavior disorders are often not identified until the student begins school. Although parents may be aware their child is different than peers, they often receive the identification of the learning or behavior disorder from the school. Special education teachers play a critical role in communicating assessment and educational planning information to parents. They are also the professionals who communicate most frequently with

parents regarding the daily progress of their child. This section presented suggestions for facilitating family adjustment as well as procedures for facilitating parent involvement in the placement and programming for their child.

The third part of the chapter presented the special education teacher's role in working with other professionals. Working with professionals is particularly important for teachers of students with learning and behavior problems as their students are frequently mainstreamed for part of the school day. Often the special education teacher serves as the primary consultant for the regular classroom teacher, who may have few skills in effectively teaching students with special needs. Barriers that may interfere with successful mainstreaming were discussed. Establishing effective working relationships with the school principal is an important role for the special education teacher. The school principal sets the tone in the building for the acceptance of students with special needs.

Although teachers may be effective in providing the academic and social instruction their students require, unless they are equally effective in communicating with parents and professionals, they will be unsuccessful. The special education teacher spends relatively little time with the student, compared to the time the child spends with others. When all persons who interact with the student are working cooperatively to advance educational and social goals, the child's progress is assured.

References

Aaronson, S. (1975). Notetaking improvement: A combined auditory, functional and psychological approach. *Journal of Reading, 19,* 8–12.

Abroms, K. I., and Kodera, T. L. (1979). Acceptance hierarchy of handicaps: Validation of Kirk's statement, "Special education often begins where medicine stops." *Journal of Learning Disabilities, 12*(1), 15–20.

Abt Associates (1976). *Education as experimentation: A planned variation model* (Vol. 3). Boston: Abt Associates.

Achenbach, T. M., and Edelbrock, C. S. (1978). The child behavior profile: II. Boys aged 12–16 and girls aged 6–11 and 12–16. *Journal of Consulting and Clinical Psychology, 41,* 223–233.

Ackerman, P. T., and Dykman, R. A. (1982). Automatic and effortful information-processing deficits in children with learning and attention disorders. *Topics in Learning and Learning Disabilities, 2,* 12–22.

Adams, A., Carnine, D., and Gersten, R. (1982). Instructional strategies for studying context area texts in the intermediate grades. *Reading Research Quarterly, 18*(1), 27–55.

Allen, R. R., and Brown, K. L. (1977). *Developing communication competence in children.* Skokie, Ill.: National Textbook.

Allen, R. V. (1976). *Language experiences in communication.* Boston: Houghton Mifflin.

Allen, R. V., and Allen, C. (1966–68). *Language experiences in reading* (Levels I, II, and III). Chicago: Encyclopedia Britannica.

Allen, R. V., and Allen, C. (1982), *Language experience activities* (2nd ed.). Boston: Houghton Mifflin.

Alexander, F. (1987). The California reading initiative. In B. E. Cullinan (Ed.), *Children's literature in the reading program.* Newark, Del.: International Reading Association, pp. 139–148.

Alley, G. R., and Deshler, D. D. (1979). *Teaching the learning disabled adolescent: Strategies and methods.* Denver: Love Publishing.

Alsup, R. (1982). *WH-questions.* Allen, Tex.: DLM.

Altwerger, B., Edelsky, C., and Flores, B. M. (1987). Whole language: What's new? *The Reading Teacher, 41,* 144–154.

Amish, P. L., Gesten, E. L., Smith, J. K., Clark, H. B., and Stark, C. (1988). Social problem-solving training for severely emotionally and behaviorally disturbed children. *Behavioral Disorders, 13*(3), 175–186.

Anders, P. L., and Bos, C. S. (1984). In the beginning: Vocabulary instruction in content classroom. *Topics in Learning and Learning Disabilities, 3*(4), 53–65.

Anders, P. L., and Bos, C. S. (1986). Semantic feature analysis: An interactive strategy for vocabulary development and text comprehension. *Journal of Reading, 29*(7), 610–616.

Anders, P. L., Bos, C. S., Jaffe, L. E., and Filip, D. (April 1986). *Comparison of semantic feature analysis and direct instruction of word meaning for improving reading comprehension.* Paper presented at the annual meeting of the American Educational Research Association, San Francisco.

Anders, P. L., and Mitchell, J. N. (May 1980). *Pilgrims, Indians, the Mayflower, and freedom: Interactions among readers, texts, concepts, and questions.* Paper presented at the International Reading Association Convention, St. Louis, Mo.

Anderson, J. R. (1980). *Cognitive psychology and its implications.* San Francisco: W. H. Freeman.

Anderson, L., Brubaker, N., Alleman-Brooks, J., and Duffy, G. (1986). A qualitative study of seatwork in first-grade classrooms. *Elementary School Journal, 86,* 123–140.

Anderson, R. C. (1977). The notion of schemata and the educational enterprise. In R. C. Anderson, R. J. Spiro, and W. E. Montague (Eds.), *Schooling and the acquisition of knowledge*. Hillsdale, N.J.: Erlbaum, pp. 415–431.

Anderson, R. C., and Freebody, P. (1981). Vocabulary knowledge. In J. T. Guthrie (Ed.), *Comprehension and reading: Research reviews*. Newark, N.J.: International Reading Association.

Anderson, R. C., Hiebert, E., Scott, J., and Wilkinson, I. (1985). *Becoming a nation of readers: The Report on the Commission on Reading*. Washington, D.C.: National Institute of Education.

Anderson, R. C., and Pearson, P. D. (1984). A schema-theoretic view of basic processes in reading comprehension. In P. D. Pearson (Ed.), *Handbook of reading research*. New York: Longman.

Anderson, R. C., Reynolds, R. E., Schallert, D. L., and Goetz, E. T. (1977). Frameworks for comprehending discourse. *American Educational Research Journal, 14*, 367–382.

Anderson, R. C., Wilson, P. T., and Fielding, L. G. (1988). Comparison in reading and how children spend their time outside of school. *Reading Research Quarterly, 23*, 285–303.

Anderson, R. P., Halcomb, C. G., and Doyle, R. B. (1973). The measurement of attentional deficits. *Exceptional Children, 39*, 534–539.

Anderson, S., and Messick, S. (1974). Social competency in young children. *Developmental Psychology, 10*(2), 282–293.

Anderson, T. H., and Armbruster, B. B. (1984). Content area textbooks. In R. C. Anderson, J. Osborn, and R. J. Tierney (Eds.), *Learning to read in American schools: Basal readers and content texts*. Hillsdale, N.J.: Erlbaum, pp. 193–226.

Andolina, C. (1980). Syntactic maturity and vocabulary richness of learning disabled children at four age levels. *Journal of Learning Disabilities, 13*, 27–32.

Anglin, J. (1970). *The growth of meaning*. Cambridge, Mass.: MIT Press.

Archer, A., and Edgar, E. (1976). Teaching academic skills to mildly handicapped children. In S. Lowenbraun and J. Q. Affect (Eds.), *Teaching mildly handicapped children in regular classes*. Columbus, Ohio: Merrill.

Armbruster, B. B., and Anderson, T. H. (1988). On selecting "considerate" content area textbooks. *Remedial and Special Education, 9*(1), 47–52.

Ashton-Warner, S. (1958). *Spinster*. New York: Simon and Schuster.

Ashton-Warner, S. (1963). *Teacher*. New York: Simon and Schuster.

Ashton-Warner, S. (1972). *Spearpoint*. New York: Alfred A. Knopf.

Atwell, N. (1985). Writing and reading from the inside out. In J. Hansen, T. Newkirk, and D. Graves (Eds.), *Breaking ground: Teachers relate reading and writing in the elementary school*, Portsmouth, N.H.: Heinemann, pp. 147–168.

Ausubel, D. P., and Robinson, F. G. (1969). *School learning: An introduction to education psychology*. New York: Holt, Rinehart and Winston.

Axelrod, L. (1982). Social perception in learning disabled adolescents. *Journal of Learning Disabilities, 15*, 610–613.

Axline, V. (1947). *Play therapy*. Boston: Houghton Mifflin.

Baker, G. A. (1977). *A comparison of traditional spelling with phonemic spelling of fifth and sixth grade students*. Unpublished doctoral dissertation, Wayne State University, Detroit.

Bandura, A. (1977). *Social learning theory*. Englewood Cliffs, N.J.: Prentice-Hall.

Barney, L. (1973). The first and third R's. *Today's Education, 62*, 57–58.

Barrett, T. (1976). Taxonomy of reading comprehension. In R. Smith and T. Barrett (Eds.), *Teaching reading in the middle grades*. Reading, Mass.: Addison-Wesley.

Barron, R., and Earle, R. (1973). An approach for vocabulary development. In H. L. Herber and P. L. Sanders (Eds.), *Research in reading in the content areas: Second report*. Syracuse, N.Y.: University of Syracuse, Reading and Language Arts Center.

Bartlett, R. C. (1932). *Remembering*. Cambridge, Eng.: Cambridge University Press.

Battle, J., and Blowers, T. (1982). A longitudinal comparative study of the self-esteem of students in regular and special education classes. *Journal of Learning Disabilities, 15*(2), 100–102.

Bauer, R. H. (1987). Control processes as a way of understanding, diagnosing, and remediating learning disabilities. In H. L. Swanson (Ed.), *Advances in learning and behavioral disabilities* (Supplement 2). Greenwich, Conn.: JAI Press, pp. 41–81.

Baumann, J. F., and Serra, J. K. (1984). The frequency and placement of main ideas in children's social studies textbooks: A modified replication of Braddock's research on topic sentences. *Journal of Reading Behavior, 16,* 27–40.

Beck, J., and McKeown, M. G. (1981). Developing questions that promote comprehension: The story map. *Language Arts, 58,* 913–918.

Becker, W. C. (1977). Teaching reading and language to the disadvantaged—What we have learned from field research. *Harvard Educational Review, 44*(4), 518–543.

Becker, W. C., and Englemann, S. E. (1976). Technical report 1976–1. Eugene: University of Oregon.

Becker, W. C., and Gersten, R. (1982). A follow-up on Follow Through: The later effects of the direct instruction model on children in fifth and sixth grades. *American Education Research Journal, 19,* 75–92.

Behrmann, M. M., and Levy, S. A. (1986). Computers and special education children. In J. L. Hoot (Ed.), *Computers in early childhood education: Issues and practices.* Englewood Cliffs, N.J.: Prentice-Hall, pp. 104–127.

Bender, W. N. (1989). Generalization and setting specificity of behavioral deficits among learning disabled students. *Learning Disabilities Research, 4*(2), 96–100.

Bergerud, D., Lovitt, T. C., and Horton, S. (1988). The effectiveness of textbook adaptations in life science for high school students with learning disabilities. *Journal of Learning Disabilities, 21,* 70–76.

Berler, E. S., Gross, A. M., and Drabman, R. S. (1982). Social skills training with children: Proceed with caution. *Journal of Applied Behavioral Analysis, 15,* 41–53.

Berliner, D. C. (1983). The executive who manages classrooms. In B. J. Fraser (Ed.), *Classroom management.* South Bentley: Western Australian Institute of Technology.

Berres, F., and Eyer, J. T. (1970). In A. J. Harris (Ed.), *Casebook on reading disability.* New York: David McKay, pp. 25–47.

Betts, E. A. (1946). *Foundations of reading instruction.* New York: American Book.

Bickett, L. G., and Milich, R. (April 1987). *First impressions of learning disabled and attention deficit disordered boys.* Paper presented at the Biennial Meeting of the Society for Research in Child Development, Baltimore, Md.

Bierman, K. L., and Furman, W. (1984). The effects of social skills training and peer involvement on the social adjustment of preadolescents. *Child Development, 55,* 151–162.

Bitter, G. G. (1984). Hardware and software selection and evaluation. *Computers in the Schools, 1*(1), 13–28.

Black, F. (1974). Self-concept as related to achievement and age in learning disabled children. *Child Development, 45,* 1137–1140.

Blackman, S., and Goldman, K. M. (1982). Cognitive styles and learning disabilities. *Journal of Learning Disabilities, 15,* 106–115.

Blankenship, C. S. (1984). Curriculum and instruction: An examination of models in special and regular education. In J. F. Cawley (Ed.), *Developmental teaching of mathematics for the learning disabled.* Rockville, Md.: Aspen.

Blankenship, C. S., and Lovitt, T. C. (1976). Story problems: Merely confusing or downright befuddling. *Journal for Research in Mathematics Education, 7,* 290–298.

Bley, N. S., and Thornton, C. A. (1981). *Teaching mathematics to the learning disabled.* Rockville, Md.: Aspen.

Bloom, L., and Lahey, M. (1978). *Language development and language disorders.* New York: John Wiley.

Bloom, L., Miller, P., and Hood, L. (1975). Variation and reduction as aspects of competence in language development. In A. Pick (Ed.), *Minnesota symposium on child psychology* (Vol. 9). Minneapolis: University of Minnesota.

Bloomer, R. H. (1962). The cloze procedure as a remedial reading exercise. *Journal of Developmental Reading, 5,* 173–181.

Bloomfield, L., and Barnhart, C. L. (1961). *Let's read: A linguistic approach.* Detroit: Wayne State University Press.

Bloomfield, L., Barnhart, C. L., and Barnhart, R. K. (1963). *Let's read: Part I.* Bronxville, N.Y.: C. L. Barnhart.

Borkowski, J. G., Weyhing, R. S., and Carr, M. (1988). Effects of attributional retraining on strategy-based reading comprehension in learning-disabled students. *Journal of Educational Psychology, 80*(1), 46–53.

Borkowski, J. G., Weyhing, R. S., and Turner, L. A. (1986). Attributional retraining and the teaching of strategies. *Exceptional Children, 53*(2), 130–137.

Bos, C. S. (1979). *Inferential operations in the reading comprehension of educable mentally retarded and average students.* Doctoral dissertation, University of Arizona, Tucson.

Bos, C. S. (1982). Getting past decoding: Using modeled and repeated readings as a remedial method for learning disabled students. *Topics in Learning and Learning Disabilities, 1,* 51–57.

Bos, C. S. (October 1983). *Using computers to put learning disabled students in the driver's seat.* Paper presented at the annual meeting of the Arizona Association for Children with Learning Disabilities Conference, Phoenix.

Bos, C. S. (1985). *Formalized planning: Its role in the writing process.* Paper presented at the annual meeting of the National Reading Conference, San Diego, Calif.

Bos, C. S. (October 1987). *Promoting story comprehension using a story retelling strategy.* Paper presented at the Teachers Applying Whole Language Conference, Tucson, Ariz.

Bos, C. S. (1988). Academic interventions for learning disabilities. In K. A. Kavale (Ed.), *Learning disabilities: State of the art and practice.* Boston: Little, Brown—College Hill, pp. 98–122.

Bos, C. S., Allen, A. A., and Scanlon, D. J. (1989). Vocabulary instruction and reading comprehension with bilingual learning disabled students. In S. McCormick and J. Zutell (Eds.), *Cognitive and social perspectives for literacy research and instruction* (Thirty-eighth yearbook). Chicago: National Reading Conference, pp. 173–180.

Bos, C. S., and Anders, P. L. (1987). Semantic feature analysis: An interactive teaching strategy for facilitating learning from text. *Learning Disabilities Focus, 3,* 55–59.

Bos, C. S., and Anders, P. L. (1990a). Effects of interactive vocabulary instruction on the vocabulary learning and reading comprehension of junior-high learning disabled students. *Learning Disability Quarterly, 13,* 31–42.

Bos, C. S., and Anders, P. L. (1990b). Toward an interactive model: Teaching text-based concepts to learning disabled students. In H. L. Swanson and B. Keogh (Eds.), *Learning disabilities: Theoretical and research issues.* Hillsdale, N.J.: Erlbaum, pp. 247–261.

Bos, C. S., Anders, P. L., Filip, D., and Jaffe, L. E. (1989). The effects of an interactive instructional strategy for enhancing learning disabled students' reading comprehension and content area learning. *Journal of Learning Disabilities, 22,* 384–390.

Bos, C. S., Anders, P. L., Jaffe, L. E., and Filip, D. (1985). Semantic feature analysis and long-term learning. In J. A. Niles (Ed.), *Issues in literacy: A research perspective* (Thirty-fourth yearbook). Rochester, N.Y.: National Reading Conference, pp. 42–46.

Bos, C. S., and Filip, D. (1984). Comprehension monitoring in learning disabled and average students. *Journal of Learning Disabilities, 17*(4), 229–233.

Bos, C. S., and Grimm, D. (in progress). *Increasing reading comprehension and writing through a story retelling strategy.* Unpublished manuscript.

Bos, C. S., and Van Reusen, A. K. (1986). *Effects of teaching a strategy for facilitating student and parent participation in the IEP process* (Partner Project Final Report G008400643). Tucson: University of Arizona, Department of Special Education.

Bos, C. S., and Vaughn, S. (1988) *Strategies for teaching students with learning and behavior problems.* Boston: Allyn and Bacon.

Bos, C. S., Vaughn, S. R., and Harrell, J. (in progress). *Hispanic and non-Hispanic parents' involvement in the initial placement conference.* Unpublished manuscript.

Boston Herald (November 10, 1984), pp. 1, 7.

Bradley, C. A. (1985). The relationship between students' information-processing styles and Logo programming. *Journal of Educational Computing Research, 1,* 427–433.

Bradley, L., and Bryant, P. (1985). *Rhyme and reason in reading and spelling.* Ann Arbor: University of Michigan Press.

Bragstad, B. J., and Stumpf, S. M. (1982). *A guidebook for teaching: Study skills and motivation.* Boston: Allyn and Bacon.

Bransford, J. D., and Johnson, M. D. (1972). Contextual prerequisites for understanding: Some investigations of comprehension and recall. *Journal of Verbal Learning and Verbal Behavior, 11,* 717–726.

Brewer, W. R., and Nakamura, G. V. (1984). *The nature and functions of schemas* (Tech. Rep. 325). Champaign: University of Illinois, Center for the Study of Reading.

Bridge, C. A., and Burton, B. (1982). Teaching sight vocabulary through patterned language materials. In J. A. Niles and L. A. Harris (Eds.), *New inquiries in reading research and instruction* (Thirty-first yearbook), Washington, D.C.: National Reading Conference, pp. 119–223.

Bridge, C. A., Winograd, P. N., and Haley, D. (1983). Using predictable materials vs. preprimers to teach beginning sight words. *The Reading Teacher, 36*(9), 884–891.

Briggs, D. (1970) Influence of handwriting on assessment. *Educational Research, 13,* 50–55.

Brown, A. L. (1980). Metacognitive development and reading. In R. J. Spiro, B. C. Bruce, and W. F. Brewer (Eds)., *Theoretical issues in reading comprehension,* Hillsdale, N.J.: Erlbaum, pp. 453–482.

Brown, A. L., and Palincsar, A. S. (1982). Including strategic learning from texts by means of informed, self-control training. *Topics in Learning and Learning Disabilities, 2*(1), 1–17.

Brown, A. L., Palinscar, A. S., and Armbruster, B. B. (1984). Instructing comprehension-fostering activities in interactive learning situations. In H. Mandl, N. L. Stein, and T. Trabasso (Eds.), *Learning and comprehension of text.* Hillsdale, N.J.: Erlbaum, pp. 255–286.

Brown, R. (1973). *A first language: The early stages.* Cambridge, Mass.: Harvard University Press.

Bruck, M. (1986). Social and emotional adjustments of learning disabled children: A review of the issues. In S. J. Ceci (Ed.), *Handbook of cognitive, social, and neuropsychological aspects of learning disabilities.* Hillsdale, N.J.: Erlbaum, pp. 361–380.

Bruininks, V. L. (1978). Peer status and personality characteristics of learning disabled and nondisabled students. *Journal of Learning Disabilities, 11*(8), 29–34.

Bryan, J. H., Bryan, T. H., and Sonnefeld, L. J. (1982). Being known by the company we keep! The contagion of first impressions. *Learning Disability Quarterly, 5*(3), 228–293.

Bryan, J. H., and Perlmutter, B. (1979). Immediate impressions of LD children by female adults. *Learning Disability Quarterly, 2,* 80–88.

Bryan, J. H., and Sherman, R. (1980). Immediate impressions of nonverbal ingratiation attempts by learning disabled boys. *Learning Disabilities Quarterly, 3,* 19–29.

Bryan, J. H., Sonnefeld, L. J., and Grabowski, B. (1983). The relationship between fear of failure and learning disabilities. *Learning Disability Quarterly, 6*(2), 217–222.

Bryan, T., Pearl, R., and Fallon, P. (1989). Conformity to peer pressure by students with learning disabilities: A replication. *Journal of Learning Disabilities, 22*(7), 458–459.

Bryan, T. H. (1986). Self-concept and attributions of the learning disabled. *Learning Disabilities Focus, 1*(2), 82–89.

Bryan, T. H., and Bryan, J. H. (1978). Social interactions of learning disabled children. *Learning Disability Quarterly, 1,* 33–38.

Bryan, T. H., and Pflaum, S. (1978). Social interactions of learning disability children: A linguistic, social, and cognitive analysis. *Learning Disability Quarterly, 1,* 70–78.

Bryan, T. S. (1974). An observational analysis of classroom behaviors of children with learning disabilities. *Journal of Learning Disabilities, 7*(1), 35–43.

Bryan, T. S. (1976). Peer popularity of learning disabled children: A replication. *Journal of Learning Disabilities, 9,* 307–311.

Bryant, N. D., Drabin, I. R., and Gettinger, M. (1981). Effects of varying unit size on spelling ahcievement in learning disabled children. *Journal of Learning Disabilities, 14*(4), 200–203.

Buchanan, C. O. (1968). *Sullivan Associates programmed reading.* New York: Sullivan Press, Webster Division—McGraw-Hill.

Buckley, N., Siegel, L. S., and Ness, S. (1979). Egocentrism, empathy, and altruistic behavior in children. *Developmental Psychology, 15*(3), 329–330.

Budoff, M., Thormann, J., and Gras, A. (1984). *Microcomputers in special education.* Cambridge, Mass.: Brookline Books.

Bulgren, J. A. (in progress). *Models for concept teaching routines.* Lawrence, Kans.: University of Kansas, Institute for Research in Learning Disabilities.

Bulgren, J., Schumaker, J. B., and Deshler, D. D. (1988). Effectiveness of a concept teaching routine in enhancing the performance of LD students in secondary-level mainstream classes. *Learning Disability Quarterly, 11,* 3–17.

Bullock, J., Pierce, S., Strand, L., and Branine, K. (1981). *Touch math teachers manual.* Colorado Springs, Colo.

Camarata, S. M., Hughes, C. A., and Ruhl, K. L. (1988). Mild/moderate behaviorally disordered students: A population at risk for language disorders. *Language, Speech, and Hearing Services in Schools, 19,* 191–200.

Cambourne, B. (1988). *The whole story: Natural learning and the acquisition of literacy in the class-room.* Auckland, N.Z.: Ashton Scholastic.

Camp, B. W., and Bash, M. A. S. (1981). *The think aloud series: Increasing social and cognitive skills.* Champaign, Ill: Research Press.

Camp, B. W., Blom, G. E., Herbert, F., and Van Doorninck, W. J. (1977). "Think around": A program for developing self-control in young aggressive boys. *Journal of Abnormal Child Psychology, 5,* 157–169.

Campione, J., Brown, A., and Ferrara, R. (1982). Mental retardation and intelligence. In R. J. Sternberg (Ed.), *Handbook of human intelligence.* New York: Cambridge University Press, pp. 392–473.

Carbo, M. (1978). Teaching reading with talking books. *The Reading Teacher, 32,* 267–273.

Carman, R. A., and Adams Jr., W. R. (1972). *Study skills: A student's guide for survival.* New York: Wiley.

Carnine, D. (1989). Teaching complex content to learning disabled students: The role of technology. *Exceptional Children, 55,* 524–533.

Carnine, D., Silbert, J., and Kameenui, E. J. (1990). *Direct instruction reading* (2nd ed.). Columbus, Ohio: Merrill.

Carpenter, R. L. (1985). Mathematics instruction in resource rooms: Instruction time and teacher competence. *Learning Disability Quarterly, 8,* 95–100.

Carpenter, D., and Miller, L. J. (1982). Spelling ability of reading disabled LD students and able readers. *Learning Disability Quarterly, 5*(1), 65–70.

Carr, E., and Ogle, D. (1987). K-W-L plus: A strategy for comprehension and summarization. *Journal of Reading, 30,* 626–631.

Carrier, C. A. (1983). Notetaking research: Implications for the classroom. *Journal of Instructional Development, 6*(3), 19–25.

Carrier, C. A., and Newell, K. (1983). *What dental hygiene undergraduates think about notetaking in lecture classes: Report of a survey.* Unpublished manuscript, University of Minnesota, Minneapolis.

Carroll, J. (1964) *Language and thought.* Englewood Cliffs, N.J.: Prentice-Hall.

Carrow, E. (1973). *Test of auditory comprehension of language.* Austin, Tex.: Urban Research Group.

Cawley, J. F. (1984). An integrative approach to needs of learning disabled children: Expanded use of mathematics. In J. F. Cawley (Ed.), *Developmental teaching of mathematics for the learning disabled.* Rockville, Md.: Aspen.

Cawley, J., Fitzmaurice, A. M., Sedlak, R., and Althaus, V. (1976) *Project math.* Tulsa, Okla.: Educational Progress.

Cawley, J. F. and Miller, J. H. (1986). Selected views on metacognition, arithmetic problem solving, and learning disabilities. *Learning Disabilities Focus, 2*(1), 36–48.

Cawley, J. F., and Miller, J. H. (1989). Cross-sectional comparisons of the mathematical performance of children with learning disabilities: Are we on the right track toward comprehensive programming? *Journal of Learning Disabilities, 22,* 250–254, 259.

Chaffin, J. D., Maxwell, B., and Thompson, B. (1982). ARC-ED curriculum: The applications of video game formats to educational software. *Exceptional Children, 49,* 173–178.

Chalfant, J. C. (1987). Providing services to all students with learning problems: Implications for policy and programs. In S. Vaughn and C. Bos (Eds.), *Research in learning disabilities: Issues and future trends.* Boston: College-Hill, Little Brown, pp. 239–251.

Chalfant, J. C. (1989). Learning disabilities: Policy issues and promising approaches. *American Psychologist, 44,* 392–398.

Chalfant, J. C., and Pysh, M. V. (November 1981). Teacher assistance teams: A model for within-building problem solving. *Counterpoint.*

Chalfant, J. C., and Pysh, J. (1983). Teacher assistance teams. In C. Collin (Ed.), *Keys to success.* Monographs of the Michigan ACLD Conference. Garden City, Mich.: Quality Printers.

Chalfant, J. C., and Pysh, M. V. (1989). Teacher assistance teams: Five descriptive studies on 96 teams. *Remedial and Special Education, 10*(6), 49–58.

Chalfant, J. C., and Pysh, M. V. (in press). Teacher assistance teams: Implications for the gifted. In C. J. Maker (Ed.), *Critical issues in gifted education: Vol III—Gifted students in the regular classroom.* Austin, Tex.: Pro-Ed.

Chalfant, J. C., Pysh, M. V., and Moultrie, R. (1979). Teacher assistance teams: A model for within-building problem solving. *Learning Disability Quarterly, 2,* 85–96.

Chall, J. S. (1983). *Learning to read: The great debate* (2nd ed.), New York: McGraw-Hill.

Chapman, J. W., and Boersman, F. J. (1980). *Affective correlates of learning disabilities*. Lisse: Swets & Zeitlinger.

Cheek, E. H., and Lindsey, J. D. (1986). Principal's roles and teacher conflict: A recapitulation. *Journal of Learning Disabilities, 19*(5), 280–284.

Cherkes-Julkowski, M. (1985). Metacognitive considerations in mathematics for the learning disabled. In J. Cawley (Ed.), *Cognitive strategies and mathematics for the learning disabled*. Rockville, Md.: Aspen.

Chiang, B., Thorpe, H. W., and Lubke, M. (1984). LD students tackle the LOGO language: Strategies and implications. *Journal of Learning Disabilities, 17*, 303–304.

Chomsky, C. (1969). *The acquisition of syntax in children from 5 to 10*. Cambridge, Mass.: MIT Press.

Chomsky, C. (1972). Stages in language development and reading exposure. *Harvard Educational Review, 42*, 1–33.

Chomsky, C. (1976). After decoding: What? *Language Arts, 53*, 288–296.

Christian, B. T. (1983). A practical reinforcement hierarchy for classroom behavior modification. *Psychology in the Schools, 20*, 83–84.

Clark, F. L., Deshler, D. D., Schumaker, J. B., Alley, G. R., and Warner, M. M. (1984). Visual imagery and self-questioning: Strategies to improve comprehension of written materials. *Journal of Learning Disabilities, 17*(3), 145–149.

Clark, K. B. (1980). Empathy: A neglected topic in psychological research. *American Psychologist, 35*(2), 187–190.

Clay, M. M. (1982). *Observing young readers*. Portsmouth, N.H.: Heinemann.

Clay, M. M. (1985). *The early detection of reading difficulties* (3rd ed.). Portsmouth, N.H.: Heinemann.

Clay, M. M. (1989). Concepts about print in English and other languages. *The Reading Teacher, 42*, 268–275.

Clay, M. M., and Watson, B. (1987). *Reading Recovery book list*. Auckland, New Zealand: University of Auckland.

Clements, D. H. (1985). Research on Logo in education: Is the turtle slow but steady, or not even in the race? *Computers in the Schools, 2*(2/3), 55–71.

Clements, D. H. (1986). Logo programming in the early grades; Research and implications. In J. L. Hoot (Ed.), *Computers in early childhood education: Issues and practices*. Englewood Cliffs, N.J.: Prentice-Hall, pp. 174–197.

Coffland, J. A., and Baldwin, R. S. (1985). *Wordmath*. St. Louis: Milliken.

Cohen, M. W. (1986). Intrinsic motivation in the special education classroom. *Journal of Learning Disabilities, 19*(5), 258–261.

Cohen, V. B. (January 1983). Criteria for the evaluation of microcomputer courseware. *Educational Technology*, 9–14.

Coie, J. D., Dodge, K. A., and Coppotelli, H. (1982). Dimensions and types of social status: A cross-age perspective. *Developmental Psychology, 18*, 557–570.

Cooley, E. J., and Ayres, R. R. (1988). Self-concept and success-failure attributions of nonhandicapped students and students with learning disabilities. *Journal of Learning Disabilities, 21*(3), 174–178.

Cosden, M. A., Gerber, M. M., Semmel, D. S., Goldman, S. R., and Semmel, M. I., (1987). Microcomputer use within micro-educational environments. *Exceptional Children, 53*, 399–409.

Coterell, G. (1972). A case of severe learning disability. *Remedial Education, 7*, 5–9.

Cronbach, L., and Snow, R. (1977). *Aptitudes and instructional methods*. New York: Irvington Press.

Cullinan, B. E. (Ed.) (1987). *Children's literature in the reading program*. Newark, Del.: International Reading Association.

Cummings, R. W., and Maddux, C. D. (1985). *Parenting the learning disabled: A realistic approach*. Springfield, Ill.: Charles C. Thomas.

Cummins, J. (1981). Age on arrival and immigrant second language learning in Canada: A reassessment. *Applied Linguistics, 2*, 132–149.

Cummins, J. (1983). Bilingualism and special education: Program and pedological issues. *Learning Disability Quarterly, 6*(4), 373–386.

Cummins, J. (1984). *Bilingualism and special education: Issues in assessment and pedagogy*. San Diego, Calif.: College Hill.

Cummins, J. (1989). A theoretical framework for bilingual special education. *Exceptional Children, 56*, 111–119.

Cunningham, P. (1979). Beginning reading without readiness: Structured language experience. *Reading Horizons, 11*, 222–227.

Dale, E. (1966). The art of reading. *The Newsletter, 32*, 1–4.

Dale, E., and Chall, J. (February 1948). A formula for predicting readability. *Educational Research Bulletin, 27*, 37–54.

Darch, C., and Carnine, D. (1986). Teaching content area to learning disabled students. *Exceptional Children, 53*, 240–246.

Davison, A. (1984). Readability formulas and comprehension. In G. G. Duffy, L. R. Roehler, and J. Mason, (Eds.), *Comprehension instruction: Perspective and suggestions.* New York: Longman, pp. 128–143.

Deese, J., and Deese, E. K. (1979). *How to study* (3rd ed. rev.). New York: McGraw-Hill.

DeFeo, A. B., Grimm, D. D., and Paige, P. A. (1987). *Making conversation idiomatic.* Tucson, Ariz.: Communication Skill Builders.

Delquadri, J., Greenwood, C. R., Whorton, D., Carta, J. J., and Hall, R. V. (1986). Classwide peer tutoring. *Exceptional Children, 52*(6), 535–542.

DeMaster, V. K., Crossland, C. L., and Hasselbring, T. S. (1986). Consistency of learning disabled students' spelling performance. *Learning Disability Quarterly, 9*, 89–96.

Dembinski, R. J., and Mauser, A. J. (1977). What parents of the learning disabled really want from professionals. *Journal of Learning Disabilities, 10*(9), 49–55.

Deno, S. L. (1985). Curriculum-based measurement: The emerging alternative. *Exceptional Children, 52*, 219–232.

Deshler, D. D., and Schumaker, J. B. (1986). Learning strategies: An instructional alternative for low-achieving adolescents. *Exceptional Children, 52*, 583–590.

Deshler, D. D., and Schumaker, J. B. (1990). *Learning strategies model* (training package). Lawrence: University of Kansas, Institute for Research in Learning Disabilities.

Deshler, D. D., Schumaker, J. B., Alley, G. R., Clark, F. L., and Warner, M. M. (1981). *Multipass: A learning strategy for improving reading comprehension.* Unpublished manuscript, University of Kansas, Institute for Research in Learning Disabilities, Lawrence, Kans.

Deshler, D. D., Warner, M. M., Schumaker, J. B., and Alley, G. R. (1983). Learning strategies intervention model: Key components and current status.

In J. D. McKinney and L. Feagans (Eds.), *Current topics in learning disabilities* (Vol. 1). Norwood, N.J.: Ablex, pp. 245–283.

de Villiers, J., and de Villiers, P. (1978). *Language acquisition.* Cambridge, Mass.: Harvard University Press.

Devine, T. G. (1978). Listening: What do we know about fifty years of research and theorizing? *Journal of Reading, 21*, 296–304.

Devine, T. G. (1987). *Teaching study skills: A guide for teachers* (2nd ed.). Boston: Allyn and Bacon.

Diaz, S., Moll., L. C., and Mehan, H. (1986). Sociocultural resources in instruction: A context-specific approach. In *Beyond language: Social and cultural factors in schooling language minority students.* Sacramento, Calif.: Bilingual Education Office, California State Department of Education, pp. 187–229.

Dixon, M. E. (1983). *Questioning strategy instruction: Participation and reading comprehension of learning disabled students.* Unpublished doctoral dissertation, University of Arizona, Tucson.

Donahue, M., Pearl, R., and Bryan, T. (1980). Learning disabled children's conversational competence: Responses in inadequate messages. *Applied Psycholinguistics, 1*, 387–403.

Dorval, B., McKinney, J. D., and Feagans, L. (1982). Teacher interaction with learning disabled children and average achievers. *Journal of Pediatric Psychology, 7*(3), 317–330.

Doyle, W. (1979). Making managerial decisions in classrooms. In D. L. Duke (Ed.), *Classroom management.* Seventy-eighth yearbook of the National Society for the Study of Education, Part 2. Chicago: University of Chicago Press.

Doyle, W. (1986). Classroom organization and management. In M. C. Wittrock (Ed.), *Handbook of research on teaching* (3rd ed). New York: Macmillan, pp. 392–431.

Dreher, M. J., and Singer, H. (1980). Story grammar instruction is unnecessary for intermediate grade students. *The Reading Teacher, 34*, 261–268.

Dudley-Marling, C. C., Snider, V., and Tarver, S. G. (1982). Locus of control and learning disabilities: A review and discussion. *Perceptual and Motor Skills, 54*(2), 503–514.

Duffy, G. G., and McIntyre, L. D. (1982). A naturalistic study of instructional assistance in primary-grade reading. *Elementary School Journal, 83*(1), 15–23.

Duke, D. L., and Meckel, A. M. (1980). *Managing student behavior problems*. New York: Teachers College Press, Columbia University.

Dunn, L. M., Smith, J. O., Dunn, L. M., Horton, K. B., and Smith, D. D. (1981). *Peabody language development kits* (Rev. ed.). Circle Pines, Minn.: American Guidance Service.

Duran, R. P. (1989). Assessment and instruction of at-risk Hispanic students. *Exceptional Children, 56*, 154–159.

Durkin, D. D. (1966). *Children who read early: Two longitudinal studies*. New York: Teachers College Press.

Durkin, D. D. (1978–79). What classroom observations reveal about reading comprehension instruction. *Reading Research Quarterly, 14*(4), 481–533.

Durkin, D. D. (1983). What classroom observations reveal about reading comprehension instruction. In L. M. Gentile, M. L. Kamil, and J. S. Blanchard (Eds.), *Reading research revisited*. Columbus, Ohio: Merrill.

Durkin, D. D. (1987). *Teaching young children to read* (4th ed.). Boston: Allyn and Bacon.

D'Zurilla, T., and Goldfired, M. (1971). Problem solving and behavior modification. *Journal of Applied Psychology, 78*, 107–129.

Earle, R. (1969). Developing and using study guides. In H. L. Herber and P. L. Sanders (Eds.), *Research in reading in the content areas: First report*. Syracuse, N.Y.: Syracuse University, Reading and Language Arts Center.

Earle, R. A. (1970). *The use of vocabulary as a structured overview in seventh grade mathematics classes*. Unpublished doctoral dissertation, Syracuse University. Syracuse, N.Y.

Ehri, L. C. (1989). The development of spelling knowledge and its role in reading acquisition and reading disability. *Journal of Learning Disabilities, 22*(6), 356–365.

Ellis, E., Deshler, D., Lenz, K., Schumaker, J., and Clark, F. (in press). An instructional model for teaching learning strategies. *Focus on Exceptional Children*.

Ellis-Weismer, S., and Murray-Branch, J. (1989). Modeling vs. modeling plus evoked production training: A comparison of two language intervention methods. *Journal of Speech and Hearing Disorders, 54*, 269–281.

Emmer, E., Evertson, C., and Anderson, L. (1980). Effective classroom management at the beginning of the school year. *Elementary School Journal, 80*(5),219–231.

Engelhardt, Ashlock, and Wiebe (1984). *Helping children understand and use numerals*. Boston: Allyn and Bacon, pp. 89–149.

Engelmann, S., with Johnson, G., Hanner, S., Carinie, L., Meyers, L., Osborn, S., Haddox, P., Becker, W., Osborn, J., and Becker, J. (1988). *Corrective reading* (Chicago: Science Research Associates.

Engelmann, S., Becker, W. C., Hanner, S., and Johnson, G. (1978). *Corrective reading: Series guide*. Chicago: Science Research Associates.

Engelmann, S., and Bruner, E. C. (1973–75). *Distar reading I–III*. Chicago: Science Research Associates.

Engelmann, S., and Bruner, E. C. (1983). *Reading mastery: DISTAR reading storybook 2*. Chicago: Science Research Associates.

Engelmann, S., Bruner, E. C., Hanner, S., Osborn, J., Osborn, S., and Zoref, L. (1983–84). *Reading mastery*. Chicago: Science Research Associates.

Engelmann, S., and Carnine, D. (1972). *DISTAR arithmetic level I*. Chicago: Science Research Associates.

Engelmann, S., and Carnine, D. (1975). *DISTAR arithmetic level I*. Chicago: Science Research Associates.

Engelmann, S., and Carnine, D. (1976). *DISTAR arithmetic level II*. Chicago, Science Research Associates.

Engelmann, S., and Carnine, D. (1982). *Corrective mathematics program*. Chicago: Science Research Associates.

Engelmann, S., and Osborn, J. (1987). *DISTAR language I* (2nd ed.). Chicago: Science Research Associates.

Englert, C. S., and Raphael, T. E. (1988). Constructive well-formed prose: Process, structure, and metacognitive knowledge. *Exceptional Children, 54*, 513–520.

Englert, C. S., Raphael, T. E., Fear, K. L., and Anderson, L. M. (1988). Students' metacognitive knowledge about how to write informational texts. *Learning Disability Quarterly, 11*, 18–46.

Epstein, M. H., Cullinan, D., and Nieminen, G. (1984). Social behavior problems of learning disabled and normal girls. *Journal of Learning Disabilities, 17,* 609–611.

Erickson, R., and Schultz, J. (1981). When is a context? Some issues and methods in the analysis of social competence. In J. L. Green and C. Wallat (Eds.), *Ethnography and language in educational settings.* Norwood, N. J.: Ablex.

Estes, T. J., and Vaughan, J. L. (1978). *Reading and learning in the content classroom: Diagnostic and instructional strategies.* Boston: Allyn and Bacon.

Evans, S. (1980). The consultant role of the resource teacher. *Exceptional Children, 46*(5), 402–404.

Farrell, M. L., and Kaczka, A. (1988). Integrating the computer into resource room instruction. *Computers in the Schools, 5,* 213–223.

Ferguson, D. L. (1984). Parent advocacy network. *The Exceptional Parent, 14*(2), 41–45.

Fernald, G. M. (1943). *Remedial techniques in basic school subjects.* New York: McGraw-Hill.

Fernald, G. M. (1988). *Remedial techniques in basic school subjects.* (L. Idol, Ed.). Austin, Tex.: Pro-Ed (original edition 1943).

Feshbach, N. D. (1975). Empathy in children: Some theoretical and empirical considerations. *The Counseling Psychologist, 5*(2), 25–30.

Fisher, F. (1983). Spelling by speech synthesis: A new technology for an old problem. *Journal of Learning Disabilities, 16,* 368–369.

Fisher, J. L., and Harris, M. B. (1973). Effect of notetaking and review on recall. *Journal of Educational Psychology, 65*(3), 321–325.

Fitzsimmons, R. J., and Loomer, B. M. (1977). *Spelling: Learning and instruction—Research and practice.* Iowa City: University of Iowa.

Flavell, J. H. (1976). Metacognitive aspects of problem solving. In L. B. Resnick (Ed.), *The nature of intelligence.* Hillsdale, N.J.: Erlbaum.

Fleischner, J. E., Nuzum, M. G., and Marzola, E. S. (1987). Devising an instructional program to teach arithmetic problem-solving skills to students with learning disabilities. *Journal of Learning Disabilities, 20*(4), 214–217.

Fletcher, J. M. (1989). Nonverbal learning disabilities and suicide: Classification leads to prevention. *Journal of Learning Disabilities, 22,* 176–179.

Fletcher, R. J., and Rosenberger, N. (1987). Beware of tapping pencils. *Arithmetic Teacher, 34*(5), 6–10.

Fokes, J. (1984). *Fokes sentence builder.* Allen, Tex.: DLM.

Foster, S. L., and Ritchey, W. C. (1979). Issues in the assessment of social competence in children. *Journal of Applied Behavioral Analysis, 12,* 625–631.

Fowler, G. L., and Davis, M. (1985). The story frame approach: A tool for improving reading comprehension of EMR children. *Teaching Exceptional Children, 17*(4), 296–298.

Fowler, S. A. (1986). Peer-monitoring and self-monitoring: Alternatives to traditional teacher management. *Exceptional Children, 52*(6), 573–582.

Fox, B., and Routh, D. K. (1980). Phonemic analysis and severe reading disability in children. *Journal of Psycholinguistic Research, 9,* 115–119.

Fox, C. (1989). Peer acceptance of learning disabled children in the regular classroom. *Exceptional Children, 56*(1), 50–57.

Frayer, D. A., Frederick, W. C., and Klausmeier, H. J. (1969). *A schema for testing the level of concept mastery* (Working Paper No. 16). Madison: University of Wisconsin, Wisconsin Research and Development Center for Cognitive Learning.

Freire, P. (1985). Reading the world and reading the word: An interview with Paulo Freire. *Language Arts, 62*(1), 15–21.

Friend, M. (1984). Consultation skills for resource teachers. *Learning Disability Quarterly, 7*(3), 246–250.

Fries, C. C. (1963). *Linguistics and reading.* New York: Holt, Rinehart and Winston.

Frith, G. H., and Armstong, W. W. (1986). Self-monitoring for behavior disordered students. *Teaching Exceptional Children, 18*(2), 144–148.

Frith, U. (1980). *Cognitive processes in spelling.* London: Academic Press.

Fry, E. B. (1977). Fry's readability graph: Clarifications, validity, and extension to level 17. *Journal of Reading, 21,* 242–252.

Fry, E. B., Fountoukidis, D. L., Polk, J. K. (1985). *The new reading teacher's book of lists.* Englewood Cliffs, N.J.: Prentice-Hall.

Fuchs, L. S., Bahr, C. M., and Rieth, H. J. (1989). Effects of goal structures and performance contingencies on the math performance of adolescents with learning disabilities. *Journal of Learning Disabilities, 22,* 554–560.

Fuchs, L., Deno, S., and Mirkin, P. (1984). The effects of frequent, curriculum-based measurement and evaluation on pedagogy, student achievement, and student awareness of learning. *American Educational Research Journal, 21,* 449–460.

Gaffney, J. S., and Anderson, R. C. (in press). Two-tiered scaffolding: Congruent processes of teaching and learning. In E. H. Hiebert (Ed.), *Literacy for a diverse society.* New York: Teachers College Press.

Gagne, R., and Briggs, L. (1979). *Principles of instructional design.* New York: Holt, Rinehart and Winston.

Garret, M. K., and Crump, W. D. (1980). Peer acceptance, teacher preference and self-appraisal of social status among learning disabled students. *Learning Disability Quarterly, 3,* 42–48.

Gelfand, D. M., and Hartmann, D. P. (1984). *Child behavior analysis and therapy* (2nd ed.). New York: Pergamon Press.

Gerber, M., and Kauffman, J. (1981). Peer tutoring in academic settings. In P. Strain (Ed.), *Utilization of classroom peers as behavior change agents.* New York: Plenum Press, pp. 155–187.

German, D. (1979). Word-finding skills in children with learning disabilities. *Journal of Learning Disabilities, 12,* 176–181.

German, D. (1982). Word-finding substitutions in children with learning disabilities. *Language, Speech, and Hearing Services in Schools, 13,* 223–230.

Gettinger, M. (1984). Applying learning principles to remedial spelling instruction. *Academic Therapy, 20*(1), 41–48.

Gettinger, M., Bryant, M. D., and Fayne, H. R. (1982). Designing spelling instruction for learning disabled children: An emphasis on unit size, distributed practice, and training for transfer. *Journal of Special Education, 16*(4), 439–448.

Gibson, E. J. (1969). *Principles of perceptual learning and development.* New York: Appleton-Century-Crofts.

Gilbert, L., and Gilbert, D. (1944). The improvement of spelling through reading. *Journal of Educational Research, 37,* 458–463.

Gillingham, A., and Stillman, B. W. (1973). *Remedial training for children with specific disability in reading, spelling, and penmanship.* Cambridge, Mass.: Educators Publishing Service.

Ginther, D. W., and Williamson, J. D. (1985). Learning Logo: What is really learned? *Computers in the Schools, 2*(2/3), 73–78.

Glasser, W. (1965). *Reality therapy, a new approach to psychiatry* (1st ed.). New York: Harper & Row.

Gold, V. (1976). *The effect of an experimental program involving acquisition of phoneme-grapheme relationships incorporating criterion referenced tests with evaluative feedback upon spelling performance of third grade pupils.* Unpublished doctoral dissertation, University of Southern California, Los Angeles.

Goldman, S. R., and Pellegrino, J. W. (1987). Information processing and educational microcomputer technology: Where do we go from here? *Journal of Learning Disabilities, 20,* 144–154.

Goldman, S. R., Semmel, D. S., Cosden, M. A., Gerber, M. M., and Semmel, M. I. (1987). Special education administrators' policies and practices on microcomputer acquisition, allocation, and access for mildly handicapped children: Interfaces with regular education. *Exceptional Children, 53,* 330–339.

Goodlad, J. I. (1976). *Facing the future: Issues in education and schooling.* New York: McGraw-Hill.

Goodman, K. S. (1967). Reading: A psycholinguistic guessing game. *Journal of the Reading Specialist, 6,* 126–135.

Goodman, K. S. (1984). Unity in reading. In A. C. Purves and O. Niles (Eds.), *Becoming readers in a complex society.* Eighty-third yearbook of the National Society for the Study of Education. Chicago: University of Chicago Press, pp. 79–114.

Goodman, K. (1986). *What's whole in whole language?* Portsmouth, N.H.: Heinemann.

Goodman, K. S., and Goodman, Y. M. (1982). A whole language comprehension centered view of reading development. In L. Reed and S. Ward (Eds.), *Basic skills: Issues and choices* (Vol. 2). St. Louis, Mo.: CEMREL, pp. 125–134.

Goodman, K. S., Goodman, Y. M., and Hood, W. J. (Eds.) (1989). *The whole language evaluation book.* Portsmouth, N.H.: Heinemann.

Goodman, K. S., Smith, E. G., Meredith, R., and Goodman, Y. M. (1987). *Language and thinking in school: A whole-language curriculum* (3rd ed.). New York: Richard C. Owen.

Goodstein, H. A. (1981). Are the errors we see the true errors? Error analysis in verbal problem solving. *Topics in Learning and Learning Disabilities, 1*(3), 31–45.

Gottlieb, J., Alter, M., and Gottlieb, B. W. (1983). Mainstreaming mentally retarded children. In J. L. Matson and J. A. Mulich (Eds.), *Handbook of mental retardation,* New York: Pergamon, pp. 67–77.

Graham, S. (1983). The effect of self-instructional procedures on LD students' handwriting performance. *Learning Disability Quarterly, 6*(2), 231–244.

Graham, S., and Freeman, S. (1986). Strategy training and teacher- vs. student-controlled study conditions: Effects on LD students' spelling performance. *Learning Disability Quarterly, 9,* 15–22.

Graham, S., and Harris, K. R. (1988). Instructional recommendations for teaching writing to exceptional students. *Exceptional Children, 54,* 506–512.

Graham, S., and Harris, K. R. (1989a). Components analysis of cognitive strategy instruction: Effects on learning disabled students' compositions and self-efficacy. *Journal of Educational Psychology, 81,* 353–361.

Graham, S., and Harris, K. R. (1989b). Improving learning disabled students' skills at composing essays: Self-instructional strategy training. *Exceptional Children, 56,* 201–214.

Graham, S., and Miller, L. (1979). Spelling research and practice: A unified approach. *Focus on Exceptional Children, 12*(2), 1–16.

Graham, S., and Miller, L. (1980). Handwriting research and practice: A unified approach. *Focus on Exceptional Children, 13*(2), 1–16.

Graves, A. W. (1986). Effects of direct instruction and metacomprehension training on finding main ideas. *Learning Disabilities Research, 1*(2), 90–100.

Graves, D. (1985). Personal correspondence.

Graves, D. H. (1983). *Writing: Teachers and children at work.* Portsmouth, N.H.: Heinemann Educational Books.

Graves, D. H. (1985). All children can write. *Learning Disability Focus, 1*(1), 36–43.

Graves, D. H., and Hansen, J. (1983). The author's chair. *Language Arts, 60,* 176–183.

Gray, B., and Ryan, B. (1973). *A language program for the nonlanguage child.* Champaign, Ill.: Research Press.

Greif, E. B., and Hogan, R. (1973). The theory and measurement of empathy. *Journal of Counseling Psychology, 20*(3), 280–284.

Gresham, F. M. (1982). Misguided mainstreaming: The case for social skills training with handicapped children. *Exceptional Children, 48,* 422–433.

Grice, H. P. (1975). Logic and conversation. In P. Cole and J. Morgan (Eds.), *Studies in syntax and semantics: Speech acts* (Vol. 3). New York: Academic Press.

Grimm, J. A., Bijou, S. W., and Parsons, J. A. (1973). A problem solving model for teaching remedial arithmetic to handicapped children. *Journal of Abnormal Child Psychology, 1,* 26–39.

Grottenthaler, J. A. (1970). *A comparison of the effectiveness of three programs of elementary school spelling.* Unpublished doctoral disseration, University of Pittsburgh.

Guerney, B. G. (1977). *Relationship enhancement: Skills training programs for therapy, problem prevention, and enrichment.* San Francisco: Jossey Bass.

Guice, B. M. (1969). The use of the cloze procedure for improving reading comprehension of college students. *Journal of Reading Behavior, 1,* 81–92.

Guszak, F. J. (1967). Teaching questioning and reading. *The Reading Teacher, 21,* 227–234, 252.

Guszak, F. J. (1972). *Diagnostic reading instruction in the elementary school.* New York: Harper & Row.

Guthrie, J. T., Burnham, N. A., Caplan, R. I., and Seifert, M. (1974). The maze technique to assess and monitor reading comprehension. *The Reading Teacher, 28,* 161–168.

Hagen, D. (1984). *Microcomputer resource book for special education.* Reston, Va.: Reston Publishing.

Hagin, R. A. (1983). Write right or left: A practical approach to handwriting. *Journal of Learning Disabilities, 16*(5), 266–271.

Hall, R. V. (1975). *Behavior modification: Basic principles, managing behavior (Part 2)* (Rev. ed.). Lawrence, Kans.: H & H Enterprises.

Hallahan, D. P., Hall, R. J., Ianna, S. O., Kneedler, R. D., Lloyd, J. W., Loper, A. B., and Reeve, R. E. (1983). Summary of research findings at the University of Virginia Learning Disabilities Research Institute. *Exceptional Education Quarterly, 4*(1), 95–114.

Hallahan, D. P., Keller, C. E., McKinney, J. D., Lloyd, J. W., and Bryan, T. (1988). Examining the research base of the regular education initiative: Efficacy studies and the adaptive learning environments model. *Journal of Learning Disabilities, 21,* 29–34, 55.

Hallahan, D. P., Lloyd, J., Kosiewicz, M. M., Kauffman, J. M., and Graves, A. W. (1979). Self-monitoring of attention as a treatment for learning disabled boy's off-task behavior. *Learning Disability Quarterly, 2,* 24–32.

Hallahan, D. P., Tarver, S. G., Kauffman, J. M., and Graybeal, N. L. (1978). A comparison of the effects of reinforcement and response cost on the selective attention of learning disabled children. *Journal of Learning Disabilities, 11*(7), 430–438.

Halliday, M. (1975). *Learning how to mean: Explorations in the development of language.* London: Edward Arnold.

Halliday, M. A. K., and Hassan, R. (1976). *Cohesion in English.* London: Longman.

Halpern, N. (1981). Mathematics for the learning disabled. *Journal of Learning Disabilities, 14*(9), 505–506.

Hanover, S. (1983). Handwriting comes naturally? *Academic Therapy, 18,* 407–412.

Hansen, J. (1981). The effect of inference training and practice on young children's reading comprehension. *Reading Research Quarterly, 16*(3), 391–417.

Hansen, J. (1985). Skills. In J. Hansen, T. Newkirk, and D. Graves (Eds.), *Breaking ground: Teachers relate reading and writing in the elementary school,* Portsmouth, N.H.: Heinemann, pp. 147–168.

Hansen, J., and Hubbard, R. (1984). Poor readers can draw inferences. *The Reading Teacher, 37*(7), 586–590.

Hansen, J., Newkirk, T., and Graves, D. (Eds.). (1985). *Breaking ground: Teachers relate reading and writing in the elementary school.* Portsmouth, N.H.: Heinemann.

Hansen, J., and Pearson, P. D. (1983). An instructional study: Improving the inferential comprehension of good and poor fourth grade readers. *Journal of Educational Psychology, 75*(6), 821–829.

Haring, N. G., Liberty, K. A., and White, O. R. (1980). Rules for data-based strategy decisions in instructional programs. Current research and instructional implications. In W. Sailor, B. Wilcox, and L. Brown (Eds.), *Methods of instruction for severely handicapped students.* Baltimore: Paul H. Brookes.

Harris, A. J., and Sipay, E. R. (1985). *How to increase reading ability* (8th ed). New York: Longman.

Harris, K. R. (1982). Cognitive-behavior modification: Application with exceptional students. *Focus on Exceptional Children, 15*(2), 1–16.

Harris, K. R., (1985). Conceptual, methodological, and clinical issues in cognitive behavior assessment. *Journal of Abnormal Child Psychology, 13,* 373–390.

Harris, K. R., and Graham, S. (1985). Improving learning disabled students' composition skills: Self-control strategy training. *Learning Disability Quarterly, 8,* 27–36.

Harste, J. (1990). Jerry Harste speaks on reading and writing. *The Reading Teacher, 43,* 316–318.

Harste, J., Woodward, V., and Burke, C. (1984). *Language stories and literacy lessons.* Portsmouth, N.H.: Heinemann.

Hasselbring, T. S., Goin, L. I., and Bransford, J. D. (1988). Developing mathematics automaticity in learning handicapped children: The role of computerized drill and practice. *Focus on Exceptional Children, 20*(6), 1–7.

Hawton, K. (1982). Attempted suicide in children and adolescents. *Journal of Child Psychology and Psychiatry, 23*(4), 497–503.

Hazel, J. S., Schumaker, J. B., Sherman, J. A., and Sheldon-Wildgen, J. (1981). *ASSET: A social skills program for adolescents.* Champaign, Ill: Research Press.

Hazel, J. S., Schumaker, J. B., Sherman, J. A., and Sheldon, J. (1982). Application of a group training program in social skills and problem solving to learning disabled and non–learning disabled youth. *Learning Disability Quarterly, 5,* 398–409.

Heald-Taylor, G. (1987). How to use predictable books for K–2 language arts instruction. *The Reading Teacher, 40*(7), 656–663.

Heckelman, R. G. (1969). A neurological-impress method of remedial-reading instruction. *Academic Therapy Quarterly, 4,* 227–282.

Hembree, R. (1986). Research gives calculators a green light. *Arithmetic Teacher, 34*(1), 18–21.

Herman, P. A. (1985). The effect of repeated readings on reading rate, speech pauses, and word recognition memory. *Reading Research Quarterly, 20,* 553–574.

Herman, P. A., Anderson, R. C., Pearson, P. D., and Nagy, W. E. (1987). Incidental acquisition of word meaning from expositions with varied text features. *Reading Research Quarterly, 22,* 263–284.

Hirsch, E., and Niedermeyer, F. C. (1973). The effects of tracing prompts and discrimination training on kindergarten handwriting performance. *Journal of Education Research, 67*(2), 81–86.

Hofmann, R. (1985). Educational software: Evaluation? No! Utility? Yes! *Journal of Learning Disabilities, 18*, 358–360.

Hofmeister, A. (1982). Microcomputers in perspective. *Exceptional Children, 49*, 115–121.

Hofmeister, A. M., and Lubke, M. M. (1988). Expert systems: Implications for the diagnosis and treatment of learning disabilities. *Learning Disability Quarterly, 11*, 287–291.

Holdaway, D. (1979). *The foundations of literacy.* Portsmouth, N.H.: Heinemann.

Holland, A. (1975). Language therapy for children: Some thoughts on context and content. *Journal of Speech and Hearing Disorders, 40*, 514–523.

Hollingsworth, P. M. (1978). An experimental approach to the impress method of teaching reading. *The Reading Teacher, 24*, 112–114, 187.

Homan, D. R. (1970). The child with a learning disability in arithmetic. *The Arithmetic Teacher, 18*, 199–203.

Horn, E. (1937). *Methods of instruction in the social studies.* New York: Scribners.

Horowitz, E. C. (1981). Popularity decentering ability and role taking skills in learning disabled and normal children. *Learning Disability Quarterly, 4*, 23–30.

Horton, S. V., Lovitt, T. C., and Bergerud, D. (1990). The effectiveness of graphic organizers for three classifications of secondary students in content area classes. *Journal of Learning Disabilities, 23*, 12–22, 29.

Hoskins, B. (1987). *Conversations: Language intervention for adolescents.* Allen, Tex.: Developmental Learning Materials.

Hoskins, B. (1990). Language and literacy: Participating in the conversation. *Topics in Language and Language Disorders, 10*(2), 46–62.

Howe, M. L., Brainerd, C. J., and Kingma, J. (1985). Storage-retrieval process of normal and learning disabled children: A stages-of-learning analysis of picture-word effects. *Child Development, 56*, 1120–1133.

Howell, R. (1985). *Logo and kids: Some research findings.* Unpublished manuscript, Ohio State University, Columbus.

Howell, R., Sidorenko, E., and Jurica, J. (1987). The effects of computer use on the acquisition of multiplication facts by a learning disabled student. *Journal of Learning Disabilities, 20*, 336–341.

Hubbell, R. (1977). On facilitating spontaneous talking in young children. *Journal of Speech and Hearing Disorders, 42*, 216–231.

Hudson, P. J. (1987). *The pause procedure: A technique to help mildly handicapped students learn lecture content.* Unpublished doctoral dissertation, University of Florida, Gainesville.

Hughes, C. A., Schumaker, J. B., Deshler, D. D., and Mercer, C. D. (1988). *The test-taking strategy.* Lawrence, Kans.: Edge Enterprises.

Hummel, J. W., and Balcom, F. W. (1984). Microcomputers: Not just a place for practice. *Journal of Learning Disabilities, 17*, 432–434.

Hummel, J. W., Mather, N., and Senf, G. M. (1985). *Microcomputers in the classroom: Courseware reviews.* New York: Professional Press.

Hummel, J. W., and Senf, G. M. (1985). The courseware review process. *Journal of Learning Disabilities, 18*, 486–494.

Hunt, E. B. (1985). Verbal ability. In R. J. Sternberg (Ed.), *Human abilities: An information processing approach.* New York: Freeman, pp. 63–100.

Hunter, B. (1985). Problem solving with data bases. *The Computing Teacher, 12*(8), 20–27.

Hutton, J. B., and Palo, L. (1976). A sociometric study of learning disability children and type of teaching strategy. *Group Psychotherapy, Psychodrama and Sociometry, 29*, 113–121.

Idol, L., Paolucci-Whitcomb, P., and Nevin, A. (1986). *Collaborative consultation.* Austin, Tex.: Pro-Ed.

Idol, L. (1987a). A critical thinking map to improve content area comprehension of poor readers. *Remedial and Special Education, 8*(4), 28–40.

Idol, L. (1987b). Group story mapping: A comprehension strategy for both skilled and unskilled readers. *Journal of Learning Disabilities, 20*(4), 196–205.

Idol, L., and Croll, V. J. (1987). Story-mapping training as a means of improving reading comprehension. *Learning Disability Quarterly, 10*, 214–229.

Idol-Maestas, L. (1983). *Special educator's consultation handbook.* Rockville, Md.: Aspen.

Imber, S. C., Imber, S. C., and Rothstein, C. (1979). Modifying independent work habits: An effective teacher-parent communication program. *Exceptional Children, 46*, 218–221.

Isaacson, S. (1988). Assessing the writing product: Qualitative and quantitative measures. *Exceptional Children, 54,* 528–534.

Ives, J. P., Bursuk, L. Z., and Ives, S. A. (1979). *Word identification techniques.* Chicago: Rand McNally College Publishing.

Jackson, H. J., and Boag, P. G. (1981). The efficacy of self control procedures as motivational strategies with mentally retarded persons; A review of the literature and guidelines for future research. *Australian Journal of Developmental Disabilities, 7,* 65–79.

Jay, T. B. (January 1983). The cognitive approach to computer courseware design and evaluation. *Educational Technology,* 22–26.

Johns, J., and McNamara, L. (1980). The SQ3R study technique: A forgotten research target. *Journal of Reading, 23,* 705–708.

Johnson, D. D., and Baumann, J. F. (1984). Word identification. In P. D. Pearson (Ed.), *Handbook of reading research.* New York: Longman.

Johnson, D. D., and Pearson, P. D. (1984). *Teaching reading vocabulary* (2nd ed.). New York: Holt, Rinehart and Winston.

Johnson, D. D., Pittelman, S. D., and Heimlich, J. E. (1986). Semantic mapping. *The Reading Teacher, 39*(8), 778–783.

Johnson, D. J., and Myklebust, H. R. (1967). *Learning disabilities: Educational principles and practices.* New York: Grune & Stratton.

Johnson, D. W., and Johnson, R. T. (1975). *Learning together and alone.* Engelwood Cliffs, N.J.: Prentice-Hall.

Johnson, D. W., and Johnson, R. T. (1984a). Classroom learning structure and attitudes toward handicapped students in mainstream settings: a theoretical model and research evidence. In R. Jones (Ed.), *Special education in transition: Attitudes toward the handicapped.* Reston, Va.: ERIC Clearinghouse on Handicapped and Gifted Children, The Council for Exceptional Children.

Johnson, D. W., and Johnson, R. T. (1984b). Building acceptance of differences between handicapped and nonhandicapped students: The effects of cooperative and individualistic problems. *Journal of Social Psychology, 122,* 257–267.

Johnson, D. W., and Johnson, R. T. (1986). Mainstreaming and cooperative learning strategies. *Exceptional Children, 52*(6), 553–561.

Jones, D. J., Fox, M. M., Haroutun-Babigian, H. M., and Hutton, H. E. (1980). Epidemiology of anorexia nervosa in Monroe County, New York: 1960–1976. *Psychosomatic Medicine, 42*(6), 551–558.

Jones, K. M., Torgesen, J. K., and Sexton, M. A. (1987). Using computer guided practice to increase decoding fluency in learning disabled children: A study using the Hint and Hunt I program. *Journal of Learning Disabilities, 20,* 122–128.

Jongsma, E. (1971). *The cloze procedure as a teaching technique.* Newark, Del.: International Reading.

Jongsma, E. (1980). *Cloze instruction research: A second look.* Newark, Del.: International Reading.

Karlin, R. (1980). *Teaching elementary reading* (3rd ed.). New York: Harcourt Brace Jovanovich.

Kauffman, J. M. (1985). *Characteristics of children's behavior disorders* (3rd ed.). Columbus, Ohio: Merrill.

Kauffman, J., Hallahan, D., Haas, K., Brame, T., and Boren, R. (1978). Imitating children's errors to improve spelling performance. *Journal of Learning Disabilities, 11,* 33–38.

Kavale, K. A., and Forness, S. R. (1985). *The science of learning disabilities.* San Diego: College-Hill Press.

Kavanagh, J. F., and Truss, T. J., Jr. (1988). *Learning Disabilities: Proceedings of the National Conference.* Parkton, M.D.: York Press.

Keefe, C. H., and Candler, A. C. (1989) LD students and word processors: Questions and answers. *Learning Disabilities Focus, 4,* 78–83.

Keogh, B. K., and Donlon, G. McG. (1972). Field dependence, impulsivity, and learning disabilities. *Journal of Learning Disabilities, 5,* 331–336.

Keogh, B. K., Tchir, C., and Windeguth-Behn, A. (1974). Teachers' perceptions of educationally high risk children. *Journal of Learning Disabilities, 7,* 367–374.

Kimmel, M. M., and Segal, E. (1988). *For reading out loud:.* New York: Delacorte.

Kinney, G. C., Marsetta, M., and Showman, D. J. (1966). *Studies in display symbol legibility, Part XXI.* The legibility of alphanumeric symbols for digitized television (ESD-TR-66-117). Bedford, Mass.: Mitre Corporation.

Kintsch, W. (1974). *The representation of meaning in memory.* Hillsdale, N.J.: Erlbaum.

Kirk, R. N. (1986). Tape-recording poetry. *The Reading Teacher, 40*(2), 200–202.

Kirk, S. A., and Chalfant, J. C. (1984). *Academic and developmental learning disabilities.* Denver: Love.

Kirk, S. A., Kirk, W. D., and Minskoff, E. H. (1985). *Phonic remedial reading lessons.* Novato, Calif.: Academic Therapy Publications.

Kistner, J., and Osborne, M. (1987). A longitudinal study of LD children's self-evaluations. *Learning Disability Quarterly, 10,*(4), 258–266.

Klausmeier, J. H., and Sipple, T. S. (1980). *Learning and teaching process concepts: A strategy for testing applications for theory.* New York: Academic Press.

Kleiman, G., Humphrey, M., and Lindsay, P. H. (1981). Microcomputers and hyperactive children. *Creative Computing, 7*(3), 93–94.

Knight-Arest, I. (1984). Communicative effectiveness of learning disabled and normally achieving 10- to 13-year-old boys. *Learning Disability Quarterly, 7,* 237–245.

Kolligian, J., Jr., and Sternberg, R. J. (1987). Intelligence, information processing, and specific learning disabilities: A triarchic synthesis. *Journal of Learning Disabilities 20*(1), 8–17.

Kosc, L. (1981). Neuropsychological implications of diagnosis and treatment of mathematical learning disabilities. *Topics in Learning and Learning Disabilities, 1*(3), 19–30.

Koskinen, P. S., and Blum, I. H. (1985). Paired repeated reading: A classroom strategy for developing fluent reading. *The Reading Teacher, 40,* 70–75.

Kosiewicz, M. M., Hallahan, D. P., Lloyd, J. W., and Graves, A. W. (1982). Effects of self-instruction and self-correction procedures on handwriting performance. *Learning Disability Quarterly, 5*(1), 71–78.

Koziol, S. (1973). The development of noun plural rules during the primary grades. *Research in the Teaching of English, 7,* 30–50.

Krauss, R., and Glucksberg, S. (1967). The development of communication competence as a function of age. *Child Development, 40,* 255–260.

Kress, R. A., and Johnson, M. S. (1970). Martin. In A. J. Harris (Ed.), *Casebook on reading disability.* New York: David McKay, pp. 1–24.

Kreviski, J., and Linfield, J. L. (1974). *Bad speller's dictionary.* New York: Random House.

Kronik, D. (1977). A parent's thought for parents and teachers. In N. Haring and B. Bateman (Eds.), *Teaching the learning disabled child.* Englewood Cliffs, N.J.: Prentice-Hall.

Krug, R. S. (1983). Substance abuse. In C. E. Walker and McRoberts (Eds.), *Handbook of clinical child psychology.* New York: John Wiley, pp. 853–879.

Kucer, S. B. (1986). Helping writers get the "big picture." *Journal of Reading, 30*(1), 18–25.

LaBerge, D., and Samuels, S. J. (1974). Toward a theory of automatic information processing in reading. *Cognitive Psychology, 6,* 293–323.

Ladas, H. S. (1980). Notetaking on lectures: An information processing approach. *Educational Psychologist, 15*(1), 44–53.

LaGreca, A. M. (1981). Social behavior and social perception in learning-disabled children: A review with implications for social skills training. *Journal of Pediatric Psychology, 6,* 395–416.

LaGreca, A. M. (November 1982). Issues in the assessment of social skills with learning disabled children. In *Children's social skills: Future directions,* S. Beck (Chair). Paper presented at the annual meeting of the Association for the Advancement of Behavior Therapy, Los Angeles, Calif.

Langan, J. (1982). *Reading and study skills* (2nd ed.). New York: McGraw-Hill.

Langdon, H. W. (1989). Language disorder or difference? Assessing the language skills of Hispanic students. *Exceptional Children, 56,* 160–167.

Langer, J. A. (1981). From theory to practice: A prereading plan. *Journal of Reading, 25*(2), 152–156.

Langer, J. A. (1982). Facilitating text processing: The elaboration of prior knowledge. In J. A. Langer and M. T. Smith-Burke (Eds.), *Reader meets author: Bridging the gap.* Newark, Del.: International Reading Association, pp. 149–162.

Langer, J. A., and Nicolich, M. (1981). Prior knowledge and its effects on comprehension. *Journal of Reading Behavior, 13,* 375–378.

Lankford, F. G. (1974). *Some computational strategies in seventh grade pupils.* Unpublished manuscript, University of Virginia.

Larsen, S. C., Parker, R., and Trenholme, B. (1978). The effects of syntactic complexity upon arithmetic performance. *Learning Disability Quarterly, 1*(4), 80–85.

Legenza, A. (1974). *Questioning behavior of kindergarten children.* Paper presented at the 19th Annual Convention, International Reading Association.

Lenchner, O., Gerber, M. M., and Routh, D. K. (1990). Phonological awareness tasks as predictors of decoding ability: Beyond segmentation. *Journal of Learning Disabilities, 23,* 240–247.

Lenz, B. K. (1983). Promoting active learning through effective instruction: Using advance organizers. *Pointer, 27*(2), 11–13.

Lenz, B. K., Alley, G. R., and Schumaker, J. B. (1987). Activating the inactive learner: Advance organizers in the secondary content classroom. *Learning Disability Quarterly, 10*(10), 53–67.

Lenz, B. K., and Bulgren, J. A. (in press). Promoting learning in the content areas. In P. A. Cegelka and W. H. Berdine (Eds.), *Effective instruction for students with learning problems.* Boston: Allyn and Bacon.

Lenz, B. K., and Hughes, C. A. (1990). A word identification strategy for adolescents with learning disabilities. *Journal of Learning Disabilities, 23,* 149–158, 163.

Lenz, B. K., Schumaker, J. B., Deshler, D. D., and Beals, V. L. (1984). *The word identification strategy* (Learning Strategies Curriculum). Lawrence: University of Kansas.

Leon, J. A., and Pepe, H. J. (1983). Self-instructional training: Cognitive behavior modification for remediating arithmetic deficits. *Exceptional Children, 50*(1), 54–60.

Lerner, J. W. (1985). *Learning disabilities: Theories, diagnosis, and teaching strategies* (4th ed.). Boston: Houghton Mifflin.

Lewis, S. K., and Lawrence-Patterson, E. (1989). Locus of control of children with learning disabilities and perceived locus of control by significant others. *Journal of Learning Disabilities, 22,* 255–257.

Lewkowicz, N. K. (1980). Phonemic awareness training: What to teach and how to teach it. *Journal of Educational Psychology, 72,* 686–700.

Liberman, I., and Shankweiler, D. (1979). Speech, the alphabet, and teaching of reading. In L. Resnick and P. Weavers (Eds.), *Theory and practice in early reading* (Vol. 2). Hillsdale, N.J.: Erlbaum, pp. 109–132.

Liberman, I. Y., and Shankweiler, D. (1987). Phonology and the problems of learning to read and write. In H. L. Swanson (Ed.), *Advances in learning and behavioral disabilities* (Supplement 2). Greenwich, Conn.: JAI Press, pp. 203–224.

Lindfors, J. W. (1984). How children learn or how teachers teach? A profound confusion. *Language Arts, 61,* 600–614.

Link, D. (1980). *Essential learning skills and the low achieving student at the secondary level: A rating of the importance of 24 academic abilities.* Unpublished master's thesis, University of Kansas, Lawrence.

Lipscomb, S. D., and Zuanich, M. A. (1984). *Basic fun with adventure games.* New York: Avon Books.

Lloyd, J. W. (1980). Academic instruction and cognitive behavior modification: The need for attack strategy training. *Exceptional Educational Quarterly, 1*(1), 53–64.

Lloyd, J., Epstein, M. H., and Cullinan, D. (1981). Direct teaching for learning disabilities. In J. Gottlieb and S. Strickhart (Eds.), *Perspective on handicapping conditions: Current research and application in learning disabilities.* Baltimore, Md.: University Park Press.

Loban, W. (1976). *Language development: Kindergarten through grade twelve* (Res. Report #18). Urbana, Ill.: National Council of Teachers of English.

Lock, C. (1981). *Study skills.* West Lafayette, Ind.: Kappa Delta Pi.

Loftus, G., and Loftus, E. R. (1976). *Human memory.* Hillsdale, N.J.: Erlbaum.

Lorenz, L., and Vockell, E. (1979). Using the neurological impress method with learning disabled readers. *Journal of Learning Disabilities, 12,* 420–422.

Lovitt, T. C., and Curtiss, K. A. (1968). Effects of manipulating antecedent events on mathematics response rate. *Journal of Applied Behavior Analysis, 1,* 329–333.

Lundsteen, S. W. (1979). *Listening: Its impact on reading and the other language arts* (Rev. ed.). Urbana, Ill.: ERIC Clearinghouse on Reading and Communications Skills and the National Council of Teachers of English.

Luria, A. R. (1961). *The role of speech in the regulation of normal and abnormal behavior.* (J. Tizard, Trans.). New York: Liveright.

Lynch, E. W., and Stein, R. (1982). Perspectives on parent participation in special education. *Exceptional Education Quarterly, 3*(2), 56–63.

Lynch, P. (1986). *Big books and predictable books.* New York: Scholastic.

Lyon, G. R. (1985). Identification and remediation of learning disability subtypes: Preliminary findings. *Learning Disabilities Focus, 1,* 21–35.

MacArthur, C. (1984). Simulations in remedial and special education. *The Pointer, 28*(2), 36–39.

MacArthur, C. A. (1988). The impact of computers on the writing process. *Exceptional Children, 54,* 536–542.

MacArthur, C. A., and Schneiderman, B. (1986). Learning disabled students' difficulties in learning to use a word processor: Implications for instruction and software evaluation. *Journal of Learning Disabilities, 19,* 248–253.

MacWilliams, L. J. (1978). Mobility board games: Not only for rainy days. *Teaching Exceptional Children, 11*(1), 22–25.

Maddux, C. D. (1984). The educational promise of Logo. *Computers in the Schools, 1*(1), 79–89.

Maddux, C. D., and Cummings, R. E. (1985). BASIC, Logo, and Pilot: A comparison of three computer languages. *Computers in the Schools, 2*(2/3), 139–178.

Maddux, C. D., and Johnson, D. (1983). Microcomputers in LD: Boon or boondoggle? *Academic Therapy, 19,* 113–118.

Mager, R. F. (1975). *Preparing instructional objectives.* Belmont, Calif.: Fearon Publishing.

Mandler, J. M., and Johnson, N. S. (1977). Rememberance of things passed: Story structure and recall. *Cognitive Psychology, 9,* 111–151.

Mandoli, M., Mandoli, P., and McLaughlin, T. F. (1982). Effects of same-age peer tutoring on the spelling performance of a mainstreamed elementary learning disabled student. *Learning Disability Quarterly, 5*(2), 185–189.

Mann, V. A. (1986). Why some children encounter reading problems: The contribution of difficulties with language processing and phonological sophistication to early reading disability. In J. K. Torgesen and B. Y. L. Wong (Eds.), *Psychological and educational perspectives on learning disabilities.* Orlando, Fla.: Academic Press, pp. 133–159.

Mann, V. A., and Liberman, I. Y. (1984). Phonological awareness and verbal short-term memory. *Journal of Learning Disabilities, 17*(10), 592–599.

Manzo, A. V. (1969). The request procedure. *Journal of Reading, 13,* 123–126.

Manzo, A., and Manzo, U. (1990). *Content area reading: A heuristic approach.* Columbus, Ohio: Merrill.

Marcus, R. F., Tellen, S., and Roke, E. J. (1979). Relation between cooperation and empathy in young children. *Developmental Psychology, 15*(3), 346–349.

Markham, L. (1976). Influence of handwriting quality on teacher evaluation of written work. *American Educational Research Journal, 13,* 277–283.

Marsh, G. E., Price, B. J., and Smith, T. C. (1983). *Teaching mildly handicapped: Methods & materials.* St. Louis, Mo.: C. V. Mosby, pp. 243–249.

Martin, B., and Brogan, P. (1971). *Teachers guide to the instant readers.* New York: Holt, Rinehart and Winston.

Martin, B., with Brogan, P., and Archaumbault, J. (1990). *Sounds of language* (Reading Program). Allen, Tex.: DLM.

Martinez, M., and Teale, W. H. (1988). Reading in a kindergarten classroom library. *The Reading Teacher, 41,* 568–572.

Maria, K. (1989). Developing disadvantaged children's background knowledge interactively. *The Reading Teacher, 42,* 296–300.

Marvin, C. A. (1987). Consultation services: Changing roles for SLPs. *Journal of Childhood Communication Disorders, 11*(1), 1–15.

Mastropieri, M. A., and Scruggs, T. E. (1989). Reconstructive elaborations: Strategies that facilitate content learning. *Learning Disabilities Focus, 4,* 73–77.

Mastropieri, M. A., Scruggs, T. E., McLoone, B., and Levin, J. R. (1985). Facilitating learning disabled student's acquisition of science classification. *Learning Disability Quarterly, 8*(4), 299–309.

Mastropieri, M. A., Scruggs, T. E., and Mushinski Fulk, B. J. (1990). Teaching abstract vocabulary with the key word method: Effects on recall and comprehension. *Journal of Learning Disabilities, 23,* 92–96, 107.

Mather, N. (1986). Fantasy and adventure software with the learning disabled student. *Journal of Learning Disabilities, 19,* 56–58.

Mathinos, D. A. (April 1987). Communicative abilities of disabled and nondisabled children. Paper presented at the annual meeting of the Society for Research on Child Development, Baltimore, Md.

Mayer, R. E. (1979). Twenty years of research on advance organizers: Assimilation theory is still the best predictor of results. *Instructional Science, 8,* 133–167.

Mayer, S. B. (1982). Repeated reading. *Journal of Learning Disabilities, 15,* 619–623.

McConaughy, S. H., and Ritter, D. R. (1986). Social competence and behavioral problems in learning disabled boys ages 6–11. *Journal of Learning Disabilities, 19,* 39–45.

McDonough, K. M. (1989). Analysis of the expressive language characteristics of emotionally handicapped students in social interactions. *Behavior Disorders, 14,* 127–139.

McGregor, K. K., and Leonard, L. B. (1989). Facilitating word-finding skills of language-impaired children. *Journal of Speech and Hearing Disorders, 54,* 141–147.

McKeown, M. G., and Beck, I. L. (1988). Learning vocabulary: Different ways for different goals. *Remedial and Special Education, 9*(1), 42–52.

McKinney, J. D. (1984). The search for subtypes of specific learning disabilities. *Journal of Learning Disabilities, 17,* 43–51.

McKinney, J. D., and Hocutt, A. M. (1982). Public school involvement of parents of learning disabled and average achievers. *Exceptional Education Quarterly, 3*(2), 64–73.

McKinney, J. D., and Hocutt, A. M. (1988). Policy issues in the evaluation of the regular education initiative. *Learning Disabilities Focus, 4,* 15–23.

McKinney, J. D., McClure, S., and Feagans, L. (1982). Classroom behavior of learning disabled children. *Learning Disabilities Quarterly, 5,* 45–52.

McLean, J., and Snyder-McLean, L. (1978). *A transactional approach to early language training.* Columbus, Ohio: Merrill.

McLoone, B. B., Scruggs, T. E., Mastropieri, M. A., and Zucher, S. F. (1986). Memory strategy instruction and training with learning disabled adolescents. *Learning Disabilities Research, 2*(1), 45–53.

McNeill, D. (1970). *The acquisition of language: The study of developmental psycholinguistics.* New York: Harper & Row.

Meichenbaum, D. (1977). *Cognitive-behavior modification: An integrative approach.* New York: Plenum.

Meichenbaum, D. (1983). Teaching thinking: A cognitive-behavioral approach. In *Interdisciplinary voices in learning disabilities and remedial education.* Austin, Tex.: Pro-Ed.

Meichenbaum, D. (1985). *Stress inoculation training: A clinical guidebook.* Elmsford, N.Y.: Pergamon Press.

Meichenbaum, D., and Goodman, J. (1971). Training impulsive children to talk to themselves: A means of developing self-control. *Journal of Abnormal Psychology, 77,* 115–126.

Menyuk, P. (1969). *Sentences children use.* Cambridge, Mass.: MIT Press.

Menyuk, P. (1971). *The acquisition and development of language.* Englewood Cliffs, N.J.: Prentice-Hall.

Mercer, C. D., and Mercer, A. R. (1985). *Teaching students with learning problems* (2nd ed.). Columbus, Ohio: Merrill.

Mercer, C. D., Mercer, A. R., and Bott, D. A. (1984). *Self-correcting learning materials for the classroom.* Columbus, Ohio: Merrill.

Messerer, J., and Lerner, J. W. (1989). Word processing for learning disabled students. *Learning Disabilities Focus, 5*(1), 13–17.

Miller, G. A. (1956). The magical number seven, plus or minus two: Some limits on our capacity for processing information. *Psychological Review, 63,* 81–97.

Misspeller's Dictionary. (1983). New York: Simon & Schuster.

Moll, L. C., and Diaz, S. (1987). Teaching writing as communication: The use of ethnographic findings in classroom practice. In D. Bloome (Ed.), *Literacy and schooling.* Norwood, N.J.: Ablex, pp. 193–221.

Montague, M., and Bos, C. S. (1986a). Verbal math problem solving and learning disabilities: A review. *Focus on Learning Problems in Math, 8*(2), 7–21.

Montague, M., and Bos, C. S. (1986b). The effect of cognitive strategy training on verbal math problem solving performance of learning disabled adolescents. *Journal of Learning Disabilities, 19*(1), 26–33.

Montague, M., and Bos, C. S. (in press). Cognitive and metacognitive characteristics of eighth grade students' mathematical problem solving. *Learning and Individual Differences.*

Moore, J., and Fine, M. J. (1978). Regular and special class teacher' perceptions of normal and exceptional children and their attitudes toward mainstreaming. *Psychology in the Schools, 15*(2), 253–259.

Moran, M. (1980). *An investigation of the demands on oral language skills of learning disabled students in secondary classrooms* (Res. Rep. 1). Lawrence: University of Kansas, Institute for Research in Learning Disabilities.

Morgan, S. R. (1986). Locus of control in children labeled learning disabled, behaviorally disordered, and learning disabled/behaviorally disordered. *Learning Disabilities Research, 2,* 10–13.

Morocco, D. D., and Neuman, S. B. (1986). Word processors and the acquisition of writing strategies. *Journal of Learning Disabilities, 19,* 243–247.

Morrison, G. M. (1985). Differences in teacher perceptions and student self-perceptions for learning disabled and nonhandicapped learners in regular and special education settings. *Learning Disabilities Research, 1*(1), 32–41.

Murray, D. (1984). *Write to learn.* New York: Holt, Rinehart and Winston.

Murray, D. (1985). *A writer teaches writing.* Boston: Houghton Mifflin.

Muther, C. (1985). What every textbook evaluator should know. *Educational Leadership, 42,* 4–8.

Myers, C. A. (1978). Reviewing the literature on Fernald's technique of remedial reading. *Reading Teacher, 31,* 614–619.

Nagel, B. R., Schumaker, J. B., and Deshler, D. D. (1986). *The FIRST-letter mnemonic strategy* (Learning Strategies Curriculum). Lawrence, Kans.: Edge Enterprises.

National Council of Supervisors of Mathematics. (1977). *Position paper on basic mathematical skills.* Minneapolis, Minn.: National Council of Supervisors of Mathematics.

National Council of Teachers of Mathematics. (December 1974). NCTM board approves policy statement of the use of minicalculators in the mathematics classroom. *NCTM Newsletter,* p. 3.

National Research Council (1989). *Everybody counts: A report to the nation on the future of mathematics education.* Washington, D.C.: National Academy Press.

Neisser, U. (1967). *Cognitive psychology.* New York: Appleton.

Neisser, U. (1976). *Cognition and reality: Principles and implications of cognitive psychology.* San Francisco: Freeman.

Newland, E. (1932). An analytic study of the development of illegibilities in handwriting from the lower grades to adulthood. *Journal of Educational Research, 26,* 249–258.

Nippold, M. A. (Ed.) (1988). *Later language development: Ages nine through nineteen.* Boston: Little, Brown—College-Hill.

Nolan, S., Alley, G. R., and Clark, F. L. (1980). *Self-questioning strategy.* Lawrence: University of Kansas, Institute for Research in Learning Disabilities.

Novaco, R. (1975). *Anger control: The development and evaluation of an experimental treatment.* Lexington, Mass.: D. C. Heath.

Nulman, J. H., and Gerber, M. M. (1984). Improving spelling performance by imitating a child's errors. *Journal of Learning Disabilities, 17,* 328–333.

O'Connor, S. C., and Spreen, O. (1988). The relationship between parents' socioeconomic status and education level, and adult occupational and educational achievement of children with learning disabilities. *Journal of Learning Disabilities 21*(3), 148–153.

Ogle, D. M. (1986). K-W-L: A teaching model that develops active reading of expository text. *The Reading Teacher, 39,* 564–570.

Orback, S. (1986). *Hunger strike.* New York: Norton.

Osborn, S. (1984). *Reading mastery: Series guide.* Chicago: Science Research Associates.

O'Sullivan, J. T., and Pressley, M. (in press). Completeness of instruction and strategy transfer. *Journal of Experimental Child Psychology.*

Owens, R. E., Jr. (1988). *Language development: An introduction* (2nd ed.). Columbus, Ohio: Merrill.

Palincsar, A. S. (1982). Improving the reading comprehension of junior high students through the reciprocal teaching of comprehension-monitoring. Unpublished doctoral dissertation, University of Illinois, Urbana.

Palincsar, A. S. (1986). The role of dialogue in providing scaffolded instruction. *Educational Psychologist, 21*(1-2), 73–98.

Palincsar, A. S. (1988). *Reciprocal teaching instructional materials packet.* East Lansing, Mich.: Michigan State University.

Palincsar, A. S., and Brown, A. L. (1984). Reciprocal teaching of comprehension fostering and comprehension monitoring activities. *Cognition and Instruction, 1*(2), 117–175.

Palincsar, A. S., and Brown, A. L. (1986). Interactive teaching to promote independent learning from text. *The Reading Teacher, 39*(8), 771–777.

Palincsar, A. S., and Brown, D. A. (1987). Enhancing instructional time through attention to metacognition. *Journal of Learning Disabilities, 20*(2), 66–75.

Palmatier, R. A. (1971). Comparison of four note-taking procedures. *Journal of Reading, 14,* 235–240, 258.

Palmatier, R. A. (1973). A note-taking system for learning. *Journal of Reading, 17,* 36–39.

Papert, S. (1980). *Mindstorms.* New York: Basic Books.

Papert, S. (1986). New views on Logo. *Electronic Learning, 5*(7), 33–36, 63.

Paris, S. G., and Oka, E. R. (1986). Instruction and cognitive development: Coordinating communication and cues. *Exceptional Children, 53*(2), 109–117.

Parsons, J. A. (1972). The reciprocal modification of arithmetic behavior and program development. In G. Semb (Ed.), *Behavior analysis and education.* Lawrence, Kans.: University of Kansas, Department of Human Development.

Patterson, J. H., and Smith, M. S. (1986). The role of computers in higher-order thinking. In J. A. Culbertson and L. L. Cunningham (Eds.), *Microcomputers and education.* Eighty-fifth Yearbook of the National Society for the Study of Education. Chicago: University of Chicago Press, pp. 81–108.

Pattison, L. (1985). Software writing made easy. *Electronic Learning, 4*(6), 30–36.

Pauk, W. (1974). *How to study in college* (2nd ed.). Boston: Houghton Mifflin.

Pearson, P. D., Hansen, J., and Gordon, C. (1979). The effect of background knowledge on young children's comprehension of explicit and implicit information. *Journal of Reading Behavior, 11,* 201–219.

Pearson, P. D., and Johnson, D. D. (1978). *Teaching reading comprehension.* New York: Holt, Rinehart and Winston.

Pehrsson, R. S., and Robinson, H. A. (1985). *The semantic organizer approach to writing and reading instruction.* Rockville, Md.: Aspen.

Perlmutter, B. F. (1986). Personality variables and peer relations of children and adolescents with learning disabilities. In S. J. Ceci (Ed.), *Handbook of cognitive, social, and neuropsychological aspects of learning disabilities.* Hillsdale, N.J.: Erlbaum, pp. 339–359.

Personkee, C., and Yee, A. (1971). *Comprehensive spelling instruction: Theory, research, and application.* Scranton, Pa.: Intext Educational.

Peters, T., and Austin, N. (1985). *A passion for excellence.* New York: Random House.

Pinnell, G. S., DeFord, D. E., and Lyons, C. A. (1988). *Reading Recovery: Early intervention for at-risk first graders.* Arlington, Va.: Educational Research Service.

Pinnell, G. S., Fried, M. D., and Estice, R. M. (1990). Reading Recovery: Learning how to make a difference. *The Reading Teacher, 43,* 282–295.

Platt, J. J., and Spivack, G. (1972). Social competence and effective problem solving thinking in psychiatric patients. *Journal of Clinical Psychiatry, 28,* 3–5.

Pogrow, S. (1983). *Education in the computer age: Issues of policy, practice, and reform.* Beverly Hills: Sage.

Polloway, E., Epstein, M., Polloway, C., Patton, J., and Ball, D. (1986). Corrective reading program: An anlysis of effectiveness with learning disabled and mentally retarded students. *Remedial and Special Education, 7,* 41–47.

Pommer, L. T., Mark, D. S., and Hayden, D. L. (1983). Using computer software to instruct learning-disabled students. *Learning Disabilities, 2*(8), 99–110.

Premack, D. (1959). Toward empirical behavior laws. *Psychological Review, 66*(4), 219–233.

Pressley, M., Levin, J. R., Delaney, H. D. (1982). The mnemonic keyword method. *Review of Education Research, 52,* 61–92.

Prillaman, D. (1981). Acceptance of learning disabled students in the mainstream environment: A failure to replicate. *Journal of Learning Disabilities, 14,* 344–346.

Prutting, C. (1982). Pragmatics as social competence. *Journal of Speech and Hearing Disorders, 47,* 123–124.

Purkey, S. C., and Smith, M. S. (1985). School reform: The district policy implications of the effective schools literature. *Elementary School Journal, 85,* 353–389.

Raphael, T. E. (1982). Question-answering strategies for children. *The Reading Teacher, 36,* 188.

Raphael, T. E. (1984). Teaching learners about sources of information for answering comprehension questions. *Journal of Reading, 27,* 303–311.

Raphael, T. E. (1986). Teaching question-answer relationships revisited. *The Reading Teacher, 39*(6), 516–523.

Raphael, T. E., and Pearson, P. D. (1982). *The effect of metacognitive awareness training on children's question-answering behavior* (Tech. Rep. No. 238). Urbana: University of Illinois, Center for Study of Reading.

Rashotte, C. A., and Torgesen, J. K. (1985). Repeated reading and reading fluency in learning disabled children. *Reading Research Quarterly, 20*(2), 180–188.

Ratcliff, R., and McKoon, G. (1978). Priming in item recognition: Evidence for the propositional structure of sentences. *Journal of Verbal Learning and Verbal Behavior, 17,* 403–417.

Reed, V. A. (1986). *An introduction to children with language disorders.* New York: Macmillan.

Renik, M. J. (April 1987). *Measuring the relationship between academic self-perceptions and global self-worth: The self-perception profile for learning disabled students.* Presented at the Society for Research in Child Devopment, Baltimore, Md.

Reuda, R. (1989). Defining mild disabilities with language-minority students. *Exceptional Children, 56,* 121–129.

Rezmierski, V. E. (1984). Developmental interventions with behaviorally disordered youth. In J. K. Grosenick et al. (Eds.), *Social/affective interventions in behavioral disorders.* Des Moines: Project Iowa.

Rhodes, L. K. (1979). Comprehension and predictability: An analysis of beginning reading materials. In J. C. Harste and R. Carey (Eds.), *New perspectives on comprehension.* Bloomington: Indiana University, School of Education.

Rhodes, L. K. (1981). I can read! Predictable books as resources for reading and writing instruction. *The Reading Teacher, 34,* 511–518.

Rhodes, L. K., and Dudley-Marling, C. (1988). *Readers and writers with a difference.* Portsmouth, N.H.: Heinemann.

Ribner, S. (1978). The effects of special class placement on the self-concept of exceptional children. *Journal of Learning Disabilities, 11*(5), 319–323.

Richardson, J. E. (1971). *The linguistic readers.* New York: Benziger.

Ridley, C. A., and Vaughn, S. R. (1982). Interpersonal problem solving: An intervention program for preschool children. *Journal of Applied Developmental Psychology, 3,* 177–190.

Ridley, C. A., Vaughn, S. R., and Wittman, S. K. (1982). Developing empathic skills: A model for preschool children. *Child Study Journal, 3,* 177–190.

Roberts, G. H. (1968). The failure strategies of third grade arithmetic pupils. *The Arithmetic Teacher, 15,* 442–446.

Robinett, R. F., Bell, P. W., and Rojas, P. M. (1970). *Miami linguistic readers.* Lexington, Mass.: D. C. Heath.

Robinson, F. P. (1946). *Effective study.* New York: Harper and Brothers.

Rooney, K. J., and Hallahan, D. P. (1985). Future directions for cognitive behavior modification research: The quest for cognitive change. *Remedial and Special Education, 6*(2), 46–51.

Rosegrant, T. (1985). Using the microcomputer as a tool for learning to read and write. *Journal of Learning Disabilities, 18,* 113–115.

Rosegrant, T. (1986). Using the microcomputer as a scaffold for assisting beginning readers and writers. In J. L. Hoot (Ed.), *Computers in early childhood education: Issues and practices.* Englewood Cliffs, N.J.: Prentice-Hall, pp. 128–143.

Rosenblatt, L. (1978). *The reader, the text, the poem.* Carbondale, Ill.: Southern University Press.

Roser, N. L., Hoffman, J. V., and Farest, C. (1990). Language, literature, and at-risk children. *The Reading Teacher, 43,* 554–559.

Ross, A. O. (1976). *Psychological aspects of learning disabilities and reading disorders.* New York: McGraw-Hill.

Rourke, B. P., Young, G. C., and Leenaars, A. A. (1989). A childhood learning disability that predisposes those afflicted to adolescent and adult depression and suicide risk. *Journal of Learning Disabilities, 22*(3), 169–175.

Routh, D. K. (1979). Activity, attention, and aggression in learning disabled children. *Journal of Clinical Child Psychology, 8,* 183–187.

Rude, R. T., and Oehlkers, W. J. (1984). *Helping students with reading problems.* Englewood Cliffs, N.J.: Prentice-hall.

Rudel, R., Denckla, M., and Broman, M. (1981). The effect of varying stimulus context on word-finding ability: Dyslexia further differentiated from other learning disabilities. *Brain and Language, 13,* 130–144.

Ruedy, L. R. (1983). Handwriting instruction: It can be part of the high school curriculum. *Academic Therapy, 18*(4), 421–429.

Rumelhart, D. E. (1977). *Introduction to human information processing*. New York: John Wiley.

Rumelhart, D. E. (1980). Schemata: The building blocks of cognition. In R. J. Spiro, B. C. Bruce, and W. F. Brewer (Eds.), *Theoretical issues in reading comprehension*. Hillsdale, N.J.: Erlbaum, pp. 33–58.

Rumelhart, D. E. (1985). Toward an interactive model of reading. In H. Singer and R. B. Ruddell (Eds.), *Theoretical models and processes of reading* (3rd ed.). Newark, Del.: International Reading Association.

Salend, S. J., and Lutz, J. G. (1984). Mainstreaming or mainlining: A competency based approach to mainstreaming. *Journal of Learning Disabilities, 17*(1), 27–29.

Samuels, S. J. (1979). The method of repeated readings. *The Reading Teacher, 32*, 403–408.

Samuels, S. J. (1987). Information processing abilities and reading. *Journal of Learning Disabilities, 20*(1), 18–22.

Sanders, R. L., and Sanders, M. E. (1983). Evaluating microcomputer software. *Computers, Reading, and Language Arts, 1*(1), 21–25.

Sapona, R. H., Lloyd, J. W., and Wissick, C. A. (1985/86). Microcomputer use in resource rooms with learning-disabled children. *Computers in the Schools, 2*(4), 51–60.

Sargent, L. R. (1981). Resource teacher time utilization: An observational study. *Exceptional Children, 47*, 420–425.

Saville-Troike, M. (1984). What *really* matters in second language learning for academic achievement? *TESOL Quarterly, 18*, 199–219.

Scanlon, D. J., and Anders, P. L. (December, 1988). *Conceptual complexity and considerateness of vocation textbooks*. Paper presented at the annual meeting of the National Reading Conference, Tucson, Ariz.

Schank, R. C., and Abelson, R. (1977). *Scripts, plans, goals, and understanding*. Hillsdale, N.J.: Erlbaum.

Schell, L. M. (1972). Promising possibilities for improving comprehension. *Journal of Reading, 5*, 415–424.

Scheuneman, R. S., and Lambourne, J. (1981). *Study skills for school success*. Tucson, Ariz.: Study Skills for School Success.

Schiff, W. (1980). *Perception: An applied approach*. Boston: Houghton Mifflin.

Schiffman, G., Tobin, D., and Buchanan, B. (1982). Microcomputer instruction for the learning disabled. *Journal of Learning Disabilities, 15*, 557–559.

Schultz, J. B., and Turnbull, A. P. (1984). *Mainstreaming handicapped students: A guide for classroom teachers* (2nd ed.). Boston: Allyn and Bacon.

Schultz, T. (1974). Development of the appreciation of riddles. *Child Development, 45*, 100–105.

Schumaker, J. B., Denton, P. H., Deshler, D. D. (1984). *The paraphrasing strategy (Learning Strategies Curriculum)*. Lawrence: University of Kansas.

Schumaker, J. B., and Deshler, D. D. (1984). Setting demand variables: A major factor in program planning for LD adolescents. *Topics in Language Disorders, 4*(2), 22–44.

Schumaker, J. B., and Deshler, D. D. (1988). Implementing the regular education initiative in secondary schools: A different ball game. *Journal of Learning Disabilities, 21*, 36–42.

Schumaker, J. B., Deshler, D. D., Alley, G. R., and Warner, M. M. (1983). Toward the development of an intervention model for learning disabled adolescents: University of Kansas Institute. *Exceptional Education Quarterly, 4*(1), 45–74.

Schumaker, J. B., Deshler, D. D., Alley, G. R., Warner, M. M., and Denton, P. H. (1982). Multipass: A learning strategy for improving reading comprehension. *Learning Disability Quarterly, 5*(3), 295–304.

Schumaker, J. B., Deshler, D. D., and Ellis, E. S. (1986). Intervention issues related to the education of LD adolescents. In J. K. Torgesen and B. Y. L. Wong (Eds.), *Psychological and educational perspectives on learning disabilities*. Orlando, Fla.: Academic Press, pp. 329–365.

Schumaker, J. B., and Sheldon, J. (1985) *Learning strategies curriculum: The sentence writing strategy*. Lawrence: University of Kansas.

Schumaker, J. B., Sheldon-Wildgen, J., and Sherman, J. A. (1980). *An observational study of the academic and social behaviors of learning disabled adolescents in the regular classroom* (Res. Rep. 22). Lawrence: University of Kansas, Institute for Research in Learning Disabilities.

Schumaker, J. D., Wildgen, J. S., and Sherman, J. A. (1982). Social interaction of learning disabled junior high school students in their regular classrooms: An observational analysis. *Journal of Learning Disabilities, 11*, 98–102.

Schwartz, S., and Doehring, D. (1977). A developmental study of children's ability to acquire knowledge of spelling patterns. *Developmental Psychology, 13*, 419–420.

Schwartz, S. E., and Budd, D. (1981). Mathematics for handicapped learners: A functional approach for adolescents. *Focus on Exceptional Children, 13*(7), 1–12.

Scott, C. M. (1988). Producing complex sentences. *Topics in Language Disorders, 8*(2), 44–62.

Scruggs, T. E., and Mastropieri, M. A. (1988). Are learning disabled students "test-wise"?: A review of recent research. *Learning Disabilities Focus, 3*, 87–97.

Scruggs, T. E., and Mastropieri, M. A. (1989a). Mnemonic instruction of LD students: A field-based evaluation. *Learning Disability Quarterly, 12*, 119–125.

Scruggs, T. E., and Mastropieri, M. A. (1989b). Reconstructive elaborations: A model for content area learning. *American Educational Research Journal, 26*, 311–327.

Scruggs, T. E., and Richter, L. (1985). Tutoring learning disabled students: A critical review. *Learning Disability Quarterly, 8*(4), 286–298.

Seligman, M. E. P. (1975). *Helplessness: On depression, development, and death.* San Francisco: W. H. Freeman.

Senf, G. M. (1983). Learning disabilities challenge courseware. *The Computing Teacher, 10*(6), 18–19.

Shanahan, T., and Kamil, M. (1983). A further investigation of sensitivity of cloze and recall to passage organization. In J. A. Niles and L. A. Harris (Eds.), *Searches for meaning in reading/language processing and instruction.* (Thirty-second yearbook). Rochester, N.Y.: National Reading Conference.

Shanahan, T., Kamil, M., and Tobin, A. (1982). Cloze as a measure of intersentential comprehension. *Reading Research Quarterly, 17*, 229–255.

Shapero, S., and Forbes, C. R. (1981). A review of involvement programs for parents of learning disabled children. *Journal of Learning Disabilities, 14*(9), 499–504.

Sharma, M. C. (1984). Mathematics in the real world. In J. F. Cawley (Ed.), *Developmental teaching of mathematics for learning disabled.* Rockville, Md.: Aspen.

Sheare, J. B. (1978). The impact of resource programs upon the self-concept and peer acceptance of learning disabled children. *Psychology in the Schools, 15*, 406–412.

Sheras, P. L. (1983). Suicide in adolescence. In E. Walker and M. Roberts (Eds.), *Handbook of clinical child psychology.* New York: Wiley.

Shipley, K. B., and Banis, C. J. (1981). *Teaching morphology developmentally.* Tucson, Ariz.: Communication Skill Builders.

Shure, M. B., and Spivack, G. (1978). *Problem solving techniques in child-rearing.* San Francisco: Jossey Bass.

Shure, M. B., and Spivack, G. (1979). Interpersonal cognitive problem solving and primary prevention: Programming for preschool and kindergarten children. *Journal of Clinical Child Psychology, 8*, 89–94.

Shure, M. B., and Spivack, G. (1980). Interpersonal problem solving as a mediator of behavioral adjustment in preschool and kindergarten children. *Journal of Applied Developmental Psychology, 1*, 29–44.

Simon, C. S. (1980). *Communication competence: A functional-pragmatic language program.* Tucson, Ariz.: Communication Skill Builders.

Simon, C. S. (1984). *Evaluating communicative competence: A functional pragmatic procedure* (Rev. ed.). Tucson, Ariz.: Communication Skill Builders.

Simon, C. S. (Ed.) (1985). *Communication skills and classroom success: Assessment of language-learning disabled students.* San Diego, Calif.: College-Hill.

Simon, H. D. (1971). Reading comprehension: The need for a new perspective. *Reading Research Quarterly, 6*(3), 338–363.

Simpson, R. L. (1982). *Conferencing parents of exceptional children.* Rockville, Md.: Aspen.

Simpson, R. L. (1988). Needs of parents and families whose children have learning and behavior problems. *Behavioral Disorders, 14*(1), 40–47.

Singer, H., and Donlan, D. (1989). *Reading and learning from text* (2nd ed.). Hillsdale, N.J.: Erlbaum.

Siperstein, G. N., Bopp, M. J., and Bak, J. J. (1978). Social status of learning disabled children. *Journal of Learning Disabilities, 11*, 217–228.

Siperstein, G. N., and Goding, M. J. (1985). Teachers' behavior toward learning disabled and non–learning disabled children: A strategy for change. *Journal of Learning Disabilities, 18,* 139–144.

Slavin, R. E. (1987). Cooperative learning: Where behavioral and humanistic approaches to classroom motivation meet. *Elementary School Journal, 88,* 29–37.

Slavin, R. E., Stevens, R. J., and Madden, N. A. (1988). Accommodating student diversity in reading and writing instruction: A cooperative learning approach. *Remedial and Special Education, 9*(1), 60–66.

Slingerland, B. H. (1974). *A multi-sensory approach to language arts for specific language disability children.* Cambridge, Mass.: Educators Publishing Service.

Smith, D. D., and Lovitt, T. C. (1982). *The computational arithmetic program.* Austin, Tex.: Pro-Ed.

Smith, E. M., and Alley, G. R. (1981). The effect of teaching sixth graders with learning difficulties a strategy for solving verbal math problems (Research Report No. 39). Institute for Research in Learning Disabilities.

Smith, F. (1978). *Understanding reading* (2nd ed.). New York: Holt, Rinehart and Winston.

Smith, F. (1988). *Understanding reading* (4th ed.). New York: Holt, Rinehart and Winston.

Smith, F., and Goodman, K. S. (1971). On the psycholinguistic method of teaching reading. *Elementary School Journal, 71,* 177–181.

Smith, P. L., and Friend, M. (1986). Training learning disabled adolescents in a strategy for using text structure to aid recall of instructional prose. *Learning Disabilities Research, 2*(1), 38–44.

Snyder, L. S. (1984). Developmental language disorders: Elementary school age. In A. Holland (Ed.), *Language disorders in children.* San Diego, Calif: College-Hill, pp. 129–158.

Sobol, M. P., Earn, B. M., Bennett, D., and Humphries, T. (1983). A categorical analysis of the social attributions of learning disabled children. *Journal of Abnormal Child Psychology, 11*(2), 217–228.

Soenksen, P. A., Flagg, C. L., and Schmits, D. W. (1981). Social communications in learning disabled students: A pragmatic analysis. *Journal of Learning Disabilities, 14,* 283–286.

Spear, L. D., and Sternberg, R. J. (1986). An information-processing framework for understanding learning disabilities. In S. Ceci (Ed.), *Handbook of cognitive, social, and neuropsychological aspects of learning disabilities* (Vol. 2). Hillsdale, N.J.: Erlbaum, pp. 2–30.

Spencer, M., and Baskin, L. (1986). Guidelines for selecting software for children. In J. L. Hoot (Ed.), *Computers in early childhood education: Issues and practices.* Englewood Cliffs, N. J.: Prentice-Hall, pp. 22–39.

Sperling, G. A. (1960). The information available in brief visual presentation. *Psychological Monographs, 74,* whole no. 498.

Spinelli, F. M., and Ripich, D. N. (1985). Discourse and education. In D. N. Ripich and F. M. Spinelli (Eds.), *School discourse problems.* San Diego, Calif.: College Hill Press.

Spiro, R. J. (1980). Constructive processes in prose comprehension and recall. In R. J. Spiro, B. C. Bruce, and W. F. Brewer (Eds.), *Theoretical issues in reading comprehension.* Hillsdale, N.J.: Erlbaum, pp. 245–276.

Spivack, G., Platt, J. J., and Shure, M. B. (1976). *The problem solving approach to adjustment: A guide to research and intervention.* San Francisco: Jossey Bass.

Sroufe, L. A. (1975). Drug treatment of children with behavior problems. In F. D. Horowitz (Ed.), *Review of child development research* (Vol. 4). Chicago: University of Chicago Press.

Stahl, S. A., Jacobson, M. G., Davis, C. E., and Davis, R. L. (1989). Prior knowledge and difficult vocabulary in the comprehension of unfamiliar text. *Reading Research Quarterly, 24,* 27–43.

Stahl, S. A., and Vancil, S. J. (1986). Discussion is what makes semantic maps work in vocabulary instruction. *The Reading Teacher, 40*(1), 62–67.

Stallard, C. K. (1982). Computers and education for exceptional children: Emerging applications. *Exceptional Children, 49,* 102–104.

Stallings, J. S., and Kaskowitz, D. H. (1974). *Follow through classroom observation evaluation.* Menlo Park, Calif.: Stanford Research Institute.

Stanovich, K. (1986). Cognitive processes and the reading problems of learning-disabled children: Evaluating the assumption of specificity. In J. K. Torgesen and B. Y. L. Wong (Eds.), *Psychological and educational perspectives on learning disabilities.* Orlando, Fla.: Academic Press, pp. 85–131.

Stauffer, R. G. (1969). *Directing reading maturity as a cognitive process.* New York: Harper & Row.

Stauffer, R. G. (1970). *The language-experience approach to the teaching of reading.* New York: Harper & Row.

Stauffer, R. G. (1976). *Teaching reading as a thinking process.* New York: Harper & Row.

Stein, N. L., and Glenn, C. G. (1979). An analysis of story comprehension in elementary school children. In R. O. Freedle (Ed.), *New directions in discourse processing* (Vol. II). Norwood, N.J.: Ablex, pp. 53–120.

Stephens, T. (1977). *Teaching skills to children with learning and behavior problems.* Columbus, Ohio: Merrill.

Stephens, T. M. (1978). *Social skills in the classroom.* Columbus, Ohio: Cedars Press.

Stephens, T. M., Hartman, A. C., and Lucas, U. H. (1982). *Teaching children basic skills.* Columbus, Ohio: Merrill, pp. 22–23.

Stern, C. (1965). *Structural arithmetic.* Boston: Houghton Mifflin.

Stevens, K. B., and Schuster, J. W. (1987). Effects of a constant time delay procedure on the written spelling performance of a learning disabled student. *Learning Disability Quarterly, 10,* 9–16.

Stires, S. (1983). Read audiences and contexts for LD writers. *Academic Therapy, 18*(5), 561–568.

Stokes, T. F., and Baer, D. M. (1977). An implicit technology of generalization. *Journal of Applied Behavior Analysis, 10,* 349–367.

Stone, W. C., and LaGreca, A. M. (1984). Comprehension of nonverbal communication: A reexamination of the social competencies of learning disabled children. *Journal of Abnormal Child Psychology, 12*(4), 505–518.

Stone, W. L., and LaGreca, A. M. (1990). The social status of children with learning disabilities: A reexamination. *Journal of Learning Disabilities, 23* (1), 32–37.

Strickland, B. B., and Turnbull, A. P. (1990). *Developing and implementing individual education programs* (3rd ed.). Columbus, Ohio: Merrill.

Survey of CEC members' professional development needs. (1989). *Teaching Exceptional Children, 28,* 78–79.

Suydam, M. N. (1982). The use of calculators in precollege education: Fifth annual state-of-the-art review. Columbus, Ohio: Calculator Information Center. (ERIC Document Reproduction Service no. ED206454.).

Suydam, M. N., and Weaver, J. F. (1977). Research on problem solving: Implications for elementary-school classrooms. *Arithmetic Teacher, 25,* 40–42.

Swafford, K. M., and Reed, V. A. (1986). Language and learning-disabled children. In V. A. Reed (Ed.), *An introduction to children with language disorders.* New York: Macmillan, pp. 105–128.

Swanson, H. L. (1985). Verbal coding deficits in learning disabled readers. In S. J. Ceci (Ed.), *Handbook of cognitive, social and neuropsychological aspects of learning disabilities* (Vol. 1). Hillsdale, N.J.: Erlbaum, pp. 203–228.

Swanson, H. L. (1987). Information processing theory and learning disabilities: An overview. *Journal of Learning Disabilities, 20*(1), 3–7.

Swanson, H. L. (Ed.) (1987). *Advances in learning and behavioral disabilities* (Supplement 2). Greenwich, Conn.: JAI Press.

Swanson, L. (1981). Modification of comprehension deficits in learning disabled children. *Learning Disability Quarterly, 4,* 189–202.

Taber, F. M. (1983). *Microcomputers in special education.* Reston, Va.: The Council for Exceptional Children.

Tarver, S. G., Hallahan, D. P., Cohen, S. B., and Kauffman, J. M. (1977). The development of visual selective attention and verbal rehearsal in learning disabled boys. *Journal of Learning Disabilities, 10*(8), 491–500.

Tarver, S. G., Hallahan, D. P., Kauffman, J. M., and Ball, D. W. (1976). Verbal rehearsal and selective attention in children with learning disabilities: A development lag. *Journal of Experimental Child Psychology, 22,* 375–385.

Taylor, W. L. (1953). Cloze procedure: A new tool for measuring readability. *Journalism Quarterly, 30,* 415–433.

Taymans, J., and Malouf, D. (1984). A hard look at software in computer-assisted instruction in special education. *The Pointer, 28*(2), 12–15.

Test, D. W. (1985). Evaluating educational software for the microcomputer. *Journal of Special Education Technology, 7*(1), 37–46.

Tharp, R. G., and Gallimore, R. (1988). *Rousing minds to life: Teaching, learning, and schooling in social context.* New York: Cambridge University Press.

Thomas, A. (1979). Learned helplessness and expectancy factors: Implications for research in learning disabilities. *Review of Education Research, 49*(2), 208–221.

Thomas, K. (1978). The directed inquiry activity: An instructional procedure for content reading. *Reading Improvement, 15,* 138–140.

Thompkins, G. E., and Friend, M. (1986). On your mark, get set, write! *Teaching Exceptional Children, 18*(2), 82–89.

Thompson, M. (1977). *The effects of spelling pattern training on the spelling behavior of primary elementary students.* Unpublished doctoral dissertation, University of Pittsburgh.

Thornton, C. A. (1978). Emphasizing thinking strategies in basic fact instruction. *Journal for Research in Mathematics Education,* 215–227.

Thornton, C. A., and Toohey, M. A. (1985). Basic math facts; Guidelines for teaching and learning. *Learning Disabilities Focus, 1*(1), 44–57.

Thornton, C. A., Tucker, B. F., Dossey, J. A., and Bazik, E. F. (1983). *Teaching mathematics to children with special needs.* Menlo Park, Calif.: Addison-Wesley.

Thorpe, H. W., and Borden, K. F. (1985). The effect of multisensory instruction upon the on-task behavior and word reading accuracy of learning disabled students. *Journal of Learning Disabilities, 18,* 279–286.

Tierney, R. J., Readence, J. E., and Dishner, E. K. (1980). *Reading strategies and practices: Guide for improving instruction.* Boston: Allyn and Bacon.

Tierney, R. J., Readence, J. E., and Dishner, E. K. (1985). *Reading strategies and practices: A compendium* (2nd ed.). Boston: Allyn and Bacon.

Tierney, R. J., Readence, J. E., and Dishner, E. K. (1990). *Reading strategies and practices: A compendium* (3rd ed.). Boston: Allyn and Bacon.

Tobias, S. (1978). Achievement treatment interactions. *Review of Educational Research, 46,* 61–74.

Toolan, J. M. (1981). Depression and suicide in children: An overview. *American Journal of Psychotherapy, 35*(3), 311–323.

Torgesen, J. K. (1978). Performance of reading disabled children on serial memory tasks: A review. *Reading Research Quarterly, 19,* 57–87.

Torgesen, J. K. (1982). The learning disabled child as an inactive learner: Educational implications. *Topics in Learning and Learning Disabilities, 2*(1), 45–52.

Torgesen, J. K. (1985). Memory processes in reading disabled children. *Journal of Learning Disabilities, 18*(6), 350–357.

Torgesen, J. K. (1986). Using computers to help learning disabled children practice reading: A research-based perspective. *Learning Disabilities Focus, 1,* 72–81.

Torgesen, J. K., and Houck, G. (1980). Processing deficiencies in learning disabled children who perform poorly on the digit span task. *Journal of Educational Psychology, 72,* 41–60.

Torgesen, J. K., and Licht, B. G. (1983). The learning disabled child as an inactive learner: Retrospect and prospects. In J. D. McKinney and L. Feagans (Eds.), *Current topics in learning disabilities.* Norwood, N.J.: Ablex.

Torgesen, J. K., Rashotte, C. A., Greenstein, J., Houck, G., and Portes, P. (1987). Academic difficulties of learning disabled children who perform poorly on memory span tasks. In H. L. Swanson (Ed.), *Advances in learning and behavioral disabilities* (Supplement 2). Greenwich, Conn.: JAI Press, pp. 305–333.

Torgesen, J. K., and Young, K. A. (1983). Priorities for the use of microcomputers with learning disabled children. *Journal of Learning Disabilities, 16,* 234–237.

Townsend, M. A. R., and Clarihew, A. (1989). Facilitating children's comprehension through the use of advance organizers. *Journal of Reading Behavior, 21,* 15–36.

Trachtenburg, P., and Ferrugia, A. (1989). Big books from little voices: Reaching high risk beginning readers. *The Reading Teacher, 42,* 284–289.

Traub, N., and Bloom, F. (1970). *Recipe for reading.* Cambridge, Mass.: Educators Publishing Service.

Trelease, J. (1985). *The read-aloud handbook.* New York: Penguin Books.

Trelease, J. (1989a). Jim Trelease speaks on reading aloud to children. *The Reading Teacher, 43,* 200–206.

Trelease, J. (1989b). *The new read-aloud handbook.* New York: Penguin.

Tunnell, M. O., and Jacobs, J. S. (1989). Using "real" books: Research findings on literature based reading instruction. *The Reading Teacher, 42,* 470–477.

Turnbull, H. R., Turnbull, A. P., and Wheat, M. J. (1982). Assumptions about parental participation: A legislative history. *Exceptional Education Quarterly, 3*(2), 1–8.

Tyre, T. (1984). Education with PILOT. *Profiles, 2*(2), 48–54.

U.S. Department of Education. (1985–1986). *Patterns in special education service delivery and cost.* Washington, D.C.: Department of Education, Office of Special Education Programs.

Utley, B. L., Zigmond, M., and Strain, P. S. (1987). How various forms of data affect teacher analysis of student performance. *Exceptional Children 53*(5), 411–422.

Vaidya, S., and McKeeby, J. (1984). Conceptual problems encountered by children while learning Logo. *Journal of Educational Technology Systems, 13*, 33–39.

Van Reusen, A. K., and Bos, C. S. (1990). I PLAN: Helping students communicate in planning conferences. *Teaching Exceptional Children, 22*, 30–32.

Van Reusen, A. K., and Bos, C. S. (in press). *A goal-monitoring strategy.* Lawrence, Kans.: Edge Enterprises.

Van Reusen, A. K., Bos, C. S., Deshler, D. D., and Schumaker, J. B. (1987). *I PLAN: An education planning strategy.* Lawrence, Kans.: Edge Enterprises.

Van Riper, C., and Emerick, L. (1984). *Speech correction: Principles and methods* (7th ed.). Englewood Cliffs, N.J.: Prentice-Hall.

Vaughn, S. R. (1985). Why teach social skills to learning disabled students? *Journal of Learning Disabilities, 18*(10), 588–589.

Vaughn, S. R. (1987). TLC—Teaching, learning, and caring: Teaching interpersonal problem solving skills to emotionally disturbed adolescents. *Pointer, 31*, 25–30.

Vaughn, S. R., and Bos, C. S. (1987). Knowledge and perception of the resource room. The students' perspective. *Journal of Learning Disabilities, 20*, 218–223.

Vaughn, S. R., Bos, C. S., Harrell, J., and Lasky, B. (1988). Parent participation in the initial placement/IEP conference ten years after mandated involvement. *Journal of Learning Disabilities, 21* 82–89.

Vaughn, S., Bos, C. S., and Lund, K. A. (1986). . . . But they can do it in my room: Strategies for promoting generalization. *Teaching Exceptional Children, 18*, 176–180.

Vaughn, S., Cohen, J., Fournier, L., Gervasi, J., Levasseur, T., and Newton, S. (1984). Teaching interpersonal problem solving to behavior disordered adolescents. Paper presented at Council for Exceptional Children, Washington, D. C.

Vaughn, S., and Hogan, A. (1990). Social competence and learning disabilities: A prospective study. In H. L. Swanson and B. K. Keogh (Eds.), *Learning Disabilities: Theoretical and research issues.* Hillsdale, N.J.: Erlbaum, pp. 175–191.

Vaughn, S., Hogan, A., Kouzekanani, K., and Shapiro, S. (1990). Peer acceptance, self-perceptions, and social skills of LD students prior to identification. *Journal of Educational Psychology, 82*(1), 1–6.

Vaughn, S., and LaGreca, A. M. (1988). Teaching social skills to LD students. In K. A. Kavale (Ed.), *Learning disabilities: State of the art and practice.* San Diego, Calif.: College Hill–Little, Brown.

Vaughn, S., Lancelotta, G. X., and Minnis, S. (1988). Social strategy training and peer involvement: Increasing peer acceptance of a female, LD student. *Learning Disabilities Focus, 4*(1), 32–37.

Vaughn, S. R., Levine, L., and Ridley, C. A. (1986). *PALS: Problem solving and affective learning strategies.* Chicago: Science Research Associates.

Vaughn, S., McIntosh, R., and Spencer-Rowe, J. (in press). Peer rejection is a stubborn thing: Increasing peer acceptance of rejected students with learning disabilities. *Learning Disabilities Research.*

Vaughn, S. R., Ridley, C. A., and Bullock, D. D. (1984). Interpersonal problem solving skills training with aggressive young children. *Journal of Applied Developmental Psychology, 5*, 213–223.

Vaughn, S. R., Ridley, C. A., and Cox, J. (1983). Evaluating the efficacy of an interpersonal skills training program with children who are mentally retarded. *Education and Training of the Mentally Retarded, 18*(3), 191–196.

Vellutino, F. R., and Scanlon, D. M. (1987). Phonological coding, phonological awareness, and reading ability: Evidence from a longitudinal and experimental study. *Merrill-Palmer Quarterly, 33*, 321–363.

Vogel, S. (1983). A qualitative analysis of morphological ability in learning disabled and achieving children. *Journal of Learning Disabilities, 16*, 416–420.

Vygotsky, L. S. (1962). *Thought and language* (E. Hanfmann and G. Vakar, eds. and trans.). Cambridge, Mass.: MIT Press.

Vygotsky, L. S. (1978). *Mind in society: The development of higher psychological processes.* Cambridge, Mass.: Harvard University Press.

Waggoner, K., and Wilgosh, L. (1990). Concerns of families of children with learning disabilities. *Journal of Learning Disabilities, 23*(2), 97–98, 113.

Wallach, G. P. (1984). Later language learning: Syntactic structures and strategies. In G. P. Wallach and K. G. Butler (Eds.), *Language learning disabilities in school-age children.* Baltimore: Williams & Wilkins, pp. 82–102.

Wallace, G., and Kauffman, J. M. (1986). *Teaching students with learning and behavior problems* (3rd ed.). Columbus, Ohio: Merrill.

Wallach, G. P., and Miller, L. (1988). *Language intervention and academic success.* Boston: Little, Brown—College-Hill.

Warner, M. M. (1977). *Teaching learning disabled junior high students to use visual imagery as a strategy for facilitating recall of reading passages.* Unpublished doctoral dissertation, University of Kansas, Lawrence.

Warren, J. (1970). *Phonetic generalizations to aid spelling instruction at the fifth-grade level.* Unpublished doctoral dissertation, Boston University.

Warren, R. M., and Warren, R. P. (1970). Auditory illusions and confusions. *Scientific American, 223,* 30–36.

Warren, W. H., Nicholas, D. W., and Trabasso, T. (1979). Event chains and inferences in understanding narratives. In R. O. Freedle (Ed.), *New directions in discourse processing* (Vol. II). Norwood, N.J.: Ablex, pp. 23–52.

Waters, M., and Torgesen, J. K. (1985). *Effectiveness of computer administered practice in increasing sight vocabulary of learning disabled children.* Unpublished manuscript, Florida State University, Tallahassee.

Watson, D., and Crowley, P. (1988). How can we implement a whole-language approach? In C. Weaver (Ed.), *Reading process and practice.* Portsmouth, N.H.: Heinemann.

Weisberg, R. W. (1969). Sentence processing assessed through intrasentence word associations. *Journal of Experimental Psychology, 82,* 332–338.

Welch, M. (November/December 1983). Social skills in the resource room. *ACLD Newsbriefs* (No. 152).

Wells, G. (1973). *Coding manual of the description of child speech.* Bristol, Eng.: University of Bristol School of Education.

West, G. F. (1978). *Teaching reading skills in content areas: A practical guide to the construction of student exercises.* Oviedo, Fla.: Sandpiper Press.

West, J. F., and Cannon, G. S. (1988). Essential collaborative consultation competencies for regular and special educators. *Journal of Learning Disabilities, 21,* 56–63, 28.

West, J. F., and Idol, L. (1990). Collaborative consultation in the education of mildly handicapped and at-risk students. *Remedial and Special Education, 11*(1), 22–31.

West, J. F., Idol, L., and Cannon, G. (1989). *Collaboration in the schools: An inservice and preservice curriculum for teachers, support staff, and administrators.* Austin, Tex.: Pro-Ed.

White, B. (1975). Critical influences in the origins of competence. *Merrill-Palmer Quarterly, 2,* 243–266.

White, T. G., Sowell, J., Yanagihara, A. (1989). Teaching elementary students to use word-part clues. *The Reading Teacher, 42,* 302–308.

Wicks-Nelson, R., and Israel, A. L. (1984). *Behavior disorders of childhood.* Englewood Cliffs, N.J.: Prentice-Hall.

Wiig, E. H. (1982a). *Let's talk: Developing prosocial communication skills.* Columbus, Ohio: Merrill.

Wiig, E. H. (1982b). *Let's talk inventory for adolescents.* Columbus, Ohio: Merrill.

Wiig, E. H., and Bray, C. M. (1983). *Let's talk for children.* Columbus, Ohio: Merrill.

Wiig, E. H., and Fleischmann, N. (1980). Knowledge of pronominalization, reflexivization, and relativization by learning disabled college students. *Journal of Learning Disabilities, 13,* 575–576.

Wiig, E. H., and Harris. S. P. (1974). Perception and interpretation of nonverbally expressed emotions by adolescents with learning disabilities. *Perceptual and Motor Skills, 38,* 239–245.

Wiig, E. H., and Semel, E. M. (1984). *Language assessment and intervention for the learning disabled* (2nd ed.). Columbus, Ohio: Merrill.

Williams, J. P. (1986). The role of phonemic analysis in reading. In J. K. Torgesen and B. Y. L. Wong (Eds.), *Psychological and education perspective on learning disabilities*. Orlando, Fla.: Academic Press.

Williams, J. P. (1985). The case for explicit decoding instruction. In J. Osborn, P. T. Wilson, and R. C. Anderson (Eds.), *Reading education: Foundations for a literate America*. Lexington, Mass.: Lexington Books.

Williams, F., and Williams, V. (1984). *Microcomputers in elementary education: Perspectives on implementation*. Belmont, Calif.: Wadsworth.

Wilson, J. (1982). Selecting educational materials and resources. In D. D. Hammill and N. R. Bartel (Eds.), *Teaching children with learning and behavior problems* (3rd ed.). Boston: Allyn and Bacon.

Wilson, R. G., and Rudolph, M. K. (1986). *Merrill linguistic readers: Dig in*. Columbus, Ohio: Merrill.

Wilt, M. (1958). A study of teacher awareness of listening as a factor in elementary education. *Journal of Educational Research, 43*, 626–636.

Winton, P. J., and Turnbull, A. P. (1981). Parent involvement as viewed by parents of preschool handicapped children.

Wolf Nelson, N. (1989). Curriculum-based language assessment and intervention. *Language, Speech, and Hearing Services in Schools, 20*, 170–184.

Wong, B. Y. L. (1979). Increasing retention of main ideas through questioning strategies. *Learning Disability Quarterly, 2*(2), 42–47.

Wong, B. Y. L. (1980). Activating the inactive learning: Use of questions/prompts to enhance comprehension and retention of implied information in learning disabled children. *Learning Disability Quarterly, 3*, 29–37.

Wong, B. Y. L. (1986). A cognitive approach to teaching spelling. *Exceptional Children, 53*, 169–173.

Wong, B. Y. L. (1987). Directions in future research on metacognition in learning disabilities. In H. L. Swanson (Ed.), *Memory and learning disabilities: Advances in learning and behavioral disabilities* (Supplement 2). Greenwich, Conn.: JAI Press, pp. 335–356.

Wong, B. Y. L., and Jones, W. (1982). Increasing metacomprehension in learning disabled and normally achieving students through self-questioning training. *Learning Disability Quarterly, 5*, 228–240.

Wong, B. Y. L., and Wilson, M. (1984). Investigating awareness of and teaching passage organization in learning disabled children. *Journal of Learning Disabilities, 17*(8), 447–482.

Wong, B. Y. L., and Wong, R. (1980). Role taking skills in normal achieving and learning disabled children. *Learning Disability Quarterly, 3*, 11–18.

Wong, B. Y. L., and Wong, R. (1988). Cognitive interventions for learning disabilities. In K. A. Kavale (Ed.), *Learning disabilities: State of the art and practice*. Boston: Little, Brown—College Hill, pp. 141–160.

Wong, B. Y. L., Wong, R., Perry, N., and Sawatsky, D. (1986). The efficacy of a self-questioning summarization strategy for use by underachievers and learning disabled adolescents in social studies. *Learning Disabilities Focus, 2*(1), 20–35.

Wong Fillmore, L. (1983). The language learner as an individual: Implications of research on individual differences for the ESL teacher. In M. A. Clarke and J. Handscombe (Eds.), *On TESOL '82: Pacific perspectives on language learning and teaching*. Washington, D.C.: Teachers of English to Speakers of Other Languages.

Woodcock, R. W. (1987). *Woodcock Reading Mastery Test—Revised*. Circle Pines, Minn.: American Guidance Service.

Woodcock, R. W., Clark, C. R., and Davies, C. O. (1969). *The Peabody rebus reading program*. Circle Pines, Minn.: American Guidance Service.

Woodcock, R. W., and Johnson, M. B. (1977). *Woodcock Johnson psycho-educational battery*. Allen, Tex.: DLM.

Yauman, B. E. (1980). Special education placement and the self-concepts of elementary school age children. *Learning Disability Quarterly, 3*, 30–35.

Yee, A. (1969). Is the phonetic generalization hypothesis in spelling valid? *Journal of Experimental Education, 37*, 82–91.

Zinberg, N. E. (1984). *Drug, set, and setting*. New Haven, Conn.: Yale University Press.

Appendix A _____
Scope and Sequence
for Word Identification

Pre-primer

Grapheme -phoneme associations for consonants: *b, c /k/, d, f, g/g/, h, j, l, m, n, p, r, s, t, w*
Substitution: substituting initial and final consonants in known words
Context clues: using context and consonants to recognize unknown words
Morphemic analysis: inflectional endings *s* (plural marker—*dogs*) and *ed* (*called*)

Primer

Grapheme-phoneme associations:
   consonants: *k, v, y, z*
   consonant digraphs: *ch, sh, th*
   consonant blends: *pl, st, tr*
   short vowels: *a, e, i, o, u*
   spelling patterns: *er, or, ur, ar, ow, et, an, ight, at, ay, all*
Substitution: using grapheme-phoneme associations and parts of known words to recognize unknown words
Context cues: using semantic and syntactic cues to monitor responses to unknown printed words
Morphemic analysis
   inflectional endings: *s* (3rd person singular verbs—*eats*), *d (liked), es (boxes), 's* (possessive—*Ann's*), *er*
     (comparative—*faster*)
   suffix: *er* (as agent—*farmer*)

First Reader

Grapheme-phoneme associations:
   consonant: *x*
   consonant digraphs:[1] *wh, kn /n/, wr /r/, ck /k/*
   consonant blends: *br, cr, dr, fr, gr, bl, cl, fl, sl, sc, tw, ld, nd*
   short vowels: *y*
   long vowels: *a, e, i, o, u, y*
   vowel digraphs: *ay, ea /ĕ/ & /e/, ee, oa, ow /ō/*
   vowel diphthongs: *oi, oy, ow / ou/*
   spelling patterns: *alk, eigh, ind, old, ook*
   generalization: In the initial position, *y* represents a consonant sound; in other positions, a vowel sound.
Morphemic analysis:
   inflectional endings: *ing, (walking), est (fastest)*
   compound words: compounds comprised of 2 known words
   contractions: *not = n't (doesn't), will/shall = 'll (I'll)*[2]
Structural analysis:
   separating monosyllables into parts
   counting the number of vowel sounds in a word as a clue to the number of syllables

Synthesis: blending sounds into syllables; syllables into words

Second Reader

Grapheme-phoneme associations:

consonants: c / s/, g / j/

generalization: When c and g are followed by e, i, or y they usually represent their soft sounds

consonant digraphs: *ph* / f/, *tch* / ch/, *gn* / n/, *mb* / m/, *dge* / j/

consonant blends: *gl, pr, qu* / kw/, *sk, sm, sn, sp, sw, scr, sch, str, squ, thr, lk, nk*

vowel digraphs: *ai, oo* / o͞o/ & / oo/, *ey, ew, ei, ie, ue*

vowel diphthongs: *ou, au, aw*

schwa: /ə/ as represented by an initial vowel *(ago)*

r-controlled vowels: *ar, er, ir, or, ur, oor (door, poor), ear (year, earn, bear, heart), our (hour, four)*

spelling pattern: *ough (through, though, thought, rough)*

generalizations:

1) When c and g are followed by e, i, or y they usually represent soft sounds
2) A single vowel letter at the end of an accented syllable usually represents its long sound
3) A single vowel letter followed by a consonant other than r usually represents its short sound in an accented syllable
4) A single vowel letter followed by a single consonant, other than v, and a final e usually represents its long sound and the e is silent

Morphemic analysis:

inflectional endings: *s' (boys'), en (beaten)*

prefix: *un*

suffixes: *ful, fully, ish, less, ly, ness, self, y*

contraction: *have = 've (I've)*[2]

generalizations:

1) Divide between the words that form a compound; other divisions may occur in either or both parts
2) Divide between the root word and an affix; other divisions may occur in either the root or affix

recognizing words with spelling changes made by adding suffixes when: the final e has been dropped *(hide—hiding)*, y has changed to i *(baby—babies)*, and a final consonant has been doubled *(sit—sitting)*

Syllabication generalizations:

1) Usually divide between consonants that are not a digraph or blend
2) A single consonant between 2 single vowels may go with either syllable
3) Final e and the preceding consonant usually form the final syllable

Accenting: hearing and marking accented syllables

Third Reader

Grapheme-phoneme associations:

consonant blends: *spl, spr, ng, nt*

generalization: A single vowel letter or vowel combination (dangerous) represents a schwa sound in many unaccented syllables

Morphemic analysis:

prefixes: *dis, ex, im, in, post, pre, re sub, super, trans*

suffixes: *or (as agent—actor), ous, tion, sion, ment, ty, ic, al, able*

contractions: *are = 're (they're)*,[2] *would/had = 'd (I'd)*[3]

Structural analysis: syllabicating words of more than 2 syllables

Accenting generalizations:

1) Usually the first syllable in a 2-syllable word is accented
2) Usually affixes are not accented

---

[1]Silent consonants are included under consonant digraphs.

[2]More words with this contraction are likely to be encountered at higher reader levels

[3]Most contractions of *would/should* ('d) and *is/has* ('s) are likely to be encountered above the third-reader level.

Source: A. J. Harris and E. R. Sipay. *How to Increase Reading Ability,* 8th ed. New York: Longman, pp. 404–405. Copyright 1985 by Longman. Reprinted by permission.

Phonic-Based Pattern Words

Pattern	Examples
Consonant-Vowel-Consonant (CVC)—a	bad, dad, rat, sat, back, tack, bag, can, man, cap, ash, mash, last, mast, band, strand
Consonant-Vowel-Consonant (CVC)—e	bed, led, get, let, neck, wreck, mess, beg, leg, less, mess, pen, ten, best, rest, lent, spent, end, send
Consonant-Vowel-Consonant (CVC)—i	bid, lid, sit, pit, lick, sick, chip, strip, list, wrist, dish, fish, ink, think, thin, fin
Consonant-Vowel-Consonant (CVC)—o	dog, fog, sock, rock, lost, hop, chop, got, pot
Consonant-Vowel-Consonant (CVC)—u	bug, mug, but, rut, duck, truck, junk, trunk, fun, sun
Consonant-Vowel-Consonant Consonant Influenced	star, car, star, bank, thank, hang, saw, claw, haul, fault, because, walk, stalk, call, hall, ball, her, fern, stern, sir, stir, for, roll, troll, cold, hold, fur
Consonant-Vowel-Consonant-Silent E (CVCe)—a/ e	ate, skate, cave, rave, lake, stake, plane, cane, same, tame
Consonant-Vowel-Consonant-Silent E (CVCe)—e/ e	these
Consonant-Vowel-Consonant-Silent E (CVCe)—i/ e	fine, mine, bike, like, hide, slide, kite, lite, stripe, pile, smile
Consonant-Vowel-Consonant-Silent E (CVCe)—o/ e	hope, slope, choke, joke, bone, stone, pole, stole
Consonant-Vowel-Consonant-Silent E (CVCe)—u/ e	use, fuse
Consonant-Vowel-Consonant-Silent E—Consonant Influenced	care, fare, tale, here, there, fire, tire, hire, core, tore, sure, cure, nurse, purse
Consonant-Vowel-Vowel-Consonant (CVVC)—ai, ay	mail, fail, stain, rain, plain, stay, play
Consonant-Vowel-Vowel-Consonant (CVVC)—ea, ee, ei, ey	sea, pea, teach, each, weave, beat, feat, lead, read, real, steal, bee, tree, deep, keep, feet, meet, feel, steel, key
Consonant-Vowel-Vowel-Consonant (CVVC)—ie	die, lie
Consonant-Vowel-Vowel-Consonant (CVVC)—oa	boat, float, boast, roast
Consonant-Vowel-Vowel-Consonant (CVVC)—ui	fruit, suit
Consonant-Vowel-Vowel-Consonant—Consonant Influenced	air, chair, dear, fear, learn, pear, tear, cheer, leer, their, heir, pier, roar, soar
Vowel Diphthong—oo	boo, cool, food, room, tooth, soon, boost, loose, root, proof, moose book, foot, good, took, stood, shook, wood, hook
Vowel Diphthong—oi, oy	boy, toy, hoin, coin, noise, point
Vowel Diphthong—ou, ow	cow, now, plow, down, found, sound, mouse, house, cloud, owl, gown

Structural Analysis—Prefixes

Prefix	Example	Common Meaning
(a-)	atypical	not, without
(ab-)	abnormal	away, from
(ad-)	admit	to, toward, near
(ante-)	antebellum	before, prior to
(auto-)	autobiography	self
(bi-)	binocular	two
(circum-)	circumvent	around
(co-)	commingle	together, jointly
	collaborate	
	coauthor	
(counter-)	counterpoint	opposition
(de-)	defrost	opposition
(dis-)	disappear	opposition
	dishonest	not
(en-)	enslave	cause to
(ex-)	ex-president	former
(extra-)	extramarital	outside, beyond
(fore-)	forejudge	before
(hyper-)	hyperactive	overly, beyond
(im-)	immeasurable	not
(in-)	indirect	not
(inter-)	interstate	between
(intra-)	intrastate	within
(ir-)	irrational	not
(mal-)	malfunctioning	poorly, badly
(micro-)	microcomputer	small
(mid-)	midway	middle
(mis-)	miscount	wrongly, badly
(mono-)	monotone	one
(multi-)	multicolored	many
(neo-)	neoclassical	new
(non-)	nonliving	not
(poly-)	polysyllabic	many
(post-)	posttest	after
(pre-)	pretest	before
(pro-)	pro-American	for, favoring
(pseudo-)	pseudoscience	false
(re-)	rewrite	again, repeat
(retro-)	retroactive	back
(semi-)	semicolon	partly
(sub-)	subsoil	under, beneath
(super-)	superhuman	above, beyond
(syn-)	syndrome	together, with
	symbiosis	
(trans-)	transoceanic	across
(tri-)	triangular	three
(ultra-)	ultramodern	above, extremely
(un-)	unhappy	not
	untie	do opposite action
(uni-)	unicolor	one

Structural Analysis—Suffixes

Noun- and Adjective-Marketing Suffixes

Suffix	Noun Example	Adjective Example
(-able)		breakable
(-acy)	primacy	
(-age)	orphanage	
(-al)	arrival	fictional
(-an)	republican	
(-ian)	Iranian	Iranian
(-n)	American	American
(-ance)	acceptance	
(-ant)	claimant	determinant
(-ar)	scholar	
(-ary)	commentary	budgetary
(-ate)	consulate	
(-ation)	affirmation	
(-cal)		historical
(-dom)	freedom	
(-ed)		cultured
(-ee)	appointee	
(-eer)	engineer	
(-en)		given
(-ence)	preference	
(-ency)	consistency	
(-ent)	deterrent	abhorrent
(-er)	painter	
(-or)	sailor	
(-ery)	bravery	
(-ess)	authoress	
(-et)	floweret	
(-ette)	cigarette	
(-fold)		tenfold
(-ful)		peaceful
(-ing)	meeting	
(-graph)	photograph	
(-hood)	childhood	
(-ible)	convertible	
(-ic)		poetic
(-ice)	service	
(-ics)	athletics	
(-ile)		infantile
(-ine)	heroine	elphantine
(-ion)	regulation	
(-ish)		foolish
(-ism)	alcoholism	
(-ist)	racist	
(-ity)	civility	
(-ive)		creative
(-less)		lifeless
(-let)	booklet	
(-like)		childlike
(-ly)		motherly
(-ment)	development	

Structural Analysis—Suffixes

Suffix	Noun Example	Adjective Example
(-ness)	kind*ness*	
(-ology)	etym*ology*	
(-ory)	deposit*ory*	compensat*ory*
(-ous)		joy*ous*
(-ry)	citizen*ry*	
(-ship)	kin*ship*	
(-some)		burden*some*
(-ster)	young*ster*	
(-tion)	beautific*ation*	
(-ty)	certain*ty*	
(-ude)	definit*ude*	
(-ure)	fail*ure*	
(-y)	honest*y*	mess*y*

Verb-Marking Suffixes

Suffix	Example
(-ate)	activ*ate*
(-en)	short*en*
(-fy)	beauti*fy*
(-ify)	solid*ify*
(-ize)	terror*ize*

Adverb-Marking Suffixes

Suffix	Example
(-fold)	ten*fold*
(-ly)	slow*ly*
(-most)	top*most*
(-ward(s))	west*ward(s)*
(-wise)	clock*wise*

Appendix B
Instructional Activities

Oral Language

Find the Way

Objective: To provide students with practice in giving and interpreting directions.

Grades: All grades

Materials: (1) Maps of different areas. For example, use a map of the school for younger students, and use a map of the local area, the state, or the area you are studying in social studies for older students. The map should be labeled. (2) Put the names of places on the map and on small cards so the cards can be drawn during the game.

Teaching Procedures: One student is designated as "It." This student is given a map and draws a card that gives the name of the place he or she is to find. The student draws the route on his or her map. The other students are given the same map, but they do not know the destination or the route. Without showing the map to the other students, the student who is "It" must describe, by using words only, how to get to the destination. The other students are allowed to ask three questions to help clarify the directions.

To modify this exercise into a game format, each student can receive a point for each time he or she is successful in directing the other students to the location. After a student has finished, discuss how he or she was effective in giving directions and make recommendations to improve his or her language abilities.

Adaptations: A similar format can be used with one student directing the other students on a treasure hunt.

Many Meanings

Objective: To give students practice using homonyms and multiple meaning words.

Grades: Intermediate and secondary

Materials: (1) Any generic gameboard with a die or spinner and pieces to serve as players. (2) A variety of meaning cards and homonyms or words that have multiple meanings (e.g., *heal–heel, meet–meat*) written on one side.

Teaching Procedures: Have the students set up the game and clarify the rules. For each turn a student rolls the die or spins the spinner. The student then picks a card and uses each homonym in a separate sentence to show the difference between the meanings of the words or the multiple meanings. If the student's sentences reflect correct meanings, he or she moves the marker the number of spaces shown on the die or spinner. If the student is unable to make a sentence, other students may help him or her, but the student cannot move the marker. The student to reach the finish line first wins.

Adaptations: Have the students work in teams or have the students give definitions of the words rather than using them in sentences.

Surprise Pouches

Objective: To give students practice in describing objects.

Grades: Primary

Materials: (1) Cloth pouch with a drawstring. (2) Small objects that will fit in the pouch.

Teaching Procedures: Place a small object in the pouch and have one student in the group feel the object without looking in the pouch. The student cannot give the name of the object, but must describe it. The student describes what he or she feels while the rest of the students in the group try to guess what is in the pouch. When the student feeling the object thinks the other students have guessed correctly, he or she takes the object out to see if the students are right. Have the students discuss how the descriptive words helped them guess the object. For example, "Smooth and round made me think it was a ball."

Put a new object in the pouch and have another student describe the object. Each student should get several turns at describing the objects.

The Add On Game

Objective: To provide students practice in remembering and recalling lists of ideas.

Grades: Primary

Materials: Starter phrases that allow students to develop a list. For example:

> I am going on a trip to Disneyland and in my suitcase I will pack . . .
> I am going to a restaurant and I am going to eat . . .
> I went to Old McDonald's farm and saw . . .

Teaching Procedures: The students and teacher sit in a circle. A student begins the game by saying, "I am going on a trip to Disneyland and in my suitcase I will pack. . . ." This student names one article appropriate to take on the trip. The next person in the circle then repeats the sentence, listing the first item and adds another item. The next person repeats both items and adds a third, and so on. This game can be played in two ways. To play competitively, the person is eliminated from the game when he or she cannot list all the items. The last person to be "out" wins the game. To play cooperatively, the object of the game is for the group to beat the number of items remembered in previous games. In order to keep all students in the game, each student may be allowed two assists from a friend during the game (students are not "out" when incorrect). If a student has already used the two assists, then the number of items the group has correctly remembered is determined and compared to see if the group beat previous scores.

Adaptations: This can be adapted to current events or holidays (e.g., gifts for Christmas or treats you got for Halloween).

Barrier Game

Objective: To provide students practice in describing how to make something and to provide practice in listening to directions.

Grades: Elementary

Materials: (1) Colored blocks for building objects or crayons for drawing objects. (2) Some type of barrier to block the view between the two students or the student and the teacher.

Teaching Procedures: Explain the directions to the students. Have the students sit so that the barrier is between them. One student draws a simple picture or builds a simple block design. During or after the building or drawing, he or she describes to the other student how to make the design. The other student can ask questions to help. When the other student has finished, remove the barrier and have the students compare their work.

Adaptations: After the students become successful at the activity, the number of questions that can be asked can be limited.

Category Sort

Objective: To provide students practice in sorting objects or word cards by categories.

Grades: Primary

Materials: (1) Objects or word cards that can be sorted by one or more categories (e.g., colored bears, colored blocks, colored buttons, colored marbles, types of animals, types of food). (2) Word cards that represent categories. (3) Sorting boxes (i.e., small boxes into which the students can sort).

Teaching Procedure: Put a category word card next to each box. Demonstrate how to name each object or word card and then put all the like objects or cards in the same box. Once the student has sorted the objects or cards, he or she names each category and the objects or cards in each category. The student then talks about what is alike about all the objects or cards in one category.

Create a Comic

Objective: To provide students practice is using dialogue and telling stories.

Grades: Intermediate and junior high

Materials: (1) Familiar comic strips or sequences in comic books. Blank out the words in the balloons.

Teaching Procedures: Present the comic strip to the students and discuss with them what they know about the comic strip characters, what is happening, and what could be written in each of the balloons. Have the students write in the different balloons. Take turns reading the comic strip with different students reading what different characters say. The different comic strips can be put into a comic book that can be shared with other students.

Adaptations: After students are comfortable with this activity they can illustrate and dictate their own comic strips.

My Collage

Objective: To provide students with the opportunity to discuss their characteristics and to increase self-awareness.

Grades: Intermediate and junior high

Materials: (1) A variety of magazines, including teen-oriented magazines. (2) Poster board, scissors, and glue for making the collage. Cut the poster board into squares.

Teaching Procedures: Introduce the activity by having the students talk about and write down words that describe themselves. Pass out the magazines and have students find pictures, words, phrases, and sentences that describe themselves. Once the students each have about twenty pictures, words, phrases, or sentences that describe themselves, have them construct their collages.

The students then share their collages with the class and discuss why they chose different pictures, words, or phrases. Next, they write a description of themselves, again using the collage as a guide. Encourage the students to use descriptive language.

Play the Part

Objective: To provide students practice in using language during simulations of typical interactions.

Grades: Intermediate and secondary

Materials: (1) Simulation cards. Each card should describe the situation, the characters, and the goal of the language interaction. Several examples are shown in the table below.

Teaching Procedures: Explain how simulations work in that each person is to assume the described role and participate as if this were a real situation. Have the students assume the various characters and discuss what they are going to say in their role. The students then carry out the role play.

Have the students discuss how effective each person was in using his or her language to accomplish the goal.

Does It Make Sense?

Objective: To provide students practice in determining if sentences are syntactically and semantically correct and in modifying sentences to make them correct.

Grades: All grades

Materials: (1) Generic gameboard, spinner, or die, and playing pieces. (2) Does It Make Sense Cards with sentences written on them, some of which are syntactically and semantically correct and some of which are not correct. Complexity of sentences will depend on the language development level of the students participating in the activity. For example:

> Semantically and syntactically correct:
> Tamara and Jesse were walking along the road when they saw a limousine pass by.

> Semantically incorrect (nonsensical or illogical):
> Tamara and Jesse were walking along the road when they saw a limousine walk by.

> Syntactically incorrect (grammar not correct):
> Tamara and Jesse were walking along the road when they see a limousine passed by.

> Semantically and syntactically incorrect:
> Tamara and Jesse were walking along the road when they see a limousine walk by.

Situation	Characters	Goal
Introducing a new friend to an old friend and helping get the conversation started.	New friend Old friend Person making the introductions	Introduce new friend to old friend and get a conversation started between the three of you.
Describing to a stranger how to find a store located about ten blocks away (select local stores in your area).	Stranger Person giving directions	Give directions that will allow the stranger to find the store.
Persuading a friend not to shoplift (select a specific situation).	Friend Person persuading	Convince the friend not to shoplift.

Teaching Procedures: Have students set up the game and clarify the rules. For each turn a student rolls the die or spins the spinner. The student then picks a card and reads or listens to someone read the sentence. He or she then decides if the sentence "makes sense" and if not, changes the sentence so that it makes sense. If the student is correct in determining if the sentence makes sense, and is accurate in correcting an incorrect sentence, he or she moves the marker the number of spaces shown on the die or spinner. If the student is not correct, other students may help him or her, but the marker may not be moved. The student to reach the finish line first is the winner.

Listen Carefully!

Objective: To provide students practice in monitoring their comprehension as they listen and to question the integrity of the text.

Grades: Primary and intermediate

Materials: (1) Stories or expository pieces that have been modified so that they have inconsistencies in the meaning, sequence, vocabulary use, or grammar. For example:

> Beavers are brown, furry animals with long necks. They weight about forty to fifty pounds. They live in ponds on the desert.
> Sometimes they have to build their own pond. They do this by cutting down trees using their strong teeth. They put the trees on a dam they build, then they drag the trees to the pond. Finally, they pack mud and leaves in the dam so that it will hold back the water in the stream to form a pond.

(2) Stories or expository pieces that you have not modified.

Teaching Procedures: Explain to the students that you are going to read a story and that you would like them to judge how well they think the piece is written. Read the story as they listen, then ask the students if everything made sense. In the discussion, assist the students in identifying the text inconsistencies and telling why certain parts did not make sense. At the end of the discussion have the students rate how well they think the piece is written.

Adaptations: Students could read rather than listen to the pieces before they discuss them.

_____ Reading: Word Identification _____

Grocery Store

Objective: To increase the students' awareness of print in the environment and to provide practice in matching words.

Grades: Primary

Materials: (1) An area that is set up as a grocery store. (2) Commonly used packaged and canned goods with labels left on (e.g., Jello, toothpaste, corn flakes, chicken noodle soup). Remove the contents of packaged goods and reclose the box. (3) Cards with names of items written on them. (4) Baskets and/or bags children can use when shopping.

Teaching Procedures: This center can be used in a variety of ways. Word cards can be placed by each food item. When the student is shopping and selects a food item he or she also picks up the card, reads it, and matches it to the label on the box. When the child goes through checkout, he or she can read each card and hand the cashier the item that goes with it. Or the teacher and child can decide which items the child wants to buy. The teacher gives those word cards to the child, and he or she shops for those items by matching the cards to the items on the shelves.

Children can serve as stock persons by reshelving the items the other children have purchased. When a stock person reshelves an item, he or she can find the card that matches the item and then place the card next to the item.

My Sound Book

Objective: To provide the students practice in finding pictures that start with a specific consonant or vowel sound.

Grades: Primary

Materials: (1) Three-ring binder or folder into which ''Sound Pages'' can be inserted. (2) Magazines, old books, or workbooks that can be cut up. (3) Stickers, scissors, and glue.

Teaching Procedures: Explain to the students that each of them will be making a book where they can collect and keep pictures and stickers that start with various sounds. Select one sound that the students are learning and have the students write the letter representing the sound on the top of the page. Then have them look through magazines, old books, and workbooks to find pictures starting with the sound. Once they have selected the pictures, have them say the names to you so that you both can determine if the pictures represent the designated sound. Then have the students glue the pictures on the sound pages, leaving room to add other pictures they find while looking for pictures representing other sounds. Have the students put the sound page in the notebook and share his or her pictures with other students. Continue until the book is complete. As students collect stickers, you may want to encourage them to put them in the sound book.

Vowel Match

Objective: To provide the students practice in decoding words that have various vowels sounds.

Grades: Primary and intermediate

Materials: (1) One file folder that is divided into two playing areas that consist of ten boxes for each player. In each box, paste a picture that illustrates a vowel sound. (2) From thirty to forty playing cards with pictures illustrating vowel sounds.

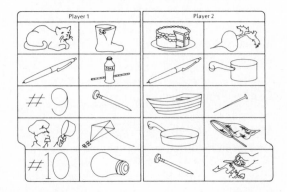

Teaching Procedures: Explain the game to the students. Shuffle and place cards face down near the players. Each student draws a card and checks to see if the vowel sound illustrated on the card matches one of the pictures on his or her side of the game folder. If it does, the player places the card over the picture on the game folder. If the picture does not match, the card is discarded. The player to cover all the boxes first wins the game.

Adaptations: This game is easily adapted to teaching rhyming words and other sounds such as consonant digraphs or blends.

Sight Word Bingo

Objective: To provide the students practice in recognizing words.

Grades: Primary and intermediate

Materials: (1) Poster board cut into 10 x 8 inch pieces to use for Bingo cards. (2) List of new words students have encountered in their reading. Such lists can be found in the back of basal readers or in books of lists such as *The New Reading Teacher's Book of Lists* (Fry, Fountoukidis, and Polk, 1985). To make the Bingo cards randomly select words from the list and write them on the card as illustrated. (3) Colored markers.

Word Bingo			
happen	should	night	enough
below	never,	complete	thought
grow	where	while	building
every	through	include	were
country	even	important	between

Teaching Procedures: One student (or the teacher) is designated as the caller. Each of the remaining students gets a Bingo card. The caller randomly selects a word from the list and says the word. The students place a colored marker on the square in which the word is written. The first person to cover all the squares in a horizontal, vertical, or diagonal row calls, "Bingo." The caller and the student then verify the words. If verified, that student wins.

Adaptations: Bingo is a generic game that can be adapted to provide practice for a variety of skills. For example:

> *Consonant Bingo:* Put pictures of objects that start with initial consonants, blends, or digraphs on the Bingo cards. The caller

says the letter(s) and the students mark the picture(s) that has the same consonant, blend, or digraph. This can also be adapted for final consonants.

> *Prefix Bingo:* Write prefixes on the Bingo cards. The caller says a word with a prefix or gives the definition of a prefix, and the students mark the prefix on their cards.

> *Math Fact Bingo:* Write the answers to math facts on the Bingo cards. The caller says a math fact and the students mark the answer.

Rotten Egg

Objective: To provide students practice in recognizing words.

Grades: Primary

Materials: (1) 30 index cards (3 x 5 inch) consisting of 15 pairs of words. Write or type the words across each end of the card so that the students can see the words as they hold the cards like playing cards. (2) One Rotten Egg card.

Teaching Procedures: Explain that the game is played like Old Maid. The dealer deals all the cards face down to the players. The players pick up the cards and match any pairs that they may have in their hands. Starting to the left of the dealer, player #1 lays down any matching pairs in his or her hand and names them. Once this student has put down any matching pairs, he or she then picks a card from the cards of another player. If it matches a card in player #1's hand, he or she names the pair and lays it down on the table. If the child cannot pronounce the word, the teacher or another student helps. The student must keep the pair of cards in his or her hand until the next turn. If the chosen card does not match one in player #1's hand, he or she keeps it. Play then proceeds to player #2 on the left and continues in the same manner until all word pairs are matched. The person left with the Rotten Egg card is the loser.

Adaptations: This game may also be played with a Happy Face card instead of a Rotten Egg card. The person ending up with the Happy Face card wins.

The game can also be adapted to other skills. For example, card pairs can be made that require the students to match initial or final sounds in words (e.g., *cat* and *cost; elephant* and *tent*), prefixes or suffixes (e.g., *repeat* and *rewind; painter* and *carpenter*), or synonyms or antonyms (e.g., *happy* and *glad; hot* and *cold*).

Silly Stories

Objective: To provide students practice in using context to decode words.

Grades: Primary and intermediate

Materials: Short stories written at the students' instructional reading levels with the adjectives and adverbs left out and replaced by blanks. For example:

The _____ farmer had a hat, an
_____, _____ hat. Oh,
how he liked that _____,
_____ hat! But one day a
_____, _____ wind took
the _____ hat right off his head.
The farmer ran _____,
_____ chasing the hat, but he just
could not catch it. . . .

Teaching Procedures: First discuss what kinds of words are left out of the story. Give each student a copy of the story and have the students read the story and decide on words that make sense. Have them read their versions of the stories to the group and discuss how different words

can go in the same blank and still make sense. Finally, as a group, create a silly story by filling in words that don't make sense.

Adaptations: Vary the parts of speech that are deleted.

Compound Concentration

Objective: To give the students practice in identifying compound words and to illustrate how words may be combined to form compound words.

Grades: Intermediate and secondary

Materials: 36 index cards (3 x 5 inch) on which the two parts of 18 compound words have been written. Make sure that each part can only be joined with one other part.

Teaching Procedure: Explain the game. Have the students shuffle the cards and place the cards face down in six rows with six cards each. Each player takes a turn at turning over two cards. The student then decides whether the two words make a compound word. If the words do not make a compound word, then the cards are again turned face down and the next player takes a turn. If the words make a compound word, then the player gets those two cards and turns over two more cards. The student continues playing until two cards are turned over that do not make a compound word. The game is over when all the cards are matched. The winner is the player with the most cards.

Adaptations: Concentration can be adapted for many skills. Students can match synonyms, antonyms, prefixes, suffixes, initial or final consonants, categories, and math facts.

Reading: Fluency and Comprehension

Critiquing Oral Reading

Objective: To provide students the opportunity to critique their oral reading.

Grades: Primary and intermediate

Materials: (1) A book or story the student is reading. (2) A tape recorder and a labeled blank tape for each student.

Teaching Procedures: Explain that the purpose of the activity is to give the students an opportunity to listen to how they read. Let the students know that they are to listen for things they do well and things they want to work on. Model the process by practicing, recording, listening, and critiquing a passage you read. Before the students read into the tape recorder, have them practice the segment. Each student should practice and then read and record a passage of about 100 to 500 words. After the students record, they should listen to their tapes and finish writing the following statements:

When I read orally, I do a really good job of _____.

One thing I could do better when I read out loud is _____.

It is important to have students start with the things they do well.

Listen to and discuss each tape and then ask the students to critique each presentation. Have the students record their oral reading every three to six weeks so that they can compare and hear how they are improving.

Adaptations: Each student can record two passages—one that has been practiced and one that is unpracticed.

Readers' Theatre

Objective: To provide students practice in oral reading and to become familiar with literature.

Grades: All grades

Materials: (1) Copies of plays, folktales, or other literature that has a great deal of dialogue. The literature will vary depending on the ages and reading abilities of the students.

Teaching Procedures: Introduce the literature piece to the students and explain the various characters and the role of the narrator. After the students select parts, prepare their copy of the literature piece (script) by highlighting the part they are to read. Tell the students to work in pairs and practice reading their parts in the scripts. Finally, have the students practice reading the script in a dress rehearsal and then a final presentation. For the final presentation, have the students read the scripts to another class and/or videotape it.

Adaptations: Students may want to develop this into a play by making costumes and memorizing their lines. Students may also want to write their own stories to read.

Story Jumble

Objective: To provide students practice in sequencing a story.

Grades: Primary and intermediate

Materials: Short stories written at the students' independent reading levels that have been cut into story parts (e.g., setting, episodes, endings), paragraphs, or sentences. Mount each segment of the story on an index card.

Teaching Procedures: Present the cards to the students and have them read each part and arrange them so that the story makes sense. Then have the students read the story again to check to see if it makes sense. If students disagree as to the order, have them explain why they prefer a certain order.

Adaptations: Students can work on this activity in groups of two or three students or individually.

Predict the Plot

Objective: To provide students practice in predicting the events and plots in stories.

Grades: Intermediate and secondary

Materials: Cartoon strips such as Peanuts, Broom-hilda, or Beetle Bailey.

Teaching Procedures: Select a cartoon strip and expose one frame at a time for the students to read. Then have them predict the plot by asking such questions as:

> What do you think is going to be pictured in the next frame? Why?
> Of the ideas we have generated, which one do you like best? Why?
> How do you think the cartoonist will end this story? Why?

Read the next frame, discussing the previous predictions and making predictions about the next frame. After the story is completed, have the students draw and write their own cartoons, using the characters presented in the strip or creating new characters. Then the students may share their cartoons with each other.

Adaptations: Mystery and adventure stories also lend themselves to this type of plot prediction. Segments of the story could be read and then predictions made. Students could also finish this activity by writing a mystery or adventure story.

Stake-Out

Objective: To give students the opportunity to arrange the paragraphs of articles in a logical order.

Grades: Intermediate and secondary

Materials: (1) At least two newspaper articles with at least four paragraphs written at the students' instructional to independent reading levels. Cut each article up by paragraphs, and mount each paragraph from the same story on the same color index card. (2) Write clues on another set of index cards that will help the students find the various paragraphs located in a given area (e.g., room, school).

Teaching Procedures: Place the paragraphs to the articles around the room or school. Divide the students into teams that consist of two or three members. Explain to the teams that their goal is to use the clues to find the various parts to their newspaper article, and then to arrange the article so that it makes sense. Explain that the parts to their article will all be on the same color index cards. Either use the rule that the first team that completes the task wins, or that a certain time limit is available for the stake-out and the team must complete it by that time if they are to win.

Give each team the clues and have them begin. When time is complete, have each group read the article. The class then determines if the order is correct. Have the students justify the order they selected.

Judge the Ad

Objective: To provide students the opportunity to think critically about advertisements.

Grades: Intermediate and secondary

Materials: Ads cut from newspapers and magazines.

Teaching Procedures: Select examples of ads that provide a fair representation of a product and ones that present a biased or unfair representation. Discuss with the students what makes the ad fair, unfair, or biased, Then have the students each select an ad for a product they know about and would like to purchase. Ask them to study the ad to determine if it is "fair." Have each student present his or her ad to the other students and build a case for why the ad is fair or unfair. Encourage the students to provide evidence for their opinions.

WH-Game

Objective: To provide students practice in answering who, what, when, where, why, and how questions.

Grades: All grades

Materials: (1) Generic gameboard, spinner or die, and markers. (2) WH Cards, which are small cards with "WH-Game" written on one side and one of the following words written on the other side: *Who, What, When, Where, Why, How.* (3) Sets of Story and Article Cards, which are copies of short stories and articles mounted on cards. There should be one copy for each player. Select topics of interest for the age level of students.

Teaching Procedures: Explain the game to the students or have them read written directions. First, the players set up the game. Next, they select a set of Story or Article Cards. All players read the story or article and place their cards face down. Then, each player takes a turn by throwing the die or spinning and selecting a WH-Card. The player must make up a question using the WH word indicated on the card and answer it correctly in order to move his or her marker the indicated number of spaces. If another player questions the validity of a player's question or answer, the players may look at the story or article card. Otherwise, these cards should remain face down during play. After ten questions have been asked using one Story or Article card, another set is selected. The students read this card and then the game continues. The first player to arrive at the finish wins.

Adaptations: Students may also work in pairs, with one person on the team making up the question and the other person answering it.

_____ Written Expression _____

Proofreading with "Scope"

Objective: To teach students a mnemonic strategy ("Scope") to help with proofreading their writing.

Grades: Intermediate and advanced

Materials: A student-generated writing piece that needs to be edited.

Teaching Procedures: Discuss with the students how they often get into difficulty because they are not sufficiently skilled at proofreading their papers before they submit them and therefore get low grades because their papers have many errors. Teach the students a mnemonic strategy, "Scope," that will assist them in proofreading their work before they submit it.

>"S"—*Spelling:* Is the spelling correct?
>
>"C"—*Capitalization:* Are the first words of sentences, proper names, and proper nouns capitalized?
>
>"O"—*Order of Words:* Is the syntax correct?
>
>"P"—*Punctuation:* Are there appropriate marks for punctuation where necessary?
>
>"E"—*Express Complete Thought:* Does the sentence contain a noun and a verb or is it only a phrase?

Next, demonstrate using "Scope" with a sample piece of writing on an overhead projector. Give the students ample practice and opportunity to apply "Scope" to their own work.

> The Life of JUAN GONZALES
> by Juan Gonzales
>
> My mother says she remembers very well the day I was born. She was at my grandmothers she said all of a sudden she had a great pain and went oh my God !! My mother knew I was going

Writing an Autobiography

Objective: To provide students practice in developing written expression and to learn more about self and family.

Grades: Adapted for all levels

Materials: Writing materials.

Teaching Procedures: During the academic year, read autobiographies to the students and discuss their contents. Ask the students what information they feel they would need to write an autobiography and how they might be able to obtain that information (e.g., students may need to interview parents and grandparents). Have the students write an autobiography, conferencing frequently with other students and teacher.

Autobiographies, with pictures, are then displayed in the classroom and school library.

Writing a Teacher Evaluation

Objective: To practice critical thinking and writing skills.

Materials: Writing materials.

Teaching Procedures: Tell the students that teachers have many opportunities to evaluate them and their work. Discuss several of the criteria used to evaluate students. Then discuss what an evaluation instrument is and how it is often used. Brainstorm some of the possible criteria and content areas that an evaluation instrument designed to assess the quality of teachers should possess.

Have the students break into small groups to write an evaluation instrument. The students then share and discuss their instruments. Then, selecting the best parts from each group's evaluation, the students construct a final version of the evaluation and complete it on selected teachers.

Interview a Classmate

Objective: To give students practice in developing and using questions as a means for obtaining more information for the piece they are writing.

Grades: Adapted for all levels

Materials: (1) Writing materials and a writing topic. (2) A list of possible questions. (3) A tape recorder (optional).

Teaching Procedures: Using the format of a radio or television interview, demonstrate and role play "mock" interviews with sport, movie, music, and political celebrities. Give the students opportunities to play both roles.

Discuss what types of questions allow the interviewee to give elaborate responses (e.g., open questions), and what types of questions do not allow the interviewee to give a very expanded answer (e.g., closed questions). Practice asking open questions.

Use a piece that you are writing as an example, and discuss who you might interview to obtain more information. For example, "In writing a piece about what it might be like to go to the St. Louis World's Fair in 1904, I might interview my grandfather, who was there, to obtain more information."

Ask the students to select an appropriate person to interview for their writing piece and to write possible questions. In pairs, the students refine their questions for the actual interview. The students then conduct the interviews and later discuss how information from the interview assisted them in writing their piece.

Who Am I?

Objective: To give students practice in writing complete sentences with correct capitalization and ending punctuation. Students will use describing words specific to themselves without describing so specifically as to "give themselves away." Students will print or write their neatest printing or manuscript so that their handwriting alone doesn't give a clue to their identity.

Grades: All levels

Materials: (1) Paper and pencil. (2) Dictionary.

Teaching Procedures: Prepare a "Who Am I?" paper and read it to the class. For example:

I have brown hair and brown eyes. I was born in
February. I have a sister and no brothers I used
to have two dogs but now I don't have any pets.
I love Mexican food, football games, and snow
skiing. My favorite color is red but I like to wear
turquoise clothes.
WHO AM I?

how many brothers or sisters you have
some of your favorites (color, sport, food,
  movie)
what you like to do for fun
your pets (but *not* their names)
DO NOT TELL YOUR NAME

Read to the class a description of someone in the
room. See if they can guess who it is. Then tell
the students to write a description of themselves.
Provide some examples they might want to use.

your hair and eye color
your age or birth month
if you are a boy or girl

Remind the students to use their neatest handwriting so that their handwriting doesn't "give
away" who they are. Then collect their descriptions and randomly distribute them so that each
student has one other than his or her own. The
students read the descriptions out loud and members of the class guess who is being described.

Adaptations: Students can be directed to write
descriptions of political leaders, historical characters, characters from their reading, and so on.

Content Area Learning and Study Skills

Dictionary Scavenger Hunt

Objective: To provide students practice in successfully utilizing a dictionary.

Grades: Intermediate and junior high

Materials: (1) Student dictionaries. (2) Scavenger Hunt Cards with questions such as:

Is a puffin a small pillow?
Is a grackle a kind of noise?
Is a poetess a man who writes poems?
Was Ceres the same God as Demeter?
Is a limerick a kind of drink?

Teaching Procedures: Divide the students into
teams. Each team draws fifteen Scavenger Hunt
Cards and places them face down in from of
them. When the signal is given, each team selects one of their cards and finds the answer in

the dictionary as quickly as possible. The answer
is written on a sheet of paper. Then the next card
is drawn and the same procedure is repeated. The
game continues until all the teams answer their
questions. Answers and cards are exchanged and
verified. The team that finishes first and gets all
the answers correct wins the game.

Jeopardy

Objective: To provide students practice in
using reference and trade books to obtain information and to generate questions.

Grades: Secondary

Materials: (1) Reference and trade books. (2)
Jeopardy board with four categories and five
answers per category. (3) Index cards to fit in the
jeopardy board.

JEOPARDY

Pop Music	Presidents	Football	Southwest
20	20	20	20
40	40	40	40
60	60	60	60
80	80	80	80
100	100	100	100

Teaching Procedures: Divide the students into three teams of two to four students. Explain to them that each team is going to make a jeopardy game for the other students to play.

To make the game, each team needs to select four categories. Then have the students use reference books, trade books, and other sources to generate five questions and answers for each category that other students could possibly answer. Have them write the questions and answers on separate index cards and order the questions and answers from easy to difficult.

Each team then takes a turn directing its jeopardy game. First, the team inserts their category names and answer cards into the jeopardy board. Then they direct the game as the two other teams compete against each other. To direct the game, one student should serve as master of ceremonies, another as timekeeper, and the rest of the students as judges.

To play, each team takes a turn selecting a category and a level underneath the category. The answer is then exposed and the team members have fifteen seconds to give the question. If the question is correct, they get the number of points indicated and are allowed to make another

selection. If the answer is incorrect, the other team has fifteen seconds to give an answer.

Study Groups

Objective: To provide students the opportunity to work in groups when studying a textbook for a test.

Grades: Secondary

Materials: (1) Content area textbook chapter or sections over which the students are going to be tested. (2) Index cards.

Teaching Procedures: Have students who are studying for tests covering the same material work in groups of two to three students. (Note: When students first do this activity the teacher will generally need to demonstrate and guide the students through the process.)

Have the students read the assigned materials together, stopping at the end of each paragraph or section to discuss the main ideas and the important vocabulary. Each main idea and important vocabulary for each section should be written on an index card. After the students finish reading the assignment using this technique, they should take all the main idea cards and arrange them in logical groupings or in a logical order. The students then take each important vocabulary card and write a simple definition that makes sense according to the text. Then they arrange the important vocabulary next to the related main idea. Next, each student copies onto paper the arrangement that was organized for the main ideas and vocabulary (with definitions). Finally, the students should study the paper and then take turns quizzing each other on the information.

Get Their Opinions

Objective: To provide students the opportunity to collect, interpret, and present information about controversial topics and to increase awareness of current topics in social studies.

Grades: Intermediate and secondary

Materials: Tape recorder and blank tapes if respondents are interviewed.

Teaching Procedures: Discuss the meanings of surveys and polls and how they are conducted. Have the students study examples of surveys to determine the topics asked and the kinds of questions asked. Tell the students to select a topic about which they want to obtain other people's opinions. Then have them develop three to five questions that one could ask someone to determine their opinion. Have them write the survey and decide who they should survey.

Discuss how to conduct a survey and how not to bias a person who is answering the survey. Next, have the students conduct the survey, recording the responses in writing or on a tape recorder. Then the students need to tabulate the results of the survey, indicating what percent of persons answered the questions in the same manner. Finally, the students report the results of the survey to the rest of the class.

Adaptations: Results can also be written as an article for a school or community newspaper.

Smell and Taste

Objective: To provide students the opportunity to learn the relationship between the two senses of smell and taste.

Grades: Elementary

Materials: (1) Fruit, bread, crackers, and other foods that are easy to prepare in a classroom. Cut food into bite-size pieces. (2) Smell and Taste Worksheet. (3) Blindfolds.

Smell and Taste Worksheet		
Food apple pear	Taste apple apple	Smell and Taste apple pear
watermelon cantaloupe honey dew	cantaloupe honey dew cantaloupe	watermelon cantaloupe honey dew
Findings:		

Teaching Procedures: Explain the instructions and pair off the students. Give each pair of students similar foods to try and a worksheet on which to record their results. Have one student in each pair hold his or her nose and close the eyes (or use a blindfold). The other student then gives the blindfolded student one type of food at a time and asks, "Is it a(n) (pear) or a(n) (apple)?" The student then records the results on the worksheet. The student who is blindfolded then releases the hold on his or her nose and the procedure is repeated. Then the students switch places and the experiment is run again.

The students then return to the general group and discuss their findings, stating the relationship between taste and smell. The findings can be written in each student's Science Idea Notebook which contains a log of the various experiments conducted and their results.

_____ *Math* _____

Two-Digit Numbers: Focus on Reversals

Objective: To help students understand and use two-digit numbers successfully. (For use with students who write 23 for 32; 41 for 14; and so on.)

Grades: Primary

Materials: Objects that can be grouped by tens (e.g., pencils, paper, chips, sticks).

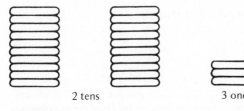

2 tens   3 ones

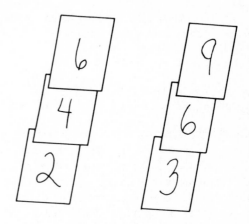

Teaching Procedures: Four steps are recommended: First, tell the children to group objects such as popsicle sticks or chips in tens, and then to *tell* the number of tens and number of ones left over. Next, the children count orally by tens and use objects to show the count (e.g., 2 tens is twenty; 6 tens is 60; and so on). When multiples of ten are established, extra ones are included (e.g., 2 tens and 3 is 23). Because of naming irregularities, teens are dealt with last.

Children then group objects by tens and write to describe the grouping. The tens-ones labels, used in early stages, are gradually eliminated. On separate sheets of paper, the students write the number that corresponds with the grouping. The children use objects (tens and ones) to help compare and sequence numbers.

"Two Up"

Objective: To practice multiplication facts by rehearsing counting by twos, threes, fours, etc.

Grades: Primary through intermediate

Prerequisite Behaviors: Counting by twos, threes, etc.

Materials: A set of forty-eight cards made by printing the multiples of two from 1 to 12, using a different color of pen for each set (e.g., 2, 4, ..., 12 in red, blue, green and brown).

Teaching Procedures: Directions for playing the game are: The cards are shuffled and dealt, giving equal number of cards to each player. The player who has the red 2 starts the game by placing the red 2 in the middle of the table. The next player must place a red 4 on top of the red

2 *or* pass. Next a red 6 is needed, and so on. Each of the players play in a similar manner. A player can only play one card each turn.

The object of the game is to play the cards from 2 on up. The first player to play all of his or her cards is the winner.

Adaptations: This game can be played with decks of threes, fours, sixes, and so on, called "Three Up," "Four Up," etc. A different deck of cards must be made for each multiple.

Bingo Clock Reading

Objective: To give the students practice in associating the time on a clock face, to its written form on a game board, to its spoken form.

Grades: Primary

Materials: (1) Cards that show times on a standard clock. (2) Large game boards with sixteen squares and with times written at the bottom of each square. (3) Sixteen "clock" chips (made by placing gummed labels on gameboard chips and drawing a clock on the face of the label). (4) Markers.

Teaching Procedures: A caller holds up a clock face. The players must decide if the time

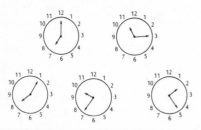

three o'clock	seven o'clock	fifteen minutes after four	twenty minutes after twelve
fifteen minutes after six	twenty minutes after twelve	twenty minutes to eleven	twenty minutes after eleven
five minutes after five	fifteen minutes after ten	twenty-five minutes after one	twenty-five minutes to eleven
nine thirty	five minutes to seven	twenty-five minutes after twelve	ten o'clock

shown by that clock is on their gameboard. If it is, the player places a marker in the square that contains the written form. The winner is the first person who completes a row in any direction and reads the time in each winning square.

Coin Concentration

Objective: To practice reading money amounts in four different notations and to reinforce coin recognition.

Grades: Primary, intermediate to high school (see adaptation for older students)

Prerequisite Behaviors: Coin value, value placement, coin recognition of dollars and cents

Materials: (1) Money picture card. (2) Money word card. (3) Money-decimal card. (4) Money-cents card.

Teaching Procedures: The game of coin concentration can be played at several levels of difficulty, with varying skill emphasis depending on specific classroom needs. At the simplest level, use only one kind of money card (make two copies of the card and cut apart on solid lines so students play with a total of twenty cards). Decide on the number and type of cards to be used, and place them face down on the table.

The first player turns over two cards, one at a time, trying to match values. If the cards match, the player keeps them. If not, he or she simply turns them back over on the table in their same location. Then the next player tries to make a match by turning over two more cards, and so on, until all the cards are matched with their pair.

The winner is the one with the most number of matched cards. For variety, ask the students to add the total value of their cards and the player with the highest value wins. To add variety and increase difficulty, put different type cards down and players can match 4¢ to $.04 or to *four cents*.

Adaptations: This activity can be used with older students by increasing the difficulty of the coin values represented and by adding a fifth card. On the fifth card is the name of an object that costs the corresponding amount. For example, if the money value is $329.00 the fifth card may have "Video Cassette Recorder" written on it.

Shopping Spree

Objective: To give students practice using money and understanding the concept of addition and subtraction with money.

Grades: Elementary-age students who are having difficulty with the money concepts. (See adaptations for use with older students.)

Materials: (1) Coins and dollar bills (when teaching the more advanced concepts). (2) Pictures of items.

Teaching Procedures: Cut out magazine pictures of things children would like to buy and put a price on the pictures. Start with easy amounts, such as 5¢, 10¢, 25¢, and then in further lessons, increase the complexity of the amounts, to such things as 63¢, 51¢, etc. For higher grades, use of dollar bills can be implemented. Have the students divide into two groups and have half the groups be storeclerks, and have the other half be shoppers. The shoppers buy picture items from the clerk. The shoppers are responsible for giving the correct amount of money. The clerks are responsible for giving the correct change. Then the children trade places.

At a later date, specific amounts of money can be distributed and the children are to select several items without going over their designated amount. Also with a specific amount of money, show two or three different items and ask which item they can afford.

Adaptations: For older students, ''pretend'' checkbooks can be made and distributed. Each student is given a specified amount in his or her checkbook and must make appropriate deductions as he or she makes purchases.

I Have . . .

Objective: To provide practice in auditory memory and application of math skills.

Grades: 3–6

Materials: (1) 3 x 5 cards. (2) Paper and pencils. (3) Pen to write word problems on each card, such as:

> I have 8. Who
> knows that times
> 5?

> Sally has 12 dogs.
> She gave 4 puppies
> away. How many
> are left?

Teaching Procedures: Shuffle the cards and take the top card and read it to the students. Then model writing the problem and answering it on the board. Next, choose another card and read it to the class. This time, the students write down the problem and answer it. You then should assist immediately any students who are making errors.

Discuss the answers with the class, and then repeat the steps until a winner obtains a predetermined number of points.

"99"

Objective: To generalize and practice adding numbers in one's head or on paper.

Grades: Intermediate to senior high

Materials: (1) Playing cards. (2) Paper and pencils.

Teaching Procedures: Explain that the objective of this game is to add cards up to a score of 99. Establish the following rules:

Jacks and Queens = 10
Kings = 99
Nines = ''free turn'' pass; to be used anytime
Fours = pass
Aces = 1
Other cards = face value

Each player is dealt three cards. The rest of the cards go face down on a draw pile. The players take turns discarding one card from their hand face up on a discard pile and drawing one card from the draw pile to put back in their hand. As a player discards his or her card, he or she must add the number from the card to any previous score acquired up to that point in the game and give the new score out loud. Note the exception: If a player plays a nine, he or she receives a free-turn pass. If a player plays a four, he or she has to pass a turn with no score. The first player to score higher than 99 loses the game.

Shopping

Objective: To provide practice in addition, subtraction, and comparing prices (problem solving).

Grades: Junior high

Materials: (1) Newspaper from which to cut out various supermarket sale ads that include price per item. Mount individual items on cardboard and cover them with clear plastic or just bring the ads. (2) Made-up shopping lists to hand out to the class. (3) Pencil and paper.

Teaching Procedures: Divide the class into small groups. Tell the students that their shopping list contains the items that they will need this week. Assign each group a designated amount for groceries (e.g., $30.00). The object is to buy everything on the list and spend the least. Place on each desk the supermarket sale ads and the name of the store. After students buy their item they record the price and the store where they bought it. (It's easier if one student in each group buys the meats, one buys the dairy products, and so on.) When the students have bought all the items on the list, tell them to total their bills and be ready to present the results.

Socialization

Please Help

Objective: To teach students a process for asking for help when needed and yet continuing to work until assistance is given. To have a record-keeping system that allows the teacher to monitor how many times each day he or she assists each student.

```
┌─────────────────────────────────┐
│    PLEASE  HELP JENNIFER         │
├──────┬──────┬───────────────────┤
│ DATE │ TIME │   COMMENTS        │
├──────┼──────┼───────────────────┤
│      │      │                   │
│      │      │                   │
│      │      │                   │
│      │      │                   │
│      │      │                   │
│      │      │                   │
│      │      │                   │
│      │      │                   │
└──────┴──────┴───────────────────┘
```

Grades: Primary and intermediate

Materials: A 6 x 8 inch card that states "Please Help _____ (student's name)" and then a place to list the date and comments.

Teaching Procedures: Construct the "Please Help _____ " card for each student, including a place to mark the date and comments. Give all the students a card and inform them that they are to place the card on their desk when they need help. They are to continue working until you or someone else is able to provide assistance.

When you or your assistant is able to provide help, mark the date and time on the card and any appropriate comments such as, "We needed to review the rules for long division," or "She could not remember the difference between long and short vowels," or "He solved the problem himself before I arrived."

Problem Box

Objective: To give students an opportunity to identify problems they are having with others and to feel their problems will be heard and attended to.

Grades: All grades

Materials: Shoe box decorated and identified as "Problem Box."

Teaching Procedures: Show the students the box that is decorated and identified as the "Problem Box." Place the box in a prominent location in the classroom. Tell the students that when they have problems with other students, teachers, or even home they can write the problems down and put them in the box. At the end of every day, you will spend a designated amount of time (e.g., fifteen minutes) reading problems and trying to solve them as a class. Be sure to tell students they do not need to identify themselves or their notes.

During the designated time, open the problem box and read a selected note. Solicit assistance from the class in solving the note. Direct students' attention to identifying the problem, suggesting solutions, evaluating the consequences of the solutions, and identifying a solution and describing how it might be implemented.

A Date by Telephone

Objective: To give students structured skills for obtaining a date by telephone.

Grades: Secondary

Materials: Two nonworking telephones.

Teaching Procedures: Discuss with the students why preplanning a telephone call with a

How Good are You at Making and Keeping Friends?

Next to each item, circle the face that best describes how well you do.

1. I tell friends the truth.
   ☺ ☺ ☹

2. I call friends on the phone.
   ☺ ☺ ☹

3. I share my favorite toys and games with friends.
   ☺ ☺ ☹

---

prospective date might be advantageous. Tell them that you are going to teach them some points to remember when calling to ask for a date. After you describe each of the following points, roll play them so the students can observe their appropriate use:

1. Telephone at an *appropriate time.*
2. Utilize an *icebreaker,* such as recalling a mutually shared experience or a recent event in school.
3. *State what you would like to do and ask him or her to do it.* Ask the person what kinds of things he or she likes to do on the weekend. After there is an initial lull in the conversation, state you would like to take her or him to the movies, state when, and to see what. Then ask the person if she or he would like to go with you.
4. If yes, *make appropriate arrangements* for day, time, and transportation. If no, ask if you can call again.

Be sure that each student has an opportunity to role play.

Making and Keeping Friends

Objective: To have students identify the characteristics of students who are successful at making and keeping friends and, after identifying these characteristics, to evaluate themselves in how well they perform.

Grades: Intermediate and secondary

Materials: Writing materials

Teaching Procedures: Ask the students to think of children they know who are good at making and keeping friends. Brainstorm what these children do that makes them successful at making and keeping friends. On an overhead projector or chalkboard, write the student-generated responses to the characteristics of children good at making and keeping friends. Then select the most agreed on characteristics and write them on a sheet of paper with smiley faces, neutral faces, and frowny faces so students can circle the face that is most like them in response to that characteristic. Finally, ask students to identify one characteristic they would like to target to increase their skills at making and maintaining friends.

Identifying Feelings

Objective: To identify the feelings of others and self, and to respond better to those feelings.

Grades: Primary and intermediate

Materials: Cards with pictures of persons in situations where their feelings can be observed or deduced.

Teaching Procedures: Select pictures that elicit feeling words such as *happy, angry, jealous, hurt, sad, mad,* and so on. Show the pictures to the students and ask them to identify the feelings of the people in the pictures. Discuss what information in the picture cued them to the emotional states of the people. Then ask the students to draw a picture of a time when they felt as the person in the picture feels. Conclude by asking students to discuss their pictures.

Appendix C
Educational Publishers

Academic Therapy Publications
20 Commercial Boulevard
Novato, CA 94947

Adapt Press
808 West Avenue North
Sioux Falls, SD 57104

Addison-Wesley Publishing
  Company
2725 Sand Hill Road
Menlo Park, CA 94025

Adston Educational Enterprises
945 East River Oaks Drive
Baton Rouge, LA 70815

Allied Education Council
P.O. Box 78
Galien, MI 49113

Allyn and Bacon
160 Gould Street
Needham Heights, MA 02194

American Association of Mental
  Deficiency
5201 Connecticut Avenue NW
Washington, DC 20015

American Book Company
450 West 33rd Street
New York, NY 10001

American Guidance Service
Publishers' Building
Circle Pines, MN 55014

American Speech and Hearing
  Association
9030 Old Georgetown Road
Washington, DC 20014

Ann Arbor Publisher
P.O. Box 338
Worthington, OH 43085

Appleton-Century-Crofts
440 Park Avenue South
New York, NY 10016

Argus Communications
P.O. Box 4000
One DLM Park
Allen, TX 75002

Association for Supervision and
  Curriculum Development
1250 N. Pitt Street
Alexandria, VA 22314

Barnell Loft
958 Church Street
Baldwin, NY 11510

Behavioral Research Laboratories
P.O. Box 577
Palo Alto, CA 94302

Bell and Howell
7100 McCormick Road
Chicago, IL 60645

Benefic Press
10300 West Roosevelt Road
Westchester, IL 60153

Biological Sciences Curriculum
  Study
P.O. Box 930
Boulder, CO 80306

Bobbs-Merrill Company
4300 West 62nd Street
Indianapolis, IN 46206

Book-Lab Inc.
1449 37th Street
Brooklyn, NY 11218

Borg-Warner Educational Systems
7450 North Natchez Avenue
Niles, IL 60648

Bowmar/Noble Publishers
4563 Colorado Boulevard
Los Angeles, CA 90039

William C. Brown Publishers
2460 Kerper Boulevard
P.O. Box 539
Dubuque, IA 52001

Childcraft Education Corp.
20 Kilmer Road
Edison, NJ 08817

Communication Skill Builders
3830 E. Bellevue
Tucson, AZ 85716

Continental Press
520 East Bainbridge Street
Elizabethtown, PA 17022

Council for Exceptional Children
1920 Association Drive
Reston, VA 22091

Creative Publications
3977 East Bayshore Road
Palo Alto, CA 94303

Cuisenaire Company of America
12 Church Street
New Rochelle, NY 10805

Curriculum Associates
5 Esquire Road
North Billerica, MA 01862

Dale Seymour Publications
P.O. Box 10888
Palo Alto, CA 94303

Developmental Learning
   Materials
P.O. Box 4000
One DLM Park
Allen, TX 75002

Devereux Foundation Press
Devon, PA 19333

DiDax, Inc
One Centennial Drive
Peabody, MA 01960

Dormac
P.O. Box 752
Beaverton, OR 97075

EBSCO Curriculum Materials
Box 11542
Birmingham, AL 35202

Economy Company
P.O. Box 25308
1901 North Walnut Street
Oklahoma City, OK 73125

Edmark Corporation
P.O. Box 3903
Bellevue, WA 98009

Educational Activities
P.O. Box 392
Freeport, NY 11520

Educational Performance
   Associates
600 Broad Avenue
Ridgefield, NJ 07657

Educational Progress
   Corporation
P.O. Box 45663
Tulsa, OK 74145

Educational Service
P.O. Box 219
Stevensville, MI 49127

Educational Teaching Aids
199 Carpenter Avenue
Wheeling, IL 60090

Educators Publishing Service
75 Moulton Street
Cambridge, MA 02138

Enrich
Mafex Associates
90 Cherry Street
Johnstown, PA 15907

Exceptional Education
P.O. Box 15308
Seattle, WA 98115

Fearon Publisher
6 Davis Drive
Belmont, CA 94002

Field Educational Publications
2400 Hanover Street
Palo Alto, CA 94302

Fisher-Price Toys
East Aurora, NY 14052

Follett Publishing Company
1010 West Washington
   Boulevard
Chicago, IL 60607

Garrard Publishing Company
1607 North Market Street
Champaign, IL 61820

General Learning Corporation
250 James Street
Morristown, NJ 07960

Ginn and Company
191 Spring Street
Lexington, MA 02173

Grosset and Dunlap
51 Madison Avenue
New York, NY 10010

Grune and Stratton
111 Fifth Avenue
New York, NY 10003

Guidance Associates
1526 Gilpin Avenue
Wilmington, DE 19806

H and H Enterprises
946 Tennessee
Lawrence, KS 66044

Harcourt Brace Jovanovich
Orlando, FL 32887

HarperCollins Publishers
10 East 53rd Street
New York, NY 10022

Haworth Press
28 East 22nd Street
New York, NY 10010

D.C. Heath and Company
125 Spring Street
Lexington, MA 02173

Heinemann
70 Court Street
Portsmouth, NH 03801

Holt, Rinehart and Winston
301 Commerce Street
Fort Worth, TX 76102

Houghton Mifflin
One Beacon Street
Boston, MA 02107

Hubbard
P.O. Box 104
Northbrook, IL 60062

Human Sciences Press
72 Fifth Avenue
New York, NY 10011

Ideal School Supply Company
11000 South Lavergne Avenue
Oak Lawn, IL 60453

Incentive Publications
P.O. Box 12522
Nashville, TN 37212

Initial Teaching Alphabet
   Publications
6 East 43rd Street
New York, NY 10017

Instruction Corp.
200 Cedar Hollow Road
Paoli, PA 19301

International Reading Association
800 Barksdale Road
Newark, DE 19711

Jamestown Publishers
Box 5643
Providence, RI 02904

Janus Books
2501 Industrial Parkway, West
Hayward, CA 94545

Jastek Associates
1526 Gilpin Avenue
Wilmington, DE 19800

Language Research Associates
P.O. Box 2085
Palm Springs, CA 92262

Learning Concepts
2501 North Lamar Blvd
Austin, TX 78705

J. B. Lippincott Co.
Educational Publishing Division
East Washington Square
Philadelphia, PA 19105

Little, Brown and Co.
34 Beacon Street
Boston, MA 02106

Longman
19 West 44th Street
New York, NY 10036

Love Publishing Co.
1777 South Bellaire Street
Denver, CO 80222

Lyons and Carnahan
407 East 25th Street
Chicago, IL 60616

Macmillan Publishing Co.
866 Third Avenue
New York, NY 10022

Mafex Associates
90 Cherry Street
Box 519
Johnstown, PA 15907

McCormick-Mathers Publishing
  Company
450 West 33rd Street
New York, NY 10001

McGraw-Hill Book Co.
1221 Avenue of Americas
New York, NY 10020

Media Materials
Department 840251
2936 Remington Avenue
Baltimore, MD 21211

Melton Book Co.
111 Leslie Street
Dallas, TX 75207

Charles E. Merrill Publishing Co.
1300 Alum Creek Drive
Columbus, OH 43216

Milton Bradley Co.
74 Park Street
Springfield, MA 01101

Minneapolis Public Schools
807 NE Broadway
Minneapolis, MN 55413

Modern Curriculum Press
13900 Prospect Road
Cleveland, OH 44136

Modern Education Corporation
P.O. Box 721
Tulsa, OK 74101

William C. Morrow
105 Madison Avenue
New York, NY 10016

National Council of Teachers of
  English
1111 Kenyon Road
Urbana, IL 61801

National Education Association
  Publications
1201 16th Street NW
Washington, DC 20036

New Readers Press
1320 Jamesville Avenue
Box 131
Syracuse, NY 13210

Noble and Noble Publishers
1 Dag Hammarskjold Plaza
New York, NY 10017

Numark Publications
104-20 Queens Blvd
Forest Hills, NY 11375

Open Court Publishing Co.
1039 Eighth Street
Box 599
LaSalle, IL 61301

Opportunities for Learning
20417 Nordhoff Street
Chatsworth, CA 91311

Orton Dyslexia Society
8415 Bellona Lane
Towson, MD 21204

Parker Brothers
P.O. Box 900
Salem, MA 01970

Phonovisual Products
12216 Parklawn Drive
Rockville, MD 20852

Prentice-Hall
Educational Books Division
Englewood Cliffs, NJ 07632

Pro-Ed
8700 Shoal Creek Blvd.
Austin, TX 78758

The Psychological Corp.
555 Academic Court
P.O. Box 9954
San Antonio, TX 78204

Rand McNally and Co.
P.O. Box 7600
Chicago, IL 60680

Random House/Singer School
  Division
201 East 50th Street
New York, NY 10022

Reader's Digest Services
Educational Division
Pleasantville, NJ 10570

Reading Joy
P.O. Box 404
Naperville, IL 60540

Recordings for the Blind
214 East 58th Street
New York, NY 10022

Research Press
Box 31773
Champaign, IL 61821

Scholastic Magazine and Book
  Service
50 West 44th Street
New York, NY 10036

Science Research Associates
155 North Wacker Drive
Chicago, IL 60606

Scott, Foresman and Company
1900 East Lake Avenue
Glenview, IL 60025

Selchow and Righter
505 East Union Street
Bay Shore, NY 11706

Select-Ed
117 North Chester
Olathe, KS 66061

L.W. Singer
A Division of Random House
201 East 50th Street
New York, NY 10022

Slosson Educational Publications
140 Pine Street
East Aurora, NY 14052

Society for Visual Education
1345 Diversey Parkway
Chicago, IL 60614

Special Learning Corp.
42 Boston Post Road
Guilford, CT 06437

Steck-Vaughn Co.
807 Brazos
P.O. Box 2028
Austin, TX 78768

Teachers College Press
Teachers College, Columbia
University
1234 Amsterdam Avenue
New York, NY 10027

Charles C. Thomas Publisher
301-27 East Lawrence Avenue
Springfield, IL 62717

Troll Associates
320 Route 17
Mahwah, NJ 07430

United States Government
Printing Office
Superintendent of Documents
Washington, DC 20025

University Park Press
233 East Redwood Street
Baltimore, MD 21202

VORT Corp.
P.O. Box 11552H
Palo Alto, CA 94306

George Wahr Publishing Co.
316 State Street
Ann Arbor, MI 41808

Walker Educational Book Corp.
750 Fifth Avenue
New York, NY 10019

Warner Educational Services
75 Rockefeller Plaza
New York, NY 10019

Webster
A Division of McGraw-Hill
Book Co.
1221 Avenue of the Americas
New York, NY 10020

John Wiley and Sons
605 Third Avenue
New York, NY 10016

The Wright Group
10949 Technology Place
San Diego, CA 92127

Xerox Education Publications
245 Long Hill Road
Middletown, CT 06457

Zaner-Bloser Co.
2500 West Fifth Avenue
P.O. Box 16764
Columbus, OH 43215

Zephyr Press Learning Materials
3865 E. 34 Street
Tucson, AZ 85713

Richard L. Zweig Associates
20800 Beach Blvd
Huntington Beach, CA 96248

Appendix D
Educational Computer Software Producers and Distributors

Academic Software
c/o Software City
22 East Quackenbush Ave
Dumont, NJ 07628

Addison-Wesley Publishing
    Company
Jacob Way
Reading, MA 01867

Advanced Ideas
2550 Ninth Street, Suite 104
Berkeley, CA 94710

American Educational Computer
525 University Avenue
Palo Alto, CA 94301

Apple Computer, Inc.
10260 Bandley Drive
Cupertino, CA 95014

Aquarius, Inc.
P.O. Box 128
Indian Rocks Beach, FL 33535

Avante-Garde Creations
P.O. Box 30160
Eugene, OR 97403

Bertamax, Inc.
3647 Stone Way North
Seattle, WA 98103

BLS/Random House School
    Division
400 Hahn Road
Westminster, MD 21157

Borg-Warner Educational System
600 West University Drive
Arlington, IL 60004

Broderbund Software
Software-Direct
17 Paul Drive
San Rafael, CA 94903

Chatterbox
29 Elk Ridge Lane
Boulder, CO 80302

Classroom Consorta Media
28 Bay Street
Staten Island, NY 10301

Communication Skill Builders
3830 E. Bellevue
Tucson, AZ 85716

Computer-Ed
1 Everett Road
Carmel, NY 10512

Computer Education
6438 West Glendale Drive
Phoenix, AZ 85069

Creative Publications
3977 East Bayshore Road
Palo Alto, CA 94303

Cross Educational Software
1802 North Trenton
Box 1536
Ruston, LA 71270

Davidson & Associates, Inc.
3135 Kashiwa Street
Torrance, CA 90505

DLM Teaching Resources
P.O. Box 4000
One DLM Park
Allen, TX 75002

Dorsett Educational Systems
Box 1226
Norman, OK 73070

Education Activities
P.O. Box 392
Freeport, NY 11520

Educational Computing Systems
106 Fairbanks
Oak Ridge, TN 37830

Educational Systems Software
23720 El Toro Road, Suite C
P.O. Box E
El Toro, CA 92630

Educational Teaching Aids
159 West Kinzie Street
Chicago, IL 60610

Edusoft
P.O. Box 2560, Dept. 50
Berkeley, CA 94702

Edu-Ware Services
28035 Dorothy Avenue
Agoura, CA 91301

Gamco Industries
Box 1911
Big Spring, TX 79720

Hartley Courseware
P.O. Box 419
Dimondale, MI 48821

Houghton Mifflin
One Beacon Street
Boston, MA 02107

Huntington Computing
P.O. Box 1297
Corcoran, CA 93212

K-12 Micromedia
172 Broadway
Woodcliff Lake, NJ 07675

Krell Software
1320 Stony Brook Road, Suite 219
Stony Brook, NY 11790

Laureate Learning Systems
One Mill Street
Burlington, VT 05401

Learning Company
4370 Alpine Road
Portola Valley, CA 94025

Learning Systems
P.O. Box 9046
Fort Collins, CO 80525

Learning Well
200 South Service Road
Roslyn Heights, NY 11577

Little Bee Educational Programs
P.O. Box 262
Massilon, OH 44648

MARCK
280 Linden Avenue
Branford, CT 06405

Media Materials
2936 Remington Avenue
Baltimore, MD 21211

Merry Bee Communications
815 Crest Drive
Omaha, NE 68046

Microcomputer Workshops
103 Puritan Drive
Port Chester, NY 10573

Micro Learningware
P.O. Box 307
Mankato, MN 56002

Milliken Publishers
100 Research Boulevard
St Louis, MO 63132

Milton Bradley Educational
  Division
443 Shaker Road
East Longmeadow, MA 01028

Mindscape, Inc.
3444 Dundee Road
Northbrook, IL 60062

Minnesota Educational
  Computing Consortium
  (MECC)
3490 Lexington Ave. North
St. Paul, MN 55112

Opportunities for Learning
20417 Nordhoff Street
Department 9
Chatsworth, CA 91311

Parrot Software
P.O. Box 1139
State College, PA 16904

Peal Software
2210 Wilshire Boulevard #806
Santa Monica, CA 90403

Queue
5 Chapell Hill Drive
Fairfield, CT 06432

Quicksoft
537 Willamette
Eugene, OR 97401

Random House School Division
2970 Brandywine Road, Suite 201
Atlanta, GA 30341

Reader's Digest Services
Educational Division
Pleasantville, NY 10570

Scholastic Inc.
730 Broadway
New York, NY 10003

Spinnaker Software
1 Kendall Square
Cambridge, MA 02139

Springboard
40005 West 65th Street, Suite 218
Edina, MN 55435

Sunburst Communications
39 Washington Avenue
Box 40
Pleasantville, NY 10570

Terrapin, Inc.
380 Green Street
Cambridge, MA 02139

Weekly Reader Software
245 Long Hill Road
Middletown, CT 06457

Zeitgeist
5150 N. 6th Street, Suite 179
Fresno, CA 93710

Index